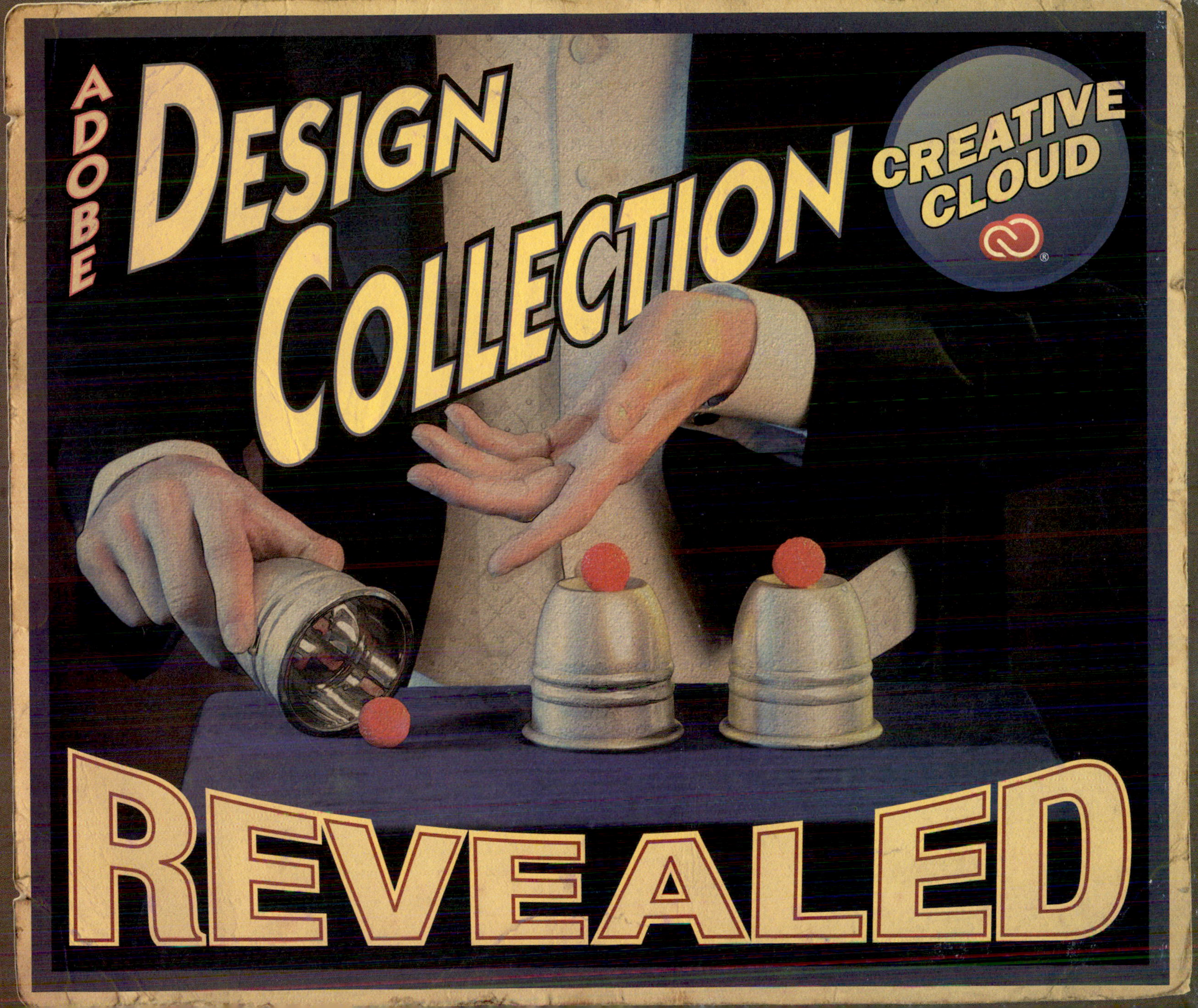

ADOBE
DESIGN
COLLECTION
CREATIVE CLOUD
REVEALED

ADOBE

DESIGN COLLECTION

CREATIVE CLOUD

Chris **BOTELLO**

Elizabeth Eisner **REDING**

REVEALED

CENGAGE
Learning·

Australia • Brazil • Mexico • Singapore • United Kingdom • United States

CENGAGE
Learning·

Design Collection Revealed Creative Cloud:
Adobe InDesign, Photoshop, and Illustrator
Chris Botello & Elizabeth Eisner Reding

Product Director: Kathleen McMahon

Senior Product Manager: Jim Gish

Senior Content Developer: Kate Mason and
    Megan Chrisman

Senior Marketing Manager: Eric LaScola

Senior Content Project Manager: Jen Feltri-George

Managing Art Director: Jack Pendleton

Manufacturing Planner: Julio Esperas

IP Analyst: Sara Crane

Senior IP Project Manager: Kathy Kucharek

Developmental Editor: Ann Fisher and Karen Stevens

Technical Editor: Tara Botelho

Production Service: Integra Software Services Pvt. Ltd.

Text Designer: Liz Kingslein

Cover Image: Cengage Learning

For product information and technology assistance,
contact us at **Cengage Learning Customer & Sales**
Support, 1-800-354-9706

For permission to use material from this text or
product, submit all requests online at
www.cengage.com/permissions.

Further permissions questions can be emailed to
permissionrequest@cengage.com.

Adobe Photoshop®, Adobe® InDesign®, Adobe® Illustrator®,
Adobe® Flash®, Adobe® Dreamweaver®, Adobe® Edge®,
and Adobe® Creative Suite® are trademarks or registered
trademarks of Adobe Systems, Inc. in the United States and/
or other countries. Third party products, services, company
names, logos, design, titles, words, or phrases within these
materials may be trademarks of their respective owners.

Adobe product screenshot(s) reprinted with permission
from Adobe Systems Incorporated.

The Adobe Approved Certification Courseware logo is
a proprietary trademark of Adobe. All rights reserved.
Cengage Learning and Adobe Illustrator Creative Cloud—
Revealed are independent from ProCert Labs, LLC and
Adobe Systems Incorporated, and are not affiliated with
ProCert Labs and Adobe in any manner. This publication
may assist students to prepare for an Adobe Certified
Expert exam, however, neither ProCert Labs nor Adobe
warrant that use of this material will ensure success in
connection with any exam.

Library of Congress Control Number: 2014948592

ISBN-13: 978-1-305-26361-1
ISBN-10: 1-305-26361-8

Cengage Learning
20 Channel Center Street
Boston, MA 02210
USA

Cengage Learning is a leading provider of customized
learning solutions with office locations around the globe,
including Singapore, the United Kingdom, Australia,
Mexico, Brazil, and Japan. Locate your local office at
www.cengage.com/global.

Cengage Learning products are represented in Canada by
Nelson Education, Ltd.

To learn more about Cengage Learning Solutions, visit
www.cengage.com.

Purchase any of our products at your local college store or
at our preferred online store **www.cengagebrain.com.**

Printed in the United States of America

Print Number: 01   Print Year: 2014

Revealed Series Vision

The Revealed Series is your guide to today's hottest digital media applications. For years, the Revealed Series has kept pace with the dynamic demands of the digital media community, and continues to do so with the publication of six exciting titles covering the latest Adobe Creative Cloud products. Each comprehensive book teaches not only the technical skills required for success in today's competitive digital media market, but the design skills as well. From animation, to web design, to digital image-editing and interactive media skills, the Revealed Series has you covered.

We recognize the unique learning environment of the digital media classroom, and we deliver textbooks that include:

- Comprehensive step-by-step instructions
- In-depth explanations of the "Why" behind a skill
- Creative projects for additional practice
- Full-color visuals for a clear explanation of concepts
- Comprehensive online material offerring additional instruction and skills practice

- **NEW** icons to highlight features that are new since the previous release of the software

With the Revealed Series, we've created books that speak directly to the digital media and design community—one of the most rapidly growing computer fields today.

—The Revealed Series

New to This Edition!

The latest edition of the Design Collection Revealed covers exciting new features, including:

- Using Creative Cloud apps and services
- Isolation Mode Layer Filtering
- Smarter Smart Guides
- Font Search

A CourseMate is available to accompany *Design Collection Creative Cloud Revealed*, which helps you make the grade!

This CourseMate includes:

- An interactive eBook, with highlighting, note-taking, and search capabilities
- Interactive learning tools including:
  - Chapter quizzes
  - Flash cards
  - Crossword puzzles
  - And more!

Go to login.cengagebrain.com to access these resources.

AUTHORS' VISION

I am thrilled to have written this book on Adobe InDesign Creative Cloud and Adobe Illustrator Creative Cloud. Illustrator was the first Adobe program I learned—back in 1988! Since then it's been my favorite program, even though I seem to spend most of my time in Photoshop. When doing this update and learning the new features of Creative Cloud, like live corners and path segment reshaping, I'm quietly amazed at how far this program has come.

It's also been a pleasure to watch InDesign evolve into the smart, strategic layout package that it is today. And it's exciting to see that Adobe is developing the software both for print and interactive uses. As new media evolves, InDesign remains positioned with a central role in that evolution, and that's exciting.

Thank you to Ann Fisher for her intelligence and dedication as the developmental editor on this title. Many thanks to Kate Mason, the senior content developer. Kate shepherded this book through to completion with her combination of patience, persistence, and clarity of vision. I also want to acknowledge technical editor Tara Botelho for her input. Such dedication in a technical editor allows an author to sleep a little more soundly.

—Chris Botello

To the reader, a book magically appears on the shelf with each software revision, but to those of us "making it happen" it means not only working under ridiculous deadlines (which we're used to), but it also means working with slightly different teams with slightly different ways of doing things.

Karen Stevens and I have worked together before on this project that has spanned more years than we care to admit. With this revision, we welcomed Megan Chrisman, Brooke Baker, Gillian Daniels, and Toni Toland to the team. Thanks also to Jim Gish, Kathy Kucharek, Glenn Castle, and Meaghan Tomaso. Special thanks to Shanthi Guruswamy, who quickly became part of the team and Ann Fisher, who oversees and compiles the Instructor Resources. Most of us have never met face-to-face, yet once again we managed to work together in a professional manner, while defying the time-space continuum with its many time zones, cultural holidays, and countless vacation plans.

I would also like to thank my husband, Michael, who is used to my disappearing acts when I'm facing deadlines, and to Bix and Jet, who know when it's time to take a break for food, water, and some good old-fashioned head-scratching.

—Elizabeth Eisner Reding

Introduction to the Design Collection

Welcome to the *Design Collection Revealed Creative Cloud*. This book offers creative projects, concise instructions, and coverage of basic to intermediate InDesign, Photoshop, and Illustrator skills, helping you to create polished, professional-looking layouts, photographs, and illustrations. Use this book both in the classroom and as your own reference guide. It also includes many of the new features of Adobe Creative Cloud. This edition is written for the 2014 CC release.

This text is organized into 17 chapters, including an integration chapter. In these chapters, you will learn many skills, including how to move among the Creative Cloud programs, which all have familiar functionality. The first five chapters cover InDesign, where you'll work extensively with InDesign features and use both Illustrator and Photoshop files as you create quality layouts. The next six chapters

cover additional Photoshop-specific skills, and then you will learn some of the finer points of Adobe Illustrator. The book ends with an integration chapter, which combines the features and benefits of all three applications and shows you how to use them together effectively.

What You'll Do

A What You'll Do figure begins every lesson. This figure gives you an at-a-glance look at what you'll do in the chapter, either by showing you a page or pages from the current project or a tool you'll be using.

Comprehensive Conceptual Lessons

Before jumping into instructions, in-depth conceptual information tells you "why" skills are applied. This book provides the "how" and "why" through the use of professional examples. Also included in the text are tips and sidebars to help you work more efficiently and creatively, or to teach you a bit about the history or design philosophy behind the skill you are using.

Step-by-Step Instructions

This book combines in-depth conceptual information with concise steps to help you learn InDesign, Photoshop, and Illustrator. Each set of steps guides you through a lesson where you will create, modify, or enhance a Creative Cloud file. Step references to large colorful images and quick step summaries round out the lessons. The Data Files for the steps are provided on CengageBrain.com.

Figure 50 *Pompom with the pseudo-stroke effect*

Figure 51 *Completed illustration*

Create pseudo-strokes

1. Select the **pompom**, copy it, then paste in back.
2. Apply a black fill to the copy.

   TIP The copy is still selected behind the original white pompom, making it easy to apply the black fill.

3. Click the **white pompom**, then remove the stroke.
4. Lock the white pompom.
5. Using the Direct Selection tool, select the **bottom anchor point** on the black copy.
6. Use the arrow keys to move the anchor point 5 pts down.

   The black copy is increasingly revealed as its size is increased beneath the locked white pompom.

7. Move the left anchor point 4 pts to the left.
8. Move the top anchor point 2 pts up, then deselect.

   Your work should resemble Figure 50.

9. Using the same methods and Figure 51 as a reference, create distorted black copies behind all the remaining elements except the torso, the mouth, and the eyebrow.
10. Save your work, then close Snowball Assembled.

You created black copies behind each element, then distorted them, using the Direct Selection tool and the arrow keys, to create the illusion of uneven black strokes around the object.

© 2015 Cengage Learning®

Lesson 6   Stroke Objects for Artistic Effect

ILLUSTRATOR 3-25

32. Name the new layer **Stamp Visible**, then set its blending mode to Overlay.
33. Compare your artwork to Figure 33.
34. Save your work, then close Jazz 2096.

Create an InDesign output file.

1. Open ID 1-7.indd, then save it as **Jazz 2096 Output**.
2. Verify that the Control panel is showing.
3. Click the Rectangle tool, then draw a rectangle anywhere on the page.
4. On the Control panel, with the rectangle still selected, click the upper-left reference point.

5. Type **-.125** in the X Location text box, type **-.125** in the Y Location text box, type **10.25** in the W text box, type **6.25** in the H text box, then press Enter (Win) or return (Mac).
6. Verify that the rectangle has no fill or stroke.
7. Click File on the Menu bar, click Place, navigate to the folder where you store your Data Files, then click the Jazz 2096.psd file.
8. Click Object on the Menu bar, point to Fitting, then click Fit Content to Frame.
9. Hide the guides.

10. Save your work.
11. Click File on the Menu bar, then click Export.
12. Click the Save as type list arrow (Win) or the Format list arrow (Mac), then click Adobe PDF (Print). (Hint: By default, the filename changes to Jazz 2096 Output.pdf.)
13. Click Save.
14. Click the Adobe PDF Preset list arrow, then click [High Quality Print].
15. Click the View PDF after Exporting check box.
16. In the left-hand column, click Compression.

Figure 33 *Completed Skills Review, Part 1*

DESIGN COLLECTION 1-44

Integrating Illustrator, Photoshop, and InDesign

Projects

This book contains a variety of end-of-chapter materials for additional practice and reinforcement. The Skills Review contains hands-on practice exercises that mirror the progressive nature of the lesson material. The chapter concludes with four projects: two Project Builders, one Design Project, and one Portfolio Project. The Project Builders and the Design Project require you to apply the skills you've learned in the chapter. Portfolio Projects encourage you to address and solve challenges based on the content explored in the chapter. Projects you create can be added to your portfolio as proof of your Adobe skills.

What Instructor Resources Are Available with this Book?

The Instructor Resources are Cengage's way of putting the resources and information needed to teach and learn effectively into your hands. All the resources are available for both Macintosh and Windows operating systems. These resources can be found online at: **http://login.cengage.com**. Once you login or create an account, search for the title under 'Add a product to your Instructor Resource Center' using the ISBN. Then select the instructor companion site resources and click 'Add Selected to Instructor Resource Center.'

Instructor's Manual

The Instructor's Manual includes chapter overviews and detailed lecture topics for each chapter, with teaching tips.

Sample Syllabus

The Sample Syllabus includes a suggested syllabus for any course that uses this book.

PowerPoint Presentations

Each chapter has a corresponding PowerPoint presentation that you can use in lectures, distribute to your students, or customize to suit your course.

Data Files for Students

To complete most of the chapters in this book, your students will need Data Files, which are available online. Instruct students to use the Data Files List at the end of this book. This list gives instructions on organizing files.

To access the Data Files for this book, take the following steps:

1. Open your browser and go to http://www.cengagebrain.com.
2. Type the author, title, or ISBN of this book in the Search window. (The ISBN is listed on the back cover.)
3. Click the book title in the list of search results.
4. When the book's main page is displayed, click the Access Now button under Free Materials.
5. To download Data Files, select a chapter number and then click on the Data Files tab on the left navigation bar to download the files.

Solutions to Exercises

Solution Files are Data Files completed with comprehensive sample answers. Use these files to evaluate your students' work. Or distribute them electronically so students can verify their work. Sample solutions to lessons and end-of-chapter material are provided, with the exception of some Portfolio Projects.

Cengage Learning

Cengage Learning Testing Powered by Cognero is a flexible, online system that allows you to:

- Author, edit, and manage test bank content from multiple Cengage Learning solutions
- Create multiple test versions in an instant
- Deliver tests from your LMS, your classroom or wherever you want

Start Right Away!

Cengage Learning Testing Powered by Cognero works on any operating system or browser.

- No special installs or downloads needed
- Create tests from school, home, the coffee shop—anywhere with Internet access

What Will You Find?

- Simplicity at every step. A desktop-inspired interface features drop-down menus and familiar, intuitive tools that take you through content creation and management with ease.
- Full-featured test generator. Create ideal assessments with your choice of 15 question types (including true/false, multiple choice, and essay). Multilanguage support, an equation editor and unlimited metadata help ensure your tests are complete and compliant.
- Cross-compatible capability. Import and export content into other systems.

BRIEF CONTENTS

INDESIGN

Chapter 1   Getting to Know InDesign

Lesson 1   Explore the InDesign Workspace   1-4
2   View and Modify Page Elements   1-12
3   Navigate Through a Document   1-24
4   Work with Objects and Smart Guides   1-28

Chapter 2   Working with Text

Lesson 1   Format Text   2-4
2   Format Paragraphs   2-16
3   Create and Apply Styles   2-24
4   Edit Text   2-30
5   Create Bulleted and Numbered Lists   2-34

Chapter 3   Setting Up a Document

Lesson 1   Create a New Document and Set Up a
Master Page   3-4
2   Create Text on Master Pages   3-24
3   Apply Master Pages to Document Pages   3-34
4   Modify Master Pages and Document
Pages   3-38
5   Place and Thread Text   3-44
6   Create New Sections and Wrap Text   3-50

Chapter 4   Working with Frames

Lesson 1   Align and Distribute Objects on a Page   4-4
2   Stack and Layer Objects   4-20
3   Work with Graphics Frames   4-32
4   Work with Text Frames   4-46

Chapter 5   Working with Color

Lesson 1   Work with Process Colors   5-4
2   Apply Color   5-12
3   Work with Spot Colors   5-24
4   Work with Gradients   5-30

PHOTOSHOP

Chapter 1　　**Getting Started with Adobe Photoshop CC**

Lesson 1　Start Adobe Photoshop CC 2014　1-4

　　2　Learn How to Open and Save an Image　1-8

　　3　Examine the Photoshop Window　1-16

　　4　Close a File and Exit Photoshop　1-24

　　5　Learn About Design Principles and Copyright Rules　1-26

Chapter 2　　**Learning Photoshop Basics**

Lesson 1　Use Organizational and Management Features　2-4

　　2　Use the Layers and History Panels　2-12

　　3　Learn About Photoshop by Using Help　2-16

　　4　View and Print an Image　2-22

Chapter 3　　**Working with Layers**

Lesson 1　Examine and Convert Layers　3-4

　　2　Add and Delete Layers　3-8

　　3　Add a Selection from One Image to Another　3-14

　　4　Organize Layers with Layer Groups and Colors　3-18

Chapter 4　　**Making Selections**

Lesson 1　Make a Selection Using Shapes　4-4

　　2　Modify a Marquee　4-14

　　3　Select Using Color and Modify a Selection　4-18

　　4　Add a Vignette Effect to a Selection　4-24

Chapter 5　　**Incorporating Color Techniques**

Lesson 1　Work with Color to Transform an Image　5-4

　　2　Use the Color Picker and the Swatches Panel　5-10

　　3　Place a Border Around an Image　5-16

　　4　Blend Colors Using the Gradient Tool　5-18

　　5　Add Color to a Grayscale Image　5-22

　　6　Use Filters, Opacity, and Blending Modes　5-26

　　7　Match Colors　5-32

Chapter 6　　**Placing Type in an Image**

Lesson 1　Learn About Type and How it is Created　6-4

　　2　Change Spacing and Adjust Baseline Shift　6-8

　　3　Use the Drop Shadow Style　6-12

　　4　Apply Anti-Aliasing to Type　6-16

　　5　Modify Type with Bevel and Emboss and Extrude to 3D　6-20

　　6　Apply Special Effects to Type Using Filters　6-24

　　7　Create Text on a Path　6-28

ILLUSTRATOR

Chapter 1   Getting to Know Illustrator

Lesson 1   Explore the Illustrator Workspace 1-4
2   View and Modify Artboard Elements 1-14
3   Work with Objects and Smart Guides 1-26
4   Create Basic Shapes 1-40
5   Apply Fill and Stroke Colors to Objects 1-44
6   Select, Move, and Align Objects 1-48
7   Transform Objects 1-52
8   Make Direct Selections 1-58
9   Work with Multiple Artboards 1-66

Chapter 2   Creating Text and Gradients

Lesson 1   Create Point Text 2-4
2   Flow Text into an Object 2-10
3   Position Text on a Path 2-14
4   Manipulate Text with the Touch Type Tool 2-18
5   Create Colors and Gradients 2-22
6   Apply Colors and Gradients to Text 2-28
7   Adjust a Gradient and Create a Drop Shadow 2-32
8   Apply Gradients to Strokes 2-38

Chapter 3   Drawing and Composing an Illustration

Lesson 1   Draw Straight Lines 3-4
2   Draw Curved Lines 3-10
3   Draw Elements of an Illustration 3-18
4   Apply Attributes to Objects 3-24
5   Assemble an Illustration 3-28
6   Stroke Objects for Artistic Effect 3-30
7   Use Image Trace 3-36
8   Use the Live Paint Bucket tool 3-46
9   Explore Alternate Drawing Techniques 3-58

Chapter 4   Transforming and Distorting Objects

Lesson 1   Transform Objects 4-4
2   Offset and Outline Paths 4-16
3   Create Compound Paths 4-20
4   Work with the Pathfinder Panel 4-24
5   Apply Round Corners to Objects 4-36
6   Use the Shape Builder Tool 4-42
7   Create Clipping Masks 4-46

Chapter 5   Working with Layers

Lesson 1   Create and Modify Layers 5-4
2   Manipulate Layered Artwork 5-12
3   Work with Layered Artwork 5-20
4   Create a Clipping Set 5-26

INTEGRATION

Chapter 1   Integrating Illustrator, Photoshop, and Indesign

Lesson 1   Copy and Paste from Illustrator to Photoshop 1-4
2   Export Layers from Illustrator to Photoshop 1-8
3   Create a Chisel Hard Emboss Layer Style 1-12
4   Create a Stamp Visible Layer 1-16
5   Create a Smooth Emboss Layer Style 1-18
6   Create and Apply a Gradient Overlay to a Layer Style 1-22
7   Create a Pillow Emboss Layer Style 1-26
8   Copy Layer Styles Between Layers 1-30
9   Add an Outer Glow Layer Style 1-32
10   Apply Blending Modes 1-34
11   Create an InDesign Output File 1-36

Glossary 1
Index 17

CONTENTS

CONTENTS

CHAPTER 1: GETTING TO KNOW INDESIGN

INTRODUCTION 1-2

LESSON 1
Explore the InDesign Workspace 1-4

Looking at the InDesign Workspace 1-4
Exploring the Tools Panel 1-5
Working with Panels 1-6
Tasks   Explore the Tools panel 1-9
            Work with panels 1-10

LESSON 2
View and Modify Page Elements 1-12

Using the Zoom Tool 1-12
Accessing the Zoom Tool 1-12
Using the Hand Tool 1-13
Working with Rulers, Grids, and Guides 1-14
Hiding and Showing Frame Edges 1-15
Choosing Screen Modes 1-15
Understanding Preferences 1-15
Working with Multiple Open Documents 1-16
Tasks   Use the Zoom tool and the Hand tool 1-17
            Hide and show rulers and set units and increments
                preferences 1-18
            Hide and show ruler guides, frame edges, and the
                document grid 1-19
            Toggle between screen modes 1-21
            Work with multiple documents 1-22

LESSON 3
Navigate Through a Document 1-24

Navigating to Pages in a Document 1-24
Applying Thumbnail Color Labels 1-25
Tasks   Navigate to pages in a document 1-26
            Apply color labels to page thumbnails 1-27

LESSON 4
Work with Objects and Smart Guides 1-28

Resizing Objects 1-28
Copying Objects 1-29
Hiding, Locking and Grouping Objects 1-29
Working with Smart Guides 1-30
Tasks   Resize a text object 1-31
            Copy and duplicate objects 1-32
            Hide, lock, and group objects 1-33
            Work with Smart Guides 1-35

CHAPTER 2: WORKING WITH TEXT

INTRODUCTION 2-2

LESSON 1
Format Text 2-4

Creating Text 2-4
Using the Character Panel 2-4
Understanding Leading 2-5
Scaling Text Horizontally and Vertically 2-6
Kerning and Tracking Text 2-6
Creating Superscript Characters 2-7
Creating Subscript Characters 2-7
Underlining Text 2-7
Searching for Fonts on the Character Panel 2-8
Tasks   Modify text attributes 2-11
              Track and kern text 2-12
              Create superscript characters 2-13
              Underline text 2-13
              Use enhanced font search options 2-14

LESSON 2
Format Paragraphs 2-16

Using the Paragraph Panel 2-16
Avoiding Typographic Problems 2-18
Understanding Returns 2-18
Tasks   Use the Paragraph panel and Character panel to
              modify leading and alignment 2-20
              Apply vertical spacing between paragraphs 2-21
              Apply paragraph indents 2-22
              Apply drop caps and soft returns 2-23

LESSON 3
Create and Apply Styles 2-24

Working with Character and Paragraph Styles 2-24
Choosing the Next Style 2-25
Using Quick Apply 2-25
Tasks   Create character styles 2-26
              Apply character styles 2-27
              Create paragraph styles 2-28
              Apply paragraph styles 2-29

LESSON 4
Edit Text 2-30

Using the Find/Change Command 2-30
Checking Spelling 2-30
Using Dynamic Spell Checking 2-31
Correcting Text Automatically 2-31
Tasks   Use the Find/Change command 2-32
              Check spelling 2-33

LESSON 5
Create Bulleted and Numbered Lists 2-34

Creating Bulleted and Numbered Lists 2-34
Modifying Bulleted and Numbered Lists 2-34
Tasks   Create a bulleted and a numbered list 2-36
              Convert numbers to text 2-37

INTRODUCTION 3-2

LESSON 1
Create a New Document and Set Up a Master Page 3-4

Creating a New Document 3-4
Setting the Starting Page Number 3-5
Modifying Margins and Columns 3-6
Understanding Master Pages 3-6
Creating Master Items on Master Pages 3-7
Creating Guides 3-7
Changing the Color of Guides, Margins, and Columns 3-8
Locking Column Guides 3-8
Choosing Default Colors for Guides, Margins, and
    Columns 3-8
Using the Transform Panel 3-8
Using the Control Panel 3-9
Using the Line Tool 3-10
Transforming Objects 3-10
Using the Transform Again Command 3-11
Tasks   View a multi-page document 3-12
        Create a new document 3-12
        Modify margins and the number of columns on a
            master page 3-14
        Add guides to a master page 3-15
        Create placeholder text frames 3-17
        Change the color of guides, margins, and
            columns 3-18
        Create color tint frames 3-19
        Use the Line tool 3-21
        Use the Transform Again command 3-22

LESSON 2
Create Text on Master Pages 3-24

Creating a New Master Page 3-24
Loading Master Pages 3-25
Creating Automatic Page Numbering 3-25
Inserting Space Between Characters 3-26
Inserting Em Dashes and En Dashes 3-26
Creating a New Master Page Based on Another 3-27
Tasks   Add placeholders for headlines 3-28
        Create automatic page numbering and insert white
            space between characters 3-29
        Create a new master page spread based on another
            master page spread 3-30
        Create a new blank master page spread 3-32

LESSON 3
Apply Master Pages to Document Pages 3-34

Applying Master Pages to Document Pages 3-34
Tasks   Apply master pages to document pages 3-36

LESSON 4
Modify Master Pages and Document Pages 3-38

Modifying Master Pages 3-38
Overriding Master Items on Document Pages 3-38
Detaching Master Items 3-39
Tasks   Override master items on a document page 3-40
        Modify master items on a master page 3-40
        Remove local overrides and detach master
            items 3-43

LESSON 5
Place and Thread Text 3-44

Placing Text 3-44
Threading Text 3-44
Tasks   Place text on document pages 3-46
        Thread text through multiple text frames 3-48

LESSON 6
Create New Sections and Wrap Text 3-50

Creating Sections in a Document 3-50
Wrapping Text Around a Frame 3-51
Tasks   Create sections in a document 3-52
        Wrap text around a frame 3-54

INTRODUCTION 4-2

LESSON 1
Align and Distribute Objects on a Page 4-4

Applying Fills and Strokes 4-4
Using the Step and Repeat Command 4-6
Aligning Objects 4-7
Distributing Objects 4-8
Using the Live Distribute Technique 4-10
Using the Gap Tool 4-11
Tasks Apply fills and strokes 4-12
    Use the Step and Repeat command 4-13
    Use the Live Distribute technique 4-14
    Use the Gap tool 4-16
    Align objects 4-17
    Distribute objects 4-18

LESSON 2
Stack and Layer Objects 4-20

Understanding the Stacking Order 4-20
Understanding Layers 4-20
Working with Layers 4-21
Manipulating Layers and Objects on Layers 4-22
Selecting Artwork on Layers 4-23
Selecting Objects Behind Other Objects 4-23
Tasks Use the Arrange commands to change the stacking
    order of objects 4-24
    Create new layers on the Layers panel 4-26
    Position objects on layers 4-27
    Change the order of layers on the Layers panel 4-29
    Group items on layers 4-30

LESSON 3
Work with Graphics Frames 4-32

Placing Graphics in a Document 4-32
The Graphic vs. the Graphics Frame 4-33
Selecting Graphics and Frames 4-33
Using the Content Indicator 4-34
Moving a Graphic Within a Frame 4-34
Copying and Pasting a Graphic 4-35
Resizing a Graphic 4-35
Using the Fitting Commands 4-36
Wrapping Text Around Graphics with Clipping Paths 4-36
Tasks Place graphics in a document 4-38
    Move a graphic in a graphics frame 4-39
    Resize graphics frames and graphics 4-41
    Wrap text around a graphic 4-43

LESSON 4
Work with Text Frames 4-46

Semi-Autoflowing Text 4-46
Autoflowing Text 4-46
Inserting a Column Break 4-47
Inserting a "Continued on page..." Notation 4-47
Tasks Autoflow text 4-49
    Reflow text 4-50
    Add a column break 4-52
    Insert a page continuation notation 4-53

CHAPTER 5: WORKING WITH COLOR

INTRODUCTION 5-2

LESSON 1
Work with Process Colors 5-4

Understanding Process Colors 5-4
Understanding Tints 5-4
Creating Tint Swatches 5-6
Working with Unnamed Colors 5-6
Tasks   Create process color swatches 5-8
            Create a tint swatch and modify the original color
                swatch 5-9
            Use the Color panel 5-10
            Save an unnamed color on the Swatches panel 5-11

LESSON 2
Apply Color 5-12

Applying Color to Objects 5-12
Understanding the Paper Swatch 5-14
Applying Color to Text 5-15
Creating Black Shadow Text 5-16
Modifying and Deleting Swatches 5-16
Tasks   Drag and drop colors onto objects 5-18
            Use the Swap Fill and Stroke and Default Fill and
                Stroke buttons 5-19
            Apply color to text 5-20
            Create black shadow text 5-21
            Modify and delete swatches 5-23

LESSON 3
Work with Spot Colors 5-24

Understanding Spot Colors 5-24
Creating Spot Color Swatches 5-25
Importing Graphics with Spot Colors 5-25
Tasks   Create a spot color swatch 5-26
            Import graphics with spot colors 5-27

LESSON 4
Work with Gradients 5-30

Creating Gradients 5-30
Applying Gradients 5-32
Modifying a Gradient Fill Using the Gradient Panel 5-32
Tasks   Create a linear gradient swatch 5-33
            Create a radial gradient swatch 5-34
            Apply gradient swatches and use the Gradient
                Swatch tool 5-35
            Use the Gradient Swatch tool to extend a gradient
                across multiple objects and modify a
                gradient 5-36

INTRODUCTION 1-2

Using Photoshop and the Creative Cloud 1-2
Understanding Platform User Interfaces 1-2
Understanding Sources 1-2

LESSON 1
Start Adobe Photoshop CC 2014 1-4

Defining Image-Editing Software 1-4
Understanding Images 1-4
Using Photoshop Features 1-4
Starting Photoshop and Creating a File 1-5
Tasks Start Photoshop (Windows 7, 8, or 8.1) 1-6
Start Photoshop (Mac OS) 1-7

LESSON 2
Learn How to Open and Save an Image 1-8

Opening and Saving Files 1-8
Customizing How You Open Files 1-8
Browsing Through Files 1-9
Understanding the Power of Bridge 1-10
Getting There with Mini Bridge 1-10
Using Save As Versus Save 1-10
Getting images into Photoshop 1-11
Tasks Open a file using the Menu bar 1-12
Open a file using the Folders panel in Adobe
Bridge 1-12
Open a file using Mini Bridge 1-13
Use the Save As command 1-13
Change from Tabbed to Floating Documents 1-14
Rate and filter with Bridge 1-15

LESSON 3
Examine the Photoshop Window 1-16

Learning About the Workspace 1-16
Finding Tools Everywhere 1-17
Using Tool Shortcut Keys 1-18
Customizing Your Environment 1-18
Tasks Select a tool 1-19
Select a tool from the Tool Preset picker 1-20
Add a tool to the Tool Preset picker 1-21
Change the default display, theme color, and
document display 1-21
Show and hide panels 1-22
Create a customized workspace 1-23

LESSON 4
Close a File and Exit Photoshop 1-24

Concluding Your Work Session 1-24
Closing Versus Exiting 1-24
Task Close a file and exit Photoshop 1-25

LESSON 5
**Learn About Design Principles and Copyright
Rules 1-26**

Print Design Versus Web Design 1-26
Composition 101 1-26
Arranging Elements 1-27
Overcoming the Fear of White Space 1-27
Balancing Objects 1-28
Considering Ethical Implications 1-28
Understanding Copyright Terms 1-29
Licensing Your Work with Creative Commons 1-31

CHAPTER 2: LEARNING PHOTOSHOP BASICS

INTRODUCTION 2-2

Working Magic with Photoshop 2-2
Using Management Tools 2-2
Learning to Love Layers 2-2
Finding Help when You Need It 2-2
Viewing and Printing 2-2

LESSON 1
Use Organizational and Management Features 2-4

Learning About the Creative Cloud 2-4
Managing the Creative Cloud 2-4
Using Behance 2-6
Using Adobe Exchange 2-7
Adobe Typekit 2-7
Reusing Housekeeping Tasks in Bridge and Mini Bridge 2-8
Understanding Metadata 2-8
Assigning Keywords to an Image 2-8
Tasks   Assigning a keyword 2-10
          Filtering with Bridge 2-11

LESSON 2
Use the Layers and History Panels 2-12

Learning About Layers 2-12
Understanding the Layers Panel 2-12
Filtering Layers 2-12
Displaying and Hiding Layers 2-13
Using the History Panel 2-13
Tasks   Hide and display a layer 2-14
          Move a layer on the Layers panel and delete a state
          on the History panel 2-15

LESSON 3
Learn About Photoshop by Using Help 2-16

Understanding the Power of Help 2-16
Using Help Topics 2-16
Tasks   Find information in Adobe reference titles 2-18
          Get help and support 2-19
          Find information using Search 2-20
          Learning what's new in Photoshop CC 2-21

LESSON 4
View and Print an Image 2-22

Getting a Closer Look 2-22
Viewing an Image in Multiple Views 2-22
Printing Your Image 2-23
Understanding Color Handling in Printing 2-23
Using the Photoshop File Info Dialog Box 2-24
Tasks   Use the Zoom tool 2-25
          Modify print settings 2-26
          Create a PDF with Bridge 2-27
          Save a PDF output file 2-28
          Create a Web Gallery with Bridge 2-29

CHAPTER 3: WORKING WITH LAYERS

INTRODUCTION 3-2

Layers Are Everything 3-2
Understanding the Importance of Layers 3-2
Using Layers to Modify an Image 3-2

LESSON 1
Examine and Convert Layers 3-4

Learning About the Layers Panel 3-4
Recognizing Layer Types 3-4
Organizing Layers 3-5
Converting Layers 3-6
Task   Convert an image layer into a Background layer 3-7

LESSON 2
Add and Delete Layers 3-8

Adding Layers to an Image 3-8
Generating Assets from Layers 3-9
Naming a Layer 3-10
Isolation Mode Layer Filtering 3-10
Deleting Layers from an Image 3-11
Tasks   Modifying a workspace 3-12
            Add a layer using the Layer menu 3-12
            Delete a layer 3-13
            Add a layer using the Layers panel 3-13

LESSON 3
Add a Selection from One Image to Another 3-14

Understanding Selections 3-14
Making and Moving a Selection 3-14
Understanding Color Range Command 3-15
Defringing Layer Contents 3-15
Tasks   Make a color range selection 3-16
            Move a selection to another image 3-17
            Defringe the selection 3-17

LESSON 4
Organize Layers with Layer Groups and Colors 3-18

Understanding Layer Groups 3-18
Organizing Layers into Groups 3-18
Identifying a Layer with Color 3-19
Flattening an Image 3-19
Understanding Layer Comps 3-20
Using Layer Comps 3-20
Tasks   Create a layer group 3-21
            Move layers to the layer group 3-21
            Rename a layer and adjust opacity 3-22
            Create layer comps 3-22
            Flatten an image 3-23

CHAPTER 4: MAKING SELECTIONS

INTRODUCTION 4-2

Combining Images 4-2
Understanding Selection Tools 4-2
Understanding Which Selection Tool to Use 4-2
Combining Imagery 4-2

LESSON 1
Make a Selection Using Shapes 4-4

Selecting by Shape 4-4
Creating a Selection 4-4
Using Fastening Points 4-5
Selecting, Deselecting, and Reselecting 4-5
Placing a Selection 4-6
Using Guides 4-7
Tasks   Create a selection with the Rectangular
              Marquee tool 4-9
          Position a selection with the Move tool 4-10
          Deselect a selection 4-11
          Create a selection with the Magnetic Lasso tool 4-12
          Move a complex selection to an existing image 4-13

LESSON 2
Modify a Marquee 4-14

Changing the Size of a Marquee 4-14
Modifying a Marquee 4-14
Moving a Marquee 4-14
Using the Quick Selection Tool 4-15
Tasks   Move and enlarge a marquee 4-16
          Use the Quick Selection tool 4-17

LESSON 3
Select Using Color and Modify a Selection 4-18

Selecting with Color 4-18
Using the Magic Wand Tool 4-18
Using the Color Range Command 4-19
Transforming a Selection 4-19
Understanding the Healing Brush Tool 4-19
Using the Healing Brush Tool 4-19
Tasks   Select using Color Range 4-20
          Select using the Magic Wand and the Quick
              Selection tools 4-21
          Flip a selection 4-22
          Fix imperfections with the Healing Brush tool 4-23

LESSON 4
Add a Vignette Effect to a Selection 4-24

Understanding Vignettes 4-24
Creating a Vignette 4-24
Task   Create a vignette 4-25

INTRODUCTION 5-2

Using Color 5-2
Understanding Color Modes and Color Models 5-2
Displaying and Printing Images 5-2

LESSON 1
Work with Color to Transform an Image 5-4

Learning About Color Models 5-4
Lab Color Mode 5-5
HSB Color Model 5-5
RGB Model 5-5
CMYK Model 5-6
Understanding the Bitmap and Grayscale Modes 5-6
Changing Foreground and Background Colors 5-6
Tasks   Set the default foreground and background
            colors 5-7
          Change the background color using the Color
            panel 5-8
          Change the background color using the
            Eyedropper tool 5-9

LESSON 2
Use the Color Picker and the Swatches Panel 5-10

Making Selections from the Color Picker 5-10
Using the Swatches Panel 5-11
Tasks   Select a color using the Color Picker dialog box 5-12
          Select a color using the Swatches panel 5-12
          Add a new color to the Swatches panel 5-13
          Use Kuler from a web browser 5-14
          Use Kuler from Photoshop 5-15

LESSON 3
Place a Border Around an Image 5-16

Emphasizing an Image 5-16
Locking Transparent Pixels 5-16
Task   Create a border 5-17

LESSON 4
Blend Colors Using the Gradient Tool 5-18

Understanding Gradients 5-18
Using the Gradient Tool 5-18
Customizing Gradients 5-19
Tasks   Create a gradient from a sample color 5-20
          Apply a gradient fill 5-21

LESSON 5
Add Color to a Grayscale Image 5-22

Colorizing Options 5-22
Converting Grayscale and Color Modes 5-22
Tweaking Adjustments 5-22
Colorizing a Grayscale Image 5-23
Tasks   Change the color mode 5-24
          Colorize a grayscale image 5-25

LESSON 6
Use Filters, Opacity, and Blending Modes 5-26

Manipulating an Image 5-26
Understanding Filters 5-26
Choosing Blending Modes 5-27
Understanding Blending Mode Components 5-27
Softening Filter Effects 5-27
Balancing Colors 5-28
Tasks   Adjust brightness and contrast 5-29
          Work with a filter, a blending mode, and an
            opacity setting 5-30
          Adjust color balance 5-31

LESSON 7
Match Colors 5-32

Finding the Right Color 5-32
Using Selections to Match Colors 5-32
Task   Match a color 5-33

INTRODUCTION 6-2

Learning About Type 6-2
Understanding the Purpose of Type 6-2
Getting the Most Out of Type 6-2

LESSON 1
Learn About Type and How It Is Created 6-4

Introducing Type Types 6-4
Getting to Know Font Families 6-4
Measuring Type Size 6-4
Acquiring Fonts 6-5
Tasks   Create and modify type 6-6
            Change type color using an existing color in
                the image 6-7

LESSON 2
Change Spacing and Adjust Baseline Shift 6-8

Adjusting Letter Spacing 6-8
Understanding Character and Line Spacing 6-8
Using the Character Panel 6-8
Understanding Type Styles 6-8
Adjusting the Baseline Shift 6-9
Tasks   Kern characters 6-10
            Shift the baseline 6-11

LESSON 3
Use the Drop Shadow Style 6-12

Adding Effects to Type 6-12
Applying a Style 6-13
Using the Drop Shadow 6-13
Controlling a Drop Shadow 6-13
Tasks   Add a drop shadow 6-14
            Modify drop shadow settings 6-15

LESSON 4
Apply Anti-Aliasing to Type 6-16

Eliminating the "Jaggies" 6-16
Knowing When to Apply Anti-Aliasing 6-16
Understanding Anti-Aliasing 6-17
Tasks   Apply anti-aliasing 6-18
            Undo anti-aliasing 6-19

LESSON 5
Modify Type with Bevel and Emboss
and Extrude to 3D 6-20

Using the Bevel and Emboss Style 6-20
Understanding Bevel and Emboss Settings 6-20
Learning About 3D Extrusion 6-21
Tasks   Add the Bevel and Emboss style with the
                Layer menu 6-22
            Modify Bevel and Emboss settings and apply
                3D Extrusion 6-23

LESSON 6
Apply Special Effects to Type Using Filters 6-24

Understanding Filters 6-24
Producing Distortions 6-24
Using Relief 6-24
Blurring Imagery 6-24
Tasks   Apply a filter to a type layer 6-26
            Modify filter settings 6-27

LESSON 7
Create Text on a Path 6-28

Understanding Text on a Path 6-28
Creating Text on a Path 6-28
Task   Create a path and add type 6-29

INTRODUCTION
Getting to Know Illustrator 1-2

LESSON 1
Explore the Illustrator Workspace 1-4

Looking at the Illustrator Workspace 1-4
Exploring the Tools Panel 1-5
Working with Panels 1-8
Creating Customized Tools Panels 1-10
Tasks   Explore the Tools panel 1-11
            Work with panels 1-12

LESSON 2
View and Modify Artboard Elements 1-14

Using the Zoom Tool 1-14
Accessing the Zoom Tool 1-14
Using the Hand Tool 1-16
Working with Rulers, Grids, and Guides 1-16
Hiding and Showing Selection Marks 1-17
Choosing Screen Modes 1-18
Understanding Preferences 1-19
Working with Multiple Open Documents 1-19
Using Shortcut Keys to Execute View Commands 1-20
Tasks   Use the Zoom tool and the Hand tool 1-21
            Hide and show rulers and set units and increments
                preferences 1-22
            Hide and show ruler guides, selection marks, and the
                document grid 1-23
            Toggle screen modes and work with multiple
                documents 1-24

LESSON 3
Work with Objects and Smart Guides 1-26

Working with Preferences 1-26
Resizing Objects 1-27
Copying Objects 1-28
Hiding, Locking, and Grouping Objects 1-29
Working with Smart Guides 1-30
Tasks   Set essential preferences 1-31
            Resize objects 1-32
            Copy and duplicate objects 1-34
            Hide, lock, and group objects 1-37
            Work with smart guides 1-39

LESSON 4
Create Basic Shapes 1-40

Getting Ready to Draw 1-40
Bitmap Images and Vector Graphics 1-40
Tasks   Use the Rectangle tool 1-42
            Use the Rectangle dialog box 1-43

LESSON 5
Apply Fill and Stroke Colors to Objects 1-44

Activating the Fill or Stroke 1-44
Applying Color with the Swatches Panel 1-45
Tasks   Apply fill and stroke colors 1-46

LESSON 6
Select, Move, and Align Objects 1-48

Selecting and Moving Objects 1-48
Making a Marquee Selection 1-49
Tasks   Move and position objects with precision 1-50
            Duplicate objects using drag and drop 1-51

LESSON 7
Transform Objects 1-52

Transforming Objects 1-52
Repeating Transformations 1-53
Tasks   Use the Scale and Rotate tools 1-54
            Use the Transform Again command 1-55
            Create a star and a triangle, and use the Reflect
                tool 1-56

LESSON 8
Make Direct Selections 1-58

Using the Direct Selection Tool 1-58
Adding Anchor Points 1-58
Turning Objects into Guides 1-59
Working with the Stacking Order 1-60
Tasks   Make guides and direct selections 1-61
            Add anchor points 1-62
            Use the Draw Behind drawing mode 1-63
            Create a simple special effect utilizing a direct
                selection 1-65

LESSON 9
Work with Multiple Artboards 1-66

Understanding Multiple Artboards 1-66
Managing Multiple Artboards 1-66
Creating, Editing, and Arranging Artboards 1-69
Printing Multiple Artboards 1-70
Using the Artboards Panel 1-71
Pasting Artwork on Multiple Artboards 1-71
Tasks   Create a new document with
                multiple artboards 1-72
            Create and name artboards 1-73
            Resize and arrange artboards 1-76
            Paste artwork between artboards 1-77

CHAPTER 2: CREATING TEXT AND GRADIENTS

INTRODUCTION
Creating Text and Gradients 2-2

Working with Text 2-2
Creating and Applying Gradient Fills 2-2

LESSON 1
Create Point Text 2-4

Creating Text 2-4
Formatting Text 2-4
Adjusting and Applying Hyphenation 2-5
Hiding Objects While Working with Text 2-5
Tasks Create text 2-6
      Format text 2-7
      Track and kern text 2-8
      Create vertical type 2-9

LESSON 2
Flow Text into an Object 2-10

Filling an Object with Text 2-10
Tasks Fill an object with text 2-12
      Format text in an object 2-12

LESSON 3
Position Text on a Path 2-14

Using the Path Type Tools 2-14
Tasks Flow text on a path 2-16
      Move text along a path 2-16

LESSON 4
Manipulate Text with the Touch Type Tool 2-18

Using the Touch Type Tool 2-18
Entering the Touch Type Tool 2-19
Tasks Use the Touch Type tool 2-20

LESSON 5
Create Colors and Gradients 2-22

Using the Gradient Panel 2-22
Using the Color Panel 2-23
Changing Color Stops 2-23
Adding Colors and Gradients to the Swatches Panel 2-23
Tasks Create a gradient and a color 2-24
      Add gradients and colors to the Swatches panel 2-26

LESSON 6
Apply Colors and Gradients to Text 2-28

Applying Fills and Strokes to Text 2-28
Converting Text to Outlines 2-28
Tasks Apply color to text 2-30
      Create outlines and apply a gradient fill 2-31

LESSON 7
Adjust a Gradient and Create a Drop Shadow 2-32

Using the Gradient Tool with Linear Gradient Fills 2-32
Applying Gradient Fills to Multiple Objects 2-33
Using the Gradient Tool with Radial Gradient Fills 2-34
Adding a Drop Shadow 2-35
Tasks Use the Gradient tool 2-36
      Add a drop shadow to text 2-36

LESSON 8
Apply Gradients to Strokes 2-38

Applying a Gradient to a Stroke 2-38
Tasks Apply gradients to strokes 2-40

INTRODUCTION
Drawing and Composing an Illustration 3-2

Drawing in Illustrator 3-2

LESSON 1
Draw Straight Lines 3-4

Viewing Objects on the Artboard 3-4
Drawing Straight Segments with the Pen Tool 3-4
Aligning and Joining Anchor Points 3-5
Tasks   Create new views 3-6
          Draw straight lines 3-7
          Close a path and align the anchor points 3-8
          Join anchor points 3-9

LESSON 2
Draw Curved Lines 3-10

Defining Properties of Curved Lines 3-10
Converting Anchor Points 3-12
Toggling Between the Pen Tool and Selection Tools 3-13
Tasks   Draw and edit a curved line 3-14
          Convert anchor points 3-15
          Draw a line with curved and straight segments 3-16
          Reverse direction while drawing 3-17

LESSON 3
Draw Elements of an Illustration 3-18

Starting an Illustration 3-18
Drawing from Scratch 3-18
Tracing a Scanned Image 3-19
Tasks   Draw a closed path using smooth points 3-20
          Begin and end a path with a corner point 3-21
          Redirect a path while drawing 3-22
          Place a scanned image 3-23

LESSON 4
Apply Attributes to Objects 3-24

Using the Eyedropper Tool 3-24
Adding a Fill to an Open Path 3-25
Tasks   Apply new attributes to closed paths 3-26
          Copy attributes with the Eyedropper tool 3-27

LESSON 5
Assemble an Illustration 3-28

Assembling an Illustration 3-28
Tasks   Assemble the illustration 3-29

LESSON 6
Stroke Objects for Artistic Effect 3-30

Defining Joins and Caps 3-30
Defining the Miter Limit 3-31
Creating a Dashed Stroke 3-31
Improving the Appearance of a
    Dashed Stroke 3-32
Creating Pseudo-Stroke Effects 3-32
Tasks   Modify stroke attributes 3-33
          Create a dashed stroke 3-34
          Create pseudo-strokes 3-35

LESSON 7
Use Image Trace 3-36

Using Image Trace 3-36
Tracing a Line-Art Sketch 3-39
Tracing a Photograph 3-40
Expanding a Traced Graphic 3-41
Embedding Placed Images 3-43
Tasks   Use Image Trace to trace a sketch 3-44
          Use Image Trace to trace a photo 3-45

LESSON 8
Use the Live Paint Bucket Tool 3-46

Using the Live Paint Features 3-46
Live Painting Regions 3-48
Painting Virtual Regions 3-49
Inserting an Object into a Live Paint Group 3-50
Expanding a Live Paint Group 3-50
Live Painting Edges 3-51
Tasks   Use the Live Paint Bucket tool 3-52
          Use the Live Paint Bucket tool to paint an
              illustration 3-55

LESSON 9
Explore Alternate Drawing Techniques 3-58

Reshape Path Segments with the Anchor Point Tool 3-58
Drawing with the Pencil Tool 3-59
Tasks   Reshape path segments with the Anchor
              Point tool 3-62
          Draw with the Pencil tool 3-63

CHAPTER 4: TRANSFORMING AND DISTORTING OBJECTS

INTRODUCTION
Transforming and Distorting Objects 4-2

Putting it All Together 4-2

LESSON 1
Transform Objects 4-4

Defining the Transform Tools 4-4
Defining the Point of Origin 4-5
Working with the Transform Again Command 4-7
Using the Transform Each Command 4-7
Using the Free Transform Tool 4-8
Using the Transform Panel 4-9
Tasks   Rotate an object around a defined point 4-10
          Use the Shear tool 4-12
          Use the Reflect tool 4-13
          Use the Free Transform tool to distort in
              perspective 4-14

LESSON 2
Offset and Outline Paths 4-16

Using the Offset Path Command 4-16
Using the Outline Stroke Command 4-17
Tasks   Offset a path 4-18
          Convert a stroked path to a closed path 4-19

LESSON 3
Create Compound Paths 4-20

Defining a Compound Path 4-20
Tasks   Create compound paths 4-22
          Create special effects with compound paths 4-23

LESSON 4
Work with the Pathfinder Panel 4-24

Defining a Compound Shape 4-24
Understanding Essential Shape Modes and Pathfinders 4-24
Using the Pathfinder Panel 4-26
Applying Shape Modes 4-26
Releasing and Expanding Compound Shapes 4-27
Tasks   Apply the Unite shape mode 4-28
          Apply the Minus Front shape mode 4-29
          Apply the Intersect shape mode 4-31
          Apply the Divide pathfinder 4-32
          Create compound shapes using the Pathfinder
              panel 4-33
          Create special effects with compound shapes 4-34

LESSON 5
Apply Round Corners to Objects 4-36

Applying Round Corners 4-36
Tasks   Apply corners to an object 4-38
          Apply specific corner measurements
              to individual points on an object 4-40

LESSON 6
Use the Shape Builder Tool 4-42

Understanding the Shape Builder Tool 4-42
Tasks   Create objects with the Shape Builder tool 4-44
          Delete objects with the Shape Builder tool 4-45

LESSON 7
Create Clipping Masks 4-46

Defining a Clipping Mask 4-46
Using Multiple Objects as a Clipping Mask 4-46
Creating Masked Effects 4-47
Using the Draw Inside Drawing Mode 4-47
Tasks   Create a clipping mask 4-48
          Apply a fill to a clipping mask 4-49
          Use text as a clipping mask 4-51
          Use a clipping mask for special effects 4-51
          Use the Draw Inside drawing mode 4-52

CHAPTER 5: WORKING WITH LAYERS

INTRODUCTION
Working with Layers 5-2

Designing with Layers 5-2

LESSON 1
Create and Modify Layers 5-4

Creating Layers and Sublayers 5-4
Duplicating Layers 5-5
Setting Layer Options 5-6
Selecting Artwork on Layers and Sublayers 5-6
Selecting All Artwork on a Layer 5-6
Tasks   Create a new layer 5-8
          Name a layer and change a layer's selection
              color 5-9
          Select items on a layer and lock a layer 5-10
          Show and hide layers 5-11

LESSON 2
Manipulate Layered Artwork 5-12

Changing the Order of Layers and Sublayers 5-12
Merging Layers 5-12
Defining Sublayers 5-12
Working with Sublayers 5-13
Dragging Objects Between Layers 5-13
Tasks   Change the hierarchy of layers 5-14
          Merge layers 5-15
          Work with sublayers 5-16
          Create new sublayers 5-17
          Move objects between layers 5-18

LESSON 3
Work with Layered Artwork 5-20

Using the View Buttons on the Layers Panel 5-20
Importing a Photoshop File with Layers 5-20
Locating an Object on the Layers Panel 5-21
Reversing the Order of Layers 5-21
Making Layers Nonprintable 5-21
Exporting Illustrator Layers to Photoshop 5-21
Tasks   Explore view options on the Layers panel 5-22
          Locate, duplicate, and delete layers 5-23
          Dim placed images 5-24
          Exclude specific layers from printing 5-25

LESSON 4
Create a Clipping Set 5-26

Working with Clipping Sets 5-26
Flattening Artwork 5-26
Tasks   Create clipping sets 5-27
          Copy a clipping mask and flatten artwork 5-28

INTRODUCTION 1-2

LESSON 1
Copy and Paste from Illustrator to Photoshop 1-4

Moving Graphics Between Programs 1-4
Task Copy and paste from Illustrator to Photoshop 1-5

LESSON 2
Export Layers from Illustrator to Photoshop 1-8

Task Export layers from Illustrator to Photoshop 1-9

LESSON 3
Create a Chisel Hard Emboss Layer Style 1-12

Task Create a Chisel Hard Emboss layer style 1-13

LESSON 4
Create a Stamp Visible Layer 1-16

Task Create a Stamp Visible layer 1-17

LESSON 5
Create a Smooth Emboss Layer Style 1-18

Task Create a Smooth Emboss layer style 1-19

LESSON 6
Create and Apply a Gradient Overlay to a Layer Style 1-22

Task Create and apply a Gradient Overlay to a layer style 1-23

LESSON 7
Create a Pillow Emboss Layer Style 1-26

Task Create a Pillow Emboss layer style 1-27

LESSON 8
Copy Layer Styles Between Layers 1-30

Task Copy layer styles between layers 1-31

LESSON 9
Add an Outer Glow Layer Style 1-32

Task Add an Outer Glow layer style 1-33

LESSON 10
Apply Blending Modes 1-34

Task Add adjustment layers and blending modes 1-35

LESSON 11
Create an InDesign Output File 1-36

Tasks Create a new InDesign document 1-37
Import artwork 1-38
Export a PDF 1-39

GLOSSARY 1

INDEX 17

InDesign

Measurements

Text attributes are given in points. Measurements on the artboard and measurements referring to an object are given in inches, not points or picas. In order to follow the exercises, it's important that the General Units Preference in the Preferences dialog box be set to Inches. To set this preference, click Edit (Win) or Illustrator (Mac) on the Menu bar, point to Preferences, and then click Units.

You may or may not prefer to work with rulers showing. You can make rulers visible by clicking View on the Menu bar, then clicking Show Rulers, or by pressing [Ctrl][R] (Win) or [⌘] [R] (Mac). You can hide visible rulers by clicking View on the Menu bar, then clicking Hide Rulers or by pressing [Ctrl][R] (Win) or [⌘] [R] (Mac).

Document Color Mode

Generally, CMYK Color (Cyan, Magenta, Yellow, and Black) is the color mode used for print projects, and RGB Color (Red, Green, and Blue) is the color mode used for projects that will appear on a screen. In InDesign, you can choose Print, Web, or Digital Publishing from the Intent menu in the New Document dialog box. Depending on what you choose, the color mode will update automatically. For example, if you select Web, the color mode will change to RGB. After a document is created, you can change the Intent by clicking File on the Menu bar and then selecting Document Setup.

Fonts

Whenever fonts are used in Data and Solution Files, they are chosen from a set of very common typefaces that you will most likely have available on your computer. If any of the fonts in use are not available on your computer, please make a substitution. For variety and typographic appeal, we have used other typefaces in Data and Solution Files that are not standard; however, we have converted those fonts to outlines. When a font is converted to an outline, the letterform is simply a vector graphic, like all other vector graphics.

Quick Keys

Quick keys are keyboard shortcuts that can be used in place of clicking the command on the Menu bar. [Ctrl][X], for example, is the quick key for Cut on the PC platform. Mastering basic quick keys is essential for a smooth work flow in Illustrator. It's a good idea to start with the commands on the Edit and Object menus as candidates for quick keys.

Photoshop

Intended Audience

This text is designed for the beginner or intermediate user who wants to learn how to use InDesign, Photoshop, and Illustrator Creative Cloud. The book is designed to provide basic and in-depth material that not only educates, but also encourages you to explore the nuances of these exciting programs. Features new to Creative Cloud and covered in this book are indicated by a New icon.

Approach

The text allows you to work at your own pace through step-by-step tutorials. A concept is presented and the process is explained, followed by the actual steps. To learn the most from the use of the text, you should adopt the following habits:

- Proceed slowly: Accuracy and comprehension are more important than speed.
- Understand what is happening with each step before you continue to the next step.

- After finishing a skill, ask yourself if you could do it on your own, without referring to the steps. If the answer is no, review the steps.

General

Throughout the initial chapters, students are given precise instructions regarding saving their work. Students should feel that they can save their work at any time, not just when instructed to do so. Students are also given precise instructions regarding magnifying/reducing their work area. Once the student feels more comfortable, he/she should feel free to use the Zoom tool to make their work area more comfortable.

Icons, Buttons, and Pointers

Symbols for icons, buttons, and pointers are shown in the step each time they are used. Once an icon, button, or pointer has been used on a page, the symbol will be shown for subsequent uses on that page *without* showing its name.

Skills Reference

As a bonus, a Power User Shortcuts table is included at the end of the Photoshop chapters.

This table contains the quickest method for completing tasks covered in the chapter. It is meant for the more experienced user, or for the user who wants to become more experienced. Tools are shown, not named. Brief directions are given, with no tool or command locations.

Fonts

The Data Files contain a variety of commonly used fonts, but there is no guarantee that these fonts will be available on your computer. In a few cases, fonts other than those common to a PC or a Macintosh are used. If any of the fonts in use is not available on your computer, you can make a substitution, realizing that the results may vary from those in the book.

Windows and Macintosh

Adobe Photoshop Creative Cloud works virtually the same on Windows and Macintosh operating systems. In those cases where there is a significant difference, the abbreviations (Win) and (Mac) are used.

Preference Settings

The learning process will be much easier if you can see the file extensions for the files you will use in the lessons. To do this in Windows, open Windows Explorer, click Organize, Folder and Search Options, click the View tab, and then uncheck the Hide Extensions for Known File Types check box. To do this for a Mac, go to the Finder, click the Finder menu, and then click Preferences. Click the Advanced tab, and then select the Show all file extensions check box.

System Requirements

For a Windows operating system:

- Processor: Intel® Pentium® 4 processor or AMD Athlon® 64 processor (2 GHz or faster)
- Operating System: Microsoft® Windows 7 (with Service Pack 1), 8, or 8 .1
- Memory: 1 GB of RAM
- Storage space: 2.5 GB of available hard-disk space
- Monitor: 1024 × 768 resolution (1280 × 800 recommended)
- Video: 16-bit or higher OpenGL 2.0 video card; 512 MB RAM (1 GB recommended)
- Broadband Internet connection required for activation, Creative Cloud membership validation, and access to online services

For a Macintosh operating system:

- Processor: Multicore Intel® processor with 64-bit support
- Operating System: Mac OS X 10.7, v10.8, or v10.9
- Memory: 1 GB of RAM
- Storage space: 3.2 GB of available hard-disk space
- Monitor: 1024 × 768 or greater monitor resolution (1280 × 800 recommended)
- Video: 16-bit or greater OpenGL 2.0 video card; 512 MB of VRAM (1 GB recommended)
- Broadband Internet connection required for software activation, Creative Cloud membership validation, and access to online services

File Identification

Instead of printing a file, the owner of a Photoshop image can be identified by reading the File Info dialog box.

Use the following instructions to add your name to an image:

1. Click File on the Menu bar, then click File Info.
2. Click the Description, if necessary.
3. Click the Author text box.
4. Type your name, course number, or other identifying information.
5. Click OK.

There are no instructions with this text to use the File Info feature other than when it is introduced in Chapter 1. It is up to each user to use this feature so that his or her work can be identified.

Measurements

When measurements are shown, needed, or discussed, they are given in pixels. Use the following instructions to change the units of measurement to pixels:

1. Click Edit (Win) or Photoshop (Mac) on the Menu bar, point to Preferences, then click Units & Rulers.
2. Click the Rulers list arrow, then click pixels.
3. Click OK. You can display rulers by clicking View on the Menu bar, and then clicking Rulers, or by pressing [Ctrl][R] (Win) or ⌘ [R] (Mac). A check mark to the left of the Rulers command indicates that the Rulers are displayed. You can hide visible rulers by clicking View on the Menu bar, then clicking Rulers, or by pressing [Ctrl] [R] (Win) or ⌘ [R] (Mac).

Menu Commands in Tables

In tables, menu commands are abbreviated using the following format:

Edit ➢ Preferences ➢ Units & Rulers

This command translates as follows: Click Edit on the Menu bar, point to Preferences, and then click Units & Rulers.

Grading Tips

Many students have web-ready accounts where they can post their completed assignments. The instructor can access the student accounts using a browser and view the images online. Using this method, it is not necessary for the student to include his/her name on a type layer, because all of their assignments are in an individual password-protected account.

Creating a Portfolio

One method for students to submit and keep a copy of all of their work is to create a portfolio of their projects that is linked to a simple web page that can be saved on a CD-ROM or a cloud-based drive. If it is necessary for students to print completed projects, work can be printed and mounted at a local copy shop; a student's name can be printed on the back of the image.

Data Files and Online Content

To complete most of the chapters in this book, your students will need Data Files, which are available online. Instruct students to use the Data Files List at the end of this book. This list gives instructions on organizing files.

To access the Data Files for this book, take the following steps:

1. Open your browser and go to http://www.cengagebrain.com
2. Type the author, title, or ISBN of this book in the Search window. (The ISBN is listed on the back cover.)
3. Click the book title in the list of search results.
4. When the book's main page is displayed, click the Access button under Free Study Tools.
5. To download Data Files, select a chapter number and then click on the Data Files tab on the left navigation bar to download the files.

Illustrator

Measurements

Text attributes are given in points. Measurements on the artboard and measurements referring to an object are given in inches, not points or picas. In order to follow the exercises, it's important that the General Units Preference in the Preferences dialog box be set to Inches. To set this preference, click Edit (Win) or Illustrator (Mac) on the Menu bar, point to Preferences, and then click Units.

You may or may not prefer to work with rulers showing. You can make rulers visible by clicking View on the Menu bar, then clicking Show Rulers, or by pressing [Ctrl][R] (Win) or [⌘][R] (Mac). You can hide visible rulers by clicking View on the Menu bar, then clicking Hide Rulers or by pressing [Ctrl][R] (Win) or [⌘][R] (Mac).

Document Color Mode

Generally, CMYK Color (Cyan, Magenta, Yellow, and Black) is the color mode used for print projects, and RGB Color (Red, Green, and Blue) is the color mode used for projects that will appear on a screen. The Profile menu in the New Document dialog box allows you to specify the type of document you need. You can choose Print, Web, Devices, Video and Film, as well as Basic CMYK or Basic RGB. You can also change a document's color mode by clicking File on the Menu bar, then clicking Document Color Mode. The color mode for each document is identified in the title bar at the top of the Illustrator window.

Whenever you are asked to create a new document, the color mode will be specified. Many menu commands, such as those under the Effect menu, are available only in RGB mode. If you run into a situation in which a specified menu command is not available, first check the color mode.

Fonts

Whenever fonts are used in Data and Solution Files, they are chosen from a set of very common typefaces that you will most likely have available on your computer. If any of the fonts in use are not available on your computer, please make a substitution.

For variety and typographic appeal, we have used other typefaces in Data and Solution Files that are not standard; however, we have converted those fonts to outlines. When a font is converted to an outline, the letterform is simply a vector graphic, like all other vector graphics.

Quick Keys

Quick keys are keyboard shortcuts that can be used in place of clicking the command on the Menu bar. [Ctrl][X], for example, is the quick key for Cut on the PC platform. Mastering basic quick keys is essential for a smooth work flow in Illustrator. It's a good idea to start with the commands on the Edit and Object menus as candidates for quick keys.

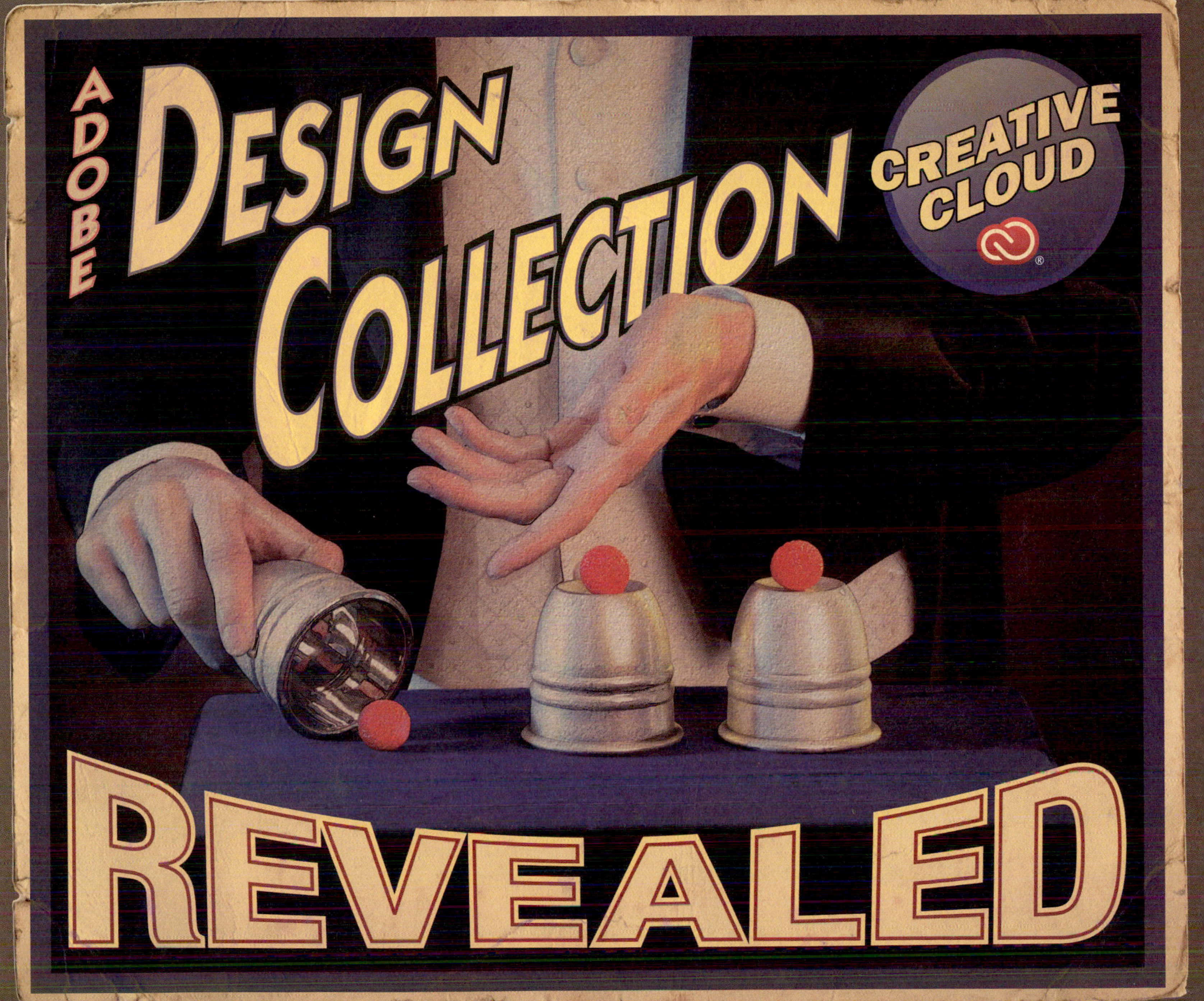
ADOBE
DESIGN
COLLECTION
CREATIVE
CLOUD
REVEALED

CHAPTER **1**

GETTING TO KNOW
INDESIGN

1. Explore the InDesign workspace
2. View and modify page elements
3. Navigate through a document
4. Work with objects and Smart Guides

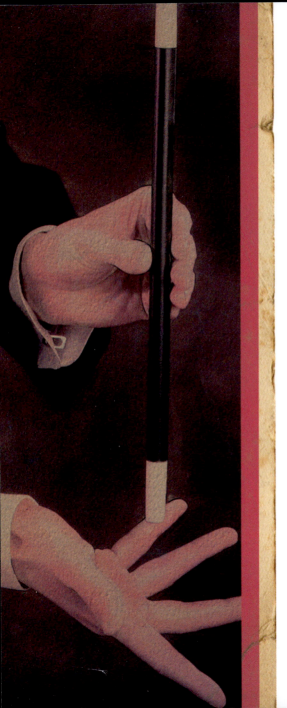

CHAPTER 1

GETTING TO KNOW INDESIGN

Introduction

Adobe InDesign is a comprehensive software program that allows you to create output-ready layouts for anything, including simple coupons, full-color magazines, interactive PDFs, splash pages for websites, and magazines for your iPad. What's even better is that, with InDesign, Adobe Systems has created a layout program that interfaces seamlessly with Adobe Photoshop and Illustrator.

If you love those two applications, you'll love InDesign too. In terms of its concept and its intuitive design, InDesign is pure Adobe. You'll feel right at home. In fact, at times, you may need to remind yourself that you're working in InDesign, not Photoshop or Illustrator.

The key word to keep in mind regarding InDesign is "layout." Even with all its other abilities, layout is InDesign's primary function. And everything you need to do it well is there—along with some pleasant surprises. With InDesign, you can build tables quickly and easily. The table of contents and index features are fun and easy to learn. And try to remember that you're not using Illustrator when you're positioning that text on a curved path!

Together, InDesign, Photoshop, and Illustrator are a formidable trifecta of design, with InDesign emerging as the best and most powerful layout utility ever devised.

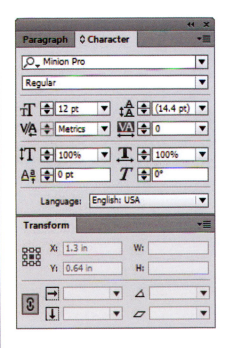

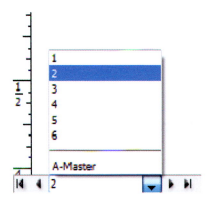

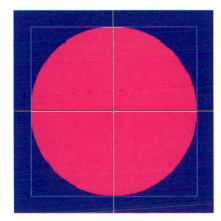

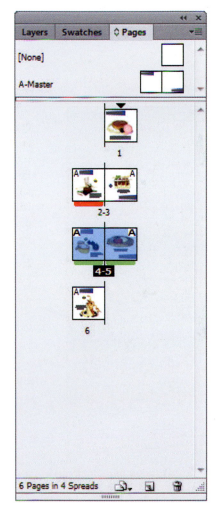

Explore the
INDESIGN WORKSPACE

What You'll Do

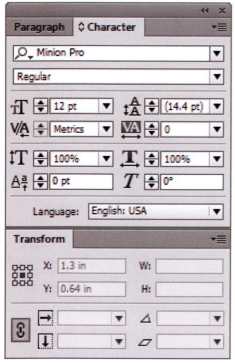

In this lesson, you will start Adobe InDesign and explore the workspace.

Looking at the InDesign Workspace

The arrangement of windows and panels that you see on your monitor is called the **workspace**. The InDesign workspace features the following areas: the document window, the pasteboard, the Menu bar, the Control panel, the Tools panel, and a stack of collapsed panels along the right side of the pasteboard. Figure 1 shows the default workspace, which is called Essentials.

InDesign offers a number of pre-defined workspaces that are customized for different types of tasks. Each workspace is designed so that panels with similar functions are grouped together. For example, the Typography workspace shows the many type- and typography-based panels that are useful for working with type. You can switch from one workspace to another by clicking Window on

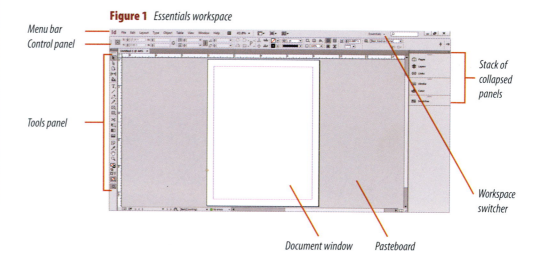

Figure 1 *Essentials workspace*

Menu bar
Control panel
Tools panel
Stack of collapsed panels
Workspace switcher
Document window
Pasteboard

the Menu bar, pointing to Workspace, and then clicking one of the available workspaces. Or you can use the workspace switcher on the Menu bar.

You can customize the workspace, including predefined workspaces, to suit your working preferences. For example, you can open and close whatever panels you want and change the location of any panel. You can save a customized workspace by clicking Window on the Menu bar, pointing to Workspace, then clicking New Workspace. Once the new workspace is named, it will appear in the Workspace menu.

The **pasteboard** is the area surrounding the document. The pasteboard provides space for extending objects past the edge of the page (known as "creating a bleed"), and it also provides space for storing objects that you may or may not use in the document. Objects that are positioned wholly on the pasteboard, as shown in Figure 2, do not print.

Exploring the Tools Panel

As its name implies, the Tools panel houses all the tools that you will work with in InDesign. The first thing that you should note about the Tools panel is that not all tools are visible; many are hidden. Look closely and you will see that some tools have small black triangles beside them. These triangles indicate that other tools are hidden behind them. To access hidden tools, point to the visible tool on the Tools panel, then press and hold the mouse button; this will reveal a menu of hidden tools. The small black square to the left of a tool name in the menu indicates the tool that is currently visible on the Tools panel, as shown in Figure 3.

Figure 2 *Using the pasteboard*

Object that "bleeds" onto the pasteboard on two sides

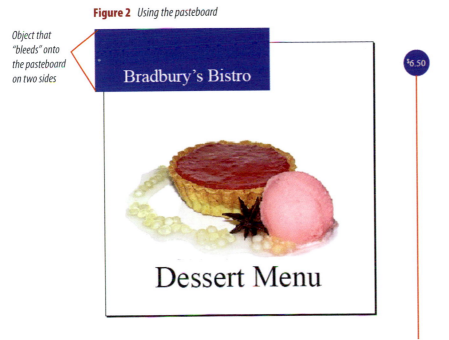

This object is on the pasteboard and will not print

Figure 3 *Hidden tools on the Tools panel*

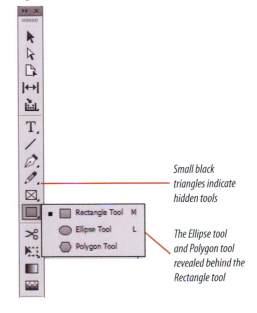

Small black triangles indicate hidden tools

The Ellipse tool and Polygon tool revealed behind the Rectangle tool

As shown in Figure 4, you can view the Tools panel as a single column, a double column, or even a horizontal row of tools. Simply click the Collapse to Icons button at the top of the Tools panel to toggle between the different setups.

Horizontal lines divide the Tools panel into eight sections. The top section contains the selection tools. The section beneath that contains item creation tools, such as the drawing, shape, and type tools. Next is a section that contains transform tools, such as the Rotate and Scale tools. The next section contains navigation tools. Here you can find the Hand tool—used to scroll through a document, and the Zoom tool, used to magnify your view of a document.

The bottom-most sections of the Tools panel contain functions for applying colors and gradients to objects and choosing different modes for viewing documents, such as the commonly used Preview mode.

To choose a tool, simply click it; you can also press a shortcut key to access a tool. For example, pressing [p] selects the Pen tool. To learn the shortcut key for each tool, point to a tool until a tooltip appears with the tool's name and its shortcut key in parentheses. Figure 5 shows the tooltip for the Type tool.

Working with Panels

Many InDesign functions are grouped into panels. For example, the Paragraph panel contains paragraph editing functions such

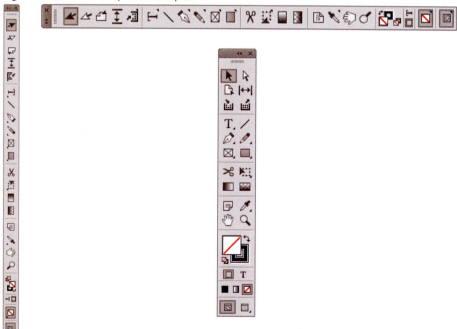

Figure 4 *Three different setups for the Tools panel*

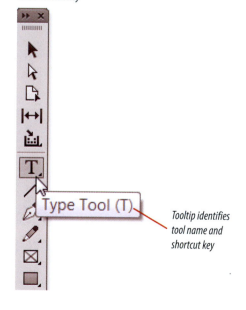

Figure 5 *Viewing tool name and shortcut key*

Tooltip identifies tool name and shortcut key

as text alignment and paragraph indents. The Character panel, shown in Figure 6, offers controls for changing the font, font size, and leading.

All panels can be accessed from the Window menu. Some panels are placed within categories on the Window menu. For example, all of the text and table-related panels, such as the Character panel and the Table panel, are listed in the Type & Tables category. When you choose a panel from the Window menu,

the panel appears in its expanded view. You can close any panel by clicking the Close button in the top right corner of the panel, and you can display panel options by clicking the Panel options button. To reduce the size of a panel, click the Collapse to Icons button, which collapses the panel to a named icon in a stack along the right side of the pasteboard. These three buttons are identified in Figure 6.

Figure 7 shows three panels grouped together. The Paragraph panel is the active panel—it is

in front of the others in the group and available for use. To better manage available workspace, it's a good idea to minimize or "collapse" panels to make them smaller but still available in the workspace. Clicking a panel icon in the stack of collapsed panels expands the panel as well as any other panels with which it is grouped. Click the thumbnail in the stack again, and it will collapse the panel you just expanded.

Figure 6 *Character panel*

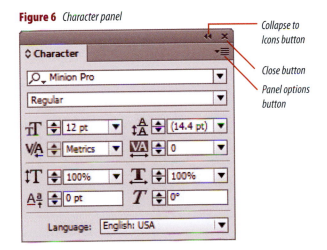

Collapse to Icons button

Close button

Panel options button

Figure 7 *Three grouped panels*

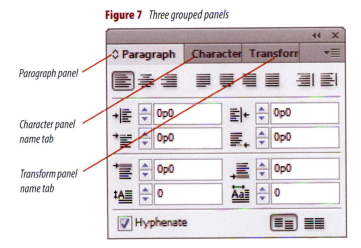

Paragraph panel

Character panel name tab

Transform panel name tab

When you have expanded a panel, the other panels grouped with it appear as tabs on the panel. You can activate these other panels by clicking their tabs. You can ungroup panels by dragging a panel's name tab away from the other panels in the group. To add a panel to a group, simply drag a panel by its name tab next to another panel name tab.

Don't confuse grouping panels with docking panels. **Docking** panels is a different function. When you dock panels, you connect the bottom edge of one panel to the top edge of another panel, so that both move together. To dock panels, first drag a panel's name tab to the bottom edge of another panel. When the bottom edge of the other panel is highlighted in bright blue, release the mouse button and the two panels will be docked. Figure 8 shows docked panels. To undock a panel, simply drag it away from its group.

Figure 8 *Docked panels*

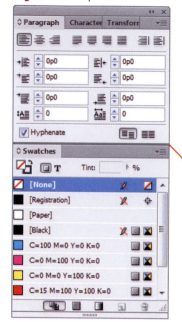

Swatches panel docked beneath Paragraph, Character, and Transform panels

Responding to Links and Font Warnings

InDesign documents often contain support files, such as graphics created in other programs like Photoshop and Illustrator. In creating this book, we included all such support files in the same folder as the InDesign data files, with which you will be working. By doing so, InDesign will be able to locate those files and update the InDesign document when you open it. When you open a document, however, you will often see a warning about missing or modified links. Unless you are instructed otherwise, you should always click Update Links when you see this warning. Likewise, we have used common fonts in the data files to minimize missing font warnings. However, should you encounter a layout that uses a font not currently loaded on your computer, you can accept the replacement font InDesign offers as an automatic replacement, or you can use the Find Font command on the Type menu to choose another font if you prefer.

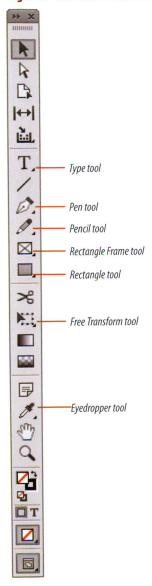

Figure 9 *Tools that contain hidden tools*

Type tool

Pen tool

Pencil tool

Rectangle Frame tool

Rectangle tool

Free Transform tool

Eyedropper tool

Explore the Tools panel

1. Launch Adobe InDesign.

2. Click **File** on the Menu bar, click **Open**, navigate to the drive and folder where your Chapter 1 Data Files are stored, click **ID 1-1.indd**, then click **Open**.

TIP If you see a warning about missing or modified links, click Update Links. If you see the Missing Fonts dialog box, you can use the font chosen by InDesign by clicking OK, or click Find Font and choose another font in the Find Font dialog box. For more information, see the Sidebar on page 1-8.

3. Click **Window** on the Menu bar, point to **Workspace**, then click **[Typography]**.

TIP If you are already working in the Typography workspace, click Window on the Menu bar, point to Workspace, then click Reset Typography to return to the default Typography workspace settings.

4. Point to the **Type tool** T̲ , then press and hold the mouse button to see the Type on a Path tool.

5. Using the same method, view the hidden tools behind the other tools with small black triangles, shown in Figure 9.

   Your visible tools may differ from the figure.

6. Position your mouse pointer over the **Selection tool** ▸ , until its tooltip appears.

7. Press the following keys and note which tools are selected with each key: **[A]**, **[P]**, **[V]**, **[T]**, **[I]**, **[H]**, **[Z]**.

(continued)

8. Press **[Tab]** to temporarily hide all open panels, then press **[Tab]** again. The panels reappear.

You explored the Tools panel, revealed hidden tools, used shortcut keys to access tools quickly, hid the panels, then displayed them again.

Work with panels

1. Click the **Paragraph panel icon** ¶ in the stack of collapsed panels to the right of the pasteboard.

   The Paragraph panel expands, but does not detach from the stack of collapsed icons. It's grouped with the Paragraph Styles panel in this Typography workspace.

2. Click the **Collapse to Icons button** ⏵⏵ at the top of the panel to collapse it, then click the **Paragraph panel icon** ¶ again to expand it.

3. Drag the **Paragraph panel name tab** to the left so it is ungrouped, as shown in Figure 10.

4. Drag the **Character panel icon** A to the blank space next to the **Paragraph panel name tab**, then release the mouse button.

   The Character panel is grouped with the Paragraph panel, as shown in Figure 11.

5. Click **Window** on the Menu bar, point to **Object & Layout**, then click **Transform**.

   The Transform panel appears expanded on the document.

   (continued)

Figure 10 *Removing the Paragraph panel from the group*

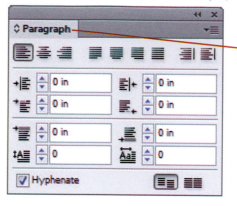

Drag a panel by its name tab

Figure 11 *Grouping the Character panel with the Paragraph panel*

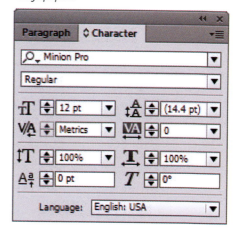

Opening InDesign CC Files in Earlier Versions of InDesign

InDesign CC documents cannot be opened in earlier versions of InDesign, such as CS5 or CS6. To open an InDesign CC document in an earlier version of InDesign, you must export the CC document in the InDesign Markup Language (IDML) format. Click File on the Menu bar, click Export, then choose InDesign Markup (IDML) as the file format. The exported document can be opened in earlier versions of InDesign. Note, however, that any new CC features applied to your document will be lost when the file is converted to the older version.

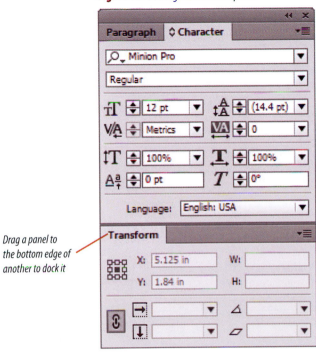

Figure 12 *Docking the Transform panel*

Drag a panel to the bottom edge of another to dock it

6. Drag the **Transform panel name tab** to the bottom edge of the Character and Paragraph panels group, then, when a blue horizontal bar appears, release the mouse button.

   The Transform panel is docked, as shown in Figure 12.

7. Click and drag the **dark gray bar** at the top of the panel group, found above the Paragraph and Character panel name tabs, in different directions.

   The Transform panel moves with the Character and Paragraph panels because it is docked.

8. Click the **Transform panel name tab**, then drag it away from the other two panels.

   The Transform panel is undocked.

9. Click **Window** on the Menu bar, point to **Workspace**, then **click Reset Typography**.

You explored methods for grouping and ungrouping panels, and you docked and undocked a panel.

Creating Custom Workspaces

With InDesign, you can customize the workspace as you like it, opening and dragging panels wherever they help make your workflow most efficient. When you are happy with the way that you have customized your workspace, click Window on the Menu bar, point to Workspace, then click New Workspace. Assign a descriptive name to your workspace, verify that the Panel Locations check box is checked, then click OK. With this option checked, the workspace will be saved with all panels in their current positions. Once you've saved a workspace, you load it by clicking Window on the Menu bar, then pointing to Workspace. You'll see your custom-named workspace in the list of workspaces.

View and Modify
PAGE ELEMENTS

What You'll Do

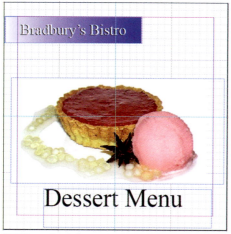

© 2015 Cengage Learning®

In this lesson, you will explore various methods for viewing the document and document elements like rulers, guides, grids and frame edges.

Using the Zoom Tool

Imagine creating a layout on a traditional pasteboard—not on your computer. For precise work, you would bring your nose closer to the pasteboard so that you could better see what you were doing. At other times, you would hold the pasteboard away from you, at arms' length, so that you could get a larger perspective of the artwork. When you're working in InDesign, the Zoom tool performs these functions for you.

When you click the Zoom tool and move the pointer over the document window, the pointer becomes the Zoom pointer with a plus sign; when you click the document with the Zoom pointer, the document area you clicked is enlarged. To reduce the view of the document, press and hold [Alt] (Win) or [option] (Mac). When the plus sign changes to a minus sign, click the document with this Zoom pointer, and the document size is reduced.

Using the Zoom tool, you can reduce or enlarge the view of the document from 5% to 4000%. Note that the current magnification level appears in the document tab and in the Zoom Level text box on the Menu bar, as shown in Figure 13.

Accessing the Zoom Tool

As you work, you can expect to zoom in and out of the document more times than you can count. The most basic way of accessing the Zoom tool is simply to click its icon on the Tools panel, however this can get very tiring. A better method for accessing the Zoom tool is to use keyboard shortcuts. When you are using the Selection tool, for example, don't switch to the Zoom tool. Instead, press and hold [Ctrl][Spacebar] (Win) or ⌘ [Spacebar] (Mac) to temporarily change the Selection tool into the Zoom tool. Click the document to zoom in. When you release the keys, the Zoom tool changes back to the Selection tool.

To Zoom out using keyboard shortcuts, press and hold [Ctrl][Alt][Spacebar] (Win) or ⌘ [option][Spacebar] (Mac).

QUICK TIP

Double-clicking the Zoom tool on the Tools panel changes the document view to 100% (actual size).

In addition to the Zoom tool, InDesign offers a number of other ways to zoom in and out of your document. One of the quickest and easiest is to press [Ctrl] [+] (Win) or ⌘ [+] (Mac) to enlarge the view and [Ctrl][-] (Win) or ⌘ [-] (Mac) to reduce the view. You can also use the Zoom In and Zoom Out commands on the View menu.

Using the Hand Tool

When you zoom in on a document—when you make it appear larger—eventually the document will be too large to fit in the window. Therefore, you will need to scroll to see other areas of it. You can use the scroll bars along the bottom and the right sides of the document window or you can use the Hand tool to scroll through the document, as shown in Figure 14.

The best way to understand the concept of the Hand tool is to think of it as your own hand. Imagine that you could put your hand up to the document on your monitor, then move the document left, right, up, or down, like a paper on a table or against a wall. This is analogous to how the Hand tool works.

The Hand tool is often a better choice for scrolling than the scroll bars. Why? Because you can access the Hand tool using a keyboard shortcut. Simply press and hold [Spacebar] to access the Hand tool. Release

Figure 13 *A reduced view of the document*

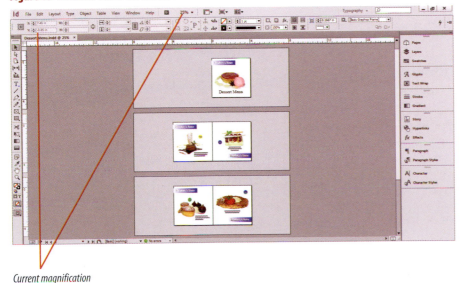

Current magnification

© 2015 Cengage Learning®

Figure 14 *Scrolling through a document*

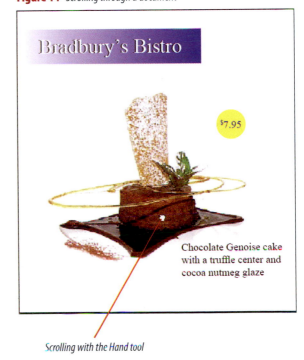

Scrolling with the Hand tool

[Spacebar] to return to the tool you were using, without having to choose it again.

Working with Rulers, Grids, and Guides

Designing and working with page layouts involves using measurements to position and align elements in your documents. You'll find that InDesign is well-equipped with a number of features that help you with these tasks.

Figure 15 shows various measurement utilities. **Rulers** are positioned at the top and left side of the pasteboard to help you align objects. Simply click Show Rulers/Hide Rulers on the View menu. Rulers (and all other measurement utilities in the document) can display measurements in different units, such as inches, picas, or points. You determine the units and increments with which you want to work in the Preferences dialog box. On the Edit menu, point to Preferences, then click Units & Increments to display the dialog box shown in Figure 16.

Ruler guides are horizontal and vertical rules that you can position anywhere in a layout as a reference for positioning elements. **Margin guides** are guides that you specify to appear at a given distance within the page, usually to maintain visual consistency from page to page or as a reminder to keep text or other

Figure 15 *Various measurement utilities*

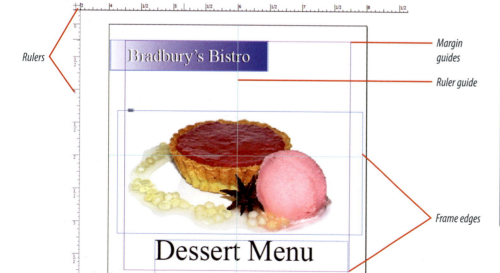

Rulers

Margin guides

Ruler guide

Frame edges

Figure 16 *Units & Increments Preferences dialog box*

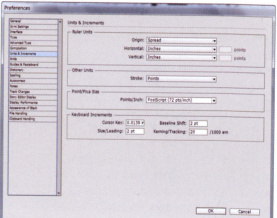

important elements from getting too close to the edge of the page. In addition to guides, InDesign offers a **document grid** for precise alignment. With the "snap" options on, objects that you move around on the page automatically align themselves with guides or with the grid quickly and easily.

Hiding and Showing Frame Edges

InDesign is a frame-based application. **Frames** are rectangular, oval, or polygonal shapes that you use for a variety of purposes, such as creating a colored area on the document or placing text and graphics. All frames have visible **frame edges**, and when a frame is selected, those edges automatically highlight.

While you're working on designing your layout, you'll often want to have frame edges visible; but once you're done designing, you'll want to see your layout without the frame edges in the way. To hide or show frame edges, click the Hide/Show Edges command on the View menu.

Keep in mind that when you hide or show guides, grids or frame edges in a document, none of these settings is saved with it. For example, say you showed frame edges in Dessert Menu, then saved and closed it. You then opened a second document right after, and hid the frame edges while you worked. If you were to open Dessert Menu again, its frame edges would be hidden too, because that is the most current display status in the InDesign window.

Choosing Screen Modes

Screen Modes are options for viewing your documents. The two basic screen modes in InDesign are Normal and Preview. You'll work in **Normal mode** most of the time. In Normal mode, you can see any and all page elements, including margin guides, ruler guides, frame edges, and the pasteboard.

Preview mode shows you what your page would look like with all non-printing elements removed. When you switch to Preview mode, all guides, grids, and frame edges become invisible to give you an idea of what your document would look like printed or as a PDF file. Even the pasteboard is hidden and becomes gray; thus, any objects on the pasteboard—or any objects that extend off of your document page—become invisible. You can think of Preview mode as showing you a "cropped" view of your page—only that which is on the page is visible.

QUICK **TIP**

Preview mode doesn't hide panels or the Menu bar.

The View menu offers commands for switching between Normal and Preview modes, but it's much faster and easier to press the [W] key on your keypad to toggle between the two modes.

Presentation mode presents a view of your document as though it were being showcased on your computer monitor. In Presentation mode, your document goes full screen against a black background and is centered and

sized so that the entire document fits in your monitor window. All other InDesign elements, including panels and the Menu bar, disappear.

When would you use Presentation mode? When you are giving a presentation! Let's say you have a multi-page document and your client is coming to your office to view it. Rather than show her the document in Normal or Preview modes with distracting menu bars and panels, show it to her in Presentation mode for a cleaner and more professional look.

To toggle Presentation mode on and off, press [Shift] [W] on your keypad.

When in Presentation mode, you'll have no tools or menus whatsoever to navigate through a multi-page document, but you can use the following keys in Table 1 to move around in it:

TABLE 1: PRESENTATION MODE NAVIGATION KEYS	
→ or [Pg Dn]	Next Spread
← or [Pg Up]	Previous Spread
[Home]	First Spread
[End]	Last Spread
[Esc]	Exit Presentation Mode

© Cengage Learning®

Understanding Preferences

All Adobe products come loaded with preferences. Preferences are options you have for specifying how certain features of the application behave. The Preferences dialog box houses the multitude of InDesign preferences available. Figure 17 shows the Interface preferences for InDesign. Note the long list of other preference categories on the left. Getting to know available preferences is a smart approach to mastering InDesign. Many preferences offer important choices that will have significant impact on how you work.

Working with Multiple Open Documents

On many occasions, you'll find yourself working with multiple open documents. For example, let's say you're into scrapbooking. If you were designing a new document to showcase a recent trip to Italy, you might also have the file open for the scrapbook you created last year when you went to Hawaii. Why? For any number of reasons. You might want to copy and paste layout elements from the Hawaii document into the new document. Or, you might want the Hawaii document open simply as a reference for typefaces, type sizes, image sizes, and effects like drop shadows that you used. When you're working with multiple open documents, you can switch from one to the other simply by clicking on the title bar of each document.

InDesign offers a preference for having multiple open documents available as tabs in the document window. With this preference selected, a tab will appear for each open document showing the name of the document. Simply click the tab and the document becomes active. This can be useful for keeping your workspace uncluttered, though at times

it might be inhibiting, because when working with multiple documents, the tabbed option allows you to view only one document at a time.

You indicate in the Interface Preferences dialog box whether or not you want open documents to appear as tabs. Click Edit (Win) or InDesign (Mac) on the Menu bar, point to Preferences, then click Interface. Click the Open Documents as Tabs check box to select it, as shown in Figure 17, then click OK.

Figure 17 *Interface Preferences dialog box*

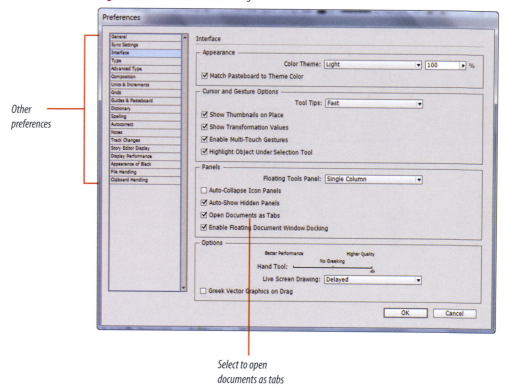

Other preferences

Select to open documents as tabs

Getting to Know InDesign

Figure 18 *Scrolling with the Hand tool*

The Hand tool will become a fist when you click and drag

Use the Zoom tool and the Hand tool

1. Press **[Z]** to access the Zoom tool.

2. Position the Zoom tool over the document window, click twice to enlarge the document, press **[Alt]** (Win) or **[option]** (Mac), then click twice to reduce the document.

3. Click the **Zoom Level list arrow** on the Menu bar, then click **800%**.

   Note that 800% is now listed in the document tab.

4. Double-click **800%** in the Zoom Level text box, type **300**, then press **[Enter]** (Win) or **[return]** (Mac).

5. Click the **Hand tool** on the Tools panel, then click and drag the **document window** so that the image in the window appears as shown in Figure 18.

6. Double-click the **Zoom tool button** on the Tools panel. The magnification changes to 100% (actual size).

7. Click the **Selection tool**, point to the center of the document window, then press and hold **[Ctrl][Spacebar]** (Win) or ⌘ **[Spacebar]** (Mac).

   The Selection tool changes to the Zoom tool.

8. Click three times, then release [Ctrl][Spacebar] (Win) or ⌘ [Spacebar] (Mac).

9. Press and hold **[Spacebar]** to access the Hand tool, then scroll around the image.

(continued)

10. Press and hold **[Ctrl] [Alt] [Spacebar]** (Win) or ⌘ **[option] [Spacebar]** (Mac), then click the mouse button multiple times to reduce the view to 25%.

11. Your document window should resemble Figure 19.

You explored various methods for accessing and using the Zoom tool for enlarging and reducing the document. You also used the Hand tool to scroll around an enlarged document.

Hide and show rulers and set units and increments preferences

1. Click **View** on the Menu bar, note the shortcut key on the Fit Page in Window command, then click **Fit Page in Window**.

   Most commonly used commands in InDesign list a shortcut key beside the command name. Shortcut keys are useful for quickly accessing commands without stopping work to go to the menu. Make a mental note of helpful shortcut keys and incorporate them into your work. You'll find that using them becomes second nature.

2. Click **View** on the Menu bar, then note the Rulers command and its shortcut key.

   The Rulers command is set to either Hide Rulers or Show Rulers, depending on your current status.

3. Click the **pasteboard** to escape the View menu, then press **[Ctrl] [R]** (Win) or ⌘ **[R]** (Mac) several times to hide and show rulers, finishing with rulers showing.

4. Note the units on the rulers.

   Depending on the preference you have set, your rulers might be showing inches, picas, or another unit of measure.

   (continued)

Figure 19 *A reduced view of the document*

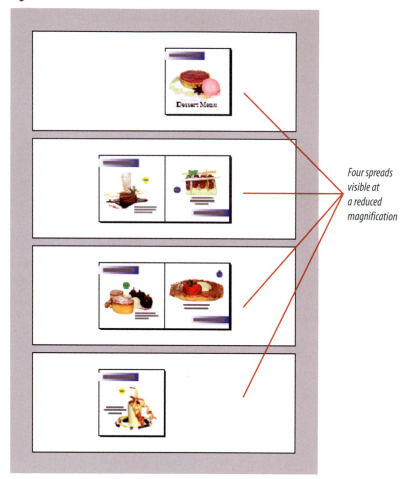

Four spreads visible at a reduced magnification

Getting to Know InDesign

Figure 20 *Setting the Units & Increments ruler units to Picas*

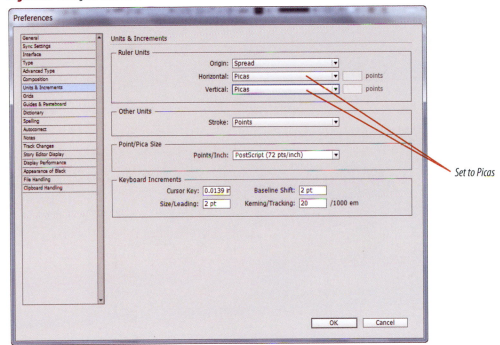

Set to Picas

5. Click **Edit** (Win) or **InDesign** (Mac) on the Menu bar, point to **Preferences**, then click **Units & Increments**.

6. In the Ruler Units section, click the **Horizontal list arrow** to see the available measurement options.

7. Set the Horizontal and Vertical fields to Picas so that your dialog box resembles Figure 20, then click **OK**.

   The horizontal and vertical rulers change to pica measurements. Picas are a unit of measure used in layout design long before the advent of computerized layouts. One pica is equal to 1/6 an inch. It's important you understand that the unit of measure you set in the Preferences dialog box is a global choice. It will affect all measurement utilities in the application, such as those on the Transform panel, in addition to the ruler increments.

8. Reopen the Units & Increments Preferences dialog box, change the Horizontal and Vertical fields to Inches, then click **OK**.

You used shortcut keys to hide and show rulers in the document. You used the Units & Increments Preferences dialog box to change the unit of measure for the document.

Hide and show ruler guides, frame edges, and the document grid

1. Click **View** on the Menu bar, point to **Extras**, then note the Show/Hide Frame Edges command and its shortcut key.

   The Frame Edges command is set to either Hide Frame Edges or Show Frame Edges depending on your current status.

(continued)

2. Click the **pasteboard** to escape the View menu, then press **[Ctrl] [H]** (Win) or ⌘ **[H]** (Mac) several times to toggle between hiding and showing frame edges, finishing with frame edges showing.

TIP The Hide Frames shortcut key is easy to remember if you think of H for Hide. Remember though, that this shortcut key only hides and shows frame edges, not other elements, like ruler guides, which use different shortcut keys.

3. Click **View** on the Menu bar, point to **Grids & Guides**, then note the Show/Hide Guides command and its shortcut key.

The Guides command is set to either Hide Guides or Show Guides depending on your current status.

4. Click the **pasteboard** to escape the View menu, then press **[Ctrl] [;]** (Win) or ⌘ **[;]** (Mac) several times to toggle between hiding and showing guides, finishing with guides showing.

Horizontal and vertical ruler guides alternately hide and show. In addition, purple margin guides hide and show .25" within the perimeter of the page, as shown in Figure 21.

TIP Make note of the difference between the Hide/Show guides shortcut key and the Hide/Show Frame Edges shortcut key.

5. Click **View** on the Menu bar, point to **Grids & Guides**, then note the Show/Hide Document Grid command and its shortcut key.

(continued)

Figure 21 *Viewing frame edges and guides*

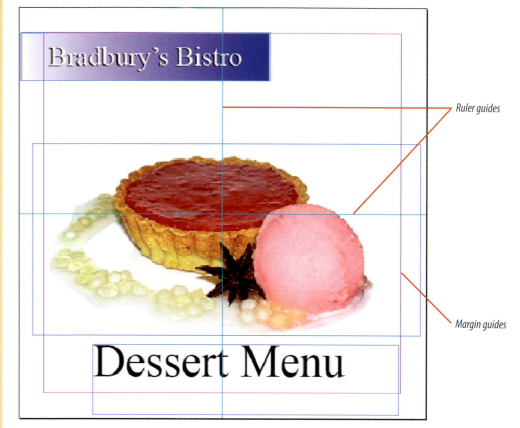

Ruler guides

Margin guides

TABLE 2: SHORTCUT KEYS FOR VIEWING COMMANDS

	Windows	Mac
Hide/Show Guides	Ctrl+;	⌘+;
Hide/Show Edges	Ctrl+H	[Ctrl] ⌘+H
Hide/Show Rulers	Ctrl+R	⌘+R
Activate/Deactivate Smart Guides	Ctrl+U	⌘+U
Fit Page in Window	Ctrl+0 (zero)	⌘+0
Fit Spread in Window	Alt+Ctrl+0 (zero)	Option+⌘+0
Toggle Normal and Preview Screen Modes	W	W
Toggle Presentation Mode On/Off	Shift+W	Shift+W

© Cengage Learning®

Setting up Document and Frame-Based Grids

Sometimes ruler guides just aren't enough, so designers choose to work with grids. Grids are multiple guides positioned to create a grid pattern across the layout. Grids help you align objects quickly and precisely. Every InDesign file you create has a default Document Grid, which you can hide or show using the Hide or Show Document Grid command in the Guides & Grids options on the View menu. You can modify the color and spacing increments of the default document grid using the Grids command in the Preferences options on the Edit menu. Choose Snap to Document Grid in the Grids and Guides options on the View menu to force objects to align to the Document Grid.

Sometimes you'll want to use a grid in a specific text frame as opposed to across the entire document. You can set up a grid for a text frame in the Text Frame Options dialog box. Select the frame, click the Object menu, then click Text Frame Options. Click the Baseline Options tab at the top of the dialog box, then enter specifications for the frame-based grid.

The Document Grid command is set to either Hide Document Grid or Show Document Grid depending on your current status.

6. Click the **pasteboard** to escape the View menu, then press **[Ctrl] [']** (Win) or ⌘ **[']** (Mac) several times to toggle between hiding and showing the document grid.

   Table 2 includes frequently used Viewing command shortcut keys.

TIP Make note of the difference between the Hide/Show Guides shortcut key and the Hide/Show Document Grid shortcut key—they're just one key away from each other.

7. Click **View** on the Menu bar, point to **Grids & Guides**, then note the Snap to Guides and Snap to Document Grid commands.

   The Snap to Guides and Snap to Document Grid commands are on/off commands. When they're active, a check mark is visible to the left of the command.

8. Click the **pasteboard** to escape the View menu.

You used shortcut keys to hide and show frame edges, ruler guides, and the document grid. You noted the location of the Snap to Guides and Snap to Document Grid commands in the View menu.

Toggle between screen modes

1. Click **View** on the Menu bar, point to **Screen Mode**, then click **Preview**.

   All guides and frame edges are hidden and the pasteboard is now gray. The Menu bar and panels remain visible.

2. Press **[W]** on your keypad several times to toggle between Preview and Normal modes, finishing with your document in Normal mode.

(continued)

3. Click **View** on the Menu bar, point to **Screen Mode**, then click **Presentation**.

As shown in Figure 22, the window changes to full-screen, and the full document appears against a black background. Guides, grids, frame edges, panels, and the Menu bar are no longer visible.

4. Press the ↓ on your keypad to scroll through the document to the last page.

5. Press the ↑ on your keypad to scroll up to the first page.

6. Press **[Esc]** to leave Presentation mode.

7. Press **[Shift] [W]** to switch to Presentation mode.

8. Press **[Shift] [W]** again to return to Normal mode.

You used menu commands and keyboard keys to toggle among Normal, Preview, and Presentation modes. When in Presentation mode, you used keyboard keys to navigate through the document.

Work with multiple documents

1. Click **Edit** (Win) or **InDesign** (Mac) on the Menu bar, point to **Preferences**, click **Interface**, click the **Open Documents as Tabs check box** to select it if it is unchecked, then click **OK**.

2. Save ID 1-1.indd as **Dessert Menu**.

3. Open ID 1-2.indd, then click the **tabs** of each document several times to toggle between them, finishing with Dessert Menu as the active document.

4. Position the mouse pointer over the bottom-right corner of the document, then click and drag downward and to the right to try to resize it.

If you are using Windows, you cannot resize the tabbed document.

(continued)

Figure 22 *Viewing the document in Presentation mode*

Getting to Know InDesign

Figure 23 *"Tabbing" the floating document*

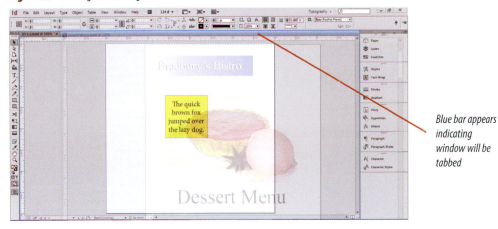

*Blue bar appears
indicating
window will be
tabbed*

5. Drag the **Dessert Menu tab** straight down
   approximately 1/2 inch.

   When you drag a tabbed document down,
   it becomes "untabbed" and becomes a
   "floating" document.

6. Position the mouse pointer over the bottom-right
   corner of the document window, then click and
   drag towards the center of the monitor window to
   reduce the window to approximately half its size.

7. Position the mouse pointer over the title bar
   of the document, then click and drag to move
   Dessert Menu half way down towards the bottom
   of your monitor screen.

   A "floating" document window can be positioned
   so that part of it is off-screen.

8. Position the mouse pointer over the title bar of
   Dessert Menu, click and drag to position it at the
   top of the window beside the ID 1-2.indd tab,
   then release the mouse button when you see a
   horizontal blue bar, as shown in Figure 23.

   The document is tabbed once again.

9. Close ID 1-2.indd without saving changes if you
   are prompted.

*You selected the Open Documents as Tabs option in the
Preferences dialog box. You opened a second document and
noted that it was tabbed and couldn't be resized. You removed
the document from its tabbed position, resized it, moved it
around, then returned it to its tabbed status.*

Navigate Through
A DOCUMENT

What You'll Do

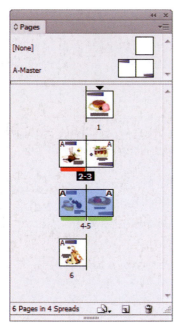

Navigating to Pages in a Document

When you create a layout for a magazine, book, or brochure, you create a document that has multiple pages. **Spreads** are two pages that face each other—a left page and a right page in a multi-page document.

You have a variety of methods at your disposal for navigating to pages or spreads in your document. The Go to Page command in the Layout menu offers you the option to enter the page to which you want to go. You can also use the scroll bars on the bottom and right sides of the document window or choose a page from the Page menu in the lower-left corner of the document window. There are also First Spread, Previous Spread, Next Spread, and Last Spread buttons at the bottom of the document window, which you can click to navigate to designated spreads, as shown in Figure 24. These navigation buttons have corresponding menu commands on the Layout menu.

Figure 24 *Page buttons and the Page menu*

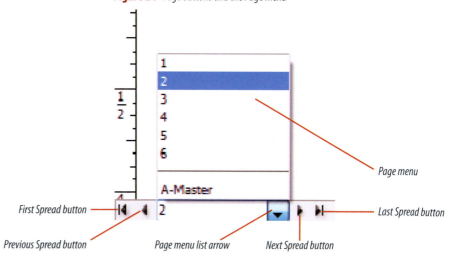

Getting to Know InDesign

The Pages panel, shown in Figure 25, is a comprehensive solution for moving from page to page in your document. The Pages panel shows icons for all of the pages in the document. Double-clicking a single page icon brings that page into view. The icon representing the currently visible page appears in blue on the panel. Click the Pages panel options button to display the Pages panel menu. This menu contains a number of powerful commands that you can use to control all of your page navigation in InDesign.

Double-clicking the numbers under the page icons representing a spread, as shown in Figure 26, centers the spread in the document window. In this case, both icons representing the spread appear blue on the Pages panel.

Applying Thumbnail Color Labels

You can apply one of fifteen color labels to a page thumbnail on the Pages panel. Color labels can be useful for organizing your own work or for working with others on a document. For your own work, you might

want to assign color labels to different types of pages. For example, you might want to assign a color label to pages in a document that contain imported Photoshop graphics. Or you might want to assign a specific color to pages that have been approved by your client. When working with others, color labels can be effective as status codes. For example, you can apply a specific color to all pages that are

proofed and approved. This way, at a glance, your whole team can see what's done and what needs to be done.

To apply color labels, simply click the Pages panel options button, point to Page Attributes, point to Color Label, then choose a color. The color that you choose will appear as a small solid rectangle beneath the thumbnail.

Figure 25 *Pages panel*

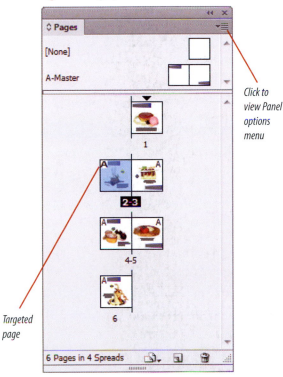

Click to view Panel options menu

Targeted page

Figure 26 *A selected two-page spread*

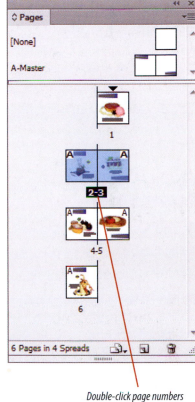

Double-click page numbers to target a spread

Navigate to pages in a document

1. Click the **Page menu list arrow** at the bottom-left of the document window, then click **3**.

   The document view changes to page 3.

2. Click **View** on the Menu bar, then click **Fit Spread in Window**.

3. Click the **Next Spread button** 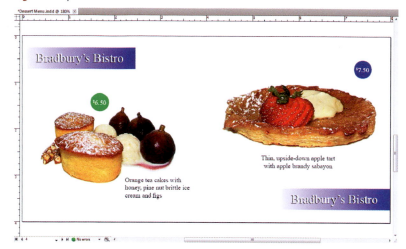.

   Your screen should resemble Figure 27.

4. Click the **Previous Spread button** twice.

5. Click the **Pages panel icon** to display the Pages panel, if necessary.

   TIP If you do not see the Pages panel icon in the stack of collapsed panels, click Window on the Menu bar, then click Pages.

6. Double-click the **page 6 icon** on the Pages panel.

   The document view changes to page 6, and the page 6 icon on the Pages panel becomes highlighted, as shown in Figure 28.

7. Double-click the **page 3 icon** on the Pages panel.

   The right half of the spread—page 3—is centered in the document window.

8. Double-click the numbers **2-3** beneath the icons for Pages 2 and 3 on the Pages panel.

   TIP Double-clicking numbers below the icons on the Pages panel centers the full spread in the document window.

(continued)

Figure 27 *Spread 4-5*

Figure 28 *Targeting Page 6 on the Pages panel*

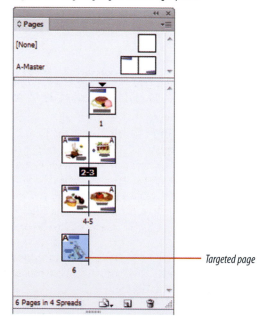

Targeted page

© 2015 Cengage Learning®

Getting to Know InDesign

Figure 29 *Color labels on the Pages panel*

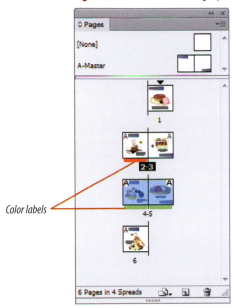

Color labels

Pages Panel Options

To customize the Pages panel, click the Pages panel options button, then click Panel Options. This opens the Panel Options dialog box. In the Pages and Masters sections of the dialog box, you can choose a size for page and master icons by clicking the Size list arrow, then clicking a size ranging from Extra Small to Jumbo. The Show Vertically and Show Thumbnails check boxes in the Pages and Masters sections control how the icons on the panel are displayed. If you remove the Show Vertically check mark, the page icons on the Pages panel will be displayed horizontally and you will only be able to resize the width of the Pages panel, not the height. If you remove the Show Thumbnails check mark, the page icons will be blank on the Pages panel. The Icons section of the dialog box defines which additional icons appear next to the page icons. For example, if the Transparency check box is checked, a small transparency icon that looks like a checkerboard appears next to the page icon where transparency has been applied to master items. In the Panel Layout section, you can choose whether you want masters on top or document pages on top of the Pages panel.

9. Click **Layout** on the Menu bar, then click **First Page**.

10. Press **[Ctrl] [J]** (Win) or ⌘ **[J]** (Mac) to open the Go to Page dialog box, enter **5**, then press **[Enter]** (Win) or **[return]** (Mac).

TIP Make a point of remembering this command—*J for Jump*. It is one of the fastest ways to jump to a specific page, especially in long documents with lots of pages on the Pages panel.

You navigated to pages using the Page menu, the Next Spread and Previous Spread buttons, page icons on the Pages panel, the Layout menu, and the Go to Page dialog box.

Apply color labels to page thumbnails

1. Click the **page 2 thumbnail** on the Pages panel.

2. Click the **Pages panel options button** ▾≡, point to **Page Attributes**, point to **Color Label**, then click **Red**.

   A red bar appears beneath the page thumbnail.

3. Click the **page numbers 4-5** on the Pages panel to select both thumbnails.

4. Click the **Pages panel options button** ▾≡, point to **Page Attributes**, point to **Color Label**, then click **Green**.

   Your Pages panel should resemble Figure 29.

5. Save the file, then close Dessert Menu.indd.

You applied a color label to a single page thumbnail and a spread thumbnail.

Work with Objects
AND SMART GUIDES

What You'll Do

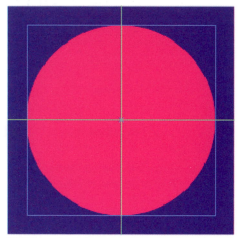

© 2015 Cengage Learning®

 In this lesson, you will work with objects with Smart Guides.

Resizing Objects

Objects are text or graphic elements, such as images, blocks of color, and even simple lines, that are placed in an InDesign document. As mentioned earlier, all objects in InDesign are in frames.

When you select an object's frame, its handles become highlighted, as shown in Figure 30.

Figure 30 *Viewing frame handles on a text frame*

The yellow square handle on a frame is an extra handle that is used to create corner effects on frames. This is covered extensively in Chapter 8.

You can click and drag the handles to change the shape and size of the frame. InDesign offers three basic keyboard combinations that you can use when dragging frame handles to affect how the frame and its contents are affected, as shown in Table 3.

TABLE 3: DRAGGING FRAME HANDLES WITH KEYBOARD COMBINATIONS		
Windows	**Mac**	**Result**
Shift-drag a handle	Shift-drag a handle	The frame is resized in proportion; its shape doesn't change; contents of the frame are not scaled
Alt-drag a handle	Option-drag a handle	Resizes the object from its center point
Ctrl-drag a handle	⌘-drag a handle	Resizes the object and its contents

© Cengage Learning®

© 2015 Cengage Learning®

These keyboard combinations can themselves be combined. For example, if you hold [Shift] and [Ctrl], then drag a handle, you can resize an object and its contents, while ensuring that you retain the proportions of the object's shape.

You can resize multiple objects just as easily. Simply select multiple objects and handles will appear around all the selected objects, as shown in Figure 31. You can then drag those handles to affect all the objects simultaneously.

Copying Objects

At any time, you can copy and paste an object. That's pretty standard program functionality. InDesign also offers the Paste in Place command on the Edit menu. This is useful for placing a copy of an object exactly in front of the original object. Simply select an object, copy it, then click the Paste in Place command.

You can also copy objects while dragging them. Press and hold [Alt] (Win) or [option] (Mac), then drag to create a copy of the object.

Hiding, Locking, and Grouping Objects

The Hide, Lock, Group, and Ungroup commands on the Object menu are essential for working effectively with layouts, especially complex layouts with many objects. Hide objects to get them out of your way. They won't print, and nothing you do changes the location of them as long as they are hidden. Lock an object to make it immovable—you will not even be able to select it. Lock your objects when you have them in a specific location and you don't want them accidentally moved or deleted. Don't think this is being

Figure 31 *Viewing frame handles around two objects*

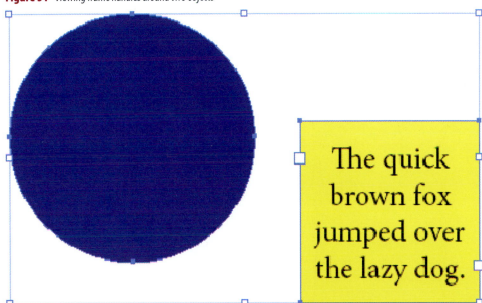

The quick brown fox jumped over the lazy dog.

© 2015 Cengage Learning®

overly cautious; accidentally moving or deleting objects—and being unaware that you did so—happens all the time in complex layouts.

You group multiple objects with the Group command under the Object menu. Grouping objects is a smart and important strategy for protecting the relationships between multiple objects. When you click on grouped objects with the Selection tool, all the objects are selected. Thus, you can't accidentally select a single object and move or otherwise alter it independently from the group. However, you *can* select individual objects within a group by double-clicking an object with the Selection tool. Double-clicking one item in the group temporarily ungroups the grouped objects until you double-click one of the objects again to re-establish the original group. If a group is not selected, you can click one item in the group with the Direct Selection tool—that's how the tool got its name. Even if you select and alter a single object within a group, the objects are not ungrouped.

Working with Smart Guides

When aligning objects, you will find **Smart Guides** to be really effective and, well, really smart. When the Smart Guides feature is activated, Smart Guides appear automatically when you move objects in the document. Smart Guides give you visual information for positioning objects precisely—in relation to the page or in relation to other objects. For example, you can use Smart Guides to align objects to the edges and centers of other objects and to the horizontal and vertical centers of the page.

You enable Smart Guide options as a preference. You use the View menu to turn them on and off. Figure 32 shows Smart Guides at work.

Figure 32 *Smart Guides aligning the top edges of two objects*

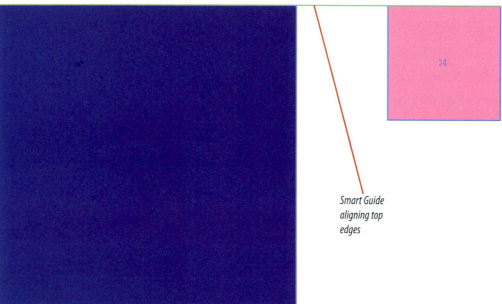

Smart Guide aligning top edges

Getting to Know InDesign

Figure 33 *Resized object and contents*

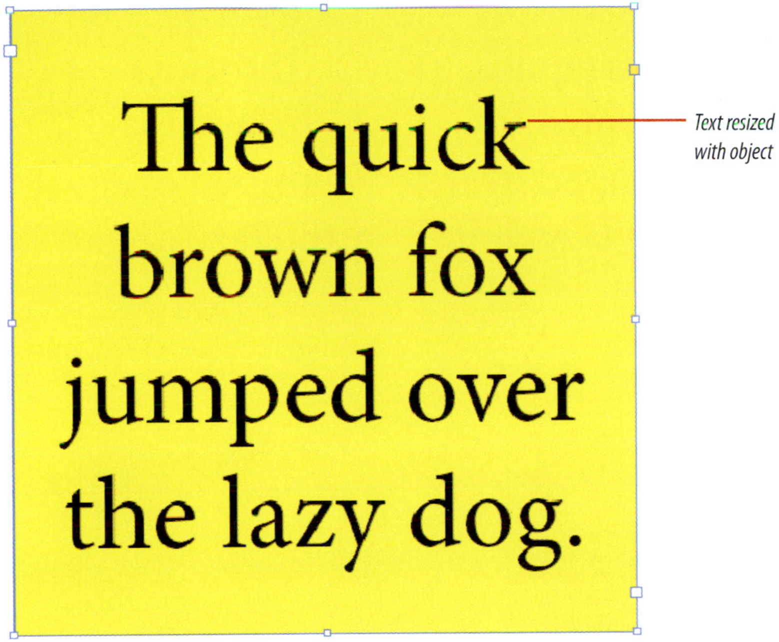

The quick brown fox jumped over the lazy dog.

Text resized with object

Resize a text object

1. Open ID 1-2.indd, then save it as **Objects**.

2. Click the **Selection tool** ▸, then click the **yellow text box** to select it.

3. Click and drag **various handles** and note how the object is resized.

4. When you are done experimenting, undo all of the moves you made.

   The Undo command is at the top of the Edit menu.

5. Press and hold **[Shift]**, then drag the **top left corner handle** to the left edge of the document.

   The object is resized proportionately. The text reflows within the resized object, but the text itself is not enlarged.

6. Undo the move.

7. Press and hold **[Alt]** (Win) or **[option]** (Mac), then click and drag **any corner handle**.

   The object is resized from its center. The text is not resized.

8. Undo the move.

9. Press and hold **[Ctrl]** (Win) or ⌘ (Mac), then click and drag **any corner handle**.

   The object and the text are resized.

TIP If this were a picture frame containing an image, the image would be resized.

10. Undo the move.

11. Press and hold **[Shift] [Ctrl] [Alt]** (Win) or **[Shift]** ⌘ **[option]** (Mac), then drag **any corner handle**.

    As shown in Figure 33, the object and the text in the object are resized proportionately from the object's center.

(continued)

12. Click **File** on the Menu bar, click **Revert**, then click **Yes** (Win) or **Revert** (Mac) if you are prompted to confirm.

    Reverting a file returns it to its status when you last saved it.

You explored various options for resizing an object and its contents, then you reverted the file.

Copy and duplicate objects

1. Select the **text frame**, then copy it, using the [Ctrl] [C] (Win) or ⌘ [C] (Mac) shortcut keys.

2. Click **Edit** on the Menu bar, then click **Paste in Place**.

    A copy of the text frame is placed in front of the original in the exact location.

3. Drag the **copy** of the object to the right so that your screen resembles Figure 34.

4. Select the left object.

(continued)

Figure 34 *Repositioning the pasted copy*

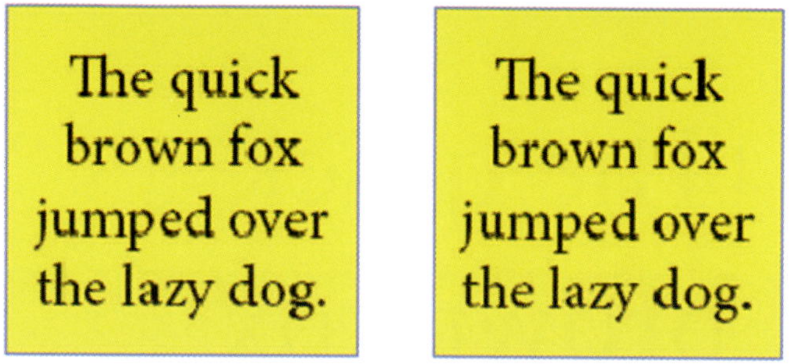

The quick brown fox jumped over the lazy dog.

The quick brown fox jumped over the lazy dog.

Getting to Know InDesign

Figure 35 *Dragging a copy*

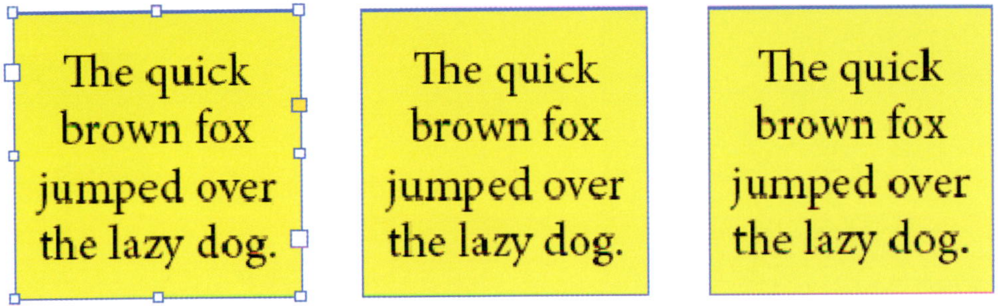

The quick brown fox jumped over the lazy dog.

The quick brown fox jumped over the lazy dog.

The quick brown fox jumped over the lazy dog.

5. Press and hold **[Alt]** (Win) or **[option]** (Mac), then drag a **copy of the object** to the left so that your screen resembles Figure 35.

TIP This method for creating a copy is referred to as "drag-and-drop" a copy.

6. Select all three objects.

   Handles appear around all three objects.

7. Click and drag **various handles** to resize all three objects.

8. Click **Edit** on the Menu bar, then click **Cut**.

9. Save the file.

You duplicated an object in two different ways, first with the Copy and Paste in Place command combination, then with the drag-and-drop technique. You resized multiple objects, and cut them from the document.

Hide, lock, and group objects

1. Click **Object** on the Menu bar, then click **Show All on Spread**.

   This document was originally saved with hidden objects. Three objects appear. They are unselected.

2. Select all three objects, click **Object** on the Menu bar, then click **Group**.

3. Click the **Selection tool** , click the **pasteboard** to deselect all, then click the **pink circle**.

   (continued)

As shown in Figure 36, all three objects are selected because they are grouped. The dotted line around the objects is a visual indication that they are grouped.

4. Click the **pasteboard** to deselect all, click the **Direct Selection tool** 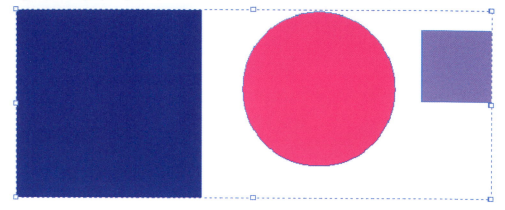, then click the **pink circle**.

   Only the circle is selected, because the Direct Selection tool selects individual objects within a group.

5. Select all, click **Object** on the Menu bar, click **Ungroup**, then click the **pasteboard** to deselect all.

6. Click the **Selection tool** , select **the small square**, click **Object** on the Menu bar, then click **Lock**.

   The object's handles disappear and a Lock icon appears; the object can no longer be selected.

7. Click **Object** on the Menu bar, then click **Unlock All on Spread**.

   The small square is unlocked.

8. Select all, click **Object** on the Menu bar, then click **Hide**.

   All selected objects disappear.

9. Click **Object** on the Menu bar, then click **Show All on Spread**.

   The three objects reappear in the same location that they were in when they were hidden.

TIP Memorize the shortcut keys for Hide/Show, Group/Ungroup, and Lock/Unlock. They are fairly easy to remember and extremely useful. You will be using these commands over and over again when you work in InDesign.

(continued)

Figure 36 *Three grouped objects*

Getting to Know InDesign

Figure 37 *Guides & Pasteboard Preferences dialog box*

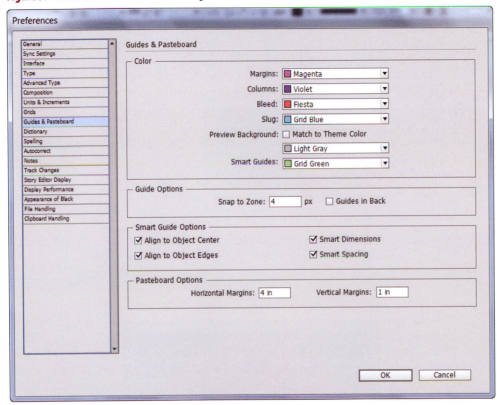

10. Hide the pink circle and the small square.

11. Save the file.

You revealed hidden objects, grouped them, then used the Direct Selection tool to select individual objects within the group. You ungrouped the objects, locked them, unlocked them, and hid them.

Work with Smart Guides

1. Click **Edit** on the Menu bar, point to **Preferences** (Win) or **InDesign** (Mac), then click **Guides & Pasteboard**.

2. Verify that your Smart Guide Options section matches Figure 37, then click **OK**.

3. Click **View** on the Menu bar, point to **Grids & Guides**, then click **Smart Guides**, if necessary, to activate it.

4. Click the **blue rectangle**, then try to center it visually on the page.

(continued)

Using the Smart Cursor

One of the Smart Guides options is the Smart Cursor. With the Smart Cursor activated, a small gray window appears beside your cursor and displays the X/Y coordinates of an object you're moving, resizing, rotating, or otherwise manipulating. To turn the Smart Cursor on and off, activate or deactivate the Show Transformation Values option in the Interface Preferences dialog box.

5. Release the mouse button when both the horizontal and vertical Smart Guides appear, as shown in Figure 38.

Both the horizontal and the vertical pink Smart Guides appear when the object's center point is aligned with the center point of the document. By default, Smart Guides that show the relationship between objects and the document are pink.

TIP The gray box beside the cursor shows the location coordinates of the object on the page. You will learn a lot more about location coordinates in Chapter 3.

6. Show the hidden objects, then hide the small blue square.

7. Using the same method, align the center of the pink circle with the center of the large blue square.

When the center points of the two object are aligned, your Smart Guides will resemble Figure 39.

(continued)

Figure 38 *Centering the square on the page*

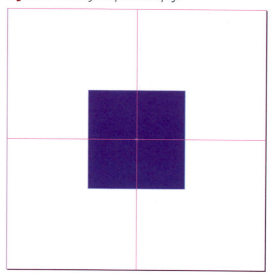

Figure 39 *Centering the circle on the square*

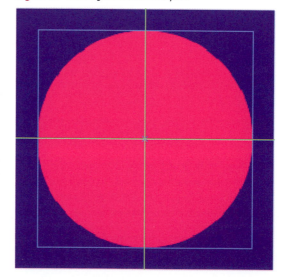

Figure 40 *Aligning the top edges of the two squares*

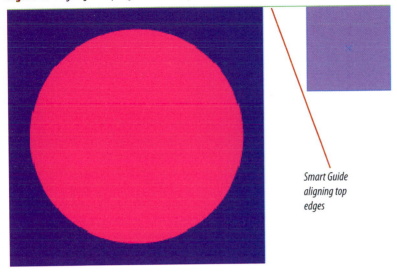

Smart Guide
aligning top
edges

Figure 41 *Aligning the bottom edges of the two squares*

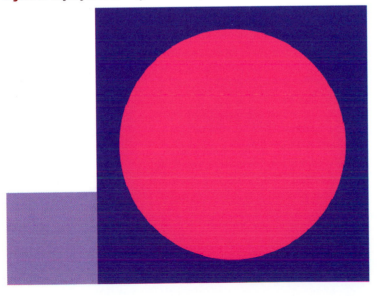

Lesson 4   Work with Objects and Smart Guides

8. Show the hidden small square.

9. Use Smart Guides to align the top of the small square with the top of the large square, as shown in Figure 40.

10. "Snap" the left edge of the small square to the right edge of the large square.

11. Position the small square as shown in Figure 41.

12. Save, then close the file.

You aligned an object at the center of the document and created precise relationships among three objects, using Smart Guides.

Explore the InDesign workspace.

1. Launch Adobe InDesign.
2. Click File on the Menu bar, click Open, navigate to the drive and folder where your Chapter 1 Data Files are stored, click ID 1-3.indd, then click Open.
3. Save the file as **Hana.indd**.
4. Click Window on the Menu bar, point to Workspace, then click [Essentials].

TIP If you are already working in the Essentials workspace, click Window on the Menu bar, then click Reset Essentials to return to the default Essentials workspace settings.

5. Point to the Type tool, then press and hold the mouse button to see the Type on a Path tool.
6. Using the same method, view the hidden tools behind the other tools with small black triangles.
7. Position your mouse pointer over the Selection tool until its tooltip appears.
8. Press the following keys and note which tools are selected with each key: [A], [P], [V], [T], [I], [H], [Z].
9. Press [Tab] to temporarily hide all open panels, then press [Tab] again. The panels reappear.

View and modify page elements.

1. Click the Color panel icon in the stack of collapsed panels in the right of the workspace to expand the Color panel.
2. Click the Collapse to Icons button at the top of the Color panel to minimize the panel, then click the Color panel icon again to expand the panel again.
3. Drag the Color panel name tab to the left so it is ungrouped from the Stroke panel.
4. Drag the Swatches panel name tab to the blank space next to the Color panel name tab, then release the mouse button.
5. Click Window on the Menu bar, point to Object & Layout, then click Transform.
6. Drag the Transform panel name tab to the bottom edge of the Swatches and Color panels group, then release the mouse button.
7. Click and drag the dark gray bar at the top of the panel group, above the Color and Swatches panel tabs.
8. Click the Transform panel name tab, then drag it away from the other two panels.
9. Click Window on the Menu bar, point to Workspace, then click Typography.
10. Press [z] to access the Zoom tool.
11. Position the Zoom tool over the document window, click three times to enlarge the document, press [Alt] (Win) or [option] (Mac), then click three times to reduce the document.
12. Click the Zoom Level list arrow on the Menu bar, then click 1200%.
13. Double-click 1200% in the Zoom Level text box, type 350, then press [Enter] (Win) or [return] (Mac).
14. Click the Hand tool on the Tools panel, then click and drag the document window to scroll around the page.
15. Double-click the Zoom tool.
16. Click the Selection tool, point to the center of the document window, then press and hold [Ctrl] [Spacebar] (Win) or [⌘] [Spacebar] (Mac).
17. Click three times, then release [Ctrl] [Spacebar] (Win) or [⌘] [Spacebar] (Mac).
18. Press and hold [Spacebar] to access the Hand tool, then scroll around the image.
19. Press and hold [Ctrl] [Alt] [Spacebar] (Win) or [⌘] [option] [Spacebar] (Mac), then click the mouse button multiple times to reduce the view to 25%.
20. Click View on the Menu bar, note the shortcut key on the Fit Page in Window command, then click Fit Page in Window.
21. Click View on the Menu bar, then note the Rulers command and its shortcut key.
22. Click the pasteboard to escape the View menu, then press [Ctrl] [R] (Win) or [⌘] [R] (Mac) several times to hide and show rulers, finishing with rulers showing.
23. Note the units on the rulers.
24. Click Edit on the Menu bar, point to Preferences, then click Units & Increments.
25. In the Ruler Units section, click the Horizontal list arrow to see the available measurement options.
26. Set the Horizontal and Vertical fields to Picas.
27. Reopen the Units & Increments Preferences dialog box, change the Horizontal and Vertical fields to Inches, then click OK.
28. Click View on the Menu bar, point to Extras, then note the Frame Edges command and its shortcut key.

29. Click the pasteboard to escape the View menu, then enter [Ctrl] [H] (Win) or [Ctrl] ⌘ [H] (Mac) several times to hide and show frame edges, finishing with frame edges showing.

30. Click View on the Menu bar, point to Grids & Guides, then note the Guides command and its shortcut key.

31. Click the pasteboard to escape the View menu, then enter [Ctrl] [;] (Win) or ⌘ [;] (Mac) several times to hide and show guides, finishing with guides showing.

32. Click View on the Menu bar, point to Grids & Guides, then note the Document Grid command and its shortcut key.

33. Click the pasteboard to escape the View menu, then enter [Ctrl] ['] (Win) or ⌘ ['] (Mac) repeatedly to hide and show the document grid.
    Click View on the Menu bar, point to Grids & Guides, then note the Snap to Guides and Snap to Document Grid commands.

34. Click the pasteboard to escape the View menu.

35. Click the View menu, point to Screen Mode, then click Preview.

36. Press [W] on your keypad to toggle between Preview and Normal modes, finishing in Normal mode.

37. Click View on the Menu bar, point to Screen Mode, then click Presentation.

38. Press the ↓ on your keypad to scroll through the document to the last page.

39. Press the ↑ on your keypad to scroll up to the first page.

40. Press [Esc] to leave Presentation mode.

41. Press and hold [Shift], then press [W] to switch to Presentation mode.

42. Still holding [Shift], press [W] again to return to Normal mode.

43. Click Edit (Win) or InDesign (Mac) on the Menu bar, point to Preferences, click Interface, click the Open Documents as Tabs check box if it is unchecked, then click OK.

44. Open ID 1-2.indd, then click the tabs to toggle between viewing both documents, finishing with Hana as the active document.

45. Position your mouse pointer over the right edge or the bottom-right corner of the document, then click and drag to try to resize it. Because it is a tabbed document, the window is "fixed" and can't be resized.

46. Drag the Hana tab straight down approximately 1/2 inch.

47. Position your mouse pointer over the bottom-right corner, then click and drag towards the center of the monitor window to reduce the window to approximately half its size.

48. Position the mouse pointer over the title bar of the document, then click and drag to move Hana half way down towards the bottom of your monitor screen.

49. Float the mouse pointer over the title bar of Hana, click and drag to position it at the top of the window beside ID 1-2.indd tab, then release the mouse button when you see a horizontal blue bar.

50. Close ID 1-2.indd without saving changes if you are prompted.

Navigate through a document.

1. Click the Page menu list arrow at the bottom-left of the document window, then click 3.

2. Click View on the Menu bar, then click Fit Spread in Window.

3. Click the Next Spread button.

4. Click the Previous Spread button twice.

5. Click the Pages icon in the stack of collapses panel to expand the Pages panel if it is not already expanded.

6. Double-click the page 6 icon on the Pages panel.

7. Double-click the page 3 icon on the Pages panel.

8. Double-click the numbers 2-3 beneath the page 2 and page 3 icons on the Pages panel.

9. Click Layout on the Menu bar, then click First Page.

10. Enter [Ctrl] [J] (Win) or ⌘ [J] (Mac) to open the Go to Page dialog box, enter 5, then press [Enter] (Win) or [return] (Mac).
11. Save the file.
12. Click the page 5 thumbnail on the Pages panel.
13. Click the Pages panel options button, point to Page Attributes, point to Color Label, then click Blue.
14. Click the page numbers 2-3 on the Pages panel to select both thumbnails.
15. Click the Pages panel options button, point to Page Attributes, point to Color Label, then click Orange. Your Pages panel should resemble Figure 42.
16. Save the file.

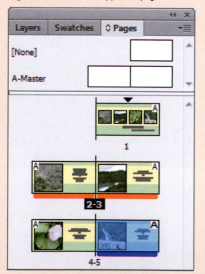

Figure 42 *Color labels applied to pages*

Work with objects and Smart Guides.

1. Open ID 1-4.indd, then save it as **Skills Objects**.
2. Click the Selection tool, then click to select the object.
3. Click and drag various handles and note how the object is resized.
4. Undo all of the moves you made.
5. Press and hold [Shift], then drag the top left corner handle towards the left edge of the document.
6. Undo the move.
7. Press and hold [Alt] (Win) or [option] (Mac), then click and drag any corner handle.
8. Undo the move.
9. Press and hold [Ctrl] (Win) or ⌘ (Mac), then click and drag any corner handle.
10. Undo the move.
11. Press and hold [Shift] [Ctrl] [Alt] (Win) or [Shift] ⌘ [option] (Mac), then drag any corner handle.
12. Click File on the Menu bar, click Revert, then click Yes (Win) or Revert (Mac) if you are prompted to confirm.
13. Select the text frame, then copy it.

14. Click Edit on the Menu bar, then click Paste in Place.
15. Drag the copy to the right so that it is beside the original object.
16. Select the left object.
17. Press and hold [Alt] (Win) or [option] (Mac), then drag a copy of the object to the left so that your screen resembles Figure 43.
18. Select all three objects.
19. Click and drag various handles to resize all three objects.
20. Click Edit on the Menu bar, then click Cut.
21. Save the file.
22. Click Object on the Menu bar, then click Show All on Spread.
23. Select all three objects, click Object on the Menu bar, then click Group.
24. Click the Selection tool, click anywhere on the pasteboard to deselect all, then click the green diamond.
25. Click the pasteboard to deselect all, click the Direct Selection tool, then click the green diamond.

Figure 43 *Text frame copied and duplicated*

© 2015 Cengage Learning®

26. Select all, click Object on the Menu bar, then click Ungroup.
27. Click the Selection tool, select the small circle, click Object on the Menu bar, then click Lock.
28. Click Object on the Menu bar, then click Unlock All on Spread.
29. Select all, click Object on the Menu bar, then click Hide.
30. Click Object on the Menu bar, then click Show All on Spread.
31. Hide the green diamond and the small blue circle.
32. Save the file.

33. Click Edit (Win) or (InDesign) Mac on the Menu bar, point to Preferences, then click Guides & Pasteboard.
34. Verify that your Smart Guide Options section shows the two left options checked and the two right objects unchecked, then click OK.
35. Click View on the Menu bar, point to Grids & Guides, then click Smart Guides, if necessary, to activate it.
36. Click the yellow circle, then try to center it visually on the page.

37. Release the mouse button when both the horizontal and vertical Smart Guides appear, as shown in Figure 44.
38. Show the hidden objects, then hide the small circle.
39. Using the same method, align the center of the green diamond with the center of the yellow circle.
40. Show the hidden small circle.
41. Referring to Figure 45, align the vertical center of the small circle with the right point of the green diamond.
42. Save, then close the file.

Figure 44 *Horizontal and vertical Smart Guides*

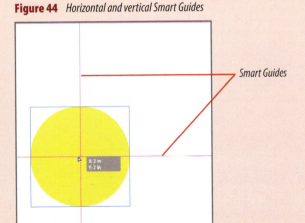

Smart Guides

Figure 45 *Completed Skills Review*

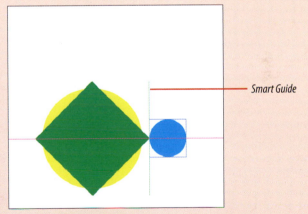

Smart Guide

You work at a local design studio. Your boss has informed you that the studio will be switching to Adobe InDesign for its layout software. She tells you that she wants you to spend the day investigating the software and creating simple layouts. You decide first to group and dock panels in a way that you think will be best for working with type and simple layouts.

1. Start Adobe InDesign.
2. Without creating a new document, group the Paragraph and Character panels together, then click the Paragraph panel name tab so that it is the active panel.
3. Dock the Pages panel to the bottom of the Paragraph panel group.
4. Group the Layers panel with the Pages panel, then click the Layers panel name tab so that it is the active panel.
5. Dock the Swatches panel below the Layers panel group.
6. Group the Color, Stroke, and Gradient panels with the Swatches panel, then click the Gradient panel name tab so that it is the active panel.
7. Dock the Align panel below the Gradient panel group. (*Hint*: The Align panel is in the Object & Layout section of the Window menu.)
8. Group the Transform and the Effects panels with the Align panel, then click the Transform panel name tab so that it is the active panel. (*Hint*: The Transform panel is in the Object & Layout section of the Window menu.)
9. Compare your panels with Figure 46.

Figure 46 *Completed Project Builder 1*

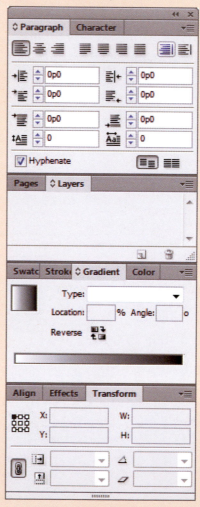

You are the creative director at a design studio. The studio has recently switched to Adobe InDesign for its layout software. You will be conducting a series of in-house classes to teach the junior designers how to use InDesign. Before your first class, you decide to practice some basic skills for viewing a document.

1. Open ID 1-5.indd.
2. Click the Selection tool if it is not active, then press [Ctrl] [Spacebar] (Win) or ⌘ [Spacebar] (Mac) to access the Zoom tool.
3. Position the Zoom tool slightly above and to the left of the left eye, click and drag the Zoom tool pointer to draw a dotted rectangle around the eye, then release the mouse button.
4. Press [Spacebar], then scroll with the Hand tool to the right eye.
5. Press [Ctrl] [Alt] [Spacebar] (Win) or [option] ⌘ [Spacebar] (Mac), then click the Zoom tool five times on the dog's right eye.
6. Move the image with the Hand tool so that both of the dog's eyes and his snout are visible in the window and your screen resembles Figure 47. (Your magnification may differ from that shown in the figure.)
7. Close ID 1-5.indd without saving any changes.

Figure 47 *Completed Project Builder 2*

You will be teaching a small, in-house class on making grids and targets in InDesign. You decide to set up a test exercise for your students to practice duplicating objects and aligning them with one another and with the document.

1. Open ID 1-6.indd, then save it as **Squares and Targets**.
2. Use the techniques you learned in this chapter to recreate the layout in Figure 48. Try it on your own, then go through the following steps and compare your results with those in the figure.
3. Verify that Smart Guides are activated.
4. Align the large yellow circle to the center of the page.
5. Center the large green circle in the large yellow circle.
6. Center the remaining three circles.
7. Copy the smallest yellow circle, then apply the Paste in Place command.
8. Center the pasted circle in the blue square.
9. Group the yellow circle and the blue square.
10. Click the Selection tool.
11. Drag and drop three copies of the group at the four corners of the document.
12. Save your work, then close the file.

Figure 48 *Completed Design Project*

© 2015 Cengage Learning®

In this project, you will examine the layout that you worked with in the lessons of this chapter. You are encouraged to critique the layout from a design perspective, to comment on the elements that you think are effective, and to suggest ways that the presentation may be improved.

1. Open ID 1-7.indd.
2. Click View on the Menu bar, point to Display Performance, then click High Quality Display.
3. Use the Pages panel to move from page to page, viewing each page at least one time, as shown in Figure 49.
4. What do you think of the photographs? Are they effective? Does the fact that they are "silhouetted" against a white background make them more effective, or do you think it would be better if they were photographed in context, such as on a plate or on a table in a restaurant setting?
5. How does the clean white background affect the look and feel of the piece, given that this is a layout about food?
6. Move through all the pages again. The layout changes from page to page. Though the restaurant's name doesn't move from one spread to another and the desserts are all positioned at the center of the page, the location of the menu descriptions changes, as does the location of the prices. Also, the circle behind the prices changes color. What do you think about these changes from page to page? Would the layout be improved if all items were consistent from page to page?
7. Should the prices be in a bold typeface?
8. None of the pages features a title of the food item; the food is described only in the menu description. Do you think it would be better if a title appeared on every page? If so, would you be willing to discard the restaurant's name in the upper-left corner in favor of a title?
9. Submit your answers to these three questions in a document called Design Critique.
10. Close ID 1-7.indd without saving any changes.

Figure 49 *ID 1-7.indd*

CHAPTER 2 WORKING WITH TEXT

1. Format text
2. Format paragraphs
3. Create and apply styles
4. Edit text
5. Create bulleted and numbered lists

CHAPTER 2 WORKING WITH TEXT

Introduction

Earth, air, fire, and water were considered the four essential elements of our world by the ancients. Another quartet—text, color, illustration, and imagery—are considered the four essential elements of layout by designers. Take a moment to read them again and make a mental note. We will use these four elements as categories throughout this book to approach the myriad features InDesign offers.

In this chapter, we will focus on working with text. Like Proteus, the mythological figure who could change his outer form at will, text in a layout can appear in a variety of ways. It is *protean*, or, versatile. As display text it can be a bold, dramatic headline at the center of a page or a miniscule footnote tucked away unobtrusively. As paragraphs of text, it can be flowed as body copy, or it can appear as simple page numbers at the lower corner of a page.

You will be pleased to find that InDesign is a first-rate application for generating and editing text. Everything you want to do can be done. With InDesign, your ability to generate functional, readable text and beautiful typographic artwork is without limitation.

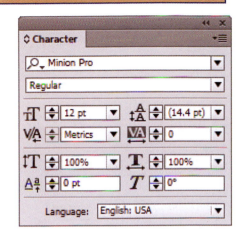

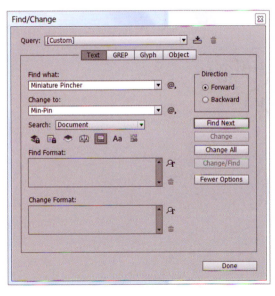

Format
TEXT

What You'll Do

Introducing the Min-Pin
by Christopher Smith

© 2015 Cengage Learning®

 In this lesson, you will use the Character panel and various keyboard commands to modify text attributes.

Creating Text

In InDesign, when you create text, you do so by first creating a text frame. Click the Type tool on the Tools panel, then click and drag the Type tool anywhere on the page to create a text frame. You'll see a blinking cursor in the frame; then just start typing.

All InDesign text is in a text frame. You use the Character and Paragraph panels to format the text in the frame. You can also use the Text Frame Options command, located on the Object menu, to format the text frame itself.

Using the Character Panel

The Character panel, shown in Figure 1, is the command center for modifying text. The Character panel works hand-in-hand with the Paragraph panel, which is why it's wise to keep them grouped together. While the Paragraph panel, as its name implies, focuses on manipulating paragraphs or blocks of text, the Character panel focuses on more specific modifications, such as font, font style, and font size.

In addition to these basic modifications, the Character panel offers other controls for manipulating text. You can use the panel to modify leading, track and kern text, apply a horizontal scale or a vertical scale to text, perform a baseline shift, or skew text. To select text quickly for editing, you can use the methods shown in Table 1: Keyboard Commands for Selecting Text, on the next page.

QUICK TIP

You can set the font list on the Character panel to show font names or font names and samples of each font. To enable or disable this feature, click Edit on the Menu bar, point to Preferences, click Type, then click to add or remove a check mark in the Font Preview Size check box. Notice also that you can click the Font Preview Size list arrow and choose Small, Medium, or Large.

Pasting Text Without Formatting

When you copy text, then paste it, it is, by default, pasted with all of its formatting—its typeface, type style, type size, and any other formatting that has been applied. Sometimes, this can be undesirable. This is where the Paste without Formatting command comes into play. It strips the copied text of all its original formatting, then reformats it to match the formatting of the text frame where it is pasted.

Understanding Leading

Leading is the term used to describe the vertical space between lines of text. This space is measured from the baseline of one line of text to the baseline of the next line of text. As shown in Figure 2, the **baseline** is the invisible line on which text sits. Leading, like font size, is measured in points.

Figure 1 *Character panel*

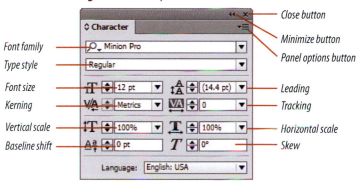

Figure 2 *Examples of leading*

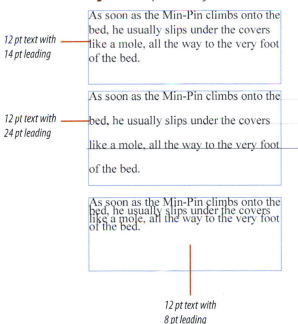

12 pt text with 14 pt leading

12 pt text with 24 pt leading

12 pt text with 8 pt leading

TABLE 1: KEYBOARD COMMANDS FOR SELECTING TEXT	
To select:	**Do the following:**
One word	Double-click word
One line	Triple-click any word in the line
One paragraph	Click any word in the paragraph four times
Entire story	Click any word in the story five times
Entire story	[Ctrl][A] (Win) or ⌘ [A] (Mac)
One character to the right of insertion point	[Shift] →
One character to the left of insertion point	[Shift] ←
One line up from insertion point	[Shift] ↑
One line down from insertion point	[Shift] ↓
One word to the right of insertion point	[Shift][Ctrl] → (Win) or [Shift] ⌘ → (Mac)
One word to the left of insertion point	[Shift][Ctrl] ← (Win) or [Shift] ⌘ ← (Mac)
One paragraph above insertion point	[Shift][Ctrl] ↑ (Win) or [Shift] ⌘ ↑ (Mac)
One paragraph below insertion point	[Shift][Ctrl] ↓ (Win) or [Shift] ⌘ ↓ (Mac)

© Cengage Learning®

Scaling Text Horizontally and Vertically

When you format text, your most basic choice is which font you want to use and at what size you want to use it. Once you've chosen a font and a font size, you can further manipulate the appearance of the text with a horizontal or vertical scale.

On the Character panel, horizontal and vertical scales are expressed as percentages. By default, text is generated at a 100% horizontal and 100% vertical scale, meaning that the text is not scaled at all. Decreasing the horizontal scale only, for example, maintains the height of the characters but decreases the width—on the horizontal axis. Conversely, increasing the horizontal scale again maintains the height but increases the width of the characters on the horizontal axis. Figure 3 shows four examples of horizontal and vertical scales.

QUICK TIP

You can also control the vertical alignment of text inside a text box by selecting the text box, clicking Object on the Menu bar, then clicking Text Frame Options. Click the Align list arrow, then click Top, Center, Bottom, or Justify.

Kerning and Tracking Text

Though your computer is a magnificent instrument for generating text in myriad fonts and font sizes, you will often want to manipulate the appearance of text after you have created it—especially if you have the meticulous eye of a designer. **Kerning** is a long-standing process of increasing or decreasing space between a pair of characters. **Tracking** is more global. Like kerning, tracking affects the spaces between letters, but it is applied globally to an entire word or paragraph.

Kerning and tracking are standard features in most word processing applications, but they are more about typography than word processing—that is, they are used for setting text in a way that is pleasing to the eye. Spacing problems with text are usually more prominent with large size headlines than with smaller body copy—this is why many designers will spend great amounts of time tracking and kerning a headline. Figures 4 and 5 show examples of kerning and tracking applied to a headline. Note, though, that kerning and tracking are also used often on body copy as a simple solution for fitting text within an allotted space.

InDesign measures both kerning and tracking in increments of 1/1000 em—a unit of measure that is determined by the current type size. In a 6-point font, 1 em equals

Figure 3 *Scaling text horizontally and vertically*

original text
50% horizontal scale
150% horizontal scale
50% vertical scale
150% vertical scale

Figure 4 *Kerning text*

No kerning

With kerning

Figure 5 *Tracking text*

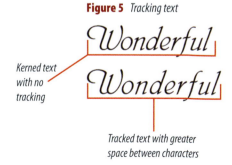

Kerned text with no tracking

Tracked text with greater space between characters

6 points; in a 12-point font, 1 em equals 12 points. It's good to know this, but you don't need to have this information in mind when kerning and tracking text. Just remember that the increments are small enough to provide you with the specificity that you desire for creating eye-pleasing text.

Creating Superscript Characters

You are already familiar with superscript characters, even if you don't know them by that term. When you see a footnote in a book or document, the superscripted character is the footnote itself, the small number positioned to the upper-right of a word. Figure 6 shows a superscripted character.

The only tricky thing about applying a superscript is remembering how to do it. The Superscript command, as shown in Figure 7, is listed in the Character panel options. Wait—there's one more tricky thing you need to remember about superscripts. If you select a 12-point character, for example, and then apply the Superscript command, the size of the character will decrease; however, its point size will still be identified on the Character panel as 12 points.

Creating Subscript Characters

The Character panel menu also offers a command for Subscript. You can think of Subscript as the opposite of Superscript. Instead of raising the baseline of the selected text, the Subscript command positions the text below its original baseline. As with Superscript, the Subscript command makes the selected text appear smaller.

Of the two, Subscript is used less often. Though it is seldom used for footnotes, many designers use Subscript for trademarks and registration marks.

Underlining Text

InDesign offers different methods for underlining text and for creating **rules**, which are horizontal, vertical, or diagonal lines. When you simply want to underline selected text, the most basic method is to use the Underline command on the Character panel menu. With this command, the weight of the underline is determined by the point size of the selected text. The greater the point size, the greater the weight of the line.

Figure 6 *Identifying a superscripted character*

Superscripted character

Superscript command

Figure 7 *Locating the Superscript command*

Hide Options	
OpenType	▶
All Caps	Shift+Ctrl+K
Small Caps	Shift+Ctrl+H
Superscript	Shift+Ctrl+=
Subscript	Alt+Shift+Ctrl+=
Underline	Shift+Ctrl+U
Strikethrough	Shift+Ctrl+/
✓ Ligatures	
Underline Options....	
Strikethrough Options...	
No Break	

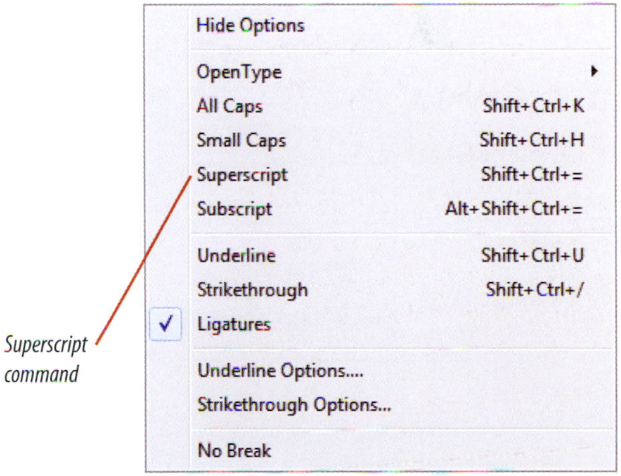

Searching for Fonts on the Character Panel

Font search enhancements in Creative Cloud make working with fonts and finding the font you want to use quick and easy. The traditional paradigm of clicking the Font family menu and choosing a font is still in place—nothing's changed there—but Creative Cloud lets you experiment with and search for fonts in powerful new ways.

QUICK **TIP**

Every function that you can perform on the Character panel can also be done on the Control panel.

As shown in Figure 8, the top field on the Character panel contains a magnifying glass icon on the left side. Think of this field as both the font search and current font field, because you can use this field to search through the available fonts on your system. Type any font name in the field—Garamond, for example— and a scrollable font menu will appear with all the Garamond typefaces on your system, grouped and listed together. You can also search for font styles such as bold, condensed, italic etc.

As shown in Figure 9, when you click the magnifying glass, you can choose between Search Entire Font Name or Search First Word only. Search First Word only is a helpful

Figure 8 *Search feature on the Character panel*

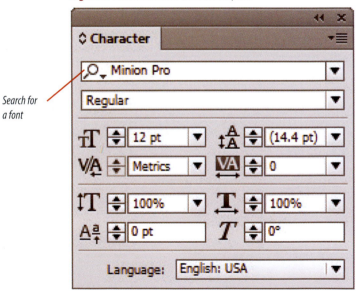

Search for a font

Figure 9 *Search options on the Character panel*

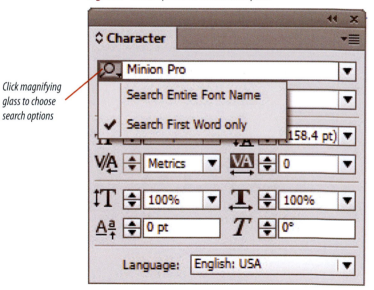

Click magnifying glass to choose search options

setting if you are unsure of the complete font name that you need.

As shown in Figure 10, if you select the contents of the field, a small x appears at the right. Click it to delete any current font listed in the field as the current search item.

If you click the Font family list arrow, you'll see the most recently used fonts at the top of the menu. As shown in Figure 11, in addition to searching through the available fonts on your system, you can also search for and download fonts from Adobe Typekit; an

Figure 11 *Font families*

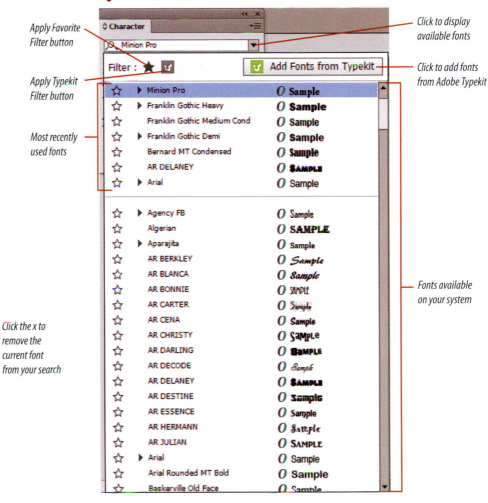

Apply Favorite Filter button

Apply Typekit Filter button

Most recently used fonts

Click to display available fonts

Click to add fonts from Adobe Typekit

Fonts available on your system

Figure 10 *Removing a font from a search*

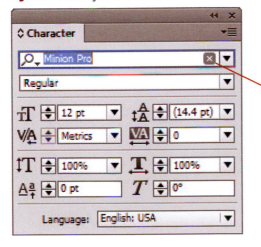

Click the x to remove the current font from your search

enormous repository of fonts that is available to Creative Cloud subscribers. Once you download a font family from Typekit, shown in Figure 12, it is available in all of your other Adobe and non-Adobe applications.

Font preview is also a powerful feature. With text selected, click the Font family list arrow on the Character panel, then use the up and down arrows on your keypad to preview how different typefaces will affect the selected text.

You can categorize fonts as favorites by clicking the star icon beside the font's name. Then, when you click the Apply Favorite Filter button at the top of the menu, only your favorite fonts will appear in the list.

Figure 12 *Adobe Typekit*

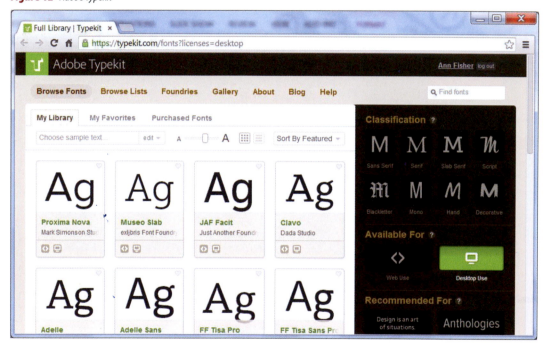

Figure 13 *Units & Increments section of the Preferences dialog box*

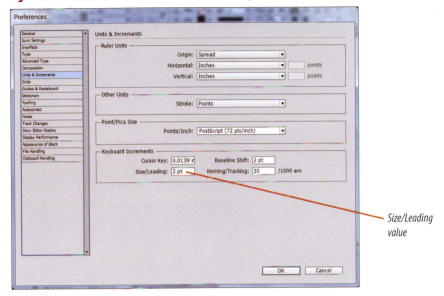

Size/Leading
value

Figure 14 *Character panel*

Font Size
list arrow

Font Family
list arrow

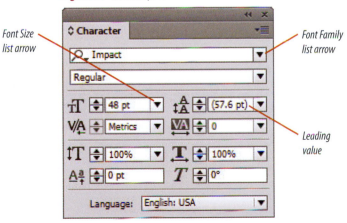

Leading
value

1. Open ID 2-1.indd, then save it as **Min-Pin Intro**.
2. Click **Edit** (Win) or **InDesign** (Mac) on the Menu bar, point to **Preferences**, then click **Units & Increments**.
3. Verify that your Preferences dialog box has the same settings shown in Figure 13, then click **OK**.
4. Click **Window** on the Menu bar, point to **Workspace**, then click [**Typography**] or **Reset Typography** if [Typography] is already checked.
5. Click the **Type tool** T, then double-click the word **Introducing** at the top of the page.
6. Open the Character panel.

   The Character panel displays the formatting of the selected text.
7. Triple-click **Introducing** to select the entire line.
8. On the Character panel, click the **Font Family list arrow**, click **Impact**, click the **Font Size list arrow**, click **48 pt**, then verify that the Leading text box contains 57.6 pt, as shown in Figure 14.
9. Press and hold [**Shift**] [**Ctrl**] (Win) or [**Shift**] ⌘ (Mac), then press [**<**] 10 times.

   The point size is reduced by one point size every time you press [**<**].
10. Press and hold [**Shift**] [**Ctrl**] (Win) or [**Shift**] ⌘ (Mac), then press [**>**] two times.

   The point size is increased by two points.
11. Triple-click **by** on the second line, change the font to Garamond or a similar font, click the **Type Style list arrow**, click **Italic**, click the **Font Size list arrow**, then click **18 pt**.

TIP If the Garamond font is not available, use a similar font.

(continued)

12. Click the **Selection tool** [cursor icon], then note that the text frame is highlighted, as shown in Figure 15.
13. Click **Object** on the Menu bar, click **Text Frame Options**, click the **Align list arrow** in the Vertical Justification section, click **Center**, then click **OK**.

You used keyboard commands and the Character panel to modify text.

Track and kern text

1. Click the **Zoom tool** [magnifier icon], click and drag the **Zoom tool pointer** around the light green text frame, then release the mouse button.

   When you drag the Zoom tool pointer, a dotted-lined selection rectangle appears. When you release the mouse button, the contents within the rectangle are magnified.

2. Click the **Type tool** [T icon], then triple-click the word **Introducing**.

3. Click the **Tracking list arrow** on the Character panel, then click **200**.

   The horizontal width of each word increases, and a consistent amount of space is applied between each letter, as shown in Figure 16.

4. Reduce the tracking value to **25**.

5. Click between the letters h and e in the word **the**, click the **Kerning list arrow**, then click **-50**.

   The space between the two letters decreases.

6. Click the **Kerning up arrow** twice to decrease the kerning value to **-30**.

7. Click the **Selection tool** [cursor icon].

   Your headline should resemble Figure 17.

You used the Character panel to modify tracking and kerning values applied to text.

Figure 15 *Selected text box*

Introducing the Min-Pin
by Christopher Smith

Text frame handles

Figure 16 *Increasing the tracking value of selected text*

Introducing the Min-Pin
by Christopher Smith

Figure 17 *Decreasing the kerning value between two letters*

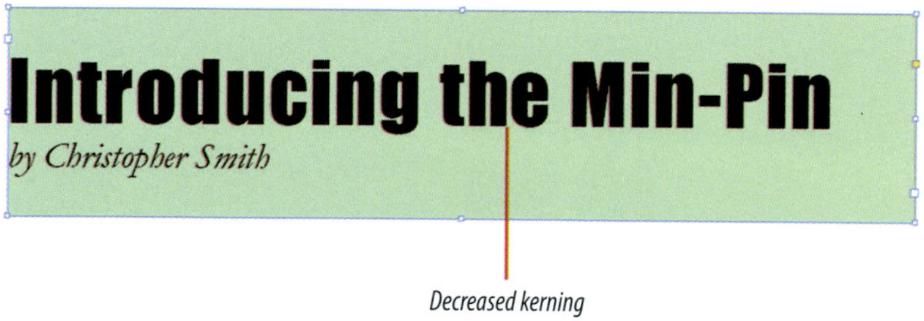

Introducing the Min-Pin
by Christopher Smith

Decreased kerning

Figure 18 *Applying the Superscript command*

Pinscher¹.

Superscript
character

Figure 19 *Using the Superscript command to format footnotes*

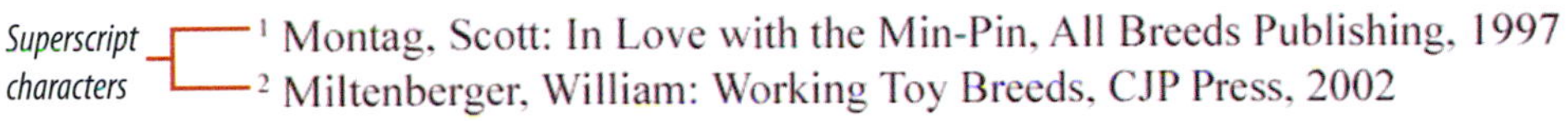

Superscript
characters

¹ Montag, Scott: In Love with the Min-Pin, All Breeds Publishing, 1997
² Miltenberger, William: Working Toy Breeds, CJP Press, 2002

Inserting Footnotes Automatically

While you can insert footnotes using the techniques in this lesson, if you have many footnotes in a document, you can use the enhanced footnote feature to insert them quickly and easily. In InDesign, a footnote consists of a reference number that appears in document text, and the footnote text that appears at the bottom of the page or column. To add a footnote, place the insertion point in the document location where you want the reference number to appear. Click Type on the Menu bar, then click Insert Footnote. The insertion point moves to the footnote area at the bottom of the page or column. Type the footnote text; the footnote area expands as you type. If the text containing a footnote moves to another page, its footnote moves with it.

Create superscript characters

1. Click **View** on the Menu bar, click **Fit Page in Window**, click the **Zoom** 🔍, then drag a selection box that encompasses all of the body copy on the page.

2. Click the **Type tool** T, then select the number **1** after the words Doberman Pinscher at the end of the fourth paragraph.

3. Click the **Character panel options button** ▾☰, then click **Superscript**.

   The character's size is reduced and it is positioned higher than the characters that precede it, as shown in an enlarged view in Figure 18.

4. Select the number **2** after the word cows in the last paragraph, then apply the Superscript command.

TIP When the Superscript command is applied to text, its designated font size remains the same.

5. Select the number **1** beside the footnote at the bottom of the page, apply the Superscript command, select the number **2** below, apply the Superscript command again, then deselect the text.

   Your footnotes should resemble Figure 19.

You applied the Superscript command to format selected text as footnotes.

Underline text

1. Click **View** on the Menu bar, click **Fit Page in Window**, click the **Zoom tool** 🔍, then drag a selection box that encompasses both footnotes at the bottom of the page.

2. Click the **Type tool** T, then select **In Love with the Min-Pin** in the first footnote.

(continued)

3. Click the **Character panel options button** ▾≣, then click **Underline**.

Only the selected text is underlined, as shown in Figure 20.

TIP The weight of the line is automatically determined, based on the point size of the selected text.

4. Select **Working Toy Breeds** in the second footnote, then apply the Underline command.

5. Select the **entire first footnote** except the number 1, double-click **12** in the Font Size text box, type **8**, then press **[Enter]** (Win) or **[return]** (Mac).

6. Select the **entire second footnote** except the number 2, change its font size to 8 pt, then click to deselect the text.

Your footnotes should resemble Figure 21.

TIP To specify how far below the baseline the underline is positioned, click the Underline Options command on the Character panel options menu, then increase or decrease the Offset value.

You selected text, then applied the Underline command from the Character panel options menu.

Use enhanced font search options

1. Click **View** on the Menu bar, then click **Fit Page in Window**.

2. Click the **Zoom tool** 🔍 on the Tools panel, then zoom in on the first three words of the first sentence, "**The Miniature Pinscher.**"

3. Click the **Type tool** T, select "**The Miniature Pinscher,**" then click in the top field of the Character panel.

(continued)

Figure 20 *Underlining text*

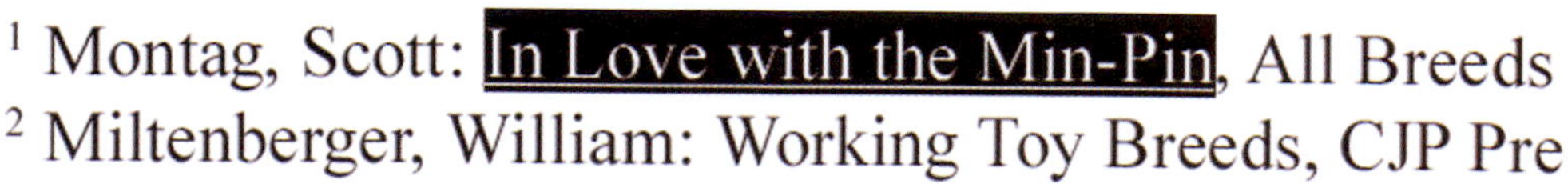

[1] Montag, Scott: <u>In Love with the Min-Pin</u>, All Breeds
[2] Miltenberger, William: Working Toy Breeds, CJP Pre

Figure 21 *Formatting footnotes*

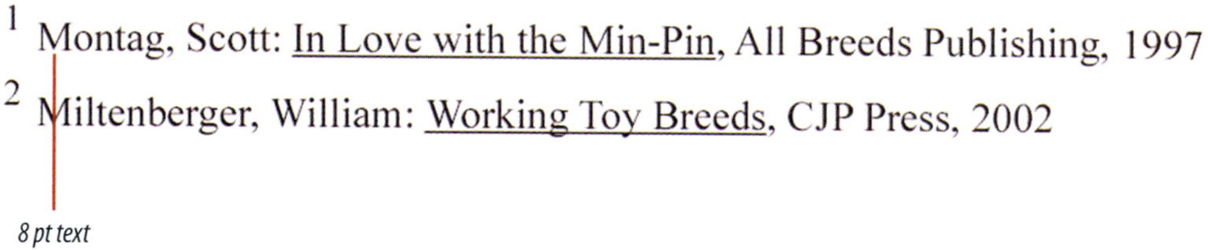

[1] Montag, Scott: <u>In Love with the Min-Pin</u>, All Breeds Publishing, 1997
[2] Miltenberger, William: <u>Working Toy Breeds</u>, CJP Press, 2002

8 pt text

Formatting Footnotes

If you use the Insert Footnote command to enter footnotes in a document, you can specify a number of formatting attributes. Click Type on the Menu bar, then click Document Footnote Options. On the Numbering and Formatting tab, you can select the numbering style, starting number, prefix, position, character style, or separator. The Layout tab lets you set the spacing above and between footnotes, as well as the rule that appears above them. Formatting changes you make to footnotes affect all existing and new footnotes.

Figure 22 *Displaying only bold fonts*

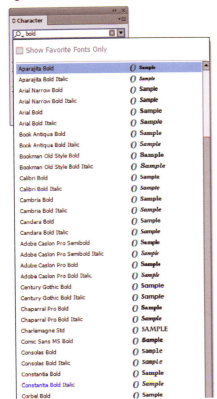

Figure 23 *Displaying favorite fonts*

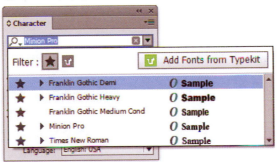

The contents of the field are automatically highlighted and an x appears at the far right.

4. Type the word **bold** in the field.

   As shown in Figure 22, the font menu appears showing only those fonts with the word "bold" in their titles.

5. Click anywhere on the page to escape the font menu.

6. Click the **Font family list arrow** next to the current font name on the Character panel, note that the most recent fonts you've used are listed at the top, then note the star icons to the left of every font name.

7. Click the **stars** beside five fonts that you use often.

8. Click the **star button** ★ (Apply Favorite Filter button) at the top of the menu.

   As shown in Figure 23, only the fonts that have been starred as favorites are listed.

9. Click the **star button** ★ again (Clear Filter button) to deactivate the feature.

10. Select "**The Miniature Pinscher**," then click the top field on the Character panel to highlight the current font.

11. Click the **up and down arrows** on your keypad.

   As you click, the next or previous font in the font menu is applied to the selected text.

12. Press [**Esc**] to escape the font menu and leave The Miniature Pinscher text unchanged.

You used the font search utility on the Character panel to find only bold fonts. You marked fonts as favorites, then specified that the font menu show only those fonts. You previewed different fonts applied to your selected text using the up and down arrows on your keypad.

Format
PARAGRAPHS

What You'll Do

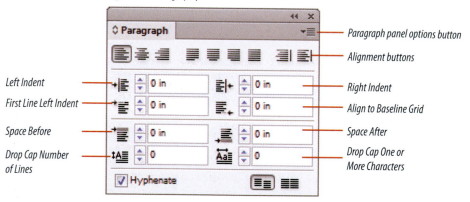

In this lesson, you will use the Paragraph panel and various keyboard commands to modify paragraph attributes.

Using the Paragraph Panel

The Paragraph panel, shown in Figure 24, is the command center for modifying paragraphs or blocks of text also known as body copy.

The Paragraph panel is divided into three main sections. The top section controls alignment. Of the nine icons offering options for aligning text, the first four—Align left, Align center, Align right, and Justify with last line aligned left—are the most common. The remaining five options include subtle modifications of justified text and two options for aligning text towards or away from the spine of a book.

The next section offers controls for indents. Use an indent when you want the first line of each paragraph to start further to the right than the other lines of text, as shown in Figure 25. This figure also shows what is commonly referred to as a **pull quote**. You have probably seen pull quotes in most magazines. They are a typographical design solution in which text is used at a larger point

Figure 24 *Paragraph panel*

Paragraph panel options button

Alignment buttons

Left Indent

First Line Left Indent

Space Before

Drop Cap Number of Lines

Right Indent

Align to Baseline Grid

Space After

Drop Cap One or More Characters

Working with Text

size and positioned prominently on the page. Note the left and right indents applied to the pull quote in Figure 25. They were created using the Left Indent and Right Indent buttons on the Paragraph panel.

The third section of the Paragraph panel controls vertical spacing between paragraphs and applying drop caps. For large blocks of text, it is often most pleasing to the eye to create either a subtle or distinct space after every paragraph. In InDesign, you create these by entering values in the Space After or the Space Before text boxes on the Paragraph panel. Of the two, the Space After text box is more commonly used. The Space Before text box, when it is used, is often used in conjunction with the Space After text box to offset special page elements, such as a pull quote.

A **drop cap** is a design element in which the first letter or letters of a paragraph are increased in size to create a visual effect. In the figure, the drop cap is measured as being three text lines in height. If you click to place the cursor to the right of the drop cap then increase the kerning value on the Character panel, the space between the drop cap and all three lines of text will be increased. Figure 26 shows a document with a drop cap and a .25 inch space after every paragraph.

Figure 25 *First line indent and left and right indents*

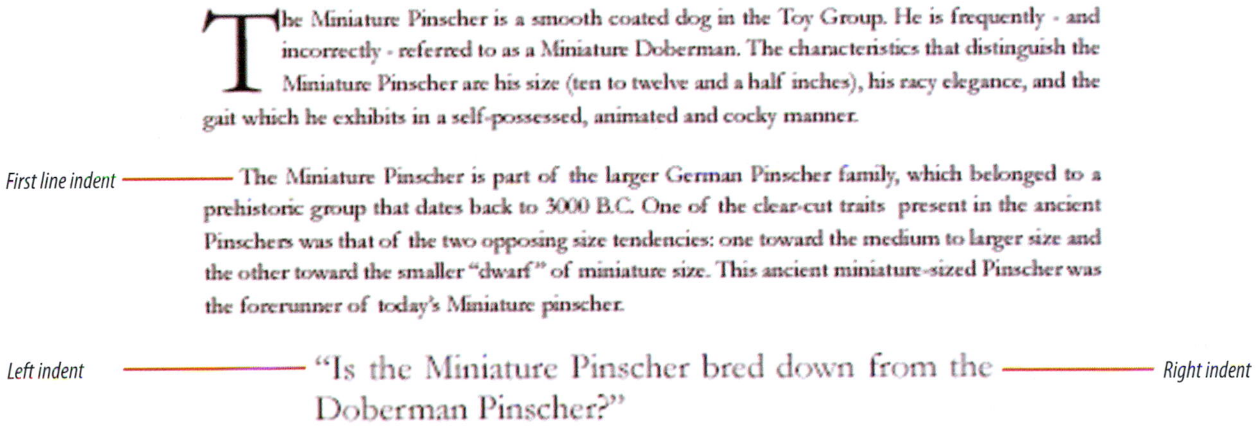

The Miniature Pinscher is a smooth coated dog in the Toy Group. He is frequently - and incorrectly - referred to as a Miniature Doberman. The characteristics that distinguish the Miniature Pinscher are his size (ten to twelve and a half inches), his racy elegance, and the gait which he exhibits in a self-possessed, animated and cocky manner.

First line indent ———— The Miniature Pinscher is part of the larger German Pinscher family, which belonged to a prehistoric group that dates back to 3000 B.C. One of the clear-cut traits present in the ancient Pinschers was that of the two opposing size tendencies: one toward the medium to larger size and the other toward the smaller "dwarf" of miniature size. This ancient miniature-sized Pinscher was the forerunner of today's Miniature pinscher.

Left indent ———— "Is the Miniature Pinscher bred down from the ———— Right indent
Doberman Pinscher?"

Using Optical Margin Alignment

Optical Margin Alignment is a great feature that controls the alignment of punctuation marks for all paragraphs within a block of type. Optical Margin Alignment forces punctuation marks, as well as the edges of some letters, to hang outside the text margins so that the type appears aligned. To override this feature, click the text box or type object, click the Paragraph panel options button, then click Ignore Optical Margin. You can also click the Paragraph Styles panel options button, click Style Options, click the Indents and Spacing category, then click the Ignore Optical Margin check box.

Avoiding Typographic Problems

Widows and **orphans** are words or single lines of text that become separated from the other lines in a paragraph. Orphans are left alone at the bottom of a page and widows at the top. The Paragraph panel options menu has a number of commands that allow you to control how text appears and flows, specifically at the end of a column or page, avoiding unsightly widows and orphans. The Keep Options command lets you highlight text that should always stay together instead of being split over two pages. The Keep Options dialog box lets you choose to keep the selected text together or choose how many lines to keep with the selected text. The Justification command opens the Justification dialog box in which you can define the percentages assigned to minimum, desired and maximum word spacing, letter spacing, and glyph scaling. You can also change the Auto Leading value and tell InDesign how to justify a one-word line. The Hyphenation Settings dialog box, which opens by clicking Hyphenation on the Paragraph panel options menu, allows you to define how words should be hyphenated. You can turn hyphenation off completely by removing the check mark in the Hyphenation check box.

Understanding Returns

Most people think of a paragraph as a block of text, but, in design language, a paragraph can be a block of text, a line of text, or even a single word, followed by a paragraph return. A **paragraph return**, also called a **hard return**, is inserted into the text formatting by pressing [Enter] (Win)

Figure 26 *A drop cap and paragraphs with vertical space applied after every paragraph*

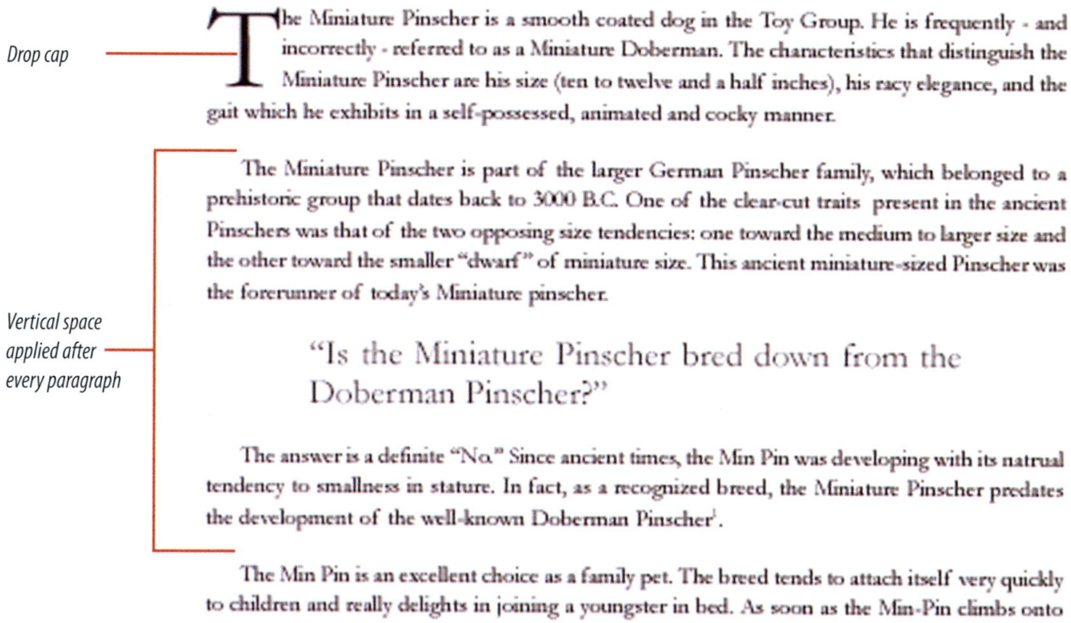

Drop cap

The Miniature Pinscher is a smooth coated dog in the Toy Group. He is frequently - and incorrectly - referred to as a Miniature Doberman. The characteristics that distinguish the Miniature Pinscher are his size (ten to twelve and a half inches), his racy elegance, and the gait which he exhibits in a self-possessed, animated and cocky manner.

The Miniature Pinscher is part of the larger German Pinscher family, which belonged to a prehistoric group that dates back to 3000 B.C. One of the clear-cut traits present in the ancient Pinschers was that of the two opposing size tendencies: one toward the medium to larger size and the other toward the smaller "dwarf" of miniature size. This ancient miniature-sized Pinscher was the forerunner of today's Miniature pinscher.

Vertical space applied after every paragraph

"Is the Miniature Pinscher bred down from the Doberman Pinscher?"

The answer is a definite "No." Since ancient times, the Min Pin was developing with its natrual tendency to smallness in stature. In fact, as a recognized breed, the Miniature Pinscher predates the development of the well-known Doberman Pinscher[1].

The Min Pin is an excellent choice as a family pet. The breed tends to attach itself very quickly to children and really delights in joining a youngster in bed. As soon as the Min-Pin climbs onto

Working with Text

or [return] (Mac). For example, if I type my first name and then enter a paragraph return, that one word—my first name—is a paragraph. When working with body copy, a paragraph is any block of text separated by a single paragraph return.

When typing body copy, designers will often want a space after each paragraph because it is visually pleasing and helps to keep paragraphs distinct. The mistake many designers make is pressing [Enter] (Win) or [return] (Mac) twice to create that space after the paragraph. Wrong! What they've done is created two paragraphs. The correct way to insert space between paragraphs is to enter a value in the Space After text box on the Paragraph panel.

QUICK TIP

When creating a first line paragraph indent, many users will press [Spacebar] 5 or 10 times and then start typing. This is incorrect formatting. Paragraph indents are created using the First Line Left Indent setting on the Paragraph panel, not by inserting multiple spaces.

As you edit text, you may encounter a "bad line break" at the end of a line, such as an oddly hyphenated word or a phrase that is split from one line to the next. In many of these cases, you will want to move a word or phrase to the next line. You can do this by entering a **soft return**. A soft return moves words down to the next baseline but does not create a new paragraph. You enter a soft return by pressing and holding [Shift], while pressing [Enter] (Win) or [return] (Mac).

You can avoid untold numbers of formatting problems by using correct typesetting behaviors, especially those regarding Space After and First Line Indent.

Using the Type on a Path Tool

Hidden behind the Type tool on the Tools panel is the Type on a Path tool. The Type on a Path tool allows you to position text on any closed or open InDesign path. For example, you could draw a closed path, such as a circle, then position text on the circular path. Or you could draw a simple curved path across the page, then flow text along the path. Simply click the Type on a Path tool on the path. A blinking cursor will appear, and you can then begin typing on the path. The path itself remains visible and selectable; you can apply stroke colors and various widths to the path. You can format the size, typeface, and type style of type on a path as well. Give it a try!

Use the Paragraph panel and Character panel to modify leading and alignment

1. Click **View** on the Menu bar, click **Fit Page in Window**, then click the first instance of **The** in the first paragraph four times.

   TIP Clicking a word four times selects the entire paragraph.

2. Click the same word five times.

   TIP Clicking a word five times selects all the text in the text frame.

3. Click the **Leading list arrow** on the Character panel, then click **30 pt**.

   The vertical space between each line of text is increased, as shown in Figure 27.

   TIP Because leading can be applied to a single selected word as well as to an entire paragraph, the Leading setting is on the Character panel (as opposed to the Paragraph panel).

4. Double-click **30** in the Leading text box, type **16**, then press **[Enter]** (Win) or **[return]** (Mac).

5. Display the Paragraph panel, then click the **Justify with last line aligned left button** ▤.

6. Click **Introducing** at the top of the document three times, then click the **Align center button** ▤ on the Paragraph panel.

7. Click **Edit** on the Menu bar, then click **Deselect All**.

   Your document should resemble Figure 28.

You modified the leading and alignment of a block of selected text.

Figure 27 *Modifying leading*

Increased leading adds more vertical space between lines of text

Figure 28 *Modifying alignment*

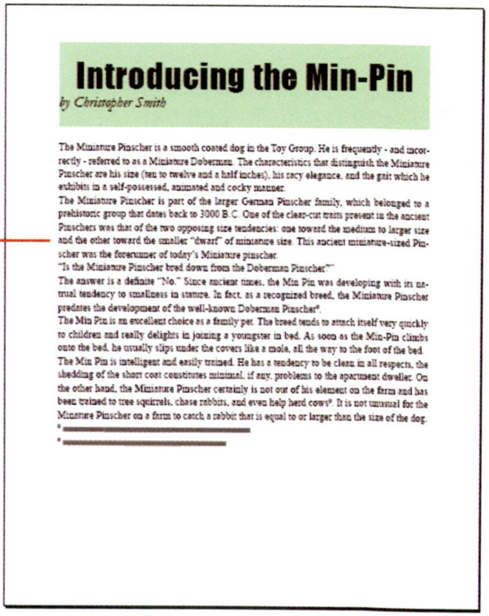

Text justified with last line aligned left

Working with Text

Figure 29 *Increasing the Space After value*

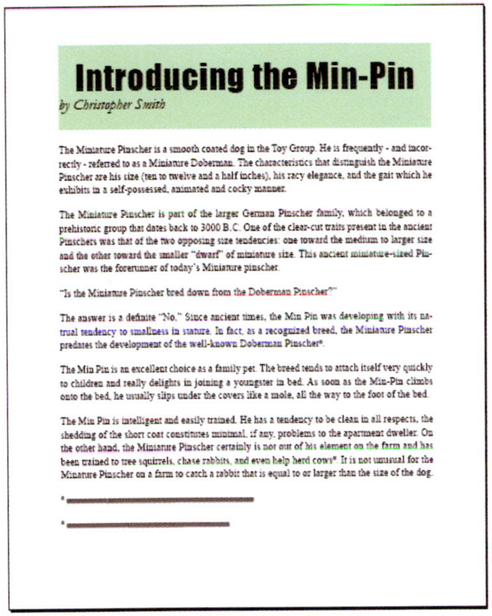

Introducing the Min-Pin
by Christopher Smith

The Miniature Pinscher is a smooth coated dog in the Toy Group. He is frequently - and incorrectly - referred to as a Miniature Doberman. The characteristics that distinguish the Miniature Pinscher are his size (ten to twelve and a half inches), his racy elegance, and the gait which he exhibits in a self-possessed, animated and cocky manner.

The Miniature Pinscher is part of the larger German Pinscher family, which belonged to a prehistoric group that dates back to 3000 B.C. One of the clear-cut traits present in the ancient Pinschers was that of the two opposing size tendencies: one toward the medium to larger size and the other toward the smaller "dwarf" of miniature size. This ancient miniature-sized Pinscher was the forerunner of today's Miniature pinscher.

"Is the Miniature Pinscher bred down from the Doberman Pinscher?"

The answer is a definite "No." Since ancient times, the Min Pin was developing with its natural tendency to smallness in stature. In fact, as a recognized breed, the Miniature Pinscher predates the development of the well-known Doberman Pinscher*.

The Min Pin is an excellent choice as a family pet. The breed tends to attach itself very quickly to children and really delights in joining a youngster in bed. As soon as the Min-Pin climbs onto the bed, he usually slips under the covers like a mole, all the way to the foot of the bed.

The Min Pin is intelligent and easily trained. He has a tendency to be clean in all respects, the shedding of the short coat constitutes minimal, if any, problems to the apartment dweller. On the other hand, the Miniature Pinscher certainly is not out of his element on the farm and has been trained to tree squirrels, chase rabbits, and even help herd cows* It is not unusual for the Miniature Pinscher on a farm to catch a rabbit that is equal to or larger than the size of the dog.

Figure 30 *Increasing Space Before value to move footnotes down*

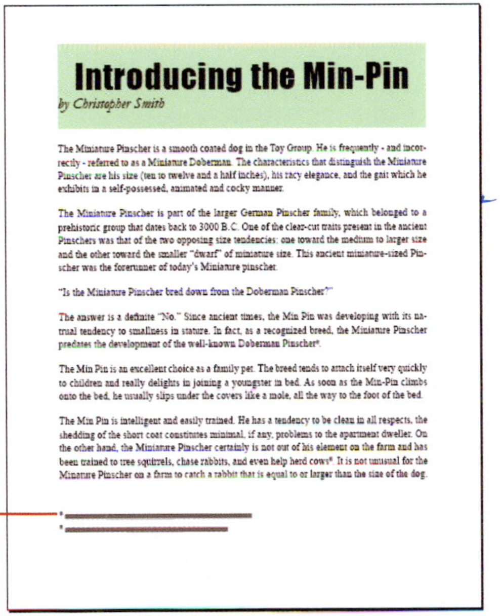

Introducing the Min-Pin
by Christopher Smith

The Miniature Pinscher is a smooth coated dog in the Toy Group. He is frequently - and incorrectly - referred to as a Miniature Doberman. The characteristics that distinguish the Miniature Pinscher are his size (ten to twelve and a half inches), his racy elegance, and the gait which he exhibits in a self-possessed, animated and cocky manner.

The Miniature Pinscher is part of the larger German Pinscher family, which belonged to a prehistoric group that dates back to 3000 B.C. One of the clear-cut traits present in the ancient Pinschers was that of the two opposing size tendencies: one toward the medium to larger size and the other toward the smaller "dwarf" of miniature size. This ancient miniature-sized Pinscher was the forerunner of today's Miniature pinscher.

"Is the Miniature Pinscher bred down from the Doberman Pinscher?"

The answer is a definite "No." Since ancient times, the Min Pin was developing with its natural tendency to smallness in stature. In fact, as a recognized breed, the Miniature Pinscher predates the development of the well-known Doberman Pinscher*.

The Min Pin is an excellent choice as a family pet. The breed tends to attach itself very quickly to children and really delights in joining a youngster in bed. As soon as the Min-Pin climbs onto the bed, he usually slips under the covers like a mole, all the way to the foot of the bed.

The Min Pin is intelligent and easily trained. He has a tendency to be clean in all respects, the shedding of the short coat constitutes minimal, if any, problems to the apartment dweller. On the other hand, the Miniature Pinscher certainly is not out of his element on the farm and has been trained to tree squirrels, chase rabbits, and even help herd cows* It is not unusual for the Miniature Pinscher on a farm to catch a rabbit that is equal to or larger than the size of the dog.

Space before value increased

Apply vertical spacing between paragraphs

1. Click the **Type tool**, click anywhere in the body copy, click **Edit** on the Menu bar, then click **Select All**.

   TIP The keyboard shortcut for Select All is [Ctrl] [A] (Win) or ⌘ [A] (Mac).

2. Click the **Space After up arrow** on the Paragraph panel three times, so that the value reads .1875 in, then deselect all.

   .1875 inches of vertical space is applied after every paragraph, as shown in Figure 29.

   TIP You may need to click the Paragraph panel options button, then click Show Options to expand the panel.

3. Click and drag to select the **two footnotes** at the bottom of the document, double-click the **Space After text box** on the Paragraph panel, type **0**, then press **[Enter]** (Win) or **[return]** (Mac).

4. Select only the first footnote, double-click the **0** in the Space Before text box on the Paragraph panel, type **.25**, then press **[Enter]** (Win) or **[return]** (Mac).

   .25 inches of vertical space is positioned above the first footnote.

5. Click **Edit** on the Menu bar, then click **Deselect All**.

   Your document should resemble Figure 30.

You used the Space After and Space Before text boxes on the Paragraph panel to apply vertical spacing between paragraphs.

Apply paragraph indents

1. Click **Type** on the Menu bar, then click **Show Hidden Characters**.

   As shown in Figure 31, hidden characters appear in blue, showing blue dots for spaces, created by pressing [Spacebar], and paragraph marks for paragraph returns.

   Be sure to memorize the keyboard command (listed beside each menu item in the menu) for hiding and showing hidden characters.

2. Select all the body copy on the page except the two footnotes, then click the **First Line Left Indent up arrow** on the Paragraph panel four times to change the value to .25 in, as shown in Figure 32.

   The first line of each paragraph is indented .25 in.

3. Select **by Christopher Smith**, then click the **Left Indent up arrow** until the value is changed to .5.

4. Click anywhere in the third paragraph, change the First Line Left Indent value to **0 in**, change the Left Indent value to **.75 in**, then change the Right Indent value to **.75 in**.

5. Click **any word in the third paragraph** three times to select the entire line, click the **Character panel name tab**, change the font size to **18 pt**, change the leading to **20 pt**, then deselect the paragraph.

   Your document should resemble Figure 33.

You showed hidden characters so that you could better identify each paragraph. You indented the first lines of every paragraph, and then you added substantial left and right indents to a paragraph and increased its point size to create a "pull quote."

Figure 31 *Showing hidden characters*

The · characteristics · that ·
— Space symbol

lf · inches), · his · racy · elegan
ocky · manner.¶
— Paragraph return symbol

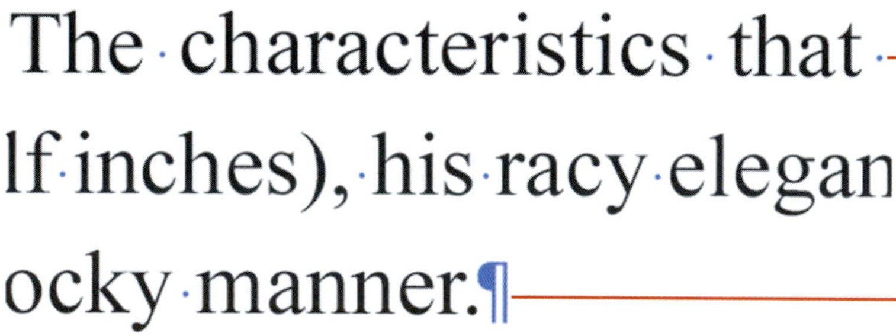

Figure 32 *Applying a first line left indent*

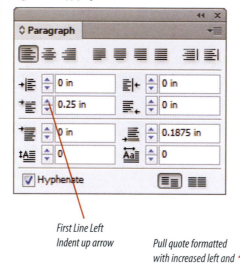

First Line Left Indent up arrow

Figure 33 *Using indents to format text as a pull quote*

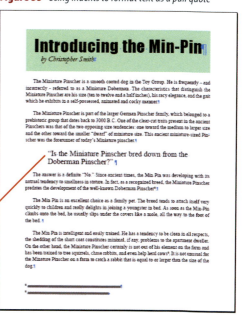

Pull quote formatted with increased left and right indents

© 2015 Cengage Learning®

Figure 34 *Creating a drop cap*

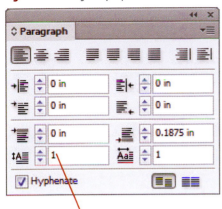

Drop Cap Number
of Lines value

Figure 35 *Viewing the finished document*

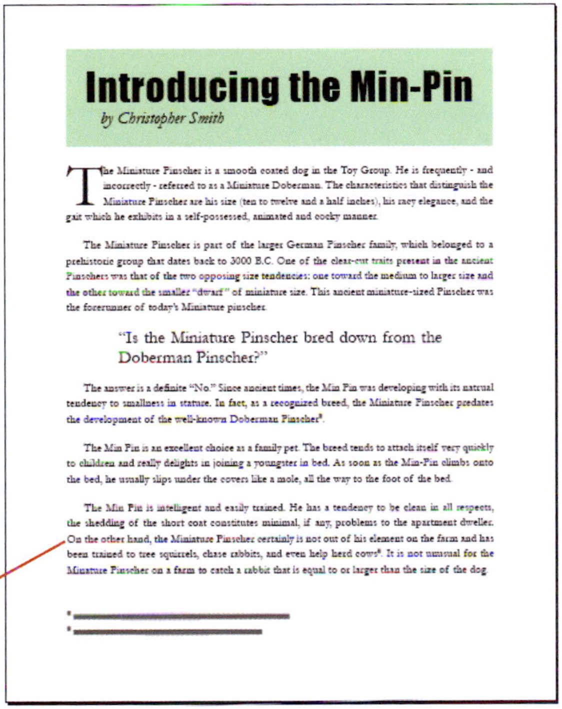

Introducing the Min-Pin
by Christopher Smith

No new
paragraph

Apply drop caps and soft returns

1. Click the **Paragraph panel name tab**, click anywhere in the first paragraph, then change the First Line Left Indent value to **0**.

2. Click the **Drop Cap Number of Lines up arrow** three times, so that the text box displays a 3, as shown in Figure 34.

   A drop cap with the height of three text lines is added to the first paragraph.

3. Select all the body copy text, including the two footnotes, then change the font to **Garamond** or a similar font.

4. Click the **Zoom tool** 🔍, then drag a selection box around the entire last paragraph.

5. Click the **Type tool** T, then click to insert the cursor immediately before the capital letter O of the word On in the third sentence of the last paragraph.

6. Press and hold **[Shift]**, then press **[Enter]** (Win) or **[return]** (Mac) to create a soft return.

   TIP Note that a new paragraph is not created.

7. Use the keyboard command to hide hidden characters.

8. Click **View** on the Menu bar, then click **Fit Page in Window**.

   Your document should resemble Figure 35.

9. Click **File** on the Menu bar, click **Save**, then close Min-Pin Intro.

You created a drop cap and a soft return, which moved text to the next line without creating a new paragraph.

Create and
APPLY STYLES

What You'll Do

Jake's Diner
Early Bird Breakfast Menu

Eggs and Bacon
Two eggs any style, two strips of lean bacon, one biscuit with our homestyle gravy, and home fries.
$5.95

French Toast
Four triangles of thick peasant bread dipped in a cinnamon-egg batter. Served with French Fries.
$6.95

Egg Sandwich
One egg over easy, served with American or Jack cheese on a soft French croissant.
$5.25

Biscuits and Gravy
Light fluffy southern biscuits served with a hearty sausage gravy.
$3.95

Belgian Waffle
A golden brown buttery waffle served with fresh-picked strawberries, raspberries and blueberries. Whipped fresh cream on request.
$4.95

Eggs Hollandaise
Three eggs lightly poached served on a bed of romaine lettuce and topped with a rich Hollandaise sauce.
$6.95

Silver Dollar Pancakes
A stack of eight golden pancakes served with fresh creamery butter and warm maple syrup.
$4.95

Steak and Eggs
A 6 oz. strip of peppered breakfast steak cooked to your liking, served with two eggs, any style.
$7.95

© 2015 Cengage Learning®

 In this lesson, you will use the Character Styles and Paragraph Styles panels to create and apply styles to text.

Working with Character and Paragraph Styles

Imagine that you are writing a book. Let's say it's a user's manual for how to care for houseplants. This book will contain seven chapters. In each chapter, different sections will be preceded by a headline that is the same font as the chapter title, but a smaller font size. Within those sections there will be subheads that, again, use the same font but in an even smaller size. Such a scenario is perfect for using styles.

A **style** is a group of formatting attributes, such as font, font size, color, and tracking, that is applied to text—whenever and wherever you want it to appear—throughout a document or multiple documents. Using styles saves you time and it keeps your work consistent. Styles are given descriptive names for the type of text to which they are applied. Figure 36 shows three styles on the Character Styles panel. You use the Character Styles panel to create styles for individual words or characters, such as a footnote, which you would want in a smaller, superscript font. You use the Paragraph Styles panel to apply a style to an entire paragraph. Paragraph styles include formatting options such as indents and drop caps. The Paragraph Styles panel is shown in Figure 37.

In the scenario of the houseplant book, if you weren't using styles, you would be required to format those chapter headlines one at time, for all seven chapter heads. You would need to remember the font size, the font style, and any tracking, kerning, scaling, or other formatting. Then you would need to do the same for every section headline, and every sub-headline. For any body copy, you'd risk inconsistent spacing, indents, and other formatting options. Using styles, you define those formats one time and one time only. A much better solution, don't you think?

Working with Text

Another important feature about styles is that they are useful when you change your mind and want to modify text. Simply modify the style, and all the text that is assigned to that style will be automatically updated—throughout the document!

Choosing the Next Style

Once you have more than one paragraph style saved on the Paragraph Styles panel, you can program which style will come next when you are currently in one style and create a new paragraph. For example, imagine you are creating a catalog and you have two styles called Item and Description. Now let's say that each time you finish typing the name of an item, you want to type the description of that item using the Description paragraph style. Then when you finish typing the description and start a new paragraph, you want to type the next item using the Item paragraph style. You can choose which style should follow which, by double-clicking a style on the Paragraph Styles panel, then clicking the Next Style list arrow and choosing the name of the style that should come next.

Using Quick Apply

A quick way to apply a character or paragraph style is to use Quick Apply. The Quick Apply button is available on the Control panel, Character Styles panel, and Paragraph Styles panel. In the Quick Apply dialog box, there is a pull-down menu showing checked items, such as Character Styles. When Character Styles is checked, you can apply a character style quickly by typing its name in the Quick Apply text box. Your style will appear in a list below. Click the name in the list and your style is applied.

Quick Apply is not limited to applying styles. You can use Quick Apply to access menu commands and run scripts. Just be sure to click the Quick Apply list arrow in the Quick Apply dialog box and select Include Scripts and Include Menu Commands.

Figure 36 *Character Styles panel*

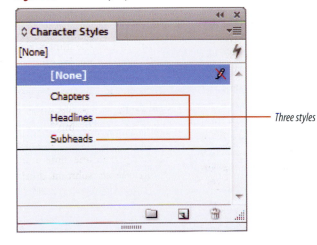

Three styles

Figure 37 *Paragraph Styles panel*

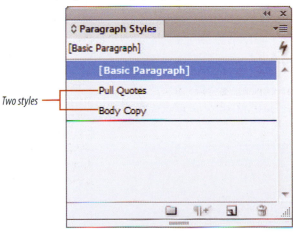

Two styles

Create character styles

1. Open ID 2-2.indd, then save it as **Jake's Diner**.

2. Display the Character Styles panel.

3. Click the **Character Styles panel options button** 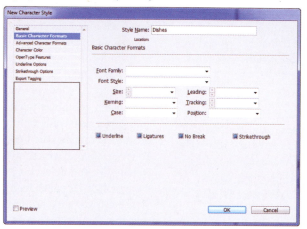, then click **New Character Style**.

4. Type **Dishes** in the Style Name text box of the New Character Style dialog box, then click **Basic Character Formats** in the left column, as shown in Figure 38.

5. Click the **Font Family list arrow**, click **Impact**, click the **Size list arrow**, click **14 pt**, click the **Leading text box**, type **16 pt**, then click **Advanced Character Formats** in the left column.

6. Type **85** in the Horizontal Scale text box, then click **OK**.

   The style "Dishes" now appears on the Character Styles panel.

7. Click the **Character Styles panel options button**, click **New Character Style**, type **Descriptions** in the Style Name text box, then click **Basic Character Formats** in the left column.

8. Click the **Font Family list arrow**, click **Garamond** or a similar font, click the **Font Style list arrow**, click **Italic**, change the font size to **10 pt**, change the leading to **12 pt**, then click **OK**.

   The style "Descriptions" now appears on the Character Styles panel.

9. Click the **Character Styles panel options button**, click **New Character Style**, type **Prices** in the Style Name text box, then click **Basic Character Formats** in the left column.

(continued)

Figure 38 *New Character Style dialog box*

Using Data Merge

InDesign lets you create documents that are customized for each recipient, much like a mail merge in a word processing program, which you can use for items like letters, name labels, and postcards. In a **data merge**, you use a data source (usually a text file) that contains **fields** (labels like "First Name") and **records** (rows representing information for each recipient, such as "Bob Jones"). A **target document** is an InDesign file containing the text that will be seen by all recipients, such as a letter, as well as placeholders representing fields, such as <<First Name>>. In a data merge, InDesign places information from each record in the appropriate places in the target document, as many times as necessary. The result is a **merged document** containing the personalized letters.

To perform a data merge, click Window on the Menu bar, point to Utilities, then click Data Merge. When the Data Merge panel opens, click the Data Merge panel options button, click Select Data Source, locate the data source file, then click Open. This displays the merge fields on the Data Merge panel. Click in a text frame and click field names to enter them in the frame. If you place placeholders on master pages, the merged document is connected to the data source, and you can automatically update the merged document with the most recent version of your data source.

To merge the document, click the Data Merge panel options button, then click Create Merged Document. Select the records to include, then click OK.

Figure 39 *Character Styles panel*

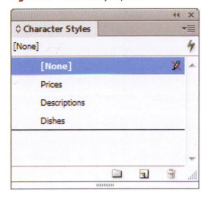

Figure 40 *Applying three different character styles*

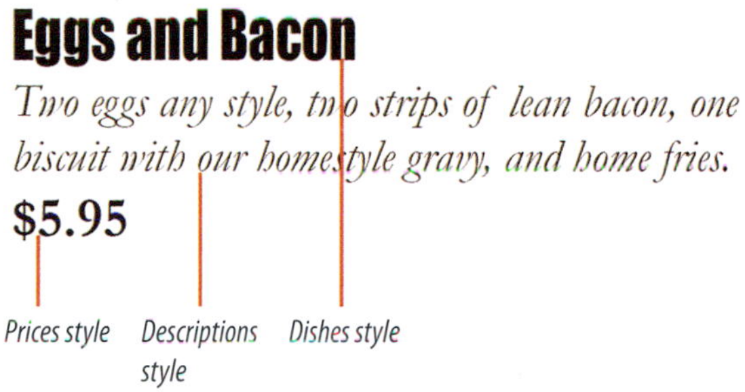

Eggs and Bacon

Two eggs any style, two strips of lean bacon, one biscuit with our homestyle gravy, and home fries.

$5.95

Prices style   Descriptions   Dishes style
              style

Figure 41 *Viewing the document with all character styles applied*

Jake's Diner
Early Bird Breakfast Menu

Eggs and Bacon
Two eggs any style, two strips of lean bacon, one biscuit with our homestyle gravy, and home fries.
$5.95
Egg Sandwich
One egg over easy, served with American or Jack cheese on a soft French croissant.
$5.25
Belgian Waffle
A golden brown buttery waffle served with fresh-picked strawberries, raspberries and blueberries. Whipped fresh cream on request.
$4.95
Silver Dollar Pancakes
A stack of eight golden pancakes served with fresh creamery butter and warm maple syrup.
$4.95

French Toast
Four triangles of thick peasant bread dipped in a cinnamon-egg batter. Served with French Fries.
$6.95
Biscuits and Gravy
Light fluffy southern biscuits served with a hearty sausage gravy.
$3.95
Eggs Hollandaise
Three eggs lightly poached served on a bed of romaine lettuce and topped with a rich Hollandaise sauce.
$6.95
Steak and Eggs
A 6 oz. strip of peppered breakfast steak cooked to your liking, served with two eggs, any style.
$7.95

© 2015 Cengage Learning®

10. Change the font to **Garamond** or a similar font, change the font style to **Bold**, change the font size to **12 pt**, change the leading to **14 pt**, then click **OK**.

    Your Character Styles panel should resemble Figure 39.

    You created three new character styles.

Apply character styles

1. Click the **Type tool**, triple-click the word **Eggs** in the first title to select the entire title "Eggs and Bacon," then click **Dishes** on the Character Styles panel.

    The Dishes character style is applied to the title.

2. Select the entire next paragraph (beginning with the word Two), then click **Descriptions** on the Character Styles panel.

3. Select the first price (**$5.95**), click **Prices** on the Character Styles panel, click **Edit** on the Menu bar, then click **Deselect All**.

    Your first menu item should resemble Figure 40. If you used a different font, your text lines may break differently.

4. Select all of the remaining text in the text frame, then apply the Descriptions style.

5. Apply the **Dishes style** to the remaining seven dish titles.

6. Apply the **Prices style** to the remaining seven prices, then deselect so that your document resembles Figure 41.

You applied character styles to format specific areas of a document.

Create paragraph styles

1. Close the Character Styles panel, then open the Paragraph Styles panel.

2. Click the **Paragraph Styles panel options button** 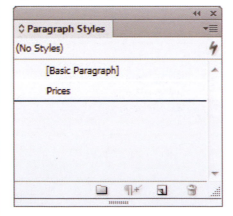, then click **New Paragraph Style**.

3. Type **Prices** in the Style Name text box, then click **Indents and Spacing** in the left column.

TIP Note that the New Paragraph Style dialog box contains Basic Character Formats and Advanced Character Formats categories—the same that you find when working in the New Character Style dialog box.

4. Click the **Alignment list arrow**, then click **Center**.

5. Type **.25** in the Space After text box, then click **Paragraph Rules** in the left column, as shown in Figure 42.

TIP The term **rules** is layout jargon for lines. Rules can be positioned on a page as a design element, or text can be underlined with rules.

6. Click the **list arrow** directly beneath Paragraph Rules, click **Rule Below**, then click the **Rule On check box** to add a check mark.

7. Type **.125** in the Offset text box, type **.25** in the Left Indent text box, type **.25** in the Right Indent text box, press **[Tab]** so that your dialog box resembles Figure 35, then click **OK**.

The paragraph style "Prices" now appears on the Paragraph Styles panel as shown on Figure 43.

You created a paragraph style, which included a center alignment, a space after value, and a paragraph rule.

Figure 42 *Paragraph Rules window in the New Paragraph Style dialog box*

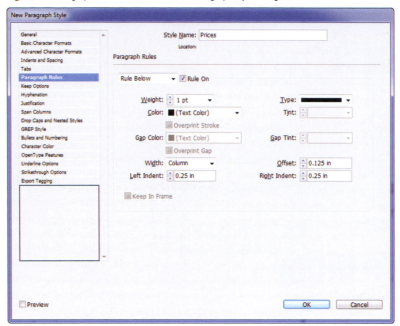

Figure 43 *Paragraph Styles panel*

Figure 44 *Applying a paragraph style to two prices*

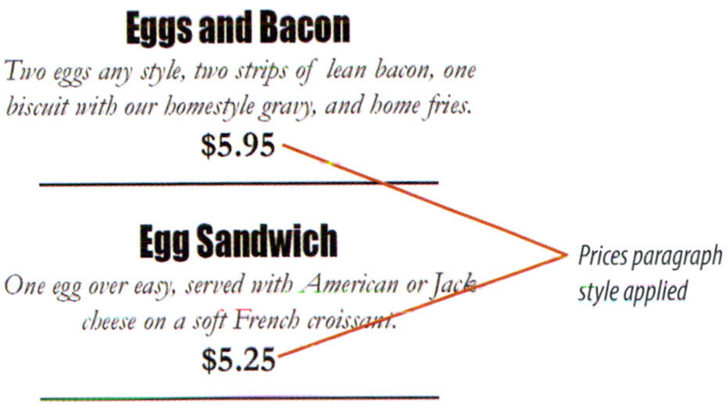

Eggs and Bacon

Two eggs any style, two strips of lean bacon, one biscuit with our homestyle gravy, and home fries.

$5.95

Egg Sandwich

One egg over easy, served with American or Jack cheese on a soft French croissant.

$5.25

Prices paragraph style applied

Figure 45 *Applying styles to all but the bottom two prices*

Eggs and Bacon	**French Toast**
Two eggs any style, two strips of lean bacon, one biscuit with our homestyle gravy, and home fries.	*Four triangles of thick peasant bread dipped in a cinnamon-egg batter. Served with French Fries.*
$5.95	$6.95
Egg Sandwich	**Biscuits and Gravy**
One egg over easy, served with American or Jack cheese on a soft French croissant.	*Light fluffy southern biscuits served with a hearty sausage gravy.*
$5.25	$3.95
Belgian Waffle	**Eggs Hollandaise**
A golden brown buttery waffle served with fresh-picked strawberries, raspberries and blueberries. Whipped fresh cream on request.	*Three eggs lightly poached served on a bed of romaine lettuce and topped with a rich Hollandaise sauce.*
$4.95	$6.95
Silver Dollar Pancakes	**Steak and Eggs**
A stack of eight golden pancakes served with fresh creamery butter and warm maple syrup.	*A 6 oz. strip of peppered breakfast steak cooked to your liking, served with two eggs, any style.*
$4.95	$7.95

Figure 46 *Viewing the final document*

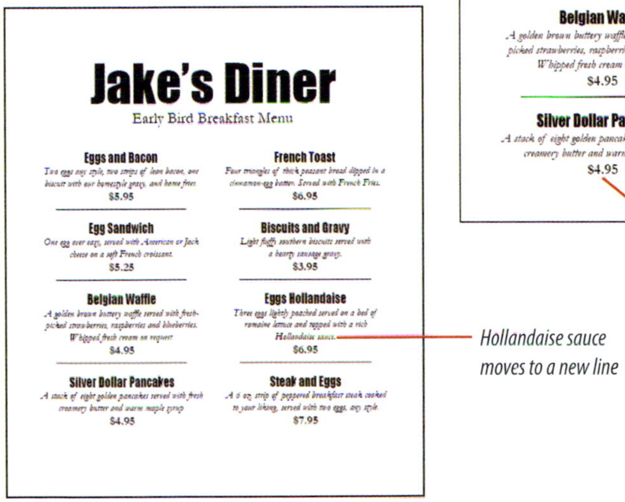

Jake's Diner
Early Bird Breakfast Menu

Eggs and Bacon	**French Toast**
Two eggs any style, two strips of lean bacon, one biscuit with our homestyle gravy, and home fries.	*Four triangles of thick peasant bread dipped in a cinnamon-egg batter. Served with French Fries.*
$5.95	$6.95
Egg Sandwich	**Biscuits and Gravy**
One egg over easy, served with American or Jack cheese on a soft French croissant.	*Light fluffy southern biscuits served with a hearty sausage gravy.*
$5.25	$3.95
Belgian Waffle	**Eggs Hollandaise**
A golden brown buttery waffle served with fresh-picked strawberries, raspberries and blueberries. Whipped fresh cream on request.	*Three eggs lightly poached served on a bed of romaine lettuce and topped with a rich Hollandaise sauce.*
$4.95	$6.95
Silver Dollar Pancakes	**Steak and Eggs**
A stack of eight golden pancakes served with fresh creamery butter and warm maple syrup.	*A 6 oz. strip of peppered breakfast steak cooked to your liking, served with two eggs, any style.*
$4.95	$7.95

Hollandaise sauce moves to a new line

You do not need dividing rules at the bottom of the menu

Apply paragraph styles

1. Click the **Type tool** T, then select all the text in the document except for the two headlines at the top of the page.

2. Click the **Align center button** on the Paragraph panel.

   For this layout, all the menu items will be aligned center. It's not necessary to create a paragraph style for all items to align center, because you can simply use the Align center button on the Paragraph panel.

3. Click the first price (**$5.95**) once, click **Prices** on the Paragraph Styles panel, click the second price (**$5.25**), then click **Prices** on the Paragraph Styles panel again.

   Your first two menu items should resemble Figure 44.

   TIP When applying paragraph styles, just place the cursor in the paragraph you want to modify.

4. Apply the Prices paragraph style to the remaining prices in the document except the Silver Dollar Pancakes and Steak and Eggs prices, then compare your document to Figure 45.

5. Click **View** on the Menu bar, point to **Grids & Guides**, then click **Hide Guides**.

6. Click before the word Hollandaise in the description text for Eggs Hollandaise, press and hold down [**Shift**], while pressing [**Enter**] (Win) or [**return**] (Mac).

   Hollandaise sauce is moved to the next line. Using the same method, add soft returns to break any other lines that you think could look better, then compare your work to Figure 46.

7. Save your work, then close Jake's Diner.

You applied a paragraph style to specific areas of the menu.

Edit
TEXT

What You'll Do

In this lesson, you will use the Find/Change and Check Spelling commands to edit the text of a document.

Using the Find/Change Command

One of the great things about creating documents using a computer is the ability to edit text quickly and efficiently. Imagine the days before the personal computer. When you finished typing a document, you needed to read through it carefully, looking for any errors. If you found any, you had three options: cover it up, cross it out, or type the whole document again.

The Find/Change dialog box, shown in Figure 47, is a powerful tool for editing a document. With this command, you can search for any word in the document, then change that word to another word or delete it altogether with a click of the mouse button. For example, imagine that you have typed an entire document about Abraham Lincoln's early years growing up in Frankfurt, Kentucky. Then you find out that Lincoln actually grew up in Hardin County, Kentucky. You could use the Find/Change command to locate every instance of the word "Frankfurt" and change it to "Hardin County." One click would correct every instance of that error, throughout the entire document.

QUICK TIP

InDesign has a number of great features in the Find/Change dialog box. The Query menu lists pre-defined search options for finding (and changing) common formatting issues. For example, the Query menu has built-in searches for finding and changing dashes to en dashes and straight single or double quotes to typographer's quotes. There's a built-in search for trailing white space—useless extra spaces at the end of paragraphs or sentences—and there's even a search for telephone number formatting.

Checking Spelling

Since the earliest days of the personal computer, the ability to check and correct spelling errors automatically has been a much-promoted benefit of creating documents digitally. It has stood the test of time. The spell checker continues to be one of the most powerful features of word processing.

InDesign's Check Spelling dialog box, shown in Figure 48, is a comprehensive utility for locating and correcting typos and other misspellings in a document. If you've done word processing before, you will find yourself on familiar turf. The spell checker identifies words that it doesn't find in its dictionary, offers you a list of suggested corrections, and asks you what you want to do. If it is indeed a misspelling, type the correct spelling or choose the correct word from the suggested corrections list, then click Change to correct that instance or click Change All to correct all instances of the misspelling throughout the document.

Sometimes the spell checker identifies a word that is not actually a misspelling. For example, say you were typing a letter about your dog whose name is Gargantua. The spell checker is not going to find that word/name in its dictionary, and it is going to ask you what you want to do with it. You have two options. You could click Ignore, which tells the spell checker to make no changes and move on to the next questionable word. However, because in the future you will probably type the dog's name in other documents, you don't want the spell checker always asking you if this word/name is a misspelling. In this case, you'd be better off clicking the Add button. Doing so adds the name Gargantua to the spell checker's dictionary, and in the future, the spell checker will no longer identify Gargantua as a misspelling.

When you click the Add button, the word in question is added to the User Dictionary, which is InDesign's main dictionary. If you use the spell checker often, you will build up a list of words that you've chosen to ignore and a list of words that you've chosen to add to the dictionary. To see those lists and modify them, click the Dictionary button in the Check Spelling dialog box.

You can create your own user dictionary in the Dictionary section of the Preferences dialog box. Click the Language list arrow to choose the language with which you want to associate your

dictionary, then click the Add User Dictionary button, then select the user dictionary file. The user dictionary file is stored on the hard drive and includes a .udc or a .not extension. When you locate it, click Open. If you can't find the dictionary file, search your hard drive to locate the .udc files (try using *.udc or *.not in the search text box). The new user dictionary is added to the list under the Language menu. Then, when you are using the spell checker, click the Dictionary button, click the Target list arrow, then choose your new user dictionary from the list. You can add words to the new user dictionary using the Add button in the Check Spelling dialog box.

Using Dynamic Spell Checking

Another spell check feature is Dynamic Spelling. As you type, the program places a squiggly red line under words that its spell checker thinks

are misspelled. To prevent the program from flagging a proper name, you can add that name to your customized dictionary. To enable dynamic spelling, click Edit on the Menu bar, point to Spelling, then click Dynamic Spelling.

Correcting Text Automatically

Autocorrect takes dynamic spell checking one step farther. Instead of flagging a misspelled word, the Autocorrect feature actually corrects the misspelled word. So if you type the word "refered" and press [Spacebar], Autocorrect will change it to "referred."

Many commonly misspelled or easily mistyped words, such as "hte" for "the," are preprogrammed into the Autocorrect feature, and you can add words that might not already be listed. To turn on the Autocorrect feature, click Edit on the Menu bar, point to Spelling, then click Autocorrect.

Figure 47 *Find/Change dialog box*

Figure 48 *Check Spelling dialog box*

Use the Find/Change command

1. Open ID 2-3.indd, then save it as **Final Edit**.

2. Click **Edit** on the Menu bar, then click **Find/Change**.

3. Type **Miniature Pincher** in the Find what text box, then type **Min-Pin** in the Change to text box, as shown in Figure 49.

4. Click **Find Next**.

   The first use of "Miniature Pincher" in the document is highlighted. As this is the first use of the term, you don't want to change it to a nickname.

   TIP Drag the dialog box out of the way if you cannot see your document.

5. Click **Find Next**, then click **Change**.

   The second use of "Miniature Pincher" is changed to "Min-Pin."

6. Click **Find Next** again, then click **Change**.

7. Click **Find Next** three times.

   You don't want to change all instances of Miniature Pincher to Min-Pin.

8. Click **Change**, then click **Done**.

9. Click **Edit** on the Menu bar, then click **Find/Change**.

10. Type **Pincher** in the Find what text box, type **Pinscher** in the Change to text box, then click **Change All**.

    A dialog box appears stating that the search is completed and 14 replacements were made.

11. Click **OK**, then click **Done**.

You used the Find/Change command to replace specific words in the document.

Figure 49 *Find/Change dialog box*

Editing Text Using Drag and Drop

InDesign has a Drag and Drop text editing feature that allows you to move text to locations within a document without having to cut and paste. This means that you can select text and simply drag it from one text frame into another text frame. You can drag and drop text between text frames on different pages. You can even drag and drop text between documents. Dragging and dropping text is usually a lot faster and easier than cutting and pasting. You can also drag and drop a copy of selected text by holding [Alt] (Win) or [option] (Mac) down when dragging. You can turn Drag and Drop text on or off in the Type window of the Preferences dialog box. In the Drag and Drop Text Editing section, check both the Enable in Layout View and the Enable in Story Editor check boxes so that the feature is activated for all of your editing methods. Give it a try!

Figure 50 *Check Spelling dialog box*

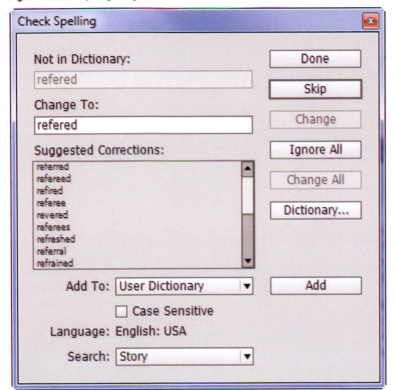

Check spelling

1. Click to the right of the drop cap T (between the T and the h) at the top of the page.

   Positioning your cursor at the top of a document forces the spell checker to begin checking for misspellings from the start of the document.

2. Click **Edit** on the Menu bar, point to **Spelling**, then click **Check Spelling**.

   As shown in Figure 50, "refered" is listed as the first word the spell checker can't find in the dictionary. Suggested corrections are listed.

3. Click **referred** in the Suggested Corrections list, then click **Change**.

   The spell checker lists "racey" as the next word it can't find in the dictionary.

4. Click **racy** in the Suggested Corrections list, then click **Change**.

   The spell checker lists "Pinscher1" as not in the dictionary because of the number 1 footnote.

5. Click **Ignore All** for all remaining queries, click **OK**, then click **Done**.

6. Save your work, then close Final Edit.

TIP Never rely on the spell checker as the sole means for proofreading a document. It cannot determine if you have used the wrong word. For example, the spell checker did not flag the word "gate" in the first paragraph, which should be spelled "gait."

You used the Check Spelling dialog box to proof a document for spelling errors.

Create
BULLETED AND NUMBERED LISTS

What You'll Do

Photoshop
Table of Contents

Chapter 1: Getting Started

1. Defining Photo Editing Software
   understanding graphics programs

2. Starting Photoshop
   getting help
   managing the workspace

3. Using the Zoom Tool and the Hand Tool
   accessing the tools

4. Saving a Document
   choosing the right file format

5. Understanding Resolution
   the difference between Image Size and file size

6. Changing Image Size
   what is "high-res" exactly

7. Creating a New Document
   using the Revert command
   introducing color models

8. Transforming the Canvas
   "rezzing up"

© 2015 Cengage Learning®

In this lesson, you will create bulleted and numbered lists, then change the typeface of the numbers.

Creating Bulleted and Numbered Lists

Creating numbered or bulleted lists is a common need in many types of layout, and InDesign allows you to do so easily. The best way to start is to type the list first, without formatting. Point to the Bulleted & Numbered Lists command in the Type menu and then choose whether you want to apply bullets or numbers to the selected text.

Bullets and numbers are like any other type of paragraph formatting. InDesign applies them to each paragraph of the selected text. At any time, you can select the text and change the marks from bullets to numbers or vice versa. You also use the same Bulleted & Numbered Lists command to remove bullets or numbers from selected text.

QUICK TIP

By default, InDesign applies bullets and numbers with the same typeface, type size, and color of the selected text in the paragraph.

Modifying Bulleted and Numbered Lists

You can think of bullets and numbers as being applied "virtually" to a paragraph. Let's use numbers as an example. When you apply numbers, you can see the numbers, but you can't select them. If you select the entire paragraph of text, the numbers won't appear to be selected. This is because the numbers are applied as a format to the paragraph. For example, let's say you had a list of nine numbered entries, and then you inserted a tenth entry between numbers 5 & 6. The new entry would automatically be numbered with a "6" and the numbers on all the following entries would be automatically updated.

Once you've finished a list, you might find that you want to modify the numbers by changing the type face, color, or size of the numbers.

To do so, you must first convert the list to text so that the numbers can be selected and modified. Click the Bulleted & Numbered Lists command, then click the Convert Bullets and Numbering to Text command, shown in Figure 51. When you do this, the numbers (or bullets) will be converted to regular text. The list will still appear to be numbered, but it will have lost the functionality of the list formatting. If you insert or remove any component of the list, the numbers won't be updated. InDesign will see it only as a block of text.

Figure 51 *Convert Bullets to Text command*

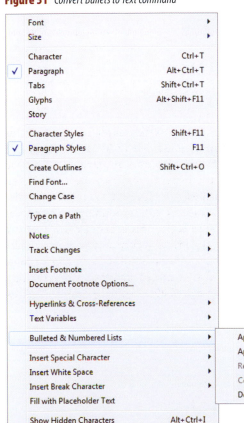

Using the Track Changes Feature

Whenever you're producing a document that involves a copy editor or more than one person making edits to copy, it becomes important that any edits made are recorded. For example, let's say you're the author of a story in a magazine. The copy editor goes through your text and makes various changes. You, as the author, will want to see what changes were made. You'll also want the option of approving or rejecting those changes, or at least the opportunity to debate whether or not the changes should be implemented.

The Track Changes feature allows for this important function within the editing process. The feature will identify each participant separately. Some of the changes that will be recorded include deleting, moving, and inserting new text. To view the changes, you use the Story Editor, accessed through the Edit menu. To accept or reject changes, use the Track Changes panel, located in the Window menu on the Editorial submenu.

Create a bulleted and a numbered list

1. Open ID 2-4.indd, then save it as **TOC**.
2. Click the **Type tool** T, then select all of the text below Chapter 1: Getting Started.
3. On the Paragraph panel, set the Space After value to **.125 in**.
4. Click **Type** on the Menu bar, point to **Bulleted & Numbered Lists**, then click **Apply Bullets**.

   A shown in Figure 52, bullets are applied at each paragraph in the selected text. The text remains selected, though the bullets themselves do not appear selected.
5. Click **Type** on the Menu bar, point to **Bulleted & Numbered Lists**, then click **Apply Numbers**.

   The bullets change to numbers that are the same type face, size, and color of the selected text.
6. Save your work.

You applied bullets to selected text, then changed the bullets to numbers.

Figure 52 *Bullets applied to text*

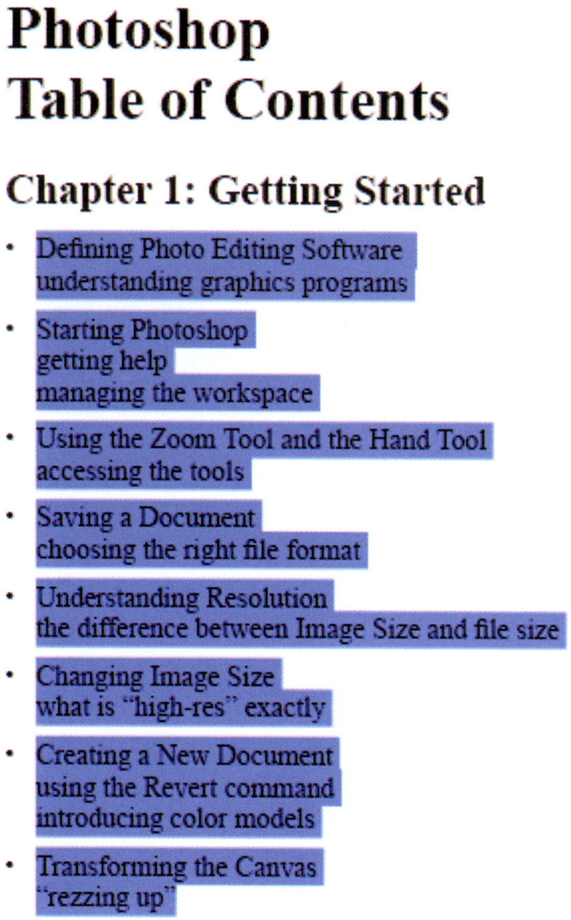

Photoshop
Table of Contents

Chapter 1: Getting Started

- Defining Photo Editing Software understanding graphics programs
- Starting Photoshop getting help managing the workspace
- Using the Zoom Tool and the Hand Tool accessing the tools
- Saving a Document choosing the right file format
- Understanding Resolution the difference between Image Size and file size
- Changing Image Size what is "high-res" exactly
- Creating a New Document using the Revert command introducing color models
- Transforming the Canvas "rezzing up"

Figure 53 *Reformatting the numbers in the list*

Photoshop
Table of Contents

Chapter 1: Getting Started

1. Defining Photo Editing Software
   understanding graphics programs

2. Starting Photoshop
   getting help
   managing the workspace

3. Using the Zoom Tool and the Hand Tool
   accessing the tools

4. Saving a Document
   choosing the right file format

5. Understanding Resolution
   the difference between Image Size and file size

6. Changing Image Size
   what is "high-res" exactly

7. Creating a New Document
   using the Revert command
   introducing color models

8. Transforming the Canvas
   "rezzing up"

Convert numbers to text

1. Verify that all of the numbered text is still selected.
2. Click **Type** on the Menu bar, point to **Bulleted & Numbered Lists**, then click **Convert Numbering to Text**.
3. Select the number 8 and the period that follows it.
4. On the Character panel, change the Type Style from Regular to Bold.
5. Change all the numbers and the periods that follow them to bold so that your list resembles Figure 53.
6. Save your work, then close TOC.indd.

You converted numbering to text so that you could format the numbers differently from the text in the list.

Format text.

1. Open ID 2-5.indd, then save it as **Independence**.
2. Click Window on the Menu bar, point to Workspace, then click Reset Typography.
3. Click the Type tool, then triple-click the word Declaration at the top of the page.
4. On the Character panel, type **80** in the Horizontal Scale text box, then press [Enter] (Win) or [return] (Mac).
5. Click the Font Family list arrow, click Impact, click the Font Size list arrow, then click 36 pt.
6. Press and hold [Shift] [Ctrl] (Win) or [Shift] [⌘] (Mac), then press [<] two times.
7. Triple-click the word July on the next line, change the type face to Garamond, if necessary, change the type style to Italic, then click the Font Size up arrow until you change the font size to 18 pt.
8. Click Object on the Menu bar, click Text Frame Options, change the Align setting to Center, then click OK.
9. Triple-click the word July, if necessary.
10. Type **100** in the Tracking text box, then press [Enter] (Win) or [return] (Mac).
11. Click between the letters r and a in the word Declaration, click the Kerning list arrow, then click 10.
12. Click View on the Menu bar, click Fit Page in Window, if necessary, click the Zoom tool, then drag a selection box that encompasses all of the body copy on the page.
13. Click the Type tool, then select the number 1 at the end of the first paragraph.
14. Click the Character panel options button, then click Superscript.
15. Select the number 1 at the beginning of the last paragraph, then apply the Superscript command.

Format paragraphs.

1. Click View on the Menu bar, click Fit Page in Window, then click the first word When in the body copy five times to select all the body copy.
2. Select (12 pt) in the Leading text box on the Character panel, type **13.25**, then press [Enter] (Win) or [return] (Mac).
3. Display the Paragraph panel, then click the Justify with last line aligned left button.
4. Click in the word Independence at the top of the document, then click the Align center button on the Paragraph panel.
5. Click the Type tool, if necessary, click anywhere in the body copy, click Edit on the Menu bar, then click Select All.
6. On the Paragraph panel, click the Space After up arrow three times, so that the value reads .1875 in, click Edit on the Menu bar, then click Deselect All.
7. Select the footnote (last paragraph of the document), double-click the Space Before text box on the Paragraph panel, type **.5**, then press [Enter] (Win) or [return] (Mac).
8. Apply the Deselect All command.
9. Click Type on the Menu bar, then click Show Hidden Characters.
10. Select all the body copy on the page except for the last paragraph (the footnote), double-click the First Line Left Indent text box on the Paragraph panel, type **.25**, then press [Enter] (Win) or [return] (Mac).
11. Select July 4, 1776 beneath the headline, then click the Align right button on the Paragraph panel.
12. Double-click the Right Indent text box on the Paragraph panel, type **.6**, then press [Enter] (Win) or [return] (Mac).
13. Click anywhere in the first paragraph, then change the First Line Left Indent value to 0.
14. Click the Drop Cap Number of Lines up arrow three times, so that the text box displays a 3.

15. Click the Zoom tool, then drag a selection box that encompasses the entire second to last paragraph in the body copy.

16. Click the Type tool, position the pointer before the word these—the second to last word in the paragraph.

17. Press and hold [Shift], then press [Enter] (Win) or [return] (Mac).

18. Click Type on the Menu bar, click Hide Hidden Characters, if necessary, click View on the Menu bar, point to Grids & Guides, then click Hide Guides.

19. Click View on the Menu bar, then click Fit Page in Window.

20. Compare your document to Figure 54, click File on the Menu bar, click Save, then close Independence.

Figure 54 *Completed Skills Review, Part 1*

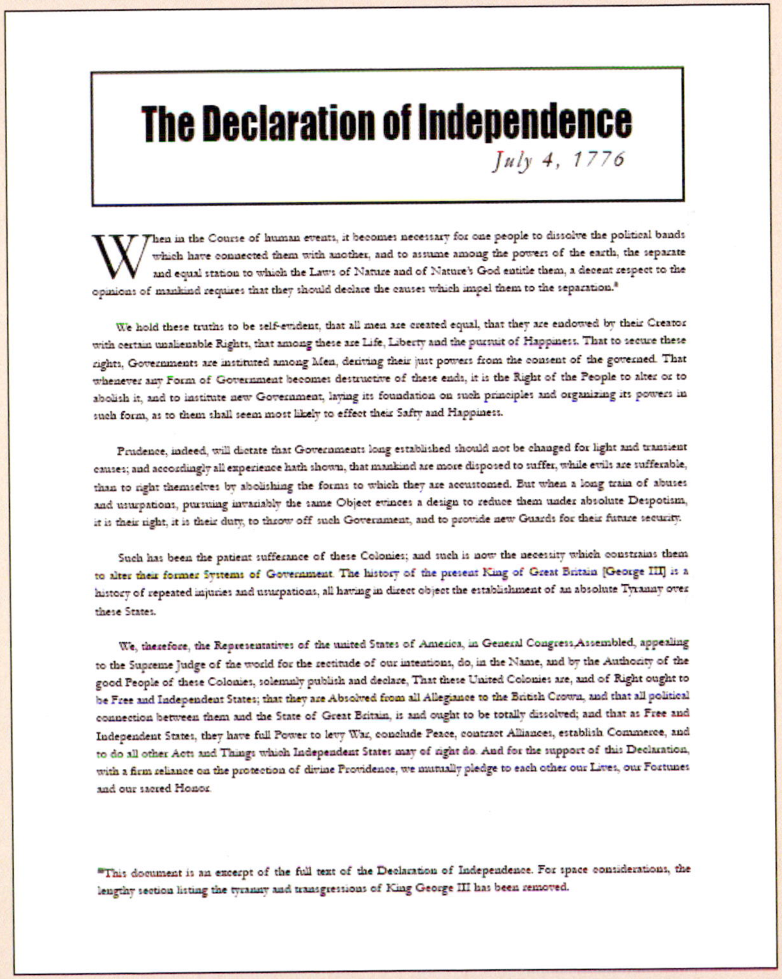

The Declaration of Independence

July 4, 1776

When in the Course of human events, it becomes necessary for one people to dissolve the political bands which have connected them with another, and to assume among the powers of the earth, the separate and equal station to which the Laws of Nature and of Nature's God entitle them, a decent respect to the opinions of mankind requires that they should declare the causes which impel them to the separation.*

We hold these truths to be self-evident, that all men are created equal, that they are endowed by their Creator with certain unalienable Rights, that among these are Life, Liberty and the pursuit of Happiness. That to secure these rights, Governments are instituted among Men, deriving their just powers from the consent of the governed. That whenever any Form of Government becomes destructive of these ends, it is the Right of the People to alter or to abolish it, and to institute new Government, laying its foundation on such principles and organizing its powers in such form, as to them shall seem most likely to effect their Safety and Happiness.

Prudence, indeed, will dictate that Governments long established should not be changed for light and transient causes; and accordingly all experience hath shown, that mankind are more disposed to suffer, while evils are sufferable, than to right themselves by abolishing the forms to which they are accustomed. But when a long train of abuses and usurpations, pursuing invariably the same Object evinces a design to reduce them under absolute Despotism, it is their right, it is their duty, to throw off such Government, and to provide new Guards for their future security.

Such has been the patient sufferance of these Colonies; and such is now the necessity which constrains them to alter their former Systems of Government. The history of the present King of Great Britain [George III] is a history of repeated injuries and usurpations, all having in direct object the establishment of an absolute Tyranny over these States.

We, therefore, the Representatives of the united States of America, in General Congress,Assembled, appealing to the Supreme Judge of the world for the rectitude of our intentions, do, in the Name, and by the Authority of the good People of these Colonies, solemnly publish and declare, That these United Colonies are, and of Right ought to be Free and Independent States; that they are Absolved from all Allegiance to the British Crown, and that all political connection between them and the State of Great Britain, is and ought to be totally dissolved; and that as Free and Independent States, they have full Power to levy War, conclude Peace, contract Alliances, establish Commerce, and to do all other Acts and Things which Independent States may of right do. And for the support of this Declaration, with a firm reliance on the protection of divine Providence, we mutually pledge to each other our Lives, our Fortunes and our sacred Honor.

*This document is an excerpt of the full text of the Declaration of Independence. For space considerations, the lengthy section listing the tyranny and transgressions of King George III has been removed.

Working with Text

Create and apply styles.

1. Open ID 2-6.indd, then save it as **Toy Breeds**.
2. Open the Character Styles panel.
3. Click the Character Styles panel options button, then click New Character Style.
4. Type **Breeds** in the Style Name text box, then click Basic Character Formats in the left column.
5. Change the font to Tahoma, change the size to 14 pt, change the leading to 16 pt, then click OK.
6. Click the Character Styles panel options button, click New Character Style, type **Info** in the Style Name text box, then click Basic Character Formats in the left column.
7. Change the font to Garamond, change the style to Italic, change the size to 10 pt, change the leading to 12 pt, then click OK.
8. Select all of the text except for the top two lines, then click Info on the Character Styles panel.
9. Double-click the Affenpinscher headline, then click Breeds on the Character Styles panel.
10. Apply the Breeds character style to the remaining seven breed headlines, then deselect all.
11. Open the Paragraph Styles panel.
12. Click the Paragraph Styles panel options button, then click New Paragraph Style.
13. Type **Info** in the Style Name text box, then click Indents and Spacing in the left column.
14. Click the Alignment list arrow, then click Center.
15. Type **.25** in the Space After text box, then click Paragraph Rules in the left column.
16. Click the list arrow directly below Paragraph Rules, click Rule Below, then click the Rule On check box.

17. Type **.1625** in the Offset text box, type **1** in the Left Indent text box, type **1** in the Right Indent text box, then click OK.
18. Select all of the text except for the top two lines, then click the Align center button on the Paragraph panel.
19. Click in the Affenpinscher description text, then click Info on the Paragraph Styles panel.
20. Apply the Info paragraph style to all the remaining descriptions except for the Pomeranian and the Pug.
21. Click View on the Menu bar, point to Grids & Guides, then click Hide Guides.

22. Click before the word bred in the Manchester Terrier description, press and hold [Shift], then press [Enter] (Win) or [return] (Mac).
23. Click before the phrase even-tempered in the Pug description, press and hold [Shift], press [Enter] (Win) or [return] (Mac), click before the word and in the "Pug" description, press and hold [Shift], then press [Enter] (Win) or [return] (Mac). (*Hint*: Your text may break differently. Correct any other bad breaks you see.)
24. Save your work, compare your screen to Figure 55, then close Toy Breeds.

Figure 55 *Completed Skills Review, Part 2*

Working with Text

Edit text.

1. Open ID 2-7.indd, then save it as **Declaration Edit**.
2. Select the Type tool, then click at the beginning of the first paragraph.
3. Click Edit on the Menu bar, then click Find/Change.
4. Type **IV** in the Find what text box, then type **III** in the Change to text box. (*Hint*: Drag the dialog box out of the way if you cannot see your document.)
5. Click Find Next. (*Hint*: You want to change the IV to III in George IV, as in George III, however, the spell checker finds all instances of "IV," such as in the word "deriving."
6. Click the Case Sensitive button in the middle of the Find/Change dialog box (*Hint*: Look for an icon with Aa), then click Find Next.
7. Click Change All, click OK in the dialog box that tells you that two replacements were made, then click Done in the Find/Change dialog box. By specifying the search to be Case Sensitive, only uppercase IV instances were found and changed.
8. Click before the drop cap in the first paragraph, click Edit on the Menu bar, point to Spelling, then click Check Spelling.
9. For the query on the word "Safty," click Safety at the top of the Suggested Corrections list, then click Change.
10. Click Ignore All to ignore the query on hath.
11. Click Ignore All to ignore all instances of III.
12. Click before the capital "S" in "States" in the Change To text box in the Check Spelling dialog box, press [Spacebar] once, then click Change.
13. Click Done.
14. Save your work, deselect, compare your screen to Figure 56, then close Declaration Edit.

Create bulleted and numbered lists.

1. Open ID 2-8.indd, then save it as **Chapter 2**.
2. Click the Type tool, then select all of the text beneath Chapter 2: Selecting Pixels.
3. On the Paragraph panel, set the Space After value to .125 in.
4. Click Type on the Menu bar, point to Bulleted & Numbered Lists, then click Apply Bullets.
5. Click Type on the Menu bar, point to Bulleted & Numbered Lists, then click Apply Numbers.
6. Click Type on the menu bar, point to Bulleted & Numbered Lists, then click Convert Numbering to Text.
7. Select the number 1 and the period that follows it.
8. On the Character panel, change the Type Style from Regular to Italic.
9. Change all the numbers and the periods that follow them to italic.
10. Save your work, then close Chapter 2.indd.

Figure 56 *Completed Skills Review, Part 3*

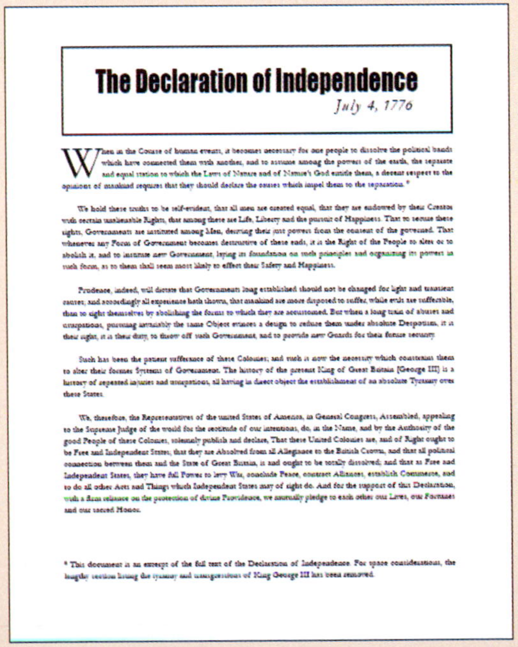

You are a freelance designer. Your client returns a document to you, telling you that she wants you to make a change to a drop cap. She wants you to format not just the first letter but the entire first word as a drop cap, so that it is more prominent on the page.

1. Open ID 2-9.indd, then save it as **Drop Cap Modifications**.
2. Click the Zoom tool, then drag a selection box around the first paragraph.
3. Click the Type tool, click after the W drop cap, double-click the 1 in the Drop Cap One or More Characters text box on the Paragraph panel, type **4**, and then press Enter.
4. Click before the word in, in the top line, then type **100** in the Kerning text box on the Character panel.
5. Select the letters HEN, click the Character panel options button, click All Caps, click the Character panel options button again, then click Superscript.
6. With the letters still selected, type **−10** in the Baseline Shift text box on the Character panel.
7. Click between the W and H in the word WHEN, then type **−60** in the Kerning text box.
8. Save your work, compare your screen to Figure 57, then close Drop Cap Modifications.

Figure 57 *Completed Project Builder 1*

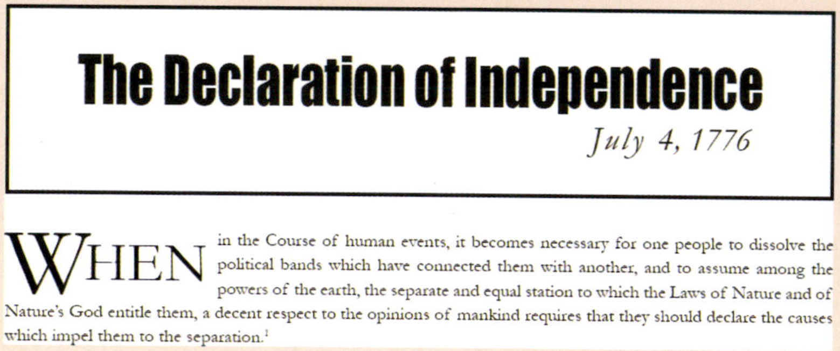

The Declaration of Independence

July 4, 1776

WHEN in the Course of human events, it becomes necessary for one people to dissolve the political bands which have connected them with another, and to assume among the powers of the earth, the separate and equal station to which the Laws of Nature and of Nature's God entitle them, a decent respect to the opinions of mankind requires that they should declare the causes which impel them to the separation.[1]

Working with Text

You have designed a document about miniature pinschers. Your client calls you with changes. He wants to show small pictures of miniature pinschers in the document, one beside each paragraph. He asks you to reformat the document to create space where the small pictures can be inserted.

1. Open ID 2-10.indd, then save it as **Hanging Indents**.
2. Select the four paragraphs of body copy, then change the first line left indent to 0.
3. Change the left indent to 2 in, then change the right indent to .5 in.
4. Create a half-inch space after each paragraph.
5. Type **−1.5** in the First Line Left Indent text box, then deselect all.
6. Save your work, compare your screen to Figure 58, then close Hanging Indents.

Figure 58 *Completed Project Builder 2*

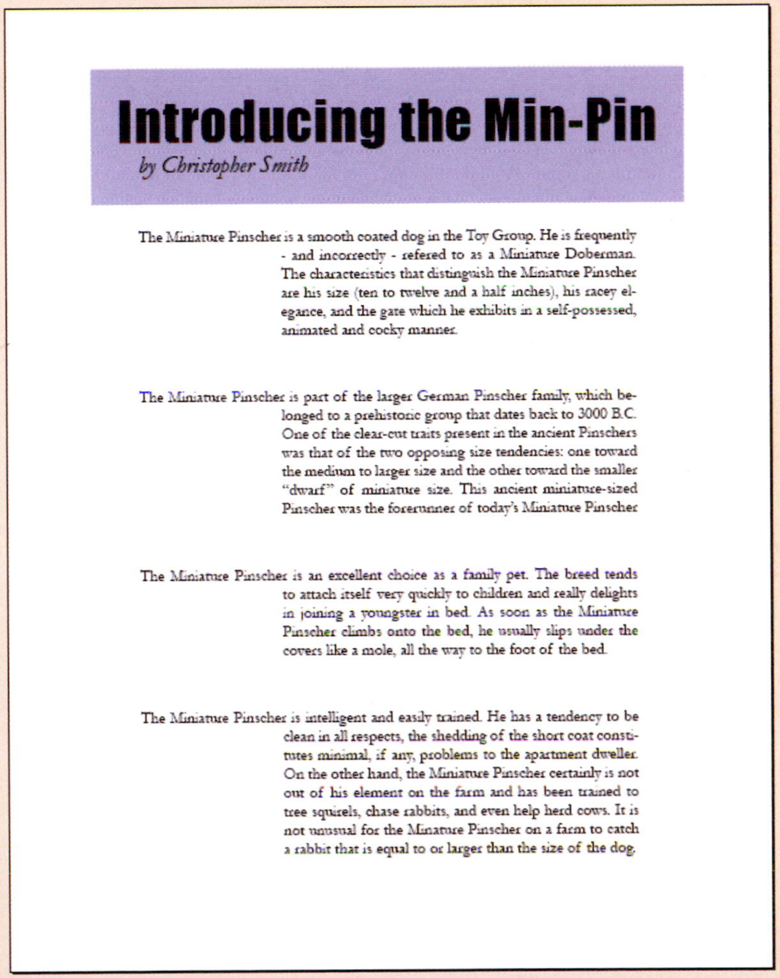

Introducing the Min-Pin
by Christopher Smith

The Miniature Pinscher is a smooth coated dog in the Toy Group. He is frequently - and incorrectly - refered to as a Miniature Doberman. The characteristics that distinguish the Miniature Pinscher are his size (ten to twelve and a half inches), his racey elegance, and the gate which he exhibits in a self-possessed, animated and cocky manner.

The Miniature Pinscher is part of the larger German Pinscher family, which belonged to a prehistoric group that dates back to 3000 B.C. One of the clear-cut traits present in the ancient Pinschers was that of the two opposing size tendencies: one toward the medium to larger size and the other toward the smaller "dwarf" of miniature size. This ancient miniature-sized Pinscher was the forerunner of today's Miniature Pinscher

The Miniature Pinscher is an excellent choice as a family pet. The breed tends to attach itself very quickly to children and really delights in joining a youngster in bed. As soon as the Miniature Pinscher climbs onto the bed, he usually slips under the covers like a mole, all the way to the foot of the bed.

The Miniature Pinscher is intelligent and easily trained. He has a tendency to be clean in all respects, the shedding of the short coat constitutes minimal, if any, problems to the apartment dweller. On the other hand, the Miniature Pinscher certainly is not out of his element on the farm and has been trained to tree squirrels, chase rabbits, and even help herd cows. It is not unusual for the Miniature Pinscher on a farm to catch a rabbit that is equal to or larger than the size of the dog.

You are designing a title treatment for .a poster for the new music CD titled, "Latin Lingo." After typing the title, you realize immediately that the phrase poses obvious kerning challenges. You note that the central letters—TIN LIN—appear close together, but the outer letters are much further apart. You decide to kern the outer letters to bring them closer together.

1. Open ID 2-11.indd, then save it as **Latin Lingo**.
2. Using the Type tool, click between the A and T, then apply a kerning value of −105.
3. Apply a kerning value of −75 between the N and the G.
4. Apply a kerning value of −80 between the G and the O.

5. Position your cursor to the immediate left of the L in the word Lingo.
6. Apply a kerning value of −75.
7. Save your work, compare your screen to Figure 59, then close Latin Lingo.

Figure 59 *Completed Design Project*

LATIN LINGO

You have been assigned the task of designing a headline for a billboard for the movie "Crushing Impact." The client has asked for a finished design in black letters on a white background. Before you design the title, you consider the following questions.

Discussion.

1. Open ID 2-12.indd, then save it as **Crushing Impact**.
2. Look at the title for a full minute.
3. What font family might be best for the title?
4. Does the title demand a big, bold font, or could it work in a fine, delicate font?
5. Should the two words be positioned side-by-side or one on top of the other?
6. Does the title itself suggest that, visually, one word should be positioned on top of the other?

Exercise.

1. Position the word IMPACT on a second line, select all the text, change the font to Impact, then change the font size to 64 pt.

2. Select the word IMPACT, change the Horizontal Scale to 200, then change the Vertical Scale to 80.
3. Select the word CRUSHING, change the horizontal scale to 50, change the font size to 190, then change the leading to 190.

4. Select the word IMPACT, then change the leading to 44.
5. Save your work, compare your screen to Figure 60, then close Crushing Impact.

Figure 60 *Completed Portfolio Project*

CHAPTER 3 SETTING UP A DOCUMENT

1. Create a new document and set up a master page

2. Create text on master pages

3. Apply master pages to document pages

4. Modify master pages and document pages

5. Place and thread text

6. Create new sections and wrap text

CHAPTER 3

SETTING UP
A DOCUMENT

Introduction

The setup of a document is a critical phase of any design project, because you make decisions that determine the fundamental properties of the layout. When you start a new document, you specify the size, number of pages, and the basic layout of the document. At this stage, you also position columns and guides to help you plan and work with the layout. Though all of these elements can be modified, it is best if you have already determined these basic properties beforehand, so that you will not need to go back and "retro-fit" the document and its design.

Chapter 3 explores all of the basic principles and features that Adobe InDesign offers for setting up a new document. You will create a complex layout using master pages, and you will create placeholders for text, graphics, and page numbers. You will also learn how to import or place text into a document and how to "thread" text from text frame to text frame.

Along the way, you'll learn some great techniques for designing a layout, simplifying your work, avoiding time-consuming repetition of your efforts, and ensuring a consistent layout from page to page.

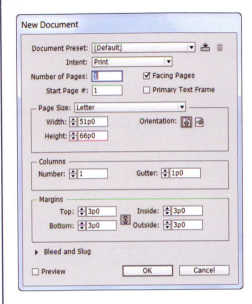

New Document

Document Preset: [Default]
Intent: Print
Number of Pages: 1   ☑ Facing Pages
Start Page #: 1   ☐ Primary Text Frame

Page Size: Letter
Width: 51p0   Orientation:
Height: 66p0

Columns
Number: 1   Gutter: 1p0

Margins
Top: 3p0   Inside: 3p0
Bottom: 3p0   Outside: 3p0

▶ Bleed and Slug

☐ Preview   OK   Cancel

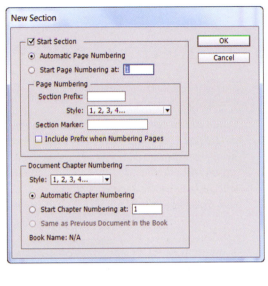

New Section

☑ Start Section
◉ Automatic Page Numbering
○ Start Page Numbering at: 1

Page Numbering
Section Prefix:
Style: 1, 2, 3, 4...
Section Marker:
☐ Include Prefix when Numbering Pages

Document Chapter Numbering
Style: 1, 2, 3, 4...
◉ Automatic Chapter Numbering
○ Start Chapter Numbering at: 1
○ Same as Previous Document in the Book
Book Name: N/A

OK
Cancel

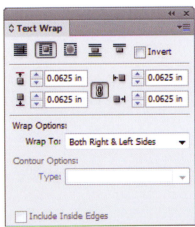

Text Wrap

☐ Invert

0.0625 in   0.0625 in
0.0625 in   0.0625 in

Wrap Options:
Wrap To: Both Right & Left Sides

Contour Options:
Type:

☐ Include Inside Edges

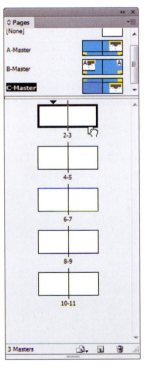

Pages
[None]
A-Master
B-Master
C-Master

2-3
4-5
6-7
8-9
10-11

3 Masters

Create a New Document
AND SET UP A MASTER PAGE

What You'll Do

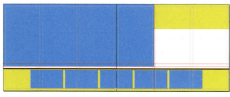

© 2015 Cengage Learning®

 In this lesson, you will create a new document, position guides on a master page, and position placeholder frames for text, tints, and graphics.

Creating a New Document

When you are ready to create a new document in InDesign, you begin in the New Document dialog box, shown in Figure 1. Here you specify the number of pages the document will contain. You also specify the **page size**, or, **trim size**—the width and height of the finished document. In addition, you specify whether or not the document will have **facing pages**. When you choose this option, the document is created with left and right pages that *face* each other in a spread, such as you would find in a magazine. If this option is not selected, each page stands alone, like a *stack* of pages.

Figure 1 *New Document dialog box*

Enter number of pages that you want in your document here

Document Preset list arrow

Page size options

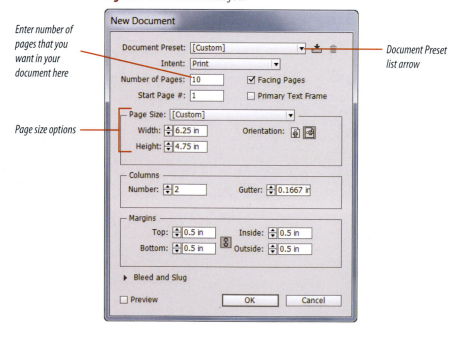

The Intent menu offers basic settings for three different types of documents: Print, Web, and Digital Publishing. For interactive presentations, choose Web when you intend the presentation to be viewed on a computer screen. Choose Digital Publishing when you intend the presentation to be viewed on a tablet device like an iPad.

The New Document dialog box also allows you to specify the width of margins on the outer edges of the page and the number of columns that will be positioned on the page. Margins and columns are useful as layout guides, and they play an important role in flowing text. When working with columns,

the term **gutter** refers to the space between the columns. Figure 2 shows margins and columns on a typical page.

When creating a document with specific settings that you plan on using again and again, you can save the settings as a preset by clicking the Save Document Preset button next to the Document Preset list in the New Document dialog box. Your named preset will then become available in the Document Preset list in the New Document dialog box.

Setting the Starting Page Number

Imagine that you are holding a closed book in your hands—perhaps this book—and

you open the front cover. The first page of the book is a single right-hand page. If you turn the page, the next two pages are pages 2-3, which face each other in a spread. Now imagine closing the book and flipping it over so that you are looking at the back cover. If you open it, the last page is a single left-hand page.

With the above in mind, consider that, by default, whenever you create a multiple page document with facing pages, InDesign automatically creates the first page on a single right-hand page and the last page on a single left-hand page. Figure 3 shows how InDesign, by default, would create a four-page

Figure 2 *Identifying margins and columns*

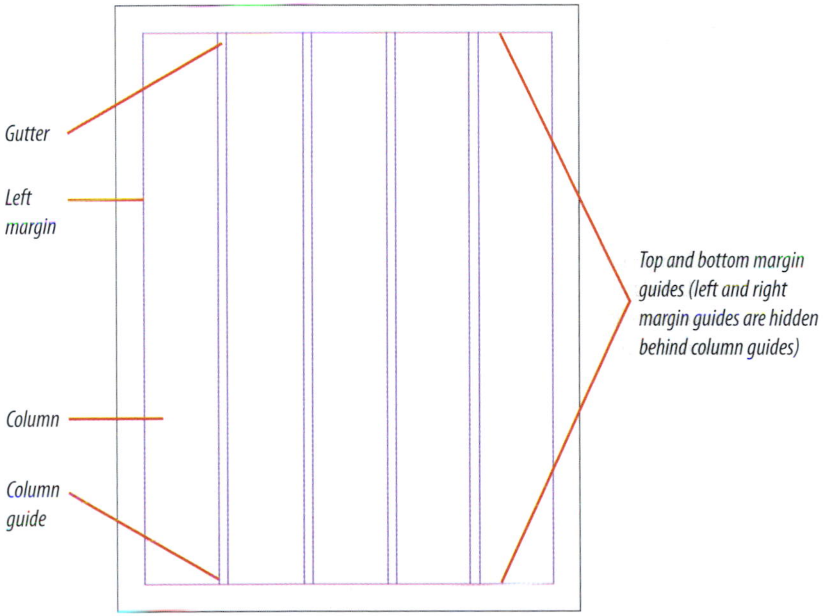

Gutter

Left
margin

Column

Column
guide

Top and bottom margin
guides (left and right
margin guides are hidden
behind column guides)

Figure 3 *Four page document with default page layout*

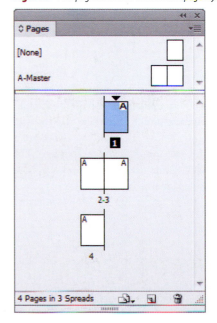

document: with a single right-hand page as the first page and a single left-hand page as the last page.

But what if you wanted to design those four pages as two spreads—what if you wanted the first page to be a left page?

You accomplish this in the Start Page # text box in the New Document dialog box. The number that you enter in this text box determines the page number of the first page and whether it is a left-hand or a right-hand page. If you enter a 2 (or any other even number), the first page will be a left-hand page. Figure 4 shows the same four-page document set up as two spreads. Note that the first page is page 2. It is a left-hand page. There is no page 1 in the document.

Modifying Margins and Columns

The New Document dialog box offers you options for specifying measurements for margins and for the number of columns in the document. Once you click OK though, you cannot return to the New Document dialog box to modify those settings. The Document Setup dialog box allows you to change the page size and the number of pages, among other choices, but it does not offer the option to modify margins or the number of columns. Don't worry though; once you've created a document, you can modify margins and columns with the Margins and Columns command on the Layout menu.

Understanding Master Pages

Imagine that you are creating a layout for a book and that every chapter title page will have the same layout format. If that book had 20 chapters, you would need to create that chapter title page 20 times. And you'd need to be careful to make the layout consistent every time you created the page. Now imagine that you've finished your layout, but your editor wants you to change the location of the title on the page. That would mean making the same change—20 times!

Not so with master pages. **Master pages** are templates that you create for a page layout. Once created, you simply apply the master page to any document pages you want based on that layout. With master pages, you create a layout one time, then use it as many times as you like. Working with master pages spares you time-consuming repetition, and it offers consistency between document pages that are meant to have the same layout.

Figure 4 *Four-page document set up as two spreads*

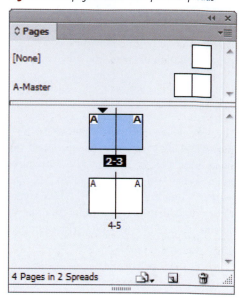

So what happens when your editor asks for that change in location of the title? Simply make the change to the master page, and the change will be reflected on all the document pages based on that master.

When you create a new document, one default master page is created and listed on the Pages panel, as shown in Figure 5. The Pages panel is command central for all things relating to pages and master pages. You use the Pages panel to add, delete, and apply master pages to document pages.

Creating Master Items on Master Pages

In InDesign, text is positioned in **text frames** and graphics are positioned in **graphics frames**. You use the Rectangle, Ellipse, or Polygon tools to create graphics frames.

When you create a frame for text or graphics on a master page, it is referred to as a **master item**. All objects on a master page are called master items and function as a "placeholder" where objects on the document pages are to be positioned. For example, if you had a book broken down into chapters and you created a master page for the chapter title pages, you would create a text frame placeholder for the chapter title text. This text frame would appear on every document page that uses the chapter title master page. Working this way— with the text frame placeholder on the master page—you can feel certain that the location

of the chapter title will be consistent on every chapter title page in the book.

Creating Guides

Guides, as shown in Figure 6, are horizontal or vertical lines that you position on a page. As their name suggests, guides are used to help guide you in aligning objects on the page. You have a number of options for creating guides. You can create them manually by "pulling" them out from the horizontal and vertical rulers. You can also use the Create Guides

command on the Layout menu. Once created, guides can be selected, moved, and deleted, if necessary. You can also change the color of guides, which sometimes makes it easier to see them, depending on the colors used in your document.

> **QUICK TIP**
>
> Press and hold [Ctrl] (Win) or ⌘ (Mac), then drag a guide from the horizontal ruler to create a guide that covers a spread instead of an individual page in a spread.

Figure 5 *Default pages on the Pages panel*

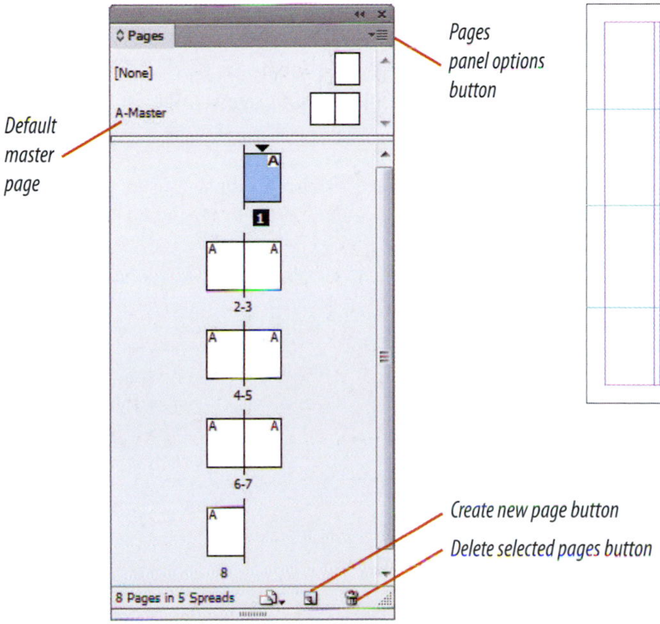

Pages panel options button

Default master page

Figure 6 *Identifying guides*

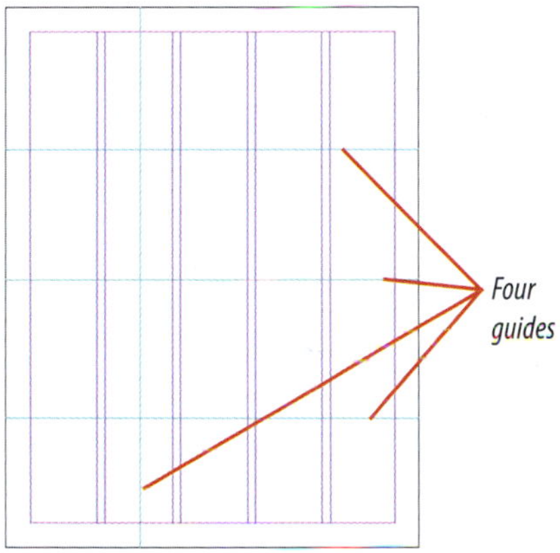

Four guides

Create new page button

Delete selected pages button

Changing the Color of Guides, Margins, and Columns

By default, guides are cyan, column guides are violet, and margin guides are magenta. Depending on your preferences and on the color of objects in the layout you are creating, you may want to change their colors.

In InDesign, you modify individual guide colors by selecting them, then clicking the Ruler Guides command on the Layout menu. Choosing a new color in the Ruler Guides dialog box affects only the selected guides. When you create more guides, they will be created in the default color.

You modify the default color of margins and columns in the Guides & Pasteboard section of the Preferences dialog box. Once you've modified the color of margins and columns, each new page you create in an existing document will appear with those colors. However, when you create a new document, the margins and columns will appear in their default colors.

Locking Column Guides

InDesign lets you lock Column Guides independently from any ruler guides you create. Click View on the Menu bar, point to Grids & Guides, and then click Lock Column Guides to add or remove the check mark, which toggles the lock on or off. By default, column guides are locked.

Choosing Default Colors for Guides, Margins, and Columns

When you choose colors for guides, margins, and columns, you may want those choices to affect every document you create. You do so by making the color changes in the appropriate dialog boxes without any documents open. The new colors will be applied in all new documents created thereafter. Remember, if you change default colors when a document is open, the changes are only applied to that document.

Using the Transform Panel

The Transform panel identifies a selected object's width and height, and its horizontal and vertical locations on the page. As shown in Figure 7, the width and height of the selected object appears in the Width and Height text boxes of the Transform panel.

When you position an object on a page, you need some way to describe that object's position on the page. InDesign defines the position of an object using X and Y Location values on the Transform panel. To work with X and Y locations, you first need to understand that the **zero point** of the page is, by default, at the top-left corner of the page. X and Y locations are made in reference to that zero point.

There are nine reference points on the Transform panel that correspond to the nine points available on a selected item's bounding box. Clicking a reference point tells InDesign that you wish to see the horizontal and vertical locations of that point of the selected object.

When an object is selected, the X Location value is the horizontal location—how far it is across the page—and the Y Location value is the vertical location—how far it is down the page. The selected object in Figure 8 has an X Location of 1 inch and a Y Location of 1 inch. This means that its top-left point is 1 inch across the page and 1 inch down.

Figure 7 *Transform panel shows coordinates and size of selected frame*

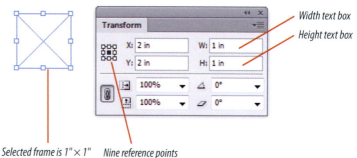

Width text box

Height text box

Selected frame is 1" × 1"   Nine reference points

Why the top-left point? Because that is the reference point chosen on the Transform panel, also shown in Figure 8.

Be sure to note that the text boxes on the Transform panel are interactive. For example, if you select an object and find that its X Location value is 2, you can enter 3 in the X Location text box, press [Enter] (Win) or [return] (Mac), and the object will be relocated to the new location on the page. You can also change the width or height of a selected object by changing the value in the Width or Height text boxes.

Using the Control Panel

You can think of the Control panel, docked at the top of the document window by default, as InDesign's "super panel." The Control panel mimics all the other panels, housing a wide variety of options for working with text and objects. Rather than always moving from one panel to another, you can usually find the option you are looking for on the Control panel.

The options on the Control panel change based on the type of object selected. For example, if a block of text is selected, the Control panel changes to show all of the type-related options for modifying text, such as changing the font or font size. When any object is selected, the Control panel display is similar to the Transform panel. It offers X/Y coordinate reference points and text boxes and the same options for modifying a selected object. For example, you can change the width and height of a frame using the Control panel, just as you can with the Transform panel.

Unlike the Transform panel, the Control panel offers a multitude of additional options for working with frames, making the Control panel perhaps the most-used panel in InDesign.

In Figure 9, the Control panel shows options for a selected graphics frame.

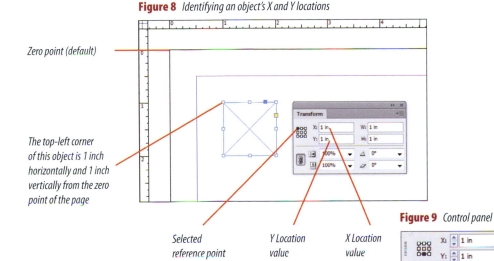

Figure 8 *Identifying an object's X and Y locations*

Zero point (default)

The top-left corner of this object is 1 inch horizontally and 1 inch vertically from the zero point of the page

Selected reference point

Y Location value

X Location value

Figure 9 *Control panel*

© 2015 Cengage Learning®

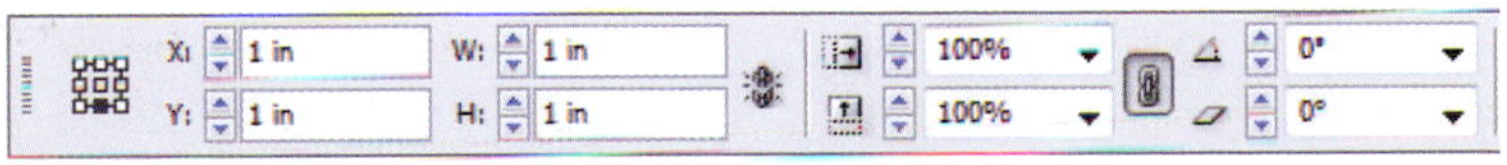

Using the Line Tool

The Line tool makes lines—no surprise there. Use the Line tool to make horizontal, vertical, and diagonal lines in your layouts. When you click the Line tool, the Fill/Stroke colors at the bottom of the Tools panel default to a fill of None and a stroke color of black. You can apply a fill color to a line, but generally speaking, you only want to stroke a line with color. You specify the weight of a line with the Stroke panel, and you can use the Line Length text box on the Control and Transform panels to specify the length. You can use all nine reference points on the Control and Transform panels to position a line in your layout.

Transforming Objects

"Transform" is a term used to describe the act of moving, scaling, skewing, or rotating an object. You can do all of the above on the Transform or Control panels. Figure 10 shows a rectangular frame that is 3" wide and 1.5" tall. Its center point is identified on the Transform panel, because the center reference

Figure 10 *A rectangle with its center point identified*

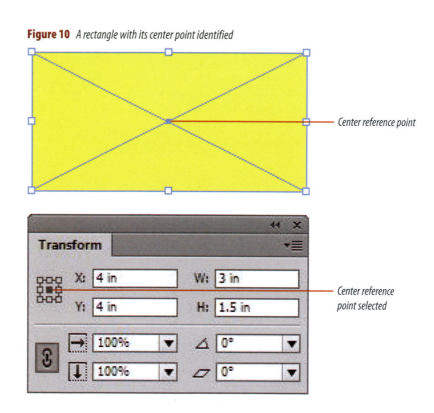

Center reference point

Center reference point selected

point is selected on the Transform panel. In Figure 11, the same frame has been rotated 90 degrees—note the 90° value in the Rotation Angle text box on the Transform panel. Note also that the object was rotated at its center point. This is because the center reference point was selected when the transformation was executed. The center point of the rectangle was the **point of origin** for the transformation. Think of the point of origin as the point from which the transformation happens. Whichever reference point is selected determines the point of origin for the transformation of the selected object.

In Figure 12, the object has not been moved. The top-left reference point on the Transform panel has been selected, so the X/Y text boxes now identify the location of the top-left corner of the rectangle.

Don't trouble yourself trying to guess ahead of time how the choice of a point of origin in conjunction with a transformation will affect an object. Sometimes it will be easy to foresee how the object will be transformed; sometimes you'll need to use trial and error. The important thing for you to remember is that the point of origin determines the point from which the transformation takes place.

Using the Transform Again Command

The Transform Again command is a powerful command that repeats the last transformation executed. For example, let's say you rotate a text frame. If you select another text frame and apply the Transform Again command, the same rotation will be applied to the second object. The Transform Again command is useful for creating multiple objects at specified distances.

Figure 11 *Rectangle rotated 90 degrees at its center point*   **Figure 12** *X/Y text boxes identify top-left corner of rectangle*

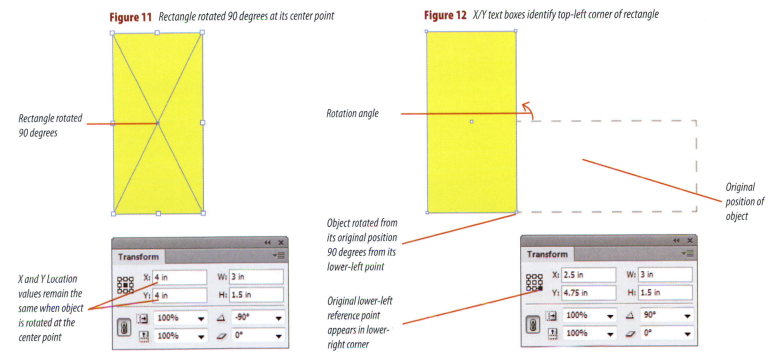

Rectangle rotated 90 degrees

X and Y Location values remain the same when object is rotated at the center point

Rotation angle

Original position of object

Object rotated from its original position 90 degrees from its lower-left point

Original lower-left reference point appears in lower-right corner

© 2015 Cengage Learning®

View a multi-page document

1. Open ID 3-1.indd.

TIP You can ignore prompts to update links for this exercise.

2. Press **[Shift] [W]** to enter Presentation mode.

3. Use the right and left arrow keys on your computer keypad to view all of the pages in the document.

   The document is composed of five two-page spreads for a total of ten pages. The document has been designed as a pamphlet for a travel company advertising destinations for a tour of Italy. Page numbers are visible at the bottom of every spread. The five spreads are based on three layout versions. The layout will be used for both a printed piece and for an interactive PDF that can be emailed.

4. Press **[Esc]** to leave Presentation mode.

5. Press **[Tab]** to show panels if necessary, then show the Pages panel.

   The first page of the document is page 2, and it is a left-hand page.

6. View spread 4-5.

   Spread 4-5, shown in Figure 13 along with other spreads, is the basis for the document you will build using master pages in this chapter.

7. Close the file without saving changes.

You viewed a finished document that will be the basis for the document you will build in this chapter.

Create a new document

1. Verify that no documents are open.

2. Click **Edit** (Win) or **InDesign** (Mac) on the Menu bar, point to **Preferences**, then click **Units & Increments**.

(continued)

Figure 13 *Layout used as the basis for this chapter*

© 2015 Cengage Learning®. Images courtesy of Chris Botello.

Figure 14 *Settings in the New Document dialog box*

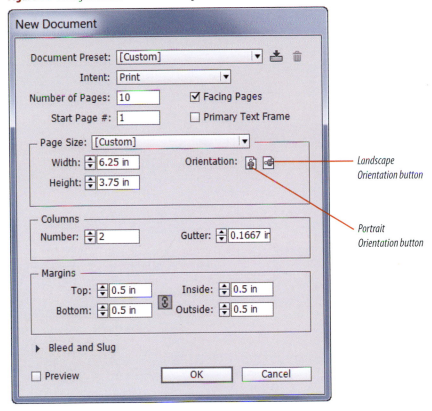

Landscape
Orientation button

Portrait
Orientation button

3. Click the **Horizontal list arrow**, click **Inches**, click the **Vertical list arrow**, click **Inches**, then click **OK**.

4. Click **File** on the Menu bar, point to **New**, then click **Document**.

5. Verify that the Intent is set to Print.

6. Type **10** in the Number of Pages text box, verify that the Facing Pages check box is checked, then verify that the Start Page # is set to 1.

7. Type **6.25** in the Width text box, press **[Tab]**, type **4.75** in the Height text box, then click the **Landscape Orientation button**.

TIP   Press [Tab] to move your cursor forward from text box to text box. Press [Shift][Tab] to move backward from text box to text box.

8. Type **2** in the Number text box in the Columns section, then verify that the Gutter text box is set to .1667 in.

9. Type **.5** in the Top Margins text box, then verify that the Make all settings the same button 🔗 is activated.

10. Compare your dialog box to Figure 14, click **OK**, then look at the Pages panel.

    Page 1 is a single right-hand page, and page 10 is a single left hand page.

11. Click **File** on the Menu bar, then click **Document Setup**.

    Note that the Margins and Columns sections are not available in the Document Setup dialog box.

12. Change the Start Page # to **2**, click **OK**, then compare your Pages panel to Figure 15.

    The document is now composed of five two-page spreads, numbered 2-11.

(continued)

13. Save the document as **Setup**.

You set the Units & Increments preferences to specify that you will be working with inches for horizontal and vertical measurements. You then created a new document using the New Document dialog box. You specified the number of pages in the document, the page size for each page, and the number of columns on each page. You then modified the start page number in the Document Setup dialog box to start the document on a left-hand page.

Modify margins and the number of columns on a master page

1. Set the workspace to **Essentials**.

2. Double-click the word **A-Master** on the Pages panel, note that both master pages in the Pages menu become blue, then note that the page menu at the lower-left corner of the document window lists A-Master.

A-Master is now the active page. You will modify the margins and the number of columns on a master page so that your changes will be applied to all ten document pages.

3. Click **Layout** on the Menu bar, then click **Margins and Columns**.

The Margins and Columns dialog box opens.

4. Set the number of columns to **3**.

5. Reduce the width of the margins on all four sides to **.125 in**, then click **OK**.

Note that the width and height of the columns change to fill the area within the margins.

6. Save the file.

You changed the number of columns and the width of margins on a master page.

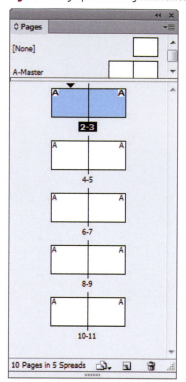

Figure 15 *Pages panel showing document starting on a left-hand page*

Using the Move Pages Command

If you have a multiple-page document, you can change the sequence of pages simply by moving them around on the Pages panel. Easy enough. But for documents with more pages—let's say 100 pages—dragging and dropping page icons on the Pages panel isn't so simple. Imagine, for example, trying to drag page 84 so that it follows page 14. Whew! With InDesign's powerful Move Pages command, you can specify which pages you want to move and where you want to move them. Click the Pages panel options button, click Move Pages, then specify options in the Move Pages dialog box. Be sure to check it out.

Figure 16 *Using the Control panel to position a guide*

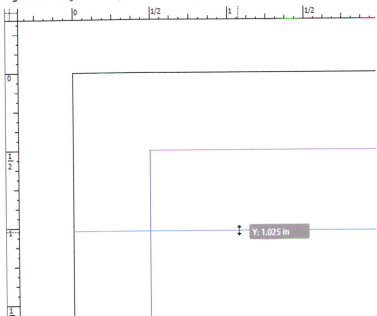

Y: 1.025 in

1. If rulers are not visible at the top and left of the document window, click **View** on the Menu bar, then click **Show Rulers**.

2. Click the **Selection tool** , position the pointer over the horizontal ruler, then click and slowly drag down a guide, releasing it anywhere on the page.

   A guide is positioned only on the left page of the spread.

   TIP As you drag the new guide onto the page, the value in the Y Location text box on the Control panel continually changes to show the guide's current location. See Figure 16.

3. Click **Edit** on the Menu bar, then click **Undo Add New Guide.**

4. Press and hold **[Ctrl]** (Win) or ⌘ (Mac), then drag down a **guide** from the horizontal ruler, releasing it anywhere on the page.

   The guide extends across the entire spread.

5. Type **2.5** in the Y Location text box on the Control panel, then press **[Enter]** (Win) or **[return]** (Mac).

   The guide jumps to the specific vertical location you entered: 2.5" from the top of the page.

   TIP For this entire chapter, you can use the Transform panel interchangeably with the Control panel.

6. While pressing **Ctrl** (Win) or ⌘ (Mac), drag a **second spread guide** from the horizontal ruler, drop the guide anywhere on the spread, then set its Y Location to **3.5 in**.

7. Click **Edit** (Win) or **InDesign** (Mac), point to **Preferences**, then click **Units & Increments**.

   (continued)

8. In the Ruler Units section, verify that Origin is set to Spread, then click **OK**.

   With the Origin value set to spread, the ruler and all X values are continuous across the entire spread. In other words, there's one ruler across both pages, as opposed to one ruler for the left page and another for the right page.

9. Drag a **guide** from the vertical ruler on the left side of the document window, then use the Control panel to position its X value at **8.35 in**.

10. Using the Selection tool 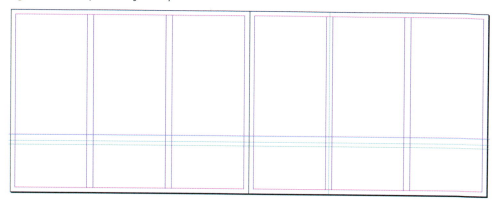, click the **first horizontal guide** you positioned at 2.5 inches to select it, double-click the **Y Location text box** on the Transform panel, type **3.4**, then press **[Enter]** (Win) or **[return]** (Mac).

   The guide is moved to the new location.

TIP   Selected guides appear darker blue.

11. Position a third horizontal spread guide at 3.25" from the top of the page.

12. Compare your spread and guides to Figure 17, then save your work.

You positioned guides on the master page by dragging them from the horizontal and vertical rulers. You used the Control panel to position them at precise locations.

Figure 17 *Master spread with guides in position*

Working with Conditional Text

Using conditional text is a great way to create different versions of the same InDesign document. You create conditional text by first creating conditions and then applying them to text. Later, you hide or show the text that has the condition applied to it by hiding or showing conditions using the Conditional Text panel. Showing and hiding conditions works just like showing and hiding layers on the Layers panel. You assign a new condition to text, and then hide it by clicking the "Eye" (visibility) icon on the Conditional Text panel. When you have many conditions, you can create a **condition set**, which is a snapshot of the current visibility of the applied conditions. Click the Conditional Text panel options button, then click Show Options. On the Conditional Text panel, click the Set list arrow, then click Create New Set. Name the set, then click OK. Instead of turning individual conditions on or off on the panel, you can choose a condition set to do the same job in one step.

Figure 18 *Positioning the text frame*

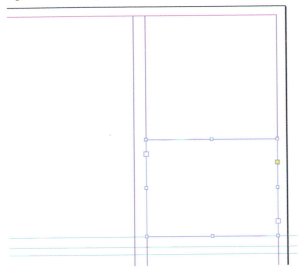

Figure 19 *Duplicated text frame*

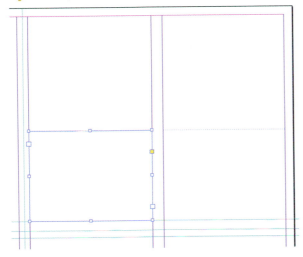

Create placeholder text frames

1. Verify that the Fill and Stroke buttons on the Tools panel are both set to None.

2. Click the **Type tool** T , then drag to create a small text frame anywhere in the rightmost column above the horizontal guides.

3. Click the **Selection tool** ▸ , drag the left and right handles of the text frame so that it is the full width of the column.

4. Drag the **bottom handle** down until it snaps to the topmost horizontal guide.

5. Click the **bottom-center reference point** on the Control panel, type **1.375** in the Height text box on the Transform panel, then press **[Enter]** (Win) or **[return]** (Mac).

   Your right page should resemble Figure 18. The bottom of the text frame did not move with the change in height.

6. Press and hold **[Shift] [Alt]** (Win) or **[Shift] [option]** (Mac), then drag and drop a copy of the text frame into the column to the left so that your page resembles Figure 19.

   Note that the new text frames are difficult to distinguish from the ruler guides.

7. Save your work.

You created two text frames, which will be used as placeholders for body copy in the document.

Change the color of guides, margins, and columns

1. Click **Edit** (Win) or **InDesign** (Mac) on the Menu bar, point to **Preferences**, then click **Guides & Pasteboard**.

2. Verify that the Guides in Back check box is unchecked.

   When this option is deactivated, guides appear in front of all items on the document, rather than hidden behind them.

3. In the Color section, click the **Margins list arrow**, then click **Light Gray**.

4. Click the **Columns list arrow**, then click **Light Gray**.

5. Click **OK**.

6. Click the **Selection tool** , click the **vertical guide** to select it, press and hold **[Shift]**, then click the three **horizontal guides**, so all the guides you created are selected.

   All four guides appear dark blue.

7. Click **Layout** on the Menu bar, then click **Ruler Guides**.

8. Click the **Color list arrow**, click **Red**, then click **OK**.

9. Click the **pasteboard** to deselect the guides, then compare your page to Figure 20.

You changed the color of margins, columns, and guides to improve your ability to distinguish text frames from page guides.

Figure 20 *Viewing changed guide colors*

Figure 21 *Viewing the copied frame*

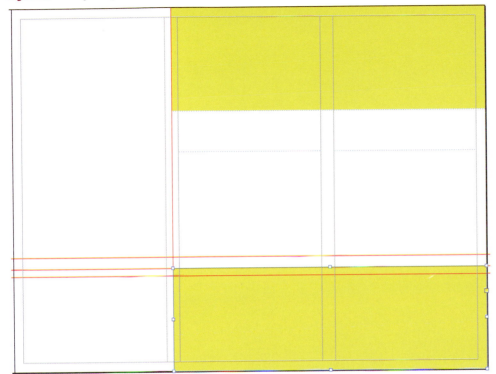

Create color tint frames

1. Verify that the Fill and Stroke buttons on the Tools panel are both set to None.

   TIP You will learn much more about fills and strokes in Chapters 4 and 5.

2. Click the **Rectangle tool** , then drag a small **rectangle** anywhere above the two text frames in the two rightmost columns.

3. Click the **Selection tool** , click **Window** on the Menu bar, point to **Object & Layout**, then click **Transform**.

   The Transform panel appears.

4. Drag the **left handle** of the frame so that it snaps to the red vertical guide.

   TIP To verify that Snap to Guides is activated, click View on the Menu bar, then point to Grids & Guides.

5. Drag the **right handle** of the frame so that it snaps to the right edge of the document.

   The Width text box on the Transform panel should read 4.15 in.

6. Drag the **top handle** of the frame so that it snaps to the top edge of the document.

7. Click the **top-center reference point** on the Transform panel, then verify that the Y text box on the Transform panel reads 0.

   If the top edge of the frame is aligned to the top edge of the page, its Y coordinate must be zero.

8. Change the Height value on the Transform panel to **1.35** in.

   Because the Units & Increments preferences are set to Inches, you do not need to—nor should

   (continued)

you—type the abbreviation for inches in the text box. Just type the number.

TIP Don't deselect the frame.

9. Click the **Fill button** on the Swatches panel so that it is in front of the Stroke button.

10. Open the Swatches panel, then click the **yellow swatch**.

   The frame fills with the yellow tint.

11. Drag and drop a copy of the yellow frame to the bottom of the page, as shown in Figure 21.

12. Drag the **top edge** of the bottom frame down so that it aligns with the bottommost of the three guides, then drag the **left edge** to align with the left edge of the document.

   The Width & Height text boxes on the Transform panel should read 12.5 in and 1.25 in, respectively.

13. Deselect all, then click the **light blue swatch** on the Swatches panel.

   The Fill button changes to the light blue color.

14. Create a small rectangle anywhere in the upper-left section of the document.

   The new rectangle is created with the light blue fill.

15. Click the **top-left reference point** on the Transform panel, enter **0** in the X text box, press **[Tab]**, enter **0** in the Y text box, press **[Tab]**, type **8.35** in the Width text box, press **[Tab]**, then enter **3.4** in the Height text box.

   Your spread should resemble Figure 22.

16. Save your work.

You created three color-filled frames on the page and used the Transform panel to position them and modify their sizes.

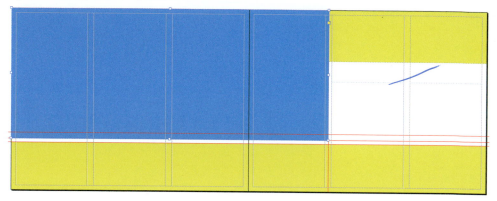

Figure 22 *Viewing tints on the spread*

Figure 23 *Viewing the line*

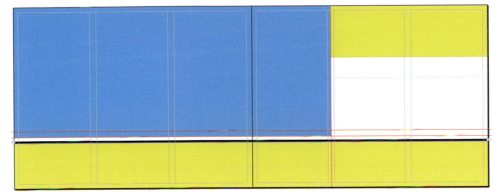

Use the Line tool

1. Close the Transform panel, click anywhere in the pasteboard to deselect all, then click the **Line tool** ⁄ .

2. On the Tools panel, set the Fill to **None** and the Stroke to **Black**.

3. Position the cursor at the left edge of the document, press and hold **[Shift]**, then click and drag to create a line of any length.

   Pressing and holding [Shift] constrains the line so that it is straight.

4. Expand the Stroke panel, then increase the weight of the stroke to 4 pt.

5. Click the **middle-left reference point** on the Control panel, type **0** in the X text box, press **[Tab]**, type **3.5** in the Y text box, press **[Tab]**, then type **12.5** in the L (length) text box so that your spread resembles Figure 23.

6. Save your work.

You created a line with the Line tool, specified its weight in the Stroke panel, then positioned it on the spread and specified its length with the Control panel.

Use the Transform Again command

1. Click the **Rectangle tool** 🔲 , then draw a small rectangle in the first column anywhere at the bottom of the page.

2. Click the **top-left reference point** on the Control panel, type **0** in the X text box, type **3.6** in the Y text box, type **1.8** in the Width text box, then type **1** in the Height text box.

3. Press **[I]** on your keypad to access the Eyedropper tool 🖊 , then click the **large blue frame** at the top of the page.

   The Eyedropper tool samples the fill and stroke colors from the large frame; the small rectangle takes on the same fill and stroke color.

4. Press **[V]** to access the Selection tool ▸ , press and hold **[Shift] [Alt]** (Win) or **[Shift] [option]** (Mac), then drag a copy approximately 1/8" to the right of the original, as shown in Figure 24.

(continued)

Figure 24 *Duplicating the frame*

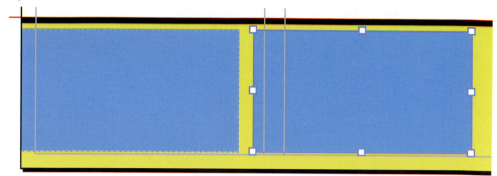

Figure 25 *Viewing five frames centered horizontally on the spread*

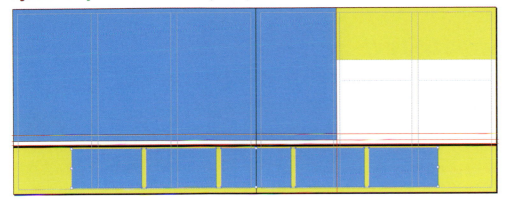

5. Click **Object** on the Menu bar, point to **Transform Again**, then click **Transform Again**.

   The last transformation you made—dragging and dropping the copy—is duplicated.

6. Apply the Transform Again command two more times.

7. Select all five of the small blue rectangles.

8. Click the **center reference point** on the Control panel.

   With the center reference point selected, the X/Y coordinates on the Control panel now identify the center point of all five boxes as a unit.

9. Change the X value on the Control panel to 6.25.

   6.25 is half of the full horizontal width of 12.5," thus the five boxes, as a unit, are centered horizontally on the page.

10. Compare your layout to Figure 25, then save your work.

You created a single rectangle, then changed its fill and stroke color with the Eyedropper tool. You duplicated it with the drag-and-drop method, used the Transform Again command three times. You used the Control panel to center all five rectangles as a unit.

Create Text
ON MASTER PAGES

What You'll Do

© 2015 Cengage Learning®

 In this lesson, you will position two headlines on a master page, create automatic page numbering, and create two new master pages.

Creating a New Master Page

You create new master pages by clicking the New Master command on the Pages panel menu. When you create a new master page, you have the option of giving the master page a new name. This is useful for distinguishing one master page from another. For example, you might want to use the name "Body Copy" for master pages that will be used for body copy and then use the name "Chapter Start" for master pages that will be used as a layout for a chapter title page. Figure 26 shows three named master pages on the Pages panel.

When you create a new master page, you have the option of changing the values for the margins and for the number of columns on the new master page.

Figure 26 *Three master pages on the Pages panel*

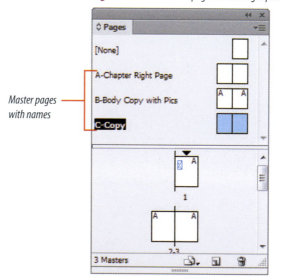

Master pages with names

Loading Master Pages

You can load master pages from one InDesign document to another by simply clicking the Pages panel options button, pointing to Master Pages, then clicking Load Master Pages. You will be prompted to navigate to the file that has the master pages you wish to load. Select the InDesign document, then click Open. The master pages are added to the Pages panel. You will be prompted to rename master pages that have the same name or replace the existing master pages.

Creating Automatic Page Numbering

When you create a document with multiple pages, chances are you'll want to have page numbers on each page. You could create a text frame on every page, then manually type the page number on every page, but think of what a nightmare that could turn out to be! You would have to create a text frame of the same size and in the same location on every page. Imagine what would happen if you were to remove or add a page to the middle of the document: you'd need to go back and renumber your pages!

Fortunately, InDesign offers a solution for this. You can create placeholder text frames for page numbers on your master pages. Click inside the text frame, click Type on the Menu bar, point to Insert Special Character, point to Markers, then click Current Page Number. A letter will appear in the text frame, as shown in Figure 27.

Figure 27 *A text frame on a master page containing an auto page number character*

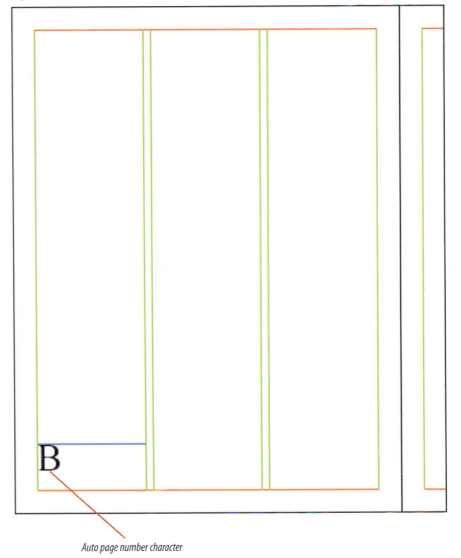

Auto page number character

That letter represents the page number. You can format it using any font, size, and alignment that you desire. On document pages based on that master, the letter in the text frame will appear as the number of the page. Page numbering is automatic. This means that the page number is automatically updated when pages are added or removed from the document.

When you work with multiple master pages, make sure that each page number placeholder is the same size, in the same location, and formatted in the same way on each master page. This will make the appearance of page numbers consistent throughout the document, regardless of the master upon which a particular document page is based.

Inserting Space Between Characters

In Chapter 2, you learned that you should not press the spacebar more than once to create extra spacing between characters. However, sometimes a single space does not provide enough space between words or characters. You may want to insert additional space to achieve a certain look. You could tab the text or, as you'll learn in this lesson, you can insert white space.

The Type menu contains commands for inserting white space between words or characters. The two most-used white spaces are **em space** and **en space**. The width of an em space is equivalent to that of the lowercase letter m in the current typeface at that type size. The width of an en space is narrower—that of the lowercase letter n in that typeface

at that type size. Use these commands—not the spacebar—to insert white space. To insert an em space or an en space, click Type on the Menu bar, point to Insert White Space, then click either Em Space or En Space. Figure 28 shows an em space between a page number placeholder and a word.

Inserting Em Dashes and En Dashes

Sometimes you'll want to put a dash between words or characters and you'll find that the dash created by pressing the hyphen key is not wide enough. That's because hyphens are shorter than dashes.

InDesign offers two types of dashes to insert between words or characters—the em dash and the en dash. The width of an em dash is

Rotating the Spread View

Sometimes, with certain layouts, not all of your content will be right-side-up on your page spread. For example, you might be designing a poster that will fold four ways, so when the poster is laid out flat in your InDesign document, some of the content will be rotated on its side—or maybe even upside down! Whatever the case, when you're working with these types of layouts, you don't need to lie on your side or do a headstand to see your work right-side-up. Instead, use the Rotate Spread View command on the Pages panel (it's a sub-menu of Page Attributes) or the Rotate Spread command on the View menu. These commands rotate the view of the spread so that you can work right-side-up. They don't actually affect the content on the page—just the view.

Figure 28 *Identifying an em space*

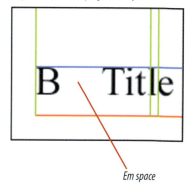

Em space

Setting Up a Document

equivalent to that of the lowercase letter m in the current typeface at that type size. The width of an en dash is narrower—that of the lowercase letter n in that typeface at that type size. To insert an em dash or an en dash, click Type on the Menu bar, point to Insert Special Character, point to Hyphens and Dashes, then click either Em Dash or En Dash. Figure 29 shows an example of an en dash.

Creating a New Master Page Based on Another

Imagine that you've created a master page for a magazine layout. The master contains master items for the headline, the body copy, and the page number. It also contains master items for pictures that will appear on the page. Now imagine that you need to create another master page that will be identical to

this master page, with the one exception that this new master will not contain frames for graphics. You wouldn't want to duplicate all of the work you did to create the first master, would you?

To avoid repeating efforts and for consistency between masters, you can create a new master page based on another master page. The new master would appear identical to the first. You would then modify only the elements that you want to change on the new master, keeping all of the elements that you don't want to change perfectly consistent with the previous one.

Basing a new master on another master is not the same thing as duplicating a master. Duplicating a master creates a copy, but the original and the copy have no relationship.

When you base a new master on another, any changes you make to the first master will be updated on masters based on it. Think of how powerful this is. Let's say that your editor tells you to change the type size of the page numbers. Making a change in only one place offers you a substantial savings in time and effort and provides you with the certainty that the page numbers will be consistent from master to master.

Remember that all master items on new master pages will also be locked by default. To unlock a master item, you must press and hold [Shift] [Ctrl] (Win) or [Shift] ⌘ (Mac) to select those objects on the new master. InDesign does this so that you don't accidentally move or delete objects from the new master or the original master.

Figure 29 *Identifying an en dash*

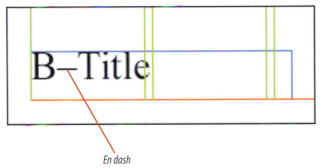

En dash

Add placeholders for headlines

1. Verify that the Fill and Stroke buttons on the Tools panel are both set to None.

2. Click the **Type tool** T , then drag a small **rectangle** anywhere in the two rightmost columns above the two text frames already there.

3. Click the **Selection tool** , then drag the **left handle** of the frame so that it snaps to the red vertical guide.

4. Drag the **right handle** of the frame so that it snaps to the right edge of the document.

   The Width text box on the Control panel should read 4.15 in.

5. Click the **bottom-center reference point** on the Control panel, then enter **1.35** in the Y text box.

   The text frame moves to align its bottom edge to the Y coordinate.

6. Change the height value on the Control panel to **1.2**.

7. Click the **Type tool** T , click inside the new frame, then type **LOCATION** in all caps.

8. On the Control panel, center the text, select the text, set the typeface to **Hobo Std Medium**, set the type size to **60 pt**, then set the Horizontal Scale to **75%**.

9. Enter **[Ctrl] [B]** (Win) or ⌘ **[B]** (Mac) to open the Text Frame Options dialog box, click the **Align list arrow**, click **Bottom**, then click **OK**.

10. Deselect, then compare your text to Figure 30.

11. Click the **Selection tool** , press and hold **[Shift] [Alt]** (Win) or **[Shift] [option]** (Mac), then drag and drop a **copy of the text frame** anywhere straight down below the original.

(continued)

Figure 30 *Formatted headline on a master page*

Figure 31 *Formatted sub-headline on a master page*

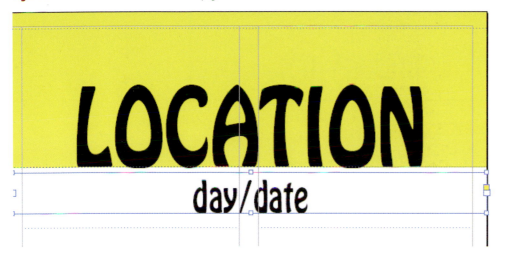

Figure 32 *The inserted page number*

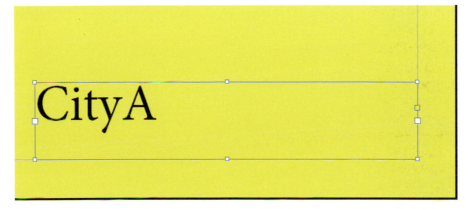

12. Click the **Type tool** , select the duplicated text, reduce the type size to 24 pt, then type **day/date** in all lowercase letters.

13. Click the **Selection tool** , then verify that the bottom-center reference point on the Control panel is selected.

14. Type **1.75** in the Y text box, type **.35** in the Height text box, then compare your layout to Figure 31.

15. Save your work.

You created and positioned two text frames on the master page, then formatted text in each.

Create automatic page numbering and insert white space between characters

1. Click the **Type tool** , draw a text frame anywhere in the lower-right corner of the spread, set its width to **1.25"**, then set its height to **.25"**.

2. Position the text frame in the lower-right corner of the spread, inside the margin guide.

3. Type the word **City** in the text frame with no space after the word, choose any typeface and size you like, then verify that the text cursor is blinking to the right of the word.

4. Click **Type** on the Menu bar, point to **Insert Special Character**, point to **Markers**, then click **Current Page Number**.

   As shown in Figure 32, the letter A appears in the text frame. This letter will change on document pages to reflect the current document page. For example, on page 4, the A will appear as the number 4.

(continued)

5. Click the cursor between the y and the A, click **Type** on the Menu bar, point to **Insert White Space**, then click **Em Space**.

6. On the Control panel, set the text to **Align Right**, click **Object** on the Menu bar, click **Text Frame Options**, then set the Vertical Justification to **Bottom**.

Your text box should resemble Figure 33.

7. Copy the **selected text frame**, paste it in place, click the **bottom-left reference point** on the Control panel, then change the X value to **.125**.

The text frame moves to the left page, inside the margin guide.

8. Reformat the text so that the copied text frame resembles Figure 34.

TIP You copy/paste the em space just like any other character.

9. Save your work.

You created automatic page numbering on the right and left pages of the master page and inserted em spaces.

Create a new master page spread based on another master page spread

1. Expand the Pages panel if necessary, click the **Pages panel options button** , then click **New Master**.

2. Click the **Based on Master list arrow**, click **A-Master**, then click **OK**.

As shown in Figure 35, the B-Master page icons on the Pages panel display an A, because B-Master is based on A-Master.

(continued)

Figure 33 *Formatted text on the right-hand page*

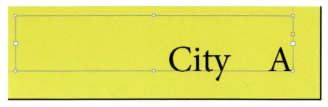

Figure 34 *Reformatted text on the left-hand page*

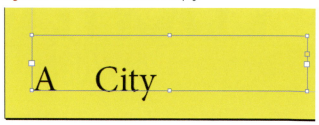

Figure 35 *Viewing the new master on the Pages panel*

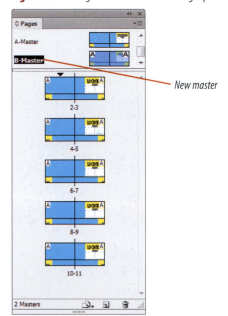

New master

© 2015 Cengage Learning®

Figure 36 *Selecting specific page elements*

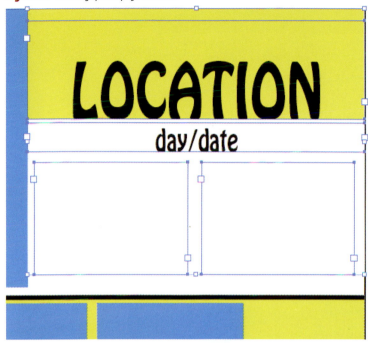

Figure 37 *Five frames centered horizontally on the spread*

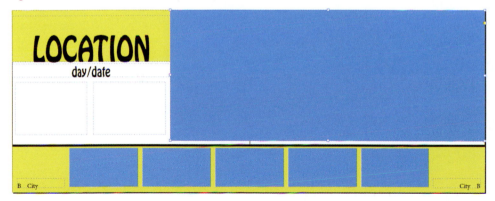

© 2015 Cengage Learning®

3. Double-click **B-Master** on the Pages panel to view the B-Master master page.

   If necessary, change the view to Fit Spread in Window. B-Master is identical to A-Master, except that the automatic page number reads B rather than A.

4. Hide guides.

5. Click the **Selection tool** , then try to select objects on the page.

   Objects on a master page based on another master cannot be selected in the standard way.

6. Press and hold **[Shift] [Ctrl]** (Win) or **[Shift]** ⌘ (Mac), then drag a **marquee** to select the elements shown in Figure 36.

   TIP Make sure you start dragging on the pasteboard and not on the document or you might accidentally select and move an object on the master.

7. Click the **middle-left reference point** on the Control panel, then set the X value to **0**.

8. Select the **large blue frame**, click the **middle-right reference point** on the Control panel, then set the X value to **12.5**.

   Your B-Master spread should resemble Figure 37.

9. Save your work.

You created a new master spread based on the A-Master spread. You modified the location of elements on the new master to differentiate it from the original.

Create a new blank master page spread

1. Click the **Pages panel options button**, then click **New Master**.

2. Click the **Based on Master list arrow**, then verify that None is selected so that your New Master dialog box resembles Figure 38.

3. Click **OK**.

   C-Master appears as two page thumbnails on the Pages panel.

4. Double-click the words **A-Master** in the top part of the Pages panel to view the A-Master spread, select all, then copy.

5. Double-click **C-Master** to view the C-Master spread, click **Edit** on the Menu bar, click **Paste in Place**, then deselect all.

   As shown in Figure 39, the A-Master layout is pasted into the C-Master spread. The only change is that the automatic page numbering reads C.

6. Click the **Selection tool**, if necessary, then select the **five blue frames** at the bottom of the page as well as the **yellow frame** behind them.

   Because C-Master is not based on A-Master, the items are not locked.

7. Click the **top-center reference point** on the Control panel, then set the Y value to **0**.

8. Click **Object** on the Menu bar, then click **Hide**.

   (continued)

Figure 38 *New Master dialog box*

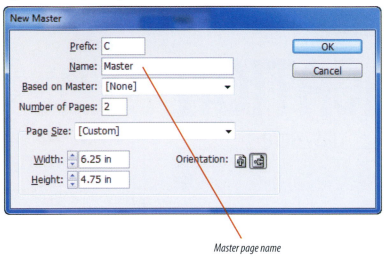

Master page name

Figure 39 *A-Master pasted into C-Master*

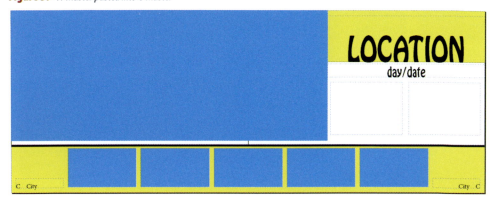

Figure 40 *Modified layout in C-Master*

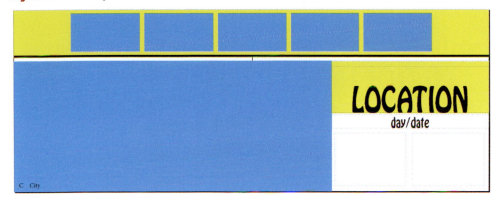

LOCATION
day/date

C City

9. Select all the objects above the horizontal black line, click the **bottom-center reference point** on the Control panel, then set the Y value to **4.75**.

10. Delete the automatic numbering text frame at the bottom of the right-hand page.

    Pages based on C-Master will have page numbers only on the left page of the spread.

11. Show the hidden frames, then deselect all.

12. Select the **large yellow frame** at the top of the page, click the **bottom-center reference point** on the Control panel, then note the Y value.

13. Select the **horizontal black line**, then set the Y value to be the same as that of the large yellow frame.

    Your C-Master spread should resemble Figure 40.

14. Save your work.

You created a new blank master spread not based on any other master. You modified the location of elements on the new master to differentiate it from the original.

Apply Master Pages
TO DOCUMENT PAGES

What You'll Do

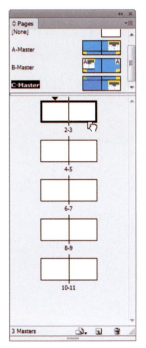

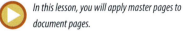

In this lesson, you will apply master pages to document pages.

Applying Master Pages to Document Pages

Once you have created master pages, you then use the Pages panel to apply them to the document pages. One method for applying master pages is the "drag and drop" method. Using this method, you drag the master page icon or the master page name, in the top section of the Pages panel, down to the page icons in the lower section of the Pages panel. To apply the master to a single page, you drag the master onto the page icon, as shown in Figure 41. To apply the master to a spread, you drag the master onto one of the four corners of the left and right page icons until you see a dark border around both pages in the spread, as shown in Figure 42.

When you apply a master page to a document page, the document page inherits all of the layout characteristics of the master.

QUICK TIP

You can apply the default None master page to a document page when you do not want the document page to be based on a master.

A second method for applying master pages to document pages is to use the Apply Master to Pages command on the Pages panel menu. The Apply Master dialog box, shown in Figure 43, allows you to specify which master you want to apply to which pages. This method is a good choice when you want to apply a master to a series of consecutive pages—it's faster than dragging and dropping.

Figure 41 *Applying C-Master to page 2*

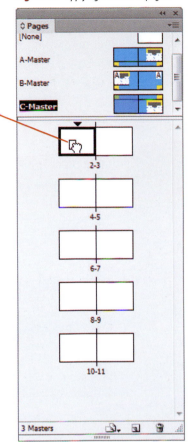

Dragging master page icon onto a single page

Figure 42 *Applying C-Master to pages 2 & 3*

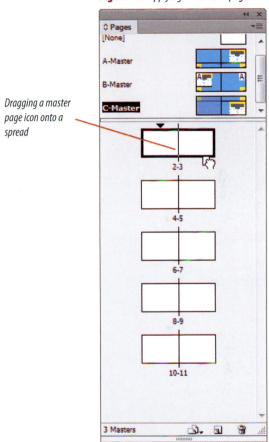

Dragging a master page icon onto a spread

Figure 43 *Using the Apply Master dialog box*

Apply master pages to document pages

1. Click the **Pages panel options button** 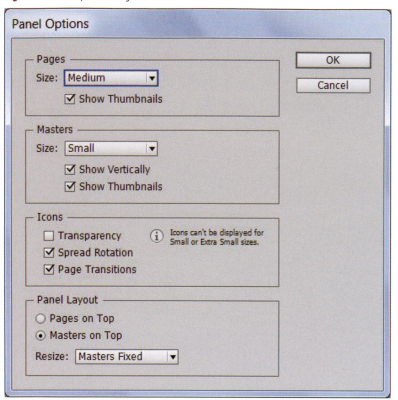, then click **Panel Options**.

2. Verify that your Pages section matches Figure 44, then click **OK**.

   Because the three master pages are similar in color, having page thumbnails hidden and only page icons showing will make it easier to see which masters have been applied to which spreads.

3. Scroll through the document and note that the A-Master has been automatically applied to all the pages in the document.

   (continued)

Figure 44 *Panel Options dialog box*

Figure 45 *Applying the master to the document spread*

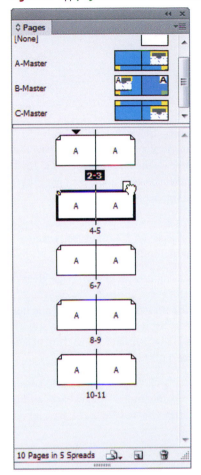

Figure 46 *Pages panel reflecting applied masters*

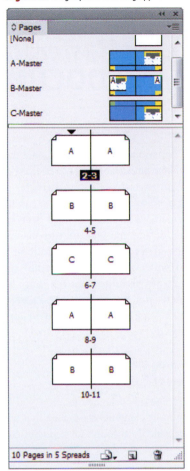

4. On the Pages panel, drag **B-Master** to the upper-right corner of spread 4-5 until a black frame appears around both thumbnails, as shown in Figure 45, then release the mouse button.

5. Using the same method, apply the C-Master to spread 6-7.

6. Click the **Pages panel options button**, then click **Apply Master to Pages**.

7. Click the **Apply Master list arrow**, then click **B-Master**.

8. Type **10-11** in the To Pages text box, then click **OK**.

   The master is applied to the spread. Your Pages panel should resemble Figure 46.

9. Navigate to page 2, then switch to Presentation mode.

10. Navigate through the spreads to see the masters applied and the automatic page numbering.

11. Exit Presentation mode, then save your work.

You applied master spreads to document spreads using the drag-and-drop method and the Apply Master to Pages command.

Modify Master Pages
AND DOCUMENT PAGES

What You'll Do

 In this lesson, you will make modifications to both master pages and document pages and explore how each affects the other.

Modifying Master Pages

When you modify a master item on a master page, that modification will be reflected on all document pages based on that master page. This is a powerful option. Let's say that you have created a layout for a 36-page book, and you decide that you want to change the typeface of all the headlines. If they were created on master pages, you could simply reformat the headline in the text frame placeholder on the master pages, and every document page in the book based on it would be updated.

Overriding Master Items on Document Pages

Master pages are designed to allow you to lay out the basic elements for a page that will be used repeatedly throughout a document. In most cases, however, you will want to make modifications to the document page once it is created—you might even want to delete some objects on the document page that were created on the master page.

Master page items on document pages are fixed objects and cannot be selected with normal methods.

You can modify a master page item on a document page, however, by **overriding**. You override a master item by pressing and holding [Shift] [Ctrl] (Win) or [Shift] ⌘ (Mac), then clicking a master item. This makes the item selectable.

You very well might find that fixed master items on document pages are annoying! Long after the master page has served its purpose, you will find—especially with long documents—that the inability to just simply select master items with the Selection tool impedes your progress. You can quickly override all master items on a targeted document page on the Pages panel options menu, by clicking Override All Master Page Items.

Making changes to a document page is often referred to as making a local change. When you override a master item, that item nevertheless maintains its status as a master item and will still be updated with changes to the master page. For example, if you resize a master item on a document page, but you do not change its color, it will retain its new size, but if the color of the master item is changed on the master page, the master item's color will be updated on the document page.

Once a master item has been released from its fixed position, it remains selectable. You can return a master item on a document page back to its original state by selecting the item, clicking the Pages panel options button, then clicking Remove Selected Local Overrides.

Detaching Master Items

When you are sure you no longer want a master item to be affected by updates made to the associated master page, you can detach a master item. To detach a master item, you must first override it by pressing and holding [Shift] [Ctrl] (Win) or [Shift] [⌘] (Mac) while selecting it. Next, click the Pages panel options button, point to Master Pages, then click Detach Selection from Master.

That's the official move. Note though, that when you modify text in a text frame on a document page, the relationship between the text on the document page and the text on the master page tends to detach automatically. Therefore, when it comes to text, it's a smart idea to use master pages for the placement of text frames on the page, but use character and paragraph styles for global formatting of the text itself.

Override master items on a document page

1. Verify that the document has been saved.

2. Double-click the **page 3 icon** on the Pages panel, click the **Selection tool** 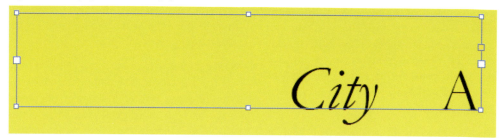, then try to select any of the objects on the page.

   Because all objects on page 3 are master items, they're fixed and cannot be selected with standard methods.

3. Press and hold **[Shift] [Ctrl]** (Win) or **[Shift]** ⌘ (Mac), then click the word **LOCATION**.

4. Click the **Type tool** T , select the **text**, type **MANAROLA**, then click the **pasteboard** to deselect.

5. Save your work.

You overrode a master item on a document page.

Modify master items on a master page

1. View the right-hand page in the A-Master, select the word **city**, the **em space**, and the **automatic page icon**, then change the type size and typeface to 12 pt Garamond.

2. Select only the word **City**, then change its typeface to Garamond Italic.

   Your text should resemble Figure 47.

   (continued)

Figure 47 *Modifying text on a master page*

City   A

Figure 48 *Stroke button on the Swatches panel*

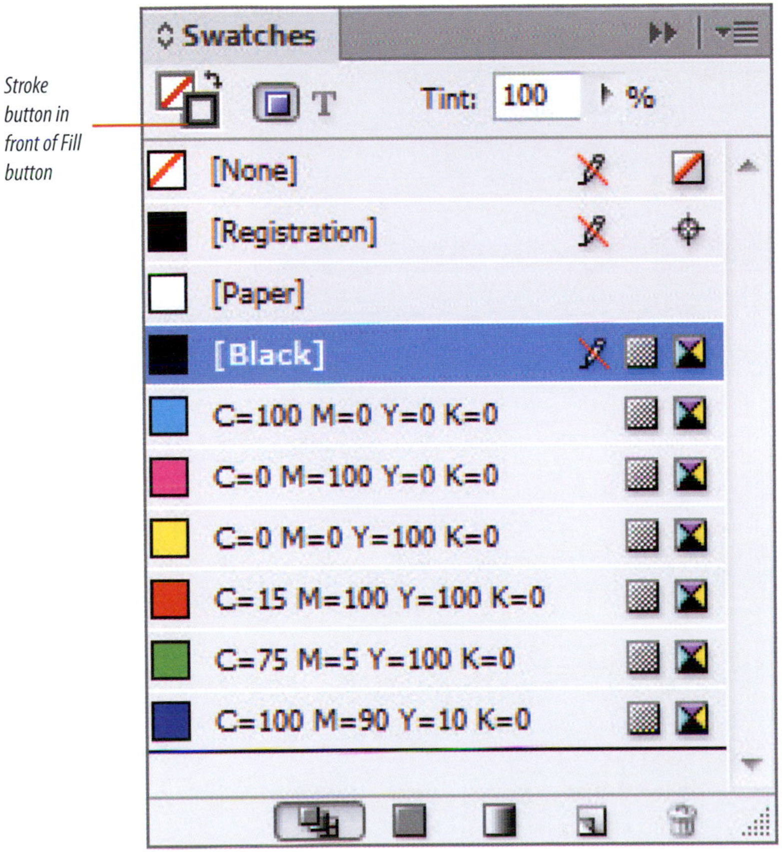

Stroke button in front of Fill button

Swatches

Tint: 100 %

[None]

[Registration]

[Paper]

[Black]

C=100 M=0 Y=0 K=0

C=0 M=100 Y=0 K=0

C=0 M=0 Y=100 K=0

C=15 M=100 Y=100 K=0

C=75 M=5 Y=100 K=0

C=100 M=90 Y=10 K=0

3. Make the same changes to the text on the bottom of the left-hand page of the spread.

4. Double-click the word **LOCATION** to select it, click the **Swatches panel**, then click **Paper**.

The Fill color of the text changes to white.

5. Click the **Selection tool**, then select the **two yellow frames** on the page.

6. Click the **green swatch** on the Swatches panel.

The fill changes to green.

7. Select the **black horizontal line**, then click the **Stroke button** at the top of the Swatches panel so that it is in front of the Fill button, as shown in Figure 48.

(continued)

8. Click the **red swatch**, then compare your layout to Figure 49.

9. Double-click **B-Master**.

All of the changes you made to A-Master, except one, are reflected on B-Master because B-Master was created based on A-Master. Note though that the headline on B-Master is still black. Type tends to behave unpredictably on master pages. The fact that this frame has been relocated from its original position when it was created as a duplicate of A-Master might explain why it didn't update.

10. Double-click **C-Master** to view the spread.

None of the changes from A-Master affect C-Master.

11. View spread 8-9.

All of the changes you made on the master page, including the white headline, are reflected on the spread. No items on this page have been touched since the page was created.

12. View spread 2-3.

All of the changes you made on the master page, except the white headline, are reflected on the spread.

You modified document pages by editing text within text frames created from master items.

Figure 49 *A-Master modifications*

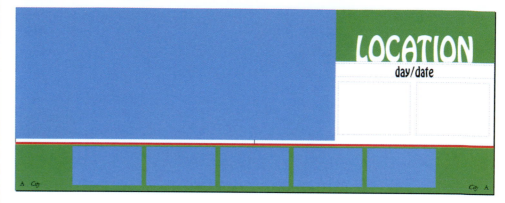

Figure 50 *Change reflected on spread 4-5*

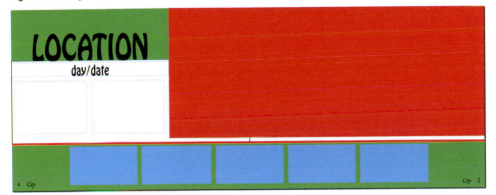

1. View spread 10-11, then select the **large blue frame**.

2. Click the **Pages panel options button**, point to **Master Pages**, then click **Detach Selection from Master**.

3. Double-click **B-Master**, then change the fill color on the large blue frame to **red**.

4. Double-click **page 4** on the Pages panel, then scroll through the document to note the changes.

   The change is reflected on spread 4-5, but not on spread 10-11.

5. Navigate to page 3 in the document, then select the **text frame of MANAROLA**.

6. Click the **Pages panel options button**, point to **Master Pages**, then click **Remove Selected Local Overrides**.

   The modified headline changes to reflect that which is on the A-Master, as shown in Figure 50.

7. Save your work, then close Setup.indd.

You detached a frame from its master. You then modified the master, noting that the change did not affect the detached frame. You selected a modified master item on a document page, then used the Remove Selected Local Overrides command to restore the item's relationship to its master.

Place
AND THREAD TEXT

What You'll Do

MANAROLA

tuesday august 9

Lorem ipsum dolor sit amet, consect etuer adipiscing elit, sed diam no nummy nibh euismod tincidunt ut laoreet dolore magna aliquam volutpat. Ut wisi enim ad veniam, quis nostrud exerci ullamcorper suscipit lobortis aliquip ex ea commodo conseq Duis autem vel eum iriure dolor hendrerit in vulputate velit esse molestie consequat, vel illum dolore

© 2015 Cengage Learning®

 In this lesson, you will place text, thread text from frame to frame, then view text threads.

Placing Text

Once you have created a text frame—either on a master page or on a document page—you can type directly into the frame, or you can place text from another document into it. When creating headlines, you usually type them directly into the text frame. When creating body copy, however, you will often find yourself placing text from another document, usually a word processing document.

Placing text in InDesign is simple and straightforward. Click the Place command on the File menu, which opens the Place dialog box. Find the text document that you want to place, then click Open.

The pointer changes to the loaded text icon. With a loaded text icon, you can drag to create a text frame or click inside an existing text frame. Position the loaded text icon over an existing text frame, and the icon appears in parentheses, as shown in Figure 51. The parentheses indicate that you can click to place the text into the text frame. Do so, and the text flows into the text frame, as shown in Figure 52.

Threading Text

InDesign provides many options for **threading text**—linking text from one text frame to another. Text frames have an **in port** and an **out port**. When threading text, you use the text frame ports to establish connections between the text frames.

In Figure 53, the center text frame is selected, and the in port and out port are identified.

Figure 51 *Loaded text icon positioned over a text frame*

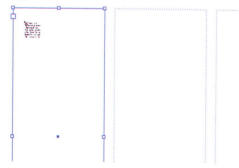

© 2015 Cengage Learning®

The in port represents where text would flow into the text frame, and the out port represents from where text would flow out.

In the same figure, note that the out port on the first text frame is red and has a plus sign in its center. This indicates the presence of **overset text**—more text than can fit in the frame.

To thread text manually from the first to the second text frame, first click the Selection tool, then click the frame with the overset text so that the frame is highlighted. Next, click the out port of the text frame. When you position your cursor over the next text frame, the cursor changes to the link icon, as shown in Figure 54. Click the link icon and the text flows into the frame, as shown in Figure 55. When the Show Text Threads command on the View menu is activated, a blue arrow appears between any two text frames that have been threaded, as shown in Figure 56.

Figure 52 *Text placed into a text frame*

Text placed in text frame

Figure 53 *Identifying in ports and out ports*

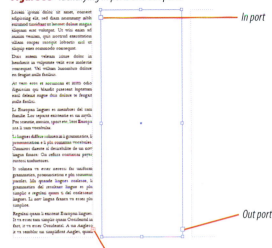

In port

Out port

Red out port of first text frame
indicates overset text

Figure 55 *Threading text between frames*

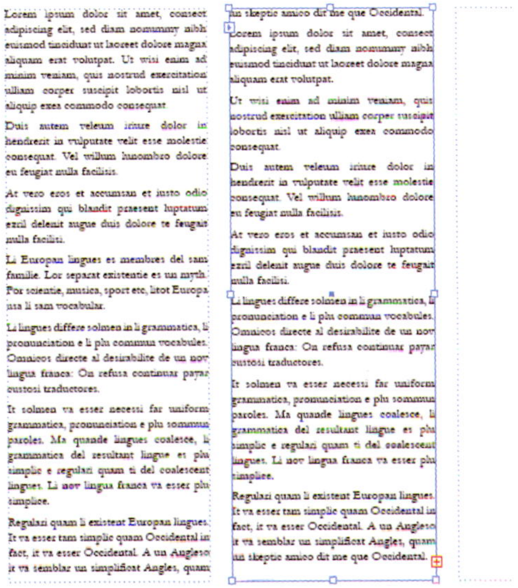

Figure 54 *Link icon*

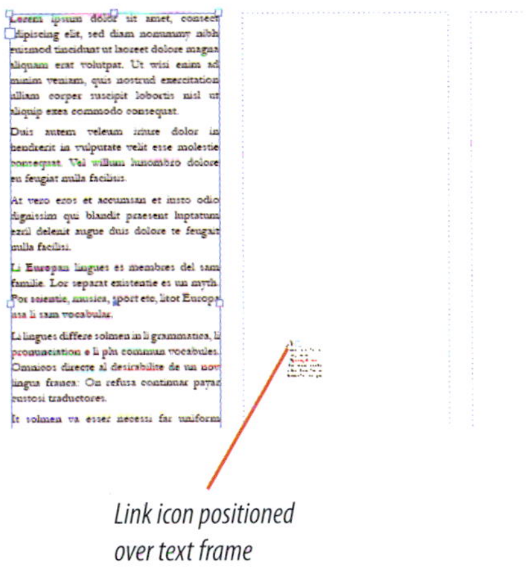

Link icon positioned
over text frame

Figure 56 *Showing text threads*

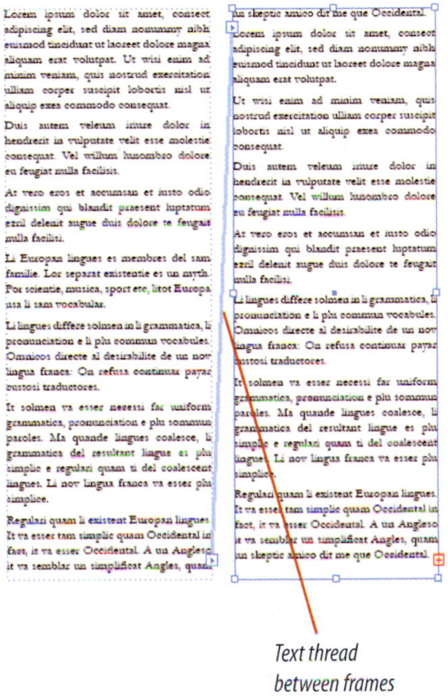

Text thread
between frames

Place text on document pages

1. Open ID 3-2.indd, then save it as **Wraps and Sections**.

   This data file has the same parameters as the document you created at the start of this chapter. The only changes are that the local document pages have been colorized and the headlines and dates have been filled in. Also, small blue frames are positioned over the text frames on each spread.

2. Click the **workspace switcher**, then click **Typography**.

3. Double-click the **page 3 icon** on the Pages panel to go to page 3.

4. Click **File** on the Menu bar, click **Place**, navigate to the drive and folder where your Data Files are stored, then double-click **Greek text**.

5. Point to the interior of the left text frame.

   As shown in Figure 57, the loaded text icon appears in parentheses, signalling that you can insert the loaded text into the text frame.

6. Click the loaded text icon in the left text frame.

   As shown in Figure 58, text flows into the frame. The red out port with the plus sign indicates that there is overset text—more text than can fit in the text frame.

   (continued)

Figure 57 *Loaded text icon*

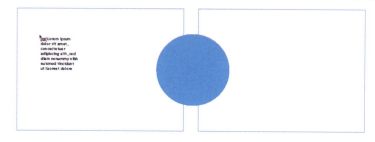

Figure 58 *Text placed into a frame*

Setting Up a Document

Figure 59 *Loaded text icon with a link icon*

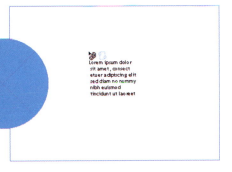

MANAROLA

tuesday august 9

Lorem ipsum dolor sit amet, consect
etuer adipiscing elit, sed diam no
nummy nibh euismod tincidunt ut
laoreet dolore magna aliquam
volutpat. Ut wisi enim ad
veniam, quis nostrud exerci
ullamcorper suscipit lobortis
aliquip ex ea commodo conse
Duis autem vel eum iriure dolor
hendrerit in vulputate velit esse
molestie consequat, vel illum dolore

Lorem ipsum dolor
sit amet, consect
etuer adipiscing elit
sed diam no nummy
nibh euismod
tincidunt ut laoreet

Using Smart Text Reflow

Smart Text Reflow is a feature that adds pages automatically when needed to accommodate text overflow. Let's say you create a single page document with a single text frame and you begin typing. If you type so much that you get to the end of the available space in the text frame, Smart Text Reflow will automatically add a new page with a new frame so that you can continue typing. This also works in reverse: If you delete the overflow text, the new page will be deleted. To work with Smart Text Reflow, open the Type Preferences dialog box, then verify that the Smart Text Reflow check box is checked. This preference works especially well with Primary Text Frames. When you create a new document, the New document dialog box offers you the option to create a primary text frame, which is essentially a text frame that appears automatically when you create a page—as though you had a text frame on a master page. In Smart Text Reflow, click Limit to Primary Text Frames and the reflow will occur only when you max out a primary text frame.

7. Click the **Type tool** [T], click **any word** five times to select all the text in the frame, set the typeface to **Garamond**, set the type size to **8 pt**, set the leading to **9 pt**, then set the alignment to **Justify with last line aligned left**.

TIP Clicking five times selects even the text that is not currently visible in the frame. If you only select the text that is visible, only that text will be affected by your format change.

8. Click the **Selection tool** [arrow], click the **red out port**, then position the loaded text icon over the right text frame.

As shown in Figure 59, a link icon appears in the loaded text icon, indicating you are about to flow text from one frame to another. The red out port turns blue when you click it.

TIP To unlink text frames, double-click the blue out port.

(continued)

9. Click in the right text frame.

   As shown in Figure 60, the text flows into the right text frame, and a new red out port appears at the bottom-right of the right frame.

   You used the Place command to load text into a text frame, then threaded text from that frame into another.

Thread text through multiple text frames

1. Click **View** on the Menu bar, point to **Extras**, then click **Show Text Threads** if necessary.

   With the Show Text Threads command activated, blue arrows appear between threaded text frames when they are selected.

2. Reduce the view of the document to 75% so that you can see more than one spread in your monitor window.

3. Click the **Selection tool**, then click the **out port** of the right text frame.

   The loaded text icon appears.

4. Scroll so that you can see both pages 3 & 4 in the monitor window.

   (continued)

Figure 60 *Text flowed from one frame to another*

Mapping Style Names when Importing Word or RTF Files

When you place a Word document or RTF text in InDesign you have a number of options to choose from regarding how text is imported. After you click Place on the File menu and find the Word or RTF document that you want to place, click the Show Import Options check box, then click Open. The Import Options dialog box opens. In this dialog box you can choose to include or not include footnotes, endnotes, table of contents text, and index text. You can also choose to remove any previous styles applied to text, and any table formatting. Conversely you can opt to retain styles and table formatting applied to incoming text. You can import styles automatically by clicking the Import Styles Automatically option button and then tell InDesign how to deal with conflicts when incoming styles have the same names as existing styles in InDesign. Finally, you can map style names from the placed text file to specific styles in InDesign by clicking the Customize Style Import option button, then clicking the Style Mapping button. The Style Mapping dialog box opens and allows you to choose which InDesign style to map to each incoming text style. For example, you can specify that the Normal style in Word is mapped to the [Basic Paragraph] style in InDesign.

Figure 61 *Text threads showing text flowing from one spread to another*

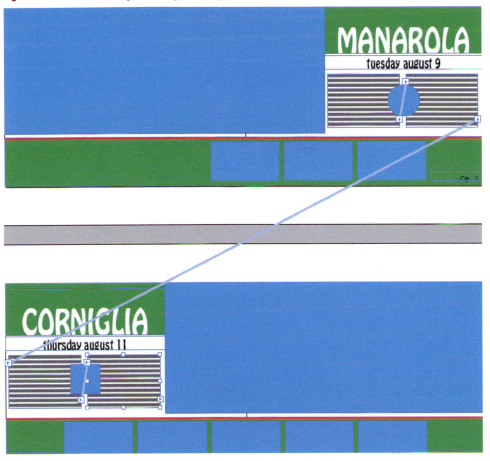

5. Press and hold **[Alt]** (Win) or **[option]** (Mac), position the loaded text icon over the left text frame on page 4, click, and do not release the **[Alt]/[option] key**.

 With the [Alt]/[option] key pressed, the loaded text icon remains active. To continue threading, you don't need to click the out port of the left text frame.

6. Position the pointer over the right text frame, then click.

 As shown in Figure 61, the text is threaded through both frames on page 4.

7. Using the same process, thread text through the remaining pages of the document. When you're done threading, you will still have loaded text.

8. Save your work.

You used a keyboard command to thread text more quickly and easily between multiple text frames.

Create New Sections
AND WRAP TEXT

What You'll Do

 In this lesson, you will create two different numbering sections and create two text wraps around graphics frames.

Creating Sections in a Document

Sections are pages in a document where page numbering changes. For example, sometimes in the front pages of a book, in the introduction or the preface, the pages will be numbered with lowercase Roman numerals, then normal page numbering will begin with the first chapter.

You can create as many sections in a document as you wish. You determine the page on which the new section will start by clicking that page icon on the Pages panel. Choose the Numbering & Section Options command on the Pages panel menu, which opens the New Section dialog box, shown in Figure 62.

QUICK **TIP**

The first time you choose a type of page numbering for a document, the Numbering & Section Options dialog box opens instead of the New Section dialog box.

Figure 62 *New Section dialog box*

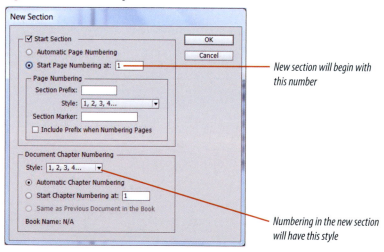

New section will begin with this number

Numbering in the new section will have this style

Wrapping Text Around a Frame

When you position a text frame or a graphics frame near another frame that contains text, you can apply a text wrap to the overlapping frame in order to force the underlying text to wrap around it. InDesign offers many options for wrapping text around a frame. One quick method is to click the Wrap around bounding box button on the Text Wrap panel, shown in Figure 63.

Figure 64 shows a rectangular frame using the No text wrap option on the Text Wrap panel. Figure 65 shows that same frame using the Wrap around bounding box option on the Text Wrap panel.

QUICK TIP

To turn off text wrap in a text frame, select the text frame, click Object on the Menu bar, click Text Frame Options, click the Ignore Text Wrap check box, and then click OK.

When you choose the Wrap around bounding box option, you can control the **offset**—the distance that text is repelled from the frame—by entering values in the Top, Bottom, Left, and Right Offset text boxes on the panel. Figure 66 shows the frame with a .125-inch offset applied to all four sides of the frame.

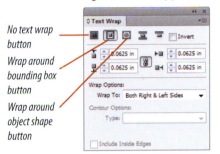

No text wrap button

Wrap around bounding box button

Wrap around object shape button

Figure 63 *Text Wrap panel*

No text wrap button

Selected text frame

Figure 64 *A frame using the No text wrap option*

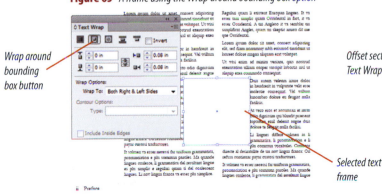

Wrap around bounding box button

Selected text frame

Figure 65 *A frame using the Wrap around bounding box option*

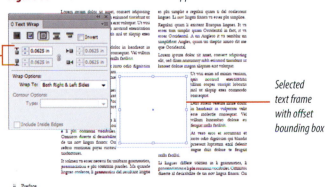

Offset section of Text Wrap panel

Selected text frame with offset bounding box

Figure 66 *A frame with a .125-inch offset applied to all sides*

Create sections in a document

1. Double-click the **page 8 icon** on the Pages panel.

   The document has been designed so that page 8 represents a new section in the document. The color theme changes to red and blue, and the city is Firenze.

2. Click the **Pages panel options button** 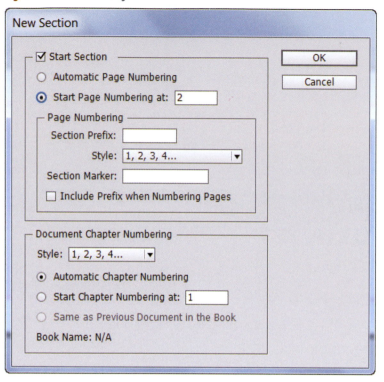, then click **Numbering and Section Options**.

   The New Section dialog box opens.

3. Verify that the Start Section check box is checked.

4. Click the **Start Page Numbering at option button**, then type **2**.

   Your dialog box should resemble Figure 67. With these choices, you are starting a new section at page 8, renumbered as page 2.

   (continued)

Figure 67 *New Section dialog box*

Figure 68 *Viewing renumbered pages on the Pages panel*

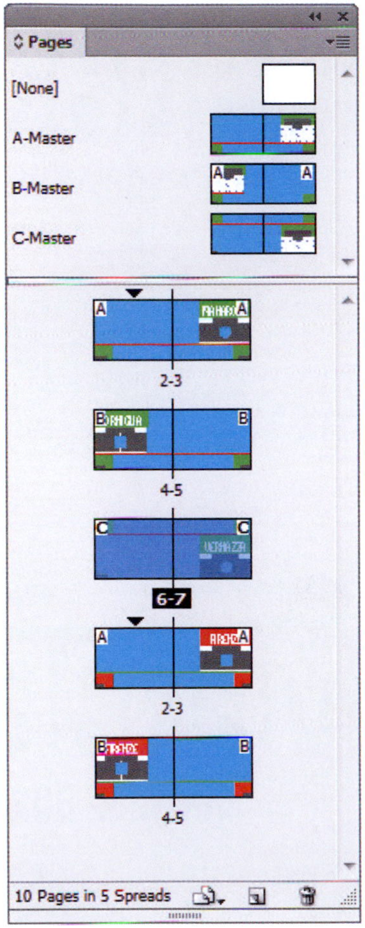

5. Click **OK**, then compare your Pages panel to Figure 68.

TIP If you get a warning that a page number in this section already exists in another section, click OK.

The pages are renumbered. Spread 8-9 is now spread 2-3.

6. Note that the automatic page numbering has updated to reflect the new numbering in the new section.

7. Save the file.

You used the New Section dialog box to change the sequence of the automatic page numbering in the document.

Wrap text around a frame

1. Double-click the **original page 3 icon** on the Pages panel, click the **Selection tool** 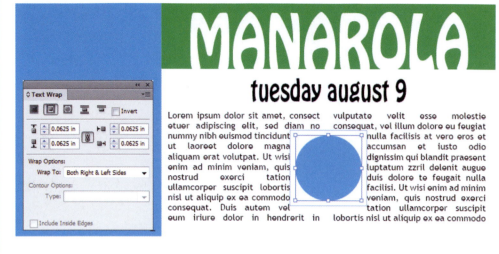, then select the **small blue ellipse frame**.

2. Show the Text Wrap panel.

3. Click the **Wrap around bounding box button** at the top of the panel.

   The text wraps around the rectangular bounding box, as shown in Figure 69.

4. Click the **Wrap around object shape button** , then type **.125** in the Top Offset text box on the Text Wrap panel.

   The text wraps around the ellipse, as shown in Figure 70.

5. Navigate to page 4, select the **small blue rectangular frame**, then click the **Wrap around bounding box button** on the Text Wrap panel.

6. Click the **Make all settings the same button** to deactivate it if necessary.

   The deactivated Make all settings the same button looks like this: .

   (continued)

Figure 69 *Text wrapped around the ellipse's bounding box*

Figure 70 *Text wrapped around the object shape*

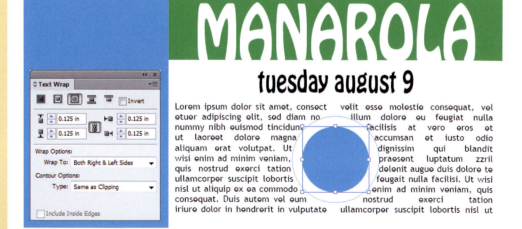

© 2015 Cengage Learning®

Setting Up a Document

Figure 71 *Text wrapped at different offset values*

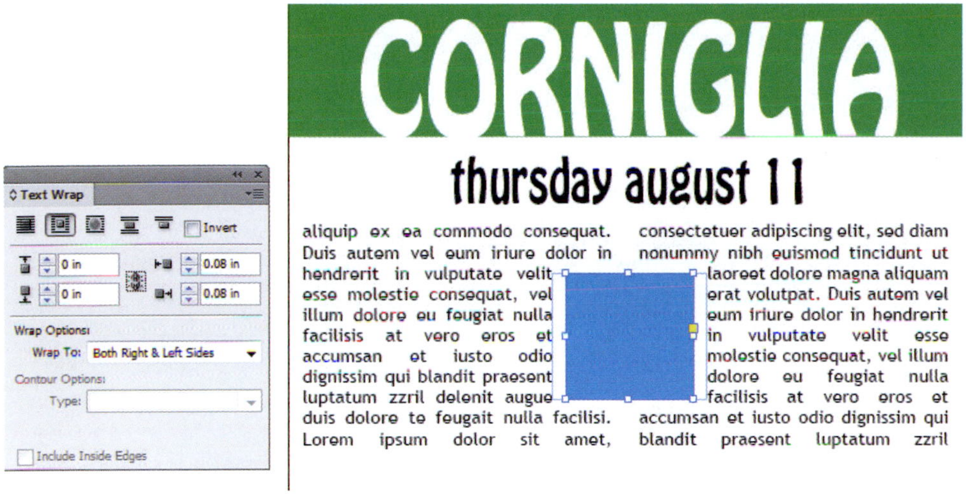

Text Wrap
Invert
0 in
0 in
0.08 in
0.08 in
Wrap Options:
Wrap To:
Both Right & Left Sides
Contour Options:
Type:
Include Inside Edges
CORNIGLIA
thursday august 11
aliquip ex ea commodo consequat. Duis autem vel eum iriure dolor in hendrerit in vulputate velit esse molestie consequat, vel illum dolore eu feugiat nulla facilisis at vero eros et accumsan et iusto odio dignissim qui blandit praesent luptatum zzril delenit augue duis dolore te feugait nulla facilisi. Lorem ipsum dolor sit amet,
consectetuer adipiscing elit, sed diam nonummy nibh euismod tincidunt ut laoreet dolore magna aliquam erat volutpat. Duis autem vel eum iriure dolor in hendrerit in vulputate velit esse molestie consequat, vel illum dolore eu feugiat nulla facilisis at vero eros et accumsan et iusto odio dignissim qui blandit praesent luptatum zzril

7. Set the Top Offset text box and the Bottom Offset text box to **0**.
8. Set the Left Offset text box and the Right Offset text box to **.08**.
9. Compare your result to Figure 71.
10. Save your work, then close Wraps and Sections.

You used the Text Wrap panel to flow text around two graphics frames.

Create a new document and set up a master page.

1. Start Adobe InDesign.
2. Without creating a new document, click Edit (Win) or InDesign (Mac) on the Menu bar, point to Preferences, then click Guides & Pasteboard.
3. In the Guide Options section, click the Guides in Back check box to select, if necessary, click Units & Increments in the Preferences list on the left side of the dialog box, verify that the Horizontal and Vertical ruler units are set to inches, then click OK.
4. Click File on the Menu bar, point to New, then click Document.
5. Type **8** in the Number of Pages text box, press [Tab], then verify that the Facing Pages check box is checked.
6. Type **5** in the Width text box, press [Tab], then type **5** in the Height text box.
7. Using [Tab] to move from one text box to another, type **1** in the Number text box in the Columns section.
8. Type **.25** in the Top, Bottom, Inside, and Outside Margins text boxes.
9. Click OK, then save the document as **Skills Review**.
10. Click the workspace switcher on the Menu bar, then click Advanced, if necessary.
11. Double-click the words A-Master on the Pages panel to center both pages of the master in your window.
12. Click Window on the Menu bar, point to Object & Layout, then click Transform.
13. Click the Selection tool, press and hold [Ctrl] (Win) or ⌘ (Mac), create a guide across the spread using the horizontal ruler, releasing the mouse pointer when the Y Location text box on the Transform panel reads 2.5 in.
14. Create a guide on the left page using the vertical ruler, releasing the mouse pointer when the X Location text box on the Transform panel reads 2.5 in.
15. Click Edit (Win) or InDesign (Mac) on the Menu bar, point to Preferences, click Units & Increments, click the Origin list arrow, click Page, then click OK.
16. Create a vertical guide on the right page, releasing the mouse pointer when the X Location text box on the Transform panel reads 2.5 in.
17. Verify that the Fill and Stroke buttons on the Tools panel are set to None, click the Rectangle Frame tool, then draw a rectangle anywhere on the left page.
18. Click the top-left reference point on the Transform panel.
19. With the rectangle frame selected, type **0** in the X Location text box on the Transform panel, type **0** in the Y Location text box, type **5** in the Width text box, type **5** in the Height text box, then press [Enter] (Win) or [return] (Mac).
20. Using the same method, create an identical rectangle on the right page.
21. If necessary, type **0** in the X Location text box on the Transform panel, type **0** in the Y Location text box, then press [Enter] (Win) or [return] (Mac).
22. Click the Pages panel options button, then click New Master.
23. Type **Body** in the Name text box, click the Based on Master list arrow, click A-Master, then click OK.
24. Click the Selection tool, press and hold [Shift][Ctrl] (Win) or [Shift] ⌘ (Mac), select both rectangle frames, then delete them.
25. Double-click B-Body on the Pages panel to center both pages of the master in your window.
26. Click Layout on the Menu bar, then click Margins and Columns.
27. Type **2** in the Number text box in the Columns section, then click OK.

Create text on master pages.

1. Click the Type tool, create a text frame of any size anywhere in the right column on the left page, then click the Selection tool.
2. Verify that the top-left reference point is selected on the Transform panel, type **2.6** in the X Location text box, type **.25** in the Y Location text box, type **2.15** in the Width text box, type **4.5** in the Height text box, then press [Enter] (Win) or [return] (Mac).

3. Click Edit on the Menu bar, click Copy, click Edit on the Menu bar again, then click Paste in Place.

4. Press and hold [Shift], then drag the copy of the text frame onto the right page, releasing the mouse button when it "snaps" into the left column on the right page.

5. Click the Type tool, then draw a small text box anywhere on the left page of the B-Body master.

6. Select the text frame, and verify that the top-left reference point is selected on the Transform panel, type **.25** in the X Location text box, type **4.5** in the Y Location text box, type **1.65** in the Width text box, type **.25** in the Height text box, then press [Enter] (Win) or [return] (Mac).

7. Select the Type tool, click in the text frame, click Type on the Menu bar, point to Insert Special Character, point to Markers, then click Current Page Number.

8. Click Type on the Menu bar, point to Insert Special Character, point to Hyphens and Dashes, then click En Dash.

9. Type the word **Title**.

10. Click the Selection tool, select the text frame if necessary, click Edit on the Menu bar, click Copy, click Edit on the Menu bar again, then click Paste in Place.

11. Press and hold [Shift], then drag the copy of the text frame so that it is positioned in the lower-right corner of the right page of the master page.

12. Open the Paragraph panel, click the Align right button, then delete the B and the dash after the B.

TIP Switch your workspace to Typography to access the Paragraph panel if necessary.

13. Click after the word Title, click Type on the Menu bar, point to Insert Special Character, point to Hyphens and Dashes, then click En Dash.

14. Click Type on the Menu bar, point to Insert Special Character, point to Markers, then click Current Page Number.

Apply master pages to document pages.

1. Double-click the page 2 icon on the Pages panel.

2. Drag the B-Body master page title to the bottom-left corner of the page 2 icon until you see a black rectangle around the page 2 and 3 icons, then release the mouse button.

3. Drag the word B-Body from the top of the Pages panel to the bottom-left corner of the page 4 icon until you see a black rectangle around the page 4 icon, then release the mouse button.

4. Click the Pages panel options button, then click Apply Master to Pages.

5. Click the Apply Master list arrow, click B-Body if necessary, type **6-8** in the To Pages text box, then click OK.

6. Double-click the page 2 icon on the Pages panel.

7. Hide guides.

Place and thread text.

1. Click File on the Menu bar, click Place, navigate to the drive and folder where your Data Files are stored, then double-click Skills Review Text.

2. Click anywhere in the text frame in the right column on page 2.

3. Click View on the Menu bar, point to Extras, then click Show Text Threads.

4. Click the Selection tool, then click the out port of the text frame on page 2.

5. Click the loaded text icon anywhere in the text frame on page 3.

Modify master pages and document pages.

1. Double-click the page 6 icon on the Pages panel.

2. Click the bottom-middle reference point on the Transform panel.

3. Click the Selection tool, press and hold [Shift] [Ctrl] (Win) or [Shift] ⌘ (Mac), then click the large text frame.

4. Type **.3** in the Height text box on the Transform panel, then press [Enter] (Win) or [return] (Mac).

5. Double-click A-Master in the top of the Pages panel, then select the graphics placeholder frame on the left page.

6. Click the center reference point on the Transform panel.

7. On the Transform panel, type **3** in the Width text box, type **3** in the Height text box, then press [Enter] (Win) or [return] (Mac).

8. Double-click the right page icon of the A-Master on the Pages panel, then select the graphics placeholder frame on the right page.

9. On the Transform panel, type **2** in the Width text box, type **4** in the Height text box, then press [Enter] (Win) or [return] (Mac).

10. View the two right-hand pages on the Pages panel that are based on the A-Master right-hand page to verify that the modifications were updated.

11. Double-click B-Body on the Pages panel, click the Rectangle Frame tool, then create a frame anywhere on the left page of the B-Body master page.

12. Click the center reference point on the Transform panel, then type **2** in the X Location text box, type **2.6** in the Y Location text box, type **2.25** in the Width text box, type **1.5** in the Height text box, then press [Enter] (Win) or [return] (Mac).

Create new sections and wrap text.

1. Double-click the page 1 icon on the Pages panel, click the Pages panel options button, then click Numbering & Section Options.

2. In the Page Numbering section, click the Style list arrow, click the lower-case style letters (a, b, c, d), click OK, then note the changes to the pages on the Pages panel and in the document.

3. Double-click the page e icon on the Pages panel, click the Pages panel options button, then click Numbering & Section Options.

4. In the Page Numbering section, click the Start Page Numbering at option button, type **5** in the text box, then verify that the Style text box in the Page Numbering section shows ordinary numerals (1, 2, 3, 4). (If it does not, click the Style list arrow and select that style.)

5. Click OK, then view the pages in the document, noting the new style of the page numbering on the pages and on the Pages panel.

6. Double-click the page b icon on the Pages panel, click the Selection tool, press and hold [Shift] [Ctrl] (Win) or [Shift] ⌘ (Mac), then select the rectangular graphics frame.

7. Click Window on the Menu bar, then click Text Wrap.

8. Click the Wrap around bounding box button on the Text Wrap panel.

9. Type **.125** in the Right Offset text box on the Text Wrap panel, then press [Enter] (Win) or [return] (Mac).

10. Click View on the Menu bar, click Fit Spread in Window, then click anywhere to deselect any selected items.

11. Compare your screen to Figure 72, save your work, then close Skills Review.

Figure 72 *Completed Skills Review*

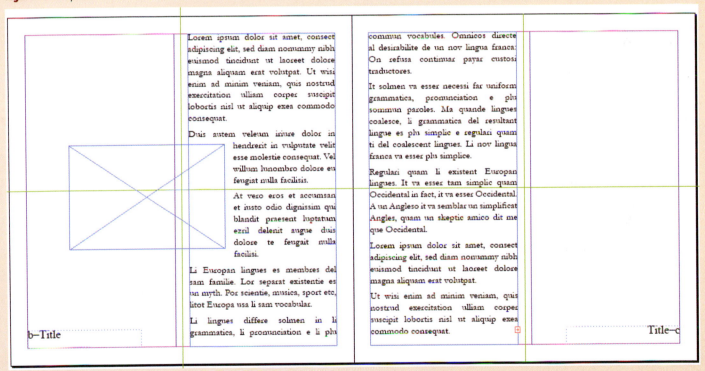

You are a graphic designer working out of your home office. A local investment company has contracted you to design their monthly 16-page newsletter. You've sketched out a design and created a new document at the correct size, and now you need to add automatic page numbering to the document.

1. Open ID 3-3.indd, then save it as **Newsletter**.
2. Double-click A-Master on the Pages panel.
3. Click the Type tool, then draw a text frame about one inch tall and one column wide.
4. Position the text frame at the bottom of the center column, being sure that the bottom edge of the text frame snaps to the bottom margin of the page.
5. Set the Preference settings so that the guides are sent to the back of the layout—so that all four sides of the text frame are visible.
6. Click the Type tool, then click inside the text box.
7. Click Type on the Menu bar, point to Insert Special Character, point to Hyphens and Dashes, then click Em Dash.
8. Click Type on the Menu bar, point to Insert Special Character, point to Markers, then click Current Page Number.
9. Click Type on the Menu bar, point to Insert Special Character, point to Hyphens and Dashes, then click Em Dash.
10. Select all three text elements and change their font size to 20 pt.
11. Click the Align center button on the Paragraph panel.
12. Click the dark blue swatch on the Swatches panel.

13. Click the Selection tool, click the bottom-center reference point on the Transform panel, double-click the Height text box on the Transform panel, type **.25**, then press [Enter] (Win) or [return] (Mac).

14. Double-click the page 5 icon on the Pages panel, compare your page 5 to Figure 73, save your work, then close Newsletter.

Figure 73 *Completed Project Builder 1*

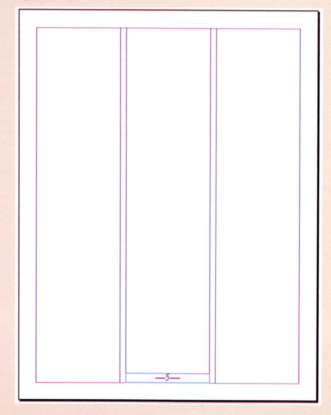

You work in the design department for a bank, and you are responsible for creating a new weekly bulletin, which covers various events within the bank's network of branches. You have just finished creating three master pages for the bulletin, and now you are ready to apply the masters to the document pages.

1. Open ID 3-4.indd, then save it as **Bulletin Layout**.
2. Apply the B-Master to pages 2 and 3.
3. Click the Pages panel options button, then click Apply Master to Pages.
4. Apply the C-Master to pages 4 through 6, then click OK.
5. Place Bulletin text.doc in the text frame on page 1.
6. Select the text frame, click the out port on the text frame, double-click page 2 on the Pages panel, then click anywhere in the text frame on page 2.
7. Thread the remaining text through each page up to and including page 6 in the document.
8. Click the Preview button, deselect any selected items, then compare your page 6 to Figure 74.
9. Save your work, then close Bulletin Layout.

Figure 74 *Completed Project Builder 2*

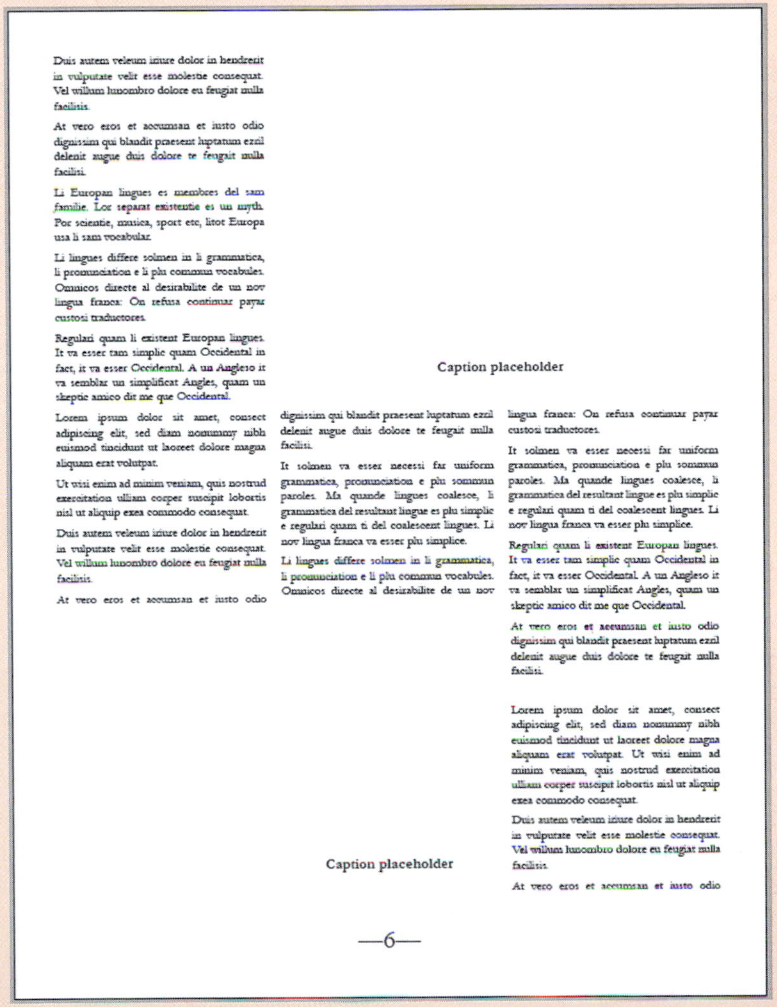
Duis autem veleum iriure dolor in hendrerit in vulputate velit esse molestie consequat. Vel willum lunombro dolore eu feugiat nulla facilisis.

At vero eros et accumsan et iusto odio dignissim qui blandit praesent luptatum ezril delenit augue duis dolore te feugait nulla facilisi.

Li Europan lingues es membres del sam familie. Lor separat existentie es un myth. Por scientie, musica, sport etc, litot Europa usa li sam vocabular.

Li lingues differe solmen in li grammatica, li pronunciation e li plu commun vocabules. Omnicos directe al desirabilite de un nov lingua franca: On refusa continuar payar custosi traductores.

Regulari quam li existent Europan lingues. It va esser tam simplic quam Occidental in fact, it va esser Occidental. A un Angleso it va semblar un simplificat Angles, quam un skeptic amico dit me que Occidental.

Caption placeholder

Lorem ipsum dolor sit amet, consect adipiscing elit, sed diam nonummy nibh euismod tincidunt ut laoreet dolore magna aliquam erat volutpat.

Ut wisi enim ad minim veniam, quis nostrud exercitation ulliam corper suscipit lobortis nisl ut aliquip exea commodo consequat.

Duis autem veleum iriure dolor in hendrerit in vulputate velit esse molestie consequat. Vel willum lunombro dolore eu feugiat nulla facilisis.

At vero eros et accumsan et iusto odio dignissim qui blandit praesent luptatum ezril delenit augue duis dolore te feugait nulla facilisi.

It solmen va esser necessi far uniform grammatica, pronunciation e plu sommun paroles. Ma quande lingues coalesce, li grammatica del resultant lingue es plu simplic e regulari quam ti del coalescent lingues. Li nov lingua franca va esser plu simplice.

Li lingues differe solmen in li grammatica, li pronunciation e li plu commun vocabules. Omnicos directe al desirabilite de un nov lingua franca: On refusa continuar payar custosi traductores.

It solmen va esser necessi far uniform grammatica, pronunciation e plu sommun paroles. Ma quande lingues coalesce, li grammatica del resultant lingue es plu simplic e regulari quam ti del coalescent lingues. Li nov lingua franca va esser plu simplice.

Regulari quam li existent Europan lingues. It va esser tam simplic quam Occidental in fact, it va esser Occidental. A un Angleso it va semblar un simplificat Angles, quam un skeptic amico dit me que Occidental.

At vero eros et accumsan et iusto odio dignissim qui blandit praesent luptatum ezril delenit augue duis dolore te feugait nulla facilisi.

Lorem ipsum dolor sit amet, consect adipiscing elit, sed diam nonummy nibh euismod tincidunt ut laoreet dolore magna aliquam erat volutpat. Ut wisi enim ad minim veniam, quis nostrud exercitation ulliam corper suscipit lobortis nisl ut aliquip exea commodo consequat.

Duis autem veleum iriure dolor in hendrerit in vulputate velit esse molestie consequat. Vel willum lunombro dolore eu feugiat nulla facilisis.

At vero eros et accumsan et iusto odio

Caption placeholder

—6—

Your client has provided you with a page layout that she wants you to use for the background of a design project. Knowing that she'll want you to use this background design for multiple pages, you decide to tweak her document to be sure that the background elements are the same size and aligned evenly.

1. Open ID 3-5.indd, then save it as **Four Square**.
2. Click File on the Menu bar, click Document Setup, note the width and height of the page, then close the Document Setup dialog box.
3. Hide the guides and the frame edges if necessary, then verify that only the Transform panel and the Tools panel are visible.
4. Click the Selection tool, then click the top-left reference point on the Transform panel.
5. Click the top-left square on the page, type **0** in the X Location text box, type **0** in the Y Location text box, type **7.75** in the Width text box, then press [Enter] (Win) or [return] (Mac).
6. Click to place the insertion point after the number 7.75 in the Width text box, type **/2**, then press [Tab].
7. Type **3.875** in the Height text box, then press [Enter] (Win) or [return] (Mac).
8. Click the top-right square, type **3.875** in the X Location text box, type **0** in the Y Location text box, type **3.875** in the Width and Height text boxes, then press [Enter] (Win) or [return] (Mac).
9. Click the lower-left square, type **0** in the X Location text box, type **3.875** in the Y Location text box, type **3.875** in the Width and Height text boxes, then press [Enter] (Win) or [return] (Mac).
10. Click the lower-right square, type **3.875** in the X Location text box, type **3.875** in the Y Location text box, type **3.875** in the Width and Height text boxes, press [Enter] (Win) or [return] (Mac), then deselect all.
11. Compare your screen to Figure 75, save your work, then close Four Square.

Figure 75 *Completed Design Project*

© 2015 Cengage Learning®

In this Portfolio Project, you're going to work on a fun puzzle that will test your problem-solving skills when using X and Y locations. You will open an InDesign document with two pages. On the first page are four 1-inch squares at each corner of the page. On the second page, the four 1-inch squares appear again—this time forming a large red square that is positioned at the exact center of the 7.75-inch × 7.75-inch document page. Just looking at the second page, your challenge will be to write down the X and Y coordinates of each of the four boxes at the center of the page. Then, you will test out your answers with the boxes on the first page.

Setup.

1. Open ID 3-6.indd, then save it as **Center Squares**.
2. On page 1, verify that each red square is 1" × 1", then deselect all.
3. Go to page 2, then press [Tab] to hide all panels.
4. Do not select any of the squares at the center.
5. Write down what you think is the X/Y coordinate of the top-left point of the top-left square.
6. Write down what you think is the X/Y coordinate of the top-right point of the top-right square.
7. Write down what you think is the X/Y coordinate of the bottom-right point of the bottom-right square.

8. Write down what you think is the X/Y coordinate of the center point of the bottom-left square.
9. Press [Tab] to show all hidden panels.
10. Go to page 1, select the top-left square, then click the top-left reference point on the Transform panel.
11. Enter the X/Y coordinates that you wrote down for this point, then press [Enter] (Win) or [return] (Mac).

12. Using the same method, test out the X/Y coordinates you wrote down for the other three boxes. (*Hint*: Be sure to click the appropriate reference point on the Transform panel for each of the three remaining boxes.)
13. When you are done, does your page 1 match page 2 exactly as shown in Figure 76?

Figure 76 *Completed Portfolio Project*

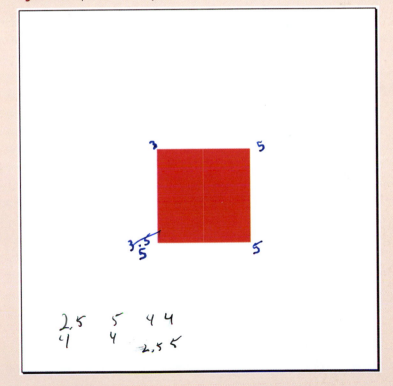

CHAPTER **4** WORKING WITH
FRAMES

1. Align and distribute objects on a page
2. Stack and layer objects
3. Work with graphics frames
4. Work with text frames

CHAPTER 4 WORKING WITH FRAMES

Introduction

When you position objects on a page, they are positioned in text frames or graphics frames. Chapter 4 focuses on frames and various techniques for working with them.

The first lesson gives you the chance to pause and explore basic options for aligning and distributing frames on the page, including Live Distribute and the Gap tool.

In the second lesson, you'll learn how to manipulate the stacking order of frames, and you'll get a thorough tour of the Layers panel. After going through these lessons, you'll feel confident in your ability to position frames precisely on a page and get them to overlap the way you want.

The third lesson is an immersion into the world of placing graphics in graphics frames. Put on your thinking caps. There's a lot going on here—all of it interesting. You'll learn the specifics of placing graphics and the all-important difference between the graphics frame and the graphic itself. Finally, you'll finish by working with text frames and exploring the power of autoflowing text in a document. Watch InDesign create dozens of text frames with a click of a button!

Gap Tool

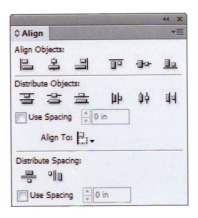

Align and Distribute
OBJECTS ON A PAGE

What You'll Do

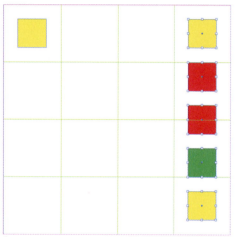

© 2015 Cengage Learning®

 In this lesson, you will explore various techniques for positioning objects in specific relationships to one another.

Applying Fills and Strokes

A **fill** is a color you apply to the inside of an object. A **stroke** is a color that you apply to the outline of an object. Figure 1 shows an object with a blue fill and a yellow stroke.

InDesign offers you a number of options for filling and stroking objects. The simplest and most direct method for doing so is to select an object and then pick a color from the Swatches panel, shown in Figure 2. The color that you choose on the Swatches panel will be applied to the selected object as a fill or as a stroke, depending on whether the Fill or the Stroke button is activated on the Tools panel.

To activate either the Fill or the Stroke button, simply click it once on the Tools panel. The Fill button is activated when it is in front of the Stroke button, as shown in Figure 3. When the Fill button is activated, clicking

Figure 1 *An object with a fill and a stroke*

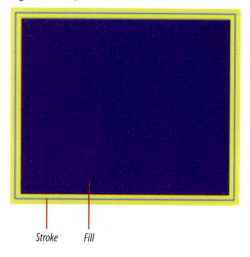

Stroke   Fill

© 2015 Cengage Learning®

a swatch on the Swatches panel applies that swatch color as a fill to the selected object(s). When the Stroke button is activated, as shown in Figure 4, the swatch color is applied as a stroke.

Once a stroke is applied, you can modify the **stroke weight**—how heavy the outline appears—using the Stroke panel. The Stroke panel is command central for all the modifications you can apply to a stroke, including making dotted and dashed strokes and varying stroke styles.

The Align Stroke section of the Stroke panel is critical for determining *where* on the object the stroke is applied. By default, a stroke is aligned to the center of the object's perimeter. This means that it's centered on the edge, halfway inside and halfway outside the object. For example, if you apply a 10 pt stroke to a rectangle, five points of the stroke will be inside the object, and five points will be outside.

Figure 2 *Swatches panel*

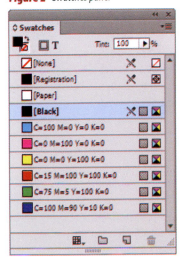

Figure 3 *Viewing the activated Fill button*

Fill button is in front of the Stroke button

Figure 4 *Viewing the activated Stroke button*

Stroke button is in front of the Fill button

The Stroke panel offers three Align Stroke options: Align Stroke to Center, Align Stroke to Inside, and Align Stroke to Outside. Figure 5 shows examples of all three. Note that in all three examples, the object itself is the same size, but the way the stroke is aligned to the object changes how much of the fill color is visible.

Using the Step and Repeat Command

Many times, when laying out a page, you will want to create multiple objects that are evenly spaced in lines or in grids. InDesign CC offers many great utilities for accomplishing this, one of which is the Step and Repeat dialog box, as shown in Figure 6.

Before you choose the Step and Repeat command, you need to decide which objects you want to copy and how many copies of it you want to create. After selecting the object, choose Step and Repeat on the Edit menu. In the Step and Repeat dialog box, you choose the number of copies. You also specify the **offset** value for each successive copy. The offset is the horizontal and vertical distance the copy will be from the original.

QUICK TIP

Click the Preview check box to see transformations before you execute them.

Figure 5 *A 10 pt stroke with three different alignments*

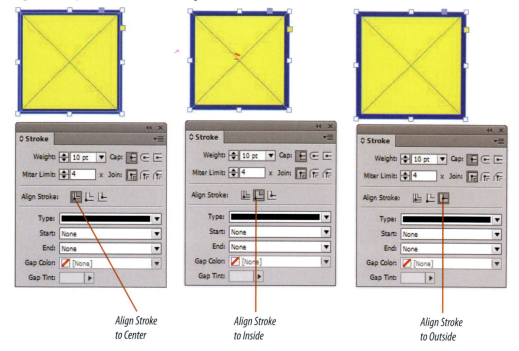

Align Stroke
to Center

Align Stroke
to Inside

Align Stroke
to Outside

Figure 6 *Step and Repeat dialog box*

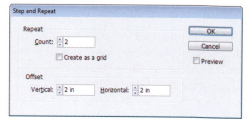

© 2015 Cengage Learning®

Working with Frames

Figure 7 shows an original 1-inch square frame and three copies created using the Step and Repeat command. The horizontal offset is two inches and the vertical offset is two inches. Thus, each copy is two inches to the right and two inches down from the previous copy.

Note that positive and negative offset values create copies in specific directions. On the horizontal axis, a positive value creates copies to the right of the original; a negative value creates copies to the left of the original. On the vertical axis, a positive value creates copies *below* the original; a negative value creates copies above the original. Figure 8 is a handy guide for remembering the result of positive and negative offset values.

Use the vertical ruler on the left side of the document page to remember positive and negative values on the vertical axis. You are used to thinking of positive as up and negative as down, but remember that in InDesign, the default (0, 0) coordinate is in the top-left corner of the page. On the ruler, positive numbers *increase* as you move *down* the ruler.

Aligning Objects

The Align panel offers quick and simple solutions for aligning and distributing multiple objects on a page. To **align** objects is to position them by their tops, bottoms, left sides, right sides or centers. To **distribute** objects is to space them equally on a page horizontally, vertically, or both. Using the top section of the Align panel, you can choose from six alignment buttons, shown in Figure 9.

Figure 7 *Results of the Step and Repeat command*

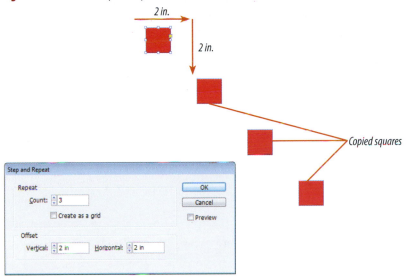

Figure 8 *Understanding positive and negative offset values*

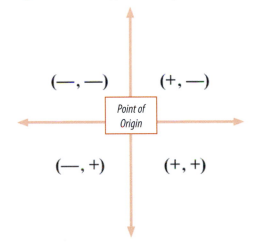

Figure 9 *Align Objects section of the Align panel*

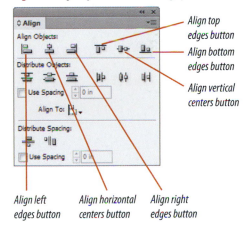

Each option includes an icon that represents the resulting layout of the selected objects, after the button has been clicked. Figure 10 shows three objects placed randomly on the page. Figure 11 shows the same three objects after clicking the Align left edges button.

Compare Figure 10 to Figure 11. Only the bottom two objects moved; they moved left to align with the left edge of the top object. This is because the top object was originally the leftmost object. Clicking the Align left edges button aligns all selected objects with the leftmost object.

Figure 12 shows the same three objects after clicking the Align top edges button. The red and yellow boxes move up so that their tops are aligned with the top of the blue box.

Distributing Objects

You use the Distribute Objects section of the Align panel to distribute objects. As stated earlier, to distribute objects is to space them equally on a page, horizontally, vertically, or both.

Figure 10 *Three objects not aligned*

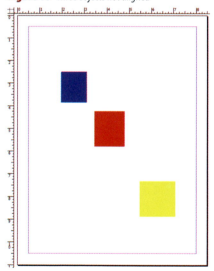

Figure 11 *Objects aligned with the Align left edges button*

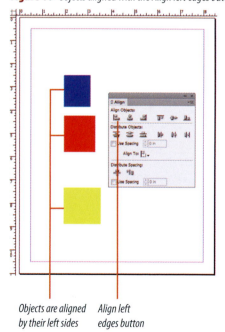

Objects are aligned by their left sides *Align left edges button*

Figure 12 *Objects aligned by top edges*

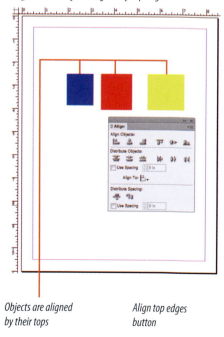

Objects are aligned by their tops *Align top edges button*

© 2015 Cengage Learning®

Figure 13 shows three objects that are not distributed evenly on either the horizontal or vertical axis. Figure 14 shows the same three objects after clicking the Distribute horizontal centers button. Clicking this button means that—on the horizontal axis—the distance between the center point of the first object and the center point of the second object is the same as the distance between the center point of the second object and the center point of the third object.

Figure 15 shows the same three objects after clicking the Distribute vertical centers button. Clicking this button means that—on the vertical axis—the distance between the center points of the first two objects is the same as the distance between the center points of the second and third objects.

Why are the Align and Distribute buttons on the same panel? Because their power is how they work in conjunction with each other. Figure 16 shows three text frames without any

Figure 13 *Three objects, positioned randomly*

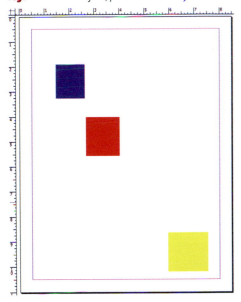

Figure 14 *Objects distributed by their horizontal centers*

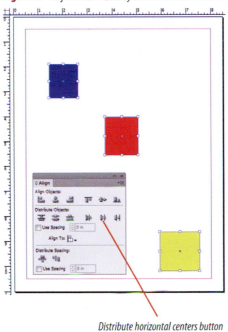

Distribute horizontal centers button

Figure 15 *Objects distributed by their vertical centers*

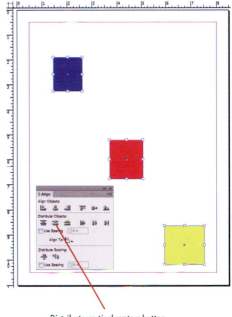

Distribute vertical centers button

Lesson 1   Align and Distribute Objects on a Page

alignment or distribution applied. Figure 17 shows the three frames after clicking the Align top edges button and the Distribute left edges button. Compare the two figures.

Using the Live Distribute Technique

When you select multiple objects, a bounding box appears around the objects. As you already know, you can drag the handles of that bounding box to transform all the selected objects. The Live Distribute option offers a different behavior. Instead of resizing the objects, you can use the Live Distribute option to proportionally resize the *space between* the objects.

To access the Live Distribute option, select multiple objects, start dragging a bounding box handle and then hold down the Spacebar as you drag. The spaces between the objects will be resized, and the alignment of the objects will change depending on where and in what direction you drag.

Figure 18 shows 20 frames aligned in a grid. Figure 19 shows the same 20 frames modified with the Live Distribute option. Note that the

Figure 16 *Three text frames, positioned randomly*

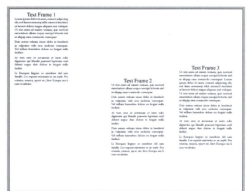

Figure 17 *Objects aligned at their top edges and distributed from left edges*

Aligned at top edge

Even horizontal distribution from left edge to left edge

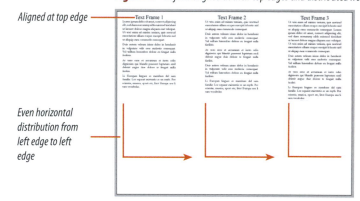

Figure 18 *20 frames*

Figure 19 *Space between frames increased proportionately with the Live Distribute option*

Working with Frames

frames haven't changed size—only the space between them has changed.

Using the Gap Tool

When you're working with multiple objects, the Gap tool offers a quick way to adjust the size of the gaps between them. It also allows you to resize several items that have commonly aligned edges at once, while maintaining the size of the gaps between them. Think of it this way: the Gap tool moves the gap.

Figure 20 shows a grid of 12 frames with the Gap tool positioned over the center gap. The shaded area indicates the length of the gap that will be modified by the tool. Figure 21 shows the result of dragging the Gap tool to the left. Note that only the gap moved; the size of the gap didn't change. The width of the associated frames changed.

You can use the Gap tool while pressing and holding various keys to perform other tasks as well, as shown in Table 1.

Figure 20 *Gap tool positioned over a grid of frames*

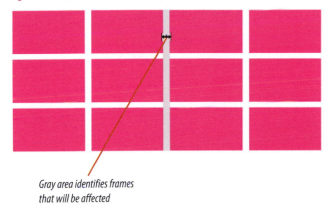

Gray area identifies frames that will be affected

Figure 21 *Result of dragging the Gap tool to the left*

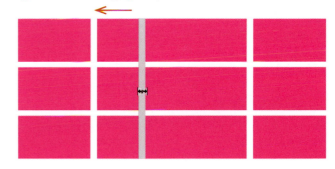

TABLE 1: GAP TOOL BEHAVIORS AND KEYBOARD COMBINATIONS		
PC	**Mac**	**Behavior**
[Shift]	[shift]	Affects the gap only between the two items nearest to the cursor
[Ctrl]	⌘	Increases the width and height of the gap
[Alt]	[option]	Moves the items with the gap instead of resizing the items

© Cengage Learning®

Apply fills and strokes

1. Open ID 4-1.indd, then save it as **Orientation**. Verify that guides are showing.
2. Click the **workspace switcher list arrow** on the Menu bar, then click **[Advanced]**.
3. Click the **Rectangle tool** 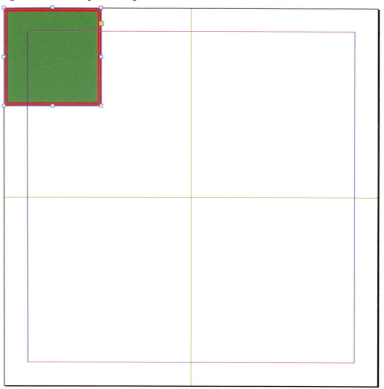, then click anywhere on the page.

TIP When a shape tool is selected on the Tools panel, clicking the document window opens the tool's dialog box, where you can enter values that determine the size of the resulting object.

4. Type **2** in the Width text box, type **2** in the Height text box, then click **OK**.
5. Switch to the Selection tool , then click **Swatches** in the stack of collapsed panels to open the Swatches panel.
6. Verify that the Fill button is activated.
7. Click **Green** on the Swatches panel. The rectangle frame fills with green.
8. Click the **Stroke button** on the Tools panel.
9. Click **Brick Red** on the Swatches panel.
10. Open the Stroke panel, type **6** in the Weight text box, then press **[Enter]** (Win) or **[return]** (Mac).
11. Click the **Align Stroke to Outside button** .
12. Click the **Align Stroke to Center button** .
13. Click the **Align Stroke to Inside button** .
14. Click the **top-left reference point** on the Control panel, type **0** in the X and Y text boxes, then press **[Enter]**(Win) or **[return]**(Mac). Your page should resemble Figure 22.

(continued)

Figure 22 *Positioning the rectangle frame*

Working with Frames

Figure 23 *Apply None button*

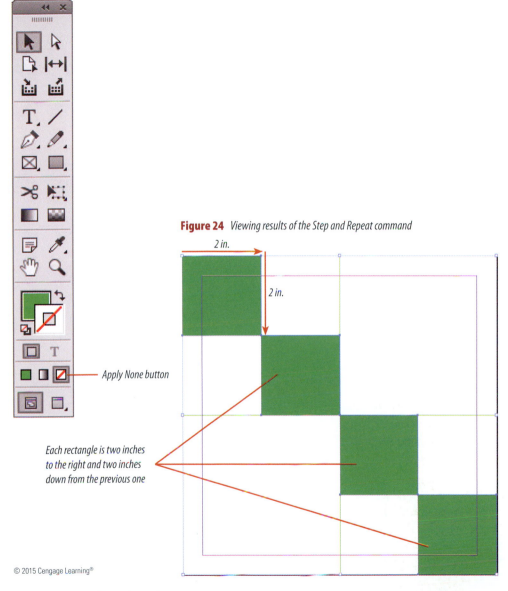

Apply None button

Figure 24 *Viewing results of the Step and Repeat command*

2 in.

2 in.

Each rectangle is two inches
to the right and two inches
down from the previous one

15. Click **File** on the Menu bar, then click **Save**.

You created a rectangle using the Rectangle dialog box. You then used the Swatches panel to choose a fill color and a stroke color for the rectangle frame. You chose a weight for the stroke and tested three options for aligning the stroke. Finally, you used the Control panel to position the square at the top-left corner of the page.

Use the Step and Repeat command

1. Make sure the green rectangle is still selected, click the **Stroke button** on the Tools panel, then click the **Apply None button** [⊘] , as shown in Figure 23.

The stroke is removed from the green rectangle. With the loss of the stroke, the rectangle is no longer aligned with the top-left corner.

2. Press **[V]** to access the Selection tool, then drag the **frame** so that its top-left corner is aligned with the top-left corner of the page.

3. Click **Edit** on the Menu bar, then click **Step and Repeat**.

4. Verify that the Horizontal and Vertical text boxes are set to **0** on the Control panel, type **3** in the Repeat Count text box, type **2** in the Vertical Offset text box, type **2** in the Horizontal Offset text box, then click **OK**.

Three new rectangles are created, each one two inches to the right and two inches down from the previous one, as shown in Figure 24.

5. Click the **Selection tool** ▶ , then click anywhere on the pasteboard to deselect.

6. Select the **top two rectangles**, click **Edit** on the Menu bar, then click **Step and Repeat**.

(continued)

7. Type **1** in the Repeat Count text box, type **0** in the Vertical Offset text box, type **4** in the Horizontal Offset text box, then click **OK**.

8. Select the **bottom two rectangles** on the page, click **Edit** on the Menu bar, then click **Step and Repeat**.

9. Type **1** in the Repeat Count text box, type **0** in the Vertical Offset text box, type **-4** in the Horizontal Offset text box, then click **OK**.

10. Press **[W]** to switch to Preview, click anywhere to deselect the new rectangles, then compare your page to Figure 25.

11. Save the file.

You used the Step and Repeat command to create a checkerboard pattern, duplicating a single rectangle multiple times.

Use the Live Distribute technique

1. Hide guides, select all, copy, then paste in place.

2. Click the **center reference point** on the Control panel, type **90** in the Rotation Angle text box on the Control panel, then press **[Enter]** (Win) or **[return]** (Mac).

3. Verify that the Fill button is in front on the Tools panel, click **Dark Blue** on the Swatches panel, then compare your screen to Figure 26.

(continued)

Figure 25 *Checkerboard created using the Step and Repeat command*

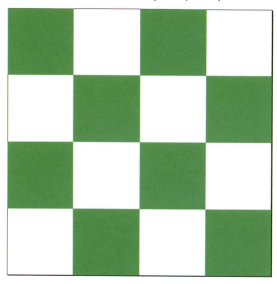

Figure 26 *Viewing the complete checkerboard*

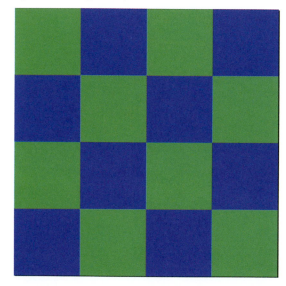

Working with Frames

Figure 27 *Scaling the checkerboard in a standard manner*

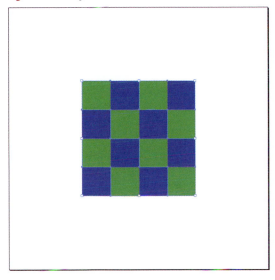

Figure 28 *Expanding the space between frames with Live Distribute*

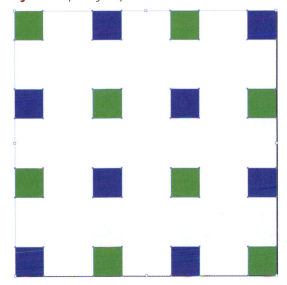

Lesson 1   Align and Distribute Objects on a Page

4. Select all, press and hold **[Shift] [Alt]** (Win) or **[Shift] [option]** (Mac), then click and drag the upper-right handle of the bounding box toward the center of the page, releasing the mouse button when your checkerboard resembles Figure 27.

    The objects are scaled from their center point.

5. Click and drag the **upper-right corner** of the bounding box toward the upper-right corner of the document, then, while you are still dragging, press and hold **[Spacebar]**.

    When you press [Spacebar] while dragging, the Live Distribute option is enabled. The space between the objects is modified—larger or smaller—depending on the direction in which you drag.

6. With the Spacebar still pressed, drag the **handle** in different directions on the document.

    Regardless of the direction you drag, the frames do not change size or shape—only the space between the frames changes.

7. With the Spacebar still pressed, press and hold **[Shift] [Alt]** (Win) or **[Shift] [option]** (Mac), then drag the **handle** to the upper-right corner of the document and release the mouse button.

    Pressing and holding [Spacebar] [Shift] [Alt] (Win) or [Spacebar][Shift][option] (Mac) when dragging enlarges the space between the frames in proportion from the center. Your page should resemble Figure 28.

8. Begin dragging the **upper-right handle** of the bounding box slowly toward the center of the document.

    (continued)

9. As you're dragging, press **[Spacebar]** to activate Live Distribute, then press **[Shift] [Alt]** (Win) or **[Shift] [option]** (Mac) and continue dragging toward the center until your artwork resembles Figure 29.

10. Deselect all, then save your work.

You pasted and rotated a copy of the squares to create a complete checkerboard. You selected all the frames, then dragged a bounding box handle to reduce all the objects in a standard manner. You then used the Live Distribute technique to modify the space between the objects.

Use the Gap tool

1. Click the **Gap tool** |↔| on the Tools panel.

2. Position the Gap tool over the middle-vertical gap, then click and drag left so that your grid resembles Figure 30.

3. Position the Gap tool over the bottom-horizontal gap, then click and drag up so that your grid resembles Figure 31.

4. Position the Gap tool over the gap between the top two frames in the upper-right corner, press and hold **[Shift]**, then click and drag to the left so that your grid resembles Figure 32.

5. Press and hold **[Ctrl]** (Win) or ⌘ (Mac), then click and drag the **left edge** of the grid to the left.

   The width of the four frames on the left is increased.

6. Press and hold **[Alt]** (Win) or **[option]** (Mac), position the Gap tool over the **bottom-horizontal gap**, then click and drag down.

(continued)

Figure 29 *Reducing the space between frames with Live Distribute*

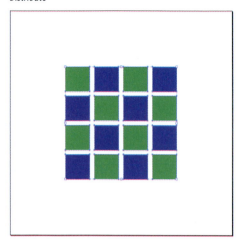

Figure 30 *Moving the vertical gap*

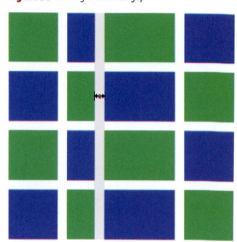

Figure 31 *Moving the horizontal gap*

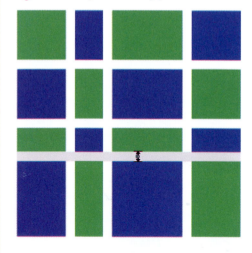

Figure 32 *Moving the gap only between two rectangles*

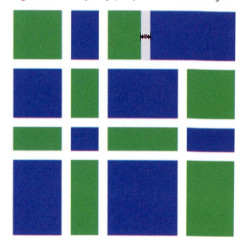

Working with Frames

Figure 33 *Moving frames with the Gap tool*

Figure 34 *Aligning three objects by their top edges*

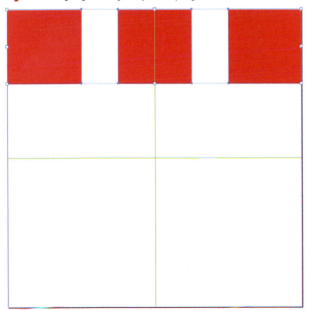

As shown in Figure 33, the frames on both sides of the gap move. Neither the frames nor the gap are resized—only relocated.

7. Save your work, then close Orientation.

You used the Gap tool with various key combinations to affect the gaps in a grid of frames.

Align objects

1. Open ID 4-2.indd, then save it as **Alignment**.

2. Click **Window** on the Menu bar, point to **Object & Layout**, then click **Align**.

   The Align panel opens.

3. Press **[Ctrl] [A]** (Win) or ⌘ **[A]** (Mac) to select all three objects on the page, then click the **Align left edges button** in the Align Objects section of the Align panel.

   The frames are aligned to the leftmost of the three.

4. Click **Edit** on the Menu bar, then click **Undo Align**.

5. Click the **Align top edges button** on the Align panel.

   As shown in Figure 34, the top edges of the three frames are aligned to the topmost of the three.

6. Undo the previous step, then click the **Align horizontal centers button**.

7. Click the **Align vertical centers button**.

   The three frames are stacked, one on top of the other, their center points aligned both horizontally and vertically.

8. Save your work, then close Alignment.

You used the buttons in the Align Objects section of the Align panel to reposition frames with various alignments.

Distribute objects

1. Open ID 4-3.indd, then save it as **Distribution**. Verify that guides are showing.

2. Select the **top two yellow squares** and the **two red squares**, then click the **Align top edges button** 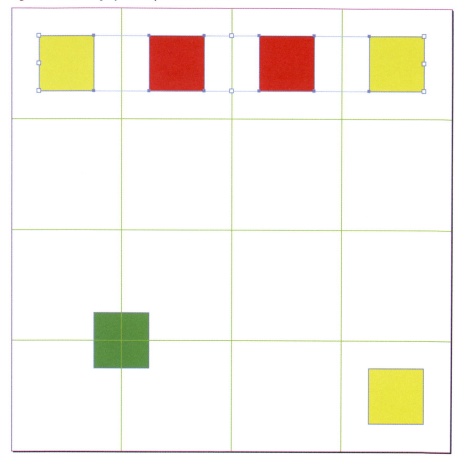 in the Align Objects section of the Align panel.

   The four objects are aligned by their top edges.

3. Click the **Distribute horizontal centers button** in the Distribute Objects section of the Align panel.

   The center points of the two red squares are distributed evenly on the horizontal axis between the center points of the two yellow squares, as shown in Figure 35.

4. Click **Edit** on the Menu bar, click **Deselect All**, select the **top-left yellow square**, select the **two red squares**, then select the **bottom-right yellow square**.

   (continued)

Figure 35 *Distributing objects evenly on the horizontal axis*

© 2015 Cengage Learning®

Working with Frames

Figure 36 *Distributing 4 objects evenly on the vertical axis*

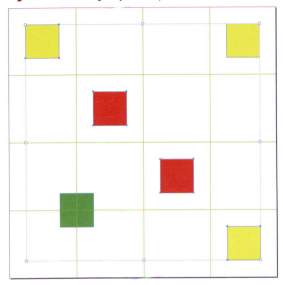

Figure 37 *Distributing 5 objects evenly on the vertical axis*

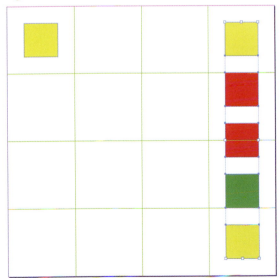

5. Click the **Distribute vertical centers button** , then compare your screen to Figure 36.

6. Select the **green square**, the **two red squares** and the **bottom yellow square**, then click the **Align right edges button** .

7. Press and hold **[Shift]**, then click the **top-right yellow square** to add it to the selection.

8. Click the **Distribute vertical centers button** .

   The center points of the five squares are distributed evenly on the vertical axis, as shown in Figure 37.

9. Save your work, then close Distribution.

You spaced objects evenly on the horizontal and vertical axes.

Stack
AND LAYER OBJECTS

What You'll Do

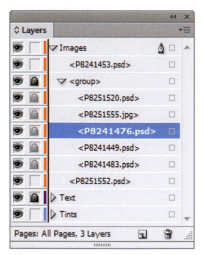

 In this lesson, you will manipulate the stacking order of objects on the page, and you'll use the Layers panel to control how objects are layered.

Understanding the Stacking Order

The **stacking order** refers to how objects are arranged in hierarchical order. When you create multiple objects, it is important for you to remember that every object is on its own level. For example, if you draw a square frame, and then draw a circle frame, the circle frame is automatically created one level in front of the square, whether or not they overlap. If they did overlap, the circle would appear in front of the square.

QUICK TIP

Use the word "level" when discussing the hierarchy of the stacking order, not the word "layer," which has its own specific meaning in InDesign.

You control the stacking order with the four commands on the Arrange menu. The Bring to Front command moves a selected object to the front of the stacking order. The Send to Back command moves a selected object to the back of the stacking order. The Bring Forward command moves a selected object one level forward in the stacking order, and the Send Backward command moves a selected object one level backward in the stacking order.

Using these four commands, you can control and arrange how every object on the page overlaps other objects.

Understanding Layers

The Layers panel, as shown in Figure 38, is a smart solution for organizing and managing elements of a layout. The Layers panel in InDesign is very similar to the Layers panel in Adobe Illustrator. It includes options for locking and hiding individual objects on a layer.

By default, every document you create in InDesign has one layer. You can create new layers and give them descriptive names to help you identify a layer's content. For example, if you were working on a layout that contained both text and graphics, you might want to create a layer for all of the text frames called Text and create another layer for all of the graphics called Graphics.

Why would you do this? Well, for one reason, you have the ability to lock layers on the Layers panel. Locking a layer makes its contents non-editable until you unlock it. In the example, you could lock the Text layer while you work on the graphic elements of the layout. By doing so, you can be certain that you won't make any inadvertent changes to the text elements. Another reason is that you have the ability to hide layers. You could temporarily hide the Text layer, thus providing yourself a working view of the graphics that is unobstructed by the text elements.

You can also duplicate layers. You do so by clicking the Duplicate Layer command on the Layers panel menu or by dragging a layer on top of the Create new layer icon on the Layers

panel. When you duplicate a layer, all of the objects on the original layer are duplicated and will appear in their same locations on the new layer.

Layers are a smart, important solution for organizing your work and improving your workflow, especially for complex layouts. Invest some time in learning layers—it will pay off with lots of saved time and fewer headaches.

Working with Layers

You can create as many layers on the Layers panel as you need to organize your work. Figure 39 shows the Layers panel with three

layers. Notice the Lock icon on Layer 2. The Lock icon indicates that this layer cannot be edited. All objects on Layer 2 are locked. Clicking the Lock icon will unlock the layer, and the lock icon will disappear.

Think of layers on the Layers panel as being three-dimensional. The topmost layer is the front layer; the bottommost layer is the back layer. Therefore, it follows logically that objects on the topmost layer are *in front* of objects on any other layer. Layers themselves are transparent. If you have a layer with no objects on it, you can see through the layer to the objects on the layers behind it.

Figure 38 *Layers panel*

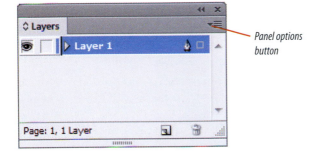

Panel options button

Figure 39 *Layers panel with three layers*

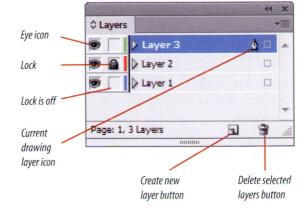

Eye icon

Lock

Lock is off

Current drawing layer icon

Create new layer button

Delete selected layers button

Note that each layer contains its own stacking order. Let's say that you have three layers, each with five objects on it. Regardless of the stacking order of the top layer, all the objects on that layer are in front of any objects on the other layers. In other words, an object at the back of the stacking order of the top layer is still in front of any object on any layer beneath it.

One great organizational aspect of layers is that you can assign a selection color to a layer. When you select an object, its bounding box appears in the selection color of the layer on which it is placed, as shown in Figure 40.

You determine a layer's selection color by selecting the layer, clicking the Layers panel options button, clicking Layer Options for the name of the selected layer, then choosing a new color from the Color menu. When you are working with a layout that contains numerous objects, this feature is a great visual aid for keeping track of objects and their relationships to other objects.

Manipulating Layers and Objects on Layers

Once you have created layers in a document, you have many options for manipulating objects on the layers and the layers themselves. You can move objects between layers, and you can reorder the layers on the Layers panel.

Clicking a layer on the Layers panel to select it is called **targeting** a layer. The layer that you click is called the **target layer**. When you create a new object, the object will be added to whichever layer is targeted on the

Layers panel. The pen tool icon next to a layer's name on the Layers panel is called the Current drawing layer icon. This icon will help remind you that anything placed or drawn will become part of that layer.

You can select any object on the page, regardless of which layer is targeted. When you

select the object, the layer that the object is on is automatically targeted on the Layers panel.

When one or more objects are selected, a small, square icon on the far right of a layer on the Layers panel, fills with color to show that items on the layer are selected as shown

Figure 40 *Assigning a selection color to a layer*

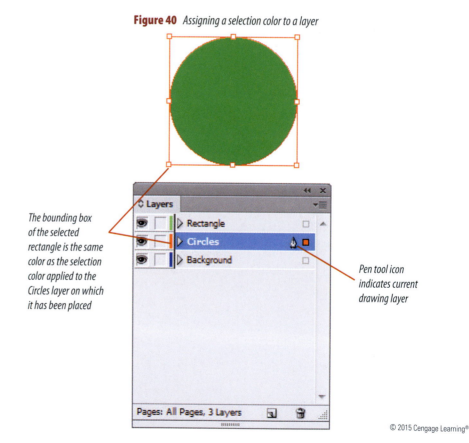

The bounding box of the selected rectangle is the same color as the selection color applied to the Circles layer on which it has been placed

Pen tool icon indicates current drawing layer

© 2015 Cengage Learning®

Working with Frames

in Figure 41. That small button, called the Selected items icon, represents the selected objects. When you click and drag the Selected items icon and move it to another layer, the selected objects move to that layer. Therefore, you should never feel constrained by the layers you have chosen for objects; it's easy to move them from one layer to another.

You can also change the order of layers on the Layers panel by dragging a layer up or down on the panel. As you drag, a heavy black line indicates the new position for the layer when you release the mouse button. In Figure 42, the Rectangles layer is being repositioned under the Circles layer.

Selecting Artwork on Layers

Let's say you have three layers in your document, each with six objects. That means your document has a total of 18 objects. If you apply the Select All command on the Edit menu, all 18 objects will be selected, regardless of which layer is targeted on the Layers panel.

In many situations, you'll want to select all the objects on one layer only. The easiest way to do this is with the Selected items icon. Even when nothing is selected, the icon is available on every layer—as a hollow square. Click that icon, and all objects on that layer will be selected. This is a powerful and useful option—make note of it.

Selecting Objects Behind Other Objects

When you have multiple overlapping objects on a page, objects behind other objects can sometimes be difficult to select. Pressing and holding [Ctrl] (Win) or [⌘] (Mac) allows you to "click through the stacking order" to select objects behind other objects. Simply click the top object, press and hold [Ctrl] (Win) or [⌘] (Mac), then click the top object again, which will select the object immediately behind it. Click the top object again and the next object down in the stacking order will be selected.

Figure 41 *Viewing the Selected items icon*

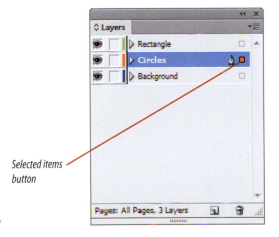

Selected items button

Figure 42 *Changing the order of two layers on the Layers panel*

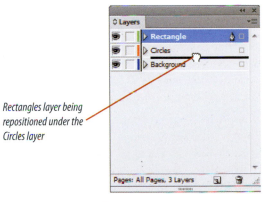

Rectangles layer being repositioned under the Circles layer

Use the Arrange commands to change the stacking order of objects

1. Open ID 4-4.indd, then save it as **Stack and Layer**.

2. Press **[V]** to access the Selection tool, then click the **yellow rectangle**.

3. Click **Object** on the Menu bar, point to **Arrange**, then click **Bring Forward**.

   The yellow rectangle moves forward one level in the stacking order.

4. Click the **red square**, click **Object** on the Menu bar, point to **Arrange**, then click **Bring to Front**.

5. Select both the **yellow rectangle** and the **blue circle**, click **Object** on the Menu bar, point to **Arrange**, then click **Bring to Front.**

   Both objects move in front of the red square, as shown in Figure 43.

6. Click the **green circle**, click **Object** on the Menu bar, point to **Arrange**, then click **Bring to Front**.

7. Select all, then click the **Align horizontal centers button** 🔲 on the Align panel.

   The blue circle is completely behind the green circle.

   (continued)

Figure 43 *Using the Bring to Front command with two objects selected*

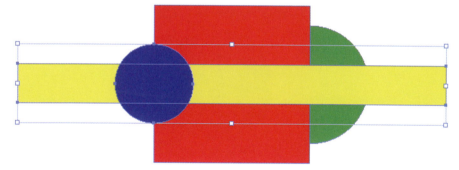

Working with Frames

Figure 44 *Sending the green circle backward one level in the stacking order*

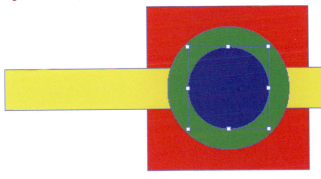

8. Deselect all, then click the center of the green circle.

9. Press and hold **[Ctrl]** (Win) or ⌘ (Mac), then click the center of the green circle again.

   The blue circle behind the green circle is selected.

10. Click **Object** on the Menu bar, point to **Arrange**, then click **Bring Forward**.

    As shown in Figure 44, the blue circle moves forward one level in the stacking order, in front of the green circle.

11. Deselect all, select the **blue circle**, press and hold **[Ctrl]** (Win) or ⌘ (Mac), then click the **blue circle center** again to select the green circle behind it.

12. Still pressing and holding [Ctrl] (Win) or ⌘ (Mac), click the **blue circle center** again to select the yellow rectangle, then click the **blue circle center** once more to select the red square.

    TIP Commit this selection technique to memory, as it is useful for selecting overlapping objects.

13. Save your work, then close Stack and Layer.

You used the Arrange commands to manipulate the stacking order of four objects.

Create new layers on the Layers panel

1. Open ID 4-5.indd, save it as **Layers Intro**, then click **Layers** in the stack of collapsed panels to open the Layers panel.

   As shown in Figure 45, the Layers panel has one default layer named Layer 1. All the objects on the spread are on Layer 1.

2. Double-click **Layer 1** on the Layers panel.

   The Layer Options dialog box opens. In this box you can change settings for Layer 1, such as its name and selection color.

3. Type **Tints** in the Name text box, then click **OK**.

4. Click the **Create new layer button** ▣ on the Layers panel, then double-click **Layer 2**.

5. Type **Images** in the Name text box, click the **Color list arrow**, click **Orange**, then click **OK**.

6. Click the **Layers panel options button** ▾≡, then click **New Layer**.

7. Type **Text** in the Name text box, click the **Color list arrow**, click **Purple**, then click **OK**.

   Your Layers panel should resemble Figure 46.

You renamed Layer 1, then created two new layers on the Layers panel.

Figure 45 *Layers panel with Layer 1*

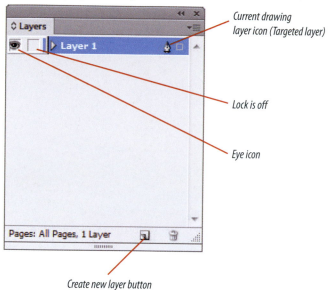

Current drawing layer icon (Targeted layer)

Lock is off

Eye icon

Create new layer button

Figure 46 *Layers panel with three layers*

Figure 47 *Seven images moved to the Images layer*

Figure 48 *Text frames moved to Text layer*

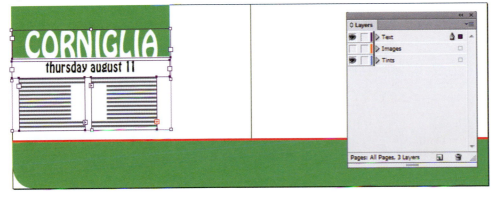

© 2015 Cengage Learning®. Images courtesy of Chris Botello.

1. Press **[V]** to access the Selection tool if it is not already active, then select the **seven images** on the spread.

   The Tints layer on the Layers panel is highlighted and the Selected items icon appears next to the layer name.

2. Click and drag the **Selected items button** from the Tints layer up to the Images layer.

   The seven images are moved to the Images layer. As shown in Figure 47, the selection edges around the frames are now orange, the color assigned to the Images layer.

3. Click the **Eye icon** on the Images layer to hide that layer.

4. Select the **four text frames** on the left page, then drag the **Selected items icon** up to the Text layer.

   As shown in Figure 48, the text frames are moved to the Text layer and the selection marks are now purple. Note that the text wrap is still affecting the text, even though the Images layer containing the images is hidden.

5. Show the Images layer, then click the **Selected items icon** on the Images layer.

   All objects on the Images layer are selected, and all the objects on the Text layer are deselected.

6. Click the **Text layer** on the Layers panel, click the **Rectangle tool** , then draw a small rectangle anywhere on the page.

   Because the Text layer was selected on the Layers panel, the new rectangle is positioned on the Text layer.

(continued)

7. Verify that the Fill button is active on the Tools panel, click **Tan** on the Swatches panel, then remove any stroke if necessary.

8. Click the **top-left reference point** on the Control panel, enter **0** in the X text box, enter **0** in the Y text box, enter **12.5** in the W text box, then enter **4.75** in the H text box.

   The rectangle should cover the entire spread. Because the rectangle is the newest object created, it is at the top of the stacking order on the Text layer.

9. Click **Object** on the Menu bar, point to **Arrange**, click **Send to Back**, then compare your spread to Figure 49.

   The rectangle is at the back of the stacking order of the Text layer. But because the Text layer is at the top of the Layers panel, the rectangle is in front of all images and all tints on the layers below.

10. Drag the **Selected items button** down to the Tints layer.

    The rectangle is moved to the Tints layer. It is at the top of the stacking order on the Tints layer, so the green tints are not visible.

11. Click **Object** on the Menu bar, point to **Arrange**, then click **Send to Back**.

    As shown in Figure 50, the tan rectangle is at the bottom of the stacking order on the Tints layer.

12. Save your work.

You used the Layers panel to move selected objects from one layer to another. You targeted a layer, then created a new object, which was added to that layer. You then pasted objects into a targeted layer.

Figure 49 *Rectangle moved to back of the stacking order on Text layer*

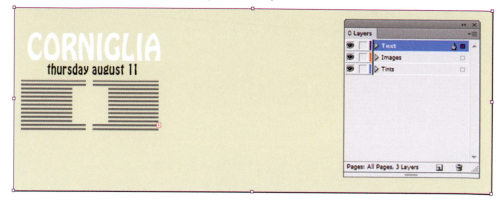

Figure 50 *Rectangle moved to back of the stacking order on Tints layer*

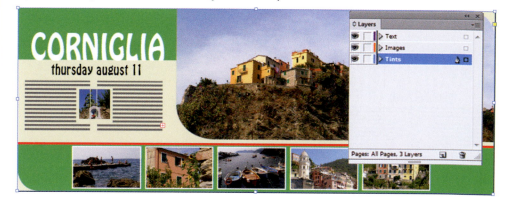

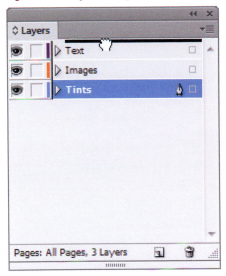

Figure 51 *Moving the Tints layer*

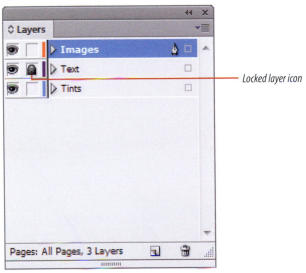

Figure 52 *Text layer, reordered and locked*

Locked layer icon

Change the order of layers on the Layers panel

1. Switch to the Selection tool ![pointer], deselect all, then click and drag the **Tints layer** to the top of the Layers panel.

   As shown in Figure 51, a thick line appears indicating where the layer will be positioned when dragged.

2. Drag the **Text layer** to the top of the Layers panel.

3. Drag the **Images layer** to the top of the Layers panel.

4. Click the **empty square** next to the Text layer name to lock the layer, then compare your Layers panel to Figure 52.

   The Lock icon appears when it is clicked, indicating the layer is now locked.

5. Save the file.

You changed the order of layers and locked the Text layer.

Group items on layers

1. Click the **triangle** next to Images on the Layers panel, then see Figure 53.

   Clicking the triangle expands the layer to show the objects on the layer. The seven frames are listed on the layer with the name of the images pasted into them.

2. Select the first four small frames at the bottom of the layout.

   The Selected items icon becomes activated for each individual object that is selected.

3. Click **Object** on the Menu bar, then click **Group**.

   The four selected objects are moved into a folder named Group.

4. Click the **triangle** to expand the group folder, select the **fifth thumbnail frame** on the layout, then compare your screen to Figure 54.

   The Selected items icon is activated beside the fifth thumbnail layer on the Layers panel. Because this image is not part of the group, it is not within the group folder.

   (continued)

Figure 53 *Expanding a layer on the Layers panel*

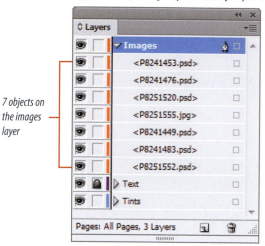

7 objects on the images layer

Figure 54 *Four objects in a group folder*

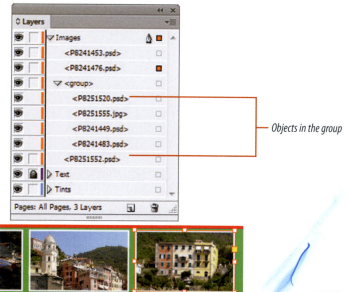

Objects in the group

© 2015 Cengage Learning®. Image courtesy of Chris Botello.

Working with Frames

Figure 55 *Dragging the ungrouped thumbnail into the group*

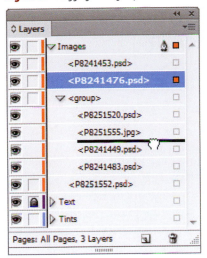

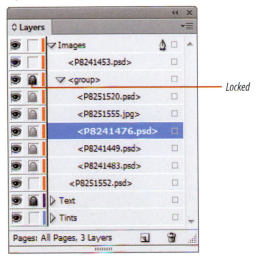

Figure 56 *Locking the group on the layer*

Locked

5. Click and drag the **fifth thumbnail layer** into the middle of the group folder, as shown in Figure 55.

6. Deselect all, then click the leftmost of the five thumbnails on the layout with the Selection tool.

   You can see by the selection marks, that the fifth thumbnail is now part of the group.

7. Lock the group folder so that your Layers panel resembles Figure 56.

   When you expand a layer, you can lock and hide individual objects on a layer. In this example, the Images layer has seven images on it, but only five of them are locked.

8. Save your work, then close Layers Intro.

You modified a group using layers. You grouped four of five frames. You then added the fifth frame to the group by dragging the fifth frame into the group folder on the Layers panel.

Work with GRAPHICS FRAMES

What You'll Do

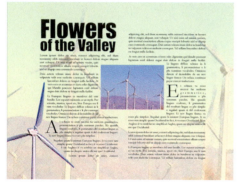

© 2015 Cengage Learning®

In this lesson, you will create graphics frames, resize them, and manipulate graphics that you import into them.

Placing Graphics in a Document

The term **graphic** is quite broad. In its most basic definition, a graphic is an element on the page that is not text. A simple square with a fill color could be called a graphic. However, when you are talking about placing graphics in an InDesign document, the term "graphic" usually refers to bitmap images or vector graphics. **Bitmap images** are images that consist of pixels. They are either created in a program like Adobe Photoshop, scanned in, or downloaded from the Internet or a digital camera. **Vector graphics** are artwork comprised of geometrically defined paths and curves, usually illustrations created and imported from drawing programs like Adobe Illustrator.

There are two essential methods for placing a graphic in a document. The first is to create a graphics placeholder frame using any of the InDesign's shape tools—Rectangle, Ellipse, or Polygon. Once you have created the frame and it is selected on the page, you use the Place command on the File menu to locate the graphic you want to import into the document. The graphic will appear in the graphics frame.

The second method is to place a graphic without first creating a graphics frame. If you click the Place command and then locate the graphic you want to import, you will see the loaded graphics icon when you position the pointer over the page. See Figure 57.

Figure 57 *Loaded graphics icon*

Loaded graphics icon

© 2015 Cengage Learning®. Image courtesy of Chris Botello.

Click the loaded graphics icon on the page to place the graphic. The graphic will be placed on the page in a graphics frame whose top-left corner will be positioned at the location where you clicked the loaded graphics icon.

Which is the better method? It depends on what you want to do with the graphic. If the size and location of the graphics frame is important, it's probably better to create and position the frame first, then import the graphic and make it fit into the frame. If the size and location of the frame are negotiable, you might want to place the graphic anywhere in the layout and then modify its size and location.

The Graphic vs. the Graphics Frame

One of the essential concepts in InDesign is the distinction between the graphics frame and the graphic itself. Think of the graphics frame as a window through which you see the placed graphic. Sometimes, the graphic will be smaller than the frame and will fit entirely within the frame. At other times, the graphic will be larger than the frame that contains it. In that case, you see only the areas of the graphic that fit in the frame. The other areas of the graphic are still there, you just can't see them because they are outside of the frame.

Selecting Graphics and Frames

The difference between the graphics frame and the graphic itself is reflected on the Tools panel. Anything you want to do to a graphics

frame, you do with the Selection tool. Anything you want to do to the contents—to a graphic itself—you do with the Direct Selection tool. This concept is the key to manipulating graphics within a graphics frame.

Figure 58 shows a graphics frame selected with the Selection tool. The Transform panel shows the X and Y locations of the frame and the width and height of the frame. In this figure, the Transform panel shows no information about the placed image.

Figure 59 shows the same object, but this time it has been selected with the Direct Selection tool. The graphic itself is selected. The selection frame is brown, which is the default color for a selected graphic. The selected frame around the image is called the bounding box. The **bounding box**—always rectangular—is the frame that defines the horizontal and vertical dimensions of the graphic itself—not the graphics frame. Finally, note that even though you can see the entire bounding box, there are parts of the graphic that you can't see. That's because the graphic is being cropped by the graphics frame.

It's important to note that the notations on the Transform panel are different. The + signs beside the X and Y text boxes are a visual indication that the Transform panel is now referring to the graphic, not the frame. The X and Y values are *in relation to the top-left corner of the frame*. Let's explore this: The upper-left reference point on the Transform panel is selected. The X/Y coordinates on the

Transform panel refer to the location of the upper-left corner of the graphic. The upper-left corner of the graphic is .04" above and 1.07" to the left of the top-left corner *of the frame*.

Figure 58 *Selected frame*

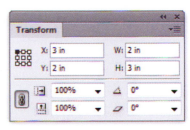

This is illustrated in Figure 60, which shows the graphic positioned at an X/Y value of 0/0.

Using the Content Indicator

When you're working with lots of graphics in lots of frames, you'll want a quicker solution for selecting graphics and frames. The quickest and easiest solution is to double-click the image. Double-clicking the image toggles between the frame and the graphic being selected.

The content indicator is the donut-shaped circle shown in Figure 61, and its available whenever you float over a graphic placed in a frame. If you click the content indicator with the Selection tool, the graphic will be selected. Thus, the content indicator allows you to select the graphic with the Selection tool without having to switch to the Direct Selection tool.

You'll just need to make sure that when you intend to select a frame, you don't accidentally select the content indicator and, thus, the graphic. Then it's easy to make modifications to the graphic, when you really mean to modify the frame.

Moving a Graphic Within a Frame

When you want to move a graphic within a frame, select the graphic by any method you prefer, then click and drag it. You can also move the selected graphic using the arrow keys on the keypad. When you click and drag the graphic to move it, you see a ghosted image of the areas that are outside the graphics frame, as shown in Figure 62. The ghosted image is referred to as a **dynamic preview**.

Figure 59 *Selected graphic*

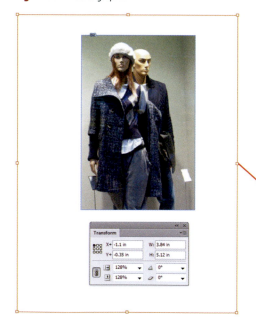

Bounding box of graphic

Figure 60 *X/Y values of the selected graphic at 0/0*

X/Y of graphic is 0/0 aligned with top-left corner of frame

Figure 61 *The content indicator*

Content indicator

Once you release the mouse button, the graphic will be repositioned within the frame. Remember, though, that regardless of where you move the graphic within the frame, the frame crops the graphic.

Copying and Pasting a Graphic

When designing layouts, you'll often find that you want to copy and paste a graphic from one frame to another. This is easy to do. First, select the graphic (not the frame), then copy it. Select the frame where you want to paste the copy, then choose the Paste Into command on the Edit menu.

Resizing a Graphic

When you select a graphic with the Direct Selection tool, you can then resize the graphic within the frame. Changes that you make to the size of the graphic do not affect the size of the graphics frame.

You can scale a selected graphic by dragging its handles or changing values in the Scale X Percentage and the Scale Y Percentage text boxes on the Transform or Control panels, as shown in Figure 63. You can also use the Transform/Scale command on the Object menu to scale the graphic. Remember, when the graphic is selected with the Direct Selection tool, only the graphic will be scaled when you use this command.

Figure 62 *Dynamic preview of the entire graphic*

© 2015 Cengage Learning®. Images courtesy of Chris Botello.

Figure 63 *Using the Control panel to scale the graphic*

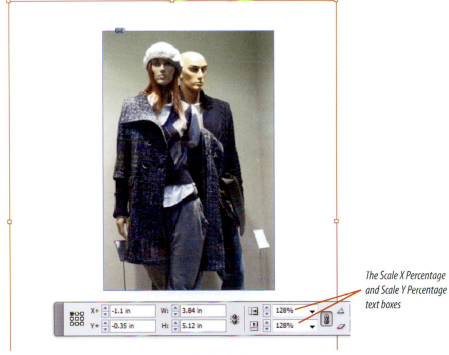

The Scale X Percentage and Scale Y Percentage text boxes

Using the Fitting Commands

While it's not difficult to select a graphic with the Direct Selection tool and then scale it using the Transform panel, there are a lot of steps in the process.

For a quick solution, you can use the Fitting commands, located on the Object menu. The Fitting commands offer different options for positioning the graphic in the frame. These commands are smart and useful but beware—they're easy to confuse with one another. It's important that you keep each command straight in your head, because one of the commands distorts the image to fit the frame. See Table 2.

Of all the fitting commands, the Fill Frame Proportionally command is the one you're likely to use most often, because it resizes the placed graphic to a size that is guaranteed to fit the frame, with no negative space in the frame. This means that some of the graphic may not be visible if it exceeds the size of the frame, but you can be confident that it will not be distorted to fit the frame.

Wrapping Text Around Graphics with Clipping Paths

In Chapter 3, you learned how to use the Text Wrap panel to wrap text around a bounding box using the Wrap around bounding box button. You can also wrap text around a graphic inside the frame, as shown in Figure 64.

The Text Wrap panel offers a number of methods for doing so. In this chapter, you will focus on wrapping text around an image that was saved with a named clipping path in Photoshop. Figure 65 shows a Photoshop image with a clipping path drawn around a man. A **clipping path** is a graphic that you draw in Photoshop that outlines the areas of the image you want to show when the file is placed in a layout program like InDesign.

Figure 64 *Wrapping text around a graphic*

The text is able to enter the graphics frame to wrap around the picture

Figure 65 *A Photoshop image with a clipping path*

Clipping path created in Photoshop

TABLE 2: FITTING COMMANDS		
Command	**Result**	**Proportion Issues**
Fill Frame Proportionally	The graphic is scaled proportionally to the minimum size required to fill the entire frame.	No proportion issues. The graphic is scaled in proportion.
Fit Content Proportionally	The graphic is scaled proportionally to the largest size it can be without exceeding the frame. Some areas of the frame may be empty.	No proportion issues. The graphic is scaled in proportion.
Fit Frame to Content	The frame is resized to the exact size of the graphic.	No proportion issues. The graphic is not scaled.
Fit Content to Frame	The content is resized to the exact size and shape of the frame.	The content will almost always be distorted with this fitting command.
Center Content	The center point of the graphic will be aligned with the center point of the frame.	No proportion issues. The graphic is not scaled.

When you save the Photoshop file, you name the clipping path and save it with the file.

When you place a graphic that has a named clipping path saved with it into your layout, InDesign is able to recognize the clipping path. With the graphic selected, click the Wrap around object shape button on the Text Wrap panel, click the Type list arrow in the Contour Options section of the panel, and then choose Photoshop Path, as shown in Figure 66. When you do so, the Path menu will list all the paths that were saved with the graphic file. (Usually, you will save only one path with a file.) Choose the path that you want to use for the text wrap.

QUICK TIP

To define the way text wraps around a graphic, click the Wrap To list arrow in the Wrap Options section, then choose one of the available presets.

Remember, in every case, you can always manually adjust the resulting text wrap boundary. Though the clipping path is created in Photoshop, the text wrap itself is created in InDesign—and it is editable. As shown in Figure 67, you can relocate the path's anchor points using the Direct Selection tool. You can also use the Add Anchor Point and Delete Anchor Point tools to add or delete points to the path as you find necessary. Click the Add Anchor Point tool anywhere on the path to add a new point and increase your ability to manipulate the path. Click any anchor point with the Delete Anchor Point tool to remove it. Changing the shape of the path changes how text wraps around the path.

© 2015 Cengage Learning®. Image courtesy of Chris Botello.

Figure 66 *Choosing the Wrap around object shape button*

Wrap around object shape button

Top Offset value (applies to entire path)

Click Type list arrow to choose Photoshop Path

Click Path list arrow to choose a named path saved with the Photoshop file

Figure 67 *Manipulating the text wrap path*

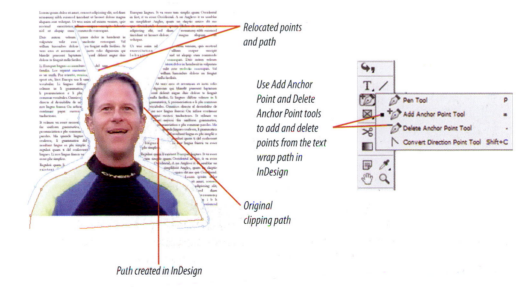

Relocated points and path

Use Add Anchor Point and Delete Anchor Point tools to add and delete points from the text wrap path in InDesign

Original clipping path

Path created in InDesign

Place graphics in a document

1. Open ID 4-6.indd, then save it as **Flowers**.

2. On the Layers panel, click the **empty square** next to the Text layer name to lock the Text layer, as shown in Figure 68.

   TIP When a layer is locked, the contents of the layer cannot be modified; this is a smart way to protect the contents of any layer from unwanted changes.

3. Click the **Background layer** to target it, click the **Rectangle Frame tool** ⊠, then draw a graphics frame in the center of the page that is approximately the size shown in Figure 69.

   The bounding box of the graphics frame is orange because orange is the selection color applied to the Background layer.

4. Click **File** on the Menu bar, click **Place**, navigate to the drive and folder where your Data Files are stored, then double-click **Windmills Ghost.psd**.

   Because the frame was selected, the graphic is placed automatically into the frame, as shown in Figure 70.

5. Click the **Selection tool** ▶, click anywhere to deselect the frame, click the **Eye icon** 👁 on the Background layer to hide it, then click the **Images layer** to target it on the Layers panel.

6. Click **File** on the Menu bar, click **Place**, navigate to the drive and folder where your Data Files are stored, click **Windmills Color.psd**, then click **Open**.

   (continued)

Figure 68 *Locking the Text layer*

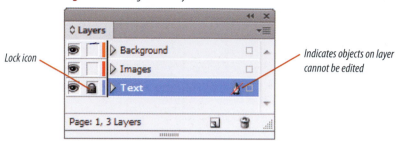

Lock icon

Indicates objects on layer cannot be edited

Figure 69 *Drawing a graphics frame*

Figure 70 *Viewing the placed graphic*

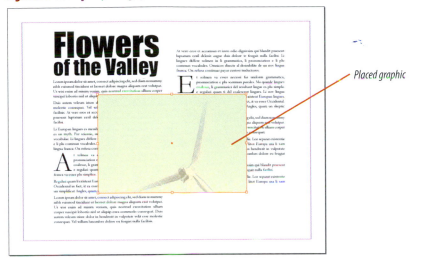

Placed graphic

Figure 71 *Viewing the graphic placed with the loaded graphics icon*

Top-left corner of placed graphic located at same spot where loaded graphics icon was clicked

TIP You can also access the Place command by pressing [Ctrl][D] (Win) or ⌘ [D] (Mac).

7. Position the pointer over the document.

   The pointer changes to the loaded graphics icon and shows a thumbnail of the graphic.

8. Click the loaded graphics icon on the **F** in the word Flowers.

   As shown in Figure 71, the graphic is placed in a new graphics frame whose top-left corner is located where the loaded graphics icon was clicked.

You imported two graphics using two subtly different methods. You created a graphics frame then used the Place command to place a graphic in that frame. You used the Place command to load a graphic file then clicked the loaded graphics icon to create a new frame for the new graphic.

Move a graphic in a graphics frame

1. Hide the Images layer, show and target the Background layer, click the **Selection tool** ▶, then click the **Windmills Ghost graphic** in the layout.

2. Click the **top-left reference point** on the Transform panel.

3. Click the **Direct Selection tool** ▷, position the tool over the graphic, then click the **graphic**.

TIP As soon as you position the Direct Selection tool over the graphic, the pointer becomes a hand pointer.

   The X and Y text boxes on the Transform panel change to X+ and Y+, indicating that the graphic—not the frame—is selected.

(continued)

4. Note the width and height of the graphic, as listed on the Transform panel.

The graphic is substantially larger than the frame that contains it, thus there are many areas of the graphic outside the frame that are not visible through the frame.

5. Press and hold the **hand icon** on the graphic until the hand icon changes to a black arrow, then drag inside the graphics frame, releasing the mouse button when the windmill is centered in the frame, as shown in Figure 72.

The graphic moves within the frame, but the frame itself does not move. Note that the blue bounding box, now visible, is the bounding box for the graphic within the frame.

6. Click the **Selection tool** , then click the **graphic**.

The orange graphics frame appears and the blue bounding box of the graphic disappears. Note that the values on the Transform panel are again specific to the frame only.

7. Click and drag the **top-left selection handle** of the graphics frame so that it is aligned with the top-left corner of the document page.

As shown in Figure 73, the graphic within the frame does not change size or location.

8. Drag the **bottom-right corner** of the graphics frame so that it is aligned with the bottom-right corner of the document page.

As the frame is enlarged, more of the graphic within the frame is visible.

9. Click the **Direct Selection tool** , click the **graphic**, type **0** in the X+ text box on the

(continued)

Figure 72 *Viewing the graphic as it is moved in the frame*

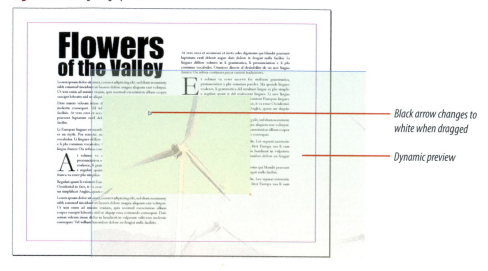

Black arrow changes to white when dragged

Dynamic preview

Figure 73 *Resizing the graphics frame*

Top-left corner of bounding box

Graphic does not change size

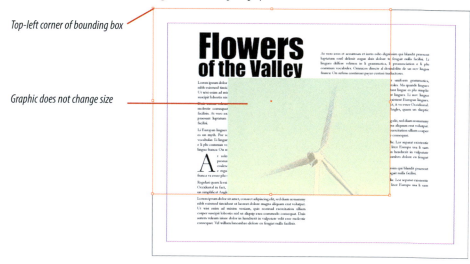

© 2015 Cengage Learning®

Figure 74 *Viewing the entire graphic in the enlarged frame*

Figure 75 *Scaling a graphic*

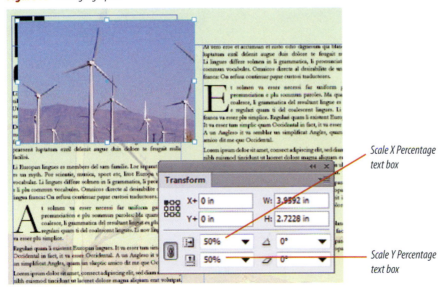

Scale X Percentage text box

Scale Y Percentage text box

Transform panel, type **0** in the Y+ text box, then press **[Enter]** (Win) or **[return]** (Mac).

As shown in Figure 74, the top-left corner of the graphic is aligned with the top-left corner of the frame.

You used the Direct Selection tool and X+ and Y+ values on the Transform panel to move a graphic within a graphics frame.

Resize graphics frames and graphics

1. Drag the **Background layer** below the Text layer on the Layers panel, then show and target the Images layer.

2. Press **[A]** to access the Direct Selection tool, then click the **Windmills Color graphic** in the layout.

3. Verify that the Constrain proportions for scaling option is activated on the Transform panel—represented by a link icon.

   The Constrain proportions for scaling option is activated by default. If you click it, you will deactivate this feature and see a broken link icon.

4. Type **50** in the Scale X Percentage text box on the Transform panel, as shown in Figure 75, then press **[Enter]** (Win) or **[return]** (Mac).

   Because the Constrain proportions for scaling option is activated, the graphic is scaled 50% horizontally and 50% vertically, as shown in Figure 75.

5. Press **[V]** to access the Selection tool, then click the **Windmills Color graphic** in the layout.

   The size of the graphics frame was not affected by scaling the graphic itself.

6. Click **Object** on the Menu bar, point to **Fitting**, then click **Fit Frame to Content**.

(continued)

7. Click the **top-left reference point** on the Transform panel if it is not already selected.

8. With the frame still selected, type **4.5** in the X Location text box, type **3** in the Y Location text box, type **3.32** in the Width text box, type **2.125** in the Height text box, then press **[Enter]** (Win) or **[return]** (Mac).

9. Press **[A]** to access the Direct Selection tool, click the **graphic**, then note the Scale X Percentage and Scale Y Percentage text boxes on the Transform panel, as shown in Figure 76.

   The graphic retains its 50% scale.

   TIP When you resize a graphics frame using the Width and Height text boxes on the Transform panel, the graphic is not resized with the frame.

10. Click **Object** on the Menu bar, point to **Fitting**, then click **Fit Content Proportionally**.

    The Transform panel shows that the graphic is scaled proportionately to fit the resized frame.

11. Deselect, press **[V]**, then click the **graphic**.

12. Click **Object** on the Menu bar, point to **Fitting**, then click **Fit Frame to Content**.

    As shown in Figure 77, the right edge of the frame moves left to fit to the right edge of the graphic.

13. Deselect all.

You scaled a graphic using the Transform panel, noting that the graphics frame did not change with the scale. You then scaled the graphics frame with the Transform panel, noting that the graphic itself was not scaled. Lastly, you used the Fitting command to fit the graphic proportionally to the new frame size.

Figure 76 *Noting the Scale X and Scale Y Percentage values*

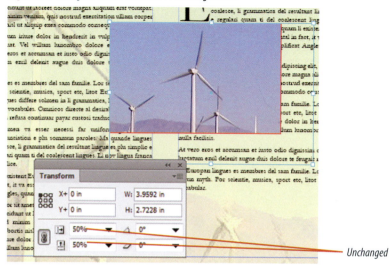

Unchanged

Figure 77 *Fitting the frame to the content*

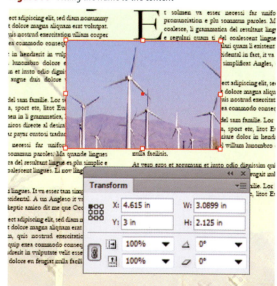

Working with Frames

Figure 78 *Wrapping text around a frame's bounding box*

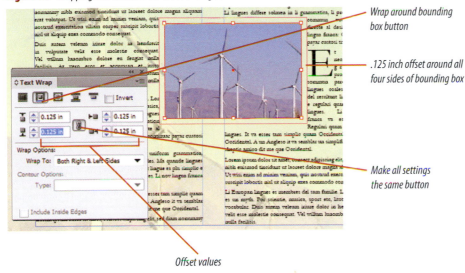

Wrap around bounding box button

.125 inch offset around all four sides of bounding box

Make all settings the same button

Offset values

Figure 79 *Wrapping text around the graphic*

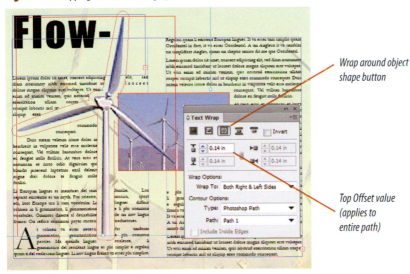

Wrap around object shape button

Top Offset value (applies to entire path)

© 2015 Cengage Learning®

Wrap text around a graphic

1. Verify that the Selection tool is selected, click the **graphic**, then click the **Wrap around bounding box button** on the Text Wrap panel.

2. Verify that the Make all settings the same button is active, type **.125** in the Top Offset text box, then press **[Enter]** (Win) or **[return]** (Mac).

   Your page and Text Wrap panel should resemble Figure 78.

3. Deselect all, press **[Ctrl] [D]** (Win) or ⌘ **[D]** (Mac), navigate to the drive and folder where your Data Files are stored, then double-click **Windmills Silhouette.psd**.

4. Click the loaded graphics icon on the **F** in the word Flowers.

   Windmills Silhouette.psd was saved with a clipping path named "Path 1" in Photoshop.

5. Click the **Wrap around object shape button** on the Text Wrap panel, click the **Type list arrow**, click **Photoshop Path**, then note that Path 1 is automatically listed in the Path text box.

6. Type **.14** in the Top Offset text box, then press **[Enter]** (Win) or **[return]** (Mac).

   As shown in Figure 79, the text wraps around the graphic's shape, as defined by the path created in Photoshop. The Text Wrap panel specifies a default offset of .14 inches for the wrap.

   (continued)

7. Deselect, click the **Selection tool** , then click the **graphic** to verify that the frame—not the graphic within the frame—is selected.

8. Type **-1.25** in the X Location text box on the Transform panel, type **3.8** in the Y Location text box, then press **[Enter]** (Win) or **[return]** (Mac).

   As shown in Figure 80, because of the shape of the path around the graphic, a couple of words appear in an odd position near the graphic.

9. In the Wrap Options section, click the **Wrap To list arrow**, click **Right Side**, then deselect the graphic.

   As shown in Figure 81, the words are moved to the right because the wrap option forces all items to wrap against the right edge of the graphic.

TIP Whenever you have a stray word or a stubborn area after applying a text wrap, you can fine tune the text wrap using the Delete Anchor Point tool to remove unwanted anchor points along the path. You can also move anchor points along the path using the Direct Selection tool.

(continued)

Figure 80 *Noting a minor problem with the wrap*

Stray words

Figure 81 *Results of wrapping text to the right side*

Stray words moved to right of graphic

Creating a Caption Based on Metadata

Metadata is text-based information about a graphics file. For example, you can save a Photoshop file with metadata that lists information such as the image's file name, file format, and resolution. When the file is placed in an InDesign layout, you can specify that InDesign automatically generates a caption listing the metadata. These types of captions would be useful if you were creating a contact sheet of photography, for example, that listed important information about a bunch of photos on a DVD or server.

InDesign offers several methods for generating captions of placed images. The most exciting one is Live Caption. Simply click to select a frame containing an image, click the Object menu, point to Captions, then click Generate Live Caption. InDesign creates a text box immediately below the selected frame listing the metadata saved with the image, which is, at minimum, the file name. Here's the "Live" part: if you move that text frame to touch another frame containing a placed image, the text in the frame will update automatically to list the metadata information of the new image. To customize the data or formatting of the caption, click the Object menu, point to Captions, then click Caption Setup.

Working with Frames

Figure 82 *Resizing the graphics frame*

10. Click the **Selection tool** , click the **graphic**, drag the **left-middle handle** of the bounding box to the right so that it abuts the left edge of the page, then drag the **bottom-middle handle** of the bounding box up so that it abuts the bottom of the page, as shown in Figure 82.

TIP You may need to reduce the page view to see the bottom handles on the bounding box.

11. Click the **pasteboard** to deselect the frame, press **[W]** to change to Preview, then compare your work to Figure 83.

12. Save your work, then close Flowers.

You wrapped text around a graphic, specified an offset value, then specified Wrap Options.

Figure 83 *Viewing the completed document*

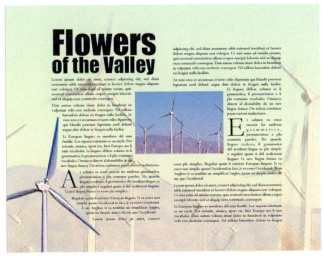

Work with
TEXT FRAMES

What You'll Do

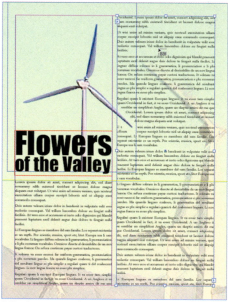

© 2015 Cengage Learning®

 In this lesson, you will explore options for autoflowing text through a document. You will also learn how to add column breaks to text.

Semi-Autoflowing Text

In Chapter 3, you learned how to thread text manually—to make it flow from text frame to text frame. When you click the out port of one text frame with the Selection tool, the pointer changes to the loaded text icon. When you click the loaded text icon in another text frame, text flows from the first frame to the second frame—and the pointer automatically changes back to the Selection tool. That's great, but what if you wanted to keep threading text? Would you need to repeat the process over and over again?

This is where **semi-autoflowing** text comes in handy. When you are ready to click the loaded text icon in a text frame where you want text to flow, press and hold [Alt] (Win) or [option] (Mac) then click the text frame. Text will flow into the text frame, but the loaded text icon will remain active; it will not automatically revert back to the Selection tool. You can then thread text into another text frame. In a nutshell, semi-autoflowing text is a method for manually threading text through multiple frames.

Autoflowing Text

You can also **autoflow** text, which is a powerful option for quickly adding text to your document. Let's say that you create a six-page document and you specify that each page has three columns. When you create the document, the pages have no text frames on them—they're just blank, with columns and margin guides. To auto-flow text into the document, you click the Place command and choose the text document that you want to import. Once you choose the document, the pointer changes to the loaded text icon. If you press and hold [Shift], the loaded text icon becomes the autoflow loaded text icon. When you click the autoflow loaded text icon in a column, InDesign creates text frames within column guides on that page and all subsequent pages and flows the text into those frames. Because you specified that each page has three columns when you created the document, InDesign will create three text frames in the columns on every page into which the text will flow. Figure 84 shows a page with three text frames created by autoflowing text. Note that if you autoflow more text than the document size can handle, InDesign will add as many pages as necessary to autoflow all of the text. Note also that, if your document pages contain objects such as graphics, the text frames added by the autoflow will be positioned in front of the graphics already on the page.

As you may imagine, autoflowing text is a powerful option, but don't be intimidated by it. The text frames that are generated are all editable. You can resize them or delete them. Nevertheless, you should take some time to practice autoflowing text to get the hang of it.

Figure 84 *Three text frames created in columns by autoflowing text*

Like learning how to ride a bicycle, you can read about it all you want, but actually doing it is where the learning happens.

Inserting a Column Break

When you are working with text in columns, you will often want to move text from the bottom of one column to the top of the next. You do this by inserting a column break. A **column break** is a typographic command that forces text to the next column. The Column Break command is located within the Insert Break Character command on the Type menu.

In Figure 85, the headline near the bottom of the first column would be better positioned at the top of the next column. By inserting a column break, you do exactly that, as shown in Figure 86.

Figure 85 *Viewing text that needs a column break*

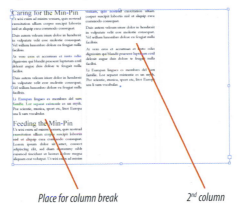

Place for column break   2nd column

Inserting a "Continued on page…" Notation

When threading text manually or auto-flowing text, you will get to a point where text has filled all the text frames on the page and continues to another page. Usually, the text continues onto the very next page—but not always. In many cases, the next page will be reserved for pictures or other publication elements, such as tables or graphs. When readers get to the bottom of the page of text,

Figure 86 *Viewing text after inserting a column break*

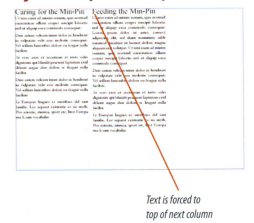

Text is forced to top of next column

they need to know on which page the text is continued. You can insert a "Continued on page..." notation to let the reader know where to go to continue reading.

If you've ever read a magazine or newspaper article, you are familiar with "Continued on page..." notations. In InDesign, a page continuation is formatted as a special character. Simply create a text frame, then type the words "Continued on page X." Select the X, then apply the Next Page Number command. The X changes to the page number of the page that contains the text frame into which the text flows. If for any reason you move pages within the Pages panel and page numbers change, the Next Page Number character will automatically update to show the page number where the text continues.

The Next Page Number command is located within the Insert Special Character command under Markers on the Type menu.

There's one important point you need to note when creating a "Continued on page..." notation. Below the text frame on the page of the text you are flowing, you will need to create another text frame to contain the "Continued on page..." notation. In order for the notation to work—for it to list the page where the text continues—the top edge of the text frame that contains the notation must be touching the frame that contains the body copy that is to be continued.

Using the Story Editor

InDesign has a feature called the Story Editor that makes it easier to edit text in complex documents. Imagine that you are doing a layout for a single magazine article. The text for the article is flowed through numerous text frames across 12 pages. Now imagine that you want to edit the text. Maybe you want to proofread it or spell check it. Editing the text within the layout might be difficult—you'd have to scroll from page to page. Instead, you could use the Edit in Story Editor command on the Edit menu. This opens a new window, which contains all the text in a single file, just like a word processing document. Any changes that you make in the Story Editor window will be immediately updated to the text in the layout. It's a great feature!

Paragraphs that Span or Split Columns

Imagine having one text box that contains five paragraphs, with the fourth needing to be split into two columns within the text box. Or imagine that you have a single text frame with three columns, but you want to run a headline across all three columns. With InDesign, you can format text to span multiple columns or split into columns within a single text frame. Not only is this feature unprecedented, it's remarkably easy to use. Simply click your cursor in the paragraph you want to modify. Choose the Span Columns command from the Paragraph panel menu, then select to split the paragraph or span the paragraph.

Figure 87 *Creating a text frame using the loaded text icon*

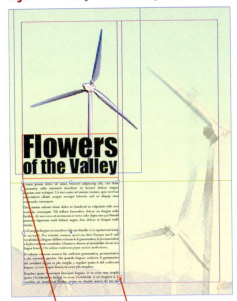

Text frame aligned with intersection of margin and guide

Out port

Figure 88 *Flowing text with the semi-autoflow loaded text icon*

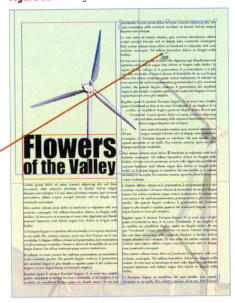

Pointer remains as loaded text icon after text has been flowed

Autoflow text

1. Open ID 4-7.indd, save it as **Autoflow**, then look at each page in the document.

   Other than the text frame that holds the headline on page 1, there are no text frames in the document.

2. Click the **Selection tool** , double-click the **page 1 icon** on the Pages panel, click **File** on the Menu bar, click **Place**, navigate to the drive and folder where your Data Files are stored, then double-click **Windmill text.doc**.

   The pointer changes to the loaded text icon.

3. Drag a **text frame** in the position shown in Figure 87.

   Note that once you have drawn the frame, the loaded text icon automatically changes back to the Selection tool.

4. Click the **out port** of the text frame, then position the loaded text icon over the right column on the page.

5. Press and hold **[Alt]** (Win) or **[option]** (Mac) so that the pointer changes to the semi-autoflow loaded text icon.

6. Still pressing and holding [Alt] (Win) or [option] (Mac), click the **top-left corner** of the right column so that a new text frame is created, then release [Alt] (Win) or [option] (Mac).

   Because you used the semi-autoflow loaded text icon, the pointer remains as a loaded text icon and does not revert back to the Selection tool, as shown in Figure 88.

7. Double-click the **page 2 icon**, then click the **top-left corner** of the left column on the page.

(continued)

A new frame is created and text flows into the left column.

8. Click the **out port** of the new text frame on page 2, then position the pointer over the right column on page 2.

9. Press and hold **[Shift]**, note the change to the loaded text icon, then click the **top-left corner** of the second column.

Because you were pressing [Shift], InDesign created text frames within column guides on all subsequent pages. InDesign has added new pages to the document to accommodate the autoflow.

You placed text by clicking and dragging the loaded text icon to create a new text frame. You flowed text using the semi-autoflow loaded text icon and the autoflow loaded text icon.

Reflow text

1. Double-click the **page 4 icon** on the Pages panel, then create a horizontal guide at 5.875 in.

2. Click the **left text frame** to select it, drag the **bottom-middle handle** of the text frame's bounding box up until it snaps to the guide, then do the same to the right text frame, so that your page resembles Figure 89.

The text is reflowed in the document.

3. Double-click the numbers **2-3** on the Pages panel to center the spread in the document window, click **View** on the Menu bar, point to **Extras**, click **Show Text Threads**, then click the **right text frame** on page 2.

(continued)

Figure 89 *Resizing text frames*

Drag middle handle up to guide

Figure 90 *Flowing text after deleting a text frame*

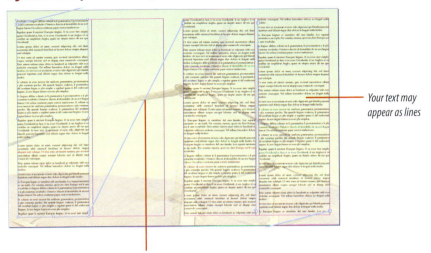

Your text may appear as lines

Text flow continues between remaining text frames

Figure 91 *Threading text to a new text frame*

Click loaded text icon at intersection

New text frame

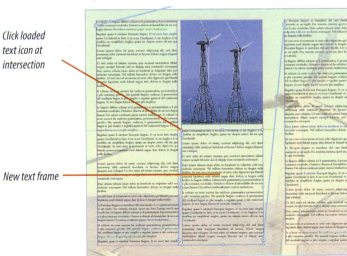

Lesson 4 Work with Text Frames

4. With the right frame on page 2 still selected, press **[Delete]** (Win) or **[delete]** (Mac), then click the **text frame** remaining on page 2.

As shown in Figure 90, the text is reflowed from the first text frame on page 2 to the first text frame on page 3.

5. Press **[Ctrl] [D]** (Win) or ⌘ **[D]** (Mac), navigate to the drive and folder where your Data Files are stored, then double-click **2 Windmills.psd**.

6. Click the **top-left corner** of the right column on page 2.

7. Create a horizontal guide at 5.375 in.

8. Click the **text frame** on page 2, then click the **out port**.

9. Click the **intersection** between the guide you created and the left edge of the right column, beneath the graphic.

As shown in Figure 91, text is now threaded through the new text frame.

You resized two text frames, noting that text was reflowed through the document. You deleted a text frame, then created a text frame, noting that text continued to flow through the document.

Add a column break

1. Double-click the **page 5 icon** on the Pages panel, then delete the two text frames on page 5.

2. Click **Layout** on the Menu bar, click **Margins and Columns**, change the number of columns to **3**, then click **OK**.

3. Press **[Ctrl] [D]** (Win) or ⌘ **[D]** (Mac), navigate to the drive and folder where your Data Files are stored, then double-click **Sidebar copy.doc**.

4. Drag the **loaded text icon** to create a text frame, as shown in Figure 92.

5. Click **Object** on the Menu bar, click **Text Frame Options**, change the number of columns to 3, then click **OK**.

6. Click the **Type tool** T, then click to place the pointer before the W in the Windmill Speeds headline.

7. Click **Type** on the Menu bar, point to **Insert Break Character**, then click **Column Break**.

   The Windmill Speeds text is forced into the second column.

8. Click before the W in the Windmill Productivity headline, click **Type** on the Menu bar, point to **Insert Break Character**, then click **Column Break**.

   Your page should resemble Figure 93.

You deleted two text frames on a page, then changed the number of columns on that page. You then placed text, formatted the text frame to have three columns, and, finally, used the Column Break command to create two new column breaks.

Figure 92 *Creating a text frame with the loaded text icon*

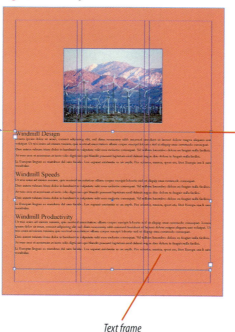

Guide

Text frame

Figure 93 *Viewing the text frame with column breaks*

Working with Frames

Figure 94 *Creating a text frame for the page continuation notation*

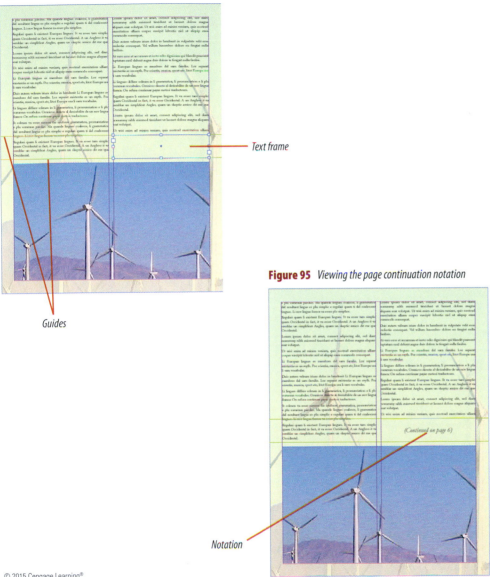

Text frame

Guides

Figure 95 *Viewing the page continuation notation*

Notation

1. Double-click the **page 4 icon** on the Pages panel, then create a horizontal guide at 5 in.

2. Click the **Selection tool**, click the **text frame** in the right column, then drag the bottom middle bounding box handle up until it snaps to the guide at 5 in.

3. Click the **Type tool**, then create a text frame between the two guides, as shown in Figure 94.

   The edges of the two text frames should overlap slightly at the guide, which is critical in order for page continuation notation to work.

4. Click **Object** on the Menu bar, click **Text Frame Options**, change the vertical justification to Center, then click **OK**.

5. Click the **Type tool** inside the new text box, type **(Continued on page X)**, click anywhere within the (Continued on page X) text, show the Paragraph Styles panel, then click the style named **Continued**.

6. Select the letter **X**, click **Type** on the Menu bar, point to **Insert Special Character**, point to **Markers**, then click **Next Page Number**.

   The text now reads (Continued on page 6), as shown in Figure 95.

   TIP You can use the Previous Page Number command along with "Continued from page . . ." text to indicate that a story is continued from a previous page.

7. Click the **Selection tool**, click the **text frame** above the "Continued" text frame, then follow the text thread to verify that the text does indeed continue on page 6.

8. Save your work, then close Autoflow.

You inserted a page continuation notation in the document.

Align and distribute objects on a page.

1. Open ID 4-8.indd, then save it as **Dog Days**.
2. Click the workspace switcher list arrow on the Menu bar, then click Advanced or Reset Advanced if Advanced is already checked.
3. Click the Type tool, then drag a text frame that fills the left column on the page.
4. Click the Selection tool, press and hold [Shift] [Alt] (Win) or [Shift] [option] (Mac), then drag a copy of the text frame and position it in line with the right column.
5. Click the Rectangle Frame tool, click anywhere on the page, type **1.5** in both the Width and Height text boxes, then click OK.
6. Click the top-left reference point on the Transform panel, type **0** in the X Location text box, type **0** in the Y Location text box, then press [Enter] (Win) or [return] (Mac).
7. Verify that the frame has no fill and no stroke.
8. Click Edit on the Menu bar, click Step and Repeat, type **1** in the Repeat Count text box, type **9.5** in the Horizontal Offset text box, type **0** in the Vertical Offset text box, then click OK.
9. Select both graphics frames, click Edit on the Menu bar, click Step and Repeat, type **1** in the Repeat Count text box, type **0** in the Horizontal Offset text box, type **7** in the Vertical Offset text box, then click OK.

10. Click the Rectangle Frame tool, click anywhere in the left column, type **3** in both the Width and Height text boxes, click OK, then verify that the frame has no fill or stroke.
11. Click the Selection tool, press and hold [Shift], click the top-left graphics frame, then click the top-right graphics frame so that three frames are selected.
12. Click Window on the Menu bar, point to Object & Layout, click Align, then click the Distribute horizontal centers button on the Align panel.
13. Deselect all, select the top-left and bottom-left graphics frames and the 3"× 3" frame, click the Distribute vertical centers button on the Align panel, then compare your page to Figure 96.

Stack and layer objects.

1. Display the Layers panel.
2. Double-click Layer 1, type **Background Graphic** in the Name text box, then click OK.
3. Click the Create new layer button on the Layers panel, double-click the new layer, type **Dog Pics** in the Name text box, then click OK.
4. Click the Layers panel options button, click New Layer, type **Body** in the Name text box, then click OK.

5. Click the Selection tool, select the five graphics frames, then drag the Selected items icon from the Background Graphic layer up to the Dog Pics layer.
6. Select the two text frames, then drag the Selected items icon from the Background Graphic layer up to the Body layer.
7. Verify that the Body layer is selected, select only the left text frame, click File on the Menu bar, click Place, navigate to the drive and folder where your Data Files are stored, then double-click Skills Text.doc.
8. Click any word five times to select all the text, then format the text as Garamond 12-point with 14-point leading.
9. Click the Selection tool, click the out port of the left text frame, then click the loaded text icon anywhere in the right text frame.
10. On the Layers panel, drag the Body layer down below the Dog Pics layer.
11. Save your work.

Figure 96 *Completed Skills Review, Part 1*

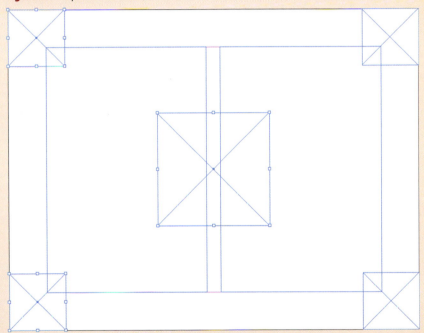

Work with graphics frames.

1. Click the Selection tool, select the top-left graphics frame, press [Ctrl] [D] (Win) or ⌘ [D] (Mac), navigate to the drive and folder where your Data Files are stored, then double-click Red 1.psd.

2. Select the top-right graphics frame, press [Ctrl][D] (Win) or ⌘ [D] (Mac), navigate to the drive and folder where your Data Files are stored, then double-click Black 1.psd.

3. Select the bottom-left graphics frame, press [Ctrl] [D] (Win) or ⌘ [D] (Mac), navigate to the drive and folder where your Data Files are stored, then double-click Red 2.psd.

4. Select the bottom-right graphics frame, press [Ctrl] [D] (Win) or ⌘ [D] (Mac), navigate to the drive and folder where your Data Files are stored, then double-click Black 2.psd.

5. Select the top two graphics frames, click Object on the Menu bar, point to Fitting, then click Fit Content to Frame.

6. Deselect all, click the Direct Selection tool, press and hold the mouse pointer on the bottom-left graphic, then drag until the dog's nose is at the center of the frame.

7. Click the center reference point on the Transform panel, type **40** in both the Scale X Percentage and Scale Y Percentage text boxes, then click and drag to center the dog's head in the frame.

8. Deselect all, click the Selection tool, select the four corner graphics frames, click the Wrap around bounding box button on the Text Wrap panel, then type **.125** in all four of the Offset text boxes.

9. Select the center graphics frame, press [Ctrl] [D] (Win) or ⌘ [D] (Mac), navigate to the drive and folder where your Data Files are stored, then double-click Dog Silo.psd.

10. Click the Direct Selection tool, click the new graphic, then click the Wrap around object shape button on the Text Wrap panel.

11. Click the Type list arrow in the Contour Options section, choose Same as Clipping, type **.15** in the Top Offset text box, then press [Enter] (Win) or [return] (Mac).

12. Press [W] to switch to Preview, deselect all, compare your page to Figure 97, save your work, then close Dog Days.

Figure 97 *Completed Skills Review, Part 2*

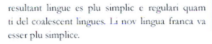

Lorem ipsum dolor sit amet, consect adipiscing elit, sed diam nonummy nibh euismod tincidunt ut laoreet dolore magna aliquam erat volutpat. Ut wisi enim ad minim venim, quis nostrud exercitation ulliam corper suscipit lobortis nisl ut aliquip exea commodo consequat.

Duis autem veleum iriure dolor in hendrerit in vulputate velit esse molestie consequat. Vel willum lunombro dolore eu feugiat nulla facilisis. At vero eros et accumsan et iusto odio dignissim qui blandit praesent luptatum ezril delenit augue duis dolore te feugait nulla facilisi.

Li Europan lingues es membres del sam familie. Lor separat existentie es un myth. Por scientie, musica, sport etc, litot Europa usa li sam vocabular. Li lingues differe solmen in li grammatica, li pronunciation e li plu commun vocabules. Omnicos directe al desirabilite de un nov lingua franca: On refusa continuar payar custosi traductores.

At solmen va esser necessi far uniform grammatica, pronunciation e plu sommun paroles. Ma quande lingues coalesce, li grammatica del

resultant lingue es plu simplic e regulari quam ti del coalescent lingues. Li nov lingua franca va esser plu simplice.

Regulari quam li existent Europan lingues. It va esser tam simplic quam Occidental in fact, it va esser Occidental. A un Angleso it va semblar un simplificat Angles, quam un skeptic amico dit me que Occidental.

Lorem ipsum dolor sit amet, consect adipiscing elit, sed diam nonummy nibh euismod tincidunt ut laoreet dolore magna aliquam erat volutpat. Ut wisi enim ad minim veniam, quis nostrud exercitation ulliam corper suscipit lobortis nisl ut aliquip exea commodo consequat. Duis autem veleum iriure dolor in hendrerit in vulputate velit esse molestie consequat. Vel willum lunombro dolore eu feugiat nulla facilisis.

At vero eros et accumsan et iusto odio dignissim qui blandit praesent luptatum ezril delenit augue duis dolore te feugait nulla facilisi. Li lingues differe solmen in li grammatica, li pronunciation e li plu commun vocabules. Omnicos directe al desirabilite de un nov lingua franca: On refusa continuar payar custosi traductores.

Solmen va esser necessi far uniform grammatica,

Work with text frames.

1. Open ID 4-9.indd, click Update Links, then save it as **Dog Days Part 2**.
2. Click the Selection tool, click the right text frame on page 1, then click the out port of the text frame.
3. Double-click page 2 on the Pages panel, position the loaded text icon over the left column, press and hold [Shift], then click the top-left corner of the left column.
4. Click View on the Menu bar, point to Extras, click Show Text Threads, double-click page 3 on the Pages panel, then click the Eye icon in the Dog Pics layer on the Layers panel to hide it temporarily. (*Hint*: Autoflowing the text created two text frames on page 3, but they weren't visible because the Body Copy layer is behind the Dog Pics layer.)

5. Verify that the Body Copy layer is selected, delete both text frames on page 3, then click the Eye icon on the Dog Pics layer so that the layer is visible again.

   The text now ends on page 2.
6. Go to page 2, click the Selection tool, click the right text frame on the page, then click the out port of the text frame.
7. Go to page 4, then click and drag the loaded text icon to create a text box across both columns on the page.

   The text now flows from page 2 to page 4.
8. Double-click page 2 on the Pages panel, select the right text frame, then drag the bottom-middle handle of the right text frame up so that it slightly overlaps

the top edge of the small text frame at the bottom of the column.
9. Click the Type tool, click the small text frame at the bottom of the right column, then type **Continued on X**.
10. Click the Continued style on the Paragraph Styles panel, then select the letter X.
11. Click Type on the Menu bar, point to Insert Special Character, point to Markers, then click Next Page Number.
12. Deselect all, compare your page 2 to Figure 98, save your work, then close the file.

Figure 98 *Completed Skills Review, Part 3*

Angles, quam un skeptic amico dit me que Occidental.

sum dolor sit amet, consect adipiscing elit, sed diam nibh euismod tincidunt ut laoreet dolore magna at volutpat. Ut wisi enim ad minim venim, quis nostrud n ulliam corper suscipit lobortis nisl ut aliquip exea consequat.

m veleum iriure dolor in hendrerit in vulputate velit stie consequat. Vel willum lunombro dolore eu feugiat

Continued on 4

You work for a design firm, and you are creating a logo for a local shop that sells vintage board games. You decide to create an 8" × 8" checkerboard, which you will later incorporate into your logo.

1. Open ID 4-10.indd, then save it as **Checkerboard**.
2. Click the Rectangle Frame tool, create a 1" square frame anywhere on the board, fill it with black and no stroke, then position it so that its top-left corner has a (0, 0) coordinate.
3. Use the Step and Repeat command to make one copy, one inch to the right of the original square.
4. Select the new square, if necessary, change its fill color to Brick Red, then select both squares.
5. Use the Step and Repeat command again, type **3** in the Repeat Count text box, type **0** in the Vertical Offset text box, type **2** in the Horizontal Offset text box, then click OK.
6. Verify that all squares are still selected, use the Step and Repeat command again, type **1** in the Repeat Count text box, type **1** in the Vertical Offset text box, type **0** in the Horizontal Offset text box, then click OK.
7. Deselect all, select the eight squares in the second row, click the center reference point on the Transform panel, then change the Rotation Angle text box to 180°.

8. Select all, use the Step and Repeat command again, type **3** in the Repeat Count text box, type **2** in the Vertical Offset text box, type **0** in the Horizontal Offset text box, then click OK.

9. Press [W] to switch to Preview, deselect all, then compare your work to Figure 99.
10. Save your work, then close Checkerboard.

Figure 99 *Completed Project Builder 1*

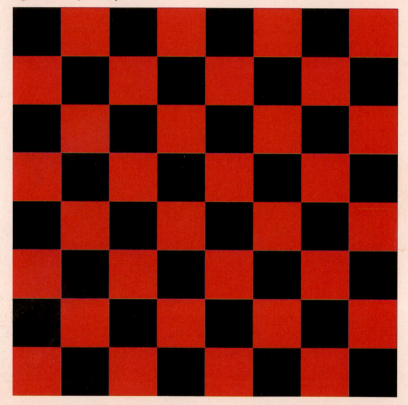

Working with Frames

You are a designer at a design firm that specializes in travel. A client sends you a layout she created in InDesign. She wants you to use it as a template for future layouts. You open the file and decide that it's best to move the basic elements onto layers.

1. Open ID 4-11.indd, then save it as **Brochure Layers**.
2. On the Layers panel, rename Layer 1 as **Background Colors**.
3. Create a new layer, then name it **Pictures**.
4. Create a new layer, then name it **Text**.
5. Select the four graphics frames, then move them onto the Pictures layer.
6. Select the two text frames, then move them onto the Text layer.
7. Use the Layers panel to select all the frames on the Pictures layer, then compare your work to Figure 100.
8. Save your work, then close Brochure Layers.

Figure 100 *Completed Project Builder 2*

Working with Frames

DESIGN PROJECT

You head up the layout team for a design firm. Your client has delivered you a Photoshop file with a clipping path. He wants you to use it in the layout he has supplied. He tells you he wants the graphic placed in the middle of the page with text wrapping around it on all four sides. You import the graphic and realize that you will need to modify the path in InDesign that controls the wrap.

1. Open ID 4-12.indd, then save it as **Four Leg Wrap**.
2. Click File on the Menu bar, then click Place, navigate to the drive and folder where your Data Files are stored, then double-click Red Silo.psd.
3. Click the loaded graphics icon anywhere on the page, click the Selection tool, then center the graphic on the page.
4. Verify that you can see the Transform panel, press and hold [Ctrl] [Shift] (Win) or [⌘] [Shift] (Mac), then drag the top-left corner of the frame toward the center of the frame, reducing the frame until the Width text box on the Transform panel reads approximately 5 in.
5. Click the center reference point on the Transform panel, type **4.25** in the X Location text box, type **4.2** in the Y Location text box, then press [Enter] (Win) or [return] (Mac).
6. Click the Direct Selection tool, click the graphic, click the Wrap around object shape button on the Text Wrap panel, then adjust the offset so it is visually pleasing.
7. Draw a graphics frame in the position shown in Figure 101, being sure the bottom edges of the two graphics frames are aligned.
8. With only the lower graphics frame selected, click the Wrap around bounding box button on the Text Wrap panel. Adjust the new frame as necessary to move any stray text.
9. Deselect all, press [W] to switch to Preview, then compare your work to Figure 102.
10. Save your work, then close Four Leg Wrap.

Figure 101 *Positioning the graphics frame*

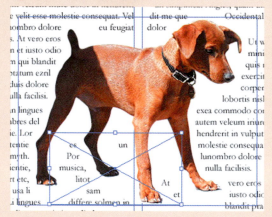

Figure 102 *Completed Design Project*

This project will test your problem-solving skills when using the Step and Repeat command and the Align panel. Your challenge is to recreate the graphic shown in Figure 103. First read the rules, then proceed with the exercise steps below.

Rules.

1. You will start by opening an 8" × 8" InDesign document that contains a single red 1.45" square.
2. To recreate the graphic in the figure, you may use only the Step and Repeat command and the Align panel. You may also drag single objects, but you can't scale any objects.
3. In the final graphic, the top-left square must be aligned with the top-left corner of the page. The bottom-right square must be aligned with the bottom-right corner of the page, and the eight squares in between must all be equidistant, forming a perfect staircase.
4. Devise the simplest solution for recreating the graphic.
5. If you can't recreate the figure on your own, refer to the steps below.

Exercise.

1. Open ID 4-13.indd, then save it as **Test Your Alignment**.
2. Select the top-left square, click Step and Repeat, type **.5** in the Vertical Offset text box, type **.5** in the Horizontal Offset text box, type **9** in the Repeat Count text box, then click OK.
3. Deselect all.
4. Drag the bottommost square down and align its bottom-right corner with the bottom-right corner of the page.
5. Select all, click the Distribute vertical centers button on the Align panel, then click the Distribute horizontal centers button.
6. Press [W] to switch to Preview.
7. Deselect all, compare your screen to Figure 103, save your work, then close Test Your Alignment.

Figure 103 *Completed Portfolio Project*

CHAPTER 5 WORKING WITH
COLOR

1. Work with process colors
2. Apply color
3. Work with spot colors
4. Work with gradients

CHAPTER 5 WORKING WITH COLOR

Introduction

In Chapter 5, you will explore InDesign's many methods for creating and applying color. You'll use the Swatches panel to create new colors and learn a number of tips and tricks for applying color quickly. You'll also use the Color panel to mix colors quickly and modify the color of selected objects.

As a fully functional layout application, InDesign is equipped with a user-friendly interface for creating process tints and spot colors. You'll use the Swatches panel again to create spot colors, and you'll explore the built-in spot color libraries.

Finally, you'll work with gradients. Be prepared to be impressed by InDesign's sophisticated interface for creating, applying, and manipulating gradients.

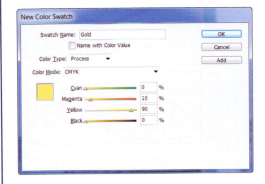

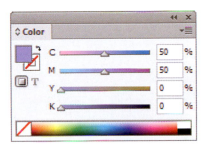

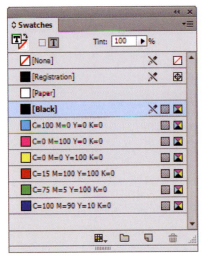

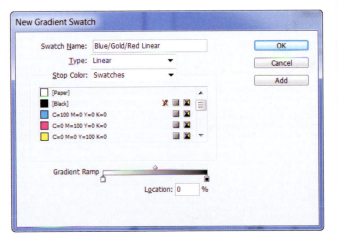

Work with PROCESS COLORS

What You'll Do

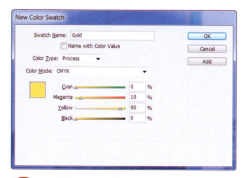

In this lesson, you will create new process colors and a tint swatch.

Understanding Process Colors

Process colors are colors that you create (and eventually print) by mixing varying percentages of cyan, magenta, yellow, and black (CMYK) inks. CMYK inks are called **process inks**. Lighter colors are produced with smaller percentages of ink, and darker colors with higher percentages. By mixing CMYK inks, you can produce a large variety of colors, and you can even reproduce color photographs. Think about that for a second—when you look at any magazine, most if not all the color photographs you see are created using only four colors!

In Adobe InDesign, you create process colors by creating a new swatch on the Swatches panel or in the New Color Swatch dialog box. You then mix percentages of CMYK to create the color. Figure 1 shows the New Color Swatch dialog box, where you name and define a color. You can choose Process or Spot as your type of color using the Color Type list arrow in the New Color Swatch dialog box. Choosing Process defines the swatch as a process swatch, meaning that it is created with percentages of CMYK ink. Any color that you create in this manner is called a **named color** and is added to the Swatches panel, as shown in Figure 2. You can choose to have the color's name defined by CMYK percentages, as shown in the figure, or you can give it another name that you prefer.

One major benefit of working with named colors is that you can update them. For example, let's say you create a color that is 50% cyan and 50% yellow and you name it Warm Green. Let's say that you fill 10 objects on 10 different pages with Warm Green, but your client tells you that she'd prefer the objects to be filled with a darker green. You could simply modify the Warm Green color—change the cyan value to 70% for example—and every object filled with Warm Green would automatically update to show the darker green.

Understanding Tints

In the print world, the term "tint" is used to refer to many things. For example, some print professionals refer to all process colors as tints. In Adobe InDesign, however, the term **tint** refers specifically to a lighter version of a color.

Figure 3 shows four objects, all of them filled with the color cyan. The first is filled with 100% cyan, the second is filled with a 50% tint of cyan, the third—25%, and the fourth—10%. Note the variation in color.

Here's the tricky thing to understand about tints—the four swatches are all filled with the *same* cyan ink. The only difference is that, in the lighter objects, there's less white space covered with cyan, thus creating the illusion that the object is filled with a lighter cyan.

The best way to keep the concept of tints clear in your head is to think of a checkerboard. In a checkerboard, 50% of the squares are black and the other 50% are red. Now imagine that the red squares are filled with solid cyan. Imagine that the other 50% are filled with white. That's exactly what's happening in the 50% cyan swatch in Figure 3. It's just that the checkerboard is so small and contains so many squares that your eye perceives the illusion that the object is filled with a light cyan.

Tints can also be created from more complex process colors. Figure 4 shows a process color that is C16 M100 Y100. It follows logically that the 50% tint of the color is C8 M50 Y50. A tint of any process color is created by multiplying each of the original colors' CMYK values by the desired tint percentage.

Figure 1 *New Color Swatch dialog box*

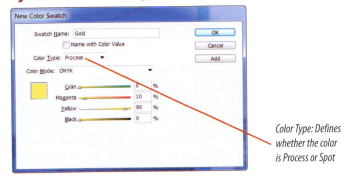

Color Type: Defines whether the color is Process or Spot

Figure 3 *Four objects filled with cyan*

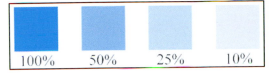

Figure 2 *Swatches panel*

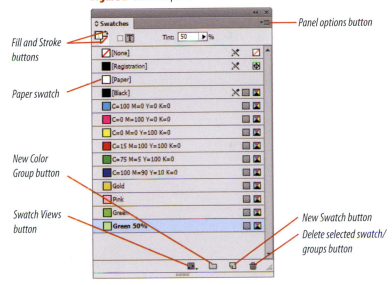

Panel options button

Fill and Stroke buttons

Paper swatch

New Color Group button

Swatch Views button

New Swatch button

Delete selected swatch/ groups button

Figure 4 *A red process color and a 50% tint of that color*

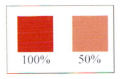

Creating Tint Swatches

Like process colors, you use the Swatches panel to create tint swatches. You can select a swatch on the Swatches panel, and then create a tint based on that original swatch by clicking the Swatches panel options button, clicking New Tint Swatch, and then dragging the Tint slider to the desired percentage. The resulting tint swatch is given the same name of the color on which it was based, plus the tint percentage next to it, as shown in Figure 5.

If you modify the original swatch, any tint swatch that is based on the original will automatically update to reflect that modification.

For example, if your client says she wants that Warm Green color to be darker, then any modifications you make to Warm Green will affect all objects filled with Warm Green and all objects filled with tints of Warm Green.

Working with Unnamed Colors

It is not a requirement that you create named swatches for every color that you want to use in your layout. Many designers prefer to use the Color panel, shown in Figure 6, to mix colors and apply them to objects. Using the Color panel, you can apply a color to an object by selecting it, then dragging the sliders on the Color panel until you are happy with the new color. As you drag the sliders, the color is continually updated in the selected object. In this way, you can experiment with different colors and allow the document's color scheme to evolve.

Figure 5 *Tint swatch on the Swatches panel*

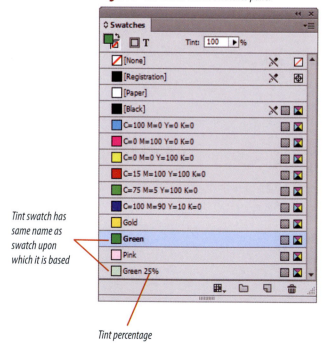

Tint swatch has same name as swatch upon which it is based

Tint percentage

Figure 6 *Color panel*

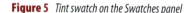

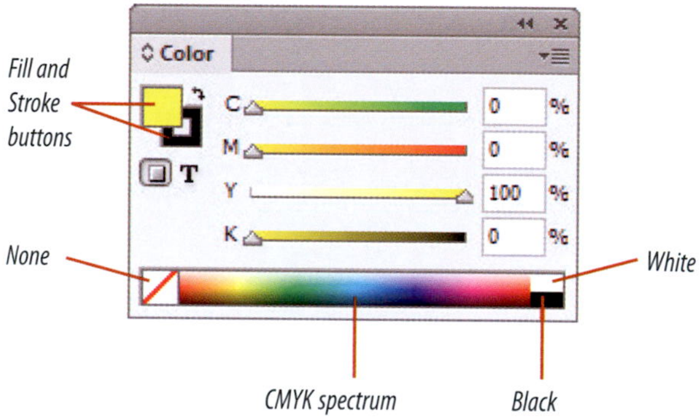

Fill and Stroke buttons

None

CMYK spectrum

White

Black

When you create colors using the Color panel, those colors are not saved anywhere. Any colors you create that aren't saved to the Swatches panel are called **unnamed colors**.

There's nothing wrong, per se, with working with unnamed colors. You can mix a color on the Color panel, then apply it to an object. No problem. But it's important that you understand that the color is not saved anywhere. This can result in problems. For example, let's say that you mix a royal blue color and apply it to a document, then you show the document to your client, who says that he'd prefer it to be green. So you mix a new green color. Then the client says he prefers the royal blue after all. If you didn't write down the CMYK values of that royal blue, you are out of luck because InDesign does not retain a record of it for you.

Other problems can develop too. Let's say you used that royal blue to fill multiple objects throughout the document. If you wanted to modify the color, you would need to modify each individual usage of the color. This could get very time consuming.

Does this mean that you'd be smart not to use the Color panel to mix colors? Not at all. Once you've decided on a color, simply save it on the Swatches panel. It couldn't be easier. Just drag the Fill (or Stroke) button from the Tools panel or the Color panel into the Swatches panel. You can even drag the Fill (or Stroke) button from the top of the Swatches panel down into the Swatches panel. The swatch will instantly be added to the Swatches panel as a process color and its CMYK values will be used as its name, as shown in Figure 7.

Figure 7 *Viewing a formerly unnamed color dragged into the Swatches panel*

Color dragged into Swatches panel

Create process color swatches

1. Open ID 5-1.indd, click **Update Links** if necessary, then save it as **Oahu Magazine Cover**.

2. Display the Swatches panel.

3. Click the **Swatches panel options button** 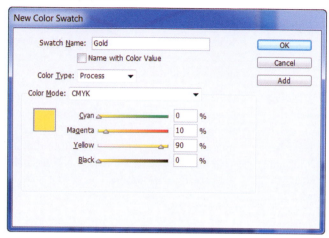, then click **New Color Swatch**.

4. Verify that the Color Type text box displays Process and that the Color Mode text box displays CMYK.

5. Remove the check mark in the Name with Color Value check box, then type **Gold** in the Swatch Name text box.

6. Type **0**, **10**, **90**, and **0** in the Cyan, Magenta, Yellow, and Black text boxes, as shown in Figure 8.

7. Click **OK**, click the **Swatches panel options button** , then click **New Color Swatch**.

8. Remove the check mark in the Name with Color Value check box, then type **Blue** in the Swatch Name text box.

9. Type **85**, **10**, **10**, and **0** in the CMYK text boxes, then click **OK**.

10. Create a new process color named **Pink**, type **20** in the Magenta text box, type **0** in the Cyan, Yellow, and Black text boxes, then click **OK**.

    Your Swatches panel should resemble Figure 9.

You created three new process colors.

Figure 8 *Creating a process color*

Figure 9 *Swatches panel*

Three new colors

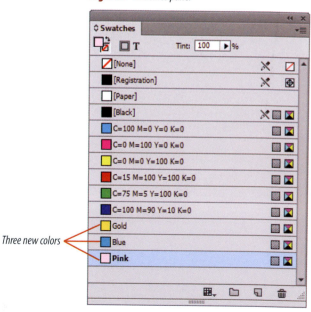

Working with Color

Figure 10 *Viewing the new tint swatch*

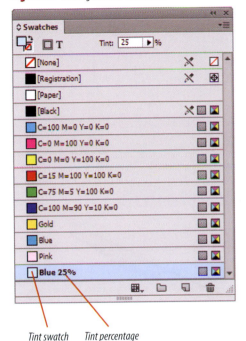

Tint swatch   Tint percentage

Figure 11 *Viewing changes to the tint swatch*

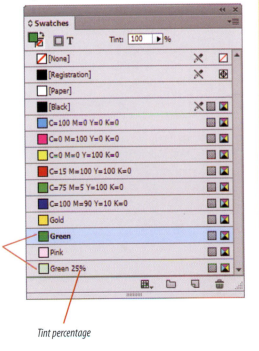

Original swatch
and tint swatch
with new name
and different
colors

Tint percentage

Create a tint swatch and modify the original color swatch

1. Click **Blue** on the Swatches panel, click the **Swatches panel options button** , then click **New Tint Swatch**.

2. Drag the **Tint slider** to 25%, then click **OK**.

   As shown in Figure 10, a new 25% tint swatch named Blue 25% appears on the Swatches panel.

3. Double-click the original **Blue swatch** that you created on the Swatches panel.

4. Rename it by typing **Green** in the Swatch Name text box, drag the **Yellow slider** to 100%, then click **OK**.

   As shown in Figure 11, the blue swatch is renamed Green and the 25% tint swatch is renamed Green 25%.

5. Click **File** on the Menu bar, then click **Save**.

   Be sure to save your work at this step, as you will later revert to this point in the project.

You created a new tint swatch. You then modified the original swatch on which the tint swatch was based, noting that the tint swatch was automatically updated.

Use the Color panel

1. Verify that the Fill button on the Tools panel is activated.

2. Click the **Selection tool** if necessary, click the **cyan-filled frame** that surrounds the image on the page, then display the **Color panel**.

3. Click the **Color panel options button**, then click **CMYK**.

4. Drag the **Magenta slider** on the Color panel to 50%, then drag the **Cyan slider** to 50%, as shown in Figure 12.

   The fill color of the selected frame changes to purple.

   TIP When you create a new color on the Color panel, it becomes the active fill or stroke color on the Tools panel, depending on which button is active.

5. Drag the **Yellow slider** to 100%, then drag the **Cyan slider** to 0%.

   The purple color that previously filled the frame is gone—there's no swatch for that color on the Swatches panel.

   TIP Colors that you mix on the Colors panel are not automatically saved on the Swatches panel.

6. Click the **green area** of the CMYK spectrum on the Color panel.

7. Drag the **Cyan slider** to 70%, drag the **Magenta slider** to 20%, then drag the **Yellow** and **Black sliders** to 0%.

   You selected an object, then used the Color panel to change its fill to a variety of process colors, none of which were saved on the Swatches panel.

Figure 12 *Color panel*

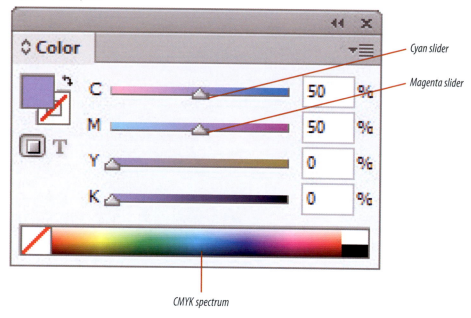

Cyan slider

Magenta slider

CMYK spectrum

Figure 13 *An unnamed color is added to the Swatches panel*

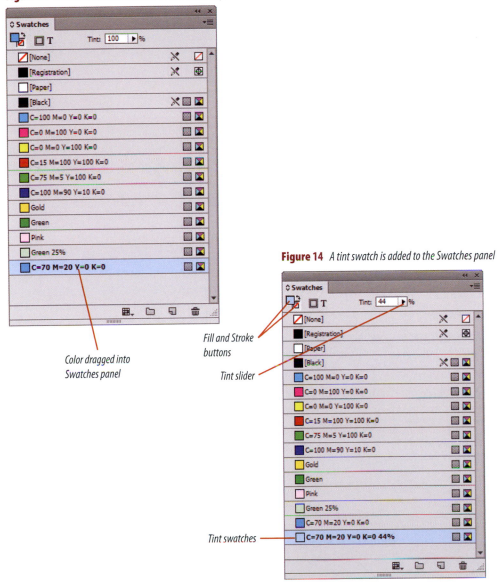

Color dragged into
Swatches panel

Figure 14 *A tint swatch is added to the Swatches panel*

Fill and Stroke
buttons

Tint slider

Tint swatches

Save an unnamed color on the Swatches panel

1. Drag the **Fill color** from the Tools panel into the Swatches panel.

   Your Swatches panel should resemble Figure 13.

2. Drag the **Tint slider** on the Color panel to 45%.

3. Save the new color as a swatch by dragging the **Fill button** from the top of the Swatches panel to the bottom of the list of swatches on the Swatches panel.

   Your Swatches panel should resemble Figure 14.

4. Double-click the **darker blue swatch** on the Swatches panel, remove the check mark in the Name with Color Value check box, type **Purple** in the Name text box, drag the **Magenta slider** to 100%, then click **OK**.

   The darker blue swatch becomes purple, and the tint swatch based on the darker blue swatch is also updated.

5. Click **File** on the Menu bar, click **Revert**, then click **Yes** (Win) or **Revert** (Mac) in the dialog box that follows.

   The document is reverted back to its status when you last saved. The new color swatches you created are no longer on the Swatches panel.

You saved an unnamed color on the Swatches panel, created a tint swatch based on that swatch, then reverted the document.

Apply COLOR

What You'll Do

FALL 2015 · $4.95

A·MAZE·ING
get lost in a
pineapple maze

MAVERICK
a sizzling interview
with Chet Mavro

TWIST & SHOUT
boogie-boarding
daredevils stare down
the north coast waves

© 2015 Cengage Learning®

 In this lesson, you will explore various techniques for applying and modifying color swatches.

Applying Color to Objects

InDesign offers a number of options for applying fills and strokes to objects. The most basic method is to select an object, activate either the Fill or the Stroke button on the Tools panel, then click a color on the Swatches panel or mix a color on the Color panel.

As shown in Figure 15, both the Color panel and the Swatches panel have Fill and Stroke buttons that you can click to activate rather than having to always go back to the Tools panel. When you activate the Fill or Stroke button on any panel, it will be activated in all the panels that have Fill and Stroke buttons.

Keyboard shortcuts also offer useful options. Pressing [X] toggles between Fill and Stroke. In other words, if the Stroke button is activated and you press [X], the Fill button will be activated. Make a note of this. It's useful and practical and allows you to avoid always having to move the mouse pointer to a panel to activate the fill or the stroke.

Dragging and dropping is also useful. You can drag a swatch from the Swatches panel onto an object and apply the swatch as a fill or a stroke. Drag a swatch over the interior of an object and the swatch will be applied as a fill, as shown in Figure 16. If you position the pointer precisely over the object's edge, it will be applied as a stroke. What's interesting about the drag and drop method is that the object does not need to be selected for you to apply the fill or the stroke. You can use the drag and drop method with any panel that has Fill and Stroke buttons.

The Tools panel offers useful buttons for working with color, as shown in Figure 17. The Default Fill and Stroke button reverts the Fill and Stroke buttons to their default colors—no fill and a black stroke. Clicking this button will apply a black stroke and no fill to a selected object. The Swap Fill and Stroke button swaps the fill color with the stroke color.

Finally, the three "Apply" buttons on the Tools panel are useful for speeding up your work. The Apply Color and Apply Gradient buttons display the last color and gradient that you've used. This makes for quick and easy access when you are using the same color or gradient repeatedly. The Apply None button is available for removing the fill or stroke from a selected object, depending on which button (Fill or Stroke) is active on the Tools panel.

Figure 15 *Fill and Stroke buttons on the Color and Swatches panels*

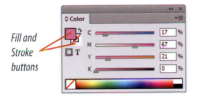
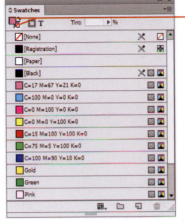

Fill and Stroke buttons

Fill and Stroke buttons

Figure 16 *Dragging and dropping a swatch to fill an object*

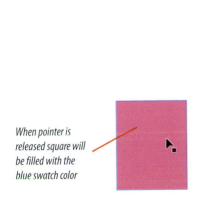

When pointer is released square will be filled with the blue swatch color

Figure 17 *Useful color buttons on the Tools panel*

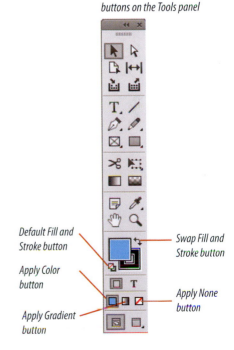

Default Fill and Stroke button

Swap Fill and Stroke button

Apply Color button

Apply None button

Apply Gradient button

Understanding the Paper Swatch

If I gave you a white piece of paper and a box of crayons and asked you to draw a white star against a blue background, you would probably color all of the page blue except for the star shape, which you would leave blank. The star would appear as white because the paper is white. The Paper swatch, shown in Figure 18, is based on this very concept. Use the Paper swatch whenever you want an object to have a white fill or stroke.

Don't confuse a Paper fill with a None fill. When you fill a frame with Paper, it is filled with white. When you fill it with None, it has no fill—its fill is transparent. Figure 19 illustrates this distinction. In the figure, two text frames are positioned in front of a frame with a yellow fill. The text frame on the left has None as its fill; therefore the yellow frame behind the text frame is visible. The text frame on the right has Paper as its fill.

Figure 18 *Paper swatch*

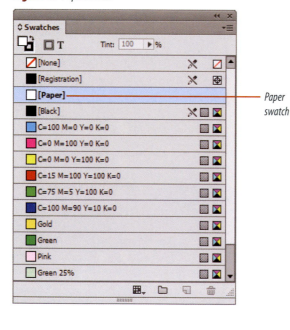

Paper swatch

Figure 19 *Understanding a Paper fill*

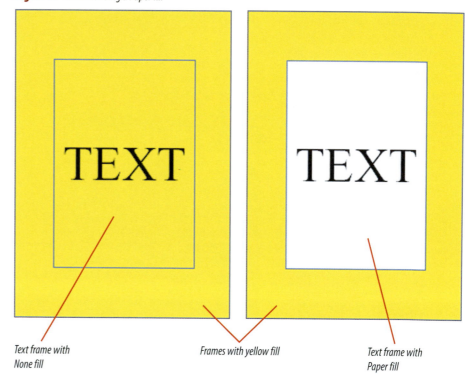

Text frame with None fill

Frames with yellow fill

Text frame with Paper fill

Working with Color

Applying Color to Text

Applying color to text is easy. There are two different methods for applying color to text, depending on whether you are using the Type tool or the Selection tool to select the text.

When you select text with the Type tool, the Fill and Stroke buttons on the Tools panel display the letter T, as shown in Figure 20. This is a visual indication that you are filling or stroking text. Click a swatch on the Swatches panel or mix a color on the Color panel and the text will be filled or stroked with that color.

QUICK TIP

The color of the T on the Fill and Stroke buttons is always the same color as the selected text.

When you select a text frame with the Selection tool, you need to tell InDesign what you want to do—apply a fill or stroke to the frame itself or apply a fill or stroke to the text in the frame. If you want to apply color to the text, click the Formatting affects text button on the Tools panel, as shown in Figure 21. If you want to apply color to the frame, click the Formatting affects container button. It's that simple. Note that the two buttons can also be found on the Swatches and Color panels.

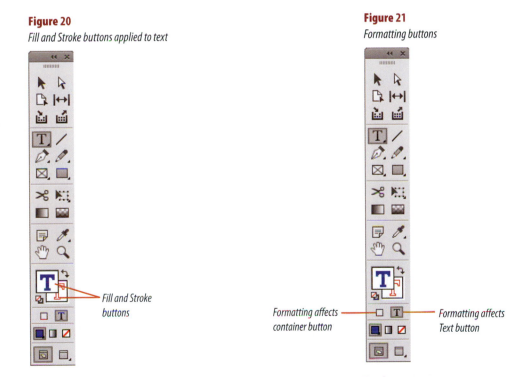

Figure 20
Fill and Stroke buttons applied to text

Fill and Stroke buttons

Figure 21
Formatting buttons

Formatting affects container button

Formatting affects Text button

Creating Black Shadow Text

When you position text against a background color or against a photographic image, sometimes it's not easy to see the text, as shown in Figure 22. To remedy this, many designers use the classic technique of placing a black copy of the text behind the original text, as shown in Figure 23. This trick adds much-needed contrast between the text and the image behind it.

Modifying and Deleting Swatches

Once you've created a swatch or added a swatch to the Swatches panel, it is a named color and will be saved with the document. Any swatch can be modified simply by double-clicking it, which opens the Swatch Options dialog box, as shown in Figure 24. Any modifications you make to the swatch will be updated automatically in any frame that uses the color as a fill or a stroke.

You can also delete a swatch from the Swatches panel by selecting the swatch, then clicking the Delete selected swatch/groups button on the Swatches panel or clicking the Delete Swatch command on the Swatches

Figure 22 *Text positioned against an image*

Figure 23 *Text with a black copy behind it*

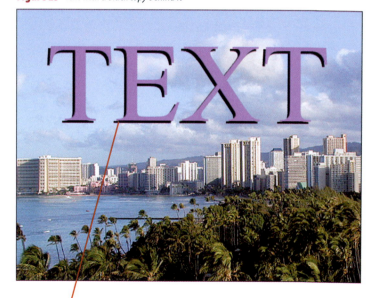

Black text placed behind purple text

panel menu. If you are deleting a swatch that is used in your document, the Delete Swatch dialog box opens, as shown in Figure 25.

You use the Delete Swatch dialog box to choose a color to replace the deleted swatch. For example, if you've filled (or stroked) a number of objects with the color Warm Green and then you delete the Warm Green swatch, the Delete Swatch dialog box wants to know what color those objects should be. You choose another named color that is already on the Swatches panel by clicking the Defined Swatch list arrow, clicking a color, and then clicking OK. When you do so, all the objects with a Warm Green fill or stroke will change to the named color you chose. Note that this can be a very quick and effective method for changing the fill (or stroke) color of multiple objects simultaneously.

If you click the Unnamed Swatch option button in the Delete Swatch dialog box, all the objects filled or stroked with the deleted color will retain their color. However, since that color is no longer on the Swatches panel, those objects are now filled with an unnamed color.

Figure 24 *Swatch Options dialog box*

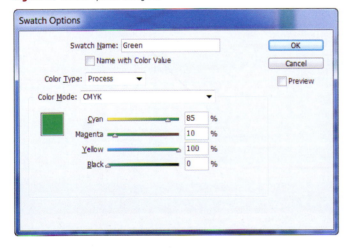

Figure 25 *Delete Swatch dialog box*

Drag and drop colors onto objects

1. Click **View** on the Menu bar, point to **Extras**, then click **Hide Frame Edges**.

2. Drag and drop the **Green swatch** on top of the blue frame, then release the mouse button.

   The frame is filled with green , as shown in Figure 26.

3. Click the **Eye icon** on the Photo layer on the Layers panel to hide the background image.

4. Drag the **Pink swatch** to the inside of the white text frame.

   The fill changes to pink.

You dragged and dropped colors from the Swatches panel to objects in the document window.

Figure 26 *Dragging and dropping a color swatch*

Using the Color Picker

In addition to using the Tools panel and the Swatches panel to apply colors, you can use the Color Picker to choose and mix colors. Select the object you want to fill, then double-click the Fill or Stroke button on the Tools panel to open the Color Picker. In the color spectrum, click or drag to select a color, drag the color slider triangles, or type values in the text boxes. To save the color as a swatch, click Add CMYK Swatch, Add RGB Swatch, or Add Lab Swatch. The color appears on the Swatches panel, displaying its color values as a name.

Figure 27 *Applying the default fill and stroke to the frame*

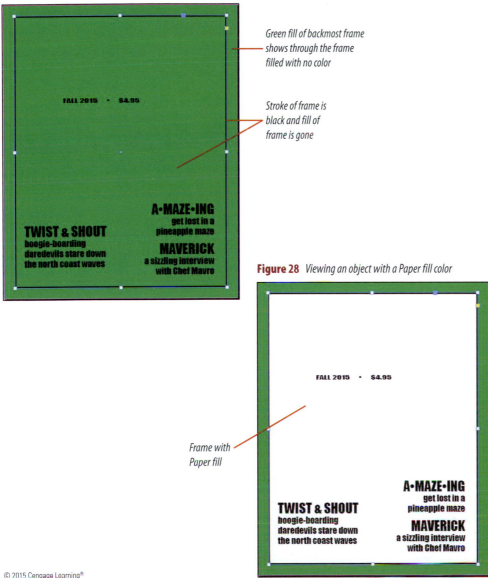

Green fill of backmost frame shows through the frame filled with no color

Stroke of frame is black and fill of frame is gone

Figure 28 *Viewing an object with a Paper fill color*

Frame with Paper fill

Use the Swap Fill and Stroke and Default Fill and Stroke buttons

1. Click the **Selection tool** if necessary, click the **center** of the pink frame, then note the Fill and Stroke buttons on the Tools panel.

   The Fill button is activated—it is in front of the Stroke button.

2. Press **[X]** to activate the Stroke button on the Tools panel, then click **Gold** on the Swatches panel.

3. Click the **Swap Fill and Stroke button** on the Tools panel.

   In the selected frame, the fill and stroke colors are swapped.

4. Click the **Default Fill and Stroke button** on the Tools panel.

   The fill color of the selected frame is removed and replaced with no fill, and the stroke changes to black as shown in Figure 27.

5. Press **[X]** to activate the Fill button, click the **Paper swatch** on the Swatches panel, then compare your work to Figure 28.

You used the Swap Fill and Stroke and Default Fill and Stroke buttons to explore ways to modify your document, and then applied the Paper swatch to the center frame.

Apply color to text

1. Click the **Selection tool** 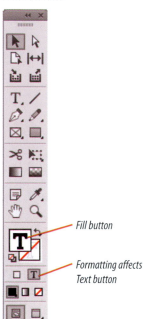, click the **TWIST & SHOUT text frame**, then click the **Formatting affects text button** T on the Tools panel.

   As shown in Figure 29, the Fill and Stroke buttons display the letter T, indicating that any color changes will affect the text in the selected frame, not the frame itself.

2. Click **Gold** on the Swatches panel.

3. Click the **A•MAZE•ING text frame**, then note that the Formatting affects container button is active on the Tools panel because you have selected a frame.

4. Click the **Type tool** T, then select all of the text in the A•MAZE•ING text frame.

   TIP When you select text with the Type tool, the Formatting affects text button on the Tools panel is automatically activated.

5. Click **Pink** on the Swatches panel.

6. Click the **Selection tool** , click the **MAVERICK text frame**, then click the **Formatting affects text button** T on the Swatches panel.

7. Click the **Green 25% swatch** on the Swatches panel so that your document resembles Figure 30.

You explored two methods for applying color to text. In the first, you selected text with the Selection tool, clicked the Formatting affects text button, then chose a new color. In the second, you selected text with the Type tool, then chose a new color.

Figure 29 *Tools panel with the Formatting affects text button activated*

Fill button

Formatting affects Text button

Figure 30 *Viewing the colors applied to text*

FALL 2015 • $4.95

A•MAZE•ING
get lost in a
pineapple maze

MAVERICK
a sizzling interview
with Chef Mavro

TWIST & SHOUT
boogie-boarding
daredevils stare down
the north coast waves

© 2015 Cengage Learning®

Working with Color

Figure 31 *Layer Options dialog box*

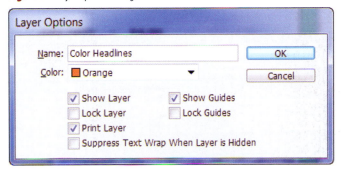

Create black shadow text

1. Click the empty box for the **Eye icon** 👁 on the Photo layer on the Layers panel to toggle on visibility, and then assess the legibility of the text in the three text frames against the background graphic.

   The text is legible, but some letters like the M in Maverick are more difficult to distinguish from the background.

2. Click the **Original Black Text layer** on the Layers panel, click the **Layers panel options button** ▾☰ , then click **Duplicate Layer "Original Black Text."**

3. Double-click the name of the new layer on the Layers panel to open the Layer Options dialog box.

4. Type **Color Headlines** in the Name text box, click the **Color list arrow**, then click **Orange**, so that your Layer Options dialog box resembles Figure 31.

5. Click **OK**, then hide the Original Black Text layer.

6. With the Color Headlines layer still selected, delete the Fall 2015 text frame on the Color Headlines layer since you will not need a duplicate of this text.

7. Hide the Color Headlines layer, then show the Original Black Text layer.

(continued)

8. Click the **Selected Items button** ☐ on the Original Black Text layer to select all the objects on the layer.

9. Click the **Formatting affects text button** **T** on the Swatches panel, apply a 100% Black fill to all the text, then deselect all.

10. Show the Color Headlines layer, then click the **Click to select items button** ☐ to select all objects on the layer.

11. Click **Object** on the Menu bar, point to **Transform**, then click **Move**.

12. Click the **Preview check box**, if necessary, type **-.04** in the Horizontal text box, type **-.04** in the Vertical text box, click **OK**, deselect all, then compare your work to Figure 32.

You duplicated a layer containing text. You changed the fill color of the text on the lower layer to Black, then repositioned the colored text on the upper layer so that the black text acts as a shadow. By doing so, you added contrast to the colored text, making it more legible against the picture on the Photo layer.

Figure 32 *Viewing the colored text with a black shadow*

Black text placed behind colored text adds contrast

© 2015 Cengage Learning®. Image courtesy of Chris Botello.

Figure 33 *Viewing modifications to the Gold swatch*

Figure 34 *Delete Swatch dialog box*

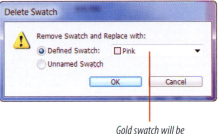

Gold swatch will be
replaced with Pink

Figure 35 *Gold swatch replaced with Pink swatch*

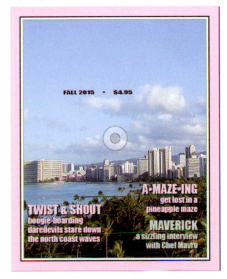

Modify and delete swatches

1. Deselect all, then drag the **Gold swatch** onto the Green frame to change its fill color to Gold.

2. Double-click the **Gold swatch** on the Swatches panel.

3. Activate the Preview option if necessary, then drag the **Black slider** to 20%.

   You may need to move the Swatch Options dialog box to see the effect on the document page.

4. Drag the **Black slider** to 5%, then drag the **Magenta slider** to 100%.

5. Click **OK**, then compare your work to Figure 33.

   All usages of the Gold swatch—the frame and the "Twist & Shout" text—are updated with the modification.

6. Drag the **Gold swatch** to the Delete selected swatch/groups button on the Swatches panel.

7. Click the **Defined Swatch list arrow** in the Delete Swatch dialog box, click **Pink**, as shown in Figure 34, then click **OK**.

   As shown in Figure 35, all usages of the Gold swatch in the document are replaced by the Pink swatch.

You modified a swatch and noted that it updated throughout the document. You then deleted the swatch, replacing all of its usages with a different swatch.

Work with
SPOT COLORS

What You'll Do

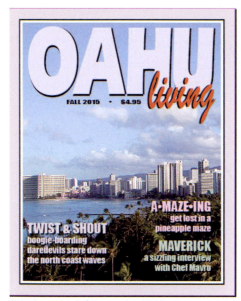

© 2015 Cengage Learning®. Image courtesy of Chris Botello.

In this lesson, you will create and apply spot colors, and import graphics that contain spot colors.

Understanding Spot Colors

Spot colors are non-process inks that are manufactured by companies. Though printing is based on the four process colors, CMYK, it is not limited to them. It is important to understand that though combinations of CMYK inks can produce a wide variety of colors—enough to reproduce any color photograph quite well—they can't produce every color. For this reason, and others, designers often turn to spot colors.

Imagine that you are an art director designing the masthead for the cover of a new magazine. You have decided that the masthead will be electric blue—vivid and eye-catching. If you were working with process tints only, you would have a problem. First, you would find that the almost-neon blue that you want to achieve is not within the CMYK range; it can't be printed. Even if it could, you would have a bigger problem with consistency issues. You would want that blue to be the same blue on every issue of the magazine, month after month. But offset printing is never perfect; variations in dot size are factored in. As the cover is printed, the blue color in the masthead will certainly vary, sometimes sharply.

Designers and printers use spot colors to solve this problem. **Spot colors** are special pre-mixed inks that are printed separately from process inks. The color range of spot colors far exceeds that of CMYK. Spot colors also offer consistent color throughout a print run.

The design and print worlds refer to spot colors by a number of names:

- Non-process inks: Refers to the fact that spot colors are not created using the process inks—CMYK.
- Fifth color: Refers to the fact that the spot color is often printed in addition to the four process inks. Note, however, that a spot color is not necessarily the "fifth" color. For example, many "two-color" projects call for black plus one spot color.
- PANTONE color: PANTONE is a manufacturer of non-process inks. PANTONE is simply a brand name.
- PMS color: An acronym for PANTONE Matching System.

A good way to think of spot colors is as ink in a bucket. With process inks, if you want red, you must mix some amount of magenta ink with some amount of yellow ink. With spot colors, if you want red, you pick a number from a chart, open the bucket, and there's the red ink—pre-mixed and ready to print.

Creating Spot Color Swatches

You create spot color swatches in Adobe InDesign using the New Color Swatch dialog box. Instead of choosing CMYK values, as you would when you create a process color, you choose Spot from the Color Type list, then choose a spot color system from one of 30 systems in the Color Mode list. After you choose a system, the related library of spot colors loads into the New Swatch dialog box, allowing you to choose the spot color you want. Figure 36 shows the PANTONE solid coated color system.

Importing Graphics with Spot Colors

When you create graphics in Adobe Illustrator or Adobe Photoshop, you can create and apply spot colors in those applications as well. For example, you can create a logo in Adobe Illustrator and fill it with a spot color.

Because InDesign, Illustrator, and Photoshop are all made by Adobe, InDesign recognizes the spot colors applied to graphics created in those applications. In the above example, when you place the graphic from Illustrator, InDesign identifies the spot color that was used and adds it to the InDesign Swatches panel. If you double-click the swatch on the Swatches panel, you will see that the swatch is automatically formatted as a spot color.

Figure 36 *Creating a spot color swatch*

Color Type: Defines whether the color is Process or Spot

Color Mode: Defines which type of Spot color system you want to use

PANTONE solid coated color system

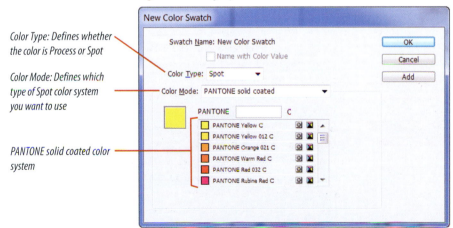

Create a spot color swatch

1. Click the **Swatches panel options button**
   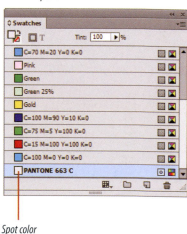, then click **New Color Swatch**.

2. Click the **Color Type list arrow**, then click **Spot**.

3. Click the **Color Mode list arrow**, then click **PANTONE + Solid Coated**.

4. Type **663** in the PANTONE text box, so that your New Color Swatch dialog box resembles Figure 37.

5. Click **OK**, then compare your Swatches panel with Figure 38.

6. Change the fill of the pink frame to PANTONE 663.

7. Change the fill of the TWIST & SHOUT text to PANTONE 663, deselect the TWIST & SHOUT text frame, then compare your document to Figure 39.

You created a spot color swatch and then applied it to elements in the layout.

Figure 37 *Creating a spot color*

Figure 39 *Viewing the document with the spot color applied*

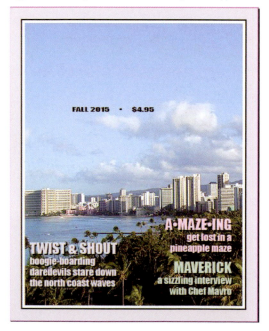

Figure 38 *Identifying a spot color on the Swatches panel*

Spot color

Figure 40 *Selecting a frame for a graphic*

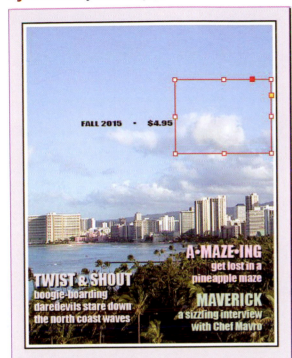

© 2015 Cengage Learning®. Image courtesy of Chris Botello.

Figure 41 *Identifying a new spot color on the Swatches panel*

PANTONE swatch added to the Swatches panel when the Illustrator graphic was imported

Import graphics with spot colors

1. Click the **Imported Graphics layer** on the Layers panel to target it, click the **Selection tool**, then select the frame shown in Figure 40.

TIP Clicking in the general area of the selected frame shown in Figure 40 will select the frame.

2. Click **File** on the Menu bar, click **Place**, navigate to the drive and folder where your Data Files are stored, click **Living Graphic.ai**, then click **Open**.

3. Click **Object** on the Menu bar, point to **Fitting**, then click **Center Content**.

   The graphic that is placed in the frame was created in Adobe Illustrator.

4. Click **View** on the Menu bar, point to **Display Performance**, then click **High Quality Display**.

5. Compare your Swatches panel to Figure 41.

   The PANTONE 159 C swatch was automatically added to the Swatches panel when the graphic was placed, since it was a color used to create the graphic.

6. Deselect the graphics frame, double-click **PANTONE 159 C** on the Swatches panel, note that PANTONE 159 C was imported as a spot color as indicated in the Color Type text box, then click **Cancel**.

   (continued)

7. Select the **frame** shown in Figure 42.

8. Click **File** on the Menu bar, click **Place**, navigate to the drive and folder where your Data Files are stored, then double-click **OAHU graphic.ai**.

   OAHU graphic.ai is an Adobe Illustrator file. The fill color of O, A, H, and U is PANTONE 663—the same PANTONE 663 fill that was created in InDesign and applied to the border and the TWIST & SHOUT text. For this reason, PANTONE 663 does not need to be added to the Swatches panel.

TIP When you import the graphic, if a dialog box appears warning you that the PANTONE color in the graphic is defined differently and asking if you want to replace it, click No.

(continued)

Figure 42 *Selecting a frame for a graphic*

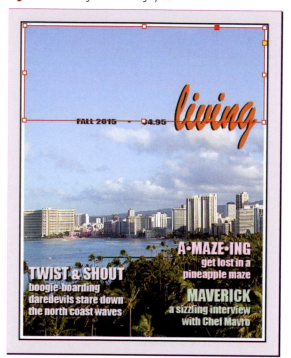

Working with Mixed Ink Swatches

When you are creating a two color job—let's say Black and PMS 100—you will want to work with more than just 100% Black and 100% PMS 100. You'll want to work with tints, such as a 70% Black and 20% PMS100 mix. These are called mixed swatches. A mixed ink group is a group of many mixed ink swatches that you can generate automatically based on the two or more inks in your color job.

You create a mixed ink group by clicking the New Mixed Ink Group command on the Swatches panel menu, which opens the New Mixed Ink Group dialog box. Use this dialog box to specify the inks involved for the mixed ink group, the initial mixture, and the increments (percentages) at which new tint swatches will be generated. All of the swatches will appear on the Swatches panel.

9. Click **Object** on the Menu bar, point to **Fitting**, then click **Center Content**.

10. Deselect all, then compare your document with Figure 43.

11. Save your work, then close OAHU Magazine Cover.

You imported a graphic that was created with a spot color in another application, then noted that the spot color was automatically added to the Swatches panel. Next, you imported a graphic that was filled with the same spot color that you had already created in InDesign.

Work with
GRADIENTS

What You'll Do

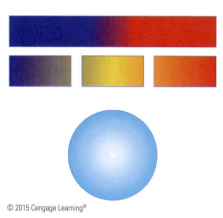

© 2015 Cengage Learning®

In this lesson, you will create gradients and explore options for applying them to frames.

Creating Gradients

A **gradient** is a graduated blend of two or more colors. By definition, every gradient must have at least two colors, which are commonly referred to as the **starting** and **ending colors** of the gradient. You can add more colors to a gradient—colors that come between the starting and ending colors. The colors that you add are called **color stops**.

In InDesign, you create gradients by clicking New Gradient Swatch on the Swatches panel menu. This opens the New Gradient Swatch dialog box, as shown in Figure 44. In this dialog box, you define all the elements of the gradient. Like new colors, you can give your gradient a descriptive name. You use the Gradient Ramp to define the starting and ending colors, as well as any intermediary colors for your gradient. You choose whether your gradient will be radial or linear using the Type list arrow. You can think of a **radial gradient** as a series of concentric circles. With a radial

Figure 44 *New Gradient Swatch dialog box*

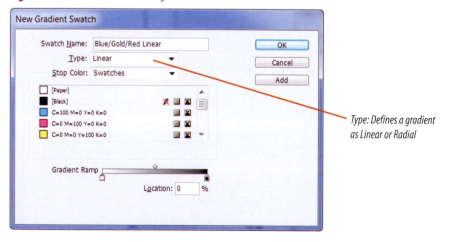

Type: Defines a gradient as Linear or Radial

gradient, the starting color appears at the center of the gradient, then radiates out to the ending color.

You can think of a **linear gradient** as a series of straight lines that gradate from one color to another (or through multiple colors). Figure 45 shows a linear and a radial gradient, each composed of three colors.

Figure 46 shows the dialog box used to create the linear gradient. The Gradient Ramp represents the gradient, and the blue color stop is selected. The sliders show the CMYK values that make the blue tint. Note that the Stop Color text box reads CMYK.

You can create gradients using swatches already on the Swatches panel as color stops.

In Figure 47, the selected color stop is a spot color named PANTONE Red 032 C. Note that the Stop Color text box reads Swatches. When you choose Swatches from the Stop Color menu, all the named colors on the Swatches panel are listed and available to be used in the gradient.

When you close the New Gradient Swatch dialog box, the new gradient swatch appears on the Swatches panel when you click the Show All Swatches button or when you click the Show Gradient Swatches button on the Swatches panel.

Figure 45 *A linear and a radial gradient*

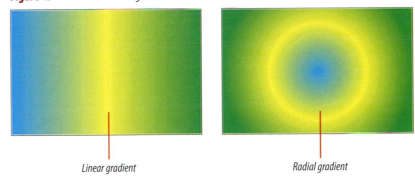

Linear gradient   Radial gradient

Figure 46 *Viewing a linear gradient*

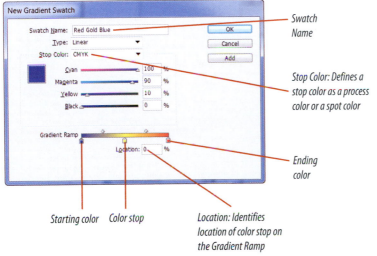

Swatch Name

Stop Color: Defines a stop color as a process color or a spot color

Ending color

Starting color   Color stop   Location: Identifies location of color stop on the Gradient Ramp

© 2015 Cengage Learning®

Figure 47 *Viewing the formatting of a gradient with a named color*

The selected stop color is defined as a named color

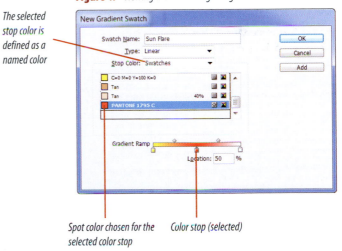

Spot color chosen for the selected color stop   Color stop (selected)

Applying Gradients

You apply a gradient to an object the same way you apply a color to an object. Simply select the object, then click the gradient on the Swatches panel. A gradient swatch can be applied as a fill or as a stroke.

If you use a gradient to fill an object, you can further control how the gradient fills the object using the Gradient Swatch tool or the Gradient Feather tool. The Gradient Swatch tool allows you to change the length and/or direction of a linear or radial gradient. You can also use it to change the angle of a linear gradient and the center point of a radial gradient. To use the Gradient Swatch tool, you first select an object with a gradient fill, then drag the Gradient Swatch tool over the object. For both linear and radial gradients, where you begin dragging and where you stop dragging determines the length of the gradient, from starting color to ending color. The Gradient Feather tool works exactly like the Gradient Swatch tool, except that it produces a softer progression of the colors in the gradient.

For linear gradients, the direction in which you drag the Gradient Swatch tool determines the angle of the blend that fills the object.

Figure 48 shows six rows of six square frames filled with rainbow gradients. The Gradient Swatch tool was dragged in varying lengths and directions across each row—represented by the black lines you see in the examples—to create different effects.

Modifying a Gradient Fill Using the Gradient Panel

Like color swatches, gradients can be modified. When you modify a gradient, all instances of the gradient used in the document will be automatically updated. Let's say you create a gradient and use it to fill 10 objects. Then you decide that, in only one of those 10 objects, you want to modify the gradient by removing one color. What do you do? If you modify the gradient swatch by removing a color stop, it's going to affect all usages of the gradient. You could, of course, duplicate the gradient swatch, remove the unwanted color stop, then apply the new gradient to the single object. But there's a better way. You can use the Gradient panel, shown in Figure 49.

When you select an object with a gradient fill, the Gradient panel shows the Gradient Ramp that you used to create the gradient in the New Gradient Swatch dialog box. You can manipulate the Gradient Ramp on the Gradient panel. You can add, move, and delete color stops. You can also select color stops and modify their color using the Color panel. And here's the great part: the modifications you make on the Gradient panel only affect the gradient fill of the selected object(s).

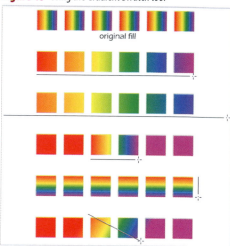

Figure 48 *Using the Gradient Swatch tool*

original fill

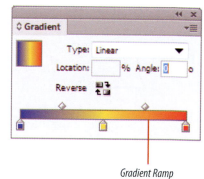

Figure 49 *Gradient panel*

Gradient Ramp

Working with Color

Figure 50 *New Gradient Swatch dialog box*

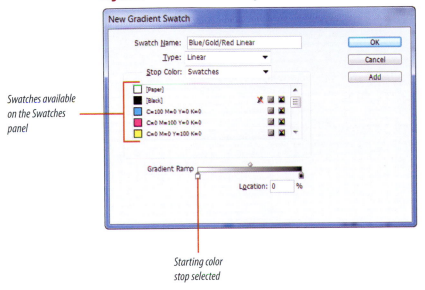

Swatches available on the Swatches panel

Starting color stop selected

Figure 51 *Creating a linear gradient swatch*

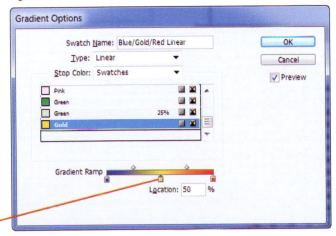

New color stop

Create a linear gradient swatch

1. Open ID 5-2.indd, then save it as **Making the Gradient**.

2. Click the **Swatches panel options button** , then click **New Gradient Swatch**.

3. In the Swatch Name text box, type **Blue/Gold/ Red Linear**.

4. Click the **left color stop** on the Gradient Ramp, click the **Stop Color list arrow**, then click **Swatches** so that your dialog box resembles Figure 50.

   When you choose Swatches, the colors on the Swatches panel are listed below.

5. Click the swatch named **Blue**.

   The left color stop on the Gradient Ramp changes to blue.

6. Click the **right color stop** on the Gradient Ramp, click the **Stop Color list arrow**, click **Swatches**, then click the swatch named **Red**.

7. Click directly below the Gradient Ramp to add a new color stop.

TIP Click anywhere to add the new color stop. You can adjust the location using the Location text box.

8. Type **50** in the Location text box, then press **[Tab]**.

   The new color stop is located at the exact middle of the Gradient Ramp.

9. Click the **Stop Color list arrow**, click **Swatches**, then click the swatch named **Gold** so that your New Gradient Swatch dialog box resembles Figure 51.

(continued)

10. Click **OK**.

The new gradient swatch is added to the Swatches panel.

You created a three-color linear gradient swatch using three named colors.

Create a radial gradient swatch

1. Click the **Swatches panel options button** ▼≡, then click **New Gradient Swatch**.

The New Gradient Swatch dialog box opens with the settings from the last created gradient.

2. In the Swatch Name text box, type **Cyan Radial**.

3. Click the **Type list arrow**, then click **Radial**.

4. Click the **center color stop**, then drag it straight down to remove it from the Gradient Ramp.

5. Click the **left color stop** on the Gradient Ramp, click the **Stop Color list arrow**, then click **CMYK**.

6. Drag each slider to **0%** so that your dialog box resembles Figure 52.

7. Click the **right color stop** on the Gradient Ramp, click the **Stop Color list arrow**, then click **CMYK**.

8. Drag the **Cyan slider** to 100%, then drag the **Magenta**, **Yellow**, and **Black sliders** to 0% so that your dialog box resembles Figure 53.

9. Click **OK**.

The new gradient swatch is added to the Swatches panel.

You created a two-color radial gradient swatch using CMYK values.

Figure 52 *Formatting the left color stop*

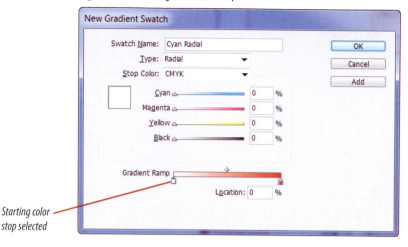

Starting color stop selected

Figure 53 *Formatting the right color stop*

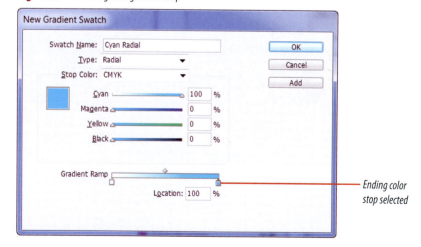

Ending color stop selected

Figure 54 *Dragging the Gradient Swatch tool straight down*

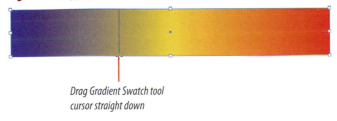

Drag Gradient Swatch tool
cursor straight down

Figure 55 *Linear gradient applied vertically to the frame*

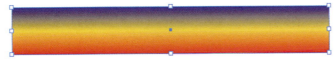

Figure 56 *Dragging the Gradient Swatch tool from left to right*

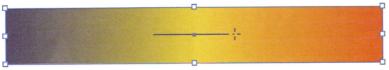

Apply gradient swatches and use the Gradient Swatch tool

1. Click the **Selection tool** ▸ , click the **border** of the top rectangular frame, verify that the Fill button is activated on the Tools panel, then click **Blue/Gold/Red Linear** on the Swatches panel.

   TIP Make sure you are in Normal view and that you are viewing frame edges.

2. Click the **Gradient Swatch tool** ▭ on the Toolbar, then, using Figure 54 as a guide, place the mouse pointer anywhere on the top edge of the rectangular frame, click and drag down, and release the mouse button at the bottom edge of the frame.

   Your frame should resemble Figure 55.

   TIP Pressing and holding down [Shift] while dragging the Gradient Swatch tool constrains the movement on a horizontal or vertical axis.

3. Drag the **Gradient Swatch tool** from the bottom-middle handle of the frame to the top-right handle.

4. Drag the **Gradient Swatch tool** from the left edge of the document window to the right edge of the document window.

5. Drag the **Gradient Swatch tool** a short distance from left to right in the center of the frame, as shown in Figure 56.

(continued)

6. Click the **Selection tool** [icon], click the edge of the circular frame, then click **Cyan Radial** on the Swatches panel.

7. Click the **Gradient Swatch tool** [icon], press and hold down **[Shift]**, then drag the **Gradient Swatch tool** from the center point of the circle up to the bottom edge of the center rectangle above the circle so that your document resembles Figure 57.

You filled two objects with two different gradients, and you used the Gradient Swatch tool to manipulate how the gradients filled the objects.

Use the Gradient Swatch tool to extend a gradient across multiple objects and modify a gradient

1. Click **Window** on the Menu bar, point to **Color**, then click **Gradient** to open the Gradient panel.

2. Deselect all, click the **Selection tool** [icon], then select the **three rectangular frames** above the circle.

3. Click **Blue/Gold/Red Linear** on the Swatches panel.

   As shown in Figure 58, the gradient fills each frame individually.

   (continued)

Figure 57 *Gradients applied to two objects*

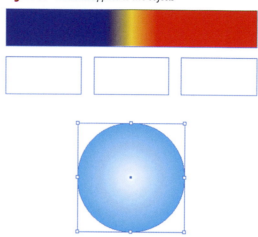

Figure 58 *A gradient fill applied individually to three objects*

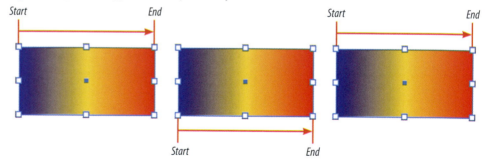

Working with Color

Figure 59 *A gradient fill gradating across three objects*

Start   End

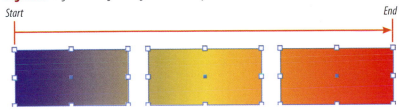

Figure 60 *Modifying a gradient on the Gradient panel*

Gold color stop
removed from
Gradient Ramp
on Gradient panel

Gold color removed
from gradient fill
in selected object

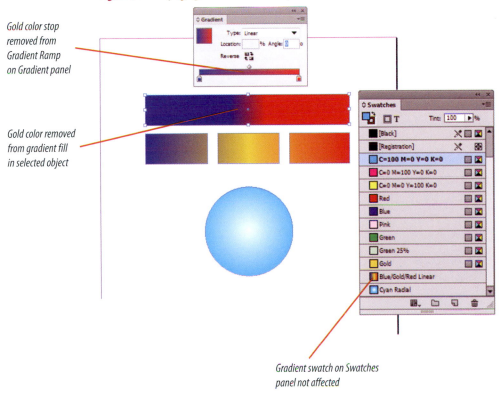

Gradient swatch on Swatches
panel not affected

4. With the three objects still selected, click the
   Gradient Swatch tool ▭ , then drag it from
   the left edge of the leftmost frame to the right
   edge of the rightmost frame.

   As shown in Figure 59, the gradient gradates
   across all three selected objects.

5. Click the **Selection tool** ▶ , then click
   the **rectangular frame** at the top of the
   document window.

6. Remove the center gold color stop from the
   Gradient Ramp on the Gradient panel.

   As shown in Figure 60, the gold color is removed
   only from the gradient fill in the *selected* frame.
   The original gradient on the Swatches panel
   (Blue/Gold/Red Linear) is not affected.

TIP In the Swatches panel, you can choose to view only
swatches, only gradients, or only color groups by
clicking the Swatch Views button on the Swatches
panel and choosing Show Color Swatches, Show
Gradient Swatches, or Show Color Groups. To view all
swatches, choose Show All Swatches.

7. Save your work, then close Making the Gradient.

*You selected three objects, applied a gradient to each of them,
then used the Gradient Swatch tool to extend the gradient
across all three selected objects. You then modified the gradient
fill of a selected object by removing a color stop from the
Gradient panel.*

Work with process colors.

1. Open ID 5-3.indd, then save it as **LAB cover**.
2. Verify that the Swatches panel is open, click the Swatches panel options button, then click New Color Swatch.
3. Verify that Process is chosen in the Color Type text box and that CMYK is chosen in the Color Mode text box.
4. Remove the check mark in the Name with Color Value check box, then type **Pink in** the Swatch Name text box.
5. Type **15** in the Cyan text box, press [Tab], type **70** in the Magenta text box, press [Tab], type **10** in the Yellow text box, press [Tab], type **0** in the Black text box, press [Tab], then click OK.
6. Display the Color panel if necessary.
7. Click the Color panel options button, click CMYK, then verify that the Fill button is activated.
8. Drag the Cyan slider on the Color panel to 50%, drag the Magenta slider to 10%, then drag the Yellow and Black sliders to 0%.
9. Drag the color from the Fill button on the Color panel to the Swatches panel.
10. Verify that the C=50 M=10 Y=0 K=0 swatch is still selected on the Swatches panel, click the Swatches panel options button, then click New Tint Swatch.
11. Drag the Tint slider to 35%, then click OK.

Apply color.

1. Duplicate the Text layer, then rename it **Colored Text**.
2. Click View on the Menu bar, point to Extras, then click Hide Frame Edges.
3. Drag and drop C=50 M=10 Y=0 K=0 from the Swatches panel to the outermost black-filled frame.

4. Click the Selection tool, click the BRUSH UP text frame, then click the Formatting affects text button on the Tools panel.
5. Click the C=50 M=10 Y=0 K=0 swatch on the Swatches panel.
6. Click the Holiday Issue text frame in the lower left corner of the cover, click the Formatting affects text button on the Swatches panel, then click the Paper swatch on the Swatches panel.
7. Click the Type tool, select all of the text in the PUPPY LOVE text frame, then click Pink on the Swatches panel.
8. Select all of the text in the FETCH text frame, then click the C=50 M=10 Y=0 K=0 35% tint swatch on the Swatches panel.
9. Click the Click to select items button on the Colored Text layer to select all the items on the layer.
10. Click Object on the Menu bar, point to Transform, then click Move.
11. Verify that there is a check mark in the Preview check box, type **-.03** in the Horizontal text box, type **-.03** in the Vertical text box, click OK, then deselect all.

Work with spot colors.

1. Click the Swatches panel options button, then click New Color Swatch.
2. Click the Color Type list arrow, then click Spot.
3. Click the Color Mode list arrow, then click PANTONE solid coated.
4. Type **117** in the PANTONE text box, then click OK.
5. Change the fill on the C=50 M=10 border to PANTONE 117 C.

6. Click the Imported Graphics layer on the Layers panel to target it, click the Selection tool, then click between the dog's eyes to select the frame for placing a new image.
7. Click File on the Menu bar, click Place, navigate to the drive and folder where your Chapter 5 Data Files are stored, click LAB.ai, then click Open. (*Hint*: LAB.ai is an Adobe Illustrator graphic filled with PANTONE 117 C.)
8. Click the Photo layer on the Layers panel, click the dog graphic in the document window, click Edit on the Menu bar, click Copy, click Edit on the Menu bar, then click Paste in Place.
9. On the Layers panel, drag the Indicates selected items button from the Photo layer up to the Imported Graphics layer.
10. Click File on the Menu bar, click Place, navigate to the drive and folder where your Chapter 5 Data Files are stored, then double-click Wally Head Silo.psd. (*Hint*: Wally Head Silo.psd is identical to the dog photo, with the exception that it was saved with a clipping path around the dog's head in order to remove the red background.)
11. Deselect all, compare your work to Figure 61, save your work, then close the document.

Work with gradients.

1. Open ID 5-4.indd, then save it as **Gradient Skills Review**.
2. Click the Swatches panel options button, then click New Gradient Swatch.

3. In the Swatch Name text box, type **Red/Golden/Green Linear**.

4. Click the left color stop on the Gradient Ramp, click the Stop Color list arrow, then click Swatches.

5. Click the swatch named Red.

6. Click the right color stop on the Gradient Ramp, click the Stop Color list arrow, click Swatches, then click the swatch named Green.

7. Position your pointer anywhere immediately below the Gradient Ramp, then click to add a third color stop.

8. Type **50** in the Location text box, then press [Tab].

9. Click the Stop Color list arrow, choose Swatches, click the swatch named Gold, then click OK.

10. Click the Selection tool, select the border of the top rectangular frame, verify that the Fill button is activated on the Tools panel, then click Red/Golden/Green Linear on the Swatches panel.

11. Click the Gradient Swatch tool, then drag from the top-middle handle of the rectangular frame down to the bottom-right handle.

12. Display the Gradient panel if necessary.

13. Click the Selection tool, deselect the top rectangular frame, then select the three lower rectangular frames.

14. Click Red/Golden/Green Linear on the Swatches panel.

15. Click the Gradient Swatch tool, and with all three objects still selected, drag the Gradient Swatch tool from the left edge of the leftmost frame to the right edge of the rightmost frame.

16. Deselect all, then compare your work to Figure 62.

17. Save your work, then close Gradient Skills Review.

Figure 61 *Completed Skills Review, Part 1*

Figure 62 *Completed Skills Review, Part 2*

Working with Color

You are a freelance graphic designer. You have recently been contracted to create a newsletter for a local financial investment company. The newsletter will be 8.5" × 11" and will be printed using the CMYK process inks. You decide on the colors you want to use, open InDesign, create a new document, then, before you start designing, create a process color and a 40% tint of that color.

1. Open ID 5-5.indd, then save it as **Process Colors**.
2. Click the Swatches panel options button, then click New Color Swatch.
3. Create a CMYK color named **Tan** using the following values: Cyan 0%, Magenta 30%, Yellow 55%, and Black 20%.
4. Create a new tint swatch based on Tan, then change the tint amount to 40%.
5. Compare your Swatches panel to Figure 63, save your work, then close Process Colors. (Don't be concerned if your swatch order differs.)

Figure 63 *Completed Project Builder 1*

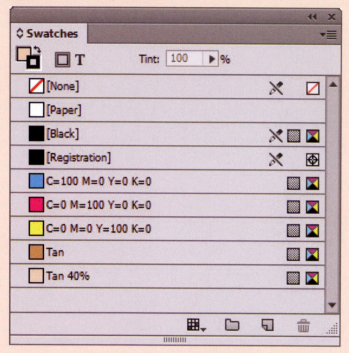

You are a freelance graphic designer. You have recently been contracted to create a cover for LAB magazine. The magazine is usually published only with one color—in black and white—but the publishers have some extra money for this issue. They want you to create a design for this cover so that it will print as a two-color job. It will be printed with black and one spot color. They provide you with the black and white version of the cover. You are free to choose the spot color and apply it in whatever way you think is best.

1. Open ID 5-6.indd, then save it as **2 Color Cover**.
2. Click the Swatches panel options button, then click New Color Swatch.
3. Click the Color Type list arrow, then choose Spot.
4. Click the Color Mode list arrow, then choose PANTONE + Solid Coated.
5. Choose PANTONE 195 C, then click OK.
6. Click the Swatches panel options button, then click New Tint Swatch.
7. Drag the Tint slider to 25%, then click OK.
8. Change the fill of the outermost frame that is filled with black to PANTONE 195 C.
9. Click the inner white border that is filled with Paper and stroked with Black, then change its fill color to PANTONE 195 C 25%.
10. Change the fill color on the three white headlines to PANTONE 195 C 25%.
11. Compare your cover to Figure 64, save your work, then close 2 Color Cover.

Figure 64 *Completed Project Builder 2*

DESIGN PROJECT

You have recently been contracted to create a logo for the Hypnotists Foundation. Their representative tells you that he wants the logo to be a circle filled with a radial gradient. Starting from the inside of the circle, the colors should go from white to black to white to black to white to black. He tells you that he wants each color to be very distinct—in other words, he doesn't want the white and black colors to blend into each other, creating a lot of gray areas in the logo.

1. Open ID 5-7.indd, then save it as **Concentric Circle Gradient**.
2. Click the Swatches panel options button, then click New Gradient Swatch.
3. Create a radial gradient named **Six Ring Radial**.
4. Add four new color stops to the Gradient Ramp, then position them so that they are equally spaced across the ramp.
5. Format the first, third, and fifth color stops as 0% CMYK (White).
6. Format the second, fourth and sixth color stops as 100% Black.
7. Close the New Gradient Swatch dialog box, then apply the new gradient to the circle.
8. Hide the frame edges, then compare your work to Figure 65.
9. Save your work, then close Concentric Circle Gradient.

Figure 65 *Completed Design Project*

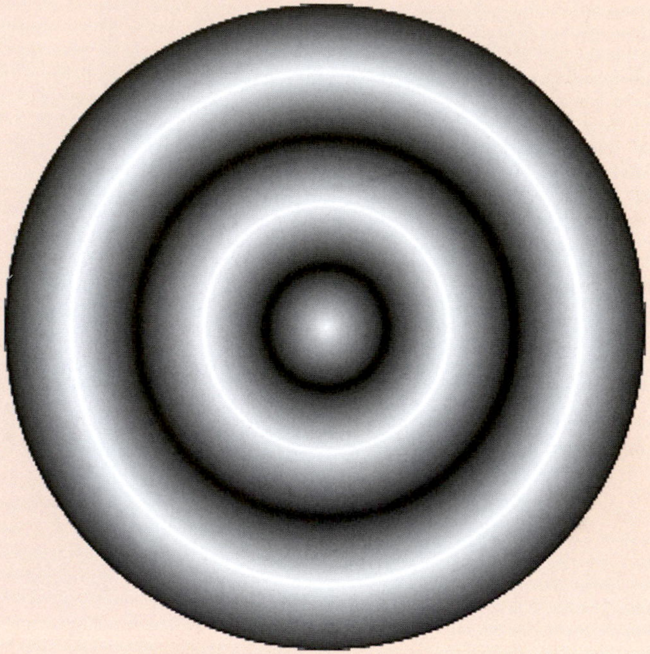

This project will test your familiarity with process colors. You will open an InDesign document that shows nine process colors. Each process color is numbered from 1 to 9. All nine colors are very basic mixes. None of the nine is composed of more than two process inks. The inks used to create the nine colors are used at either 100% or 50%. Your challenge is to guess the CMYK components of each color.

1. Open ID 5-8.indd, then save it as **Guessing Game**. The color squares are shown in Figure 66.
2. Use the Type tool to enter your guesses for each process color. You can type directly on top of each of the nine squares or directly below each, for example, **Magenta=100**.
3. When finished, double-click each color on the Swatches panel to identify the actual CMYK mix.
4. Enter the total number of your correct answers on your document window, save your work, then close Guessing Game.

Figure 66 *Portfolio Project Quiz*

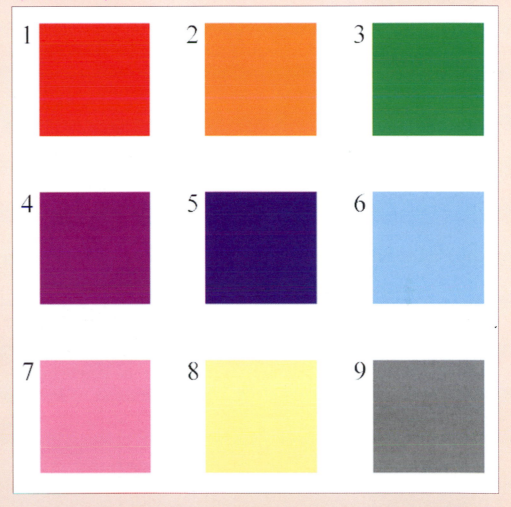

Working with Color

CHAPTER 1

GETTING STARTED WITH
ADOBE PHOTOSHOP CC

1. Start Adobe Photoshop CC 2014

2. Learn how to open and save an image

3. Examine the Photoshop window

4. Close a file and exit Photoshop

5. Learn about design principles and copyright rules

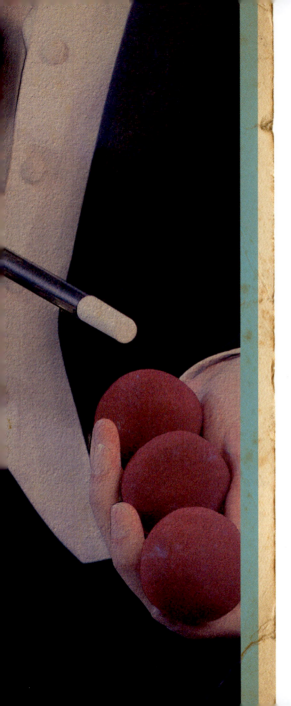

CHAPTER 1

GETTING STARTED WITH
ADOBE PHOTOSHOP CC

Using Photoshop and the Creative Cloud

Adobe Photoshop CC is an image-editing program that lets you create and modify digital images. 'CC' stands for Creative Cloud, a complete design environment. Although Adobe makes Photoshop available as a stand-alone product, it is also available as part of the Creative Cloud subscription, whether your interests lie with print design, web design, or multimedia production.

QUICK TIP

The Creative Cloud offers many constantly evolving tools (such as Bridge, Dreamweaver, Illustrator, InDesign, and Photoshop) and services (such as Typekit and Kuler).

A **digital image** is a picture in electronic form, and may be referred to as a file, document, graphic, picture, or image. Using Photoshop, you can create original artwork, manipulate images, and retouch photographs. Popular with graphics professionals, Photoshop is practical for anyone who wants to enhance existing artwork or create new masterpieces. For example, you can repair and restore damaged areas within an image, combine images, and create graphics and special effects for the web.

Understanding Platform User Interfaces

Photoshop is available for both Windows and Mac OS platforms. Regardless of which platform you use, the features and commands are similar. Some Windows and Mac OS keyboard commands use different keys. For example, the [Ctrl] and [Alt] keys are used in Windows, and the [⌘] and [option] keys are used on Macintosh computers. There are also cosmetic differences between the Windows and Mac OS versions of Photoshop due to the user interface differences found in each platform.

Understanding Sources

Photoshop allows you to work with images from a variety of sources. You can create your own original artwork in Photoshop, use images downloaded from the web, or use images that have been scanned or created using a digital camera. Whether you create Photoshop images to print in high resolution or optimize them for multimedia presentations, web-based functions, or animation projects, Photoshop is a powerful tool for communicating your ideas visually.

QUICK TIP

This book examines features in the 2014 release of Photoshop CC.

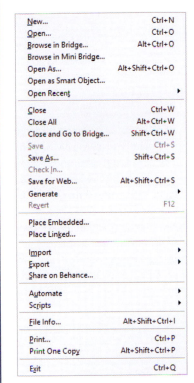

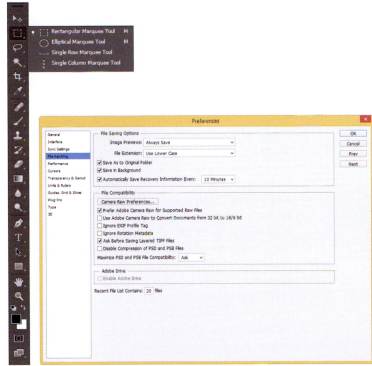

Options bar

Start Adobe
PHOTOSHOP CC 2014

What You'll Do

In this lesson, you'll start Photoshop for Windows or Mac OS, and then create a file.

Defining Image-Editing Software

Photoshop is an image-editing program. An **image-editing program** allows you to manipulate graphic images so that they can be posted on websites or reproduced by professional printers using full-color processes. Using panels, tools, menus, and a variety of techniques, you can modify a Photoshop image by rotating it, resizing it, changing its colors, or adding text. You can also use Photoshop to create and open different kinds of file formats, which enables you to create your own images, import them from a digital camera or scanner, or use files (in other formats) purchased from outside sources. Table 1 lists some of the graphics file formats that Photoshop can open and create.

Understanding Images

Every image is made up of very small squares, which are called **pixels**, and each pixel represents a color or shade. Pixels within an image can be added, deleted, or modified.

QUICK TIP

Photoshop files can become quite large. After a file is complete, you might want to **flatten** it, an irreversible process that combines all layers and reduces the file size.

Using Photoshop Features

Photoshop includes many tools that you can use to manipulate images and text. Within an image, you can add new items and modify existing elements, change colors, and draw shapes. For example, using the Lasso tool, you can outline a section of an image and drag the section onto another area of the image. You can also isolate a foreground or background image. You can extract all or part of a complex image from nearly any background and use it elsewhere.

QUICK TIP

You can create logos in Photoshop. A **logo** is a distinctive image that you can create by combining symbols, shapes, colors, and text. Logos give graphic identity to organizations such as corporations, universities, and retail stores.

You can also create and format text, called **type**, in Photoshop. You can apply a variety of special effects to type; for example, you can change the appearance of type and increase or decrease the distance between characters. You can also edit type after it has been created and formatted.

Adobe Dreamweaver CC, a web production app included in the Creative Cloud, allows you to optimize, preview, and animate images. Because Dreamweaver and Photoshop are both members of the Creative Cloud, you can jump seamlessly between the two apps.

Using these two apps, you can also quickly turn any graphics image into a gif animation.

Photoshop and Dreamweaver let you compress file size (while optimizing image quality) to ensure that your files download quickly from a web page. Using Photoshop optimization features, you can view multiple versions of an image and select the one that best suits your needs.

Starting Photoshop and Creating a File

The specific way you start Photoshop depends on whether you are using a Macintosh or Windows computer. When you start Photoshop in either platform, the computer displays a **splash screen**, which contains information about the software, and then the Photoshop window opens.

After you start Photoshop, you can create a file from scratch. You use the New dialog box to create a file. You can also use the New dialog box to set the size of the image you're about to create by typing dimensions in the Width and Height text boxes.

TABLE 1: SOME SUPPORTED GRAPHIC FILE FORMATS			
File format	**Filename extension**	**File format**	**Filename extension**
Bitmap	.bmp	PICT file	.pct, .pic, or .pict
Dicom	.dcm	Pixar	.pxr
Flash 3D	.fl3	Open EXR	.exr
Google Earth	.kmz	Radiance	.hdr, .rgbe, .xyze
Graphics Interchange Format	.gif	RAW	Varies
JPEG Picture Format	.jpg, .jpe, or .jpeg	Scitex CT	.sct
PC Paintbrush	.pcx	Tagged Image Format	.tif or .tiff
Photoshop	.psd	Targa	.tga or .vda
Photoshop EPS	.eps	Wavefront	.obj
Photoshop PDF	.pdf		

© 2013 Cengage Learning®

Start Photoshop (Windows 7, 8, or 8.1)

1. If using Windows 7, click the **Start button** 🪟 on the taskbar; if using Windows 8 or 8.1, click the **Windows logo button** ⊞ on the taskbar.

2. Type **ph**, click **Adobe Photoshop CC 2014** if necessary, as shown in Figure 1 using Windows 8.1, then click **Adobe Photoshop CC 2014**.

   If a 64-bit option is not available, click **Adobe Photoshop CC 2014**.

   TIP In Windows 7, the text will be typed in the Search programs and files text box. The results of your search will display in the box above the Start button.

3. Click **File** on the Menu bar, then click **New** to open the New dialog box.

4. Double-click the **number in the Width text box**, type **500**, click the **Width list arrow**, then click **Pixels** if it is not already selected.

5. Double-click the **number in the Height text box**, type **400**, then specify a resolution of **72** pixels/inch if necessary.

6. Click **OK**.

   TIP By default, the document window (the background of the active image) is dark gray. This color can be changed by right-clicking the background, then making a color selection.

7. Click the **menu arrow** ▶ on the status bar at the bottom of the image window, then click **Document Sizes** if it is not already selected.

You started Photoshop in Windows, then created a file with custom dimensions. Setting custom dimensions lets you specify the exact size of the image you are creating. You changed the display on the status bar to show the document size.

Figure 1 *Starting Photoshop CC (Windows)*

Your list may differ

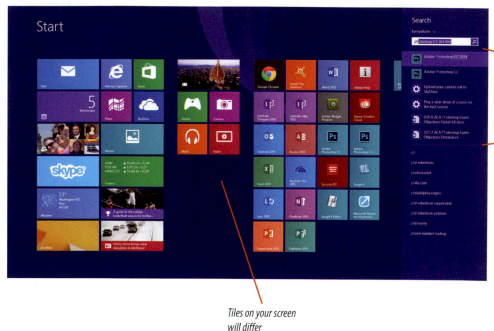

Tiles on your screen will differ

Understanding Hardware Requirements (Windows)

Adobe Photoshop CC has the following minimum system requirements:

- Processor: Intel® Pentium® 4 processor or AMD Athlon® 64 processor (2 GHz or faster)
- Operating System: Microsoft® Windows 7 (with Service Pack 1), 8, or 8 .1
- Memory: 1 GB of RAM
- Storage space: 2.5 GB of available hard-disk space
- Monitor: 1024 x 768 resolution (1280 x 800 recommended)
- Video: 16-bit or higher OpenGL 2.0 video card; 512 MB RAM (1 GB recommended)
- Broadband Internet connection required for activation, Creative Cloud membership validation, and access to online services

Figure 2 *Starting Photoshop CC (Macintosh)*

Source: Apple Inc.

Understanding Hardware Requirements (Mac OS)

Adobe Photoshop CC has the following minimum system requirements:

- Processor: Multicore Intel® processor with 64-bit support
- Operating System: Mac OS X 10.7, v10.8, or v10.9
- Memory: 1 GB of RAM
- Storage space: 3.2 GB of available hard-disk space
- Monitor: 1024 x 768 or greater monitor resolution (1280 x 800 recommended)
- Video: 16-bit or greater OpenGL 2.0 video card; 512 MB of VRAM (1 GB recommended)
- Broadband Internet connection required for software activation, Creative Cloud membership validation, and access to online services

Start Photoshop (Mac OS)

1. Click the **Launchpad icon** in the Dock, then type **ph**. (The search field does not appear in Mac OS 10.7.) Compare your screen to Figure 2.
2. Click the **Adobe Photoshop CC 2014 program icon**.
3. Click **File** on the Menu bar, then click **New**.
4. Double-click the **number in the Width text box**, type **500**, click the **Width list arrow**, then click **Pixels**.
5. Double-click the **number in the Height text box**, type **400**, then verify a resolution of **72** pixels/inch.
6. Click **OK**.

TIP The gray document window background can be turned on by clicking Window on the Menu bar, then clicking Application Frame.

7. Click the **menu arrow** ▶ on the status bar at the bottom of the image window, then click **Document Sizes** if it is not already checked.

You started Photoshop for Mac OS, then created a file with custom dimensions. You verified that the document size is visible on the status bar.

Learn How to Open
AND SAVE AN IMAGE

What You'll Do

Source: Morguefile.

 In this lesson, you'll locate and open files using the File menu, Adobe Bridge, and Mini Bridge; flag and sort files; and then save a file with a new name.

Opening and Saving Files

Photoshop provides several options for opening and saving a file. Often, the project you're working on determines the techniques you use for opening and saving files. For example, you might want to preserve the original version of a file while you modify a copy. You can open a file, and then immediately save it with a different filename, as well as open and save files in many different file formats. When working with graphic images, you can open a Photoshop file that has been saved as a bitmap (.bmp) file, and then save it as a JPEG (.jpg) file to use on a web page.

Customizing How You Open Files

You can customize how you open your files by setting preferences. **Preferences** are options you can set that are based on your work habits. For example, you can use the Open Recent command on the File menu to instantly locate and open the files that you recently worked on, or you can allow others to preview your files as thumbnails. Figure 3 shows the Windows

Figure 3 *Preferences dialog box*

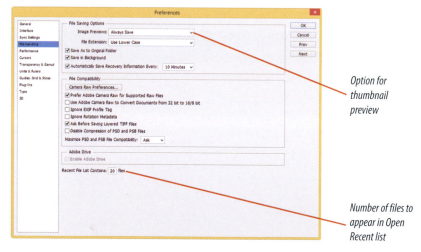

Option for thumbnail preview

Number of files to appear in Open Recent list

Getting Started with Adobe Photoshop CC

Preferences dialog box options for handling your files: the Mac dialog box differs slightly. Use the Preferences command on the Edit menu (Win) or the Photoshop menu (Mac) to open the Preferences dialog box.

Browsing Through Files

You can easily find the files you're looking for using Adobe Bridge, a separate download and stand-alone application that serves as the hub for Adobe Creative Cloud apps, or Adobe Mini Bridge, a less-powerful (and smaller) version of Bridge that opens within the Photoshop window. Mini Bridge provides less data than Bridge, but makes it easier to do simple tasks (like locating and opening files). Figure 4 shows the Magnifying Loupe tool in Adobe Bridge, the default when using the Filmstrip view. You can open Bridge or Mini Bridge using the File menu in Photoshop, but Bridge needs to be open in order to open Mini Bridge.

Figure 4 *Adobe Bridge window*
Source: Morguefile. Images © Photodisc/Getty Images. Image courtesy of Elizabeth Eisner Reding.

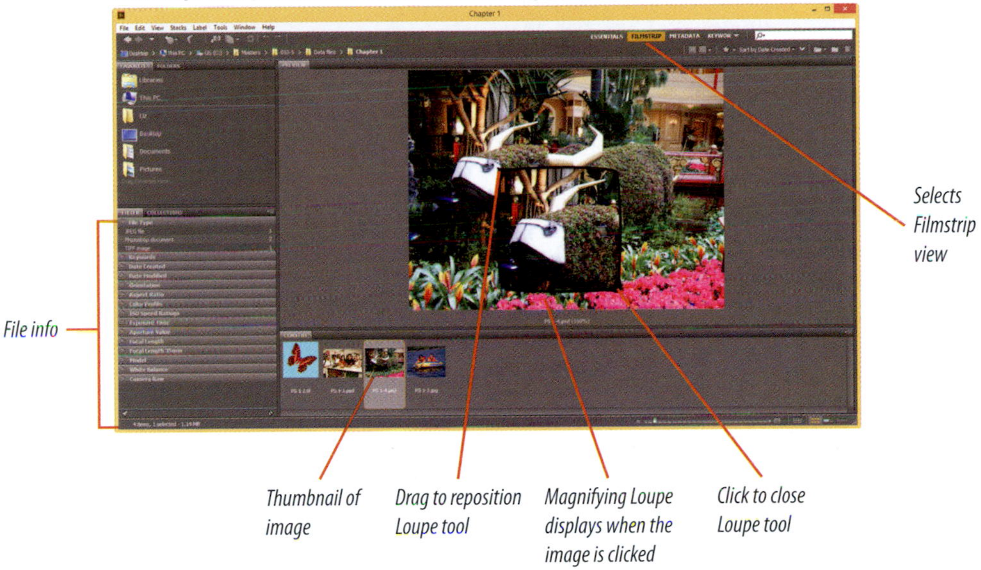

Selects Filmstrip view

File info

Thumbnail of image

Drag to reposition Loupe tool

Magnifying Loupe displays when the image is clicked

Click to close Loupe tool

DESIGNTIP

Opening Scanned Images

You can open a scanned or uploaded image in Photoshop (which usually has a .jpg extension or another graphics file format) by clicking File on the Menu bar, and then clicking Open. All Formats is the default file type, so you should be able to see all available image files in the Open dialog box. (On the Mac, the term All Readable Documents is used instead of All Formats; Enable is used instead of File Type.) Locate the folder containing your scanned or digital camera images, click the file you want to open, and then click Open. A scanned or digital camera image contains all its imagery in a single layer. You can add layers to the image, but you can only save these new layers if you save the image as a Photoshop image (with the extension .psd).

When you open Bridge, a series of panels allows you to view the files on your hard drive as hierarchical files and folders. In addition to the Favorites and Folders panels in the upper-left pane of the Bridge window, there are other important areas. Directly beneath the Favorites and Folders panels is a grouping that includes the Filter panel, which allows you to review properties of images in the (center) Content panel. In the (default) Essentials view, the right column displays the Preview panel and the Metadata and Keywords panels, which store information about a selected file (such as keywords) that can then be used as search parameters. You can use the tree structure (visible when the Folders tab is active) to find the file you are seeking. When you locate a file, you can click its thumbnail to display a larger image in the Preview panel and to see information about its size, format, and creation and modification dates in the Metadata panel. You can open a file in Photoshop from Bridge by double-clicking its thumbnail. You can close Bridge by clicking File (Win) or Adobe Bridge CC (Mac) on the (Bridge) Menu bar, and then clicking Exit (Win) or Quit Adobe Bridge CC (Mac), or by clicking the window's Close button (Win).

QUICK TIP

You can select multiple non-contiguous images by pressing and holding [Ctrl] (Win) or ⌘ (Mac) each time you click an image. You can select contiguous images by clicking the first image, and then pressing and holding [Shift] and clicking the last image in the group.

QUICK TIP

You can reset the Adobe Bridge preferences to the factory default by holding [Ctrl][Alt] (Win) or ⌘ [option] (Mac) while clicking the Launch Bridge button.

Understanding the Power of Bridge

In addition to allowing you to see all your images, Bridge can be used to rate (assign importance), sort (organize by name, rating, and other criteria), and label your images. Figure 4, on the previous page, contains images shown in Filmstrip view. There are seven potential views in Bridge (Essentials, Filmstrip, Metadata, Keywords, Light Table, Folders, and Output) that are controlled by buttons to the left of the search text box. (The Adobe Output Module and Light Table may have to be installed separately.) To assist in organizing your images, you can assign a color label or rating to one or more images regardless of your current view. Any number of selected images can be assigned a label by clicking Label on the Menu bar, and then clicking one of the Rating or Label options.

QUICK TIP

You can use Bridge to view thumbnails of all files on your computer. You can open any file for software *installed* on your computer by double-clicking its thumbnail in Bridge.

Getting There with Mini Bridge

While not as powerful as Bridge, Mini Bridge can be used to easily filter, sort, locate, and open files from *within* Photoshop. Mini Bridge is opened in the Photoshop window once Bridge is running, by clicking the Browse in Mini Bridge command on the File menu. Mini Bridge can be resized to suit your needs, and closed and reopened whenever necessary. To navigate Mini Bridge, shown in Figure 5 after being undocked and resized, you can click the arrows within the Path bar to change the file source. Clicking each arrow in the Path bar reveals the file structure in your hard drive. When you locate a file you want to open in Photoshop, double-click its thumbnail image.

QUICK TIP

So when might you use Mini Bridge? Suppose you need a file but don't know where it is. Without closing or switching out of Photoshop, you can use Mini Bridge to locate the file, and then open it by double-clicking its thumbnail.

Using Save As Versus Save

Sometimes it's more efficient to create a new image by modifying an existing one, especially if it contains elements and special effects that you want to use again. The Save As command on the File menu (in Photoshop) creates a copy of the file, prompts you to give the duplicate file a new name, and then displays the new filename in the image's title bar. You use the Save As command to name an unnamed file or to save an existing file with a new name. For example, throughout this book, you will be instructed to open your Data Files and use the Save As command. Saving your Data Files with new names keeps the original files intact in case you have to start the lesson over again or you want to repeat an exercise. When you use the Save command, you save the changes you made to the open file.

QUICK TIP

You can also create a copy of the active file by clicking Image on the Menu bar, and then clicking Duplicate. Click OK to confirm the name of the duplicate file.

Getting Images into Photoshop

There are a zillion digital cameras available in the marketplace, and each brand is a little different, but you can still easily import your images into Bridge by connecting the camera to your computer using the camera's cable. Turn the camera on and once your computer recognizes the camera, open Adobe Bridge. Click File on the (Bridge) Menu bar, then click Get Photos from Camera. This opens the Adobe Bridge CC Photo Downloader. Select the correct camera device from the

Get Photos from list arrow and choose a location for the downloaded file, then click Get Media. Your images are probably in the JPEG or RAW format, and their clarity will be the result of the megapixel capacity of your camera and the resolution setting.

Figure 5 *Mini Bridge*
Source: Morguefile. Images © Photodisc/Getty Images. Image courtesy of Elizabeth Eisner Reding.

Path bar

Click to go to Bridge

Click to sort

Drag to enlarge/reduce thumbnail size

Drag to resize the Mini Bridge window

Figure 6 *Image Size dialog box*
Source: Morguefile.

Resizing an Image

You may have created the perfect image, but the size may not be correct for your print format. Document size is a combination of the printed dimensions and pixel resolution. An image designed for a website, for example, might be too small for an image that will be printed in a newsletter. You can easily resize an image using the Image Size command on the Image menu. To use this feature, open the file you want to resize, click Image on the Menu bar, and then click Image Size. The Image Size dialog box, shown in Figure 6, opens. By changing the dimensions in the text boxes, you'll have your image resized in no time. Note the check mark next to Resample Image. With resampling checked, you can change the total number of pixels in the image and the print dimensions independently. With resampling off, you can change either the dimensions or the resolution; Photoshop will automatically adjust whichever value you ignore. The **canvas size**, which is the full editable area of an image, can be increased or decreased using the Canvas Size command on the Image menu. Decreasing an image's size crops the image whereas increasing the image's size adds to the background.

Open a file using the Menu bar

1. Click **File** on the Menu bar, then click **Open**.

2. Click the **Look in list arrow** (Win) or the **Current file location list arrow** (Mac), then navigate to the drive and folder where you store your Data Files.

3. Click **PS 1-1.psd**, as shown in Figure 7, then click **Open**.

You used the Open command on the File menu to locate and open a file.

Open a file using the Folders panel in Adobe Bridge

1. Click **File** on the Menu bar, click **Browse in Bridge**, then click the **Folders panel tab** if the Folders panel is not active.

2. Navigate through the hierarchical tree to the drive and folder where you store your Chapter 1 Data Files, verify that Sort by Type and an up arrow (^) display below the search box, then click **Essentials** on the workspace switcher if it is not already selected.

3. Click the **image of the butterfly**, then drag the **slider** (at the bottom of the Bridge window) a third of the way between the Smaller thumbnail size button ▭ and the Larger thumbnail size button ▭, then click the image of the ox *once*. Compare your screen to Figure 8.

4. Double-click the **image of a butterfly** (PS 1-2.tif). Bridge is no longer visible.

5. Click the **Close button** in the butterfly image file tab in Photoshop.

You used the Folders panel in Adobe Bridge to locate and open a file. This feature makes it easy to find which file you want to use.

Figure 7 *Open dialog box for Windows and Macintosh*
Source: Morguefile. Images © Photodisc/Getty Images.

Available folders and files may differ from your list

Selected filename

Current drive and path

Your selected view may differ

Available folders and files

Current file location list arrow

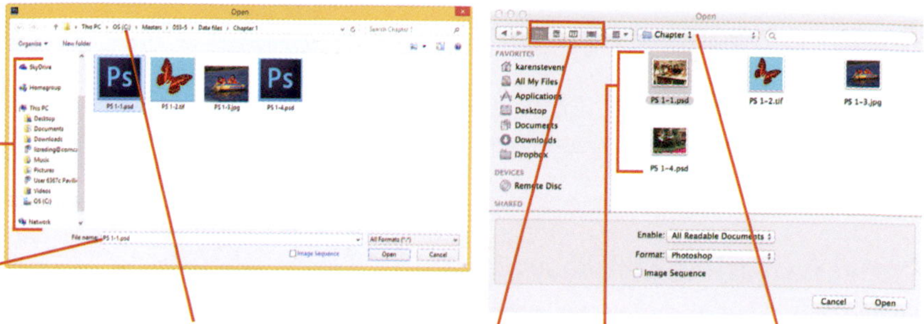

Figure 8 *Adobe Bridge window*
Source: Morguefile. Images © Photodisc/Getty Images. Image courtesy of Elizabeth Eisner Reding.

Determines whether images are sorted in ascending or descending order

Indicates how the images are sorted

Preview of selected file displays here

Click the Keywords panel tab to assign keywords to a selected file, then click any of the displayed keywords

Your list will be different

Drag to resize thumbnails

Getting Started with Adobe Photoshop CC

Figure 9 *Adobe Mini Bridge window*

Source: Morguefile. Images © Photodisc/Getty Images. Image courtesy of Elizabeth Eisner Reding.

Timeline tab displays when Mini Bridge opens

Click to change the view options

Click to sort items

Move window by dragging this bar

Click to close Mini Bridge

Click to filter items

Resize window by dragging this (or any) corner

Path bar: yours will differ

Figure 10 *Save As dialog box*

Your list of files might be different

New filename goes here

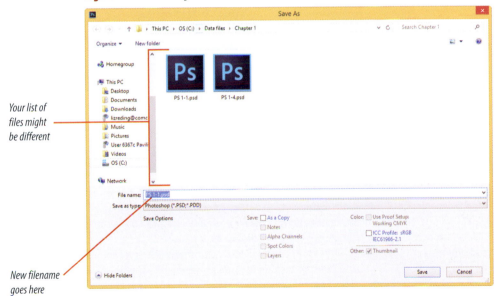

Open a file using Mini Bridge

1. Click **File** on the Menu bar, then click **Browse in Mini Bridge**.
2. Use the Path bar to locate the drive and folder where you store your Chapter 1 Data Files. See Figure 9.
3. Double-click the **image of a butterfly** (PS 1-2.tif).
4. Double-click the **Mini Bridge tab** to minimize the panel, then close PS 1-2.tif.

   By default, Mini Bridge is minimized at the bottom of the Photoshop workspace. Enlarge or minimize Mini Bridge by double-clicking its tab.

You opened Mini Bridge in Photoshop, navigated to where your Data Files are stored, opened a file, then minimized Mini Bridge.

Use the Save As command

1. Verify that the PS 1-1.psd window is active.
2. Click **File** on the Menu bar, click **Save As**, then compare your Save As dialog box to Figure 10.
3. If the drive containing your Data Files is not displayed, click the **Save in list arrow** (Win) or the **Current file location list arrow** (Mac), then navigate to the drive and folder where you store your Chapter 1 Data Files.
4. Select the current filename in the File name text box (Win) or Save As text box (Mac), type **Friends**, then click **Save**.

   TIP Click OK to close the Maximize Compatibility dialog box if it appears now and in future lessons.

You used the Save As command on the File menu to save the file with a new name. This command lets you save a changed version of an image while keeping the original file intact.

Change from Tabbed to Floating Documents

1. Click **Window** on the Menu bar, point to **Arrange**, then click **2-up Horizontal**.

   Each of the open files displays in a horizontal window.

   N-up viewing allows you to edit one image while comparing it with another. You can drag layers from one image to another in N-up view. Use N-up viewing using the Arrange command on the Window menu, and then tiling either horizontally or vertically until the images are in the configuration that works best.

   TIP You can display images in several arrangements which allows you to vary the grouping of open documents. To see these arrangements, click Window on the Menu bar, point to Arrange, then click any of the available menu choices.

   TIP The options in the Arrange menu make a temporary change to the workspace that will be in effect for the current Photoshop session.

2. Click **Window** on the Menu bar, point to **Arrange**, then click **Float All in Windows**. Compare your Friends image to Figure 11.

   TIP By default, each image is displayed in its own tab, but you can change this so each image floats in its own window.

   You temporarily changed the arrangement of open documents from consolidated, or tabbed, to a 2-up Horizontal format, and then to the Float All in Windows format where each image displays in its own window.

Figure 11 *Friends image*
Source: Morguefile.

Duplicate file has new name

Ps Friends.psd @ 100% (RGB/8#)

100%   Doc: 550.8K/550.8K

Changing File Formats

In addition to using the Save As command to duplicate an existing file, the Save As command is a handy way of changing one format into another. For example, you can open an image you created using a digital camera, and then make modifications in the Photoshop format. To do this, open a JPEG file in Photoshop, click File on the Menu bar, and then click Save As. Name the file, click the Format list arrow, click Photoshop (*.psd, *.pdd) (Win) or Photoshop (Mac), and then click Save. You can also change formats using Bridge by selecting the file, clicking Tools on the Menu bar, pointing to Photoshop, and then clicking Image Processor. Section 3 of the Image Processor dialog box lets you determine the new file format.

Figure 12 *Images in Adobe Bridge*

Source: Morguefile. Images © Photodisc/Getty Images. Image courtesy of Elizabeth Eisner Reding.

Click to change
sorting method

Rated and
Approved file

Figure 13 *Sorted files*

Source: Morguefile. Images © Photodisc/Getty Images.

Click to change how
items in the Content
panel are sorted

Filter items by rating

Rate and filter with Bridge

1. Click **File** on the Menu bar, then click **Browse in Bridge** [Br] to make the program active.

2. Click the **Folders panel tab**, then click the drive and folder where you store your Chapter 1 Data Files on the File Hierarchy tree (if necessary).

3. Verify that file **PS 1-2.tif** (the butterfly image) is selected.

4. Press and hold [**Ctrl**] (Win) or [⌘] (Mac), click **PS 1-1.psd** (the image of the friends), then release [**Ctrl**] (Win) or [⌘] (Mac).

5. Click **Label** on the Bridge Menu bar, then click **Approved**.

6. Click **PS 1-1.psd**, click **Label** on the Bridge Menu bar, then click ***. See Figure 12.

7. Click the **Sort list arrow** on the Bridge Path bar, click **By Filename**, point to **Sort**, then verify that the **Ascending Order arrow** displays to the right of the sort list arrow. Compare your screen to Figure 13.

   The order of the files is changed.

TIP You can also change the order of files in the Content panel using the Sort command on the View menu. When you click the Sort by Filename list arrow, you'll see the same sorting options as on the View menu. Click the option you want and the files in the Content panel will be rearranged.

8. Click **View** on the Menu bar, point to **Sort**, then click **By Size**.

9. Click **File** (Win) or **Adobe Bridge CC** (Mac) on the (Bridge) Menu bar, then click **Exit** (Win) or **Quit Adobe Bridge CC** (Mac) to close Bridge.

You labeled and rated files using Bridge, sorted the files in a folder, then changed the sort order. When finished, you closed Bridge.

Examine
THE PHOTOSHOP WINDOW

What You'll Do

 In this lesson, you'll arrange documents and change the default display, select a tool on the Tools panel, use a shortcut key to cycle through the hidden tools, select and add a tool to the Tool Preset picker, use the Window menu to show and hide panels in the workspace, and create a customized workspace.

Learning About the Workspace

The Photoshop **workspace** is the area within the Photoshop program window that includes the entire window, from the command menus at the top of your screen to the status bar (Win) at the bottom. Desktop items may be visible between the menu commands and the document title bar (Mac). The (Windows) workspace is shown in Figure 14.

In Windows, the area containing the Photoshop commands is called the Menu bar. On the Mac, the main menus are at the top of the desktop, but not directly attached to the options bar. If the active image window is maximized, the filename of the open unnamed file is Untitled-1, because it has not been named. The Menu bar also contains the Close button and the Minimize/Maximize and Restore buttons (Win).

You can choose a menu command by clicking it or in Windows, by pressing [Alt], and then clicking the underlined letter in the menu name. Some commands display shortcut keys on the right side of the menu. Shortcut keys provide an alternative way to activate menu commands. Some commands might appear dimmed, which means they are not currently available. A right-pointing triangle after a command indicates additional choices.

DESIGNTIP

Overcoming Information Overload

One of the most common experiences shared by first-time Photoshop users is information overload. There are just too many panels and tools to look at! When you feel your brain overheating, take a moment and sit back. Remind yourself that the active image area is the central area where you can see a composite of your work. All the tools and panels are there to help you, not to add to the confusion. The tools and features in Photoshop CC are designed to be easier to find and use, making any given task faster to complete.

Finding Tools Everywhere

The **Tools panel** contains tools associated with frequently used Photoshop commands. The face of a tool contains a graphical representation (icon) of its function; for example, the Zoom tool shows a magnifying glass. The **zoom factor** (the amount of magnification applied to the image) is shown in the document title bar and allows you to better see the area you're working on. You can place the pointer over each tool to display a tool tip, which tells you the name or function of that tool. Some tools have additional hidden tools, indicated by a small gray triangle in the lower-right corner of the tool.

QUICK TIP

You can view the Tools panel in a 2-column format by clicking the expand arrow in its upper-left corner.

The **options bar**, located directly under the Menu bar, displays the current settings for the selected tool. For example, when you click the Type tool, the default font and font size appear on the options bar, which can be changed if desired. You can move the options bar anywhere in the workspace for easier access. The first button on the options bar is the Tool preset picker, which displays the active tool. You can click the list arrow on the Tool Preset picker to select another tool without having to use the Tools panel. Two vertical docks display to the right of the Document window, the panel icon dock and the expanded panel dock. Panels not displayed in a workspace can be collapsed and expanded from the icon

dock, which also contains an area where you can assemble panels for quick access.

Panels are small windows used to access settings and modify images. By default, panels appear in stacked groups at the right side of the window. A collection of panels is called a **panel group**. A **dock** is a dark gray vertical bar that contains a collection of panels, panel groups or panel icons. The arrows in the dock are used to expand and collapse the panels. You can display a panel by simply clicking the panel tab, or making it the active panel by clicking its name in the Window menu, or by clicking its icon in the icon dock (if it's displayed). Panels can be separated

and moved anywhere in the workspace by dragging their tabs to new locations. You can dock or undock a panel by dragging its tab in or out of a dock. As you move a panel within the dock, you'll see a blue highlighted drop zone. A **drop zone** is an area where you can move a panel. You can also change the order of tabs by dragging a tab to a new location within its panel. Each panel contains a menu that you can view by clicking the Panel options button in its upper-right corner.

QUICK TIP

You can reset panels to their default locations at any time by selecting Reset Essentials in the workspace switcher.

Figure 14 *Workspace*

Double-click the Application icon to close the program

Menu bar

Options bar

Tool preset picker

Zoom factor

Status bar

Tools panel

Workspace switcher

Icon dock

Layers panel

Document window title bar

Document window

Workspace

When images are displayed as tabbed documents, the **status bar** is located at the bottom of the program window (Win) or work area (Mac). When images are floating, the status bar is located at the bottom of each individual image. It displays information, such as the file size of the active window. You can display other information on the status bar by clicking the triangle to view a menu with more options.

Rulers can help you precisely measure and position an object in the workspace. The rulers do not appear the first time you use Photoshop, but you can display them by clicking Rulers on the View menu.

Using Tool Shortcut Keys

Each tool has a corresponding shortcut key. For example, the shortcut key for the Type tool is T. After you know a tool's shortcut key, you can select the tool on the Tools panel by pressing its shortcut key. To select and cycle through a tool's hidden tools, you press and hold [Shift], and then press the tool's shortcut key until the desired tool appears.

Customizing Your Environment

Photoshop makes it easy for you to position elements just where you want them. If you move elements around to make your environment more convenient, you can always return your workspace to its original appearance by resetting the default panel locations. Once you have your work area arranged the way you want it, you can create a customized workspace by clicking the workspace switcher on the Menu bar, and then clicking New Workspace. If you want to open a named workspace, click the workspace switcher, and then click the name of the workspace you want to use. Photoshop comes with many customized workspaces that are designed for specific tasks.

You can also change the color of your workspace by clicking Edit on the Menu bar, pointing to Preferences, then clicking Interface (Win) or by clicking Photoshop on the Menu bar, pointing to Preferences, then clicking Interface (Mac). Here you can choose one of four color themes. Color themes can be changed on a permanent or temporary basis. Using the Color list arrows in the Interface panel of the Preferences dialog box, you can permanently change the color theme using the four displayed themes, or any color you choose.

Figure 15 *Keyboard Shortcuts and Menus dialog box*

Instructions to edit shortcuts

Learning Shortcut Keys and Creating Customized Keyboard Shortcuts

Keyboard shortcuts can make your work with Photoshop faster and easier. As you become more familiar with Photoshop, you'll gradually pick up shortcuts for commands and tools you use most often, such as saving a file or the Move tool. You'll notice that as you learn to use shortcut keys, your speed while working with Photoshop will increase and you'll complete tasks with fewer mouse clicks. In fact, once you discover the power of keyboard shortcuts, you may never use menus again. You can find existing keyboard shortcuts by clicking Edit on the Menu bar, and then clicking Keyboard Shortcuts. The Keyboard Shortcuts and Menus dialog box, shown in Figure 15, allows you to add shortcuts or edit those that already exist. You can also display the list of shortcuts by exporting it to an HTML file, and then printing it or viewing it in a browser.

Figure 16 *Hidden tools*
Source: Morguefile.

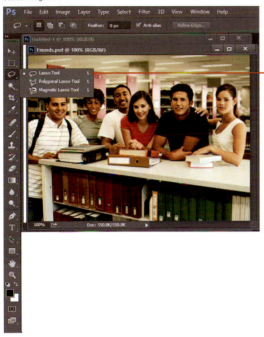

Shortcut key

Select a tool

1. Click the **Lasso tool** on the Tools panel, press and hold the **mouse button** until a list of hidden tools appears, then release the **mouse button**. See Figure 16. Note the shortcut key, L, next to the tool name.

2. Click the **Polygonal Lasso tool** on the Tools panel.

3. Press and hold [**Shift**], press [**L**] three times to cycle through the Lasso tools, then release [**Shift**]. Did you notice how the options bar changes for each selected Lasso tool?

TIP You can return the tools to their default setting by clicking the Tool Preset picker list arrow on the options bar, clicking the More Options button, then clicking Reset All Tools.

You selected the Lasso tool on the Tools panel and used its shortcut key to cycle through the Lasso tools. Becoming familiar with shortcut keys can speed up your work and make you more efficient.

64-bit Version of Photoshop

You may have heard people talking about the 64-bit version of Photoshop. What does this mean? (Here's a good analogy: Imagine a bus that can hold 64 students versus one that can only hold 32 students. Because it has a larger capacity, the bus carrying 64 students will have to make fewer trips to pick up a greater number of students.) Prior to CS5, Photoshop was only available as a 32-bit application for both Windows and Mac. With CS6 and CC, Photoshop became a 64-bit application. This meant that the architecture of the program had been redesigned to accommodate huge files (those larger than 4 GB) and make better use of RAM. The net result is that the 64-bit version of Photoshop is faster and more efficient. Some features, however, still work only in 32-bit mode (until they're updated), whereas other features, such as video, are not supported on 32-bit mode. In Windows, you can launch either version from the Windows taskbar (or pin either or both versions to the taskbar). The Mac OS version of Photoshop is only available in 64-bit.

Select a tool from the Tool Preset picker

1. Click the **Tool Preset picker list arrow** ⊞ on the options bar.

2. Deselect the **Current Tool Only check box** if checked. See Figure 17.

   The name of a button is displayed in a tool tip, the descriptive text that appears when you point to the button. Your Tool Preset picker list will differ, and may contain no entries at all. This list can be customized by each user.

3. Double-click **Magnetic Lasso 24 pixels** in the list.

TIP Double-clicking a tool selects it and closes the Tool Preset picker list.

You selected the Magnetic Lasso tool using the Tool Preset picker. The Tool Preset picker makes it easy to access frequently used tools and their settings.

Figure 17 *Using the Tool Preset picker*

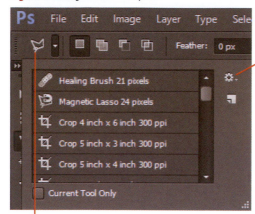

More Options button
adds new tools and
displays more options

Active tool displays
in Tool Preset picker

Figure 18 *Full Screen Mode with Menu bar*
Source: Morguefile.

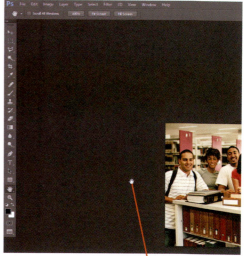

Use hand pointer
to reposition image

Using the Full Screen Mode

By default, Photoshop displays images in consolidated tabs, although you can change this on a permanent or temporary basis. This means that each image is displayed within its own tab. There are also three modes for viewing the menus, panels, and tools: Standard Screen Mode, Full Screen Mode with Menu Bar, and Full Screen Mode. And why would you want to stray from the familiar Standard Screen Mode? Perhaps your image is so large that it's difficult to see it all in Standard Screen Mode, or perhaps you want a less cluttered screen. Maybe you just want to try something different. You can switch between modes by clicking View on the Menu bar, pointing to Screen Mode, then clicking one of the three modes. You can also change modes by pressing [Shift] F. When in Full Screen Mode with Menu bar, click the Hand tool (or press the keyboard shortcut H), and you can reposition the active image, as shown in Figure 18.

Getting Started with Adobe Photoshop CC

Figure 19 *Move tool added to Tool Preset picker*

New tool added to panel

Click to display menu options

Selected check box displays only current tool

Setting Preferences

The Preferences dialog box contains several topics, each with its own settings: General; Interface; Sync Settings, File Handling; Performance; Cursors; Transparency & Gamut; Units & Rulers; Guides, Grid & Slices; Plug-Ins; Type; and 3D. To open the Preferences dialog box, click Edit (Win) or Photoshop (Mac) on the Menu bar, point to Preferences, and then click a topic that represents the settings you want to change. For example, if you move panels around the workspace or make other changes to them, those changes will be retained the next time you start the program. To reset panels to their default, click Interface on the Preferences menu, click the Restore Default Workspaces button, and then click OK.

Add a tool to the Tool Preset picker

1. Click the **Move tool** on the Tools panel.
2. Click the **Tool Preset picker list arrow** on the options bar.
3. Click the **More Options button** on the Tool Preset picker.
4. Click **New Tool Preset**, then click **OK** to accept the default name (Move Tool 1). Compare your list to Figure 19.

TIP You can display the currently selected tool alone by selecting the Current Tool Only check box.

You added the Move tool to the Tool Preset picker. Once you know how to add tools to the Tool Preset picker, you can quickly and easily customize your work environment.

Change the default display, theme color, and document display

1. Click **Edit** (Win) or **Photoshop** (Mac) on the Menu bar, point to **Preferences**, then click **Interface**.
2. Click the **far-right gray color box** (light gray).

   Did you notice that the workspace color changed?
3. Click the **far-left gray color box** (dark gray), click the **second from the right gray color box**, click the **second from the left gray color box**.

   The workspace theme display returns to the default.
4. Click the **Open Documents as Tabs check box** to deselect it, then click **OK**.

You examined each of the available color themes and changed the default display so that each time you open Photoshop, each image will display in its own window rather than in tabs.

Show and hide panels

1. If necessary, click the **Swatches tab** to make the Swatches panel active, as shown in Figure 20.
2. Click the **Collapse to Icons button** ▶▶ on the dock to collapse the panels.
3. Click the **Expand Panels button** ◀◀ on the dock to expand the panels.
4. Click **Window** on the Menu bar, then click **Swatches** to deselect it.

TIP You can hide all open panels by pressing [Shift] and [Tab] together, and then show them by pressing [Shift] and [Tab] again. To hide all open panels, the options bar, and the Tools panel, press [Tab], then show them by pressing [Tab] again. If you close a panel that is grouped with other panels, the other panels close as well.

5. Click **Window** on the Menu bar, then click **Swatches** to redisplay the Swatches panel.

You collapsed and expanded the panels, then used the Window menu to show and hide the Swatches panel. You might want to hide panels at times in order to enlarge your work area.

Figure 20 *Active Swatches panel*

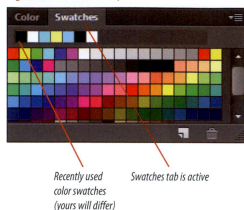

Recently used color swatches (yours will differ)

Swatches tab is active

Figure 21 *Tool Preset picker More Options menu*

New Tool Preset...
Rename Tool Preset...
Delete Tool Preset
✓ Sort by Tool
✓ Show All Tool Presets
Show Current Tool Presets
Text Only
✓ Small List
Large List
Reset Tool
Reset All Tools
Preset Manager...
Reset Tool Presets...
Load Tool Presets...
Save Tool Presets...
Replace Tool Presets...
Airbrushes
Art History
Artists' Brushes
Brushes
Crop and Marquee
DP Presets
Dry Media
Pencil Brushes
Pencils Mixer Brush
Splatter Brush Tool Presets
Text

Modifying a Tool Preset

Once you've created tool presets, you'll probably want to know how they can be deleted and renamed. To delete any tool preset, select it on the Tool Preset picker panel. Click the More Options button on the Tool Preset picker panel to view the menu, shown in Figure 21, and then click Delete Tool Preset. To rename a tool preset, click the More Options button and then click Rename Tool Preset.

Figure 22 *New Workspace dialog box*

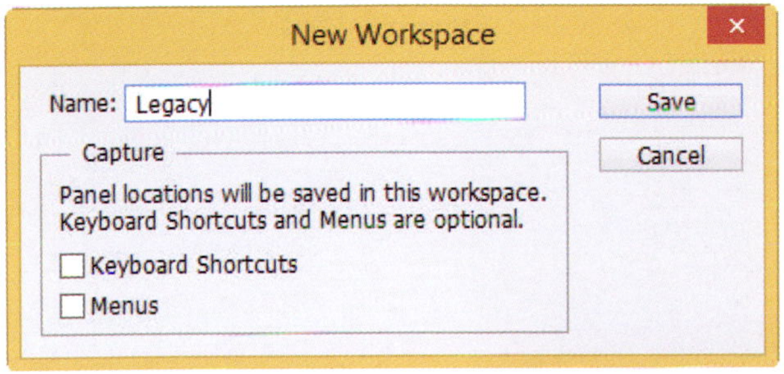

Figure 23 *Adobe Configurator 4*
Adobe Systems Incorporated.

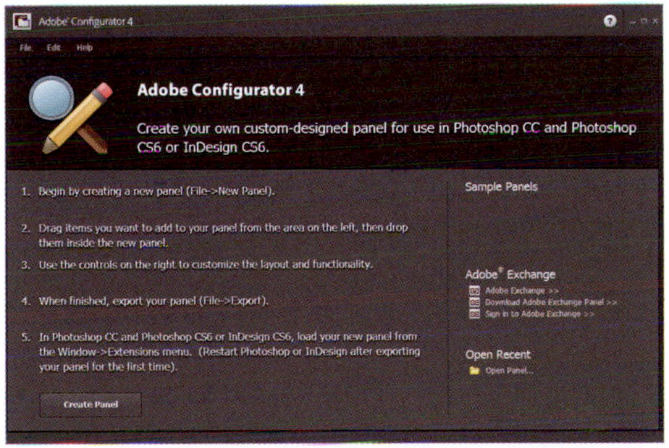

Create a customized workspace

1. Click **Window** on the Menu bar, click **History**, then drag the newly displayed panel in the dark gray line *beneath* the Swatches panel. (*Hint*: When you drag one panel into another, you'll see a light blue line, indicating that the new panel will dock with the existing panels.)

2. Click **Window** on the Menu bar, point to **Workspace**, then click **New Workspace**.

3. Type **Legacy** in the Name text box, then verify that only Panel locations will be saved, as shown in Figure 22.

4. Click **Save**.

5. Click **Window** on the Menu bar, then point to **Workspace**.

   The name of the new workspace appears on the Workspace menu.

6. Click **Essentials (Default)**.

You created a customized workspace, then reset the panel locations to the default Essentials workspace. Customized workspaces provide you with a work area that is always tailored to your needs.

Creating Your Own Panels with Adobe Configurator

You've seen how you can customize your workspace by grouping panels, and then saving the settings for future use. Configurator 4, shown in Figure 23, lets you create a customized Photoshop workspace on steroids. Configurator is a downloadable app from Adobe that lets you create your own panels. Using drag-and-drop technology, you can pick and choose from the tools, commands, actions, widgets, and containers that are at your disposal in any session of Photoshop, and arrange them in any order you choose. And the great news is that you don't have to be a master programmer to do it! Once you've created a panel, you export it using a command on the File menu, then load the panel into Photoshop using the Extensions command on the Window menu. You can download Configurator from *labs.adobe .com/downloads/configurator.html.*

Close a File
AND EXIT PHOTOSHOP

What You'll Do

New...	Ctrl+N
Open...	Ctrl+O
Browse in Bridge...	Alt+Ctrl+O
Browse in Mini Bridge...	
Open As...	Alt+Shift+Ctrl+O
Open as Smart Object...	
Open Recent	▶
Close	Ctrl+W
Close All	Alt+Ctrl+W
Close and Go to Bridge...	Shift+Ctrl+W
Save	Ctrl+S
Save As...	Shift+Ctrl+S
Check In...	
Save for Web...	Alt+Shift+Ctrl+S
Generate	▶
Revert	F12
Place Embedded...	
Place Linked...	
Import	▶
Export	▶
Share on Behance...	
Automate	▶
Scripts	▶
File Info...	Alt+Shift+Ctrl+I
Print...	Ctrl+P
Print One Copy	Alt+Shift+Ctrl+P
Exit	Ctrl+Q

 In this lesson, you'll use the Close and Exit (Win) or Quit (Mac) commands to close a file and exit Photoshop.

Concluding Your Work Session

At the end of your work session, you might have opened several files; you now need to decide which ones you want to save.

QUICK TIP

If you share a computer with other people, it's a good idea to reset Photoshop's preferences back to their default settings. You can do so when you start Photoshop by clicking Window on the Menu bar, pointing to Workspace, and then clicking Essentials (Default).

Closing versus Exiting

When you are finished working on an image, you need to save and close it. You can close one file at a time, or close all open files at the same time by exiting the program. Closing a file leaves Photoshop open, which allows you to open or create another file. Exiting Photoshop closes the file, closes Photoshop, and returns you to the desktop, where you can choose to open another program or shut down the computer. Photoshop will prompt you to save any changes before it closes the files. If you do not modify a new or existing file, Photoshop will close it automatically when you exit.

QUICK TIP

To close all open files without exiting Photoshop, click File on the Menu bar, and then click Close All.

Maintaining Adobe Creative Cloud Tools and Services

When running Photoshop, you may see a small cloud icon (as part of the Creative Cloud installation, not Photoshop specifically) indicating that you have updates to installed Creative Cloud apps, an Update dialog box might appear, prompting you to search for updates or new information on the Adobe website. If you click Yes, Photoshop will automatically notify you that a download is available; however, you do not have to select it. You can also obtain information about Photoshop from the Adobe Photoshop website (*www.adobe.com/products/photoshop.html*), where you can link to downloads, tips, training, help, resources, and other support topics. The Creative Cloud desktop app in Windows will display the number of updates available. On the Mac, the number of updates will display next to the Creative Cloud icon at the top of the screen.

Getting Started with Adobe Photoshop CC

Figure 24 *Closing a file using the File menu*

Close command

Exit command

New...	Ctrl+N
Open...	Ctrl+O
Browse in Bridge...	Alt+Ctrl+O
Browse in Mini Bridge...	
Open As...	Alt+Shift+Ctrl+O
Open as Smart Object...	
Open Recent	▶
Close	Ctrl+W
Close All	Alt+Ctrl+W
Close and Go to Bridge...	Shift+Ctrl+W
Save	Ctrl+S
Save As...	Shift+Ctrl+S
Check In...	
Save for Web...	Alt+Shift+Ctrl+S
Generate	▶
Revert	F12
Place Embedded...	
Place Linked...	
Import	▶
Export	▶
Share on Behance...	
Automate	▶
Scripts	▶
File Info...	Alt+Shift+Ctrl+I
Print...	Ctrl+P
Print One Copy	Alt+Shift+Ctrl+P
Exit	Ctrl+Q

Close a file and exit Photoshop

1. Click **File** on the Menu bar, then compare your menu to Figure 24.
2. Click **Close**.

TIP You can close an open file without closing Photoshop by clicking the Close button in the image window or tab. Photoshop will prompt you to save any unsaved changes before closing the file.

3. If asked to save your work, click **Yes** (Win) or **Save** (Mac).
4. Click **File** on the Menu bar, then click **Exit** (Win) or click **Photoshop** on the Menu bar, then click **Quit Photoshop** (Mac).
5. If asked to save your work (the untitled file), click **No** (Win) or **Don't Save** (Mac).

You closed the current file and exited the program by using the Close and Exit (Win) or Quit (Mac) commands.

DESIGNTIP

Using a Scanner and a Digital Camera

Scanners and digital cameras are two tools you can use to generate images in Photoshop. A digital camera captures images as digital files and stores them on some form of electronic medium, such as a SD/SDHC cards. After you upload the images from your camera to your computer, you can work with images in Photoshop. Digital cameras use **metering** which provides a way of compensating for a variety of lighting conditions. Examples of metering are spot metering, center-weighted average metering, average metering, partial metering, and multi-zone metering.

If you have a scanner, you can import print images, such as those taken from photographs, magazines, or line drawings, into Photoshop. Remember that images taken from magazines are owned by others and that you need permission to distribute them. There are many types of scanners, including flatbed, single-sheet feed, or handheld. Scanners are pretty commonplace, but *how* do they work? A flatbed scanner works by laying an image on a glass bed, and then a scanning array (which consists of a lamp, mirror, lens, and image sensor) moves back and forth to cover the whole surface. The image sensor may be a Charge-Coupled Device (CCD) in which a light beam is converted to an electrical signal, or a Compact Image Sensor (CIS), in which a single row of sensor elements are mounted very close to the document. Light from the lamp bounces off the original and is, with the CCD, reflected by the mirror into the lens, which focuses the image into the CCD. In the case of the CIS, the light and dark areas are picked up directly by the sensor. The CCD/CIS digitizes the results via an analog-to-digital converter, or ADC, and sends the resulting information to the scanner's own hardware, and then to the host computer.

Learn About Design Principles
AND COPYRIGHT RULES

What You'll Do

Image courtesy of Elizabeth Eisner Reding.

 In this lesson, you'll learn about various design principles, the difference between designing for print media versus designing for the web, and copyright rules that define how images may be used.

Print Design Versus Web Design

Who's going to be viewing your images, and how? Will your image be printed in a lot of 5000, or will it be viewed on a monitor? Does it matter? When you think about it, the goals of print designers are quite different from those who design for the web. Table 2 illustrates some of the differences between these two art forms.

Composition 101

What makes one design merely okay and another terrific? While any such judgment is subjective, there are some rules governing image composition. It goes without saying that, as the artist, you have a message you're trying to deliver or something you're trying to say to the viewer. This is true whether the medium is oil painting, photography, or Photoshop imagery.

Elements under your control in your composition are tone, sharpness, scale, and arrangement. (You may see these items classified differently elsewhere, but they amount to the same concepts.)

- **Tone** is the brightness and contrast within an image. By using light and shadows you can shift the focus of the viewer's eye and control the mood.
- **Sharpness** is used to direct the viewer's eye to a specific area of an image.

| TABLE 2: DIFFERENCES BETWEEN PRINT AND WEB DESIGN ||
Print	**Web**
Mass-produced product that will all be identical and can be held in someone's hand.	Will be viewed on monitors of different size and resolution, with varying colors.
Designed for a limited size and area measured in inches.	Designed for a flexible web page measured in pixels.
You want to hold the reader's attention long to deliver the message: a *passive* experience.	You want the reader to stay as long as possible on your website and click links that delve deeper: an *active* experience.
Output is permanent and stable.	Output varies with user's hardware and software and content can evolve.

© 2013 Cengage Learning®

- **Scale** is the size relationship of objects to one another.
- **Arrangement** is how objects are positioned in space, relative to one another.

Are objects in your image contributing to clarity or clutter? Are similarly-sized objects confusing the viewer? Would blurring one area of an image change the viewer's focus?

These are tools you have to influence your artistic expression. Make sure the viewer understands what you want seen.

Arranging Elements

The appearance of elements in an image is important, but of equal importance is the way in which the elements are arranged. The components of any image should form a cohesive unit so that the reader is unaware of all the different parts, yet influenced by the way they work together to emphasize a message or reveal information. For example, if a large image is used, it should be easy for the reader to connect the image with any descriptive text. There should be an easily understood connection between the text and the artwork, and the reader should be able to seamlessly connect them.

QUICK TIP

Make peace with the fact that you cannot completely control how a web page will look on every conceivable device and browser.

In a newsletter, for example, it makes sense to organize text in a columnar fashion, but would you want snaking columns in a web page? Probably not. You wouldn't want to be scrolling up and down to read all the columnar text. At the very least, good web design has to consider the following items:

- layout, navigation, and flow
- interactivity as a design element
- imagery and text as content
- scrolling and linking

Overcoming the Fear of White Space

One design element that is often overlooked is white space. It's there on every page, and it doesn't seem to be doing much, does it? Take a look at a typical page in this book. Is every inch of space filled with either text or graphics? Of course not. If it were, the page would be impossible to read and would be horribly complex and ugly. The best example of the use of white space is the margins surrounding a page. This white space acts as a visual barrier—a resting place for the eyes. Without white space, the words on a page would crowd into each other, and the effect would be a cramped, cluttered, and hard-to-read page. Thoughtful use of white space makes it possible for you to guide the reader's eye from one location on the page to another. For many, one of the first design hurdles that must be overcome is the irresistible urge to put too much stuff on a page. When you are new to design, you may want to fill each page completely. Remember, less is more. Think of white space as a beautiful frame setting off an equally beautiful image.

Balancing Objects

The **optical center** of an image or a page occurs approximately three-eighths from the top of the page and is the point around which objects on the page are balanced. Once the optical center is located, objects can be positioned around it. A page can have a symmetrical or asymmetrical balance relative to an imaginary vertical line in the center of the page. In a **symmetrical balance**, objects are placed equally on either side of the vertical line. This type of layout tends toward a restful, formal design. In an **asymmetrical balance**, objects are placed unequally relative to the vertical line. Asymmetrical balance uses white space to balance the positioned objects, and is more dynamic and informal. A page with objects arranged asymmetrically tends to provide more visual interest because it is more surprising in appearance. See Figure 25 for an image having an obvious optical center.

Considering Ethical Implications

Because Photoshop makes it so easy for you to make so many dramatic changes to images, you should consider the ethical ramifications and implications of altering images. Is it proper or appropriate to alter an image just because you have the technical expertise to do so? Are there any legal responsibilities or liabilities involved in making these alterations? Because the general public is more aware about the topic of **intellectual property** (an image or idea that is owned and retained by legal control) with the increased availability of information and content, you

should make sure you have the legal right to alter an image, especially if you plan on displaying or distributing the image to others. Know who retains the rights to an image, and if necessary, make sure you have written permission for its use, alteration, and/or distribution. Not taking these precautions could be costly.

Figure 25 *The optical center*
Image courtesy of Elizabeth Eisner Reding.

Understanding Copyright Terms

As you become more adept using Photoshop, you'll most likely obtain images from sources other than your own imagination and camera. It's of the utmost importance that you understand the legal and moral implications of using someone else's work. This means, among other things, that you have permission (verbal, or preferably, written) to use any part of the image, and that you understand terms such as copyright, fair use doctrine, intellectual property, and derivative works.

A **copyright** is protection extended to an author or creator of original work, which gives them the exclusive right to copy, distribute, and modify a thing, idea, or image. Copyright holders can give permission for others to copy, distribute, or modify their work. When something has been copyrighted, it is considered intellectual property. (The date of publication is the date the published work became generally available.) The length of time of a copyright is specific. In many cases, permission is *not* needed for education activities such as research and classroom use, but *is* required when you want to use someone else's property for profit.

Intellectual property includes ideas, inventions, or processes that derive from the work of the mind, and the corresponding body of laws, rights, and registrations relating to these properties. Intellectual property law grants certain exclusive rights to owners of intangible assets such as music, artistic works, discoveries, inventions, words, phrases, and designs. It includes the following protections: copyright, trademarks (a distinctive associated identifier), patents, design rights, and trade secrets.

Fair use doctrine allows a user to make a copy of all or part of a work, even if permission *has not* been granted, for purposes such as criticism, news reporting, research, teaching, or scholarship.

A **derivative work** is a new, original product that is based upon content from one or more previously existing works.

QUICK TIP

For copyright protection to extend to a derivative work, the derivative work must display a level of originality and new expression.

So, can you use a picture you saw on a website in a class project? **Yes**. Can you use that same picture in a project for a paying client? **No**.

Table 3 illustrates commonly used terms and an example of each.

TABLE 3: COMMONLY USED IMAGE-USE TERMS		
Term	**Definition**	**Example**
Copyright	Protection to an author of an original work, including the right to copy, distribute and adapt that work.	The author of a play (created after 1978) has copyright protection for his/her life + 70 years, after which the work passes into public domain. (The *public domain* indicates that ownership of the work is public and can be used freely by anyone.)
Intellectual property	Refers to both the products of the mind and the accompanying legal protection for these intangible assets.	Industrial icons such as the Nike swoosh, or the Lexus branding symbol.
Fair use doctrine	Conditions under which a work can be used *without* permission.	An image based on a well-known scene in the film The Godfather that appears in a newspaper article.
Derivative work	A new product created from an existing original product.	The Adobe Photoshop CC Revealed book, which is based on the pre-existing Adobe Photoshop CS6 Revealed book.

© 2013 Cengage Learning®

Licensing Your Work with Creative Commons

To many of us, the thought of dealing with lawyers or anything remotely legal makes us want to head for the hills. It is possible to license (and share) your work using licenses known as **Creative Commons licenses** without the use of lawyers or expensive fees. Creative Commons (*www.creativecommons.org*) is a nonprofit organization devoted to making it easier for people to share and build upon the works of others by offering free licenses and legal tools with which to mark creative work. Using a Creative Commons license allows you to keep your copyright, while allowing others to copy and distribute your work. You determine the conditions: you may insist that you be credited, you can decide if you will permit commercial use of your work or if your work can be modified. Figure 26 shows the Creative Commons licenses that can be applied to any work. The six licenses offered are then composed of combinations of license conditions, and consist of:

Attribution (*cc by*): The simplest of all Creative Commons licenses, in which any user (commercial or non-commercial) can distribute, modify, or enhance your work, provided you are credited.

Attribution Share Alike (*cc by-sa*): The same as Attribution, except that the new owner must create their license under the same terms you used.

Attribution No Derivatives (*cc by-nd*): Your work can be distributed by others, but not modified and in its entirety, with you being credited.

Attribution Non-Commercial (*cc by-nc*): Your work can be distributed, modified, or enhanced, with credit to you, for non-commercial purposes only. Derivative works do not have to be licensed.

Attribution Non-Commercial Share Alike (*cc by-nc-sa*): Your work can be distributed, modified, or enhanced, with credit to you, for non-commercial purposes only, but must be licensed under the identical terms. All derivative work must carry the same license, and be non-commercial.

Attribution Non-Commercial No Derivatives (*cc by-nc-nd*): This is the most restrictive license category. Redistribution is allowed as long as credit is given. The work cannot be modified or used commercially.

QUICK TIP

When determining project requirements, take into account the following criteria with respect to the audience: age, occupation, gender, education, geographic location, ethnicity, and computer literacy. Will the intended audience be able to read and comprehend the message?

Figure 26 *Creative Commons licenses conditions*
Creative Commons Attribution 4.0 International license.

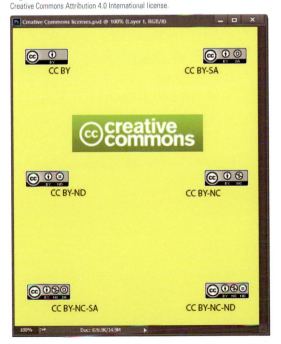

POWER USER SHORTCUTS			
To do this:	**Use this method:**	**To do this:**	**Use this method:**
Close a file	[Ctrl][W] (Win) ⌘ [W] (Mac)	Open Preferences dialog box	[Ctrl][K] (Win) ⌘ [K] (Mac)
Create a new file	[Ctrl][N] (Win) ⌘ [N] (Mac)	Reset preferences to default settings	[Shift][Alt][Ctrl] (Win) [shift][option] ⌘ (Mac)
Create a workspace	Window ➤ Workspace ➤ New Workspace or use the workspace switcher	Save a file	[Ctrl][S] (Win) ⌘ [S] (Mac)
Exit Photoshop	[Ctrl][Q] (Win) ⌘ [Q] (Mac)	Show hidden Lasso tools	[Shift] **L**
Lasso tool	♟ or **L**	Show or hide all open panels	[Shift][Tab]
		Show or hide all open panels, the options bar, and the Tools panel	[Tab]
		Show or hide Swatches panel	Window ➤ Swatches
Open a file	[Ctrl][O] (Win) ⌘ [O] (Mac)	Use Save As	[Shift][Ctrl][S] (Win) ⌘ [shift] [S] (Mac)

Key: Menu items are indicated by ➤ between the menu name and its command. Blue bold letters are shortcuts for selecting tools on the Tools panel.

Start Adobe Photoshop CC 2014.

1. Start Photoshop.
2. Create a new image that is 500 x 600 pixels, accept the default resolution, then name and save it as **Review**.

Open and save an image.

1. Open PS 1-3.jpg from the drive and folder where you store your Data Files.
2. Save it as **Rafting**. (Use the default options when saving the file using a new name. If the JPEG Options dialog box opens, click OK.)

Examine the Photoshop window.

1. Locate the image title bar and the current zoom percentage, then change the color theme to Light Gray.
2. Locate the menu you use to open an image.
3. View the Tools panel, the options bar, and the panels that are showing.
4. Click the Move tool on the Tools panel, view the Move tool options on the options bar, then reset the Essentials workspace.
5. Create, save, and display a customized workspace (based on Essentials) called **History and Layers** that captures panel locations and displays the History panel above the Color panel.
6. Open Bridge, apply the To Do label to Friends.psd, close Bridge, then return the Photoshop color theme to the default (the second from the left color box).

Close a file and exit Photoshop.

1. Compare your screen to Figure 27, then close the Rafting file.
2. Close the Review file.
3. Exit (Win) or Quit (Mac) Photoshop.

Learn about design principles and copyright rules.

1. What elements of composition are under your control?
2. How can a page be balanced?
3. Name three differences between print and web design.
4. Under what conditions can an image *not* be used in a project?

Figure 27 *Completed Skills Review*
Source: Morguefile.

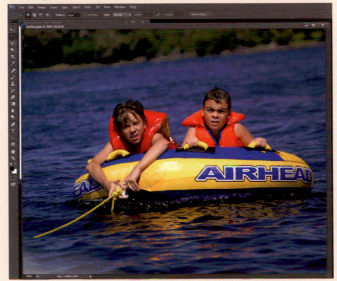

As a new Photoshop user, it's nice to know that there are so many tools to help you perform a task. Bridge and Mini Bridge seem to have many of the same features, yet Mini Bridge is available from within Photoshop and Bridge is a stand-alone program. You want to examine each of these tools to determine the best usage for each.

1. Open Photoshop, open Bridge, then open Mini Bridge.
2. Examine the folder containing the Data Files for this chapter and be prepared to discuss the differences between Bridge and Mini Bridge.
3. What are the sorting and printing limitations of Mini Bridge versus Bridge? Mini Bridge is shown in Figure 28.
4. Be prepared to discuss the best usages of Bridge and Mini Bridge.

Figure 28 *Sample Project Builder 1*

Source: Morguefile. Images © Photodisc/Getty Images. Image courtesy of Elizabeth Eisner Reding.

Getting Started with Adobe Photoshop CC

At some point in your working with Photoshop, you'll probably have direct contact with one or more clients. Rather than take a sink-or-swim approach when this inevitable time comes, you decide to be proactive and use the web to research this process.

1. Open your favorite browser and search engine and find a website with relevant information about communicating with design clients.
2. Keep track of the most relevant website and make notes of key points on the information you've found. A client meeting is shown in Figure 29.
3. Be prepared to discuss how you'll effectively interact with your design clients when the time comes.

Figure 29 *Sample Project Builder 2*
Courtesy Parker Michael Knight.

One of the best resources for learning about design principles is the web. You want to make sure you fully understand the differences between designing for print and designing for the web, so you decide to use the Internet to find out more.

1. Connect to the Internet, and use your browser to find at least two websites that have information about the differences between print and web design principles.

2. Find and download one image that serves as an example of good print design and one image of good web design. Save the images (in JPEG format) as Print design-1 and Web design-1. Figure 30 shows a sample print design.

Figure 30 *Sample Design Project*
Source: Morguefile.

Getting Started with Adobe Photoshop CC

You are preparing to work on a series of design projects to enhance your portfolio. You decide to see what information on digital imaging is available on the Adobe website. You also want to increase your familiarity with the Adobe website so that you can take advantage of product information and support, user tips and feedback, and become a more skilled Photoshop user. You'd also like to become more familiar with the concepts of intellectual property and copyright issues.

1. Connect to the Internet and go to the Adobe website at *www.adobe.com*.
2. Point to Products, then find the link for the Photoshop family, as shown in Figure 31. (Your screen may look different, as this page is updated often.)
3. Use the links on the web page to search for information about digital imaging options.
4. Print the relevant page(s).
5. Use your favorite browser and search engine to find several sites about intellectual property and copyright issues.
6. Print at least two of the sites you find the most interesting.
7. Evaluate the information in the documents, then compare any significant differences.

Figure 31 *Sample Portfolio Project*

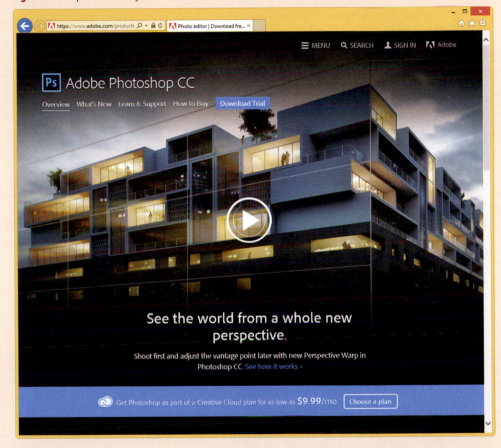

CHAPTER **2** LEARNING
PHOTOSHOP BASICS

1. Use organizational and management features
2. Use the Layers and History panels
3. Learn about Photoshop by using Help
4. View and print an image

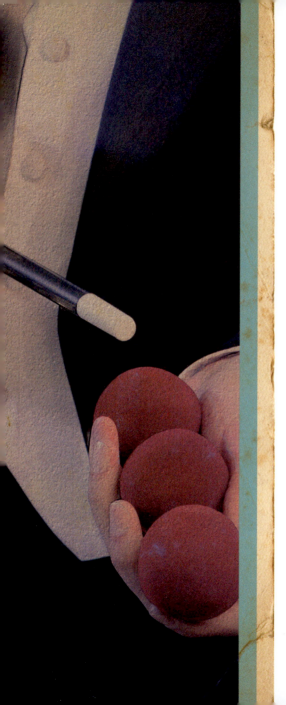

2

LEARNING
PHOTOSHOP BASICS

Working Magic with Photoshop

Working with images in Photoshop is based on an understanding of layers. Every image opened in Photoshop is made up of one or more layers, and it is within these layers that you, as an artist, work your magic. The order of layers in an image, and the effects applied to them, can make one image very different from another.

Using Management Tools

Adobe Photoshop CC is an amazingly rich program that has a variety of tools that you can use to manage your digital images. Using services such as Acrobat.com, you'll be able to increase your productivity and work more efficiently individually and with coworkers.

Learning to Love Layers

Once you become more comfortable using Photoshop, you'll understand the importance of each of the panels. Some panels, such as the Layers panel, are vital to using Photoshop. Since layers are the key to creating and manipulating Photoshop images, the Layers panel is one that we depend on most, for it tells us at-a-glance the order and type of layers within an image. And if the Layers panel is the map of the Photoshop image, the History panel provides step-by-step instructions that let us know how we got to our destination.

Finding Help when You Need It

A complex program like Photoshop needs a robust Help system. You'll find that the Help system, which is accessed using your browser, doesn't disappoint.

Viewing and Printing

While not everyone prints each one of their images, nearly everyone needs to zoom in and out to get a better look at different areas. Using the Zoom tool, you can view the areas you need to focus on in as high or as low of a magnification as you want. If you do want to print out an image, Photoshop offers great tools to do so.

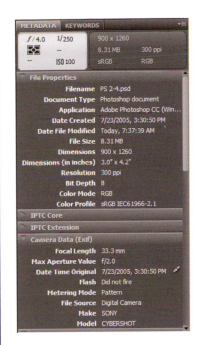

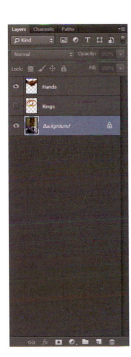

Source: Morguefile.

Use Organizational
AND MANAGEMENT FEATURES

What You'll Do

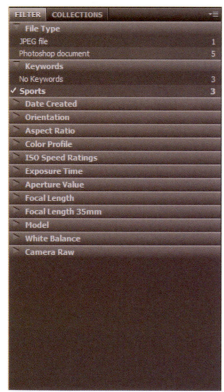

In this lesson, you'll learn about the Creative Cloud and Behance, and how to use Bridge, and Mini Bridge.

Learning About the Creative Cloud

Adobe Creative Cloud is a fee-based membership service that integrates Adobe Photoshop with apps in the Creative Cloud, as well as a variety of tools, Adobe Touch Apps, services, plus new features, products, and services as soon as they are released. Adobe Touch Apps are available for iOS and Android tablets and phones, and sync to your Creative Cloud desktop apps. With Adobe Creative Cloud, your files will be in sync regardless which device or desktop you're using. Also included is community training and support, and the opportunity to share your work and connect with peers. A Creative Cloud installation of Photoshop and Bridge, as well as some available apps is shown in Figure 1.

If you already have an Adobe ID, you can use this with Adobe Creative Cloud. Once a subscription is purchased, a redemption code is issued, which is required at installation. This code is what makes the connection between the Creative Cloud and the Photoshop program. 20 GB of cloud storage is provided with a free 30-day trial subscription, Single App, Upgrade, and Complete subscriptions.

QUICK TIP

As with any online service, the terms and instructions may change without notice.

Managing the Creative Cloud

Creative.adobe.com is a management feature of the Adobe Creative Cloud that can be used to organize your work whether you work in groups or by yourself. Adobe Creative Cloud is accessed using any browser. In addition to allowing you to share files with others in a virtual environment (also known as **cloud computing**), these services make it possible to take advantage of **file versioning**, which allows you to store multiple versions of your work. You can access creative.adobe.com using your favorite browser.

NEW If you access the Creative Cloud with multiple computers, you can duplicate settings in your personal workspace such as Preferences using the Sync feature. You can perform a sync by clicking Edit (Win) or Photoshop (Mac) on the menu bar, pointing to Sync Settings, then clicking either Upload Settings or Download Settings.

Files can be uploaded to the Creative Cloud web site (creative.adobe.com) by logging in with your Adobe ID, then dragging-and-dropping a file from your computer to the web page, or by clicking the File tab in the Creative Cloud window. Figure 2 shows sample files that have been uploaded to the Creative Cloud.

The Sync process also gives you access to the most up-to-date apps and services available and lets you sync files stored on the Creative Cloud.

Figure 1 *Sample of Creative Cloud apps*

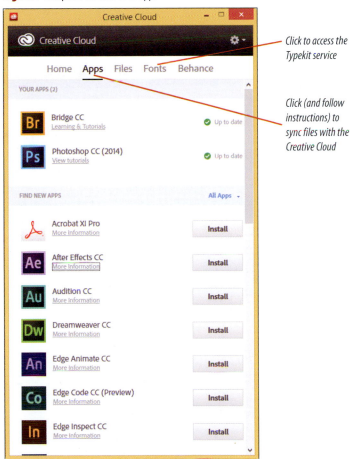

Click to access the Typekit service

Click (and follow instructions) to sync files with the Creative Cloud

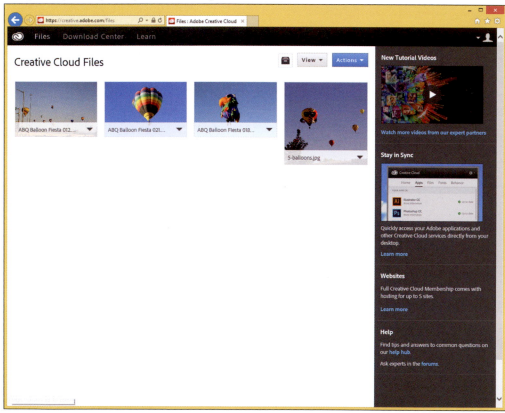 Using Behance

Behance is a social network platform dedicated to the showcasing and promotion of creative work. This platform makes it possible to display your work, gaining you global reach. While using Behance gives you a wider audience, you can also view the work of others. When you join Behance (at www.behance.net) you can log in with your Adobe ID, as well as with Facebook and other social networks. During the initial process, you will be assigned a URL you can give to others to view your work.

Participation in Behance is free for creative professionals, and there are no restrictions on the number of projects you can create and post. Once your account is created, you can find people you know by syncing your Google or Facebook accounts.

Images on the Creative Cloud can be shared with Behance by opening the image in the Creative Cloud, clicking the Share icon (in the top-right corner to the right of the image title), then clicking Post Publicly. The image will be prepared for publishing, then you will be prompted to add a title, tags, comments, viewing and thumbnail cropping options.

Figure 2 *Creative Cloud Files*

Adobe Systems Incorporated. Images courtesy of Elizabeth Eisner Reding.

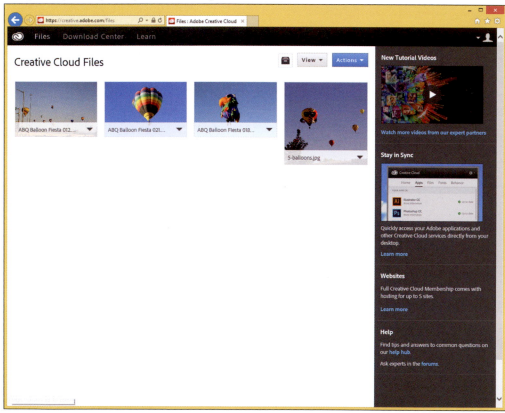

Using Adobe Exchange

Located in Photoshop in the Windows menu under the Extensions command, **Adobe Exchange** allows you to discover and install plug-ins, extensions, and other content for your Creative Cloud apps. This panel contains all sorts of free and paid content you can download.

NEW Adobe Typekit

If you're an Adobe Creative Cloud subscriber, you owe it to yourself to check out **Adobe Typekit** (located in the Fonts tab on the Creative Cloud desktop app). This service lets you select from a seemingly endless supply of really cool font families. Once downloaded, Typekit fonts can be used in any desktop applications.

When you choose fonts from the library and sync them with your desktop, the fonts will be available for use in other apps (even non-Adobe apps). Font families are organized in the Typekit website by classification, properties, or recommended usage. When you find a font family you want to use, click Use fonts, then click Sync selected fonts. Make sure you're logged into the Creative Cloud, the font sync setting is turned on in the Fonts tab in the Preferences section of the Creative Cloud desktop app and all your Typekit fonts will be ready for you. (You may have to reboot your computer for the fonts to appear in the Photoshop font list.) In Adobe apps, you'll notice a different Typekit icon next to the font name.

Figure 3 *Project Complexity triangle*
© 2013 Cengage Learning®

The Complexity of Projects

If you ask any client what they want in their project, they'll most likely say something to the effect that they want it now, they want it done well, and they want it to not cost a lot. These three variables (performance, time, and cost) that are shown in Figure 3 comprise the **project scope** and illustrate the complexity that exists in any project.

- If the project is a low price and completed quickly, will the quality be satisfactory?
- If the project is completed quickly and the quality is good, will the price be affordable?

Ask the client, and they'll say that they want all three elements. But is this a realistic expectation?

Reusing Housekeeping Tasks in Bridge and Mini Bridge

All those little housekeeping tasks you do, such as renaming files and copying files and folders from one location on your hard drive to another, can be easily carried out in Bridge and Mini Bridge. Once you select file thumbnails in Bridge or Mini Bridge, you can copy them to another location by dragging-and-dropping. Files can be renamed by clicking the filename until it is selected, typing the new name, and then pressing [Enter] (Win) or [return] (Mac).

Understanding Metadata

Metadata is descriptive standardized information about a file, and includes information such as the author's name, copyright, and keywords associated with it. In Bridge, you can also find information such as when the image was created, last modified, current size, resolution, bit depth, and color mode in the Metadata panel, shown in Figure 4. Metadata information is stored using the Extensible Metadata Platform (XMP) standard format, which was developed by Adobe and is commonly shared by their products. Sometimes metadata is stored separately in a **sidecar file**. This file can be applied to other files, making it possible to use metadata from one file as a template for another.

Assigning Keywords to an Image

The Keywords panel, as seen in Figure 5, is grouped with the Metadata panel and can be used to create your own system of identifying files based on their content.

Figure 4 *Metadata panel in Bridge*

Figure 5 *Keywords panel in Bridge*

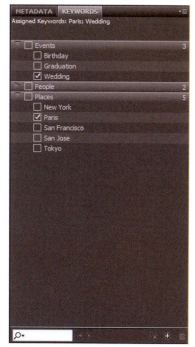

In conjunction with the options on the Filter panel (located beneath the Favorites and Folders panels on the left side of the screen in Bridge), keywords can be used to find images that meet specific criteria. Say, for example, that you have hundreds of images downloaded from your digital camera. Some could be assigned the keyword "New York," others "Paris," and still others "Rome." Viewing all images with the keyword "Rome" is as simple as making the folder containing all the images active, and then clicking the keyword Rome in the filter panel. Any file can be assigned multiple keywords, and those keywords can be renamed, deleted, or applied to other files.

Project Management Principles

Project management is the execution of a plan that brings a project to a successful completion. No longer is project management as simple as saying 'you do this' and 'I'll do that'. A good project manager has to wear many hats and needs to have a thorough understanding of many elements, including budgetary requirements, client needs, production limitations, availability of supplies (industrial and human resources), identification of deliverables (such as specifications, comps or sketches), and timeline management. Like an air traffic controller, a project manager must see what's in front, off to the side, and just around the bend.

Project management is not static: you don't get it all formulated and then just let it sit. Good project management requires periodic revisiting and revision. Without this periodic review, a project may suffer from **scope creep**, a condition to be avoided in which a project seems to have lost its way. Communication review methods vary, but can and should include periodic peer reviews and surveys, and are important feedback measurements. Scope creep can lead to budget overruns and failure to bring a product to market in a timely fashion. All too often, a project can become a victim of its own planning. Since a project plan is written down, many consider it to be 'written in stone'. In fact, a project has so many opportunities to fall off the track: project members become ill, weather becomes a limiting factor, suppliers fail to deliver when promised, or the plan may have been ill-conceived. See Table 1 for some commonly used project management terms.

TABLE 1: COMMONLY USED PROJECT MANAGEMENT TERMS		
Term	**Definition**	**Example**
Project scope	The goals and objectives of the project.	Creation of a website, including images.
Tasks	Specific goals that lead to the ultimate completion of the project.	Choose colors, collect photos, and create logo.
Due dates	When specific tasks must be completed in order to achieve the ultimate goal.	Secure image permissions before website goes live.
Resource allocation	How to best utilize resources, including budgetary constraints, human resources (including outsourcing), and supplies.	Ensure that image fees stay within budget and designer spends no more than 25% of her time.

© 2013 Cengage Learning®

Assigning a keyword

1. Launch **Bridge**.

2. Activate the **Folders tab**, if necessary, and locate the folder containing the Data Files for Chapter 2.

3. Select all the files in the folder and copy them to the folder for Solutions files for Chapter 2.

TIP It is *not necessary* to copy the files in order to complete the lesson. Copying the files just insures that the original data files are kept intact for future use.

4. Activate the **Chapter 2 folder** in the Solutions folder.

5. Click the **Sort by list arrow**, click **By Filename** if not already selected, then click the **Descending Order button** if the Ascending Order button is not already displayed.

6. Click the thumbnail in the Content panel for **PS 2-1.psd**, press and hold [**Shift**], click **PS 2-3.psd**, then release [**Shift**], as shown in Figure 6.

7. Click the **Keywords tab**, then click the **New Keyword button** ⊞ in the Keywords panel.

8. Type **Sports** in the Keywords panel text box, press [**Enter**] (Win) or [**return**] (Mac), then click the **check box** to the left of Sports.

TIP You can apply keywords to individual images, but applying them to multiple images will speed up your workflow.

You created a new keyword that you applied to three images.

Figure 6 *Files selected in Bridge*
Source: Morguefile. Images © Photodisc/Getty Images.

Click to choose ascending or descending order

Click to choose the sort parameter

Keywords tab

Repurposing in Photoshop

Just because you create a new image in Photoshop, it doesn't mean you always start from scratch. You may use part of one image that already exists in another image, or you may drag an entire existing image into a new image. The idea of repurposing is not new, in fact, Photoshop encourages and promotes it. To this end, it provides you with many tools that make it easy to reuse skills and knowledge. Presets (established settings that perform specific tasks) are available in many Photoshop tools, such as brushes, actions, video styles, and custom shapes. Templates (predesigned files that have been developed by others and generally have a specific outcome, such as a label) are available from companies such as Avery, and can be downloaded from the web.

Figure 7 *Filtered files in Bridge*
Source: Morguefile.

*Check mark means
keyword filter is on*

Filtering with Bridge

1. Click the **Keywords section** in the Filter panel, then click **Sports**.

   A check mark appears next to Sports in the Filter panel, as seen in Figure 7, and only the images with the keyword Sports are displayed.

2. Click **Sports** in the Keywords section in the Filter panel to restore all the images in the folder.

3. Close Bridge.

You used the Filter panel to see only those images that had a specific keyword applied, then you closed Bridge.

Basics of Project Management

The basics of project management include knowledge of the project scope, the tasks at hand, due dates for task completion, and effective resource allocation. And while all of this is extremely complicated, you must remember that most projects don't operate in a bubble: they are usually one of many projects competing for the same resources. In addition to competing with other projects, many tasks within a given project may be occurring simultaneously and repetitively. Not every project will have the same constraints. Some manufacturing projects, for example, may require more rigorous testing than others, and some projects may rely more heavily on outsourcing that others. Most projects will have deliverables, but the type and scope of those will vary.

Use the Layers
AND HISTORY PANELS

What You'll Do

In this lesson, you'll hide and display a layer, move a layer on the Layers panel, and then undo the move by deleting the Layer Order state on the History panel.

You can think of layers in a Photoshop image as individual sheets of clear plastic that are in a stack. It's possible for your file to quickly accumulate dozens of layers. The **Layers panel** displays all the individual layers in an open file. You can use the Layers panel to create, copy, delete, display, hide, merge, lock, group, or reposition layers.

Learning About Layers

A **layer** is a section within an image that can be manipulated independently. Layers allow you to control individual elements within an image and create great dramatic effects and variations of the same image. Layers enable you to easily manipulate individual characteristics within an image. Each Photoshop file has at least one layer, and can contain many individual layers, or groups of layers.

> **QUICK TIP**
>
> In Photoshop, using and understanding layers is the key to success.

Understanding the Layers Panel

The order in which the layers appear on the Layers panel matches the order in which they appear in the image; the top layer in the Layers panel is the top layer on the image. You can make a layer active by clicking its name on the Layers panel. When a layer is active, it is highlighted on the Layers panel, and the name of the layer appears in parentheses in the image title bar. Only one layer can be active at a time. Figure 8 shows an image with its Layers panel. Do you see that this image contains six layers? Each layer can be moved or modified individually on the panel to give a different effect to the overall image. If you look at the Layers panel, you'll see that the Finger Painting type layer is blue, indicating that it is currently active.

> **QUICK TIP**
>
> Get in the habit of shifting your eye from the image in the work area to the Layers panel. Knowing which layer is active will save you time and help you troubleshoot an image.

Filtering Layers

Layers can be filtered from within the Layers panel to build a short list of layers. This short list can be organized by Kind, Name, Effect, Mode, Attribute, Color, Smart Object, or Selected, and can be created by clicking the Filter list arrow on the Layers panel. You can also filter layers using any of the five preset filtering buttons. You can filter for layers containing images (pixel layers), adjustment layers, type layers, shape layers, and smart objects. (The different kinds of layers will be described in later chapters.)

Displaying and Hiding Layers

You can use the Layers panel to control which layers are visible in an image. You can show or hide a layer by clicking the Indicates layer visibility button next to the layer thumbnail. When a layer is hidden, you are not able to merge it with another, select it, or print it.

QUICK **TIP**

Hiding some layers can make it easier to focus on particular areas of an image.

Using the History Panel

Photoshop records each task you complete in an image on the **History panel**. This record of events, called states, makes it easy to see what changes occurred and the tools or commands that you used to make the modifications. The History panel, shown in Figure 8, displays up to 20 states by default and automatically updates the list to display the most recently performed tasks. The list contains the name of the tool or command used to change the

Figure 8 *Layers and History panels*
Image courtesy of Elizabeth Eisner Reding.

image. You can delete a state on the History panel by selecting it and dragging it to the Delete current state button. Deleting a state is equivalent to using the Undo command. You can also use the History panel to create a new image from any state.

QUICK **TIP**

When you delete a History state, you undo the state as well as all the events that followed the state.

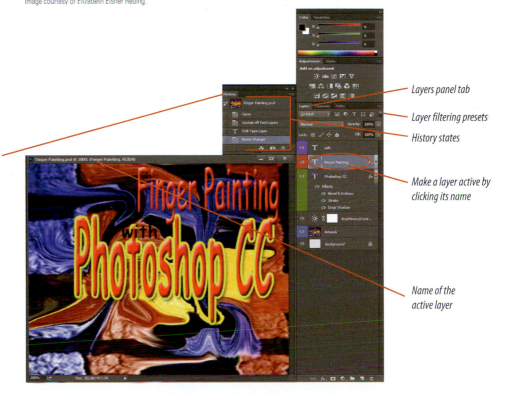

History panel tab

Layers panel tab

Layer filtering presets

History states

Make a layer active by clicking its name

Name of the active layer

Hide and display a layer

1. Open the file PS 2-4.psd, then rename it **Wedding Day.psd**.

2. Click the **Rings layer** on the Layers panel, then click the **Move tool** if necessary.

TIP Depending on the size of the window, you might only be able to see the initial characters of the layer name.

3. Verify that the **Show Transform Controls check box** on the options bar is not checked, then click the **Indicates layer visibility button** on the Rings layer to display the image, as shown in Figure 9.

TIP By default, transparent areas of an image have a checkerboard display on the Layers panel.

4. Click the **Indicates layer visibility button** on the Rings layer to hide the layer.

You made the Rings layer active on the Layers panel, then clicked the Indicates layer visibility button to display and hide the layer. Hiding layers is an important skill that can be used to remove distracting elements. Once you've finished working on a specific layer, you can display the additional layers.

Figure 9 *Wedding Day*
Source: Morguefile.

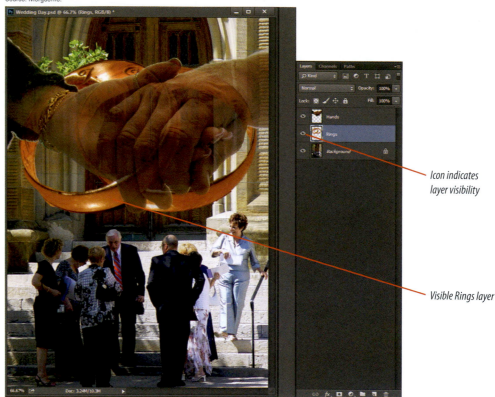

Icon indicates layer visibility

Visible Rings layer

DESIGN**TIP**

Visual Hierarchy

Projects that are visible in nature (such as a web page) should have a strong visual hierarchy. **Visual hierarchy** is the order in which the eye understands what it is seeing. For a web page, this would include fonts and font sizes, line spacing, indents, graphic images and their positioning. In graphic design, visual hierarchy is used to manipulate the reader's eye to see information in a particular location.

Learning Photoshop Basics

Figure 10 *Layer moved in Layers panel*

Figure 11 *Result of moved layer*

Source: Morguefile.

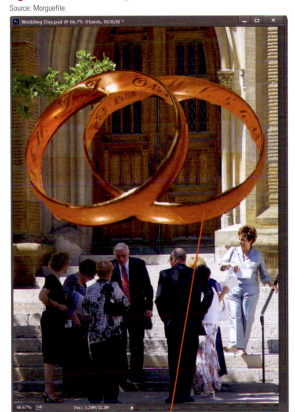

Result of moved layer

Figure 12 *Deleting a History state*

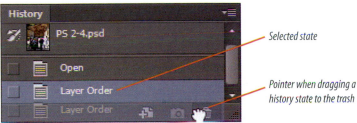

Selected state

Pointer when dragging a
history state to the trash

Move a layer on the Layers panel and delete a state on the History panel

1. Click the **Indicates layer visibility button** on the Rings layer on the Layers panel to display the layer.

2. Click on the Hands layer on the Layers panel to hide the layer.

3. Display the **Legacy workspace** you created in Chapter 1.

4. Click and drag the **Hands layer** on the Layers panel beneath the Rings layer, so your Layers panel looks like Figure 10.

   The hands are no longer visible as shown in Figure 11.

5. Click **Layer Order** on the History panel, then drag it to the **Delete current state button** on the History panel, as shown in Figure 12.

   TIP Each time you close and reopen an image, the History panel is cleared.

   The original order of the layers in the Layers panel is restored.

6. Click **File** on the Menu bar, then click **Save**.

   TIP An alternative to the deletion of history states is the Revert command. Located on the File menu, this command restores the image to its last saved state.

You moved the Hands layer beneath the Rings layer, then returned it to its original position by dragging the Layer Order state to the Delete current state button on the History panel. You can easily use the History panel to undo what you've done.

Learn About Photoshop
BY USING HELP

What You'll Do

 In this lesson, you'll open Help, and then view and find information from the available topics and the Search feature.

Understanding the Power of Help

Photoshop features an extensive Help system that you can use to access definitions, explanations, and useful tips. Help information is displayed in a browser window, so you must have web browser software installed on your computer and an Internet connection to use Photoshop Help.

QUICKTIP

Since the Help contents displays in your browser, you already know how to print. Once the content is displayed, use the Print command on your browser to print the page(s) of interest.

Using Help Topics

The Home page of the Photoshop Help/ Topics window, shown in Figure 13, displays detailed categories that you can use to retrieve information about Photoshop commands and features. The following topics are available:

- What's new
- Get started
- Workspace and workflow
- Image and color basics
- Layers
- Selecting
- Image adjustments
- Camera Raw
- Repair and restoration
- Reshaping and transforming
- Drawing and painting
- Text
- Video and animation
- Filters and effects
- Saving and exporting
- Printing
- Automation
- Web graphics
- 3D and technical imaging
- Color management
- System requirements

QUICKTIP

Due to the ever-changing nature of the Web, these categories can and will change.

When you click a link, Help takes you directly to the information you've selected. The Search feature is located in the left pane in the form of a text box. You can search the Photoshop Help System by typing your search terms in the text box, and then pressing [Enter] (Win) or [return] (Mac).

Figure 13 *Groups in Photoshop Online Help*

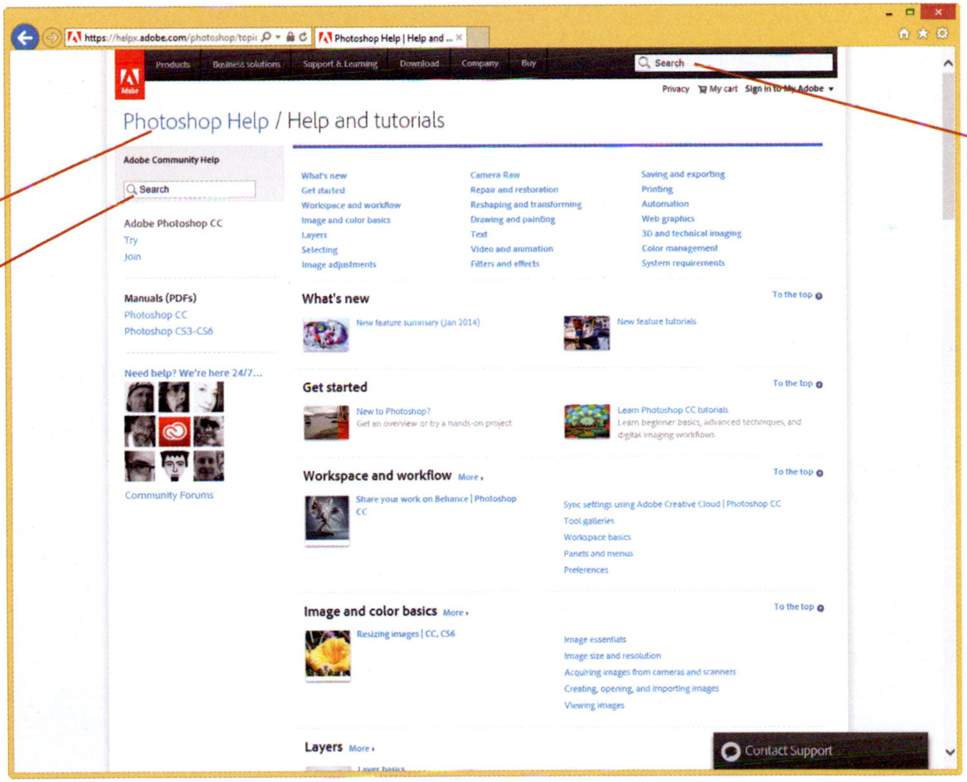

Help search box

Click text to return to Help home screen

Help community search box

Find information in Adobe reference titles

1. Click **Help** on the Menu bar, then click **Photoshop Online Help**. If the Help Manager dialog box appears, click the red Close button to close this window (Mac).

   TIP You can also open the Help window by pressing [F1] (Win) or ⌘ [/] (Mac).

2. Click **Acquiring images from cameras and scanners** in the Image and color basics group. See Figure 14.

   TIP You can maximize the window if you want to take advantage of the full screen display.

   Bear in mind that Help is web-driven and, like any website, can change as updates are made and errors and inconsistencies are found.

3. Close the Photoshop Help window.

You used the Photoshop Online Help command on the Help menu to open the Help window and view a topic.

Figure 14 *A topic in the Image and color basics group*

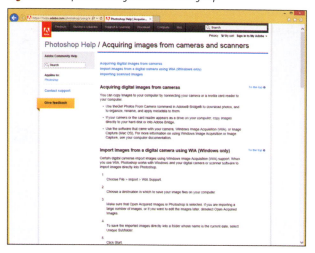

Understanding the Differences Between Monitor, Images, and Device Resolution

Image resolution is determined by the number of pixels per inch (ppi) that are printed on a page. Pixel dimensions (the number of pixels along the height and width of a bitmap image) determine the amount of detail in an image, while resolution controls the amount of space over which the pixels are printed. Think of the differences between the picture quality on a standard-definition 480i television versus a high-definition 1080i television. The high-definition image will be crisper and have more vibrant colors, whereas the standard-definition image may look weak and washed out. High resolution images show greater detail and more subtle color transitions than low resolution images. Lower resolution images can look grainy, like images in older newspapers.

Device resolution or printer resolution is measured by the ink dots per inch (dpi) produced by printers. You can set the resolution of your computer monitor to determine the detail with which images will be displayed. Each monitor should be calibrated to describe how the monitor reproduces colors. Monitor calibration is one of the first things you should do because it determines whether your colors are being accurately represented, which in turn determines how accurately your output will match your design intentions. **Screen frequency**, or *line screen*, is the number of printer dots or halftone cells per inch used to print grayscale images or color separations and is measured in lines per inch (lpi). Printer calibration ensures that what you see on your monitor is translated to paper.

Figure 15 *Photoshop Help Support Center*

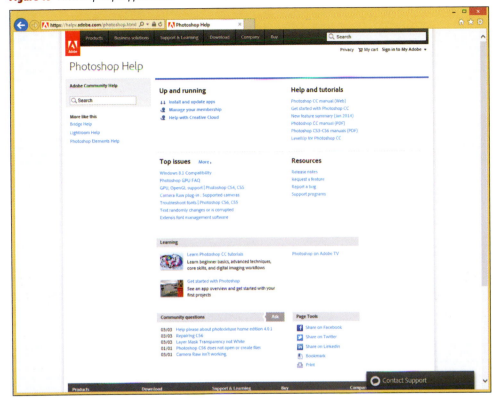

Get help and support

1. Click **Help** on the Menu bar, then click **Photoshop Support Center**.

2. Compare your Help window to Figure 15, then close the Photoshop Help window.

You accessed the Photoshop Help Support Center.

Using Help versus Support Center

So which helpful Help resource should you use? Use Help when you need instructions or basic how-to, or 'what is this' information. Use the Support Center if you want to see the latest issues and resource information on new and/or existing features.

The links listed in Figure 15 include top issues, such as operating system compatibility and troubleshooting, as well as installation and membership instructions. Also, look in this section for Release notes on new features.

Find information using Search

1. Open Photoshop Online Help, then click the **Search text box** in the browser window.

2. Type **rulers**, press [**Enter**] (Win) or [**return**] (Mac), then click the link for **Photoshop Help | Rulers**.

TIP You can search for multiple words by inserting a space.

3. Go to the top of the page, then compare your Help screen to Figure 16.

4. Close the Photoshop Help window.

You entered a search term, viewed search results, then closed the Help window.

Figure 16 *Result of a search in Help*

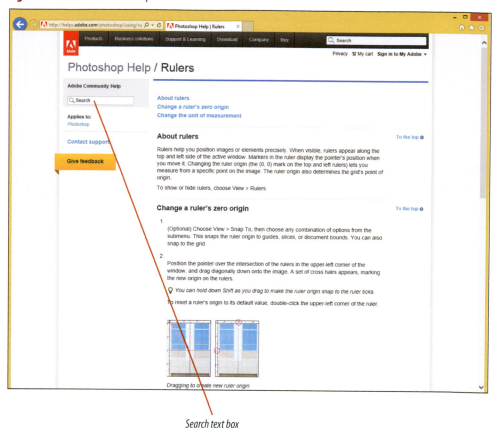

Search text box

Figure 17 *List of new features in Photoshop CC*

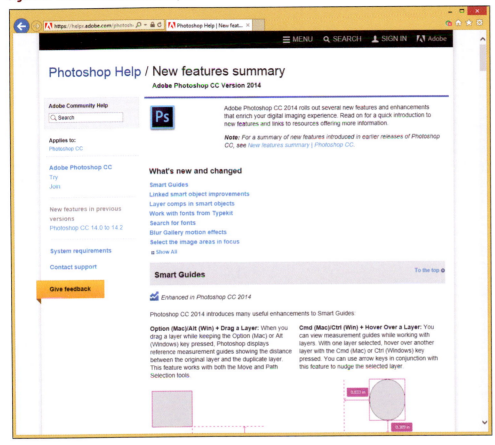

TIP If you have some experience with a previous version of Photoshop or you just want to cut-to-the-chase and find out what's new in this version, you can find a list of new features in this version of Photoshop by clicking Help on the Menu bar, clicking Photoshop Online Help, and then clicking New feature summary in the What's new group. The list of new features, shown in Figure 17, contains a brief description of each feature and a link to more information.

View and PRINT AN IMAGE

What You'll Do

Source: Morguefile.

 In this lesson, you'll use the Zoom tool on the Tools panel to increase and decrease your views of the image. You'll also change the page orientation settings in the Print dialog box, and print the image.

Getting a Closer Look

When you edit an image in Photoshop, it is important that you have a good view of the area on which you want to focus. Photoshop has a variety of methods that allow you to enlarge or reduce your current view. You can use the Zoom tool by clicking the image to zoom in on (magnify the view) or zoom out of (reduce the view) areas of your image. Zooming in or out enlarges or reduces your *view*, not the actual image. The maximum zoom factor is 3200%. The current zoom percentage appears in the document's title bar, on the Navigator panel, and on the status bar. The View menu lets you zoom in and out, fit an image to the screen, change to 100% or 200% magnification, and see the print size.

When the Zoom tool is selected, the options bar provides additional choices for changing your view, as shown in Figure 18. For example, the Resize Windows To Fit check box automatically resizes the window whenever you magnify or reduce the view. You can also change the zoom percentage using the Navigator panel or the status bar by typing a new value in the Zoom text box, and then pressing [Enter] (Win) or [return] (Mac).

Viewing an Image in Multiple Views

You can use the New Window for *filename* command (accessed by pointing to Arrange on the Window menu) to open multiple

Figure 18 *Zoom tool options bar*

Selected check box resizes window

Displays image at 100% magnification

Fits the image on the screen

views of the same image. You can change the zoom percentage in each view so you can spotlight the areas you want to modify, and then modify the specific area of the image in each view. Because you are working on the same image in multiple views, not in multiple versions, Photoshop automatically applies the changes you make in one view to all views. Although you can close the views you no longer need at any time, Photoshop will not save any changes until you save the file.

Printing Your Image

In many cases, a professional print shop might be the best option for printing a Photoshop image to get the highest quality. Lacking a professional print shop, you can print a Photoshop image using a standard black-and-white or color printer from within Photoshop, or you can switch to Bridge and then choose to send output to a PDF or Web Gallery. The printed image will be a composite of all visible layers. The quality of your printer and paper will affect the appearance of your output. The Print dialog box displays options for printing, such as paper orientation. **Orientation** is the direction in which an image appears on the page. In **portrait orientation**, the image is printed with the shorter edges of the paper at the top and bottom. In **landscape orientation**, the image is printed with the longer edges of the paper at the top and bottom.

Use the Print command when you want to print multiple copies of an image. The Photoshop Print Settings dialog box allows you to handle color values using color management and printer profiles. Use the Print One Copy command to print a single copy without making dialog box selections.

Understanding Color Handling in Printing

The Photoshop Print Settings dialog box that opens when you click Print on the File menu lets you determine how colors are output. You can click the Color Management list arrow to choose whether Photoshop or the printing device should manage the colors. If you let Photoshop determine the colors, Photoshop performs any necessary conversions to color values appropriate for the selected printer. If you choose to let the printer determine the colors, the printer will convert document color values to the corresponding printer color values. In this scenario, Photoshop does not alter the color values.

Printed Images versus On-Screen Images

Why isn't what you see on your computer screen the same as your printer output? Well, these two items are different because video monitors and printers work very differently. The most obvious difference is that you can have a tiny monitor or an enormous monitor which can display an image in any zoom factor you choose while a printed image is limited to paper size. A printed image is measured in inches or centimeters, and its size is modified on paper by scaling. Also, an image size does not vary with its scanned resolution, and printed pixels are spaced using a specified scaled resolution (dpi). On paper, several printer ink dots are used to represent the color of one image pixel.

On a video monitor, the image size is measured on the screen in pixels, the image size is modified by resampling, and the size varies with the scanned resolution. Image pixels are located at each screen pixel location. On screen, one screen pixel location contains one image pixel, and can be of any RGB value.

Using the Photoshop File Info Dialog Box

You can use the File Info dialog box to identify a file, add a caption or other text, or add a copyright notice. The Description text box, shown in Figure 19, allows you to enter text that can be printed with the image. For example, to add information to an image, click File on the Menu bar, click File Info, and then click the Description text box. (You can move from field to field by pressing [Tab] or by clicking individual text boxes.) Type your name or other identifying information in the Description text box, or click stars to assign a rating. You can enter additional information in the other text boxes, and then save all the File Info data by clicking OK. To print data from the Description field of the File Info dialog box, click File on the Menu bar, and then click Print. Scroll down and click the right-pointing triangle to expand Printing Marks, and then select the Description check box. Additional printable options are listed.

To print the filename, select the Labels check box. You can also select check boxes that let you print crop marks and registration marks. If you choose, you can even add a background color or border to your image in the Functions category. After you select the items you want to print, click Print.

Figure 20 *Navigator panel*
Source: Morguefile.

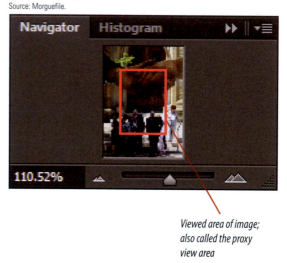

Viewed area of image; also called the proxy view area

Figure 19 *File Info dialog box*

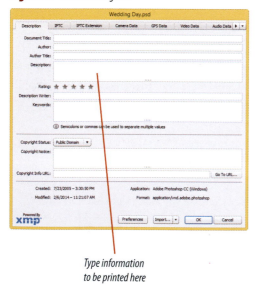

Type information to be printed here

Using the Navigator Panel

You can change the magnification factor of an image using the Navigator panel or the Zoom tool on the Tools panel. You can open the Navigator panel by clicking Window on the Menu bar, and then clicking Navigator. By double-clicking the Zoom text box on the Navigator panel, you can enter a new magnification factor, and then press [Enter] (Win) or [return] (Mac). The magnification factor—shown as a percentage—is displayed in the lower-left corner of the Navigator panel, as shown in Figure 20. The red border in the panel, called the proxy view area, defines the area of the image that is magnified. You can drag the proxy view area inside the Navigator panel to view other areas of the image at the current magnification factor.

Zoom percentage
changed

Zoom tool on the
Tools panel

Use the Zoom tool

1. Click the **Indicates layer visibility button** 👁
   on the Layers panel for the Rings layer so the
   layer is no longer displayed.

2. Click the **Indicates layer visibility button** ▢
   on the Layers panel for the Hands layer so the
   layer is visible.

3. Click the **Zoom tool** 🔍 on the Tools panel.

   TIP You can also change the magnification level by
   double-clicking the Zoom Level text box at the
   bottom-left corner of the image window and
   manually entering a zoom level.

4. Select the **Resize Windows To Fit check box**
   (if it is not already selected) on the options bar.

5. Position the **Zoom in pointer** ⊕ over the
   center of the image, then click the **image**.

   TIP Position the pointer over the part of the image you
   want to keep in view.

6. Press [**Alt**] (Win) or [**option**] (Mac), then when the
   Zoom out pointer appears, click the **center of the
   image** twice with the **Zoom out pointer** ⊖.

7. Release [**Alt**] (Win) or [**option**] (Mac), then
   compare your image to Figure 21.

   The zoom factor for the image is 50%. Your zoom
   factor may differ.

*You selected the Zoom tool on the Tools panel and used it
to zoom in to and out of the image. The Zoom tool makes it
possible to see the detail in specific areas of an image, or to see
the whole image at once, depending on your needs.*

Modify print settings

1. Click **File** on the Menu bar, then click **Print** to open the Print dialog box.

TIP If you have not selected a printer using the Print Center, a warning box might appear.

2. Click the **Print paper in landscape orientation button** 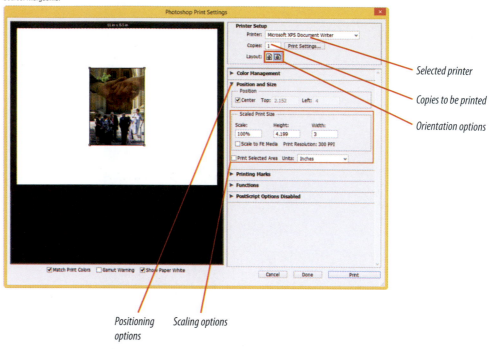.

3. Make sure that **1** appears in the Copies text box, compare your dialog box to Figure 22, click **Print**, then click **Print** after verifying that the correct printer is selected. (If you get a color-management dialog box, click OK.)

TIP You can use the handles surrounding the image preview in the Print dialog box to scale the print size.

4. Save your work.

You used the Print command on the File menu to open the Photoshop Print Settings dialog box, changed the page orientation, and then printed the image. Changing the page orientation can sometimes make an image fit better on a printed page.

Figure 22 *Print dialog box*
Source: Morguefile.

Selected printer

Copies to be printed

Orientation options

Positioning options

Scaling options

Previewing and Creating a Proof Setup

You can create and save a Proof Setup, which lets you preview your image to see how it will look when printed on a specific device. (How an image looks on specific hardware that has been calibrated and using a color management system is called a **soft proof**. The soft proof is an accurate representation of how an image will look when it has been printed.) This feature lets you see how colors can be interpreted by different devices. By using this feature, you can decrease the chance that the colors on the printed copy of the image will vary from what you viewed on your monitor. Create a custom proof by clicking View on the Menu bar, pointing to Proof Setup, and then clicking Custom. Specify the conditions in the Customize Proof Condition dialog box, and then click OK. Each proof setup has the .psf extension and can be loaded by clicking View on the Menu bar, pointing to Proof Setup, clicking Custom, and then clicking Load.

Figure 23 *PDF Output options in Bridge*

Source: Morguefile. Images © Photodisc/Getty Images.

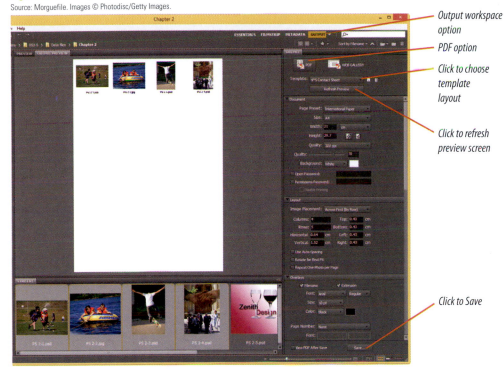

Output workspace option

PDF option

Click to choose template layout

Click to refresh preview screen

Click to Save

Create a PDF with Bridge

1. Open **Bridge**.

2. Click the **Folders tab** (if necessary), click **Chapter 2** in the location where your Data Files are stored in the Folders tab (if necessary), then verify that **Sort by Filename** is selected.

TIP Creating a PDF with Bridge requires the installation of the Adobe Output Module. If you don't see Output as a workspace option by clicking the workspace list arrow (to the left of the Bridge search text box), then the Output module has not been installed.

3. Click **Output** on the Bridge workspace switcher.

4. Click the **PDF button** in the Output tab.

5. Click **PS 2-1.psd**, hold [**Shift**], click **PS 2-4.psd** in the Content tab, then release [**Shift**].

6. Click the **Template list arrow** in the Output panel, click **4*5 Contact Sheet**, click **Refresh Preview**, then compare your screen to Figure 23. (The Generate PDF Contact Sheet dialog box will appear; the contact sheet will display in the Document window when processing is finished.)

You used Adobe Bridge to create a PDF, then selected specific images and an arrangement for the file.

DESIGN**TIP**

Installing the Adobe Output Module

When shipped, Bridge CC *might not* include the Adobe Output Module. This module allows you to create PDF presentation and web galleries. You can find this module by searching Bridge Help for Bridge CC Output. The resulting page will instruct you as to how to download and install the Adobe Output Module.

Save a PDF output file

1. Click **Save** (at the bottom of the Output panel), locate the folder where your Data Files are stored, type **your name Chapter 2 contact sheet** in the text box, then click **Save**.

2. Click **OK** to acknowledge that the contact sheet was successfully processed.

You generated a PDF that can be printed later using Adobe Acrobat, then saved and printed the PDF.

Figure 24 *Output panel in Bridge*
Source: Morguefile. Images © Photodisc/Getty Images.

Click to create output

Click to create PDF

Output preview

Selected thumbnails

Creating a PDF

Using Bridge you can create a PDF Presentation (a presentation in the PDF file format). Such a presentation can be viewed fullscreen on any computer monitor, or in Adobe Acrobat or Adobe Reader as a PDF file. You can create such a presentation by opening Bridge, locating and selecting images using the file hierarchy, and then clicking the Output button on the Bridge Menu bar. The Output panel, shown in Figure 24, opens and displays the images you have selected. You can add images by pressing [Ctrl] (Win) or ⌘ (Mac) while clicking additional images.

You can also create a PDF from a Photoshop file by clicking File on the menu bar, then clicking Print. Select Adobe PDF from the Print list arrow in the Printer Setup section of the Photoshop Print Settings dialog box, make any other necessary selections, then click Print. (These instructions are for Windows, Mac steps vary slightly.)

Learning Photoshop Basics

Figure 25 *Web Gallery options in Bridge*
Source: Morguefile.

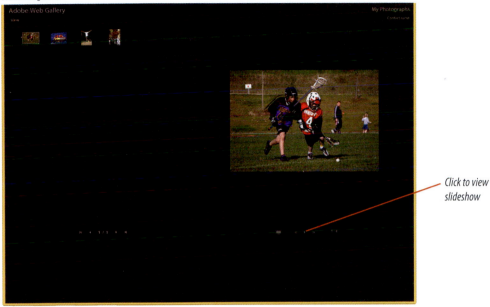

Click to view slideshow

Create a Web Gallery with Bridge

1. Verify that Bridge is open and that the images are still selected.
2. Click the **Web Gallery button** in the Output panel.
3. Click the **Preview in Browser button** in the Output Preview window, select a browser that will open the file if asked, click the **Play Slideshow button** in the browser window, then after reviewing the slideshow, click the **Pause Slideshow button**.

   Compare your screen to Figure 25.
4. Close the browser, return to Bridge, scroll down the Output panel to the Create Gallery section, click the **Save Location Browse button**, navigate to the location where your Data Files are stored if necessary, click **OK** (Win) or **Open** (Mac) in the Choose a Folder dialog box, then click **Save** at the bottom of the Output panel.
5. Click **OK** to close the Create Gallery dialog box.
6. Click **File** on the Bridge menu, then click **Exit** (Win) or click **Adobe Bridge CC** in Bridge, then click **Quit Adobe Bridge CC** (Mac).

You generated a Web Gallery using Adobe Bridge.

DESIGNTIP

Using Contrast to Add Emphasis

Contrast is an important design principle that uses opposing elements, such as colors or lines, to produce an intensified effect in an image, page, or publication. Just as you can use a font attribute to make some text stand out from the rest, you can use contrasting elements to make certain graphic objects stand out. You can create contrast in many ways: by changing the sizes of objects; by varying object weights, such as making a line surrounding an image heavier; by altering the position of an object, such as changing its location on the page or rotating it so that it is positioned on an angle; by drawing attention-getting shapes or a colorful box behind an object that makes it stand out (called a **matte**); or by adding carefully selected colors that emphasize an object.

POWER USER SHORTCUTS	
To do this:	**Use this method:**
Drag a layer	🖐
Hide a layer	👁
Open Help	[F1] (Win) ⌘ [/] (Mac)
Print File	File ➤ Print [Ctrl][P] (Win) ⌘ [P] (Mac)
Show a layer	▢
Show History panel	Window ➤ History ▣
Zoom in	🔍 [Ctrl][+] (Win) ⌘ [+] (Mac)
Zoom out	[Alt] 🔍 (Win) [option] 🔍 (Mac) [Ctrl][-] (Win) ⌘ [−] (Mac)
Zoom tool	🔍 or **Z**

Key: Menu items are indicated by ➤ between the menu name and its command. Blue bold letters are shortcuts for selecting tools on the Tools panel.

© 2013 Cengage Learning®

Use organizational and management features.

1. Open Adobe Bridge.
2. Click the Folders tab, then locate the folder that contains your Data Files.
3. Close Adobe Bridge.

Use the Layers and History panels.

1. Open PS 2-5.psd from the drive and folder where you store your Data Files.
2. Save it as **Zenith Design Logo**.
3. Display the Legacy workspace.
4. Drag the Wine Glasses layer so it is above the Zenith layer, then use the History panel to undo the state.
5. Use the Indicates layer visibility button to hide the Wine Glasses layer.
6. Make the Wine Glasses layer visible again.
7. Hide the Zenith layer.
8. Show the Zenith layer.
9. Show the Tag Line layer.

Learn about Photoshop by using Help.

1. Open the Adobe Photoshop Online Help window.
2. Display information about Image size and resolution. (*Hint*: look in the Image and color basics group.).
3. Scroll down to information about file size.
4. Use your browser to print the information you find.
5. Close the Help window.

View and print an image.

1. Make sure that all the layers of the Zenith Design Logo are visible in the Layers panel.
2. Click the Zoom tool, then make sure the setting is selected to resize the window to fit.
3. Zoom in on the wine glasses twice.
4. Zoom out to the original perspective.
5. Print one copy of the image.
6. Save your work.
7. Compare your screen to Figure 26, then close the Zenith Design Logo file.

Figure 26 *Completed Skills Review*
Images © Photodisc/Getty Images.

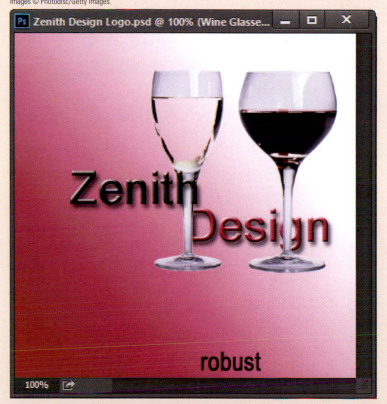

As a new Photoshop user, you are comforted knowing that Photoshop's Help system provides definitions, explanations, procedures, and other helpful information. It also includes examples and demonstrations to show how Photoshop features work. You use the Help system to learn about moving document windows, switching workspaces, and the Tools panel.

1. Open the Photoshop Online Help window.
2. Click the Workspace basics link in the Workspace and workflow group.
3. Scroll down to the section on rearranging, docking, or floating document windows and read this information.
4. Scroll back to the top of the page, then click the Save and switch workspaces link.
5. Return to the Help home page, click Tool galleries in the Workspace and workflow group, compare your screen to the sample shown in Figure 27, then close the Help window.

Figure 27 *Sample Project Builder 1*

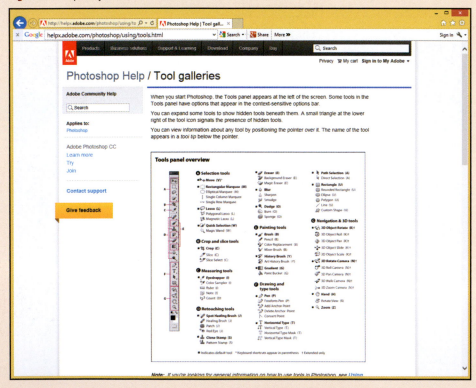

Kitchen Experience, your local specialty cooking shop, has just added herb-infused oils to its product line. They have hired you to draft a flyer that features these new products. You use Photoshop to create this flyer.

1. Open PS 2-6.psd, then save it as **Cooking**.
2. Display the Essentials workspace (if necessary).
3. Make the Measuring Spoons layer visible.
4. Drag the Oils layer so the content appears behind the Skillet layer content.
5. Drag the Measuring Spoons layer above the Skillet layer.
6. Save the file, then compare your image to the sample shown in Figure 28.

Figure 28 *Sample Project Builder 2*
Images © Photodisc/Getty Images.

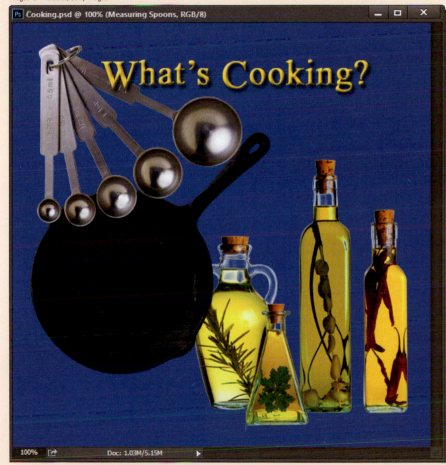

As an avid, albeit novice Photoshop user, you have grasped the importance of how layers affect your image. With a little practice, you can examine a single-layer image and guess which objects might display on their own layers. Now, you're ready to examine the images created by Photoshop experts and critique them on their use of layers.

1. Connect to the Internet, and use your browser and Behance, if possible, to find interesting artwork located on at least two websites.
2. Download a single-layer image (in its native format) from each website.
3. Start Photoshop, then open the downloaded images.
4. Save one image as **Critique-1** and the other as **Critique-2** in the Photoshop format (use the .psd extension).
5. Analyze each image for its potential use of layers.

6. Open the File Info dialog box for Critique-1.psd, then type in the Description section your speculation as to the number of layers there might be in the image, their possible order on the Layers panel, and how moving the layers would affect the image. Use the File Info dialog box to add a description for Critique-2.psd.
7. Close the dialog box.
8. Compare your image to the sample shown in Figure 29, then close the files.

Figure 29a *Sample Design Project*
Source: Morguefile.

Figure 29b *File Info dialog box for sample Design Project*

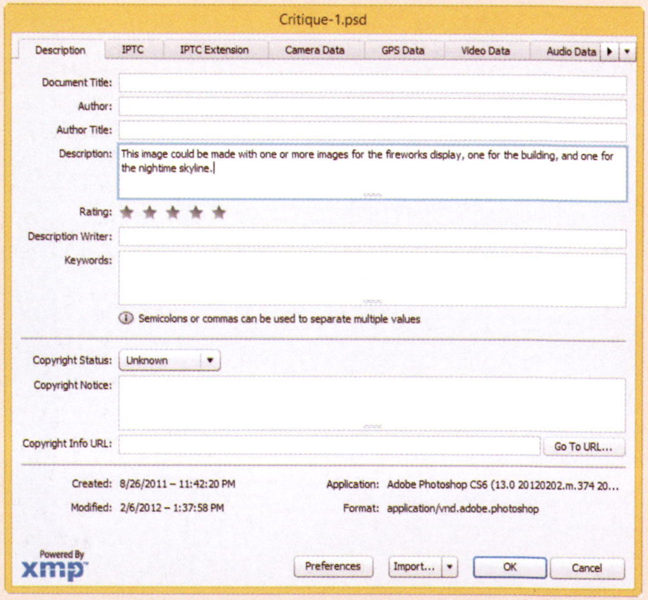

It seems that every major software manufacturer is including an element of 'cloud computing' in their latest version of their software. You've heard of it, but you're still not sure you fully understand it.

1. Connect to the Internet and use your favorite search engine to find information about cloud computing.
2. Using a sheet of paper or your favorite word processor, create a grid that contains the names of at least two or three major technology companies (such as Adobe, Microsoft, and Google) and find out about their forays into cloud computing. Figure 30 contains a sample document.
3. Print any relevant page(s).
4. Be prepared to discuss this topic and its relevance to your work in Photoshop.

Figure 30 *Sample Portfolio Project*

Cloud·Computing·Examples¶

Manufacturer¤	Name¤	Specifications¤	
Adobe·Corporation¤	Adobe·Creative·Cloud¤	An·Adobe·Creative·Cloud·subscription·gives·you·immediate·access·to·the·latest·updates·and·features.·Creative·tools·for·photography,·video,·audio,·and·design·are·all·available.·Additional·services·exist·for·file·sharing,·collaboration,·and·publishing·apps·and·websites.·Individual·subscribers·get·20GB·of·storage;·team·subscribers·get·100GB.¤	¤
Apple·Corporation¤	iCloud¤	Allows·you·to·sync·your·apps,·music,·photos,·books,·mail,·and·documents·seamlessly·on·an·iPhone,·iPad,·iPod·Touch,·Mac,·or·PC.·Included·in·iCloud·is·Photos·Sharing,·iWork,·Keychain,·Mail,·Calendar,·and·Contacts,·Backup·and·Storage,·and·iCloud.com.¤	¤
Google¤	Google·Drive¤	Google·Drive·is·a·place·where·you·can·safely·store·photos,·videos,·documents,·and·any·other·files·you·might·have·Users·get·15·GB.·Google·Drive·lets·you·edit·and·create·documents·and·spreadsheets·with·Docs·and·Sheets,·share·photos,·access·the·most·current·document·version·regardless·of·your·location,·and·make·files·available·for·offline·use.¤	¤
Microsoft·Corporation¤	OneDrive¤	OneDrive·is·free·online·storage·service·you·can·access·from·anywhere.·All·you·need·to·access·OneDrive·is·a·Microsoft·account,·such·as·Xbox,·Hotmail,·Skype,·or·Outlook.com.·¶ You·receive·7·GB·of·free·online·storage.·A·desktop·app·is·available·that·lets·you·sync·your·files·with·all·your·devices,·although·this·app·is·unnecessary·if·you're·running·Windows·8.1.·¤	¤

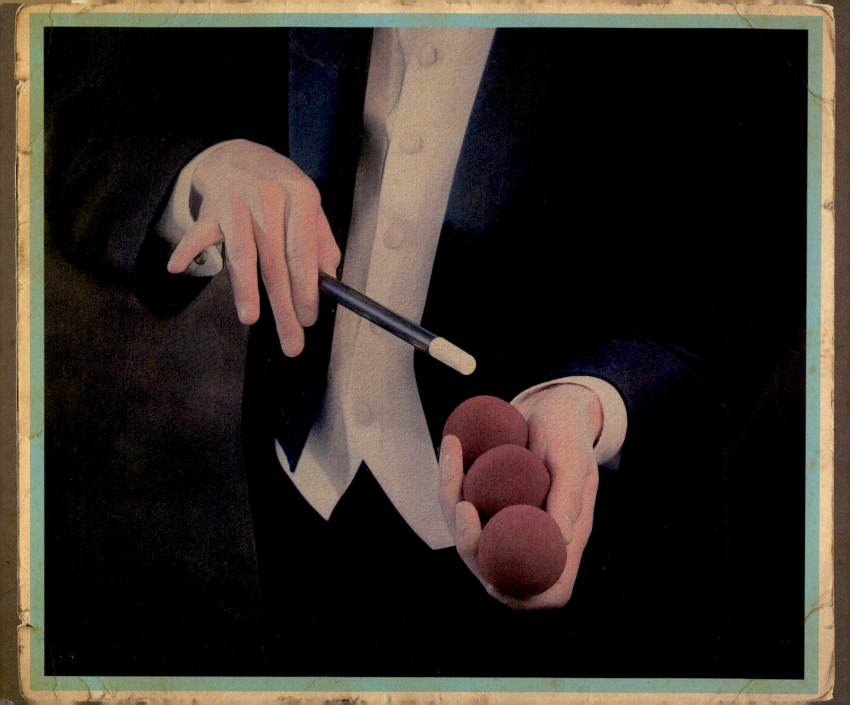

CHAPTER 3 WORKING WITH LAYERS

1. Examine and convert layers

2. Add and delete layers

3. Add a selection from one image to another

4. Organize layers with layer groups and colors

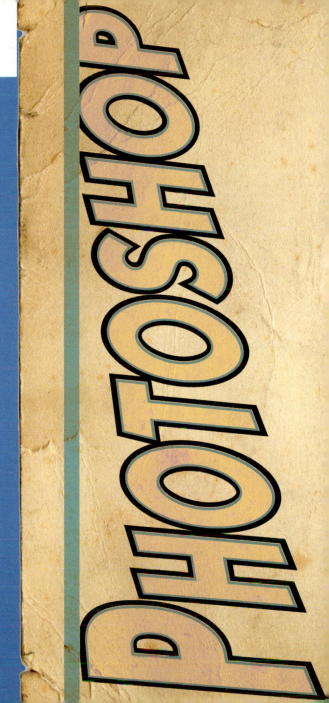

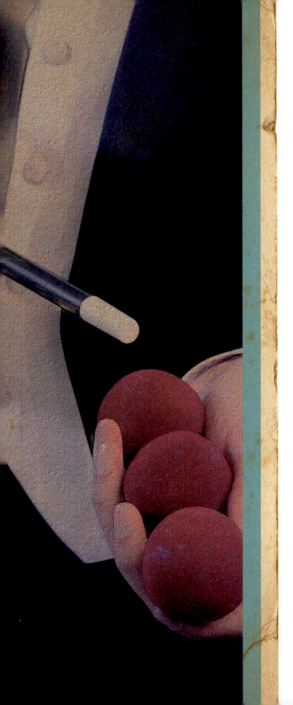

CHAPTER 3 WORKING WITH LAYERS

Layers Are Everything

You can use Photoshop to create sophisticated images in part because a Photoshop image can contain multiple layers. Each object created in Photoshop can exist on its own individual layer, making it easy to control the position and quality of each layer in the stack. Depending on your computer's resources, you can have a maximum of 8000 layers in each Photoshop image with each layer containing as much or as little detail as necessary.

Understanding the Importance of Layers

Layers make it possible to manipulate the tiniest detail within your image, which gives you tremendous flexibility when you make changes. By placing objects, effects, styles, and type on separate layers, you can modify them individually *without* affecting other layers. The advantage to using multiple layers is that you can isolate effects and images on one layer without affecting the others. The disadvantage of using multiple layers is that your file size might become very large.

However, once your image is finished, you can dramatically reduce its file size by combining all the layers into one using a process known as **flattening**.

Using Layers to Modify an Image

You can add, delete, and move layers in your image. You can also drag a portion of an image, called a **selection**, from one Photoshop image to another. When you do this, a new layer is automatically created. Copying layers from one image to another makes it easy to transfer a complicated effect, a simple image, or a piece of type. In addition to being able to hide and display each layer, you can also change its opacity. **Opacity** is the ability to see through a layer so that layers beneath it are visible. The more opacity a layer has, the less see-through (transparent) it is. You can continuously change the overall appearance of your image by changing the order of your layers, until you achieve just the look you want.

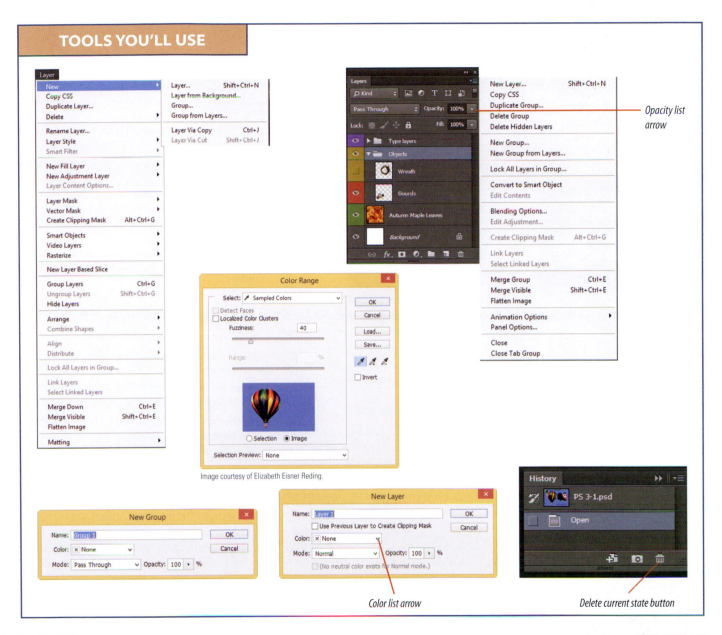

Image courtesy of Elizabeth Eisner Reding.

Opacity list arrow

Color list arrow

Delete current state button

Examine and
CONVERT LAYERS

What You'll Do

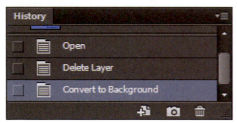

 In this lesson, you'll use the Layers panel to delete a Background layer and the Layer menu to create a Background layer from an image layer.

Learning About the Layers Panel

The Layers panel lists all the layers within a Photoshop file and makes it possible for you to manipulate one or more layers. By default, this panel is located in the lower-right corner of the screen, but it can be moved to a new location by dragging the panel's tab. In some cases, the entire name of the layer might not appear on the panel. If a layer name is too long, an ellipsis appears, indicating that part of the name is hidden from view. You can view a layer's entire name by holding the pointer over the name until the full name appears. The **layer thumbnail** appears to the left of the layer name and contains a miniature picture of the layer's content, as shown in Figure 1. To the left of the layer thumbnail, you can add color, which you can use to easily identify layers. The Layers panel also contains common buttons, such as the Delete layer button and the Create a new layer button.

Recognizing Layer Types

The Layers panel includes several types of layers: Background, type, adjustment, and image (non-type). The Background layer—whose name appears in italics—is always at the bottom of the stack. Type layers—layers that contain text—contain the type layer icon in the layer thumbnail, and image layers display a thumbnail of their contents. Adjustment layers, which affect the appearance of layers, have a variety of thumbnails depending on the kind of adjustment. Along with dragging selections from one Photoshop image to another, you can also drag objects created in other applications, such as Adobe Dreamweaver, Adobe InDesign, Adobe Illustrator, or Adobe Flash, onto a Photoshop image, which creates a layer containing the object you dragged from the other program window.

It is not necessary for a Photoshop image to have a Background layer. However, if you don't have a Background layer, the background will take on the properties of an **object layer** (a layer containing one or more images) which is more memory intensive. The *Background* layer does not support transparency, in fact, when you click on the Background layer, you'll notice that the locking tools in the Layers panel become dimmed.

Organizing Layers

One of the benefits of using layers is that you can create different design effects by rearranging their order. Figure 2 contains the same layers as Figure 1, but they are arranged differently. Did you notice that the yellow-striped balloon is in front of both the black-striped balloon and the lighthouse balloon? This image was created by dragging the layer containing the yellow balloon (named Layer 2 on the Layers panel) above the Black striped balloon layer. When organizing layers, you may find it helpful to resize the Layers panel so you can see more layers within the image.

QUICK **TIP**

Did you notice the horizontal and vertical lines in the Figure 2? Although you may find them distracting, these lines are moveable guides that you can use to help you place objects precisely. As you continue working in Photoshop, you'll find they are very useful—and soon you probably won't even notice them. You can display existing (but non-displayed) guides by clicking View on the Menu bar, pointing to Show, and then clicking Guides. (The Guides command for an image not containing guides will appear dimmed.)

Figure 1 *Image with multiple layers*
Image courtesy of Elizabeth Eisner Reding.

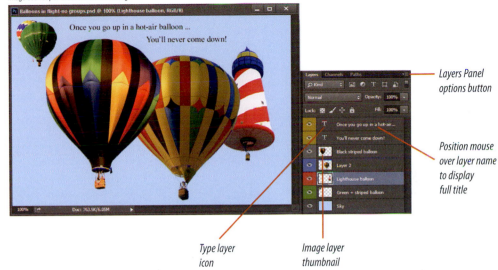

Layers Panel options button

Position mouse over layer name to display full title

Type layer icon

Image layer thumbnail

Figure 2 *Layers rearranged*
Image courtesy of Elizabeth Eisner Reding.

New layer order

Guideline   Overlapping balloons

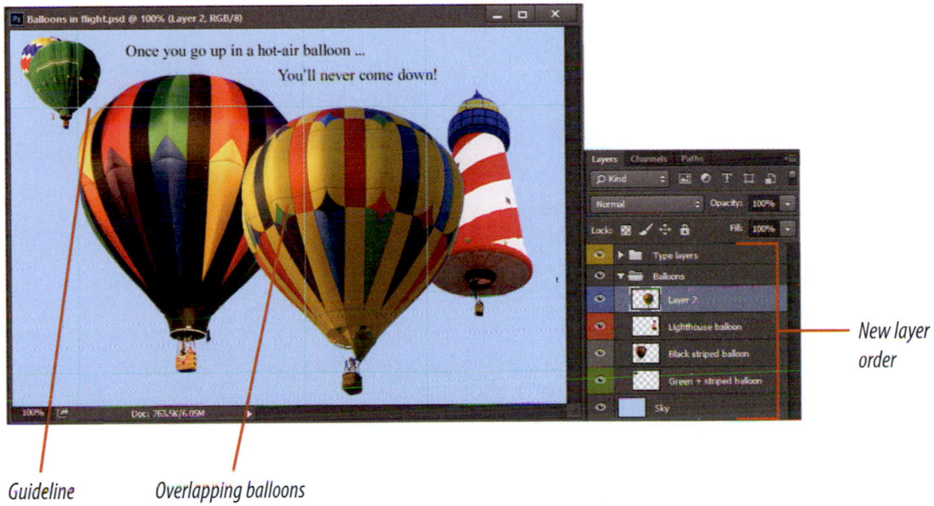

Converting Layers

When you open an image created with a digital camera, you'll notice that the entire image appears in the Background layer. The Background layer of any image is the initial layer and is always located at the bottom of the stack. You cannot change its position in the stack, nor can you change its opacity or lighten or darken its colors. You can, however, convert a Background layer into an image layer (non-type layer), and you can convert an image layer into a Background layer. You might want to convert a Background layer into an image layer so that you can use the full range of editing tools on the layer content. You might want to convert an image layer into a Background layer after you have made all your changes and want it to be the bottom layer in the stack. Note that when you convert an image layer to a Background layer, you need to modify the image layer *before* converting it.

QUICK TIP

Before you can convert an image layer to a Background layer, you must first delete the existing Background layer. You delete a Background layer by selecting it on the Layers panel, and then dragging it to the Delete layer button on the Layers panel.

Figure 3 *Changing units of measurement*
Image courtesy of Elizabeth Eisner Reding.

Right-click (Win) or [control]-click (Mac) to display measurement choices

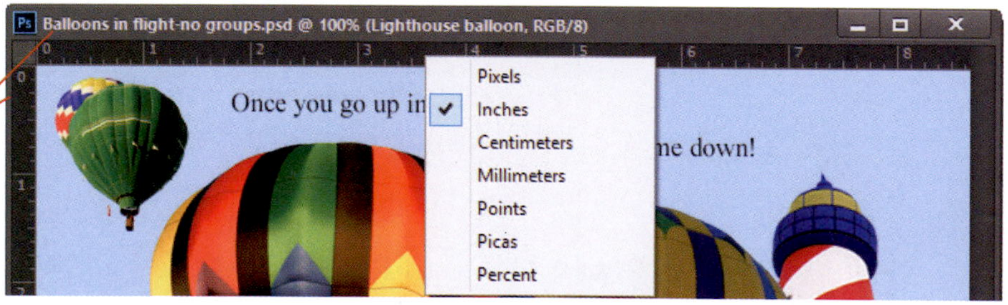

Using Rulers and Changing Units of Measurement

You can display horizontal and vertical rulers to help you better position elements. To display or hide rulers, click View on the Menu bar, and then click Rulers. (A check mark to the left of the Rulers command indicates that the rulers are displayed.)

In addition to displaying or hiding rulers, you can also choose from various units of measurement. Your choices include pixels, inches, centimeters, millimeters, points, picas, and percentages. Pixels, for example, display more tick marks and can make it easier to make tiny adjustments. You can change the units of measurement by clicking Edit [Win] or Photoshop [Mac] on the Menu bar, pointing to Preferences, and then clicking Units & Rulers. In the Preferences dialog box, click the Rulers list arrow, click the units you want to use, and then click OK. The easiest way to change units of measurement, however, is shown in Figure 3. Once the rulers are displayed, right-click (Win) or [control]-click (Mac) either the vertical or horizontal ruler, and then click the unit of measurement you want. When displayed, the Info panel shows the current X/Y coordinates of your pointer in your image, based on the units of measurement in use.

Pixel dimensions measure the number of pixels forming the width and height of an image, while *resolution* is the fineness of the detail in an image. The more pixels per inch, the greater the resolution.

Figure 4 *Warning box*

Figure 5 *Background layer deleted*

Background layer
no longer present

Figure 6 *New Background layer added to Layers panel*

History state
indicating layer
conversion

New Background
layer

Convert an image layer into a Background layer

1. Open PS 3-1.psd from the drive and folder where you store your Data Files, then save it as **Up in the air**.

TIP If you receive a warning box about maximum compatibility or a message stating that some of the text layers need to be updated before they can be used for vector-based output, click Update and/or click OK.

2. Click **View** on the Menu bar, click **Rulers** if your rulers are not visible, then make sure that the rulers are displayed in pixels.

TIP If you are unsure which units of measurement are used, right-click (Win) or [control]-click (Mac) one of the rulers, then click Pixels if it is not already selected.

3. Click **Legacy** (created in a lesson in Chapter 1) in the workspace switcher on the options bar.

4. On the Layers panel, click the **Background layer**, then click the **Delete layer button** 🗑.

5. Click **Yes** in the dialog box, as shown in Figure 4, then compare your Layers panel to Figure 5.

6. Verify that the Sky layer in the Layers panel is active, click **Layer** on the Menu bar, point to **New**, then click **Background from Layer**.

   The Sky layer has been converted into the Background layer. Did you notice that in addition to the image layer being converted to the Background layer that a state now appears on the History panel that says Convert to Background? See Figure 6.

7. Save your work.

You displayed the rulers and switched to a previously created workspace, deleted the Background layer of an image, then converted an image layer into the Background layer. You can convert any layer into the Background layer, as long as you first delete the existing Background layer.

Add and Delete
LAYERS

What You'll Do

 In this lesson, you'll create a new layer using the New command on the Layer menu, delete a layer, and create a new layer using buttons on the Layers panel.

Adding Layers to an Image

Because it's so important to make use of multiple layers, Photoshop makes it easy to add and delete layers. You can create layers in three ways:

- Use the New command on the Layer menu.
- Use the New Layer command on the Layers panel menu.
- Click the Create a new layer button on the Layers panel.

Objects on new layers have a default opacity setting of 100%, which means that objects on lower layers are not visible. Each layer has the Normal (default) blending mode

Merging Layers

You can combine multiple image layers into a single layer using the merging process. **Merging layers** is useful when you want to combine multiple layers in order to make specific edits permanent. (This merging process is different from flattening in that it's selective. Flattening merges *all* visible layers.) In order for layers to be merged, they must be visible. You can merge all visible layers within an image, or just the ones you select.

Type layers cannot be merged until they are **rasterized** (turned into a bitmapped image layer) or converted into uneditable text. To merge two layers, make sure that they are adjacent and that the Indicates layer visibility button is visible on each layer, and then click the layer in the higher position on the Layers panel. Click the Layers Panel options button, and then click Merge Down. The **active layer** (the layer that's currently selected) and the layer immediately beneath it will be combined into a single layer. To merge all visible layers, click the Layers Panel options button, and then click Merge Visible. Many layer commands that are available using the Layers Panel options button such as Merge Visible, are also available on the Layer menu.

Working with Layers

applied to it. (A **blending mode** is a feature that affects a layer's underlying pixels, and is used to lighten or darken colors. Blending modes affect how pixels in two separate layers interact with each other.)

QUICK **TIP**

See Table 1 for tips on navigating the Layers panel.

Generating Assets from Layers

Imagine that you have an image with half a dozen or so layers. And these layers may have to be used elsewhere for a website, or for use by other departments. These other users are going to need these elements as gifs or jpgs, *not* Photoshop layers. Using **Adobe Generator**, you can have Photoshop create individual files (such as GIFs or JPGs) from the layers in an image. To do this, open the file for which you want the assets generated, click File on the Menu bar, point to Generate, then click Image Assets. (This option is a toggle switch so be sure to turn this off when you're finished.)

QUICK **TIP**

Adobe Generator is created to improve workflows, particularly for web designers, screen designers, and anyone who needs to extract image assets from a Photoshop image.

On each layer that you want to create as an asset, rename the layer with a sensible name, appended by the extension of the file format you want (.gif, .png, or .jpg). Photoshop generates the image assets in a subfolder (named *filename*-assets) in the same location as the source PSD file.

TABLE 1: SHORTCUTS FOR NAVIGATING THE LAYERS PANEL	
Use the combination:	**To navigate:**
[Alt] [[] (Win) or [option] [[] (Mac)	down the Layers panel
[Alt] [[] (Win) or [option] []] (Mac)	up the Layers panel
[Ctrl] [[] (Win) or ⌘ [[] (Mac)	to move a layer down one layer*
[Ctrl] []] (Win) or ⌘ []] (Mac)	to move a layer up one layer*
[Ctrl] [Shift] [[] (Win) or ⌘ [Shift] [[] (Mac)	to move a layer to the bottom of the stack*
[Ctrl] [Shift] []] (Win) or ⌘ [Shift] []] (Mac)	to move a layer to the top of the stack*

Excluding the Background layer
© 2013 Cengage Learning®

Naming a Layer

Photoshop automatically assigns a sequential number to each new layer name, but you can rename a layer at any time. So, if you have four named layers and add a new layer, the default name of the new layer will be Layer 1. Although calling a layer "Layer 12" is fine, you might want to use a more descriptive name so it is easier to distinguish one layer from another. If you use the New command on the Layer menu, you can name the layer when you create it. You can rename a layer at any time by using either of these methods:

■ Click Layer on the Menu bar, click Rename Layer, type the new name when the existing text is selected, and then press [Enter] (Win) or [return] (Mac).

■ Double-click the name on the Layers panel, type the new name, and then press [Enter] (Win) or [return] (Mac).

Isolation Mode Layer Filtering

Suppose you are working with a complex image that has so many layers that you become distracted by them. Using this isolaton enhancement, you can filter layers in an image and focus more clearly on a specific subset of layers. You can selectively filter specific layers by clicking them (click the initial layer, then [Ctrl]-click (Win) or [command]-click (Mac) each additional layer, clicking Select on the Menu bar, then clicking Isolate Layers. Only the selected layers will be displayed in the Layers panel. To return the Layers Panel to normal, click Select on the Menu bar, then click Isolate Layers. Once the layers are selected, you can enter isolation mode by clicking the Layer Filtering list arrow in the Layers panel, then clicking Selected.

Deleting Layers from an Image

You might want to delete an unused or unnecessary layer. You can use multiple methods to delete a layer:

■ Click the name on the Layers panel, click the Layers Panel options button, and then click Delete Layer, as shown in Figure 7.

■ Click the name on the Layers panel, click the Delete layer button on the Layers panel, and then click Yes in the warning box.

■ Click the name on the Layers panel, press and hold [Alt] (Win) or [option] (Mac), and then click the Delete layer button on the Layers panel.

■ Drag the layer name on the Layers panel to the Delete layer button on the Layers panel.

■ Right-click a layer (Win) or [Ctrl]-click a layer (Mac), and then click Delete Layer.

You should be certain that you no longer need a layer before you delete it. If you delete a layer by accident, you can restore it during the current editing session by deleting the Delete Layer state on the History panel, or by clicking Edit on the Menu bar, then clicking Undo Delete Layer.

QUICK TIP

Photoshop always numbers layers sequentially, no matter how many layers you add or delete.

Figure 7 *Layers panel menu*

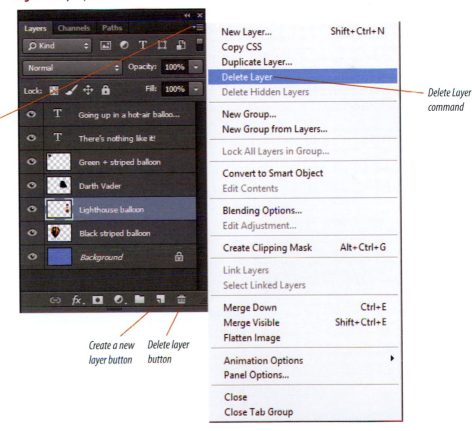

Layers Panel options button

Delete Layer command

Create a new layer button

Delete layer button

Modifying a workspace

1. Drag the History panel so it displays above the Layers panel.
2. Click **Window** on the Menu bar, point to **Workspace**, then click **New Workspace**.
3. Type **Legacy** in the Name text box, click **Save**, then click **Yes** in the New Workspace warning box.

You moved a panel in a saved workspace, then saved the change using the original name (making the change permanent).

Add a layer using the Layer menu

1. Click the **Lighthouse balloon layer** on the Layers panel.
2. Click **Layer** on the Menu bar, point to **New**, then click **Layer** to open the New Layer dialog box, as shown in Figure 8.

   A new layer will be added above the active layer.

TIP You can change the layer name in the New Layer dialog box before it appears on the Layers panel.

3. Click **OK**.

   The New Layer dialog box closes and the new layer, Layer 1, appears above the Lighthouse balloon layer on the Layers panel. The New Layer state is added to the History panel. See Figure 9.

You created a new layer above the Lighthouse balloon layer using the New command on the Layer menu. The layer does not yet contain any content.

Figure 8 *New Layer dialog box*

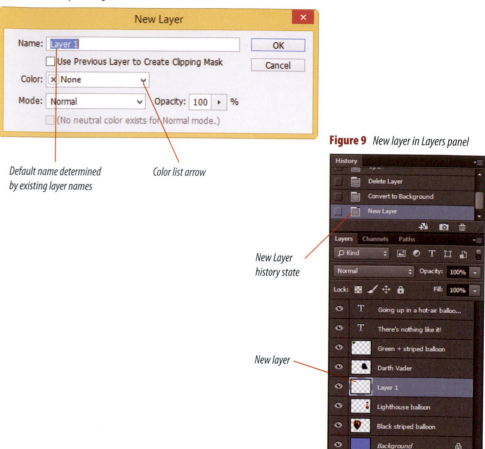

Default name determined by existing layer names

Color list arrow

Figure 9 *New layer in Layers panel*

New Layer history state

New layer

Inserting a Layer Beneath the Active Layer

When you add a layer to an image either by using the Layer menu or clicking the Create a new layer button on the Layers panel, the new layer is inserted above the active layer. But there might be times when you want to insert the new layer beneath, or in back of, the active layer. You can do so easily, by pressing [Ctrl] (Win) or [⌘] (Mac) while clicking the Create a new layer button on the Layers panel.

Figure 10 *New layer with default settings*

Default settings

Create a new layer button

Delete a layer

1. Position the **Layer selection pointer** over Layer 1 on the Layers panel.

2. Drag **Layer 1** to the **Delete layer button** on the Layers panel.

TIP You can also delete the layer by dragging the New Layer state on the History panel to the Delete current state button.

3. If the Delete the layer "Layer 1" dialog box opens, click the **Don't show again check box**, then click **Yes**.

TIP Many dialog boxes let you turn off this reminder feature by selecting the Don't show again check box. Selecting these check boxes can improve your efficiency.

You used the Delete layer button on the Layers panel to delete a layer.

Add a layer using the Layers panel

1. Click the **Lighthouse balloon layer** on the Layers panel, if it is not already selected.

2. Click the **Create a new layer button** on the Layers panel, then compare your Layers panel and History panel to Figure 10.

3. Save your work.

You used the Create a new layer button on the Layers panel to add a new layer.

Add a Selection
FROM ONE IMAGE TO ANOTHER

What You'll Do

Image courtesy of Elizabeth Eisner Reding.

 In this lesson, you'll use the Invert check box in the Color Range dialog box to make a selection, drag the selection to another image, and remove the fringe from a selection using the Defringe command.

Understanding Selections

Often the Photoshop file you want to create involves using an image or part of an image from another file. To use an image or part of an image, you must first select it. Photoshop refers to this as "making a selection." A selection is an area of an image surrounded by a **marquee**, a dashed line that encloses the area you want to edit or move to another image, as shown in Figure 11. You can drag a marquee around a selection using four marquee tools: Rectangular Marquee, Elliptical Marquee, Single Row Marquee, and Single Column Marquee. Table 2 displays the four marquee tools along with other selection tools. You can set options for each tool on the options bar when the tool you want to use is active.

Making and Moving a Selection

You can use a variety of methods and tools to make a selection, which can then be used as a specific part of a layer or as the entire layer. You use selections to isolate an area you want to alter. For example, you can use the Magnetic Lasso tool to select complex shapes by clicking the starting point, tracing an approximate outline, and then clicking the ending point. Later, you can use the Crop tool to trim areas from a selection. When you use the Move tool to drag a selection to the destination image, Photoshop places the selection in a new layer above the previously active layer.

Cropping an Image

You might find an image that you really like, except that it contains a particular portion that you don't need. You can exclude, or **crop**, certain parts of an image by using the Crop tool on the Tools panel. Cropping hides areas of an image from view *without* decreasing resolution quality. To crop an image, click the Crop tool on the Tools panel, drag the pointer around the area you *want to keep*, and then press [Enter] (Win) or [return] (Mac).

Understanding Color Range Command

In addition to using selection tools, Photoshop provides more methods for incorporating imagery from other files. You can use the Color Range command, located on the Select menu, to select a particular color contained in an existing image. Depending on the area you want, you can use the Color Range dialog box to extract a portion of an image.

For example, you can select the Invert check box, choose one color, and then Photoshop will select the portion of the image that is every color *except* the color you chose. After you select all the imagery you want from another image, you can drag it into your open file. Simply put, the Invert feature allows you to flip whatever you currently have selected to include whatever is not currently selected.

Defringing Layer Contents

Sometimes when you make a selection and move it into another image, the newly selected image contains unwanted pixels that give the appearance of a fringe, or halo. You can remove this effect using a Matting command called Defringe. This command is available by pointing to Matting on the Layer menu and allows you to replace fringe pixels with the colors of other nearby pixels. You can determine a width for replacement pixels between 1 and 200. It's magic!

Figure 11 *Marquee selections*
Image courtesy of Elizabeth Eisner Reding.

Area selected using the Rectangular Marquee tool

Specific element selected using the Magnetic Lasso tool

TABLE 2: SELECTION TOOLS			
Tool	**Tool name**	**Tool**	**Tool name**
	Rectangular Marquee tool		Quick Selection tool
	Elliptical Marquee tool		Lasso tool
	Single Row Marquee tool		Polygonal Lasso tool
	Single Column Marquee tool		Magnetic Lasso tool
	Crop tool		Slice tool
	Magic Wand tool		

© 2013 Cengage Learning®

Make a color range selection

1. Open PS 3-2.psd from the drive and folder where you store your Data Files, save it as **Yellow striped balloon**, click the **title bar**, then drag the **window** to an empty area of the workspace so that you can see both images.

TIP When more than one file is open, each has its own set of rulers. The ruler on the inactive file appears dimmed.

2. With the Yellow striped balloon image selected, click **Select** on the Menu bar, then click **Color Range**.

TIP If the background color is a solid color, when you select it and select the Invert check box, only the foreground will be selected.

3. Click the **Image option button** below the image preview, then type **100** in the Fuzziness text box (or drag the **slider** to the right until you see **100**).

4. Position the **Eyedropper pointer** 💧 in the **blue background** of the image in the Color Range dialog box, then click the **background**.

5. Select the **Invert check box**. Compare the settings in your dialog box to Figure 12.

6. Click **OK**, then compare your Yellow striped balloon.psd image to Figure 13.

You opened a file and used the Color Range dialog box to select the image pixels by selecting the image's inverted colors. Selecting the inverse is an important skill in making selections.

Figure 12 *Color Range dialog box*
Image courtesy of Elizabeth Eisner Reding.

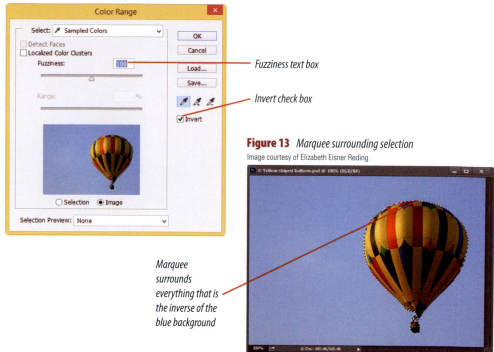

Fuzziness text box

Invert check box

Figure 13 *Marquee surrounding selection*
Image courtesy of Elizabeth Eisner Reding.

Marquee surrounds everything that is the inverse of the blue background

Using the Place Commands

You can add an image from another image to a layer using a Place command. Place an image in a Photoshop layer by clicking File on the Menu bar, clicking Place Embedded or Place Linked, then committing the changes. A file that is Place Linked will be automatically updated when the original (source) file is modified. A file that is Place Embedded is essentially a copy of the source file and will not be updated if the original file is modified. The placed artwork appears *flattened* inside a bounding box at the center of the Photoshop image. The artwork maintains its original aspect ratio; however, if the artwork is larger than the Photoshop image, it is resized to fit. The Place commands work well if you want to insert a multi-layered image in another image. (If all you want is a specific layer from an image, you should just drag the layer you want into an image and not use a Place command.)

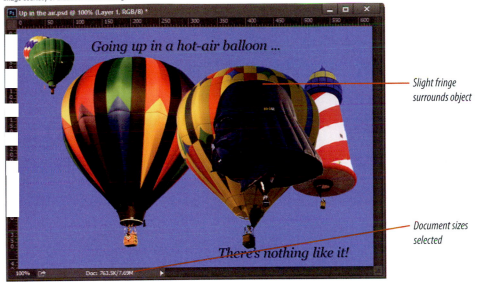

Slight fringe
surrounds object

Document sizes
selected

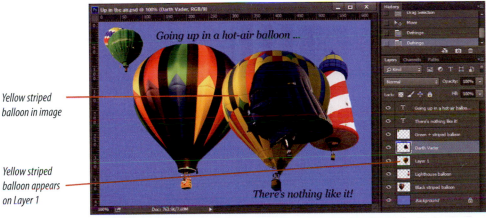

Yellow striped
balloon in image

Yellow striped
balloon appears
on Layer 1

Lesson 3   Add a Selection from One Image to Another

Move a selection to another image

1. Click the **Move tool** on the Tools panel.
2. Position the **Move tool pointer** anywhere over the selection in the Yellow striped balloon image.
3. Drag the **selection** to the Up in the air image, then release the mouse button.

   The Yellow striped balloon image moves to the Up in the air image appearing on Layer 1.
4. Use to drag the yellow striped balloon to the approximate location shown in Figure 14.

   TIP When you drag an object, a box displays showing you how many horizontal and vertical pixels the object is moving.
5. Click the **menu arrow** in the document window status bar and verify that Document Sizes is selected.

You dragged a selection from one image to another. You verified that the document size is displayed in the window.

Defringe the selection

1. With Layer 1 selected, click **Layer** on the Menu bar, point to **Matting** then click **Defringe**.

   Defringing a selection gets rid of the halo effect that sometimes occurs when objects are dragged from one image to another.
2. Type **2** in the Width text box, then click **OK**.
3. Click the **Darth Vader layer** and defringe it using a width of **2**.
4. Save your work.
5. Close **Yellow striped ballon.psd**, then compare the Up in the air image to Figure 15.

You removed the fringe from a selection and a layer.

Organize Layers with
LAYER GROUPS AND COLORS

What You'll Do

Image courtesy of Elizabeth Eisner Reding.

 In this lesson, you'll use the Layers Panel options button to create, name, and color-code a layer group, and then add layers to it. You'll add finishing touches to the image, save it as a copy, and then flatten it.

Understanding Layer Groups

A **layer group** is a Photoshop feature that allows you to organize your layers on the Layers panel. A layer group contains individual layers, which are sometimes referred to as *nested layers*. For example, you can create a layer group that contains all the type layers in your image. To create a layer group, you click the Layers Panel options button, and then click New Group. As with layers, it is helpful to choose a descriptive name for a layer group.

QUICK TIP

You can press [Ctrl][G] (Win) or [⌘] [G] (Mac) to place the selected layer in a layer group.

Organizing Layers into Groups

After you create a layer group, you simply drag layers on the Layers panel directly on top of the layer group. You can remove layers from a layer group by dragging them out of the layer group to a new location on the Layers panel or by deleting them. Some changes made to a layer group, such as blending mode or opacity changes, affect every layer in the layer group. You can choose to expand or collapse layer groups, depending on the amount of information you need to see. Expanding a layer group shows all of the layers in the layer

---

Duplicating a Layer

When you add a new layer by clicking the Create a new layer button on the Layers panel, the new layer contains default settings. However, you might want to create a new layer that has the same settings as an existing layer. You can do so by duplicating an existing layer to create a copy of that layer and its settings. Duplicating a layer is also a good way to preserve your modifications, because you can modify the duplicate layer and not worry about losing your original work. To create a duplicate layer, select the layer you want to copy, click the Layers Panel options button, click Duplicate Layer, and then click OK. The new layer will appear above the original.

group, and collapsing a layer group hides all of the layers in a layer group. You can expand or collapse a layer group by clicking the triangle to the left of the layer group icon. Figure 16 shows one expanded layer group and one collapsed layer group.

Identifying a Layer with Color

If your image has relatively few layers, it's easy to locate the layers. However, if your image contains many layers, you might need some help in organizing them. You can organize layers by color-coding them, which makes it easy to find the layer or the group you want, regardless of its location on the Layers panel. For example, you can identify all type layers with red or color-code the layers associated with a particular portion of an image with blue. To color-code the Background layer, you must first convert it to a regular layer.

QUICK TIP

You can also color-code a layer group without losing the color-coding you applied to individual layers.

Flattening an Image

After you make all the necessary modifications to your image, you can greatly reduce the file size by flattening the image. Flattening merges all visible layers into a single Background layer and discards all hidden layers. Make sure that all layers that you want to display are visible before you flatten the image. Because flattening removes an image's individual layers, it's a good idea to make a copy of the original image *before* it is flattened. The status bar displays the file's current size and the size it will be when flattened.

Figure 16 *Layer groups*

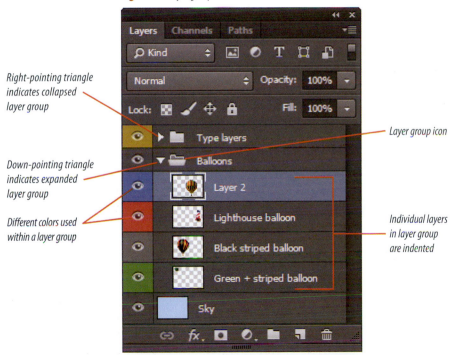

Right-pointing triangle indicates collapsed layer group

Down-pointing triangle indicates expanded layer group

Different colors used within a layer group

Layer group icon

Individual layers in layer group are indented

Understanding Layer Comps

The ability to create a **layer comp**, a variation on the arrangement and visibility of existing layers, is a powerful tool that can make your work more organized. You might, for example, want to create several variations of your single image that include different configurations of layers, and layer comps give you this ability. You open the Layer Comps panel by clicking Window on the Menu bar, and then clicking Layer Comps. Clicking the Create New Layer Comp button on the panel opens the New Layer Comp dialog box, shown in Figure 17, which allows you to name the layer comp and set parameters.

Using Layer Comps

Multiple layer comps, shown in Figure 18, make it easy to switch back and forth between variations on an image theme. The layer comp is an ideal tool for showing a client multiple layer arrangement options.

Figure 18 *Multiple layer comps in image*
Image courtesy of Elizabeth Eisner Reding.

Figure 17 *New Layer Comp dialog box*

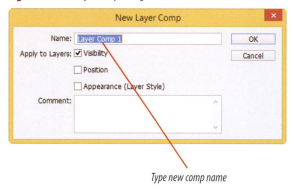

Type new comp name

Layer Comps tab

Last created layer comp

Create New Layer Comp button

Figure 19 *New Group dialog box*

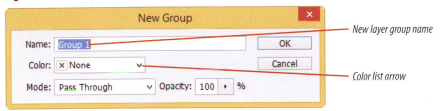

New layer group name

Color list arrow

Figure 20 *New layer group in Layers panel*

Down-pointing arrow indicates expanded layer group

New layer group

Figure 21 *Layers added to the All Type layer group*

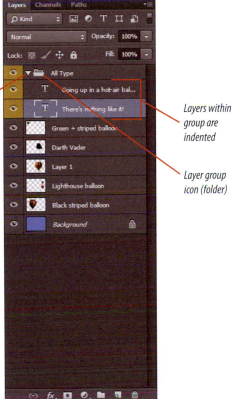

Layers within group are indented

Layer group icon (folder)

Create a layer group

1. Click the **Green + striped balloon layer**, click the **Layers Panel options button** ▤, then click **New Group**.

   The New Group dialog box opens, as shown in Figure 19.

   TIP Photoshop automatically places a new layer group above the active layer.

2. Type **All Type** in the Name text box.

3. Click the **Color list arrow**, click **Yellow**, then click **OK.**

   The New Group dialog box closes. Compare your Layers panel to Figure 20.

You used the Layers panel menu to create a layer group, then named and applied a color to it. This new group will contain all the type layers in the image.

Move layers to the layer group

1. Click the **Going up in a hot-air balloon** layer on the Layers panel, then drag it on to the **All Type layer group**.

2. Click the **There's nothing like it! layer**, drag it on to the **All Type layer group**, then compare your Layers panel to Figure 21.

   TIP If the There's nothing like it! layer is not below the Going up in a hot-air balloon layer, move the layers to match Figure 21.

3. Click the **triangle** ▼ to the left of the layer group icon (folder) to collapse the layer group.

You moved two layers into a layer group. Using layer groups is a great organizational tool, especially in complex images with many layers.

Rename a layer and adjust opacity

1. Double-click **Layer 1**, type **Yellow striped balloon**, then press [**Enter**] (Win) or [**return**] (Mac).

2. Double-click the **Opacity text box** on the Layers panel, type **85**, then press [**Enter**] (Win) or [**return**] (Mac).

3. Drag the **Yellow striped balloon layer** beneath the Lighthouse balloon layer, then compare your image to Figure 22.

4. Save your work.

You renamed the new layer, adjusted opacity, and rearranged layers.

Create layer comps

1. Click **Window** on the Menu bar, then click **Layer Comps**.

2. Click the **Create New Layer Comp button** on the Layer Comps panel.

3. Type **Green off/Yellow off** in the Name text box, as shown in Figure 23, then click **OK**.

4. Click the **Indicates layer visibility button** on the Green + striped balloon layer and the Yellow striped balloon layer.

5. Click the **Update Layer Comp button** on the Layer Comps panel. Compare your Layer Comps panel to Figure 24.

6. Save your work, then click the **Layer Comps Close button** on the icon dock to close the Layer Comps panel.

You created a Layer Comp in an existing image.

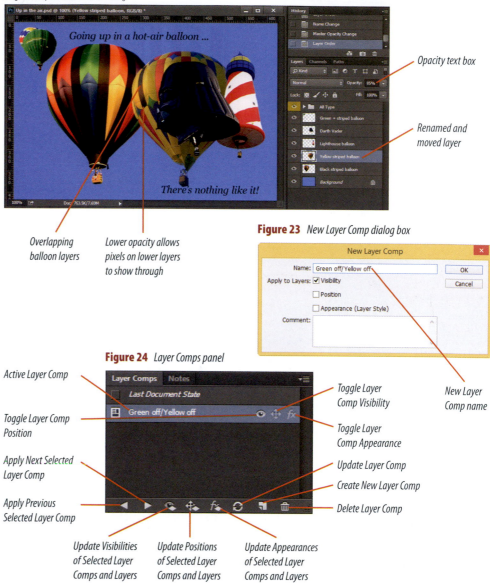

Figure 22 *Finished image*
Image courtesy of Elizabeth Eisner Reding.

Overlapping balloon layers

Lower opacity allows pixels on lower layers to show through

Opacity text box

Renamed and moved layer

Figure 23 *New Layer Comp dialog box*

Figure 24 *Layer Comps panel*

Active Layer Comp

Toggle Layer Comp Position

Apply Next Selected Layer Comp

Apply Previous Selected Layer Comp

Toggle Layer Comp Visibility

Toggle Layer Comp Appearance

New Layer Comp name

Update Layer Comp

Create New Layer Comp

Delete Layer Comp

Update Visibilities of Selected Layer Comps and Layers

Update Positions of Selected Layer Comps and Layers

Update Appearances of Selected Layer Comps and Layers

Working with Layers

Figure 25 *Save As dialog box*

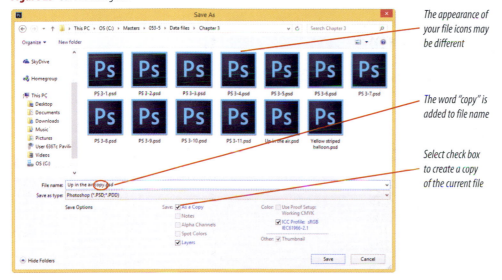

The appearance of your file icons may be different

The word "copy" is added to file name

Select check box to create a copy of the current file

Figure 26 *Flattened image layer*
Image courtesy of Elizabeth Eisner Reding.

Flattened file size

Flattened image contains one layer

Flatten an image

1. Click **File** on the Menu bar, then click **Save As**.

2. Click the **As a Copy check box** to select it, then compare your dialog box to Figure 25.

TIP   If "copy" does not display in the File name text box, click this text box and type copy to add it to the name.

3. Click **Save**, then click **OK** to Maximize Compatibility, if necessary.

    Photoshop saves and closes a copy of the file containing all the layers and effects.

4. Click **Layer** on the Menu bar, then click **Flatten Image**.

5. Click **OK** in the warning box (to discard hidden layers), then save your work.

    Compare your Layers panel to Figure 26.

6. Click the **workspace switcher** on the options bar, then click **Essentials**.

7. Close all open images, then exit Photoshop.

You saved a copy of the file, then flattened the image. The image now has a single layer.

POWER USER SHORTCUTS	
To do this:	**Use this method:**
Adjust layer opacity	Click Opacity list arrow on Layers panel
	Drag Opacity slider
	Double-click Opacity text box, type a percentage
Add a layer to a group	Drag selected layer(s) to Group folder
Change measurements	Right-click ruler (Win)
	[Ctrl]-click ruler (Mac)
Color-code a layer	Right-click layer, click color
Create a layer comp	⬛ on Layer Comps panel
Create a layer group	⬛, New Group, or [Ctrl][G] (Win)
	⌘ [G] (Mac)
Delete a layer	🗑
Defringe a selection	Layer ➤ Matting ➤ Defringe
Flatten an image	Layer ➤ Flatten Image
Use the Move tool	⬛ or **V**
Make a new Background layer from existing layer	Layer ➤ New ➤ Background from Layer
Make a new layer	Layer ➤ New ➤ Layer
	or ⬛
Rename a layer	Double-click layer name, type new name
Select color range	Select ➤ Color Range
Show/Hide Rulers	View ➤ Rulers
	[Ctrl][R] (Win)
	⌘ [R] (Mac)
Update a layer comp	⬛

Key: Menu items are indicated by ➤ *between the menu name and its command. Blue bold letters are shortcuts for selecting tools on the Tools panel.*

Examine and convert layers.

1. Start Photoshop.
2. Open PS 3-3.psd from the drive and folder where you store your Data Files, then save it as **Music Store**.
3. Make sure the rulers appear and that pixels are the unit of measurement.

TIP For now and future lessons, if you see a dialog box telling you that text layers might need to be updated, please update the layers.

4. Delete the Background layer.
5. Verify that the Rainbow blend layer is active, then convert the image layer to a Background layer.
6. Save your work.

Add and delete layers.

1. Make Layer 2 active.
2. Create a new layer above this layer using the Layer menu.
3. Accept the default name (Layer 5), and change the color of the layer to Red.
4. Delete (new) Layer 5.
5. Make Layer 2 active (if it is not already the active layer).
6. Save your work.

Add a selection from one image to another.

1. Open PS 3-4.psd.
2. Reposition this image of a horn by dragging the window to the right of the Music Store image.
3. Open the Color Range dialog box. (*Hint*: Use the Select menu.)
4. Verify that the Image option button is selected, the Invert check box is selected, and then set the Fuzziness to 0.
5. Sample the white background in the preview window in the dialog box, then click OK.
6. Use the Move tool to drag the selection into the Music Store image.
7. Position the selection so that the upper-left edge of the instrument matches the sample shown in Figure 27 on the next page.
8. Defringe the horn selection (in the Music Store image) using a 3 pixel width.
9. Close PS 3-4.psd.
10. Drag Layer 5 above the Notes layer.
11. Rename Layer 5 **Horn**.
12. Change the opacity for the Horn layer to 55%.
13. Drag the Horn layer so it is beneath Layer 2.
14. Hide Layer 1.
15. Hide the rulers.
16. Save your work.

Organize layers with layer groups and colors.

1. Create a Layer Group called **Type Layers** and assign the color Orange to the group.
2. Drag the following layers into the Type Layers folder: Allegro, Music Store, Layer 2.
3. Delete Layer 2, then collapse the Type Layers group.
4. Move the Notes layer beneath the Horn layer.
5. Create a layer comp called **Notes layer on**.
6. Update the layer comp.
7. Hide the Notes layer.
8. Create a new layer comp called **Notes layer off**, then update the layer comp.
9. Display the previous layer comp, save your work, then close the tab group. (*Hint*: Click the Layer Comps Panel options button, then click Close Tab Group.)
10. Save a copy of the Music Store file using the default naming scheme (add 'copy' to the end of the existing filename).
11. Flatten the original image. (*Hint*: Be sure to discard hidden layers.)
12. Save your work, then compare your image to Figure 27.

Figure 27 *Completed Skills Review*
Images © Photodisc/Getty Images.

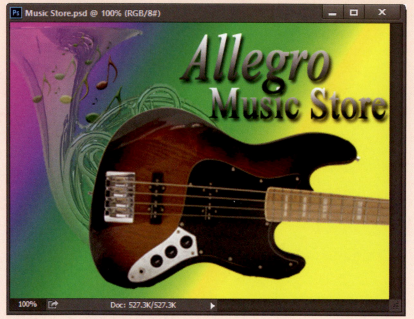

A credit union is developing a hotline for members to use to help mitigate credit card fraud as soon as it occurs. They're going to distribute ten thousand refrigerator magnets over the next three weeks. As part of their effort to build community awareness of the project, they have sponsored a contest for the magnet design. You decide to enter the contest.

1. Open PS 3-5.psd, then save it as **Combat Fraud**. The PalatinoLinotype Roman font is used in this file. Please make a substitution if this font is not available on your computer.
2. Open PS 3-6.psd, use the Color Range dialog box or any selection tool on the Tools panel to select the cell phone image, then drag it to the Combat Fraud image.
3. Rename the newly created layer **Cell Phones**, then assign a color code to the layer on the Layers panel. Make sure the Cell Phones layer is beneath the type layers.
4. Convert the Background layer to an image layer, then rename it **Banner**.
5. Change the opacity of the Banner layer to any setting you like.
6. Defringe the Cell Phones layer using the pixel width of your choice.
7. Save your work, close PS 3-6.psd, then compare your image to the sample shown in Figure 28.

Figure 28 *Sample Project Builder 1*
Source: Morguefile.

The local community can't get enough of the zoo's new giraffe exhibit, and they have hired you to create a promotional billboard commemorating this event. The Board of Directors wants the billboard to be humorous.

1. Open PS 3-7.psd, then save it as **Giraffe promotion**.
2. Open PS 3-8.psd, use the Color Range dialog box or any selection tool on the Tools panel to create a marquee around the giraffe, then drag the selection to the Giraffe promotion image.
3. Name the new layer **Giraffe**.
4. Change the opacity of the giraffe layer to 90% and defringe the layer containing the giraffe.
5. Reorder the layers so the Giraffe layer appears below the type layers.
6. Save your work, then compare your image to the sample shown in Figure 29.

Figure 29 *Sample Project Builder 2*

Images © Photodisc/Getty Images.

A friend of yours has designed a new heat-retaining coffee cup for take-out orders. She is going to present the prototype to a prospective vendor, but first needs to print a brochure. She's asked you to design an eye-catching cover.

1. Open PS 3-9.psd, then save it as **Coffee Cover**.
2. Open PS 3-10.psd, then drag the entire image to Coffee Cover.
3. Close PS 3-10.psd.
4. Rename Layer 1 with the name **Mocha**.
5. Delete the Background layer and convert the Mocha layer into a new Background layer.
6. Reposition the layer objects so they look like the sample. (*Hint*: You might have to reorganize the layers in the stack so all layers are visible. You can move type on a layer by selecting that layer, clicking the Move tool on the Tools panel, positioning the pointer over the type, then dragging until it is positioned where you want it.)
7. Create a layer group above Layer 2, name it **High Octane Text**, apply a color-code of your choice to the layer group, then drag the type layers to it. You can apply color-codes to any individual layers of your choosing.
8. Save your work, then compare your image to Figure 30.

Figure 30 *Sample Design Project*
Images © Photodisc/Getty Images.

Working with Layers

Harvest Market, a line of natural food stores, and the trucking associations in your state have formed a coalition to deliver fresh fruit and vegetables to food banks and other food distribution programs. The truckers want to promote the project by displaying a sign on their trucks. Your task is to create a design that will become the Harvest Market logo. Keep in mind that the design will be seen from a distance.

1. Open PS 3-11.psd, then save it as **Harvest Market**.
2. Obtain at least two images of different-sized produce. You can obtain images by using what is available on your computer, scanning print media, or connecting to the Internet and downloading images.

3. Open one of the produce files, select it, then drag or copy it to the Harvest Market image. (*Hint*: Experiment with some of the other selection tools. Note that some tools require you to copy and paste the image after you select it.)
4. Repeat step 3, then close the two produce image files.
5. Set the opacity of the Market layer to 80%.
6. Arrange the layers so that smaller images appear on top of the larger ones. (You can move layers to any location in the image you choose.)

7. Create a layer group for the type layers, and apply a color-code to it.
8. You can delete any layers you feel do not add to the image. (In the sample image, the Veggies layer has been deleted.)
9. Save your work, then compare your image to Figure 31.
10. What are the advantages and disadvantages of using multiple images? How would you assess the ease and efficiency of the selection techniques you've learned?

Figure 31 *Sample Portfolio Project*

Source: Morguefile. Images © Photodisc/Getty Images.

CHAPTER 4 MAKING
SELECTIONS

1. Make a selection using shapes
2. Modify a marquee
3. Select using color and modify a selection
4. Add a vignette effect to a selection

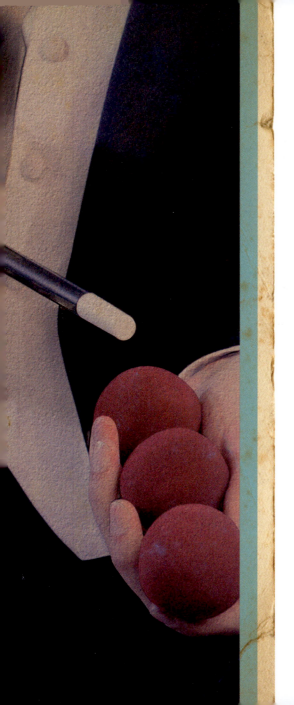

CHAPTER 4 MAKING SELECTIONS

Combining Images

Most Photoshop images are created using a technique called **compositing**—combining images from different sources. These sources include other Photoshop images, royalty-free images, pictures taken with digital cameras, and scanned artwork. How you get those multiple images into your Photoshop images is an art unto itself. You can include additional images by using tools on the Tools panel and menu commands. And to work with all these images, you need to know how to select them—or how to select the parts you want to include.

Understanding Selection Tools

The two basic methods you can use to make selections are using a tool or using color. You can use three free-form tools to create your own unique selections, four fixed area tools to create circular or rectangular selections, and a wand tool to make selections using color. In addition, you can use menu commands to increase or decrease selections that you made

with these tools, or to make selections based on color.

Understanding Which Selection Tool to Use

With so many tools available, how do you know which one to use? After you become familiar with the different selection options, you'll learn how to look at images and evaluate selection opportunities. With experience, you'll learn how to identify edges that can be used to isolate imagery, and how to spot colors that can be used to isolate a specific object.

Combining Imagery

After you decide on an object that you want to place in a Photoshop image, you can add the object to another image by cutting, copying, and pasting or dragging and dropping objects using the selection tools, the Move tool, menu commands, or using the **Clipboard**, the temporary storage area provided by your operating system.

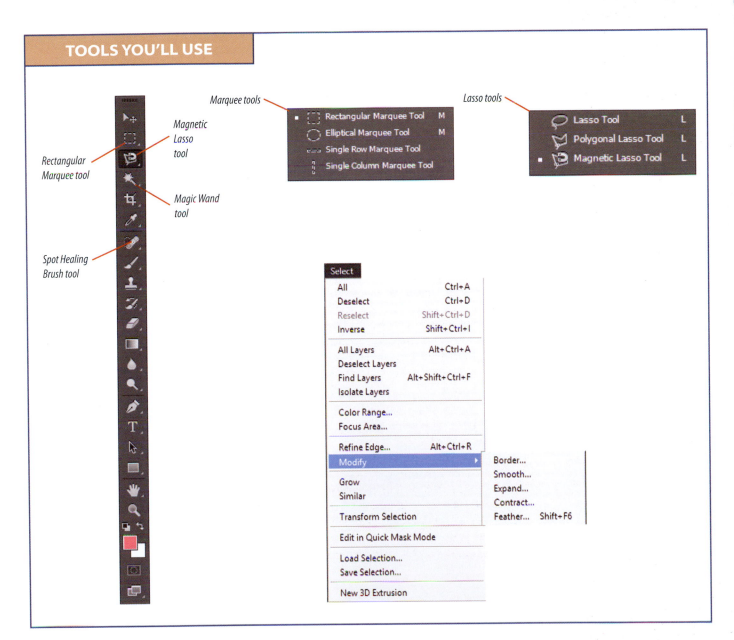

Marquee tools

Rectangular Marquee Tool   M
Elliptical Marquee Tool   M
Single Row Marquee Tool
Single Column Marquee Tool

Lasso tools

Lasso Tool   L
Polygonal Lasso Tool   L
Magnetic Lasso Tool   L

Magnetic Lasso tool

Rectangular Marquee tool

Magic Wand tool

Spot Healing Brush tool

Select

All	Ctrl+A
Deselect	Ctrl+D
Reselect	Shift+Ctrl+D
Inverse	Shift+Ctrl+I
All Layers	Alt+Ctrl+A
Deselect Layers	
Find Layers	Alt+Shift+Ctrl+F
Isolate Layers	
Color Range...	
Focus Area...	
Refine Edge...	Alt+Ctrl+R
Modify	▶
Grow	
Similar	
Transform Selection	
Edit in Quick Mask Mode	
Load Selection...	
Save Selection...	
New 3D Extrusion	

Border...
Smooth...
Expand...
Contract...
Feather...   Shift+F6

Make a Selection
USING SHAPES

What You'll Do

Source: Morguefile.

 In this lesson, you'll make selections using a marquee tool and a lasso tool, position a selection with the Move tool, deselect a selection, and drag a complex selection into another image.

Selecting by Shape

The Photoshop selection tools make it easy to select objects that are rectangular or elliptical in nature. However, it would be a boring world if every image we wanted fell into one of those categories, so fortunately they don't. While some objects are round or square, most are unusual in shape. Making selections can sometimes be a painstaking process because many objects don't have clearly defined edges. To select an object by shape, you need to click the appropriate tool on the Tools panel, and then drag the pointer around the object. The selected area is defined by a **marquee**, or series of dotted lines, as shown in Figure 1.

Creating a Selection

Drawing a rectangular marquee is easier than drawing an elliptical marquee, but with practice, you'll be able to create both types of marquees easily. Table 1 lists the tools you can use to make selections using shapes. Figure 2 shows a marquee surrounding an irregular shape.

Figure 1 *Elliptical Marquee tool used to create marquee*
Images © Photodisc/Getty Images.

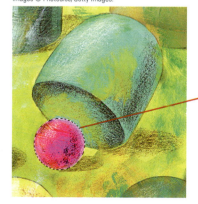

Elliptical Marquee surrounds object

Figure 2 *Marquee surrounding irregular shape*
Images © Photodisc/Getty Images.

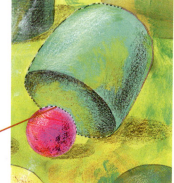

Marquee

Using Fastening Points

Each time you click one of the marquee tools, a fastening point is added to the image. A **fastening point** is an anchor within the marquee. When the marquee pointer reaches the initial fastening point (after making its way around the image), a very small circle appears on the pointer, indicating that you have reached the starting point. Clicking the pointer when this circle appears closes the marquee. Some fastening points, such as those in a circular marquee, are not visible, while others, such as those created by the Magnetic Lasso tools, are visible.

Selecting, Deselecting, and Reselecting

After a selection is made, you can move, copy, transform, or make adjustments to it.

A selection stays selected until you unselect, or **deselect**, it. You can deselect a selection by clicking Select on the Menu bar, and then clicking Deselect. You can reselect a deselected object by clicking Select on the Menu bar, and then clicking Reselect.

TABLE 1: SELECTION TOOLS BY SHAPE		
Tool	**Button**	**Effect**
Rectangular Marquee tool		Creates a rectangular selection. Press [Shift] while dragging to create a square.
Elliptical Marquee tool		Creates an elliptical selection. Press [Shift] while dragging to create a circle.
Single Row Marquee tool		Creates a 1-pixel-wide row selection.
Single Column Marquee tool		Creates a 1-pixel-wide column selection.
Lasso tool		Creates a freehand selection.
Polygonal Lasso tool		Creates straight line selections. Press [Alt] (Win) or [option] (Mac) to create freehand segments.
Magnetic Lasso tool		Creates selections that snap to an edge of an object. Press [Alt] (Win) or [option] (Mac) to alternate between freehand and magnetic line segments.

© 2013 Cengage Learning®

Placing a Selection

You can place a selection in a Photoshop image in many ways. You can copy or cut a selection, and then paste it to a different location in the same image or to a different image. You can also use the Move tool to drag a selection to a new location. The Paste In Place command (found within the Paste Special option on the Edit menu) lets you paste Clipboard contents in the same relative location in the target document or layer as it occupied in the source document or layer.

Using Guides

Guides are non-printing horizontal and vertical lines that you can display on top of an image to help you position a selection.

You can create an unlimited number of horizontal and vertical guides. You create a guide by displaying the rulers, positioning the pointer on either ruler, and then clicking and dragging the guide into position. Figure 3 shows the creation of a horizontal guide in a file that already contains guides. You delete a guide by selecting the Move tool on the Tools panel, positioning the pointer over the guide, and then clicking and dragging it back to its ruler. If the Snap feature is enabled, as you drag an object toward a guide, the object will be pulled toward the guide. To turn on the Snap feature, click View on the Menu bar, and then click Snap. A check mark appears to the left of the command if the feature is enabled.

Figure 3 *Creating guides in image*
Image courtesy of Elizabeth Eisner Reding.

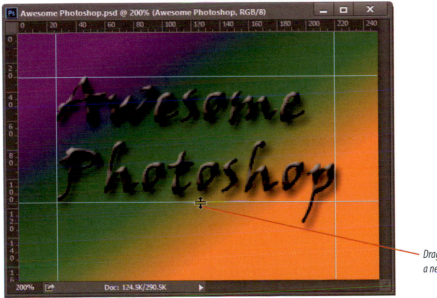

Dragging a guide to a new location

Taking Measurements

You can use any selection tool to select the object(s) you want measured. Measurements are recorded in the Measurement Log, which is grouped with the Mini Bridge and Timeline panels when it is opened. Sometimes you just need to know the dimensions of an object, such as the length, width, area, or density. Before you begin, you need to set the scale. This determines what unit of measurement will be used. You can do this by clicking the Measurement Log Panel options button, pointing to Set Measurement Scale, and then clicking Default or Custom. (The default scale uses pixel units.) Next, click Image on the Menu bar, point to Analysis, and then click Ruler Tool or Count Tool to select the measurement tool. If you select the Count Tool, the pointer will add a sequentially numbered object to the image so you can easily keep track of the count.

You can open the Measurement Log by clicking Window on the Menu bar, and then clicking Measurement Log. After you make a selection, click the Record Measurements button to record the measurement in a new row in the Measurement Log. Data in this log include label, date and time, document, source, scale, scale units, scale factor, count, length, and angle. Depending on what tool was used to define the area, measurements may also include area, perimeter, circularity, height, width, gray value (minimum), gray value (maximum), gray value (median), integrated density, and histogram. To measure a particular area, use a selection tool (including the Magic Wand or Quick Selection tool) to define an area. Click the Ruler tool, click a point on the selection area, then drag to another point on the selection area (which defines the area you want measured). Click the Record Measurements button on the Measurement Log panel and the measurement of the point-to-point area will display in the log. Repeat the process by clicking the next portion you want measured, then click Record Measurements. All your measurements will be recorded in the Measurement Log panel. You can skip the point-to-point measurement and simply collect data for a selection by clicking the Record Measurements button on the Measurement Log panel.

Figure 4 *Rectangular Marquee tool selection*
Source: Morguefile.

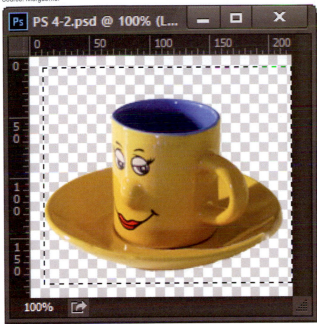

TABLE 2: WORKING WITH A SELECTION	
If you want to:	**Then do this:**
Move a selection (an image) using the mouse	Position ▶⊕ over the selection, then drag the marquee and its contents
Copy a selection to the Clipboard	Activate image containing the selection, click Edit ➤ Copy
Cut a selection to the Clipboard	Activate image containing the selection, click Edit ➤ Cut
Paste a selection from the Clipboard	Activate image where you want the selection, click Edit ➤ Paste
Delete a selection	Activate the image with the selection, then press [Delete] (Win) or [delete] (Mac)
Deselect a selection	Press [Ctrl][D] (Win) or ⌘[D] (Mac)

© 2013 Cengage Learning®

Create a selection with the Rectangular Marquee tool

1. Start Photoshop, open PS 4-1.psd from the drive and folder where you store your Data Files, save it as **Kitchen Table**, click **OK** if the Maximize compatibility dialog box displays, then reset the **Essentials workspace**.

2. Open PS 4-2.psd, then display the rulers in pixels for this image if they do not already appear.

3. Click the **Rectangular Marquee tool** ▣ on the Tools panel, then make sure the value in the Feather text box on the options bar is **0 px**.

   Feathering determines the amount of blur between the selection and the pixels surrounding it.

4. Drag the **Marquee pointer** ┼ to select the coffee cup from approximately **10 H/10 V** to **210 H/180 V**. See Figure 4.

   The first number in each coordinate refers to the horizontal ruler (H); the second number refers to the vertical ruler (V).

   TIP You can also use the X/Y coordinates displayed in the Info panel.

5. Click the **Move tool** ▶⊕ on the Tools panel, then drag the **coffee cup** to any location in the Kitchen Table image.

   The selection now appears in the Kitchen Table image on a new layer (Layer 1).

   TIP Table 2 describes methods you can use to work with selections in an image.

Using the Rectangular Marquee tool, you created a selection in an image, then you dragged that selection into another image. This left the original image intact, and created a copy of the selection in the destination image.

Position a selection with the Move tool

1. Verify that the **Move tool**  is active on the Tools panel, and display the rulers if they do not already appear.

2. If you do not see guides in the Kitchen Table image, click **View** on the Menu bar, point to **Show**, then click **Guides**.

TIP You can use the Straighten Layer button on the Ruler options bar to straighten an image to any given angle. Select the Ruler tool on the Tools panel (which is grouped with the Eyedropper tool), click and drag the pointer from one area to another, release the mouse button, then click the Straighten Layer button on the options bar. The horizontal edge of the active layer will be made parallel with the drawn line.

3. Drag the **coffee cup** so that the lower-left corner snaps to the ruler guides at approximately **220 H/520 V**. Compare your image to Figure 5.

   Did you feel the snap to effect as you positioned the selection within the guides? This feature makes it easy to properly position objects within an image.

TIP If you didn't feel the image snap to the guides, click View on the Menu bar, point to Snap To, then click Guides.

4. Rename Layer 1 **Coffee cup**.

You used the Move tool to reposition a selection in an existing image, then you renamed the layer.

Figure 5 *Rectangular selection in image*
Source: Morguefile.

Coffee cup snaps to guides

Using Smart Guides

Wouldn't it be great to be able to see a vertical or horizontal guide as you move an object? Using **Smart Guides**, you can do just that. Smart Guides are turned on/off by clicking View on the Menu bar, pointing to Show, and then clicking Smart Guides. (Smart Guides are turned on, by default.) When this feature is turned on, horizontal and vertical magenta guidelines appear automatically when you draw a shape or move an object. This feature allows you to align layer content as you move it. With the Smart Guides feature enabled, hold [Ctrl] (Win) or [command] (Mac) while dragging an object in the selected layer: as you drag, you'll see measurement guides displaying the dimensions of the active layer as well as the dimensions of nearby layers. As you move the object, the guides will also display spacing between other objects.

Figure 6 *Deselect command*

Source: Morguefile.

Shortcut can be used instead of clicking the menu

Deselect a selection

1. Click **Window** on the Menu bar, then click **PS 4-2.psd**.

TIP If you can see the window of the image you want anywhere on the screen, you can just click it to make it active instead of using the Window menu.

2. Click **Select** on the Menu bar, then click **Deselect**, as shown in Figure 6.

You made another window active, then used the Deselect command on the Select menu to deselect the object you moved. When you deselect a selection, the marquee no longer surrounds it.

Figure 7 *Save Selection dialog box*

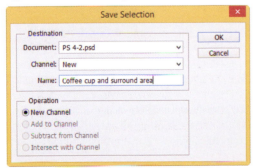

Saving and Loading a Selection

Any selection can be saved independently of the surrounding image, so that if you want to use it again in the image, you can do so without having to retrace it using one of the marquee tools. Once a selection is made, you can save it in the image by clicking Select on the Menu bar, and then clicking Save Selection. The Save Selection dialog box opens, as shown in Figure 7; be sure to give the selection a meaningful name. When you want to load a saved selection, click Select on the Menu bar, and then click Load Selection. Click the Channel list arrow to display the Channel list, click the named selection, and then click OK.

Create a selection with the Magnetic Lasso tool

1. Open PS 4-3.psd from the drive and folder where you store your Data Files.
2. Click the **Zoom tool** 🔍 on the Tools panel, then click the **tomato image** until the zoom factor is **200%**.
3. Click the **Magnetic Lasso tool** 🧲 on the Tools panel, then change the settings on the options bar so that they are the same as those shown in Figure 8. Table 3 describes Magnetic Lasso tool settings.
4. Click the **Magnetic Lasso tool pointer** 🖈 once anywhere on the edge of the tomato to create your first fastening point.

   TIP If you click a spot that is not at the edge of the tomato, press [Esc] to undo the action, then start again.

5. Drag 🖈 slowly around the tomato (clicking at the top of each leaf may be helpful) until it is almost entirely selected, then click directly over the **initial fastening point**. See Figure 9.

   TIP Zoom in or out of an image to see as much/little detail as you need.

   Don't worry about all the nooks and crannies surrounding the leaves on the tomato; the Magnetic Lasso tool will select those automatically. You will see a small circle next to the pointer when it is directly over the initial fastening point, indicating that you are closing the selection. The individual segments turn into a marquee.

   TIP If you feel that the Magnetic Lasso tool is missing some major details while you're tracing, you can insert additional fastening points by clicking the pointer while dragging. For example, click the mouse button at a location where you want to change the selection shape.

You created a selection with the Magnetic Lasso tool.

Figure 8 *Options for the Magnetic Lasso tool*

Figure 9 *Creating a selection with the Magnetic Lasso tool*
Source: Morguefile.

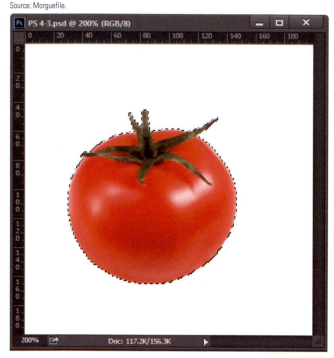

DESIGN TIP

Mastering the Art of Selections

You might feel that making selections is difficult when you first start. Making selections is a skill, and like most skills, it takes a lot of practice to become proficient. In addition to practice, make sure that you're comfortable in your work area, that your hands are steady, and that your mouse or other pointing device is working well. A non-optical mouse that is dirty will make selecting an onerous task, so make sure your mouse is well cared for and is functioning correctly.

Figure 10 *Selection dragged into image*

Source: Morguefile.

Defringing the layer reduces the amount of background that appears; your results will vary

Complex selection includes only object, no background

TABLE 3: MAGNETIC LASSO TOOL SETTINGS	
Setting	**Description**
Feather	The amount of blur between the selection and the surrounding pixels. This setting is measured in pixels and can be a value between 0 and 250.
Anti-alias	The smoothness of the selection, achieved by softening the color transition between edge and background pixels.
Width	The interior width, achieved by detecting an edge from the pointer. This setting is measured in pixels and can have a value from 1 to 40.
Contrast	The sensitivity of the tool. This setting can be a value between 1 percent and 100 percent; higher values detect high-contrast edges.
Frequency	The rate at which fastening points are applied. This setting can be a value between 0 and 100; higher values insert more fastening points.

© 2013 Cengage Learning®

Move a complex selection to an existing image

1. Click the **Move tool** on the Tools panel.

   TIP You can also click the Tool Preset picker list arrow on the options bar, then double-click the Move tool.

2. Use the **Move tool pointer** to drag the tomato selection to the Kitchen Table image, then open the **Info panel** (using the Window command on the Menu bar).

   The selection appears on a new layer (Layer 1).

3. Drag the object so that the bottom of the tomato snaps to the guide at approximately **450 Y** and the left edge of the tomato snaps to the guide at **220 X** using the coordinates on the Info panel. (The coordinates in the Info panel track the location where you clicked to drag the object.)

4. Use the Layer menu to defringe the new Layer 1 at a width of **1** pixel.

5. Close the PS 4-3.psd image without saving your changes, then collapse the Info panel to the dock.

6. Rename the new layer **Tomato** in the Kitchen Table image, then reposition the Tomato layer so it is beneath the Coffee cup layer in the Layers panel.

7. Save your work, then compare your image to Figure 10.

8. Click **Window** on the Menu bar, then click **PS 4-2.psd**.

9. Close the PS 4-2.psd image without saving your changes.

You dragged a complex selection into an existing Photoshop image. You positioned the object using ruler guides and renamed and repositioned a layer. You also defringed a selection to eliminate its white border.

Modify
A MARQUEE

What You'll Do

Source: Morguefile.

In this lesson, you'll move and enlarge a marquee, drag a selection into a Photoshop image, and then position a selection.

Changing the Size of a Marquee

Not all objects are easy to select. Sometimes, when you make a selection, you might need to change the size or shape of the marquee.

The options bar contains selection buttons that help you add to and subtract from a marquee, or intersect with a selection. The marquee in Figure 11 was modified into the one shown in Figure 12 by clicking the Add to selection button. After the Add to selection button is active, you can draw an additional marquee, and it will be added to the current marquee.

One method you can use to increase the size of a marquee is the Grow command. After you make a selection, you can increase the marquee size by clicking Select on the Menu bar, and then clicking Grow. The Grow command selects pixels adjacent to the marquee that have colors similar to those specified by the Magic Wand tool. The Similar command, also located on the Select menu, selects both adjacent and non-adjacent pixels.

Modifying a Marquee

While a selection is active, you can modify the marquee by expanding or contracting it, smoothing out its edges, or enlarging it to add a border around the selection. These five commands, Expand, Contract, Smooth Feather, and Border, are located on the Modify command submenu, which is found on the Select menu. For example, you might want to enlarge your selection. Using the Expand command, you can increase the size of the selection, as shown in Figure 13.

> **QUICK TIP**
>
> While the Grow command selects adjacent pixels that have similar colors, the Expand command increases a selection by a specific number of pixels.

Moving a Marquee

After you create a marquee, you can move the marquee to another location in the same image or to another image entirely. You might want to move a marquee if you've drawn it in the wrong image or the wrong location. Sometimes it's easier to draw a marquee elsewhere on the page, and then move it to the desired location.

> **QUICK TIP**
>
> You can always hide and display layers as necessary to facilitate making a selection.

Using the Quick Selection Tool

The Quick Selection tool lets you paint-to-select an object from the interior using a resizeable brush. As you paint the object, the selection grows. Using the Auto-Enhance check box, rough edges and blockiness are automatically reduced to give you a perfect selection. As with other selection tools, the Quick Selection tool has options to add and subtract from your selection.

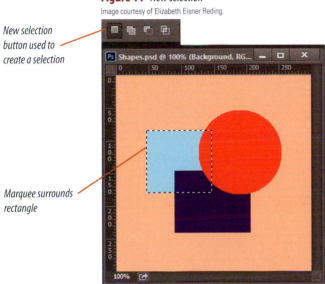

Figure 11 *New selection*
Image courtesy of Elizabeth Eisner Reding.

New selection button used to create a selection

Marquee surrounds rectangle

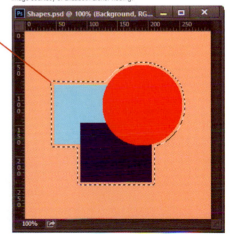

Figure 12 *Selection with additions*
Image courtesy of Elizabeth Eisner Reding.

Add to selection button adds new selection to the existing selection

Single marquee surrounds all shapes

Add to selection pointer

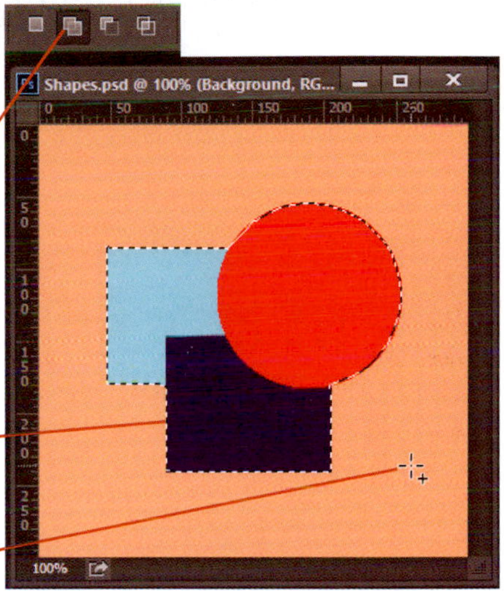

Figure 13 *Expanded selection*
Image courtesy of Elizabeth Eisner Reding.

Marquee expanded by 5 pixels

Adding To and Subtracting From a Selection

Of course knowing how to make a selection is important, but it's just as important to know how to make alterations in an existing selection. Sometimes it's almost impossible to create that perfect marquee on the first try. Perhaps your hand moved while you were tracing or you just got distracted. Using the Add to selection and Subtract from selection buttons (which appear with all selection tools), you can alter an existing marquee without having to start from scratch.

Move and enlarge a marquee

1. Open PS 4-4.psd from the drive and folder where you store your Data Files, then change the zoom factor to **200%**, enlarging the window as necessary.

2. Click the **Elliptical Marquee tool** on the Tools panel.

TIP The Elliptical Marquee tool might be hidden under the Rectangular Marquee tool.

3. Click the **New selection button** on the options bar if it is not already active.

4. Drag the **Marquee pointer** ╀ to select the area from approximately **150 X/50 Y** to **400 X/250 Y**. Compare your image to Figure 14.

5. Position the **pointer** ▷₊ in the center of the selection, then drag the **Move pointer** ▶₊ so the marquee covers the casserole, at approximately **250 X/165 Y**, as shown in Figure 15.

TIP You can also nudge a selection to move it by pressing the arrow keys. Each time you press an arrow key, the selection moves one pixel in the direction of the arrow.

6. Click **Select** on the Menu bar, then click **Similar**.

7. Click **Select** on the Menu bar, point to **Modify**, then click **Expand**.

8. Type **1** in the Expand Selection dialog box, click **OK**, then deselect the selection.

You created a marquee, then dragged the marquee to reposition it. You then enlarged a selection marquee by using the Similar and Expand commands then deselected the selection.

Figure 14 *Selection in image*
Source: Morguefile.

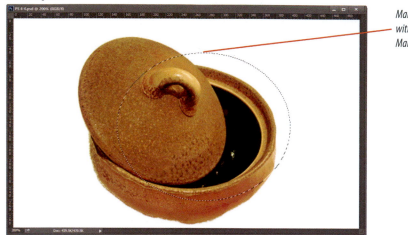

Marquee created with Elliptical Marquee tool

Figure 15 *Moved selection*
Source: Morguefile.

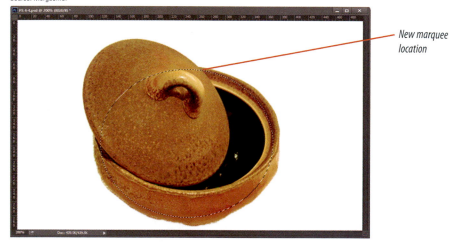

New marquee location

Figure 16 *Quick Selection tool settings*

Sample All Layers   Auto-Enhance   Refine Edge...

Click to add to selection

Figure 17 *Selection in file*
Source: Morguefile.

Figure 18 *Selection moved to the Kitchen Table image*
Source: Morguefile.

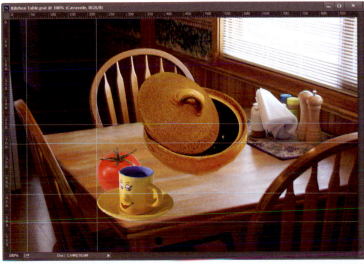

Use the Quick Selection tool

1. Click the **Quick Selection tool** on the Tools panel, then adjust your settings using Figure 16.

2. Verify that the Brush settings are 30 px diameter, 0% hardness, 1% spacing, 0° angle, 100% roundness, and Pen Pressure size.

TIP If you need to change the Brush settings, click the Brush picker list arrow on the options bar, then drag the sliders to the appropriate settings.

3. Position the pointer in the **center of the casserole**, then slowly drag the pointer to the outer edges until the object is selected. See Figure 17.

TIP Sometimes making a selection is easy, sometimes… not so much. Time and practice will hone your selection skills. It will get easier.

4. Change the zoom level to **100%**, then click the **Move tool** on the Tools panel.

5. Position the **Move pointer** over the selection, then drag the **casserole** to the Kitchen Table image.

6. Drag the **casserole** so that it is to the left of the napkins.

7. Defringe the casserole using a setting of **1** pixel.

8. Rename the new layer **Casserole**.

9. Save your work on the Kitchen Table image, then compare your work to Figure 18.

10. Make **PS 4-4.psd** active, then close PS 4-4.psd without saving your changes.

You selected an object using the Quick Selection tool, then you dragged the selection into an existing image.

Select Using Color and
MODIFY A SELECTION

What You'll Do

Source: Morguefile.

 In this lesson, you'll make selections using both the Color Range command and the Magic Wand tool. You'll also flip a selection, and then fix an image using the Healing Brush tool.

Selecting with Color

Selections based on color can be easy to make, especially when the background of an image is different from the image itself. High contrast between colors is an ideal condition for making selections based on color. You can make selections using color with the Color Range command on the Select menu, or you can use the Magic Wand tool on the Tools panel.

Using the Magic Wand Tool

When you select the Magic Wand tool, the following options are available on the options bar, as shown in Figure 19:

- The four selection buttons.
- Sample size, which defines the number of pixels sampled by the tool.

- The **Tolerance** setting, which allows you to specify how similar in color pixels must be in order to be selected. This setting has a value from 0 to 255; the lower the value, the closer in color the selected pixels will be.
- The Anti-alias check box softens the appearance of the edge of the selection.
- The Contiguous check box, which lets you select pixels that are next to one another.
- The Sample All Layers check box, which lets you select pixels from multiple layers at once.
- The Refine Edge button lets you easily improve the quality of the selection edges.

Figure 19 *Options for the Magic Wand tool*

Using the Color Range Command

You can use the Color Range command, located on the Select menu, to make the same selections as with the Magic Wand tool. When you use the Color Range command, the Color Range dialog box opens. This dialog box lets you use the pointer to identify which colors you want to use to make a selection. You can also select the Invert check box to *exclude* the chosen color from the selection. The **fuzziness** setting is similar to tolerance, in that the lower the value, the closer in color pixels must be to be selected.

QUICK **TIP**

Unlike the Magic Wand tool, the Color Range command does not give you the option of excluding contiguous pixels.

Transforming a Selection

After you place a selection in a Photoshop image, you can change its size and other qualities by clicking Edit on the Menu bar, pointing to Transform, and then clicking any of the commands on the submenu. After you select certain commands, small squares called **handles** surround the selection. To complete the command, you drag a handle until the image has the look you want, and then press [Enter] (Win) or [return] (Mac). You can also use the Transform submenu to flip a selection horizontally or vertically.

Understanding the Healing Brush Tool

If you place a selection then notice that the image has a few imperfections, you can fix the image. You can fix imperfections such as dirt, scratches, visible veins on skin, or wrinkles on a face using the Healing Brush tool on the Tools panel.

QUICK **TIP**

When correcting someone's portrait, make sure your subject looks the way he or she *thinks* they look. That's not always possible, but strive to get as close as you can to their ideal!

Using the Healing Brush Tool

This tool lets you sample an area, and then paint over the imperfections. What is the result? The less-than-desirable pixels seem to disappear into the surrounding image. In addition to matching the sampled pixels, the Healing Brush tool also matches the texture, lighting, and shading of the sample. This is why the painted pixels blend so effortlessly into the existing image. Corrections can be painted using broad strokes or using clicks of the mouse.

QUICK **TIP**

To take a sample, press and hold [Alt] (Win) or [option] (Mac) while dragging the pointer over the area you want to duplicate.

DESIGN**TIP**

Knowing Which Selection Tool to Use

The hardest part of making a selection might be determining which selection tool to use. How are you supposed to know if you should use a marquee tool or a lasso tool? The first question you need to ask yourself is, "What do I want to select?" Becoming proficient in making selections means that you need to assess the qualities of the object you want to select, and then decide which method to use. Ask yourself: Does the object have a definable shape? Does it have an identifiable edge? Are there common colors that can be used to create a selection?

Select using Color Range

1. Open PS 4-5.psd from the drive and folder where you store your Data Files.

2. Click **Select** on the Menu bar, then click **Color Range**.

3. Click the **Image option button** if it is not already selected.

4. Click the **Invert check box** to add a check mark if it does not already contain a check mark.

5. Verify that your settings match those shown in Figure 20, click anywhere in the white background area surrounding the sample image, then click **OK**.

   The Color Range dialog box closes and the teapot in the image is selected.

6. Click the **Move tool** ▸₊ on the Tools panel.

7. Drag the selection into Kitchen Table.psd, then position the selection as shown in Figure 21.

8. Rename the new layer **Teapot**.

9. Defringe the teapot using a setting of **2** pixels.

10. Activate **PS 4-5.psd**, then close this file without saving any changes.

You made a selection within an image using the Color Range command on the Select menu, and dragged the selection to an existing image.

Figure 20 *Completed Color Range dialog box*
Source: Morguefile.

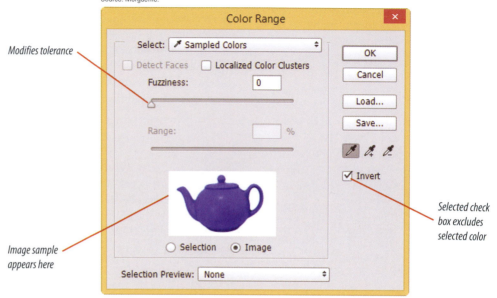

Modifies tolerance

Image sample appears here

Selected check box excludes selected color

Figure 21 *Selection in image*
Source: Morguefile.

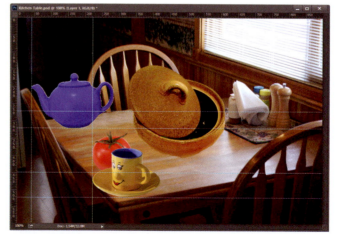

Figure 22 *Magic Wand tool settings*

Figure 23 *Selected area*

Source: Morguefile.

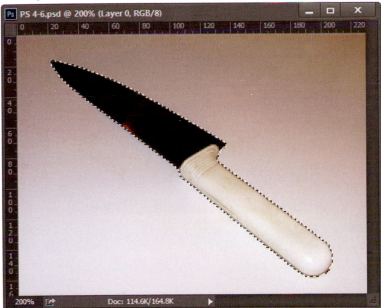

Select using the Magic Wand and the Quick Selection tools

1. Open PS 4-6.psd from the drive and folder where you store your Data Files, then change the zoom factor to **200%**.

2. Click the **Magic Wand tool** on the Tools panel.

3. Change the settings on the options bar to match those shown in Figure 22.

4. Click anywhere in the **knife blade** of the image (such as **100 x/60 Y**).

5. Click the **Quick Selection tool** on the Tools panel, click the **Add to selection button** , change the brush size to 20 (by clicking the Brush picker list arrow, dragging the Size slider to 20 px, then pressing **[Esc]**, then drag across the **knife handle**. Compare your selection to Figure 23.

TIP   If you get too many pixels in your selection, you can try using the Subtract from selection button on the options bar to modify your selection.

6. Click the **Move tool** on the Tools panel, then drag the selection into Kitchen Table.psd.

You made a selection using the Magic Wand and Quick Selection tools, then dragged it into an existing image. The Magic Wand tool is just one more way you can make a selection. One advantage of using the Magic Wand tool (versus the Color Range tool) is the Contiguous check box, which lets you choose pixels that are next to one another. Combining tools is an effective way of making selections.

Flip a selection

1. Click **Edit** on the Menu bar, point to **Transform**, then click **Flip Vertical**.

2. Rename Layer 1 as **Knife**.

3. Defringe **Knife** using a **1** pixel setting.

4. Drag the **flipped selection** with the **Move tool pointer** so it is positioned as shown in Figure 24.

5. Make **PS 4-6.psd** the active file, then close PS 4-6.psd without saving your changes.

6. Save your work.

You flipped and repositioned a selection. Sometimes it's helpful to flip an object to help direct the viewer's eye to a desired focal point.

Figure 24 *Flipped and positioned selection*
Source: Morguefile.

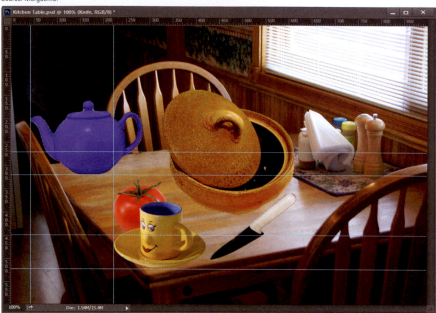

Getting Rid of Red Eye

When digital photos of your favorite people have that annoying red eye, what do you do? You use the Red Eye tool to eliminate this effect. To do this, select the Red Eye tool (which is grouped on the Tools panel with the Spot Healing Brush tool, the Healing Brush tool, and the Patch tool), and then either click a red area of an eye or draw a selection over a red eye. When you release the mouse button, the red eye effect is removed.

Figure 25 *Healing Brush tool options*

Figure 26 *Healed area*
Source: Morguefile.

Stain removed from image

Figure 27 *Image after using the Healing brush*
Source: Morguefile.

Fix imperfections with the Healing Brush tool

1. Click the **Table layer** on the Layers panel, then zoom into the area below the coffee cup until the zoom factor is **200%** and you can see the black ink stain on the table.

2. Click the **Healing Brush tool** 🖌 on the Tools panel. Change the settings on the options bar to match those shown in Figure 25.

TIP If you need to change the Brush settings, click the Brush picker list arrow on the options bar, then drag the sliders so the settings are 25 px diameter, 100% hardness, 1% spacing, 0° angle, and 100% roundness.

3. Press and hold [**Alt**] (Win) or [**option**] (Mac), click the wood to the right of the stain, such as **410 X/565 Y**, then release [**Alt**] (Win) or [**option**] (Mac).

   You sampled an area of the table that is not stained so that you can use the Healing Brush tool to paint a damaged area with the sample.

4. Click the stain (at approximately **380 X/570 Y**).

   Notice that as you move the pointer over the stain, the sample shows you how the corrected area will look when healing is applied. Compare the repaired area to Figure 26.

5. Zoom out from the center of the image until the zoom factor is **100%**.

6. Save your work, then compare your image to Figure 27.

You used the Healing Brush tool to fix an imperfection in an image.

Lesson 3   Select Using Color and Modify a Selection

Add a Vignette Effect
TO A SELECTION

What You'll Do

Source: Morguefile.

In this lesson, you'll create a vignette effect, using a layer mask and feathering.

Understanding Vignettes

Traditionally, a **vignette** is a picture or portrait whose border fades into the surrounding color at its edges. You can use a vignette effect to give an image an old-world appearance. You can also use a vignette effect to tone down an overwhelming background. You can create a vignette effect in Photoshop by creating a mask with a blurred edge. A **mask** lets you protect or modify a particular area and is created using a marquee.

Creating a Vignette

A **vignette effect** uses feathering to fade a marquee shape. The feather setting blurs the area between the selection and the surrounding pixels, which creates a distinctive fade at the edge of the selection. You can create a vignette effect by using a marquee or lasso tool to create a marquee in an image layer. After the selection is created, you can modify the feather setting (a 10- or 20-pixel setting creates a nice fade) to increase the blur effect on the outside edge of the selection.

Getting that Healing Feeling

The Spot Healing Brush tool works in much the same way as the Healing Brush tool in that it removes blemishes and other imperfections. Unlike the Healing Brush tool, the Spot Healing Brush tool does not require you to take a sample. When using the Spot Healing Brush tool, you can choose from three option types:

- proximity match—which uses pixels around the edge of the selection as a patch.
- create texture—which uses all the pixels in the selection to create a texture that is used to fix the area.
- content-aware—which compares nearby image content to fill the selection while realistically maintaining key details such as shadows and edges.

You also have the option of sampling all the visible layers or only the active layer.

Figure 28 *Marquee in image*
Source: Morguefile.

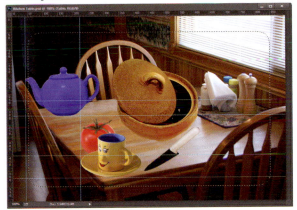

Figure 29 *Layers panel*

Feathered mask creates vignette effect

Figure 30 *Vignette in image*
Source: Morguefile.

Vignette effect fades border and reveals background

Create a vignette

1. Verify that the **Table layer** is selected.
2. Click the **Rectangular Marquee tool** on the Tools panel.
3. Change the **Feather setting** on the options bar to **20px**.
4. Create a **selection** with the **Marquee pointer** from **50 X/50 Y** to **850 X/550 Y**, as shown in Figure 28.
5. Click **Layer** on the Menu bar, point to **Layer Mask**, then click **Reveal Selection**.

   The vignette effect is added to the layer and the mask blurs the selection and the background layer.

   Compare your Layers panel to Figure 29.
6. Click **View** on the Menu bar, then click **Rulers** to hide them.
7. Click **View** on the Menu bar, then click **Clear Guides**.
8. Save your work, then compare your image to Figure 30.
9. Close the Kitchen Table image, then exit Photoshop.

You created a vignette effect by adding a feathered layer mask. Once the image was finished, you hid the rulers and cleared the guides.

POWER USER SHORTCUTS			
To do this:	**Use this method:**	**To do this:**	**Use this method:**
Copy selection	Click Edit ➤ Copy or [Ctrl][C] (Win) or ⌘ [C] (Mac)	Move tool	⊹ or **V**
Create vignette effect	Marquee or Lasso tool, create selection, click Layer ➤ Layer Mask ➤ Reveal Selection	Paste selection	Edit ➤ Paste or [Ctrl][V] (Win) or ⌘ [V] (Mac)
Cut selection	Click Edit ➤ Cut or [Ctrl][X] (Win) or ⌘ [X] (Mac)	Polygonal Lasso tool	⊬ or [Shift] **L**
Deselect object	Select ➤ Deselect or [Ctrl][D] (Win) or ⌘ [D] (Mac)	Rectangular Marquee tool	⬚ or [Shift] **M**
Elliptical Marquee tool	⬭ or [Shift] **M**	Reselect a deselected object	Select ➤ Reselect or [Shift][Ctrl][D] (Win) or [Shift] ⌘ [D] (Mac)
Flip image	Edit ➤ Transform ➤ Flip Horizontal	Select all objects	Select ➤ All or [Ctrl][A] (Win) or ⌘ [A] (Mac)
Grow selection	Select ➤ Grow	Select using color range	Select ➤ Color Range, click sample area
Increase selection	Select ➤ Similar	Select using Magic Wand tool	⟆ or [Shift] **W**, then click image
Lasso tool	⟲ or [Shift] **L**	Select using Quick Selection tool	⟆ or [Shift] **W**, then drag pointer over image
Magnetic Lasso tool	⟲ or [Shift] **L**	Single Column Marquee tool	▦
Move selection marquee	Position pointer in selection, drag ⟿ to new location	Single Row Marquee tool	▭

Key: *Menu items are indicated by ➤ between the menu name and its command. Blue bold letters are shortcuts for selecting tools on the Tools panel.*

Making Selections

Make a selection using shapes.

1. Open PS 4-7.psd from the drive and folder where you store your Data Files, update any text layers, then save it as **Lovely Felines**.
2. Select the Backdrop layer, then open PS 4-8.tif.
3. Display the rulers and any available guides in each image window if they are not displayed, and make sure that the Essentials workspace is selected.
4. Use the Rectangular Marquee tool to select the entire image in PS 4-8.tif. (*Hint*: Reset the Feather setting to 0 pixels, if necessary.)
5. Deselect the selection.
6. Use the Magnetic Lasso tool to create a selection surrounding only the block cat in the image. (*Hint*: You can use the Zoom tool to make the image larger.)
7. Drag the selection into the Powerful Felines image, positioning it so the right side of the cat is at 490 X, and the bottom of the right paw is at 450 Y.
8. Defringe the block cat, rename this new layer **Block cat**, then save your work.
9. Close PS 4-8.tif without saving any changes.

Modify a marquee.

1. Open PS 4-9.tif.
2. Use the Elliptical Marquee tool to create a marquee from 100 X/50 Y to 200 X/100 Y, using a setting of 0 in the Feather text box.
3. Use the Grow command on the Select menu.
4. Deselect the selection.
5. Use the Quick Selection tool to select the tabby cat.
6. Drag the selection into the Powerful Felines image, positioning it so the upper-left corner of the selection is near 0 X/0 Y.

7. Defringe the new layer using a width of 2 pixels.
8. Rename the layer **Tabby cat**, then save your work.
9. Close PS 4-9.tif without saving any changes.

Select using color and modify a selection.

1. Open PS 4-10.tif.
2. Use the Color Range dialog box to select only the kitten. (*Hint*: You can adjust any of the Color Range settings to get the best results.)
3. Drag the selection into the Powerful Felines image.
4. Flip the kitten image (in the Powerful Felines image) horizontally.

5. Position the kitten image so the bottom right snaps to the ruler guides at 230 X/450 y.
6. Defringe the kitten using a width of 3 pixels.
7. Rename the layer **Kitten**, then save your work.
8. Close PS 4-10.tif without saving any changes.

Add a vignette effect to a selection.

1. Use a 15-pixel feather setting and the Backdrop layer to create an elliptical selection surrounding the contents of the Powerful Felines image.
2. Add a layer mask that reveals the selection.
3. Hide the rulers and guides, then save your work.
4. Compare your image to Figure 31.

Figure 31 *Completed Skills Review project*
Images © Photodisc/Getty Images.

As a professional photographer, you often take photos of people for use in various publications. You recently took a photograph of a woman that will be used in a marketing brochure. The client is happy with the overall picture, but wants the facial lines smoothed out. You decide to use the Healing Brush tool to ensure that the client is happy with the final product.

1. Open PS 4-11.psd, then save it as **Portrait**.
2. Make a copy of the Background using the default name, or the name of your choice.
3. Use the Background copy layer and the Healing Brush tool to smooth the appearance of facial lines in this image. (*Hint*: You may have greater success if you use short strokes with the Healing Brush tool than if you paint long strokes.)
4. Create a vignette effect on the Background copy layer that reveals the selection using an elliptical marquee.
5. Reorder the layers (if necessary), so that the vignette effect is visible.
6. Save your work, then compare your image to the sample shown in Figure 32.

Figure 32 *Sample Project Builder 1*
Source: Morguefile.

The Clarksville Athletic Association, which sponsors the Clarksville Marathon, is holding a contest for artwork to announce the upcoming race. Submissions can be created on paper or computer-generated. You feel you have a good chance at winning this contest, using Photoshop as your tool.

1. Open PS 4-12.psd, then save it as **Marathon Contest**.
2. Locate at least two pieces of appropriate artwork—either on your hard disk, in a royalty-free collection, or from scanned images—that you can use in this file.
3. Use any appropriate methods to select imagery from the artwork.
4. After the selections have been made, copy each selection into Marathon Contest.
5. Arrange the images into a design that you think will be eye-catching and attractive.
6. Deselect the selections in the files you are no longer using, and close them without saving the changes.
7. Add a vignette effect to the Backdrop layer.
8. Display the type layers if they are hidden.
9. Defringe any layers, as necessary.
10. Save your work, then compare your screen to the sample shown in Figure 33.

Figure 33 *Sample Project Builder 2*

Images © Photodisc/Getty Images.

You are aware that there will be an opening in your firm's design department. Before you can be considered for the job, you need to increase your Photoshop compositing knowledge and experience. You have decided to teach yourself, using informational sources on the Internet and images that can be scanned or purchased.

1. Connect to the Internet and use your browser and favorite search engine to find information on image compositing. (Make a record of the site you found so you can use it for future reference, if necessary.)
2. Create a new Photoshop image, using the dimensions of your choice, then save it as **Sample Compositing**.
3. Locate at least two pieces of artwork—either on your hard disk, in a royalty-free collection, or from scanned images—that you can use. (The images can contain people, plants, animals, or inanimate objects.)
4. Select the images in the artwork, then copy each into the Sample Compositing image, using the method of your choice.
5. Rename each of the layers using meaningful names.
6. Apply a color-code to each new layer.
7. Arrange the images in a pleasing design. (*Hint*: Remember that you can flip any image, if necessary.)
8. Deselect the selections in the artwork, then close the files without saving the changes.
9. If desired, create a background layer for the image.
10. If necessary, add a vignette effect to a layer.
11. Defringe any images as you see necessary.
12. Save your work, then compare your screen to the sample shown in Figure 34.

Figure 34 *Sample Design Project*
Images © Photodisc/Getty Images.

At your design firm, a Fortune 500 client plans to start a 24-hour cable sports network called Total Sportz that will cover any nonprofessional sporting event. You have been asked to create some preliminary designs for the network using images from multiple sources.

1. Open PS 4-13.psd, then save it as **Total Sportz**.
2. Locate several pieces of sports-related artwork—either on your hard disk, in a royalty-free collection, or from scanned images. Remember that the images should not show professional sports figures, if possible.
3. Select imagery from the artwork and move it into the Total Sportz image.
4. Arrange the images in an interesting design. (*Hint*: Remember that you can flip any image, if necessary.)
5. Change each layer name to describe the sport in the layer image.
6. Deselect the selections in the files that you used, then close the files without saving the changes.
7. If you choose, you can add a vignette effect to a layer and/or adjust opacity.
8. Defringe any images (if necessary).
9. Save your work, then compare your image to the sample shown in Figure 35.

Figure 35 *Sample Portfolio Project*

Images © Photodisc/Getty Images.

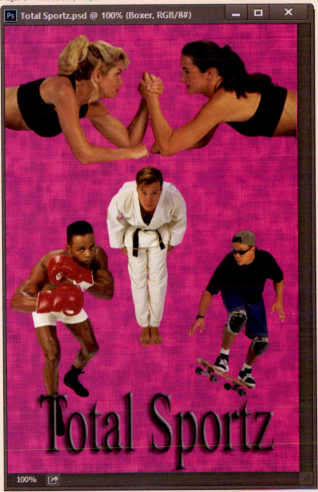

CHAPTER 5 INCORPORATING COLOR TECHNIQUES

1. Work with color to transform an image
2. Use the Color Picker and the Swatches panel
3. Place a border around an image
4. Blend colors using the Gradient tool
5. Add color to a grayscale image
6. Use filters, opacity, and blending modes
7. Match colors

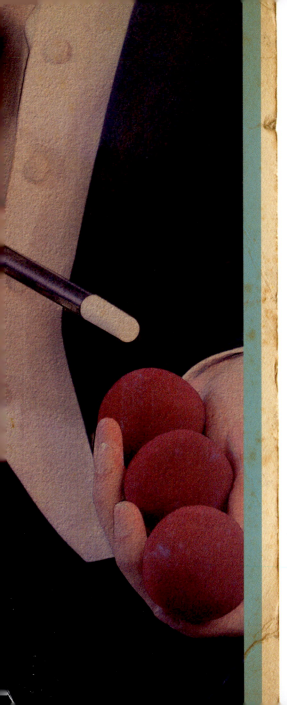

CHAPTER 5
INCORPORATING COLOR TECHNIQUES

Using Color

Color can make or break an image. Sometimes colors can draw us into an image; other times they can repel us. We all know which colors we like, but when it comes to creating an image, it is helpful to have some knowledge of color theory and be familiar with color terminology.

Understanding how Photoshop measures, displays, and prints color can be valuable whether you create new images or modify existing images. Some colors you choose might be difficult for a professional printer to reproduce or might look muddy when printed. As you become more experienced using color, you will learn which colors reproduce well and which ones do not.

Understanding Color Modes and Color Models

Photoshop displays and prints images using specific color modes. A **color mode** is the amount of color data that can be stored in a given file format, based on an established model. A **color model** determines how pigments combine to produce resulting colors. This is the way your computer or printer associates a name or number with colors. Photoshop uses standard color models as the basis for its color modes. The *color mode* determines the number and range of colors displayed, as well as which color model will be used; the *color model* interprets the color mode information by a monitor and/or printer.

Displaying and Printing Images

An image displayed on your monitor, such as an icon on your desktop, is a **bitmap**, a geometric arrangement of different color dots on a rectangular grid. Each dot, called a **pixel**, represents a color or shade. Bitmapped images are *resolution-dependent* and can lose detail—often demonstrated by a jagged appearance—when highly magnified. When printed, images with high resolutions tend to show more detail and subtler color transitions than low-resolution images.

TOOLS YOU'LL USE

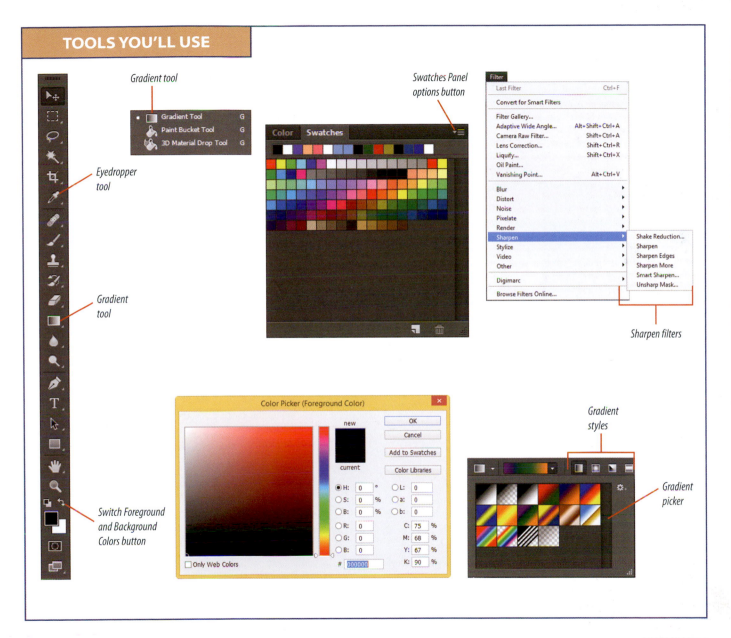

Gradient tool

Gradient Tool G
Paint Bucket Tool G
3D Material Drop Tool G

Eyedropper tool

Gradient tool

Switch Foreground and Background Colors button

Swatches Panel options button

Color   Swatches

Filter
Last Filter   Ctrl+F
Convert for Smart Filters
Filter Gallery...
Adaptive Wide Angle...   Alt+Shift+Ctrl+A
Camera Raw Filter...   Shift+Ctrl+A
Lens Correction...   Shift+Ctrl+R
Liquify...   Shift+Ctrl+X
Oil Paint...
Vanishing Point...   Alt+Ctrl+V
Blur   ▶
Distort   ▶
Noise   ▶
Pixelate   ▶
Render   ▶
Sharpen   ▶   Shake Reduction...
Stylize   ▶   Sharpen
Video   ▶   Sharpen Edges
Other   ▶   Sharpen More
                                            Smart Sharpen...
Digimarc   ▶   Unsharp Mask...
Browse Filters Online...

Sharpen filters

Color Picker (Foreground Color)
new
current
OK
Cancel
Add to Swatches
Color Libraries
H: 0 °   L: 0
S: 0 %   a: 0
B: 0 %   b: 0
R: 0   C: 75 %
G: 0   M: 68 %
B: 0   Y: 67 %
Only Web Colors   # 000000   K: 90 %

Gradient styles

Gradient picker

Work with Color
TO TRANSFORM AN IMAGE

What You'll Do

Source: Morguefile.

 In this lesson, you'll use the Color panel, the Paint Bucket tool, and the Eyedropper tool to change the background color of an image.

Learning About Color Models

Photoshop reproduces colors using models of color modes. The range of displayed colors, or **gamut**, for each model available in Photoshop is shown in Figure 1. The shape of each color gamut indicates the range of colors it can display. If a color is **out of gamut**, it is beyond the color space that your monitor can display or that your printer can print. You select the color mode from the Mode command on the Image menu. The available Photoshop color models include Lab Color, Indexed Color, RGB Color, CMYK Color, Bitmap, Duotone, Multichannel, and Grayscale. Photoshop uses color modes to determine how to display and print an image.

> **QUICK TIP**
>
> A color mode is used to determine which color model will be used to display and print an image.

> **DESIGNTIP**
>
> ### Understanding the Psychology of Color
>
> Have you ever wondered why some colors make you react a certain way? You might have noticed that some colors affect you differently than others. Color is such an important part of our lives, and in Photoshop, it's key. Specific colors are often used in print and web pages to evoke the following responses:
>
> - Blue tends to instill a feeling of safety and stability and is often used by financial services.
> - Certain shades of green can generate a soft, calming feeling, while others suggest youthfulness and growth.
> - Red commands attention and can be used as a call to action; it can also distract a reader's attention from other content.
> - White evokes the feeling of purity and innocence, looks cool and fresh, and is often used to suggest luxury.
> - Black conveys feelings of power and strength, but can also suggest darkness and negativity.

Lab Color Mode

The Lab color mode is based on the human perception of color. The numeric values describe all the colors a person with normal vision can see. The Lab color mode has one luminance (lightness) component and two chromatic components (from green to red, and from blue to yellow). Using the Lab color model has distinct advantages: you have the largest number of colors available to you and the greatest precision with which to create them. You can also create all the colors contained by other color models, which are limited in their respective color ranges. The Lab color model is device-independent—the colors will not vary, regardless of the hardware. Use this model when working with digital images so that you can independently edit the luminance and color values.

HSB Color Model

Based on the human perception of color, the HSB (Hue, Saturation, Brightness) model has three fundamental characteristics: hue, saturation, and brightness. The color reflected from or transmitted through an object is called **hue**. Expressed as a degree (between 0° and 360°), each hue is identified by a color name (such as red or green). **Saturation** (or *chroma*) is the strength or purity of the color, representing the amount of gray in proportion to hue. Saturation is measured as a percentage from 0% (gray) to 100% (fully saturated). **Brightness** is the measurement of relative lightness or darkness of a color and is measured as a percentage from 0% (black) to 100% (white). Although you can use the HSB model to define a color on the Color panel or in the Color Picker dialog box, Photoshop *does not* offer HSB mode as a choice for creating or editing images.

RGB Model

Each Photoshop color mode is based on established models used in color reproduction. Most colors in the visible spectrum can be represented by mixing various proportions and intensities of red, green, and blue (RGB) colored light known as the RGB color model. RGB images use three colors, or **channels**, to reproduce colors on screen. RGB colors are additive colors. **Additive colors** are used for lighting, video, and computer monitors; color is created by adding together red, green, and blue light. When red, green, and blue are combined at their highest value (255), the result is white; the absence of any color (when their values are zero) results in black. Photoshop assigns each component of the RGB mode an intensity value. Your colors can vary from monitor to monitor even if you are using the exact same RGB values on different computers.

Figure 1 *Photoshop color gamuts*

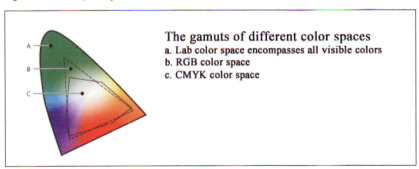

The gamuts of different color spaces
a. Lab color space encompasses all visible colors
b. RGB color space
c. CMYK color space

CMYK Model

The light-absorbing quality of ink printed on paper is the basis of the CMYK (Cyan, Magenta, Yellow, Black) mode. Unlike the **RGB mode**—in which components are combined to create new colors—the CMYK mode is based on colors being partially *absorbed* as the ink hits the paper and being partially *reflected* back to your eyes. CMYK colors are **subtractive colors**—the *absence* of cyan, magenta, yellow, and black creates white. Subtractive (CMYK) and additive (RGB) colors are complementary colors; a pair from one model creates a color in the other. When combined, cyan, magenta, and yellow absorb all color and produce black. The **CMYK mode**—in which the lightest colors are assigned the highest percentages of ink colors—is used in four-color process printing. Converting an RGB image into a CMYK image produces a **color separation** (the commercial printing process of separating colors for use with different inks). Note, however, that because your monitor uses RGB mode, you will not see the exact colors until you print the image, and even then the colors can vary depending on the printer and offset press.

Understanding the Bitmap and Grayscale Modes

In addition to the RGB and CMYK modes, Photoshop provides two specialized color modes: bitmap and grayscale. The **bitmap mode** uses black or white color values to represent image pixels, and is a good choice for images with subtle color gradations, such as photographs or painted images. The **grayscale mode** uses up to 256 shades of gray (in an 8-bit image), assigning a brightness value from 0 (black) to 255 (white) to each pixel. (The number of shades of gray in 16- and 32-bit images is much greater than 256.) The **Duotone mode** is used to create the following grayscale images: monotone, duotones (using two colors), tritones (using three colors), and quadtones (using four colors).

Changing Foreground and Background Colors

In Photoshop, the **foreground color** is black by default and is used to paint, fill, and apply a border to a selection. The **background color** is white by default and is used to make **gradient fills** (gradual blends of multiple colors) and to fill in areas of an image that have been erased. You can change foreground and background colors using the Color panel, the Swatches panel, the Color Picker, or the Eyedropper tool. One method of changing foreground and background colors is **sampling**, in which an existing color is used. You can restore the default colors by clicking the Default Foreground and Background Colors button on the Tools panel, shown in Figure 2. You can apply a color to the background of a layer using the Paint Bucket tool grouped with the Gradient tool. When you click an image with the Paint Bucket tool, the current foreground color on the Tools panel fills the active layer.

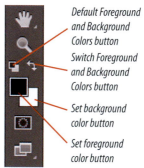

Figure 2 *Foreground and background color buttons*

Default Foreground and Background Colors button

Switch Foreground and Background Colors button

Set background color button

Set foreground color button

Figure 3 *Image with rulers displayed*
Source: Morguefile.

Figure 4 *Color Settings dialog box*

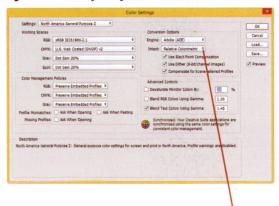

Intent list arrow

Creating a Rendering Intent

The use of a **rendering intent** determines how colors are converted by a color management system. A **color management system** is used to keep colors looking consistent as they move between devices. Colors are defined and interpreted using a **profile**. You can create a rendering intent by clicking Edit on the Menu bar, and then clicking Color Settings. Click the Intent list arrow in the Conversion Options area, shown in Figure 4, and then select one of the four rendering intent options. Since a gamut is the range of color that a color system can display or print, the rendering intent is constantly evaluating the color gamut and deciding whether or not the colors need adjusting. Although colors that fall inside the destination gamut are not changed, using a rendering intent allows colors that fall outside the destination gamut to be adjusted based on the intent you set.

Set the default foreground and background colors

1. Start Photoshop, open PS 5-1.psd from the drive and folder where you save your Data Files, then save it as **Basketball Star**.

   TIP Whenever the Photoshop Format Options dialog box appears, click OK to maximize compatibility.

2. Click the **Default Foreground and Background Colors button** ▣ on the Tools panel, then reset the Essentials workspace.

   TIP If you accidently click the Set foreground color button, the Color Picker (Foreground Color) dialog box opens.

3. Change the status bar so the document size displays, if it is not already displayed.

   TIP Document sizes will not display in the status bar if the image window is too small. Drag the lower-right corner of the image window to expand the window and display the menu arrow and document sizes.

4. Display the rulers in pixels and show the guides if they are not already displayed, then compare your screen to Figure 3.

   TIP You can right-click (Win) or [control]-click (Mac) one of the rulers to choose Pixels, Inches, Centimeters, Millimeters, Points, Picas, or Percent as a unit of measurement, instead of using the Rulers and Units Preferences dialog box.

You set the default foreground and background colors and displayed rulers in pixels.

Change the background color using the Color panel

1. Click the **Background layer** on the Layers panel.
2. Display the **Legacy workspace** (which was created in Chapter 1).
3. If necessary, display the **Color panel**.
4. Drag each **color slider** on the Color panel until you reach the values shown in Figure 5.

    The active color changes to the new color. Did you notice that this image is using the RGB mode?

TIP You can also double-click each component's text box on the Color panel and type the color values.

5. Click the **Paint Bucket tool** 🪣 on the Tools panel.

TIP If the Paint Bucket tool is not visible on the Tools panel, click the Gradient tool on the Tools panel, press and hold the mouse button until the list of hidden tools opens, then click the Paint Bucket tool.

6. Click the **image** with the **Paint Bucket pointer** ▸🪣.
7. Drag the **Paint Bucket state** on the History panel onto the Delete current state button 🗑.

TIP You can also undo the last action by clicking Edit on the Menu bar, then clicking Undo Paint Bucket.

You set new values in the Color panel, used the Paint Bucket tool to change the background to that color, then undid the change. You can change colors on the Color panel by dragging the sliders or by typing values in the color text boxes.

Figure 5 *Color panel with new color*

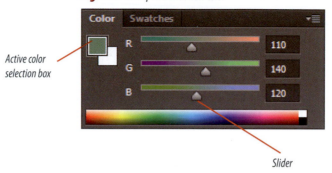

Active color selection box

Slider

Figure 6 *Info panel*

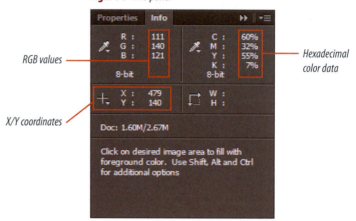

RGB values

X/Y coordinates

Hexadecimal color data

Using Ruler Coordinates

Photoshop rulers run along the top and left sides of the document window. Each point on an image has a horizontal and vertical location. These two numbers, called X and Y coordinates, appear on the Info panel (which is located with the Properties panel and can be opened with the Window menu) as shown in Figure 6. The X coordinate refers to the horizontal location, and the Y coordinate refers to the vertical location. You can use one or both sets of guides to identify coordinates of a location, such as a color you want to sample. If you have difficulty seeing the ruler markings, you can increase the size of the image; the greater the zoom factor, the more detailed the measurement hashes.

Incorporating Color Techniques

Figure 7 *New foreground color applied to Background layer*
Source: Morguefile.

New foreground color

Change the background color using the Eyedropper tool

1. Click the **Background layer** on the Layers panel, if it is not already selected.

2. Click the **Eyedropper tool** 🖋 on the Tools panel.

3. Click the **light blue area on the boy's right shoe** in the image with the **Eyedropper pointer** 🖋.

   The Set foreground color button displays the light blue color that you clicked (or sampled).

   TIP Remember to zoom in or out of any image at any time during a lesson to improve your view.

4. Click the **Paint Bucket tool** 🪣 on the Tools panel.

5. Click the **image**, then compare your screen to Figure 7.

   You might have noticed that in this instance, it doesn't matter where on the layer you click, as long as the correct layer is selected.

6. Save your work.

You used the Eyedropper tool to sample a color as the foreground color, then used the Paint Bucket tool to change the background color to the color you sampled. Using the Eyedropper tool is a convenient way of sampling a color in any Photoshop image.

Use the Color Picker
AND THE SWATCHES PANEL

What You'll Do

 In this lesson, you'll use the Color Picker and the Swatches panel to select new colors, and then you'll add a new color to the background and to the Swatches panel. You'll also learn how to download and apply color themes from Kuler.

Making Selections from the Color Picker

Depending on the color model you are using, you can select colors using the **Color Picker**, a feature that lets you choose a color from a color spectrum or numerically define a custom color. You can change colors in the Color Picker dialog box by using the following methods:

- Drag the sliders along the vertical color bar.
- Click inside the vertical color bar.

- Click a color in the Color field.
- Enter a value in any of the text boxes.

Figure 8 shows a color in the Color Picker dialog box. A circular marker indicates the active color. The color slider displays the range of color levels available for the active color component. The adjustments you make by dragging or clicking a new color are reflected in the text boxes; when you choose a new color, the previous color appears below the new color in the preview area.

Using Kuler to Coordinate Colors

Kuler®, from Adobe, is a web application from which you can download pre-coordinated color themes or design your own. These collections can be saved and shared with others. Use Kuler as a fast, effective way of ensuring that your use of color is consistent and harmonious. If you decide to select an existing Kuler theme, you'll find that there are thousands from which to choose. Kuler themes can be seen by clicking the Window menu, pointing to Extensions, and then clicking Kuler, which opens a Kuler panel within Photoshop. You can also access Kuler through your browser at *kuler.adobe.com*, using the Kuler desktop (which requires the installation of Adobe AIR), or from Adobe Illustrator (CS4 or higher). When you pass the mouse over a theme in the Kuler website, icons appear over the current theme displaying options to get info, edit, copy link, download, and make a favorite. Click Info and the colors display at the top of the window. Click Edit to view the theme's color values. As a web-based app, the Kuler user interface and its available swatches change often. *Don't be alarmed* if your screens look different than those shown in this chapter.

Using the Swatches Panel

You can also change colors using the Swatches panel. The **Swatches panel** is a visual display of colors you can choose from, as shown in Figure 9. You can add your own colors to the panel by sampling a color from an image, and you can also delete colors. When you add a swatch to the Swatches panel, Photoshop assigns a default name that has a sequential number, or you can name the swatch whatever you like. Photoshop places new swatches in the first available space at the end of the panel. You can view swatch names by clicking the Swatches Panel options button, and then clicking Small List (or Large List).

QUICK TIP

You can reset the Swatches panel to its default settings by clicking the Swatches panel option button, then clicking Reset Swatches.

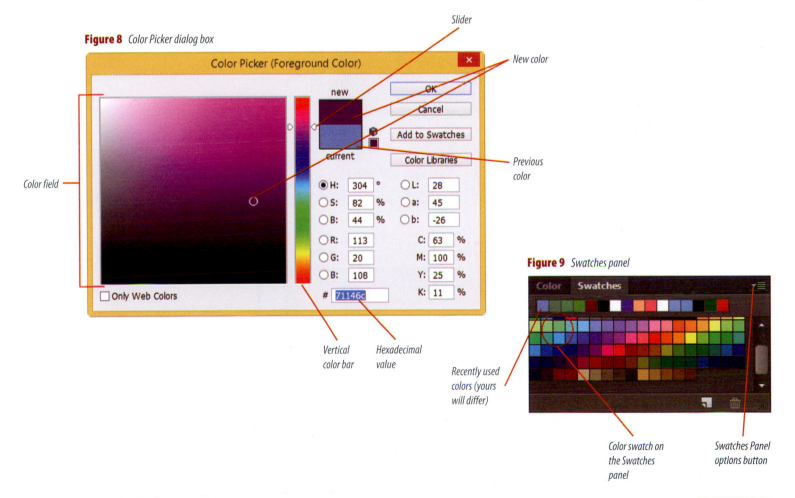

Figure 8 *Color Picker dialog box*

Slider

New color

Previous color

Color field

Vertical color bar

Hexadecimal value

Figure 9 *Swatches panel*

Recently used colors (yours will differ)

Color swatch on the Swatches panel

Swatches Panel options button

Select a color using the Color Picker dialog box

1. Click the **Set foreground color button** ■ on the Tools panel, verify that the H: option button is selected in the Color Picker dialog box, then drag the slider in the Vertical color bar to the mid-point.

2. Click the **R: option button**.

3. Click the **bottom-right corner** of the Color field (purple), as shown in Figure 10.

TIP If the Warning: out-of-gamut for printing indicator appears next to the color, then this color is outside the printable range of colors.

4. Click **OK**.

You opened the Color Picker dialog box, selected a different color mode by clicking the R option button, and then selected a new color.

Select a color using the Swatches panel

1. Click the **Swatches panel option button** ≡ , click **Reset Swatches**, then click **OK** in the warning box.

2. Click the **third swatch from the right in the second row** (Pastel Red Orange), as shown in Figure 11 (the actual location of this color swatch may differ on your Swatches panel).

    Did you notice that the foreground color on the Tools panel changed to a pastel red orange?

3. Click the **Paint Bucket tool** 🪣 on the Tools panel if necessary.

4. Click the **image** with the **Paint Bucket pointer** 🪣 , then compare your screen to Figure 12.

You selected a color from the Swatches panel, and then used the Paint Bucket tool to change the background to that color.

Figure 10 *Color Picker dialog box*

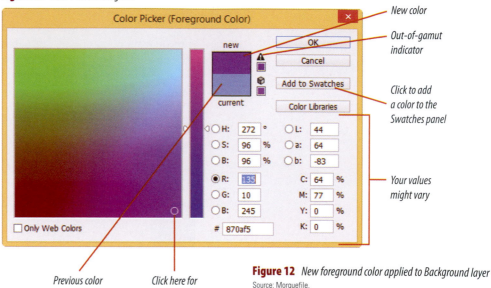

New color

Out-of-gamut indicator

Click to add a color to the Swatches panel

Your values might vary

Previous color

Click here for new color

Figure 11 *Swatches panel*

Pastel Red Orange

Your swatches on the last row might vary

Figure 12 *New foreground color applied to Background layer*
Source: Morguefile.

Figure 13 *Swatch added to Swatches panel*

*New swatch appears
in last row*

Maintaining Your Focus

Adobe Photoshop is probably unlike any other program you've used before. In other programs, there's a central area on the screen where you focus your attention. In Photoshop, there's the workspace containing your document, but you've probably already figured out that if you don't have the correct layer selected in the Layer's panel, things won't quite work out as you expected. In addition, you have to make sure you've got the right tool selected in the Tools panel. You also need to keep an eye on the History panel. As you work on your image, it might feel a lot like negotiating a grocery parking lot on the day before Thanksgiving. You've got to be looking in a lot of places at once.

Add a new color to the Swatches panel

1. Click the **Eyedropper tool** 🖊 on the Tools panel.

2. Click the **palm leaf** (on the boy's shirt) at coordinates **310 X/348 Y**.

TIP Use the Zoom tool whenever necessary to enlarge or decrease your workspace so you can better see what you're working on.

3. Scroll down the Swatches panel, then click the **empty area to the right of the last swatch** in the bottom row with the **Paint Bucket pointer** 🪣.

4. Type **Palm leaf** in the Name text box.

5. Click **OK** in the Color Swatch Name dialog box.

TIP To delete a color from the Swatches panel, press [Alt] (Win) or [option] (Mac), position the ✂ pointer over a swatch, then click the swatch.

6. Save your work, then compare the new swatch on your Swatches panel to Figure 13.

You used the Eyedropper tool to sample a color, added the color to the Swatches panel, and then gave it a descriptive name. Adding swatches to the Swatches panel makes it easy to reuse frequently used colors.

Use Kuler from a web browser

1. Open your favorite browser, type **kuler.adobe.com** in the URL text box, then press [**Enter**] (Win) or [**return**] (Mac).

   If you have an iPad, iPhone, or Android device, you can download and install a Kuler app by searching the App Store or Google Play (depending on your mobile device).

2. Click the **Sign In link**, type your **Adobe ID** and **password**, then Agree to the terms of the website if asked. (If you don't have an Adobe ID, click the Register link and follow the instructions.)

3. Click **Explore** on the Kuler menu bar, type **Johnny Cash Tribute** in the Search text box, press [**Enter**] (Win) or [**return**] (Mac). The swatches shown in Figure 14 will display, although your screen may contain other swatches.

4. Place your mouse over the swatch indicated in Figure 14 (top-right swatch), click the **Download button** 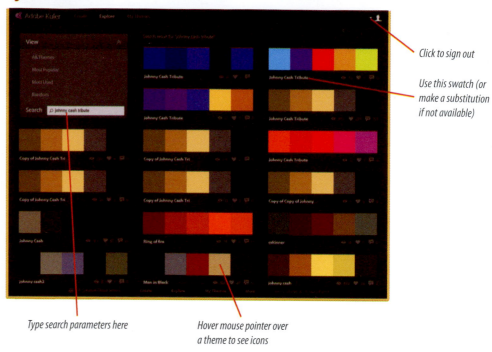, find the location where you save your Data Files in the Save As dialog box, then click **Save** (Win); on Mac OS, the downloaded file is automatically sent to the Downloads folder.

5. Click the **profile icon** in the upper-right of the screen, click the **Sign Out** button to sign out from Kuler, then activate Photoshop.

6. Click the **Swatches Panel options button**, then click **Load Swatches**.

7. Navigate to the location where you save your Data Files, (click the **Files of type button**, click **Swatch Exchange (*.ASE)** (Win)), click **Johnny Cash Tribute**, then click **Load** (Win) or **Open** (Mac).

You searched the Kuler website, downloaded a color theme, and then added it to your Photoshop Swatches panel.

Figure 14 *Themes in Kuler*

Click to sign out

Use this swatch (or make a substitution if not available)

Type search parameters here

Hover mouse pointer over a theme to see icons

Using the Kuler Mobile App

Using your iPhone, you can use the Kuler mobile app to copy colors you see when you're on the go. Imagine that you're out and about and you see a fabulous color that you'd really like to use in Photoshop. With the Kuler iPhone app and your phone's camera, you can capture the color and Kuler will not only save the color, but will also create a theme that includes complimentary colors. You can then save the theme on your phone for use in your Kuler account on your desktop. Once you've installed the Kuler mobile app and logged in, click the camera icon and point the camera at nearby images. The camera will pick up key colors within its view and create complimentary themes on-the-spot. You can then choose to see the hexadecimal values for those colors, name and save the theme (automatically added to your Kuler account), share the theme via Twitter or email, or delete the theme.

Figure 15 *Kuler panel*

Type search
criteria here

Theme to add

Adds theme to
Swatches panel

Figure 16 *Theme added to Swatches panel*

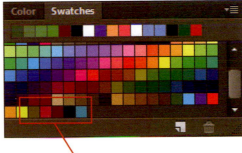

Marooned theme swatches
added to panel

Use Kuler from Photoshop

1. Click **Window** on the Menu bar, point to **Extensions**, then click **Kuler**.

2. Click the **Search text box**, type **maroon**, then press [**Enter**] (Win) or [**return**] (Mac). Compare your Kuler panel to Figure 15.

TIP Your Kuler panel may differ as themes change frequently.

3. Click the **Marooned theme** (or a similar theme if Marooned is not available), then click the **Add selected theme to swatches button**. Compare your Swatches panel to Figure 16.

4. Close the Kuler panel.

5. In the Swatches panel, click the **color box** for #F2CA80 (or the color of your choice if this color is not available) with the **Eyedropper pointer**.

TIP The locations of your color swatches may vary.

6. Verify that the Background layer is active, click the **Paint Bucket tool** on the Tools panel, then click the **image**.

7. Save your work.

You opened Kuler in Photoshop, then added a color theme to the Swatches panel. You then applied a color downloaded from Kuler to the image.

Place a Border Around
AN IMAGE

What You'll Do

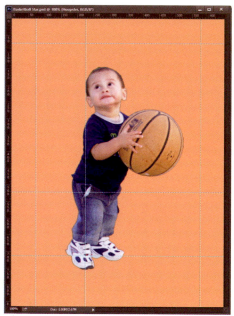

Source: Morguefile.

 In this lesson, you'll add a border to an image.

Emphasizing an Image

You can emphasize an image by placing a border around its edges. This process is called **stroking the edges**. You add a border by selecting a layer or object, clicking Edit on the Menu bar, and then clicking Stroke. The default color of the border is the current foreground color on the Tools panel. You can change the width, color, location, and blending mode of a border using the Stroke dialog box. The location option buttons in the dialog box determine where the border will be placed. If you want to change the location of the stroke, you must first delete the previously applied stroke, or Photoshop will apply the new border over the existing one.

Locking Transparent Pixels

As you modify layers, you can lock some properties to protect their contents. The ability to lock—or protect—elements within a layer is controlled from within the Layers panel, as shown in Figure 17. It's a good idea to lock transparent pixels when you add borders so that stray marks will not be included in the stroke. You can lock the following layer properties:

- Transparency: Limits editing capabilities to areas in a layer that are opaque.
- Image: Makes it impossible to modify layer pixels using painting tools.
- Position: Prevents pixels within a layer from being moved.

QUICK TIP

You can lock transparent or image pixels only in a layer containing an image, not in one containing type.

Figure 17 *Layers panel locking options*

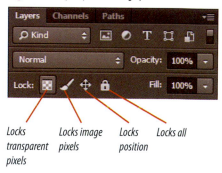

Locks transparent pixels   *Locks image pixels*   *Locks position*   *Locks all*

Figure 18 *Locking transparent pixels*

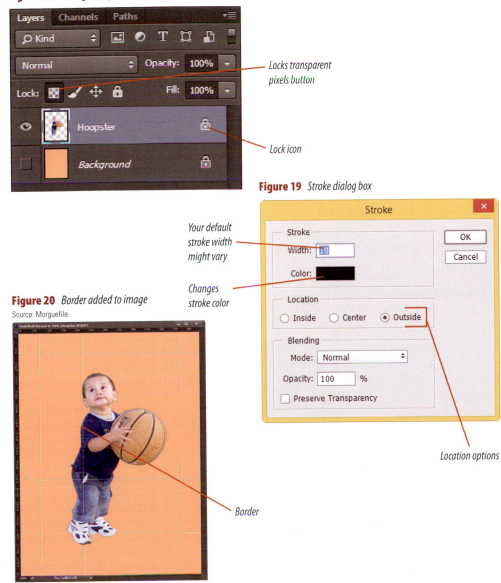

Locks transparent pixels button

Lock icon

Figure 19 *Stroke dialog box*

Your default stroke width might vary

Changes stroke color

Figure 20 *Border added to image*
Source: Morguefile.

Location options

Border

Stroke

Stroke

Width: 10

Color:

OK

Cancel

Location

◯ Inside   ◯ Center   ⦿ Outside

Blending

Mode: Normal

Opacity: 100 %

☐ Preserve Transparency

Create a border

1. Click the **Indicates layer visibility button** 👁 on the Background layer on the Layers panel to hide the layer.

TIP You can click the Indicates layer visibility button to hide distracting layers.

2. Click the **Default Foreground and Background Colors button** ◱.

   The foreground color will become the default border color.

3. Click the **Hoopster layer** on the Layers panel.

4. Click the **Lock transparent pixels button** ▥ on the Layers panel. See Figure 18.

   The border will be applied only to the pixels on the edge of the boy and the ball.

5. Click **Edit** on the Menu bar, then click **Stroke** to open the Stroke dialog box. See Figure 19.

6. Verify that **1px** displays in the Width text box, click the **Outside option button**, then click **OK**.

TIP Determining the correct border location can be confusing. The default stroke width is the setting last applied; you can apply a width from 1 to 150 pixels. Try different settings until you achieve the look you want.

7. Click the **Indicates layer visibility button** ▣ on the Background layer on the Layers panel.

8. Save your work, then compare your image to Figure 20.

You hid a layer, changed the foreground color to black, locked transparent pixels, then used the Stroke dialog box to apply a border to the image.

Blend Colors Using
THE GRADIENT TOOL

What You'll Do

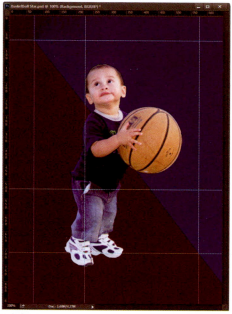

Source: Morguefile.

 In this lesson, you'll create a gradient fill from a sampled color and a swatch, and then apply it to the background.

Understanding Gradients

A **gradient fill**, or simply **gradient**, is a blend of colors used to fill a selection of a layer or an entire layer. A gradient's appearance is determined by its beginning and ending points, and its length, direction, and angle. Gradients allow you to create dramatic effects, using existing color combinations or your own colors. The Gradient picker, as shown in Figure 21, offers multicolor gradient fills and a few that use the current foreground or background colors on the Tools panel.

Using the Gradient Tool

You use the Gradient tool to create gradients in images. When you choose the Gradient tool, five gradient styles become available on the options bar. These styles—Linear, Radial,

Figure 21 *Gradient picker*

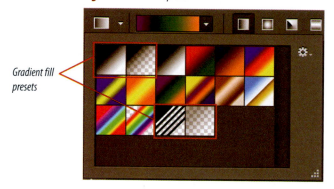

Gradient fill presets

Angle, Reflected, and Diamond—are shown in Figure 22. In each example, the gradient was drawn from 50 X/50 Y to 100 X/100 Y.

Customizing Gradients

Using the **gradient presets**—predesigned gradient fills that are displayed in the Gradient picker—is a great way to learn how to use gradients. But as you become more familiar with Photoshop, you might want to venture into the world of the unknown and create your own gradient designs. You can create your own designs by modifying an existing gradient using the Gradient Editor. You can open the Gradient Editor, shown in Figure 23, by clicking the selected gradient pattern that appears in the Gradient picker on the options bar. After it's open, you can use it to make the following modifications:

- Create a new gradient from an existing gradient.
- Modify an existing gradient.
- Add intermediate colors to a gradient.
- Create a blend between more than two colors.
- Adjust the opacity values.
- Determine the placement of the midpoint.

Figure 22 *Sample gradients*

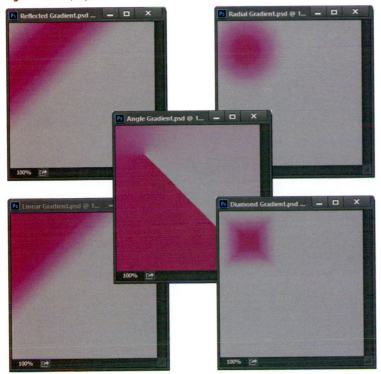

Figure 23 *Gradient Editor dialog box*

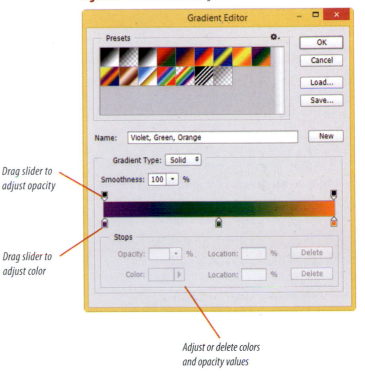

Drag slider to adjust opacity

Drag slider to adjust color

Adjust or delete colors and opacity values

Create a gradient from a sample color

1. Verify that the **Eyedropper tool** 🔲 is selected.
2. Click the **blue shirt** in the image at coordinates **250 X/300 Y**.

TIP To accurately select the coordinates, adjust the zoom factor as necessary.

3. Click the **Switch Foreground and Background Colors button** 🔲 on the Tools panel.
4. Click the **Maroon swatch** (R=102 G=0 B=51) on the Swatches panel (or one of the new swatches you added) with the **Eyedropper pointer** 🔲 .
5. Click the **Indicates layer visibility button** 🔲 on the Hoopster layer to hide it, and make sure the Background layer is active, as shown in Figure 24.
6. Click the **Paint Bucket tool** 🔲 on the Tools panel, then press and hold the mouse button until the panel of hidden tools opens.
7. Click the **Gradient tool** 🔲 on the Tools panel, then click the **Angle Gradient button** 🔲 on the options bar if it is not already selected.
8. Click the **Gradient picker list arrow** on the options bar, then double-click **Foreground to Background gradient fill** (first row, first column), as shown in Figure 25.

TIP You can close the Gradient picker by pressing [Esc].

You sampled a color on the image to set the background color, changed the foreground color using an existing swatch, selected the Gradient tool, and then chose a gradient fill and style.

Figure 24 *Hoopster layer hidden*

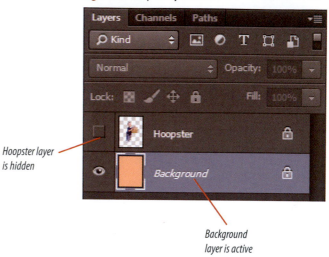

Hoopster layer
is hidden

Background
layer is active

Figure 25 *Gradient picker*

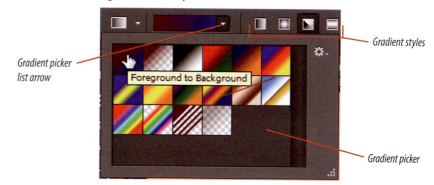

Gradient styles

Gradient picker
list arrow

Foreground to Background

Gradient picker

Incorporating Color Techniques

Figure 26 *Gradient fill applied to Background layer*

Source: Morguefile.

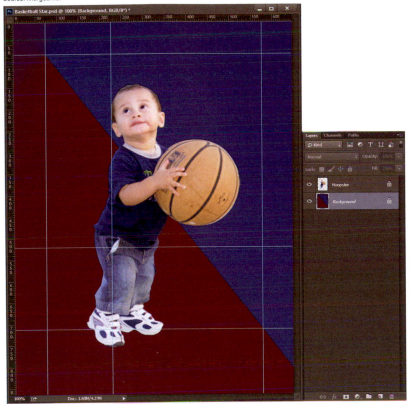

Apply a gradient fill

1. Drag the **Gradient pointer** from **75 X/75 Y** to **575 X/710 Y** using the Info panel and the guides to help you create the gradient in the work area.

2. Click the **Indicates layer visibility button** on the Hoopster layer.

   The Hoopster layer appears against the new background, as shown in Figure 26.

3. Save your work.

TIP It is a good practice to save your work early and often in the creation process, especially before making significant changes or printing.

You applied the gradient fill to the background. You can create dramatic effects using the gradient fill in combination with foreground and background colors.

Add Color
TO A GRAYSCALE IMAGE

What You'll Do

Source: Morguefile.

In this lesson, you'll convert an image to grayscale, change the color mode, and then colorize a grayscale image using the Hue/Saturation dialog box.

Colorizing Options

Grayscale images can contain up to 256 shades of gray (at 8 bits per pixel), assigning a brightness value from 0 (black) to 255 (white) to each pixel. Since the earliest days of photography, people have been tinting grayscale images with color to create a certain mood or emphasize an image in a way that purely realistic colors could not. To capture this effect in Photoshop, you convert an image to the Grayscale mode, and then choose the color mode you want to work in before you continue. When you apply a color to a grayscale image, each pixel becomes a shade of that particular color instead of gray.

Converting Grayscale and Color Modes

When you convert a color image to grayscale, the data for light and dark values—called the **luminosity**—remain, while the color information is deleted. When you change from grayscale to a color mode, the foreground and background colors on the Tools panel change from black and white to the previously selected colors.

Tweaking Adjustments

Once you have made your color mode conversion to grayscale, you may want to make some adjustments. You can fine-tune

Converting a Color Image to Black and White

Using the Black & White command, you can easily convert a color image to black and white. This command lets you quickly make the color-to-black-and-white conversion while maintaining full control over how individual colors are converted. Tones can also be applied to the grayscale by applying color tones (the numeric values for each color). To use this feature, click Image on the Menu bar, point to Adjustments, and then click Black & White. The Black & White command can also be applied as an Adjustment layer.

the Brightness/Contrast, filters, and blending modes in a grayscale image.

Colorizing a Grayscale Image

In order for a grayscale image to be colorized, you must change the color mode to one that accommodates color. After you change the color mode and adjust settings in the Hue/Saturation dialog box, Photoshop determines the colorization range based on the hue of the currently selected foreground color. If you want a different colorization range, you need to change the foreground color.

Figure 27 *Gradient Map dialog box*

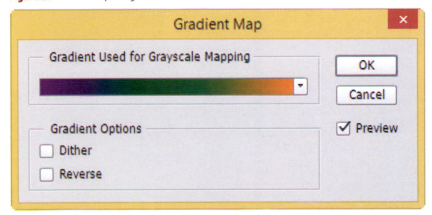

Applying a Gradient Effect

You can also use the Gradient Map to apply a colored gradient effect to a grayscale image. The Gradient Map uses gradient fills (the same ones displayed in the Gradient picker) to colorize the image, which can produce some stunning effects. You use the Gradient Map dialog box, shown in Figure 27, to apply a gradient effect to a grayscale image. You can access the Gradient Map dialog box using the Adjustments command on the Image menu.

Change the color mode

1. Open PS 5-2.psd from the drive and folder where you store your Data Files, then save it as **Basketball Star Colorized**.

2. Click **Image** on the Menu bar, point to **Mode**, then click **Grayscale**.

3. Click **Flatten** in the warning box, then click **Discard**.

   The color mode of the image is changed to grayscale, and the image is flattened so there is only a single layer. All the color information in the image has been discarded.

4. Click **Image** on the Menu bar, point to **Mode**, then click **RGB Color**.

   The color mode is changed back to RGB color, although there is still no color in the image. Compare your screen to Figure 28.

You converted the image to Grayscale, which discarded the existing color information. Then you changed the color mode to RGB color.

Figure 28 *Grayscale image converted to RGB mode*
Source: Morguefile.

Mode changed to RGB

Converting Color Images to Grayscale

Like everything else in Photoshop, there is more than one way of converting a color image into one that is black and white. Changing the color mode to grayscale is the quickest method. You can also make this conversion by converting to black and white or through desaturation by clicking Image on the Menu bar, pointing to Adjustments, and then clicking Black & White or Desaturate. Converting to Grayscale mode generally results in losing contrast, as does the desaturation method, while using the Black & White method retains the contrast of the original image.

Figure 29 *Hue/Saturation dialog box*

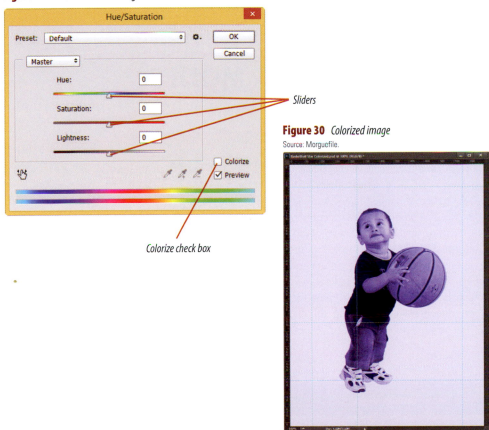

Sliders

Colorize check box

Figure 30 *Colorized image*
Source: Morguefile.

Colorize a grayscale image

1. Click **Image** on the Menu bar, point to **Adjustments**, then click **Hue/Saturation** to open the Hue/Saturation dialog box, as shown in Figure 29.

2. Click the **Colorize check box** in the Hue/Saturation dialog box to add a check mark.

3. Drag the **Hue slider** until the text box displays **240**.

   TIP You can also type values in the text boxes in the Hue/Saturation dialog box. Negative numbers must be preceded by a minus sign or a hyphen. Positive numbers can be preceded by an optional plus sign (+).

4. Drag the **Saturation slider** until the text box displays **30**.

5. Drag the **Lightness slider** until the text box displays **-10**.

6. Click **OK**.

7. Compare your screen to Figure 30, then save your work.

You colorized a grayscale image by adjusting settings in the Hue/Saturation dialog box.

Understanding the Hue/Saturation Dialog Box

The Hue/Saturation dialog box is an important tool in the world of color enhancement. Useful for both color and grayscale images, the saturation slider can be used to boost a range of colors. By clicking the Master list arrow, you can isolate which colors (all, cyan, blue, magenta, red, yellow, or green) you want to modify. Using this tool requires patience and experimentation, but gives you great control over the colors in your image.

Use Filters, Opacity,
AND BLENDING MODES

What You'll Do

Source: Morguefile.

In this lesson, you'll adjust the brightness and contrast in the Basketball Star Colorized image, apply a Sharpen filter, and adjust the opacity of the lines applied by the filter. You'll also adjust the color balance of the Basketball Star image.

Manipulating an Image

As you work in Photoshop, you might realize that some images have fundamental problems that need correcting, while others just need to be further enhanced. For example, you might need to adjust an image's contrast and sharpness, or you might want to colorize an otherwise dull image. You can use a variety of techniques to change the way an image looks. For example, you have learned how to use the Adjustments command on the Image menu to modify hue and saturation, but you can also use this command to adjust brightness and contrast, color balance, and a host of other visual effects.

Understanding Filters

Filters are Photoshop commands that can significantly alter an image's appearance. Experimenting with Photoshop's filters is a fun way to completely change the look of an image. For example, the Watercolor filter gives the illusion that your image was painted using traditional watercolors. Sharpen filters can appear to add definition to the entire image, or just the edges. Compare the

Fixing Blurry Scanned Images

An unfortunate result of scanning a picture is that the image can become blurry. You can fix this, however, using the Unsharp Mask filter. This filter both sharpens and smoothes the image by increasing the contrast along element edges. Here's how it works: the smoothing effect removes stray marks, and the sharpening effect emphasizes contrasting neighboring pixels. Most scanners come with their own Unsharp Masks built into the scanner driver, but using Photoshop, you have access to a more powerful version of this filter. You can use Photoshop's Unsharp Mask to control the sharpening process by adjusting key settings. In most cases, your scanner's Unsharp Mask might not give you this flexibility. Regardless of the technical aspects, the result is a sharper image. You can apply the Unsharp Mask by clicking Filter on the Menu bar, pointing to Sharpen, and then clicking Unsharp Mask.

different Sharpen filters applied in Figure 31. The **Sharpen More filter** increases the contrast of adjacent pixels and can focus a blurry image. Be careful not to overuse sharpening tools (or any filter), because you can create high-contrast lines or add graininess in color or brightness.

Choosing Blending Modes

A **blending mode** controls how pixels are made either darker or lighter based on colors on underlying layers. Photoshop provides a variety of commonly used blending modes, listed in Table 1, to combine the color of the pixels in the current layer with those in layer(s) beneath it. You can see a list of blending modes by clicking the Set the blending mode for the layer list arrow on the Layers panel, or by clicking Blending Options, and then clicking the Blend Mode list arrow. You can also see a list of blending modes by clicking the Mode list arrow on the options bar when the Gradient tool is selected, or by clicking Layer on the Menu bar, pointing to Layer Style, and then clicking Blending Options.

Understanding Blending Mode Components

You should consider the following underlying colors when planning a blending mode: **base color**, which is the original color of the image; **blend color**, which is the color you apply with a paint or edit tool; and **resulting color**, which is the color that is created as a result of applying the blend color.

Softening Filter Effects

Opacity can soften the line that the filter creates, but it doesn't affect the opacity of the entire layer. After a filter has been applied, you can modify the opacity and apply a blending mode using the Layers panel or the Fade dialog box. You can open the Fade dialog box by clicking Edit on the Menu bar, and then clicking the Fade command.

QUICK TIP

The Fade command appears only after a filter has been applied. When available, the command name includes the name of the applied filter.

Figure 31 *Sharpen filters*

Original image

Sharpen filter applied

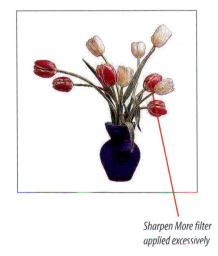

Sharpen More filter applied excessively

Images © Photodisc/Getty Images.

Balancing Colors

As you adjust settings, such as hue and saturation, you might create unwanted imbalances in your image. You can adjust colors to correct or improve an image's appearance. For example, you can decrease a color by increasing the amount of its opposite color. You open the Color Balance dialog box by clicking Image on the Menu bar, pointing to Adjustments, and then clicking Color Balance. This dialog box is used to balance the color in an image.

TABLE 1: BLENDING MODES	
Blending mode	**Description**
Dissolve mode	Dissolve mode creates a grainy, mottled appearance.
Multiply and Screen modes	Multiply mode creates semitransparent shadow effects. This mode assesses the information in each channel, and then multiplies the value of the base color by the blend color. The resulting color is always *darker* than the base color. The Screen mode multiplies the value of the inverse of the blend and base colors. After it is applied, the resulting color is always *lighter* than the base color.
Overlay mode	Dark and light values preserve the highlights and shadows of the base color while mixing the base color and blend color, dark base colors are multiplied (darkened), and light areas are screened (lightened).
Soft Light and Hard Light modes	Soft Light lightens a light base color and darkens a dark base color giving the effect of shining a diffuse spotlight on an image. The Hard Light blending mode creates the effect of a harsh spotlight, useful for adding highlights or shadows by providing a greater contrast between the base and blend colors.
Color Dodge and Color Burn modes	Color Dodge mode brightens the base color to reflect the blend color. The Color Burn mode darkens base color to reflect the blend color.
Darken and Lighten modes	Darken mode selects the base color or blend color based on whichever color is darker. The Lighten mode selects a new resulting color based on the lighter of the two colors.
Difference and Exclusion modes	The Difference mode subtracts the value of the blend color from the value of the base color, or vice versa, depending on which color has the greater brightness value. The Exclusion mode creates an effect similar to that of the Difference mode, but with less contrast between the blend and base colors.
Color and Luminosity modes	The Color mode creates a resulting color with the luminance of the base color and the hue and saturation of the blend color. The Luminosity mode creates a resulting color with the hue and saturation of the base color and the luminance of the blend color.
Hue and Saturation modes	The Hue mode creates a resulting color with the luminance and saturation of the base color and the hue of the blend color. The Saturation mode creates a resulting color with the luminance and hue of the base color and the saturation of the blend color.

Figure 32 *Brightness/Contrast dialog box*

Source: Morguefile.

Figure 33 *Shadow/Highlight dialog box*

Adjust brightness and contrast

1. Click **Image** on the Menu bar, point to **Adjustments**, then click **Brightness/Contrast** to open the Brightness/Contrast dialog box.

2. Drag the **Brightness slider** until **15** appears in the Brightness text box.

3. Drag the **Contrast slider** until **30** appears in the Contrast text box. Compare your screen to Figure 32.

TIP Any dialog box containing a Preview check box can be toggled on and off to see the effects of your changes.

4. Click **OK**.

You adjusted settings in the Brightness/Contrast dialog box. The image now looks much brighter, with a higher degree of contrast, which obscures some of the finer detail in the image.

Correcting Shadows and Highlights

The ability to correct shadows and highlights will delight photographers everywhere. This image correction feature (opened by clicking Image on the Menu bar, pointing to Adjustments, and then clicking Shadows/Highlights) lets you modify overall lighting and make subtle adjustments. Figure 33 shows the Shadows/Highlights dialog box with the Show More Options check box selected. Check out this one-stop shopping for shadow and highlight adjustments!

Work with a filter, a blending mode, and an opacity setting

1. Click **Filter** on the Menu bar, point to **Sharpen**, then click **Sharpen More**.

   The border and other features of the image are intensified.

2. Click **Edit** on the Menu bar, then click **Fade Sharpen More** to open the Fade dialog box, as shown in Figure 34.

3. Drag the **Opacity slider** until **45** appears in the Opacity text box.

   The opacity setting softened the lines applied by the Sharpen More filter.

   TIP You may have noticed the Fill list arrow (beneath the Opacity list arrow) on the Layers panel. The Fill list arrow lets you adjust the transparency of a layer (as does the Opacity setting) while ignoring any special effects (such as a drop shadow or stroke) you may have added.

4. Click the **Mode list arrow**, then click **Dissolve**.

   The Dissolve setting blends the surrounding pixels. Zoom in on the image if you need a closer look at the changes.

5. Click **OK**.

6. Save your work, then compare your image to Figure 35.

You applied the Sharpen More filter, then adjusted the opacity and changed the color mode in the Fade dialog box. The edge in the image looks crisper than before, with a greater level of detail.

Figure 34 *Fade dialog box*

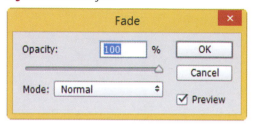

Figure 35 *Image settings adjusted*

Source: Morguefile.

Incorporating Color Techniques

Figure 36 *Color Balance dialog box*

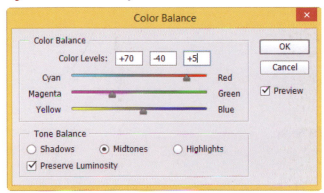

Figure 37 *Image with colors balanced*

Source: Morguefile.

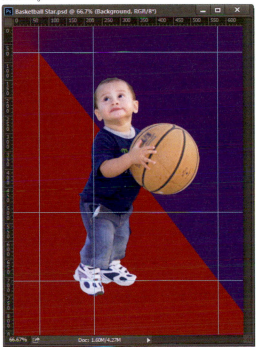

Adjust color balance

1. Switch to the **Basketball Star image**, with the Background layer active, then change the zoom factor to **66.7%**.

   The image you worked with earlier in this chapter becomes active.

2. Click **Image** on the Menu bar, point to **Adjustments**, then click **Color Balance**.

3. Drag the **Cyan-Red slider** until **+70** appears in the first text box.

4. Drag the **Magenta-Green slider** until **−40** appears in the middle text box.

5. Drag the **Yellow-Blue slider** until **+5** appears in the last text box, as shown in Figure 36.

   Subtle changes were made in the color balance in the image.

6. Click **OK**.

7. Save your work, then compare your image to Figure 37.

You balanced the colors in the Basketball Star image by adjusting settings in the Color Balance dialog box.

Match COLORS

What You'll Do

Source: Morguefile.

In this lesson, you'll make selections in source and target images, and then use the Match Color command to replace the target color.

Finding the Right Color

If it hasn't happened already, at some point you'll be working on an image and wish you could grab a color from another image to use in this one. Just as you can use the Eyedropper tool to sample any color in the current image for the foreground and background, you can sample a color from any other image to use in the current one. Perhaps the skin tones in one image look washed out; you can use the Match Color command to replace those tones with skin tone colors from another image. Or maybe the jacket color in one image would look better using a color in another image.

Using Selections to Match Colors

Remember that this is Photoshop, where everything is about layers and selections.

To replace a color in one image with one you've matched from another, you work with—you guessed it—layers and selections.

Suppose you've located the perfect color in another image. The image you are working with is the **target**, and the image that contains your perfect color is the **source**. By activating the layer on which the color lies in the source image, and making a selection around the color, you can have Photoshop match the color in the source and replace a color in the target. To accomplish this, you use the Match Color command, which is available by pointing to Adjustments on the Image menu.

Figure 38 *Selection in source image*

Images © Photodisc/Getty Images.

Selected area

Name of
target
image

Figure 39 *Match Color dialog box*

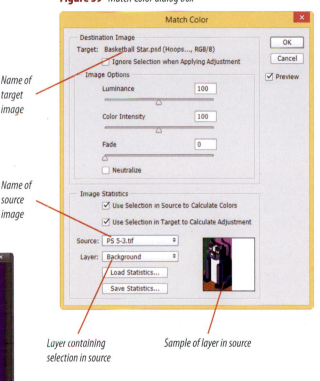

Name of
source
image

Layer containing
selection in source

Sample of layer in source

Figure 40 *Image with matched color*

Source: Morguefile.

Modified
selection

Match a color

1. Click the **Hoopster layer** on the Layers panel, then zoom (once) into the boy's shirt collar.

2. Click **Select** on the Menu bar, then click **Load Selection**.

3. Click the **Channel list arrow**, click **collar**, then click **OK**.

4. Open PS 5-3.tif from the drive and folder where you store your Data Files, zoom into the image (if necessary), select the Magic Wand tool, change the tolerance to **4**, verify that the **Anti-alias** and **Contiguous check boxes** on the options bar are selected, then click the **yellow part of the cat's eye** (at **105 X/95 Y**) with the **Magic Wand pointer** . Compare your selection to Figure 38.

5. Activate the **Basketball Star image**, click **Image** on the Menu bar, point to **Adjustments**, then click **Match Color**.

6. Click the **Source list arrow**, then click **PS 5-3.tif**. Compare your settings to Figure 39.

7. Click **OK**.

8. Deselect the selection, turn off the rulers and the guides, save your work, then compare your image to Figure 40.

9. Close all open images, display the **Essentials workspace**, then exit Photoshop.

You loaded a saved selection, then used the Match Color dialog box to replace a color in one image with a color from another image. The Match Color dialog box makes it easy to sample colors from other images, giving you even more options for incorporating color into an image.

POWER USER SHORTCUTS

To do this:	Use this method:	To do this:	Use this method:
Apply a sharpen filter	Filter ➤ Sharpen	Hide or show rulers	[Ctrl][R] (Win) or ⌘ [R] (Mac)
Balance colors	Image ➤ Adjustments ➤ Color Balance	Hide or show the Color panel	[F6]
Change color mode	Image ➤ Mode	Lock transparent pixels check box on/off	[/]
Choose a background color from the Swatches panel	[Ctrl]Color swatch (Win) or ⌘ Color swatch (Mac)	Make Swatches panel active	Window ➤ Swatches
Delete a swatch from the Swatches panel	[Alt], click swatch with ✂ (Win) [option], click swatch with ✂ (Mac)	Paint Bucket tool	or **G**
Eyedropper tool	or **I**	Return background and foreground colors to default	or **D**
Fill with background color	[Shift][Backspace] (Win) or ⌘ [delete] (Mac)	Show a layer	
Fill with foreground color	[Alt][Backspace] (Win) or [option][delete] (Mac)	Show hidden Paint Bucket/Gradient tools	[Shift] **G**
Gradient tool	or **G**	Switch between open files	[Ctrl][Tab] (Win) or [control][tab] (Mac)
Guide pointer	or	Switch foreground and background colors	or **X**
Hide a layer			

Key: Menu items are indicated by ➤ between the menu name and its command. Blue bold letters are shortcuts for selecting tools on the Tools panel.

© 2013 Cengage Learning®

Incorporating Color Techniques

Work with color to transform an image.

1. Start Photoshop.
2. Open PS 5-4.psd from the drive and folder where you store your Data Files, then save it as **Firetruck**.
3. Make sure the rulers display in pixels, and that the guides and the default foreground and background colors display.
4. Use the Eyedropper tool to sample the red color at 90 X/165 Y using the guides to help.
5. Use the Paint Bucket tool to apply the new foreground color to the Background layer.
6. Undo your last step using either the Edit menu or the History panel. (*Hint*: You can switch to another workspace that displays the necessary panels.)
7. Switch the foreground and background colors.
8. Save your work.

Use the Color Picker and the Swatches panel.

1. Use the Set foreground color button to open the Color Picker dialog box.
2. Click the R:, G:, and B: option buttons, one at a time. Note how the color panel changes.
3. With the B: option button selected, click the panel in the upper-left corner, then click OK.
4. Switch the foreground and background colors.
5. Add the foreground color (red) to the Swatches panel using a meaningful name of your choice.

Place a border around an image.

1. Make the Firetruck layer active.
2. Revert to the default foreground and background colors.
3. Create a border by applying a 2-pixel outside stroke to the firetruck.
4. Save your work.

Blend colors using the Gradient tool.

1. Change the foreground color to the fourth swatch from the left in the top row of the Swatches panel (RGB Cyan). (Your swatch location may vary.)
2. Switch foreground and background colors.
3. Use the new red swatch that you added previously as the foreground color.
4. Make the Background layer active, and verify that the blending mode is Normal.
5. Use the Gradient tool (Foreground to Background gradient fill) and the Radial Gradient style with its default settings, then using the guides to help, drag the pointer from 90 X/70 Y to 145 X/165 Y.
6. Save your work, and turn off the guides and rulers display.

Add color to a grayscale image.

1. Open PS 5-5.psd, then save it as **Firetruck Colorized**.
2. Change the color mode to RGB Color and flatten the image.
3. Open the Hue/Saturation dialog box, then select the Colorize check box.
4. Drag the sliders so the text boxes show the following values: 200, 56, and −30, then click OK.
5. Save your work.

Use filters, opacity, and blending modes.

1. Use the Sharpen filter to sharpen the image.
2. Open the Fade dialog box by using the Edit menu, change the opacity to 60%, change the mode to Overlay, then save your work.
3. Open the Color Balance dialog box.
4. Change the color level settings so the text boxes show the following values: +70, +25, and -15.
5. Turn off the guides and the rulers if necessary.
6. Save your work.

Match colors.

1. Open PS 5-6.tif, then use the Magic Wand tool to select the gray in the cat's left ear.
2. Using Firetruck.psd, select the lightest areas of the firetruck cab. (*Hint*: You can press [Shift] and click multiple areas using the Magic Wand tool.)
3. Use the Match Color dialog box to change the white in the Firetruck layer of the firetruck image to gray (in the cat's ear), then lock the Firetruck layer. Deselect the selection and compare your images to Figure 41. (The brightness of your colors may vary.)
4. Save your work.

Figure 41 *Completed Skills Review*
Image courtesy of Elizabeth Eisner Reding.

You are finally able to leave your current job and pursue your lifelong dream of opening a fix-it business. While you're waiting for business to increase, you start to work on a website design.

1. Open PS 5-7.psd, then save it as **Fix It!**.
2. Move the objects to any location to achieve a layout you think looks attractive and eye-catching.
3. Sample the blue pliers in the tool belt, then switch the foreground and background colors.
4. Sample another item in the image.
5. Use any Gradient tool to create an interesting effect on the Background layer.
6. Save the image, then compare your screen to the sample shown in Figure 42.

Figure 42 *Sample Project Builder 1*
Images © Photodisc/Getty Images.

Incorporating Color Techniques

You're working on the budget at the PB&J Preschool, when you notice a staff member struggling to redesign the school's website. Although the basic website is complete, it doesn't convey the high energy of the school. You offer to help, and soon find yourself in charge of creating an exciting background for the image.

1. Open PS 5-8.psd, then save it as **Preschool**.
2. Apply a foreground color of your choice to the Background layer.
3. Add a new layer above the Background layer, then select a background color and apply a gradient you have not used before to the layer. (*Hint*: Remember that you can immediately undo a gradient that you don't want.)
4. Add the foreground and background colors to the Swatches panel.
5. Apply a Sharpen filter to the Boy at blackboard layer and adjust the opacity of the filter.
6. Move any objects as you see fit.
7. Save your work.
8. Compare your screen to the sample shown in Figure 43.

Figure 43 *Sample Project Builder 2*
Images © Photodisc/Getty Images.

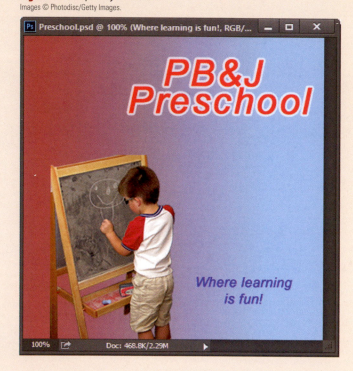

A local Top 40 morning radio show recently conducted a survey about chocolate, and discovered that only one in seven people knew about its health benefits. Now everyone is talking about chocolate. The station's web designer wants to incorporate chocolates into her fall campaign, and has asked you to create a design that will be featured on the radio station's website. You decide to highlight as many varieties as possible.

1. Open PS 5-9.psd, then save it as **Chocolate**.
2. If you choose, you can add any appropriate images that have been scanned or captured using a digital camera.
3. Activate the Background layer, then sample colors from the image for foreground and background colors. (*Hint*: Try to sample unusual colors, to widen your design horizons.)
4. Display the rulers, then move the existing guides to indicate the coordinates of the colors you sampled.
5. Add the sampled colors to the Swatches panel.
6. Create a gradient fill by using both the foreground and background colors and the gradient style of your choice.
7. Defringe the Chocolates layer, if necessary.
8. Hide the rulers and guides, save your work, then compare your image to the sample shown in Figure 44.

Figure 44 *Sample Design Project*
Source: Morguefile.

Chocolate.psd @ 100% (Background, RGB/8)

100%   Doc: 791.0K/1.83M

An educational toy and game store has hired you to create a design that will be used on the company's website to announce this year's Most Unusual Hobby contest. After reviewing the photos from last year's awards ceremony, you decide to build a design using the winner of the Handicrafts Award. You'll use your knowledge of Photoshop color modes to convert the color mode, adjust color in the image, and add a shaded background.

1. Open PS 5-10.psd, then save it as **Rubberband**.
2. Convert the image to Grayscale mode. (*Hint*: When Photoshop prompts you to flatten the layers, click Don't Flatten.)
3. Convert the image to RGB Color mode. (*Hint*: When Photoshop prompts you to flatten the layers, click Don't Flatten.)
4. Colorize the image and adjust the Hue, Saturation, and Lightness settings as desired.
5. Adjust Brightness/Contrast settings as desired.
6. Adjust Color Balance settings as desired.
7. Sample the image to create a new foreground color, then add a color of your choice as the background color.
8. Apply any Sharpen filter and adjust the opacity for that filter.
9. Add a reflected gradient to the Background layer that follows the path of one of the main bands on the ball.
10. Save your work, then compare your image to the sample shown in Figure 45.
11. Be prepared to discuss the color-correcting methods you used and why you chose them.

Figure 45 *Sample Portfolio Project*
Images © Photodisc/Getty Images.

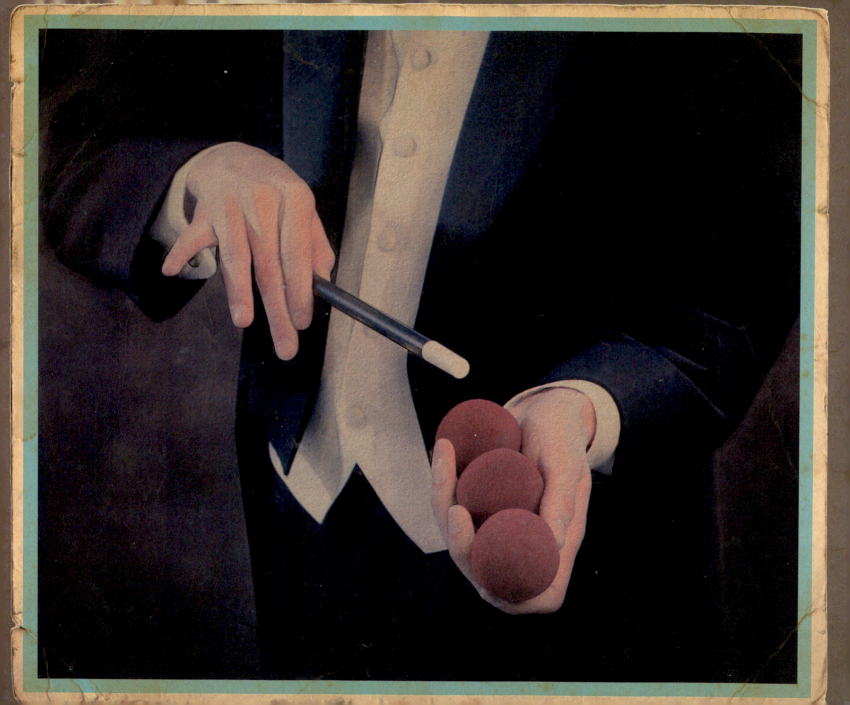

CHAPTER 6 PLACING TYPE
IN AN IMAGE

1. Learn about type and how it is created
2. Change spacing and adjust baseline shift
3. Use the Drop Shadow style
4. Apply anti-aliasing to type
5. Modify type with Bevel and Emboss and Extrude to 3D
6. Apply special effects to type using filters
7. Create text on a path

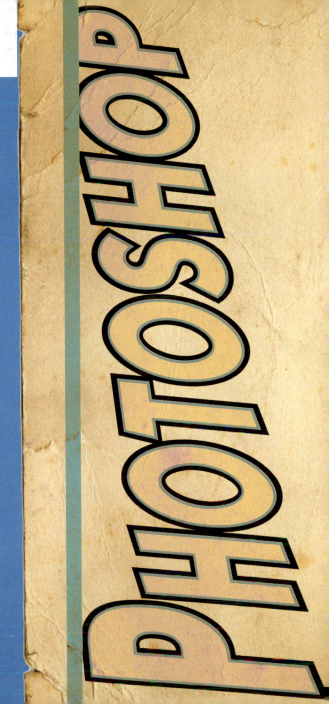

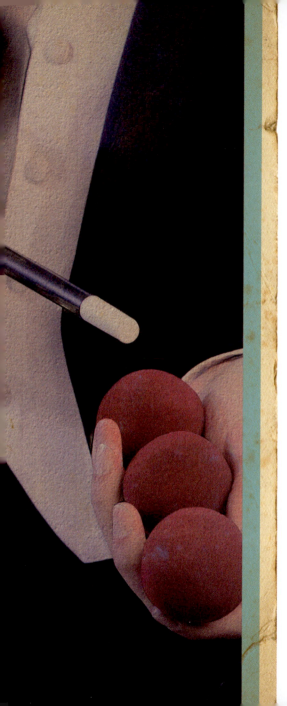

CHAPTER 6   PLACING TYPE
IN AN IMAGE

Learning About Type

Text plays an important design role when combined with images for posters, magazine and newspaper advertisements, and other graphics materials that are used to communicate detailed information. In Photoshop, text is referred to as **type**. You can use type to express the ideas conveyed in a file's imagery or to deliver an additional message. You can manipulate type in many ways to reflect or reinforce the meaning behind an image. As in other programs, type has its own unique characteristics in Photoshop. For example, you can change its appearance by using different fonts (also called **typefaces**) and colors.

Understanding the Purpose of Type

Type is typically used along with imagery to deliver a message quickly and with flare. Because type is used sparingly (often there's

not a lot of room for it), its appearance is very important; color and imagery are frequently used to *complement* or *reinforce* the message within the text. Type should be limited, direct, and to the point. It should be large enough for easy reading, but should not overwhelm or distract from the central image. For example, a vibrant and daring advertisement should contain just enough type to interest the reader, without demanding too much reading.

Getting the Most Out of Type

Words can express an idea, but the appearance of the type is what drives the point home. After you decide on the content you want to use and create the type, you can experiment with its appearance by changing its **font** (a set of characters with a similar appearance, size, and color). You can also apply special effects that make it stand out or appear to pop off the page.

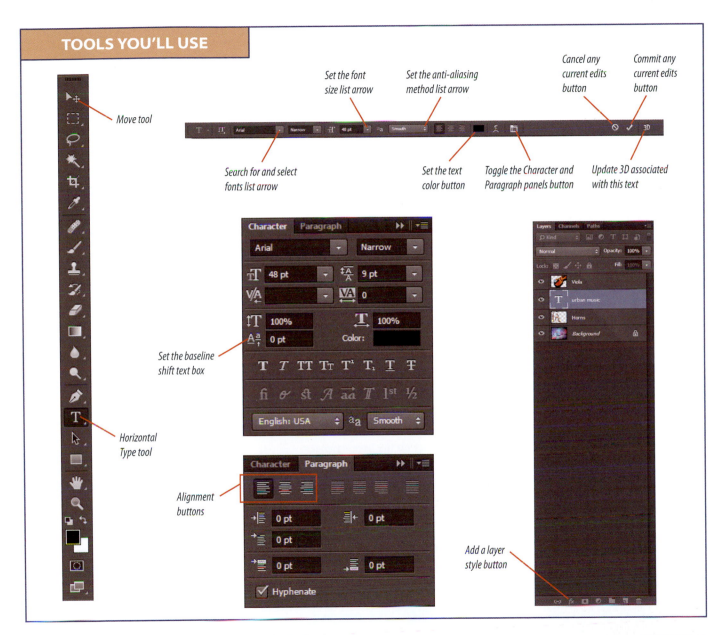

Move tool

Set the font size list arrow

Set the anti-aliasing method list arrow

Cancel any current edits button

Commit any current edits button

Search for and select fonts list arrow

Set the text color button

Toggle the Character and Paragraph panels button

Update 3D associated with this text

Set the baseline shift text box

Horizontal Type tool

Alignment buttons

Add a layer style button

Learn About Type and
HOW IT IS CREATED

What You'll Do

Source: Morguefile.

 In this lesson, you'll create a type layer, and then change the font family, size, and color of the type.

Introducing Type Types

Outline type is mathematically defined, which means that it can be scaled to any size without losing its sharp, smooth edges. Some programs, such as Adobe Illustrator, create outline type, also known as **vector fonts**. **Bitmap type** is composed of pixels, and, like bitmap images, can develop jagged edges when enlarged. The type you create in Photoshop is initially outline type, but it is converted into bitmap type when you apply special filters. Using the type tools and the options bar, you can create horizontal or vertical type and modify font size and alignment. You use the Color Picker dialog box to change type color. Each time you create type in Photoshop, it is automatically placed on a new type layer on the Layers panel.

QUICK **TIP**

Keeping type on separate layers makes it much easier to modify and change its position within the image.

Getting to Know Font Families

Each **font family** represents a complete set of characters, letters, and symbols for a particular typeface. Font families are generally divided into three categories: serif, sans serif, and

symbol. Characters in **serif fonts** have a tail, or stroke, at the ends of some characters. These tails make it easier for the eye to recognize words. For this reason, serif fonts are generally used in text passages as in the body text of this book. Emphasized text is a sans serif font. **Sans serif fonts** do not have tails and are commonly used in headlines. **Symbol fonts** are used to display unique characters (such as \$, +, or ™). Table 1 lists some commonly used serif and sans serif fonts. After you select the Horizontal Type tool, you can change font families using the options bar.

QUICK **TIP**

The Verdana typeface was designed to be readable on a computer screen.

Measuring Type Size

The size of each character within a font is measured in **points**. **PostScript**, a programming language that optimizes printed text and graphics, was introduced by Adobe in 1984. In PostScript measurement, one inch is equivalent to 72 points or six picas. Therefore, one pica is equivalent to 12 points. In traditional character measurement, one inch is equivalent to 72.27 points. The default

Photoshop type size is 12 points. In Photoshop, you have the option of using PostScript or traditional character measurement.

Acquiring Fonts

Your computer has many fonts installed on it, but no matter how many fonts you have, you can probably use more. Fonts can be purchased from private companies, individual designers, computer stores, or catalog companies. Fonts are delivered on CD, DVD, or over the Internet from services such as Typekit (as part of your Creative Cloud subscription). Using your favorite search engine and the keywords "type foundry", you can locate websites where you can purchase or download fonts. Many websites offer specialty fonts, while others offer fonts free of charge or for a nominal fee. Figure 1 shows font samples in Photoshop (your list may differ). Notice that an icon may appear to the left of the font name: this indicates the origin or manufacturer of the font.

TABLE 1: COMMONLY USED SERIF AND SANS SERIF FONTS			
Serif fonts	**Sample**	**Sans serif fonts**	**Sample**
Lucida Handwriting	*Adobe Photoshop*	Arial	Adobe Photoshop
Rockwell	**Adobe Photoshop**	Bauhaus	Adobe Photoshop
Times New Roman	Adobe Photoshop	Century Gothic	Adobe Photoshop
Georgia	Adobe Photoshop	Verdana	Adobe Photoshop

© 2015 Cengage Learning®

Figure 1 *Fonts in Photoshop*

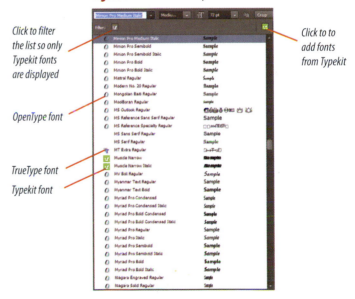

Click to filter the list so only Typekit fonts are displayed

Click to to add fonts from Typekit

OpenType font

TrueType font

Typekit font

Create and modify type

1. Start Photoshop, open PS 6-1.psd from the drive and folder where you store your Data Files, then save the file as **Urban Music**.

2. Display the document size in the status bar, guides, and rulers in pixels (if they are not already displayed), then change the workspace to **Typography**.

TIP You can quickly toggle the rulers on and off by pressing [Ctrl][R] (Win) or [⌘][R] (Mac).

3. Click the **Default Foreground and Background Colors button** ▣ on the Tools panel.

4. Click the **Horizontal Type tool** T on the Tools panel.

5. Click the **Search for and select fonts list arrow** on the options bar, click **Arial Regular** (a sans serif font), click the **Set the font style list arrow**, then click **Italic**.

TIP If Arial is not available, make a reasonable substitution.

6. Click the **Set the font size list arrow** on the options bar, then click **48 pt**.

7. Click the **image** with the **Horizontal Type pointer** ⊥ at approximately **430 X/510 Y**, then type **Live Music** as shown in Figure 2.

TIP It's okay if your text falls above or below the guide line.

You created a type layer by using the Horizontal Type tool on the Tools panel and modified the font family, font style, and font size.

Figure 2 *New type in image*
Source: Morguefile.

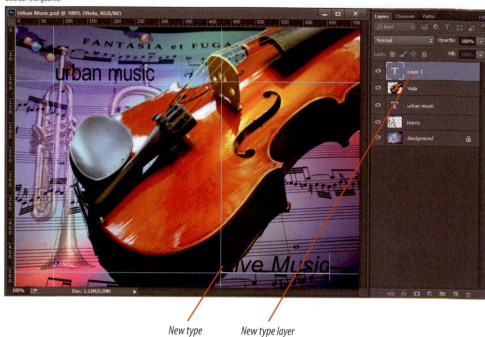

New type   New type layer

NEW **Curing the Missing Font Blues**

On occasion, you may see a dialog box telling you that the file you've opened in Photoshop contains fonts that are missing from your computer. Remember Typekit? That's the service available to Creative Cloud subscribers that contains hundreds of fonts. When you open an existing image, Photoshop automatically checks to see if any fonts within the document are available on your computer. If they are available, then everything is fine and the document opens. If they are not available, Photoshop checks Typekit to see if they (or a reasonable match) are available. If a match is found in Typekit, a dialog box will display asking if you want to replace the missing font with the Typekit font. And voilà! Your fonts are updated!

Figure 3 *Type with new color*

Source: Morguefile.

Type with
new color

Change type color using an existing color in the image

1. Press [**Ctrl**][**A**] (Win) or ⌘ [**A**] (Mac) to select all the text.
2. Click the **Search for and select fonts list arrow** on the options bar, scroll down, then click **Times New Roman Regular**.

   TIP Click *in* the Set the font family text box and you can select a different font by typing the first few characters of the font name.

3. Click the **Set the font style list arrow**, then click **Bold Italic**.
4. Click the **Set the text color button** ▬ on the options bar.

   As you position the pointer over the image, the pointer automatically becomes an Eyedropper pointer.

5. Reposition the Color Picker (Text Color) dialog box if necessary, then click the **image** with the **Eyedropper pointer** 🖋 anywhere in the orange area of the viola at approximately **250 X/250 Y**.

   The new color is now the active color in the Color Picker (Text Color) dialog box.

6. Click **OK** in the Color Picker (Text Color) dialog box.
7. Click the **Commit any current edits button** ✓ on the options bar.

   Click the Commit any current edits button to accept your changes and make them permanent.

8. Save your work, then compare your image to Figure 3.

You changed the font family, modified the color of the type by using an existing image color, and committed the current edits.

Change Spacing and
ADJUST BASELINE SHIFT

What You'll Do

Source: Morguefile.

In this lesson, you'll adjust the spacing between characters, change the baseline of type, and then apply the same style to two different characters.

Adjusting Letter Spacing

Competition for readers on the visual landscape is fierce. To get and maintain an edge over other designers, Photoshop provides tools that let you make adjustments to your type, offering you the opportunity to make your type more distinctive. These adjustments might not be very dramatic, but they can influence readers in subtle ways. For example, type that is too small and difficult to read might make the reader impatient (at the very least), and he or she might not even look at the image (at the very worst). You can make finite adjustments, called **type spacing**, to the space between characters and between lines of type. Adjusting type spacing affects the ease with which words are read.

Understanding Character and Line Spacing

Fonts in desktop publishing and word-processing programs use proportional letter spacing, whereas typewriters use monotype spacing. In **monotype spacing**, each character occupies the same amount of space. This means that wide characters such as "o" and "w" take up the same real estate on the page as narrow ones such as "i" and "l". In **proportional spacing**, each character can take up a different amount of space, depending on its width. **Kerning** controls the amount of space between two characters and can affect several characters, a word, or an entire paragraph. **Tracking** inserts a *uniform* amount of space between selected characters. Figure 4 shows an example of type before and after it has been kerned. The second line of text takes up less room and has less space between its characters, making it easier to read. You can also change the amount of space, called **leading**, between lines of type, to add or decrease the distance between lines of text.

Using the Character Panel

The **Character panel**, shown in Figure 5, helps you manually or automatically control type properties such as kerning, tracking, and leading. You open the Character panel from the Type tool options bar, the icon dock, or from the Window menu on the Menu bar.

> **QUICK TIP**
>
> Click the Search for and select fonts list arrow on the options bar or Character panel to see previews of installed fonts.

Understanding Type Styles

You've probably noticed that within any publication you'll see certain formatting

Placing Type in an Image

similarities occurring repeatedly. Since many people may be collaborating to make a publication possible, styles are often used to ensure consistency. A **style** is a collection of formatting attributes that can be saved and applied to specific characters or an entire paragraph. Perhaps a magazine has a five space indent at the start of each paragraph, or maybe sidebars that occur on certain pages have the same horizontal line spacing and justification. Photoshop allows you to define both character and paragraph styles that can be applied at any time. You can create and apply type styles by clicking Window on the Menu bar, then clicking either Character Styles or Paragraph Styles. Figure 6 shows the Paragraph Styles panel with two customized styles.

Creating a paragraph or character style is easy: for a paragraph, place your cursor anywhere within the paragraph containing the attributes you want and click the Create new paragraph style button at the bottom of the Paragraph Styles panel. The attributes in that paragraph will automatically be reflected in the Paragraph Style Options dialog box. For a character style, select type containing the attributes you want to preserve and reuse, then click the Create new character style button at the bottom of the Character Styles panel. This method is sometimes referred to as *style by example*. In the case of a new paragraph or character style, you are always free to define your attributes in the Paragraph Style Options dialog box or Character Style Options dialog box *without* first making a paragraph or character selection.

Adjusting the Baseline Shift

Type rests on an invisible line called a **baseline**. Using the Character panel, you can adjust the **baseline shift**, the vertical distance that type moves from its baseline. You can add interest to type by changing the baseline shift. Negative adjustments to the baseline move characters

below the baseline, while positive adjustments move characters *above* the baseline.

Figure 5 *Character panel*

Figure 6 *Paragraph Styles panel*

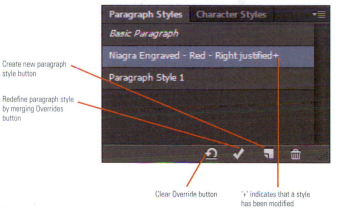

Figure 4 *Kerned characters*

Kern characters

1. Verify that the **Live Music type layer** is active and that the Horizontal Type tool is selected.

2. Click **between "L" and "i"** in the word "Live."

TIP Many of the changes you make throughout Photoshop will be subtle. Don't be disappointed when you only see slight change in your image. Those slight improvements add up, and you'll find that you might invest hours in individual details that no one notices. Taken together, these tweaks can take an image from blah to brilliant.

3. Click the **Set the kerning between two characters list arrow** 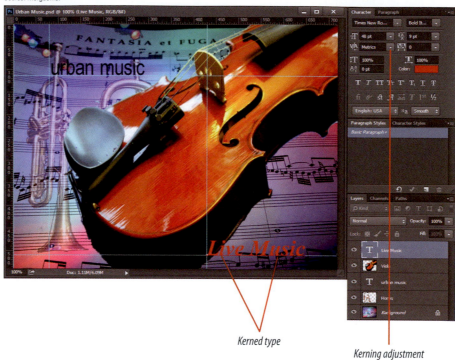 on the Character panel, then click **−50**.

   The spacing between the two characters decreases.

TIP You can close the Character panel by clicking the Panel options button in the upper-right corner of its title bar, then clicking the Close command. You can also open and close the Character panel by clicking the Character icon on the dock if it's displayed, or by clicking the Character tab in the Character panel.

4. Click **between "M" and "u"** in the word "Music," as shown in Figure 7.

5. Click the 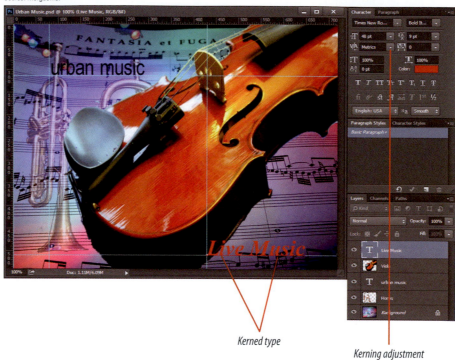 **list arrow**, then click **−25**.

6. Click the **Commit any current edits button** 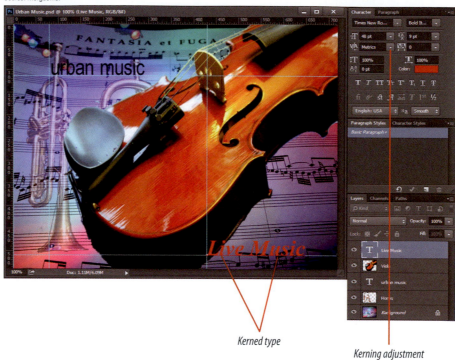 on the options bar.

You modified the kerning between characters by using the Character panel.

Figure 7 *Kerned type*
Source: Morguefile.

Kerned type

Kerning adjustment

Correcting Spelling Errors

Are you concerned that your gorgeous image will be ruined by misspelled words? Photoshop understands your pain and has included a spelling checker to make sure you are never plagued by incorrect spellings. If you want, the spelling checker will check the type on the current layer, or on all the layers in the image. First, make sure the correct dictionary for your language is selected on the Character panel. English: USA is the default, but you can choose another language by clicking the Set the language on selected characters for hyphenation and spelling list arrow at the bottom of the panel. To check spelling, click Edit on the Menu bar, and then click Check Spelling. The spelling checker will automatically stop at each word not already appearing in the dictionary. One or more suggestions might be offered, which you can either accept or reject. (Note: The spelling checker does not correct for incorrect usage, such as their, there, and they're.)

Placing Type in an Image

Figure 8 *Character Style Options dialog box*

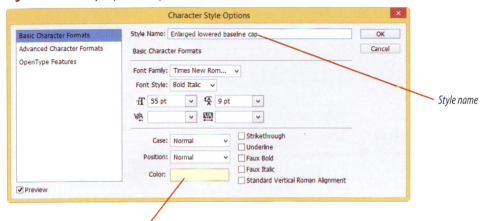

Style name

New font color

Figure 9 *Type with baseline shifted*
Source: Morguefile.

Shift the baseline

1. Use the **Horizontal Type pointer** to select the **"L"** in **"Live"**, then click the **Set the text color button** on the options bar.

2. Click **anywhere in the yellow area** in the center of the viola, such as **470 X/200**, then click **OK**.

3. Verify that the **"L"** in **"Live"** is selected, double-click **48** in the Set the font size text box on the Character panel, type **55**, double-click **0** in the Set the baseline shift text box on the Character panel, type **–5**, then click the **Commit any current edits button** on the options bar.

4. Select the **"L"** in **"Live"**, click the **Character Styles tab**, then click the **Create new Character Style button** on the Character Styles panel.

5. Double-click the name **Character Style 1** in the Character Styles panel, type **Enlarged lowered baseline cap** in the Style Name text box in the Character Style Options dialog box, as shown in Figure 8, then click **OK**.

TIP The application of a character style requires that you override the existing paragraph style by clicking the Clear Override button.

6. Select the **"M"** in **"Music"** with the **Horizontal Type pointer**, click **Enlarged lowered baseline cap** in the Character Styles panel, click **Clear Override** on the Character Styles panel, then click on the options bar.
   The "M" is *painted* with the same characteristics you created in the "L".

7. Save your work, compare your screen to Figure 9.

You changed the type color, adjusted the baseline of the first character in a word to make the first character stand out, created a character style, then applied the style to another character.

Use the
DROP SHADOW STYLE

What You'll Do

Source: Morguefile.

 In this lesson, you'll apply the drop shadow style to a type layer, and then modify drop shadow settings.

Adding Effects to Type

Layer styles (effects which can be applied to a type or image layer) can greatly enhance the appearance of type and improve its effectiveness. A type layer is indicated by the appearance of the T icon in the layer's thumbnail box on the Layers panel. When a layer style is applied to any layer, the Indicates layer effects icon (fx) appears in that layer when it is active. The Layers panel is a great source of information. You can see which effects have been applied to a layer by clicking the arrow to the right of the Indicates layer effects icon on the Layers panel whether the layer is active or inactive. Figure 10 shows a type layer that has a layer style applied to it. Layer styles are linked to the contents of a layer, which means that if a type layer is moved or modified, the layer's style will still be applied to the type.

Figure 10 *Effect applied to a type layer*

Layer styles applied

Indicates effect(s) applied in layer

Placing Type in an Image

Applying a Style

You can apply a style, such as a drop shadow, to the active layer, by clicking Layer on the Menu bar, pointing to Layer Style, and then clicking a style. The settings in the Layer Style dialog box are "sticky," meaning that they display the settings that you last used. An alternative method to using the Menu bar is to select the layer on the Layers panel that you want to apply the style to, click the Add a layer style button, and then click a style. Regardless of which method you use, the Layer Style dialog box opens. You use this dialog box to add all kinds of effects to type. Depending on which style you've chosen, the Layer Style dialog box displays options appropriate to that style.

Using the Drop Shadow

One method of placing emphasis on type is to add a drop shadow to it. A **drop shadow** creates an illusion that another colored layer of identical text is behind the selected type. The drop shadow default color is black, but it can be changed to another color using the Color Picker dialog box, or any of the other methods for changing color.

Controlling a Drop Shadow

You can control many aspects of a drop shadow's appearance, including its angle, its distance behind the type, the amount of blur it contains, and its opacity. The **angle** indicates the direction of the light source and determines where the shadow falls relative to the text, and the **distance** determines how far the shadow falls from the text. The **spread** determines the width of the shadow text, and the **size** determines the clarity of the shadow. Figure 11 shows samples of two different drop shadow effects. The first line of type uses the default background color (black), has an angle of 160 degrees, a distance of 10 pixels, a spread of 0%, and a size of five pixels. The second line of type uses a purple background color, has an angle of 120 degrees, a distance of 20 pixels, a spread of 10%, and a size of five pixels. As you modify the drop shadow, the preview window displays the changes.

Figure 11 *Sample drop shadows*

Add a drop shadow

1. Click the **layer thumbnail** on the urban music type layer.

2. Double-click **48** in the Set the font size text box in the Character panel, type **55**, then press [**Enter**] (Win) or [**return**] (Mac).

3. Click the **Add a layer style button** _fx_ on the Layers panel.

4. Click **Drop Shadow**.

5. Compare your Layer Style dialog box to Figure 12, and _do not close_ the dialog box. (The settings are Blend Mode = Multiply, Opacity = 75, Angle = 30, Distance = 5, Spread = 0, Size = 5.)

   The default drop shadow settings are applied to the type. Table 2 describes the drop shadow settings.

TIP You can also open the Layer Style dialog box by double-clicking a layer on the Layers panel.

You created a drop shadow by using the Add a layer style button on the Layers panel and the Layer Style dialog box.

Figure 12 _Drop shadow settings_
Source: Morguefile.

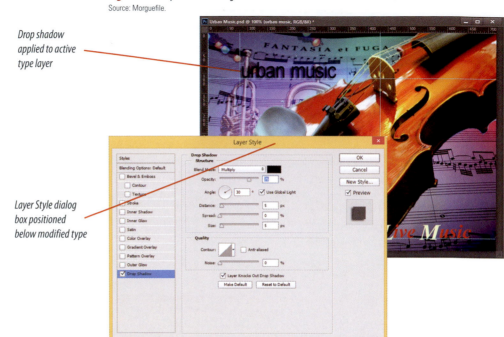

Drop shadow applied to active type layer

Layer Style dialog box positioned below modified type

TABLE 2: DROP SHADOW SETTINGS		
Setting	**Scale**	**Explanation**
Opacity	0–100%	Controls the opacity of the shadow. At 0%, the shadow is invisible.
Angle	0–360 degrees	At 0 degrees, the shadow appears on the baseline of the original text. At 90 degrees, the shadow appears directly below the original text.
Distance	0–30,000 pixels	A larger pixel size increases the distance from which the shadow text falls relative to the original text.
Spread	0–100%	A larger percentage increases the width of the shadow text.
Size	0–250 pixels	A larger pixel size increases the blur of the shadow text.

© 2015 Cengage Learning®

Figure 13 *Layer Style dialog box*

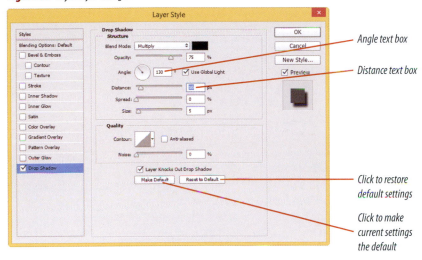

Angle text box

Distance text box

Click to restore
default settings

Click to make
current settings
the default

Figure 14 *Drop shadow added to type layer*
Source: Morguefile.

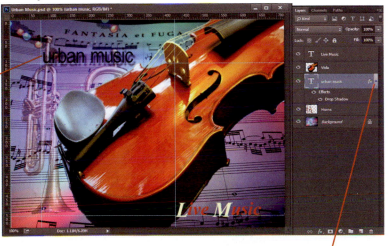

Drop shadow appears
behind text

Collapses effect(s)
applied to layer

Modify drop shadow settings

1. Double-click the **number in the Angle text box**, then type **130**.

Each style in the Layer Style dialog box shows different options in the center section. These options are displayed as you select each style from the Styles pane on the left.

TIP You can also set the angle by dragging the dial slider.

2. Double-click the **number in the Distance text box**, then type **10**. See Figure 13.

TIP You can create your own layer style in the Layer Style dialog box, by choosing your style options, clicking New Style, typing a new name or accepting the default, then clicking OK. Click Styles (at the top of the left pane), and the new style appears as a preset in the Styles list of the Layer Style dialog box. You can create a new style, rename, or delete a style from the list of presets by right-clicking the preset you want to change.

3. Click **OK**, then compare your screen to Figure 14.

4. Click the **Reveals layers effects in the panel arrow** , located to the right of the Indicates layer effects icon on the urban music layer, to collapse the list of layer styles.

5. Save your work.

You used the Layer Style dialog box to modify the settings for the drop shadow.

Apply Anti-Aliasing
TO TYPE

What You'll Do

Source: Morguefile.

 In this lesson, you'll view the effects of the anti-aliasing feature, and then use the History panel to return the type to its original state.

Eliminating the "Jaggies"

In the good old days of dot-matrix printers, jagged edges were obvious in many print ads. You can still see these jagged edges in designs produced on less sophisticated printers. To prevent the jagged edges (sometimes called "jaggies") that often accompany bitmap type, Photoshop offers an anti-aliasing feature. **Anti-aliasing** partially fills in pixel edges with additional colors, resulting in smooth-edge type and an increased number of colors in the image. Anti-aliasing is useful for improving the display of large type in print media; however, this can increase the file size.

Knowing When to Apply Anti-Aliasing

As a rule, type that has a point size greater than 12 should have some anti-aliasing method applied. Sometimes, smaller type sizes can become blurry or muddy when anti-aliasing is used. As part of the process, anti-aliasing adds intermediate colors to your image in an effort to reduce the jagged edges. As a designer, you need to weigh these three factors (type size, file size, and image quality) when determining if you should apply anti-aliasing.

DESIGN TIP

Using Type on the Web

While any typeface you use affects your reader, your choice of type has a larger impact on the web because it is more interactive than the print media. Since the goal of a website is to make your reader linger as long as possible, do you really want to offend or annoy that person with an ugly typeface? Of course not. So, you want to make sure that the typeface is not only appropriate, but can be seen as you intended.

In many cases, a typeface can only be seen on a web page if that font is installed on the reader's computer. Web-safe typefaces (which most computers can display with accuracy) are Times New Roman, Arial, Arial Black, or Helvetica (Mac), Lucida Console, Lucida Sans Unicode, Palatino Linotype, Book Antiqua, Verdana, and Comic Sans. There are other typefaces that can be downloaded from a variety of websites for free, such as Georgia and Trebuchet.

Understanding Anti-Aliasing

Anti-aliasing improves the display of type against the background. You can use five anti-aliasing methods: None, Sharp, Crisp, Strong, and Smooth. An example of each method is shown in Figure 15. The **None** setting applies no anti-aliasing, and can result in type that has jagged edges. The **Sharp** setting displays type with the best possible resolution. The **Crisp** setting gives type more definition and makes type appear sharper. The **Strong** setting makes type appear heavier, much like the bold attribute. The **Smooth** setting gives type more rounded edges.

Figure 15 *Anti-aliasing effects*

Anti-aliasing method: None

Anti-aliasing method: Sharp

Anti-aliasing method: Crisp

Anti-aliasing method: Strong

Anti-aliasing method: Smooth

Apply anti-aliasing

1. Double-click the **layer thumbnail** on the urban music layer to select the text, and verify that the Set the text color box displays yellow.

2. Click the **Set the anti-aliasing method list arrow**  on the options bar.

   TIP You've probably noticed that some items, such as the Set the anti-aliasing method list arrow, the Set the text color button, and the Set the font size list arrow are duplicated on the options bar and the Character panel. So which should you use? Whichever one you feel most comfortable using. These tasks are performed identically regardless of the feature's origin.

3. Click **Crisp**.

4. Click the **Commit any current edits button** on the options bar, then compare your work to Figure 16.

   You applied the Crisp anti-aliasing setting to see how the setting affected the appearance of type.

Figure 16 *Effect of Crisp anti-aliasing*
Source: Morguefile.

Type appearance altered

Different Strokes for Different Folks

You're probably already aware that you can use multiple methods to achieve the same goals in Photoshop. For instance, if you want to see the Type options bar so you can edit a type layer, you can either double-click a type layer thumbnail or select the type layer and then click the Horizontal Type tool. The method you use determines what you'll see in the History panel.

Figure 17 *Deleting a state from the History panel*

Dragging state to Delete current state button

Undo anti-aliasing

1. Click **Legacy** in the workspace switcher.

   The History panel is now visible.

   TIP You can also display the History panel by clicking the History icon on the dock (if it's displayed). Once displayed, you can collapse the panel by clicking the Panel options button, then clicking Close.

2. Click the **Edit Type Layer state** listed at the bottom of the History panel, then drag it to the **Delete current state button**, as shown in Figure 17.

   Various methods of undoing actions are reviewed in Table 3.

   TIP Use the Undo command to undo the last edit, while using the Step Backward command lets you undo the last 20 edits you've done, one at a time. The Step Backward command is found on the Edit menu.

3. Return the workspace to the **Typography workspace**.

4. Save your work.

You changed the workspace to complete a specific task, deleted a state in the History panel to return the type to its original appearance, then changed the workspace again. The History panel offers an easy way of undoing previous steps.

TABLE 3: UNDOING ACTIONS		
Method	**Description**	**Shortcut**
Undo	Edit ➤ Undo	[Ctrl][Z] (Win) ⌘[Z] (Mac)
Step Backward	Click Edit on the Menu bar, then click Step Backward	[Alt][Ctrl][Z] (Win) [option]⌘[Z] (Mac)
History panel	Drag state to the Delete current state button on the History panel, [Ctrl]-click or right-click state, then click [Delete], or click the Delete current state button on the History panel	[Alt] 🗑 (Win) [option] 🗑 (Mac)

© 2015 Cengage Learning®

Modify Type with Bevel and Emboss
AND EXTRUDE TO 3D

What You'll Do

Source: Morguefile.

In this lesson, you'll apply the Bevel and Emboss style, modify the Bevel and Emboss settings, and then apply 3D Extrusion to a type layer.

Using the Bevel and Emboss Style

You use the Bevel and Emboss style to add combinations of shadows and highlights to a layer and make type appear to have dimension and shine. You can use the Layer menu or the Layers panel to apply the Bevel and Emboss style to the active layer. Like all Layer styles, the Bevel and Emboss style is linked to the type layer to which it is applied.

Understanding Bevel and Emboss Settings

You can use two categories of Bevel and Emboss settings: structure and shading. **Structure** determines the size and physical properties of the object, and **shading** determines the lighting effects. The shading used in the Bevel and Emboss style determines how and where light is projected on the type. You can control a variety of settings, including the angle, altitude, and gloss contour, to create a unique appearance. The **angle** setting indicates the direction of the light source and determines where the shadow falls relative to the text, and the **altitude** setting affects the amount of visible dimension. For example, an altitude of 0 degrees looks flat, while a setting of 90 degrees has a more three-dimensional appearance. The **gloss contour** setting determines the pattern with which light is reflected, and the **highlight mode** and **shadow mode** settings determine how pigments are combined. When the Use Global Light check box is selected, *all the type* in the image will be affected by your changes.

Filling Type with Imagery

You can use the imagery from a layer in one file as the fill pattern for another image's type layer. To create this effect, open a multilayer file that contains the imagery you want to use (the source), and then open the file that contains the type you want to fill (the target). In the source file, activate the layer containing the imagery you want to use, use the Select menu to select all, and then use the Edit menu to copy the selection. In the target file, press [Ctrl] (Win) or ⌘ (Mac) while clicking the layer thumbnail to which the imagery will be applied, click Edit on the Menu bar, point to Paste Special, and then click Paste Into. The imagery will appear within the type.

Learning About 3D Extrusion

3D Extrusion, formally called Repoussé (pronounced re-poo-say) is a tool for turning a 2-dimensional object (like type) into a 3-dimensional object. Extrusion tools allow you to rotate, roll, pan, slide, and scale an object, and this feature has a number of presets that help you learn its many uses. You can apply Extrusion to a type layer or image layer using the Type command on the Menu bar or the 3D panel or the 3D workspace. (Applying Extrusion to a type layer automatically rasterizes the type, a process that is covered in more detail later in this chapter.) With a existing type layer active and the 3D workspace open, click the 3D Extrusion option button (under Create New 3D Object) in the 3D panel, then click the Create button.

Each 3D extruded object displays on the image (sometimes on a grid or mesh), shown in Figure 18. A secondary window can be toggled, showing either the text in the document or by itself. Objects within the image are clickable, and when clicked, reveal **widgets** (tools that can be used to change the 3D object). Widgets exist for light, movement, and camera, to name a few. As you click on various elements within the image, take note that the Properties panel changes to reflect the active element.

Once you are finished adjusting the 3D settings, the image must be **rendered** for those settings to be applied to the image. The rendering process may take several minutes to complete: the amount of time remaining displays in the status bar at the bottom of the document

window and a blue dotted line displays on the image indicating the rendering status.

QUICK **TIP**

Any formatting such as bold or italics, effects like a drop shadow or bevel, or warping can be applied to a 3D extrusion.

Elements with the image can be shown/hidden using the Show command on the View menu.

QUICK **TIP**

As you might imagine, 3D features are extremely memory- and hardware-intensive. 3D will not work If your computer does not have a GPU card, with a minimum of 512MB of Video RAM (VRAM). Please consult *www.adobe.com* for a list of supported video cards and requirements.

Figure 18 *3D Extrusion object*

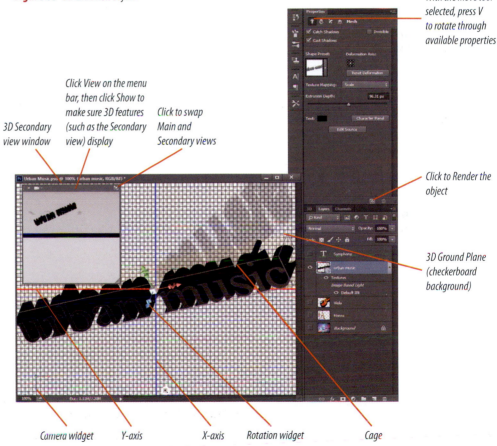

With the Move tool selected, press V to rotate through available properties

Click View on the menu bar, then click Show to make sure 3D features (such as the Secondary view) display

3D Secondary view window

Click to swap Main and Secondary views

Click to Render the object

3D Ground Plane (checkerboard background)

Camera widget   Y-axis   X-axis   Rotation widget   Cage

Add the Bevel and Emboss style with the Layer menu

1. Click the **Live Music layer** and verify that the Horizontal Type tool is active.

2. Click the **Set the text color button** ■ on the options bar, click the **pink area below the left horn** (at approximately **80 X/510 Y**), then click **OK**.

3. Click **Layer** on the Menu bar, point to **Layer Style**, click **Bevel & Emboss**.

4. Review the Layer Style dialog box shown in Figure 19, copying the settings shown to your dialog box, then move the Layer Style dialog box so that you can see the "Live Music" type, if necessary.

You applied the Bevel and Emboss style by using the Layer menu. This gave the text a three-dimensional look.

Figure 19 *Layer Style dialog box*

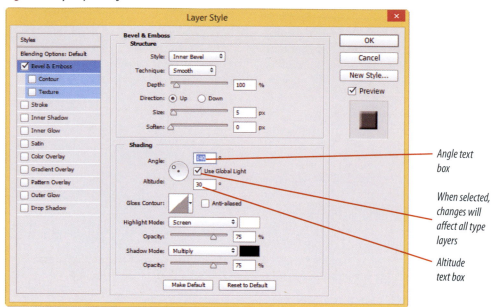

Angle text box

When selected, changes will affect all type layers

Altitude text box

Understanding GPU and OpenGL

Photoshop CC uses the GPU (graphics processing unit) rather than the main processor within your computer to speed screen redraw. (You can tell if your computer has OpenGL (Open Graphics Library) enabled by opening Preferences in Photoshop, clicking Performance, and then looking at the Graphics Processor Settings. If Use Graphics Processor is dimmed, your computer **does not** have OpenGL enabled or your graphics board may not be supported.) Once the GPU technology is detected, Photoshop automatically turns on the OpenGL technology which communicates with your display driver. OpenGL is necessary in Photoshop to operate many features, including 3D Extrusion, brush dynamic resize and hardness control, 3D overlays, 3D Acceleration, 3D Axis, Accelerated 3D Interaction via Direct to Screen, 3D Ground Plane, and 3D Selections via a Hi-light Overlay. In short, *no OpenGL means no 3D.*

Figure 20 *3D grid over type layer*
Source: Morguefile.

Figure 21 *3D Extrusion applied to type*
Source: Morguefile.

3D extrusion applied to layer

Thumbnail indicates a 3D layer

Modify Bevel and Emboss settings and apply 3D Extrusion

1. Double-click the **number in the Angle text box**, then type **165**.

   You can use the Layer Style dialog box to change the structure of the bevel by adjusting style, technique, depth, direction, size, and soften settings.

2. Double-click the **Altitude text box**, then type **20**.

3. Click **OK**, then note the expanded Live Music layer in the Layers panel.

4. Click the **urban music layer** on the Layers panel.

   If you do not have OpenGL enabled on your computer, proceed to step 9.

5. Click **Type** on the Menu bar, click **Extrude to 3D**, click **Yes** to switch to the 3D workspace, drag the Secondary view out of the way if it obscures the type, then compare your screen to Figure 20.

6. If necessary, click the **Drag the 3D Object** 🔁 on the options bar, position the pointer ✛ **between the "n" and "m"**, then drag the type horizontally **to the right** until the "m" is at approximately **250X**.

7. Click the **Render button** 🔲 at the bottom of the Properties panel.

8. Click **View** on the Menu bar, point to **Show**, deselect any 3D options, then display the **Typography workspace**.

9. Save your work, turn off the ruler display, then compare your image to Figure 21.

You modified the default settings for the Bevel and Emboss style, then applied 3D Extrusion to a layer. Experimenting with different settings is crucial to achieve the effect you want.

Apply Special Effects to Type
USING FILTERS

What You'll Do

In this lesson, you'll rasterize a type layer, and then apply a filter to it to change its appearance.

Understanding Filters

Like an image layer, a type layer can have one or more filters applied to it to achieve special effects and make your text look unique, as shown in Figure 22. Some filters are available in the Filter Gallery while others have dialog boxes with preview windows that let you see the results of the particular filter before it is applied to the layer. Other filters must be applied to the layer before you can see the results. Before a filter can be applied to a type layer, the type layer must first be **rasterized**, or converted to an image layer. After it is rasterized, the type characters *can no longer be edited* because it is composed of pixels, just like artwork. When a type layer is rasterized, the T icon in the layer thumbnail becomes an image thumbnail while the Effects icons remain. Notice that none of the original type layers on the Layers panel in Figure 22 display the T icon in the layer thumbnail.

> **QUICK TIP**
>
> Because you cannot edit type after it has been rasterized, you should save your original type by making a copy of the layer *before* you rasterize it, and then hide it from view. This allows you to use the copy if you need to make changes to the type at a later time.

Producing Distortions

Distort filters let you create waves or curves in type. Some of the types of distortions you can produce include Pinch, Polar Coordinates, Ripple, Shear, Spherize, Twirl, Wave, and Zigzag. These effects are sometimes used as the basis of a corporate logo. The Twirl dialog box, shown in Figure 23, lets you determine the amount of twirl effect you want to apply. By dragging the Angle slider, you control how much twirl effect is added to a layer. Most filter dialog boxes have Zoom in and Zoom out buttons that make it easy to see the effects of the filter.

Using Relief

Many filters let you create the appearance of textures and **relief** (the height of ridges within an object). One of the Stylize filters, Wind, applies lines throughout the type, making it appear shredded. The Wind dialog box, shown in Figure 24, lets you determine the kind of wind and its direction.

Blurring Imagery

The Gaussian Blur filter, one of the Blur filter options, softens the appearance of type by blurring its edge pixels. You can control the amount of blur applied to the type by entering high or low values in the Gaussian Blur dialog box. The higher the blur value, the blurrier the effect.

Figure 22 Sample filters applied to type

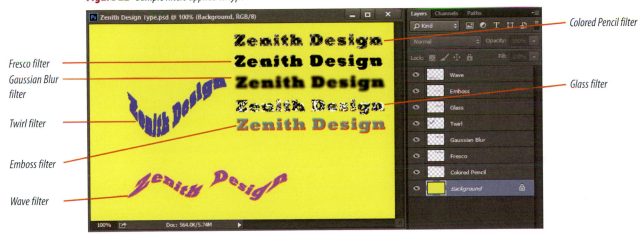

Colored Pencil filter

Fresco filter

Gaussian Blur filter

Twirl filter

Emboss filter

Wave filter

Glass filter

Figure 23 Twirl dialog box

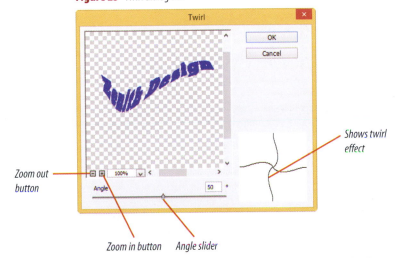

Zoom out button

Shows twirl effect

Zoom in button Angle slider

Figure 24 Wind dialog box

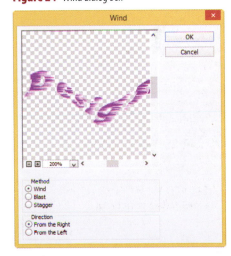

Apply a filter to a type layer

1. Click the **Live Music** layer on the Layers panel.
2. Click **Filter** on the Menu bar, point to **Stylize**, then click **Diffuse**.
3. Click **OK** to rasterize the type and close the warning box shown in Figure 25.

TIP You can also rasterize a type layer by clicking Layer on the Menu bar, pointing to Rasterize, then clicking Type.

The Diffuse dialog box opens.

You rasterized a type layer in preparation for applying a filter.

Figure 25 *Warning box*

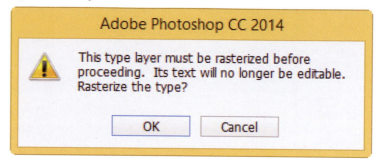

Figure 26 *Type with Diffuse filter*

Source: Morguefile.

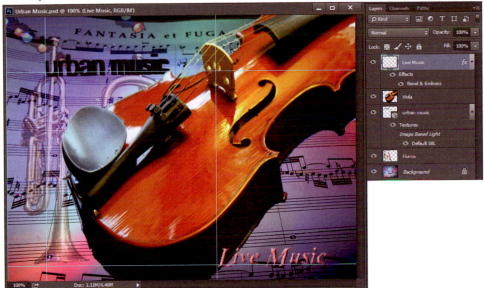

Modify filter settings

1. Drag in the preview window of the dialog box from the bottom to position the type so at least part of the type is visible.
2. Click the **Darken Only** and **Lighten Only option buttons**, notice the difference each makes, then click the **Normal option button**.
3. Click **OK**.
4. Save your work. Compare your modified type to Figure 26.

You modified the Diffuse filter settings to modify the appearance of the layer.

Creating a Neon Glow

Want to create a really cool effect that takes absolutely no time at all, and works on both type and objects? You can create a neon glow that appears to surround an object. You can apply the Neon Glow filter (one of the Artistic filters) to any flattened image. This effect works best by starting with any imagery—either type or objects—that has a solid color background. Flatten the image so there's only a Background layer. Click the Magic Wand tool on the Tools panel, and then click the solid color (in the background). Click Filter on the Menu bar, click Filter Gallery, click Artistic to expand the category, then click Neon Glow. Adjust the glow size, the glow brightness, and color, if you wish, and then click OK. (An example of this technique is used in the Design Project at the end of this chapter.)

Create Text
ON A PATH

What You'll Do

Source: Morguefile.

 In this lesson, you'll create a shape, and then add type to it.

Understanding Text on a Path

Although it is possible to create some cool type effects by adding layer styles such as bevel and emboss and drop shadow, you can also create some awesome warped text. Suppose you want type to conform to a shape, such as an oval, or a free-form outline you've drawn. No problem—just create the shape and add the text!

Creating Text on a Path

You start by creating a shape using one of the Photoshop shape tools on the Tools panel, setting the Pick tool mode to Path on the shape's options bar, and then adding type to that shape. Add type to a shape by clicking the Horizontal Type tool. When the pointer nears the path, you'll see that it changes to the Type on a Path pointer. Click the path when the Type on a Path pointer displays and begin typing. You can change fonts, font sizes, add styles, and any other interesting effects you've learned to apply with type. As you will see, the type is on a path!

QUICK **TIP**
Don't worry when you see the outline of the path on the screen. The path won't print, only the type will.

Warping Type

You can add dimension and style to your type by using the Warp Text feature. After you select the type layer you want to warp, click the Horizontal Type tool on the Tools panel. Click the Create warped text button on the options bar to open the Warp Text dialog box. If a warning box opens telling you that your request cannot be completed because the type layer uses a faux bold style, click the Character Panel options button, click Faux Bold to deselect it, and then click the Create warped text button again. You can click the Style list arrow to select from 15 available styles. After you select a style, you can modify its appearance by dragging the Bend, Horizontal Distortion, and Vertical Distortion sliders.

Figure 27 *Type on a path*
Source: Morguefile.

*Path does not display
when image is printed*

Create a path and add type

1. Turn on the ruler display, click the **Ellipse tool** on the Tools panel.

2. Click the **Pick tool mode list arrow** on the options bar, then click **Path**.

3. Drag the **Paths pointer** ⊕ to create an elliptical path on the base of the viola from **150 X/350 Y** to **430 X/460 Y**.

4. Click the **Horizontal Type tool** T on the Tools panel.

5. Change the font to **Times New Roman**, use the **Bold font style**, set the font size to **48,** then verify that the **Left align text button** is selected, and anti-aliasing is set to **Smooth**.

TIP You can change to any point size by typing the number in the Set the font size text box. You can also resize the circle by clicking Edit on the Menu bar, pointing to Transform Path, clicking Scale, then dragging the circle to make it larger.

6. Click the **Horizontal Type pointer** at approximately **200** on the ellipse.

7. Using the Color Picker, change the font color by sampling the blue at approximately **150 X/150 Y**, close the Color Picker, type **Symphony,** then commit any edits.

8. Drag the **Symphony layer** above the Viola layer, hide the rulers and guides, and return to the **Essentials workspace**. Compare your image to Figure 27.

9. Save your work, close the Urban Music.psd file, and exit Photoshop.

You created a path using a shape tool, then added type to it.

SKILLS REFERENCE

POWER USER SHORTCUTS

To do this:	Use this method:	To do this:	Use this method:
Apply anti-alias method	(aa icon)	Horizontal Type tool	(T icon) or **T**
Apply Bevel and Emboss	(fx icon), Bevel & Emboss style	Kern characters	(VA icon)
Apply blur filter to type	Filter ➤ Blur ➤ Gaussian Blur	Move tool	(move icon) or **V**
Apply Drop Shadow	(fx icon), Drop Shadow style	Save image changes	[Ctrl][S] (Win) or ⌘ [S] (Mac)
Cancel any current edits	(no icon)	See type effects (to collapse)	(down icon)
Change font family	Myriad Pro	See type effects (to expand)	(up icon)
Change font size	(T icon)	Select all text in layer	Double-click type layer icon
Change type color	(black box)	Shift baseline of type	(Aa icon)
Commit current edits	(check icon)	Step Backward	[Alt][Ctrl][Z] (Win) or [option] ⌘ [Z] (Mac)
Cycle through 3D properties	Select Move tool, press V	Toggles Character and Paragraph panels from the options bar	(panel icon)
Display/hide rulers	[Ctrl][R] (Win) or ⌘ [R] (Mac)	Undo	[Ctll][Z] (Win) or ⌘ [Z] (Mac)
Erase a History state	Select state, drag to (trash icon)	Warp type	(T warp icon)

Key: Menu items are indicated by ➤ between the menu name and its command. Blue bold letters are shortcuts for selecting tools on the Tools panel.

© 2015 Cengage Learning®

Learn about type and how it is created.

1. Open PS 6-2.psd from the drive and folder where you store your Data Files, then save it as **ZD-Logo**.
2. Display the rulers with pixels, then change to the Typography workspace.
3. Use the Horizontal Type tool to create a type layer that starts at 45 X/95 Y.
4. Use a black 35 pt Lucida Sans Regular font or substitute another font.
5. Type **Zenith**, deselect the text, then reposition the type if necessary.
6. Use the Horizontal Type tool and a 16 pt type size to create a type layer at 70 X/180 Y, then type **Always the best**.
7. Save your work.

Change spacing and adjust baseline shift.

1. Use the Horizontal Type tool to create a new type layer at 210 X/95 Y.
2. Use a 35 pt Myriad Pro Regular font.
3. Type **Design**.
4. Select the Design type.
5. Change the type color to the color used in the lower-left of the background.
6. Change the type size of the D to 50 pt.
7. Adjust the baseline shift of the D to −5.
8. Select the Z, change the type size to 50 pt and the baseline shift to -5.
9. Save your work.

Use the Drop Shadow style.

1. Activate the Zenith type layer.
2. Apply the Drop Shadow style.

3. In the Layer Style dialog box, set the angle to 150°, then close the Layer Style dialog box.
4. Save your work.

Apply anti-aliasing to type.

1. Activate the Zenith type layer if necessary.
2. Change the Anti-Alias method to Smooth (if necessary).
3. Save your work.

Modify type with Bevel and Emboss and Extrude to 3D.

1. Activate the Design type layer.
2. Apply the Bevel and Emboss style.
3. In the Layer Style dialog box, set the style to Inner Bevel.
4. Set the angle to 150° and the altitude to 30°.
5. Close the Layer Style dialog box and apply the style.
6. Activate the Zenith type layer.
7. Apply the Bevel and Emboss style.
8. Set the style to Inner Bevel.
9. Verify that the angle is set to 150° and the altitude is set to 30°.

10. Close the Layer Style dialog box and apply the style.
11. Save your work.

Apply special effects to type using filters.

1. Apply a 1.0 pixel Gaussian Blur filter to the "Always the best" layer.
2. Save your work.

Create text on a path.

1. Use the Ellipse tool with Path selected to draw an ellipse from approximately 200 X/120 Y to 370 X/185 Y.
2. Click the path with the Horizontal Type tool at 250 X/120 Y.
3. Type **Since 1972** using the orange color in the lower-left triangle of the file, in a 16 pt Arial Regular font.
4. Change the anti-aliasing method to Crisp.
5. Change the opacity of the type (using the Opacity slider in the Layers panel) on the path to 45%.
6. Turn off the ruler display.
7. Save your work, then compare your image to Figure 28.

Figure 28 *Completed Skills Review*

A local flower shop, Nature's Beauty, asks you to design its color advertisement for website that features members of a group called *Florists United*. You have already started on the image, and need to add some type.

1. Open PS 6-3.psd, then save it as **Nature's Beauty Web Promo**.

2. Using the Horizontal Type tool, click at the top of the image, then type **Nature's Beauty** using a black 60 pt Times New Roman Regular font.

3. Create a catchy phrase of your choice, using a 24 pt Verdana Regular font.

4. Apply a drop shadow style to the name of the flower shop using the following settings: Multiply blend mode, 75% Opacity, 30° Angle, 5 pixel distance, 2% spread, and 5 pixel size.

5. Apply a Bevel and Emboss style to the catch phrase using the following settings: Emboss style, Chisel Soft technique, 100% depth, Up direction, 15 pixel size, 0 pixel soften, 30° angle, 25° altitude, and using global light.

6. If your computer has OpenGL enabled, add a 3D Extrusion effect to the Nature's Beauty type created in step 2.

7. Compare your image to the sample in Figure 29.

8. Save your work.

Figure 29 *Sample Project Builder 1*
Source: Morguefile.

You are a junior art director for an advertising agency. You have been working on a print ad that promotes milk and milk products. You have started the project, but still have a few details to finish up before it is complete.

1. Open PS 6-4.psd, then save it as **Milk Promotion**.
2. Create a shape using any shape tool, then use the shape as a text path and type a snappy phrase of your choosing on the shape.
3. Use a 24 pt Arial Regular font in the style and color of your choice for the catch phrase type layer. (If necessary, substitute another font.)
4. Create a Bevel and Emboss style on the type layer, setting the angle to 100° and the altitude to 30°.
5. Compare your image to the sample in Figure 30.
6. Save your work.

Figure 30 *Sample Project Builder 2*
Source: Morguefile.

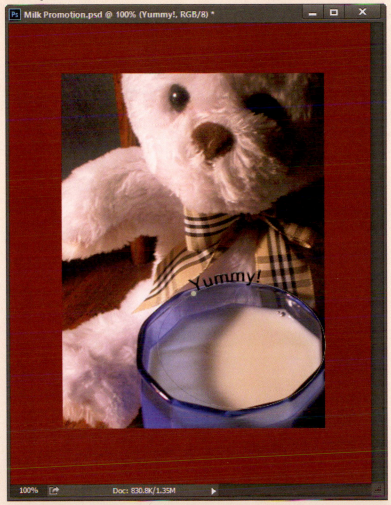

You are a freelance designer. A local clothing store, Attitude, is expanding and has hired you to work on a print advertisement. You have already created the file, and inserted the necessary type layers. Before you proceed, you decide to explore the Internet to find information on using type to create an effective design.

1. Connect to the Internet and use your browser to find information about typography. (Make a record of the site you found so you can use it for future reference, if necessary.)
2. Find information about using type as an effective design element.
3. Open PS 6-5.psd, update the layers (if necessary), then save the file as **Attitude**.
4. Modify the existing type by changing fonts, font colors, and font sizes.
5. Edit the type, if necessary, to make it shorter and clearer.
6. Rearrange the position of the type to create an effective design.
7. Add a Bevel and Emboss style using your choice of settings, then compare your image to the sample in Figure 31.
8. Save your work.

Figure 31 *Sample Design Project*
© Photodisc/Getty Images.

You have been hired by your community to create an advertising campaign that promotes tourism on its website. Decide what aspect of the community you want to emphasize. Locate appropriate imagery (already existing on your hard drive, on the web, your own creation, or using a scanner), and then add type to create a meaningful Photoshop image.

1. Create an image with any dimensions you choose.
2. Save this file as **Community Promotion**.
3. Add at least two layers of type in the image, using multiple font sizes. (Use any fonts available on your computer. You can use multiple fonts if you want.)
4. Add a Bevel and Emboss style to at least one type layer and add a Drop Shadow style to at least one layer. (*Hint*: You can add both effects to the same layer.)
5. Position type layers to create an effective design.
6. Compare your image to the sample in Figure 32.
7. Save your work.

Figure 32 *Sample Portfolio Project*
Source: Morguefile.

CHAPTER 1

GETTING TO KNOW
ILLUSTRATOR

1. Explore the Illustrator workspace

2. View and modify artboard elements

3. Work with objects and smart guides

4. Create basic shapes

5. Apply fill and stroke colors to objects

6. Select, move, and align objects

7. Transform objects

8. Make direct selections

9. Work with multiple artboards

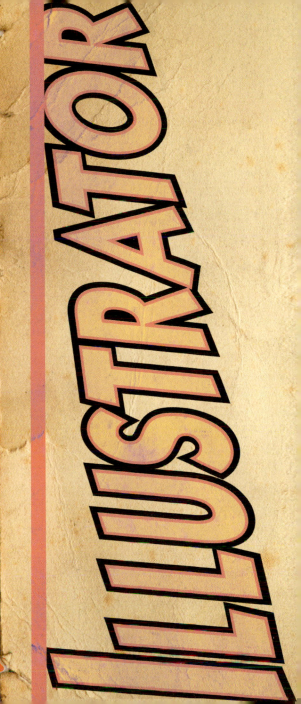

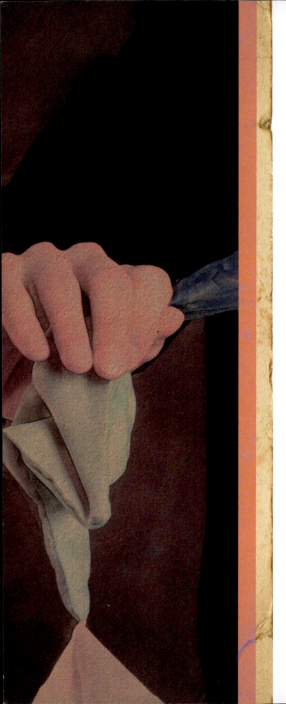

CHAPTER 1

GETTING TO
KNOW ILLUSTRATOR

Getting to Know Illustrator

Adobe Illustrator CC is a professional illustration software application created by Adobe Systems Incorporated. If this name is familiar to you, it's because Adobe is a leading producer of graphics software for the personal computer. Along with Illustrator, Adobe produces an entire suite of applications, including InDesign, Acrobat, Flash, Dreamweaver, and, of course, the revolutionary and award-winning Photoshop.

With Illustrator, you can create everything from simple graphics, icons, and text to complex and multilayered illustrations, all of which can be used within a page layout, in a multimedia presentation, or on the web.

Adobe Illustrator offers dozens of essential tools. Using them in combination with various menu commands, you have the potential to create any illustration that your imagination can dream up. With experience, you will find that your ability to create complex graphics rests on your ability to master simple, basic operations.

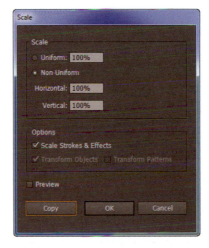

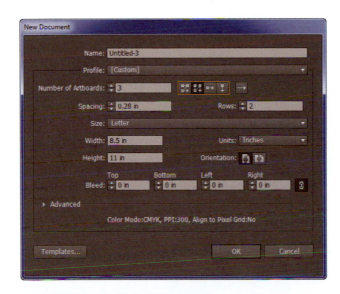

Explore the ILLUSTRATOR WORKSPACE

What You'll Do

In this lesson, you will start Adobe Illustrator and explore the workspace.

Looking at the Illustrator Workspace

The arrangement of windows and panels that you see on your monitor is called the **workspace**. The Illustrator workspace features the following areas: artboard, pasteboard, Menu bar, Control panel, Tools panel, and a stack of collapsed panels along the right side of the document window. Figure 1 shows the default workspace, which is called Essentials.

Illustrator offers a number of pre-defined workspaces that are customized for different types of tasks. Each workspace is designed so that panels with similar functions are grouped together. For example, the Typography workspace shows the many type- and typography-based panels that are useful for working with type. You can switch from one workspace to another by clicking Window

Figure 1 *Essentials workspace*

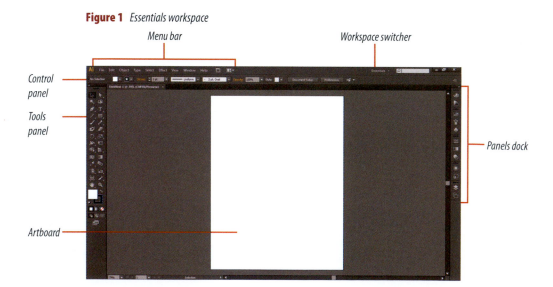

Menu bar

Workspace switcher

Control panel

Tools panel

Panels dock

Artboard

on the Menu bar, pointing to Workspace, and then choosing a workspace. Or you can use the workspace switcher on the Menu bar.

You can customize the workspace, including predefined workspaces, to suit your working preferences. For example, you can open and close whatever panels you want and change the location of any panels. You can save a customized workspace by clicking Window on the Menu bar, pointing to Workspace, then clicking New Workspace. Assign a descriptive name to your workspace, then click OK. With this option checked, the workspace will be saved with all panels in their current positions. Once you've saved a workspace, you load it by clicking Window on the Menu bar, then pointing to Workspace. You'll see your custom-named workspace in the list of workspaces.

Exploring the Tools Panel

As its name implies, the Tools panel houses all the tools that you will work with in Illustrator. The first thing that you should note about the Tools panel is that not all tools are visible; many are hidden. Look closely and you will see that some tools have small white triangles beside them. These triangles indicate that other tools are hidden behind them. To access hidden tools, point to the visible tool on the Tools panel, then press and hold the mouse button; this will reveal a menu of hidden tools. The small white square to the left of a tool name in the submenu indicates which tool is currently visible on the Tools panel, as shown in Figure 2.

When you expose hidden tools, you can click the small triangle to the right of the menu and create a separate panel for those tools, as shown in Figure 3.

Figure 2 *Viewing hidden tools*

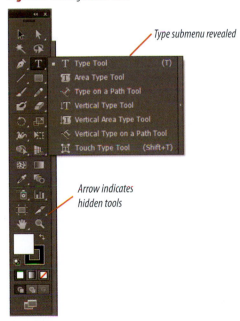

Type submenu revealed

Arrow indicates hidden tools

Figure 3 *"Detaching" hidden tools*

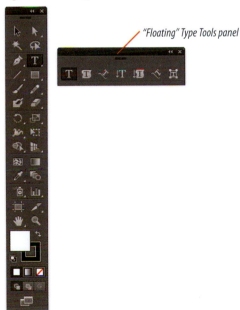

"Floating" Type Tools panel

As shown in Figure 4, you can view the Tools panel as a single column or a double column of tools. Simply click the Collapse/Expand panels button at the top of the Tools panel to toggle between the two setups.

Horizontal lines divide the Tools panel into ten sections. Figure 5 identifies a number of essential tools that you'll use all the time when you're working with Illustrator. To choose a tool, simply click it. You can also press a shortcut key to access a tool. For example, pressing [p] selects the Pen tool.

To learn the shortcut key for each tool, point to a tool until a tool tip appears with the tool's name and its shortcut key in parentheses.

Figure 4 *Two setups for the Tools panel*

Figure 5 *Essential tools*

Selection tool

Direct Selection tool

Type tool

Rectangle tool

Rotate tool

Scale tool

Free Transform tool

Eyedropper tool

Artboard tool

Zoom tool

Fill color

Stroke color

Drawing modes

Figure 6 shows the tool tip for the Type tool. Tool tips appear when they are activated in the General preferences dialog box, which you can access by clicking Edit (Win) or Illustrator (Mac) on the Menu bar, pointing to Preferences, and then clicking General.

QUICK TIP

Shortcut keys are not case-sensitive. In other words, if you press [p], you'll switch to the Pen tool regardless of whether or not Caps Lock is on.

Figure 6 *Activated tool tips preference*

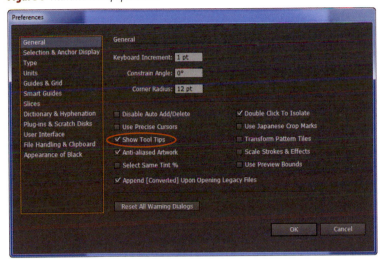

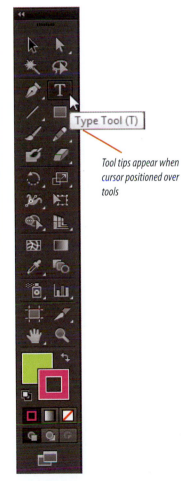

Tool tips appear when cursor positioned over tools

Working with Panels

Working in Illustrator is not only about using tools; many essential Illustrator functions are grouped into panels. For example, the Paragraph panel contains paragraph editing functions, such as text alignment and paragraph indents. The Swatches panel, shown in Figure 7, offers colors to sample as fills and strokes for objects.

You can access all panels from the Window menu. Some panels are placed within categories on the Window menu. For example, all of the text-related panels, such as the Character panel and the Paragraph panel, are listed in the Type category.

When you choose a panel from the Window menu, the panel is displayed in its expanded view. You can close any panel by clicking the Close button in the top-right corner of the panel, and you can display panel options by clicking the Panel options button. To reduce the size of a panel, click the Collapse to Icons button, which displays a panel only by its name and an icon. These three buttons are identified in Figure 8.

Figure 7 *Swatches panel*

Figure 8 *Three interactive panel buttons*

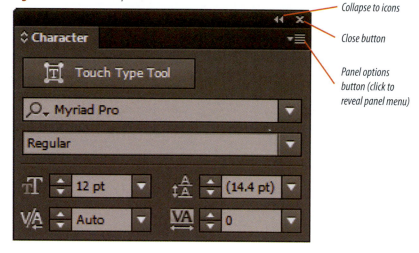

Collapse to icons

Close button

Panel options button (click to reveal panel menu)

To better manage available workspace, you can group panels. You can also minimize, or "collapse," panels to make them smaller but still available in the workspace.

Figure 9 shows two panels grouped together. The Paragraph panel is the active panel—it is in front of the Character panel in the group

and available for use. To activate the Character panel, you would simply click its tab.

Figure 10 shows the entire dock of panels minimized on the right side of the document window. Clicking a panel thumbnail, or icon, opens the panel as well as any other panels

with which it is grouped. Click the thumbnail in the stack again, and it will collapse the panel you just expanded.

Click the Expand panels button at the top of the panels dock to expand all the panels, as shown in Figure 11.

Figure 9 *Two grouped panels*

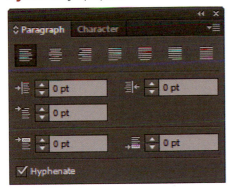

Figure 10 *Dock of panels collapsed*

Figure 11 *Dock of panels expanded*

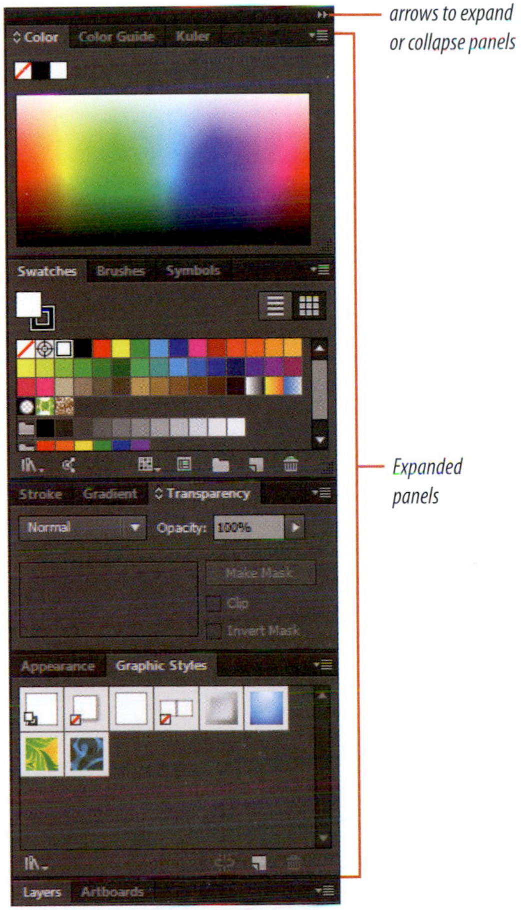

Click double arrows to expand or collapse panels

Panels minimized as icons

Expanded panels

Don't confuse grouping panels with docking panels. Docking panels is a different function. When you dock panels, you connect the bottom edge of one panel to the top edge of another panel, so that both move together. To dock panels, first drag a panel's name tab to the bottom edge of another panel. When the bottom edge of the other panel is highlighted in bright blue, release the mouse button and the two panels will be docked. Figure 12 shows docked panels. To undock a panel, simply drag it away from its group.

Creating Customized Tools Panels

The ability to create alternative, customized Tools panels is a great new feature in Illustrator Creative Cloud. Over the years, as Illustrator has become more complex and able to do more and more things, you might have noticed that the Tools panel has become quite crowded. In Creative Cloud you can create multiple Tools panels specified for different functions. For example, you could customize a Tools panel just for your favorite drawing tools or just for transforming objects. To create additional Tools panels, click the Window menu, point to Tools, then click New Tools Panel. Once you've named

the panel, it appears on the artboard beside the main Tools panel. To add tools to the new Tools panel, simply drag and drop tools from the main Tools panel. Note that all Tools panels you create are listed and accessible on the Window menu.

Figure 12 *Docked panels*

Figure 13 *Document window*

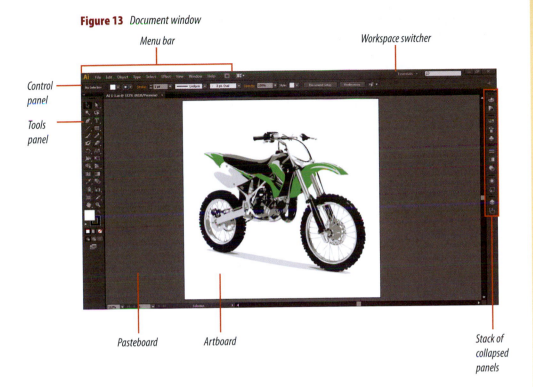

Menu bar

Workspace switcher

Control panel

Tools panel

Pasteboard

Artboard

Stack of collapsed panels

Opening Illustrator Files in Previous Versions

Illustrator is "backwards compatible," meaning that Illustrator CC can open files from previous versions. The reverse, however, isn't true; earlier versions can't open newer versions. For example, Illustrator CS6 cannot open Illustrator CC documents. This can become an issue if you send an Illustrator CC file to another designer, client, or vendor who is using an older version. To accommodate, you can "save down" to a previous version when you save the file. When you name the file and click Save, the Illustrator Options dialog box opens. Click the Version list arrow to choose the version to which you want to save it. Note that any new CC features used in your file may be lost when the file is converted to the older format.

Explore the Tools panel

1. Launch Adobe Illustrator CC.

2. Click **File** on the Menu bar, click **Open**, navigate to the drive and folder where your Chapter 1 Data Files are stored, click **AI 1-1.ai**, then click **Open**.

3. Click **Window** on the Menu bar, point to **Workspace**, then click **Essentials**.

   Compare your window to Figure 13.

   TIP If you are already working in the Essentials workspace, click **Reset Essentials** on the Workspace menu.

4. Click the **double-arrows** on the Tools panel, then click it again to switch between the two setups for the Tools panel.

   All of the figures in this book that show the Tools panel will display the panel in two rows.

5. Point to the **Type tool** [T], then press and hold the mouse button to see the Type on a Path tool.

6. View the hidden tools behind the other tools with small black triangles.

   Your visible tools may differ from the figure.

7. Click **Edit** (Win) or **Illustrator** (Mac) on the Menu bar, point to **Preferences**, click **General**, verify that Show Tool Tips is checked, then click **OK**.

8. Position your mouse pointer over the **Selection tool** [↖], until its tool tip appears.

9. Press the following keys and note which tools are selected with each key: **[a]**, **[p]**, **[v]**, **[t]**, **[i]**, **[h]**, **[z]**.

(continued)

10. Press **[Tab]** to temporarily hide all open panels, then press **[Tab]** again.

    The panels reappear.

You explored different views of the Tools panel, revealed hidden tools, used shortcut keys to access tools quickly, hid the panels, then displayed them again.

Work with panels

1. Click **Swatches** in the stack of collapsed panels to the right of the pasteboard to open the Swatches panel.

    The panel opens, but does not detach from the stack of collapsed panels. The Swatches panel is grouped with the Symbols and Brushes panels in the Essentials workspace.

2. Click the **Collapse panels button** ▸▸ at the top of the panel to minimize the panel, then click **Swatches** to open the panel again.

3. Drag the **Swatches panel name tab** to the left so it is ungrouped from the stack.

4. Click **Color** in the stack of collapsed panels to the right of the pasteboard to open the Color panel.

TIP If you do not see the CMYK sliders on the Color panel, as shown in Figure 14, click the Color Panel options button, then click Show Options.

5. Drag the **Color panel name tab** to the left so it is ungrouped from the stack.

6. Drag the **Color panel name tab** to the blank space next to the **Swatches panel name tab**, then release the mouse button.

(continued)

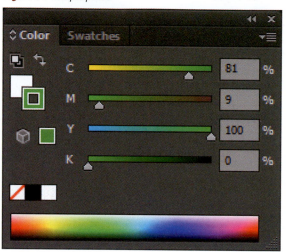

Figure 14 *Grouped panels*

Using the Document Info Panel

The Document Info panel, listed on the Window menu, contains useful information about the document and about objects in the document. Along with general file information such as filename, ruler units and color space, the panel lists specific information like the number and names of graphic styles, custom colors, patterns, gradients, fonts, and placed art. To view information about a selected object, choose Selection Only from the panel menu. Leaving this option deselected lists information about the entire document. To view artboard dimensions, click the Artboard tool, choose Document from the panel menu, and then click to select the artboard you want to view.

Figure 15 *Docked panels*

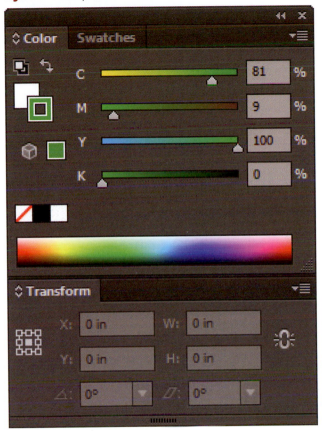

The Color panel is grouped with the Swatches panel, as shown in Figure 14.

7. Click **Window** on the Menu bar, then click **Transform**.

The Transform panel appears expanded on the document.

8. Drag the **Transform panel name tab** to the bottom edge of the Swatches and Color panels group, then, when a blue horizontal line appears, release the mouse button.

The Transform panel is docked, as shown in Figure 15.

9. Click and drag the **dark gray bar** at the top of the panel group, found above the Swatches and Color panel name tabs.

The Transform panel moves with the Swatches and Color panels because it is docked.

10. Click the **Transform panel name tab**, then drag it away from the other two panels.

The Transform panel is undocked.

11. Click **Window** on the Menu bar, point to **Workspace**, then click **Reset Essentials**.

You explored methods for grouping and ungrouping panels, then you docked and undocked a panel.

View and Modify
ARTBOARD ELEMENTS

What You'll Do

© 2015 Cengage Learning® Image courtesy of Chris Botello.

 In this lesson, you will explore various methods for viewing the document and document elements, such as rulers, guides, grids, and selection marks.

Using the Zoom Tool

Imagine creating a layout on a traditional pasteboard—not on your computer. For precise work, you would bring your nose closer to the pasteboard so that you could better see what you were doing. At other times, you would hold the pasteboard away from you at arms' length so that you could get a larger perspective of the artwork. When you're working in Illustrator, the Zoom tool performs these functions for you.

When you click the Zoom tool and move the pointer over the document window, the pointer becomes the Zoom pointer with a plus sign; when you click the document with the Zoom pointer, the document area you clicked is enlarged. To reduce the view of the document, press and hold [Alt] (Win) or [option] (Mac). When the plus sign changes to a minus sign, click the document with this Zoom pointer, and the document size is reduced.

Using the Zoom tool, you can reduce or enlarge the view of the document from 3.13% to 6400%. Note that the current magnification level appears in the document tab and in the Zoom Level text box on the Menu bar, as shown in Figure 16.

Accessing the Zoom Tool

As you work, you can expect to zoom in and out of the document more times than you can count. The most basic way of accessing the Zoom tool is simply to click it on the Tools panel, but this can get very tiring if you have to access it often.

A better method for accessing the Zoom tool is to use keyboard shortcuts. When you are using the Selection tool, for example, don't switch to the Zoom tool. Instead, press and hold [Ctrl] [Spacebar] (Win) or ⌘ [Spacebar] (Mac) to temporarily change the Selection tool into the Zoom tool. Click the document to zoom in. When you release the keys, the Zoom tool changes back to the Selection tool.

To Zoom out using keyboard shortcuts, press and hold [Ctrl] [Alt] [Spacebar] (Win) or ⌘ [option] [Spacebar] (Mac).

In addition to the Zoom tool, Illustrator offers a number of other ways to zoom in and out of your document. One of the quickest and easiest is to press [Ctrl] [+] (Win) or ⌘ [+] (Mac) to enlarge the view and [Ctrl] [-] (Win) or ⌘ [-] (Mac) to reduce the view. You can also use the Zoom In and Zoom Out commands on the View menu.

Figure 16 *Magnification levels*

© 2015 Cengage Learning® Image courtesy of Chris Botello.

Using the Hand Tool

When you zoom in on a document to make it appear larger, eventually the document will be too large to fit in the window. Therefore, you will need to scroll to see other areas of it. You can use the scroll bars along the bottom and the right sides of the document window or you can use the Hand tool to scroll through the document.

The best way to understand the concept of the Hand tool is to think of it as your own hand. Imagine that you could put your hand up to the document on your monitor, then move the document left, right, up, or down, like a paper on a table or against a wall. This is analogous to how the Hand tool works.

QUICK TIP

Double-clicking the Hand tool on the Tools panel changes the document view to fit the page (or the spread) in the document window.

The Hand tool is often a better choice for scrolling than the scroll bars. Why? Because you can access the Hand tool using a keyboard shortcut. Regardless of whatever tool you are using, simply press and hold [Spacebar] to access the Hand tool. Release [Spacebar] to return to whatever tool you were using, without having to choose it again.

QUICK TIP

When you are using the Type tool, don't use the [Spacebar] shortcut to access the Hand tool because it will add spaces to the text with which you are working. Instead, use the scroll bar.

Working with Rulers, Grids, and Guides

Many illustrations involve using measurements to position and align objects. You'll find that Illustrator is well-equipped with a number of features that help you with these tasks.

Rulers are positioned at the top and left side of the pasteboard to help you align objects. To display or hide the rulers, click View on the Menu bar, point to Rulers, then click Hide Rulers or Show Rulers. Rulers (and all other measurement utilities in the document) can display measurements in different units, such as inches, picas, or points. You determine the **units** with which you want to work in the Preferences dialog box. On the Edit (Win) or Illustrator (Mac) menu, point to Preferences, then click Units to display the dialog box shown in Figure 17.

QUICK TIP

In this book, all exercises are set up with Units set to inches.

Ruler Guides are horizontal and vertical rules that you can position anywhere in a layout as a reference for positioning elements. In addition to guides, Illustrator offers a **document grid** for precise alignment. With the "snap" options on, objects that you move around on the page automatically align themselves with guides or with the grid that they come in contact with.

Figure 17 *Units Preferences dialog box*

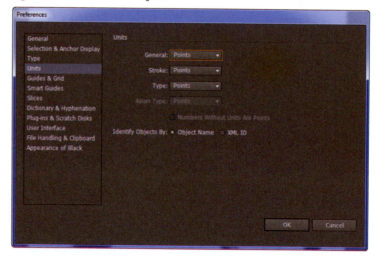

Getting to Know Illustrator

Hiding and Showing Selection Marks

All objects you create have visible selection marks or selection edges, and when an object is selected, those edges automatically highlight, showing anchor points.

While you're designing your illustration, you might want to work with selection marks hidden so that all you see is the artwork. To hide or show selection marks, click the Hide Edges or Show Edges command on the View menu.

Figure 18 shows a complex illustration with selection marks visible and hidden. In both examples, the artwork is selected, but the selection marks are not visible in the example on the right.

Figure 18 *Selection marks visible and hidden*

Choosing Screen Modes

Screen modes are options for viewing your documents. The two basic screen modes in Illustrator are Preview and Outline. You'll work in **Preview** mode most of the time. In Preview mode, you see all of your objects with fills and strokes and whatever effects you might have applied.

Outline mode displays all your objects only as hollow shapes, with no fills or strokes. Working in Outline mode can sometimes be helpful for selecting various objects that are positioned close together.

Figure 19 shows the motorcycle artwork in Outline mode.

To select objects in Preview mode, simply click anywhere on the object's fill or stroke. In Outline mode, however, you need to click the edge of the object.

Figure 19 *Artwork in Outline mode*

Getting to Know Illustrator

Understanding Preferences

All Adobe products, as most other software products, come loaded with preferences. Preferences are specifications you can set for how certain features of the application behave. The Preferences dialog box houses the multitude of Illustrator preferences available. Figure 20 shows the Type preferences for Illustrator. Getting to know available preferences is a smart approach to mastering Illustrator. Many preferences offer important choices that will have significant impact on how you work.

Working with Multiple Open Documents

On many occasions, you'll find yourself working with multiple open documents. For example, let's say you're into scrapbooking. If you were designing a new illustration to highlight a recent trip to Italy, you might also have the file open for an illustration you created last year when you went to Hawaii. Why? For any number of reasons. You might want to copy and paste art elements from the Hawaii document into the new document. Or, you might want the Hawaii document open simply as a reference for typefaces, type sizes, image sizes, and effects that you used in the document. When you're working with multiple open documents, you can switch from one to the other simply by clicking on the title bar of each document.

Figure 20 *Type Preferences dialog box*

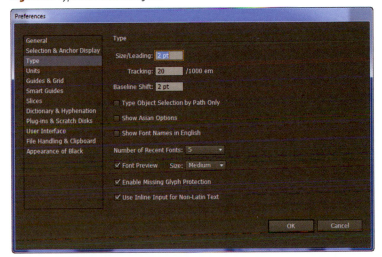

Illustrator offers a preference for having multiple open documents available as tabs in the document window. With this preference selected, a tab will appear for each open document showing the name of the document. Simply click the tab and the document becomes active. This can be useful for keeping your workspace uncluttered. However, it can sometimes be inhibiting, because when working with multiple documents, the tabbed option allows you to view only one document at a time.

You indicate in the User Interface Preferences dialog box whether or not you want open documents to appear as tabs. Click Edit on the Menu bar, point to Preferences, then click User Interface. Click Open Documents As Tabs, as shown in Figure 21, then click OK.

Using Shortcut Keys to Execute View Commands

The most commonly used commands in Illustrator list a shortcut key beside the command name. Shortcut keys are useful for quickly accessing commands without stopping work to go to the menu. Make a mental note of helpful shortcut keys and incorporate them into your work. You'll find that using them becomes second nature.

See Table 1 for shortcut keys you will use regularly for manipulating the view of your Illustrator screen.

Figure 21 *Open Documents As Tabs preference activated*

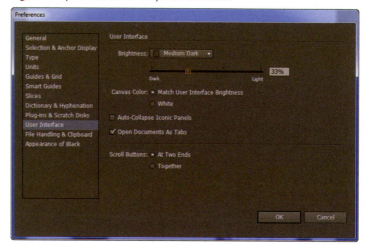

TABLE 1: SHORTCUT KEYS FOR VIEWING COMMANDS		
	Windows	**Mac**
Hide/Show Guides	Ctrl-;	Command-;
Hide/Show Edges	Ctrl-H	Command-H
Hide/Show Rulers	Ctrl-R	Command-R
Activate/Deactivate Smart Guides	Ctrl-U	Command-U
Fit Page in Window	Ctrl-0	Command-0
Fit Spread in Window	Alt-Ctrl-0	Option-Command-0
Toggle Preview and Outline Screen Modes	Ctrl-Y	Command-Y
Hide/Show Grid	Ctrl-"	Command-"

© 2015 Cengage Learning®

Figure 22 *A reduced view of the document*

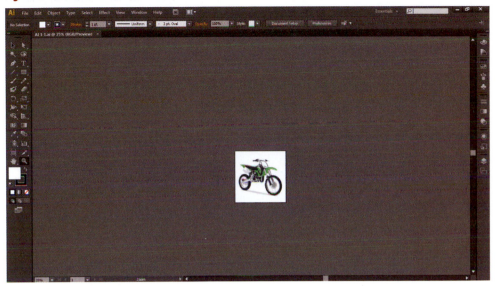

Using the Keyboard Shortcuts Dialog Box

Shortcuts are keyboard combinations you can use instead of clicking menu items to execute commands. Illustrator lets you view a list of all shortcuts, edit or create shortcuts, define your own sets of shortcuts, change individual shortcuts within a set, and switch between sets of shortcuts in the Keyboard Shortcuts dialog box. To open the Keyboard Shortcuts dialog box, click Edit on the Menu bar, then click Keyboard Shortcuts. Choose a set of shortcuts from the Set menu at the top of the Keyboard Shortcuts dialog box, then choose to modify either Menu Commands or Tools from the menu. To activate the set of shortcuts, click OK. To change a shortcut, click in the Shortcut column of the scroll list, type a new shortcut, then click OK.

Use the Zoom tool and the Hand tool

1. Press **[z]** to access the Zoom tool 🔍.

2. Position the Zoom tool over the **document window**, click twice to enlarge the document, press **[Alt]** (Win) or **[option]** (Mac), then click twice to reduce the document.

3. Click the **Zoom Level list arrow** in the lower-left corner of the document window, then click **800%**.

   Note that 800% is now listed in the document tab.

4. Double-click **800%** in the Zoom Level text box, type **300**, then press **[Enter]** (Win) or **[return]** (Mac).

5. Click the **Hand tool** ✋ on the Tools panel, then click and drag the **document window** to scroll.

6. Double-click the **Zoom tool** 🔍.

   The magnification changes to 100% (actual size).

7. Click the **Selection tool** ▶, point to the **center of the document window**, then press and hold **[Ctrl] [Spacebar]** (Win) or ⌘ **[Spacebar]** (Mac).

   The Selection tool changes to the Zoom tool.

8. Click three times, then release [Ctrl] [Spacebar] (Win) or ⌘ [Spacebar] (Mac).

9. Press and hold **[Spacebar]** to access the Hand tool, then scroll around the image.

10. Press and hold **[Ctrl] [Alt] [Spacebar]** (Win) or ⌘ **[option] [Spacebar]** (Mac), then click the mouse button multiple times to reduce the view to 25%.

11. Your document window should resemble Figure 22.

You explored various methods for accessing and using the Zoom tool for enlarging and reducing the document. You also used the Hand tool to scroll around an enlarged document.

Hide and show rulers and set units and increments preferences

1. Click **View** on the Menu bar, note the shortcut key on the Fit All in Window command, then click **Fit Artboard in Window**.

2. Click **View** on the Menu bar, point to **Rulers**, then note the Hide/Show Rulers command and its shortcut key.

   The Rulers command is listed as either Hide Rulers or Show Rulers depending on your current status.

3. Leave the View menu, then press **[Ctrl] [R]** (Win) or ⌘ **[R]** (Mac) several times to hide and show rulers, finishing with rulers showing.

4. Note the units on the rulers.

   Depending on the preference you have set, your rulers might be showing inches, picas, or another unit of measure.

5. Click **Edit** (Win) or **Illustrator** (Mac) on the Menu bar, point to **Preferences**, then click **Units**.

6. Click the **General list arrow** to see the available measurement options, then click **Picas**.

7. Click **OK**.

   The rulers change to pica measurements. Picas are a unit of measure used in layout design long before the advent of computerized layouts. One pica is equal to 1/6 an inch. It's important that you understand that the unit of measure you set as ruler units will affect all measurement utilities in the application, such as those on the Transform panel, in addition to the ruler increments.

8. Reopen the Units Preferences dialog box, click the **General list arrow**, then click **Inches**.

   Your dialog box should resemble Figure 23.

   (continued)

Figure 23 *Setting the ruler units to Inches*

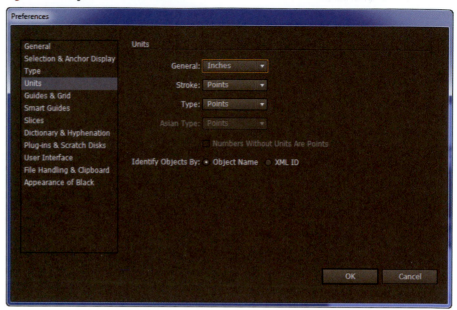

Arranging Documents

When you're working with multiple documents, you can use the Arrange Documents button to the right of the menu items in the Menu bar. If you have three separate documents open, for example, the 3-UP options in the Arrange Documents panel will tile and display all three documents as you like, in a column or a row. The Tile All In Grid option positions all of your open documents in a single window, allowing you to compare artwork from one file to another and even drag objects across documents.

Figure 24 *Viewing four guides*

9. Click **OK**.

You used shortcut keys to hide and show rulers in the document. You used the Units Preferences dialog box to change the unit of measure for ruler units.

Hide and show ruler guides, selection marks, and the document grid

1. Click **Select** on the Menu bar, then click **All**.

2. Click **View** on the Menu bar, then note the Hide/Show Edges command and its shortcut key.

   The command is listed as either Hide Edges or Show Edges, depending on your current status.

3. Leave the View menu, then press **[Ctrl] [H]** (Win) or ⌘ **[H]** (Mac) several times to switch between hiding and showing selection marks, finishing with marks showing.

   TIP The Hide Edges shortcut key is easy to remember if you think of *H for Hide*. Remember, though, that this shortcut key only hides and shows selection marks, not other elements, like ruler guides, which use different shortcut keys.

4. Click the **Select** menu, then click **Deselect**.

5. Click **View** on the Menu bar, point to **Guides**, then note the Hide/Show Guides command and its shortcut key.

   The Guides command is listed as either Hide Guides or Show Guides depending on your current status.

6. Leave the View menu, then press **[Ctrl] [;]** (Win) or ⌘ **[;]** (Mac) several times to hide and show guides, finishing with guides showing.

   Four guides are shown in Figure 24.

   TIP Make note of the difference between the Hide/Show guides shortcut key and the Hide/Show selection marks shortcut key.

   (continued)

7. Click **View** on the Menu bar, then click **Show Grid**, as shown in Figure 25.

8. Leave the View menu, then press **[Ctrl] ["]** (Win) or ⌘ **["]** (Mac) several times to hide and show the grid.

TIP Make note of the difference between the Hide/Show Guides shortcut key and the Hide/Show Document Grid shortcut key—they're just one key away from each other.

9. Hide the grid and the guides.

You used shortcut keys to hide and show selection marks, ruler guides, and the document grid.

Toggle screen modes and work with multiple documents

1. Click the **View menu**, note the shortcut key command for Outline mode, then escape the View menu.

2. Press **[Ctrl] [Y]** (Win) or ⌘ **[Y]** (Mac) repeatedly to toggle between Outline and Preview mode, finishing in Preview mode.

3. Click **Edit** (Win) or **Illustrator** (Mac) on the Menu bar, point to **Preferences**, then click **User Interface**.

4. Verify that the Open Documents As Tabs check box is checked, then click **OK**.

5. Click **File** on the Menu bar, click **Save As**, type **Motocross** in the File name box, then click the **Save button** to save the file with a new name.

TIP Each time you save a data file with a new name, the Illustrator Options dialog box will open. Click OK to close it.

(continued)

Figure 25 *Artboard with grid and guides showing*

Figure 26 *"Tabbing" the floating document*

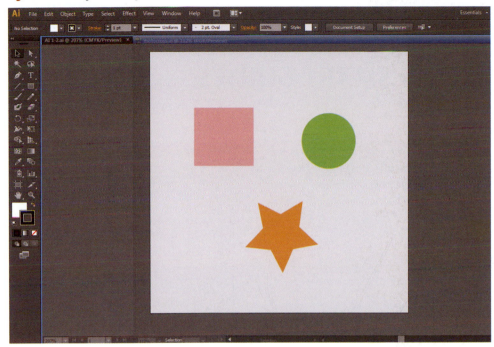

6. Open **AI 1-2.ai**, then click the **tabs** of each document several times to toggle between them, finishing with Motocross.ai as the active document.

7. Drag the **Motocross.ai tab** straight down approximately ½ inch.

   When you drag a tabbed document down, it becomes "untabbed" and a "floating" document.

8. Position your mouse pointer over the upper-right or bottom-right corner of the document window, then click and drag toward the center of the monitor window to reduce the window to approximately half its size.

9. Position your mouse pointer over the title bar of the document, then click and drag to move Motocross.ai half way down toward the bottom of your monitor screen.

   A "floating" document window can be positioned so that part if it is off-screen.

10. Position your mouse pointer over the title bar of Motocross.ai, click and drag to position it at the top of the window beside the AI 1-2.ai tab, then release the mouse button when you see a horizontal blue bar, as shown in Figure 26.

    The document is tabbed once again.

11. Close AI 1-2.ai without saving changes if you are prompted.

12. Close Motocross.ai without saving changes if you are prompted.

You verified that the Open Documents As Tabs option in the Preferences dialog box was activated. You removed the document from its tabbed position, resized it, moved it around, then returned it to its tabbed status.

Work with Objects
AND SMART GUIDES

What You'll Do

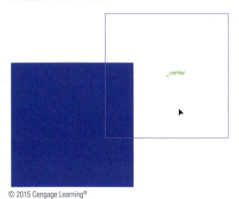

© 2015 Cengage Learning®

▶ In this lesson, you will work with objects with smart guides.

Working with Preferences

Illustrator features several preferences dialog boxes. Preferences affect many aspects of the Illustrator interface, including guides, smart guides, and rulers. You can think of preferences as the "ground rules" that you establish before doing your work. For example, you might want to specify your preferences for guide and grid colors or for hyphenation if you're doing lots of type work.

One tricky thing about preferences is that, if you're just learning Illustrator, preferences refer to things that you don't really know about. That's OK. Illustrator's preferences default to a paradigm that makes most of the work you do intuitive. But as you gain experience, it's a good idea to go back through the available preferences and see if there are any changes you want to make or with which you want to experiment.

One more thing about preferences: remember that they're there. Let's say you want to apply a 2 pt stroke to an object, but the Stroke panel is showing stroke weight in inches. First you click the Stroke panel options button to show the Stroke panel menu, but you soon find that the menu holds no command for changing the readout from inches to points. That's the point where you say to yourself, "Aha! It must be a preference."

Resizing Objects

Individual pieces of artwork that you create in Illustrator, such as squares, text, or lines, are called **objects**. All objects you create in Illustrator are composed of paths and anchor points. When you select an object, its paths and anchor points become highlighted, as shown in Figure 27.

You have many options for changing the size and shape of an object. One of your most straightforward options is to use the **bounding box**. Select any object or multiple objects, then click **Show Bounding Box** on the View menu. Eight handles appear around the selected object. See Figure 28. Click and drag the handles to change the shape and size of the object.

Figure 27 *Selected objects*

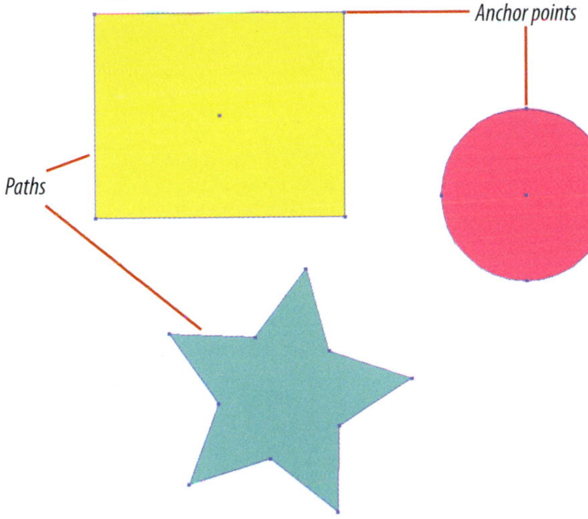

Anchor points

Paths

Figure 28 *Selected circle with bounding box showing*

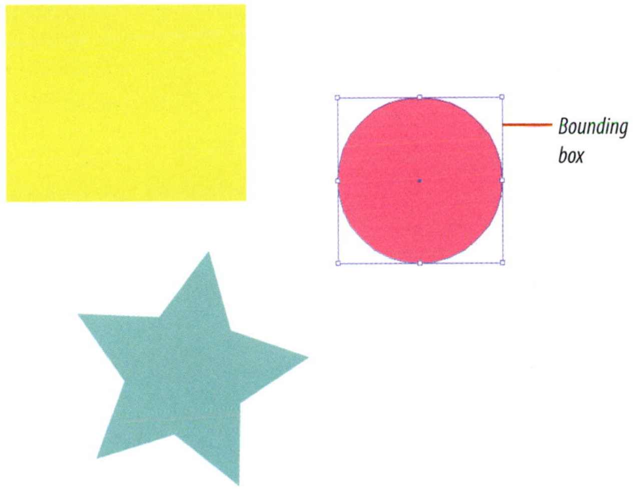

Bounding box

When you select multiple objects, a single bounding box appears around all the selected objects, as shown in Figure 29. Manipulating the bounding box will affect all the objects.

Illustrator offers two basic keyboard combinations that you can use when dragging bounding box handles as shown in Table 2.

Copying Objects

At any time, you can copy and paste an object. When you paste, the object is pasted at the center of the artboard—regardless of the position of the original. When designing, you'll often find it more desirable for the copy to be pasted in the exact same location as the original. The Edit menu offers three commands to achieve this goal. The **Paste in Front** command pastes the copy directly in front of the original. The **Paste in Back** command pastes the copy directly behind the original. Both have quick keys that are easy to remember: for Paste in Front enter [Ctrl] [F] (Win) or ⌘ [F] (Mac) and for Paste in Back, enter [Ctrl] [B] (Win) or ⌘ [B] (Mac).

QUICK TIP

In this book, you'll be asked numerous times to paste in front and paste in back. The direction will read, "Copy, then paste in back," or, "Copy, then paste in front." It would be a good idea for you to remember the quick keys.

In addition, Illustrator also offers the **Paste in Place** command on the Edit menu. The Paste In Place command functions identically to the Paste In Front command; it pastes the copy in the same location in front of the original.

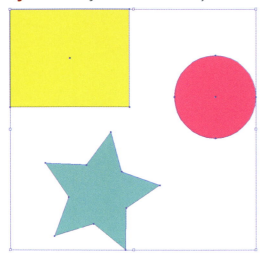

Figure 29 *Bounding box around three selected objects*

TABLE 2: OBJECT RESIZING COMBINATIONS		
Windows	**Mac**	**Result**
Shift-drag a corner handle	Shift-drag a corner handle	The object is resized in proportion; its shape doesn't change
Alt-drag a handle	Option-drag a handle	Resizes the object from its center point
Alt-Shift-drag a handle	Option-Shift-drag a handle	Resize the object from its center and in proportion

© 2015 Cengage Learning®

Getting to Know Illustrator

Be sure to make a note that you can copy objects while dragging them. Press and hold [Alt] (Win) or [option] (Mac), then drag to create a copy of the object. This behavior is referred to as **drag and drop a copy**, and it's something you'll do a lot of in Illustrator and in this book.

Hiding, Locking, and Grouping Objects

The Hide, Lock, Group, and Ungroup commands on the Object menu are essential for working effectively with layouts, especially complex layouts with many objects. **Hide** objects to get them out of your way. They won't print, and nothing you do will change the location of them as long as they are hidden. **Lock** an object to make it immovable—you will not even be able to select it. Lock your objects when you have them in a specific location and you don't want them accidentally moved or deleted. Don't think this is being overly cautious; accidentally moving or deleting objects—and being unaware that you did so—happens all the time in complex layouts. Having objects grouped strategically is also a solution for getting your work done faster.

You group multiple objects with the **Group** command on the Object menu. Grouping objects is a smart and important strategy for protecting the relationships between multiple objects. When you click on grouped objects with the Selection tool, all the objects are selected. Thus, you can't accidentally select a single object or move it or otherwise alter it independently from the group. However, you *can* select individual objects within a group with the Direct Selection tool—that's how the tool got its name. Even if you select and alter a single object within a group, the objects are not ungrouped. If you click on any of them with the Selection tool, all members of the group will be selected.

Working with Smart Guides

When aligning objects, you will find **smart guides** to be really effective and, well, really smart. When the Smart Guides feature is activated, smart guides appear automatically when you move objects in the document. They give you visual information for positioning objects precisely in relation to the artboard or to other objects. For example, you can use smart guides to align objects to the edges and centers of other objects, and to the horizontal and vertical centers of the artboard.

You enable Smart Guides options as a preference. You use the View menu to turn them on and off. Figure 30 shows smart guides at work.

Figure 30 *Smart guides aligning the top edges of two objects*

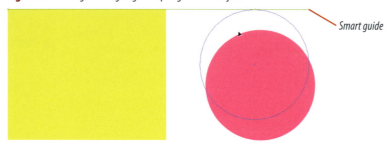

Smart guide

Getting to Know Illustrator

Figure 31 *General Preferences dialog box*

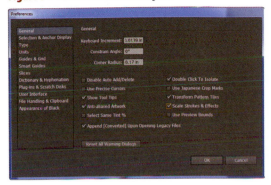

Figure 32 *Units Preferences dialog box*

Figure 33 *Setting Guides & Grid preferences*

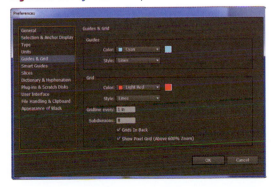

Set essential preferences

1. Click **Edit** (Win) or **Illustrator** (Mac) on the Menu bar, point to **Preferences**, then click **General**.

   For the remainder of this chapter and this book, use this combination of commands to find your preferences dialog boxes.

2. Set your General preferences to match Figure 31.

   The keyboard increment determines the distance a selected object moves when you click an arrow key on your keypad. The measurement entered, .0139" is equivalent to 1 pt. The Show Tool Tips option will reveal a tool's name when you position your cursor over it. The Scale Strokes & Effects option means that, for example, if you apply a 200% scale to an object that has a 1 pt stroke, the result will be an object with a 2 pt stroke.

TIP If you press and hold [Shift] while pressing the arrow keys, a selected object moves a distance that is 10X the keyboard increment.

3. Click **Units** on the left side of the Preferences dialog box, then make sure your settings match those shown in Figure 32.

   All the general artboard measurements in this book are based on inches. In almost all cases, you'll want to work with strokes and type in point measurements.

4. Click **Guides & Grid** on the left side of the Preferences dialog box, then make sure your settings match those shown in Figure 33.

(continued)

Note that you have options for showing your guides as dots.

5. Click **Smart Guides** on the left side of the Preferences dialog box, then enter the settings shown in Figure 34.

It's a good idea for your smart guides to be a distinctly different color than your ruler guides and artboard grid.

6. Click **User Interface** on the left side of the Preferences dialog box, then make sure your settings match those shown in Figure 35.

The Brightness slider defines how light or dark the Illustrator interface is.

7. Click **OK**.

You specified various essential preferences in different Preferences dialog boxes.

Resize objects

1. Open **A1-2.ai**, then save it as **Objects**.

2. Click **View** on the Menu bar, then verify that the Bounding Box command is set to Show Bounding Box.

3. Click the **Selection tool** , then click the **pink square** to select it.

As shown in Figure 36, the paths and the anchor points that draw the square are revealed, as is the object's center point.

4. Click **View** on the Menu bar, then click **Show Bounding Box**.

Eight "hollow" handles appear around the rectangle, as shown in Figure 37.

(continued)

Figure 34 *Setting Smart Guides preferences*

Figure 35 *Setting User Interface preferences*

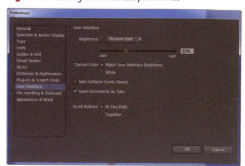

Figure 36 *Viewing paths and points on a selected object*

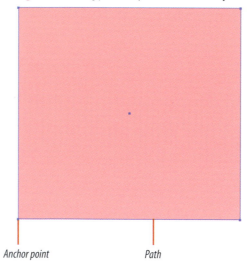

Anchor point   Path

Figure 37 *Viewing the bounding box*

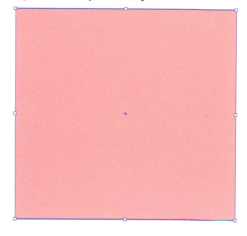

Getting to Know Illustrator

Figure 38 *All objects selected on the artboard*

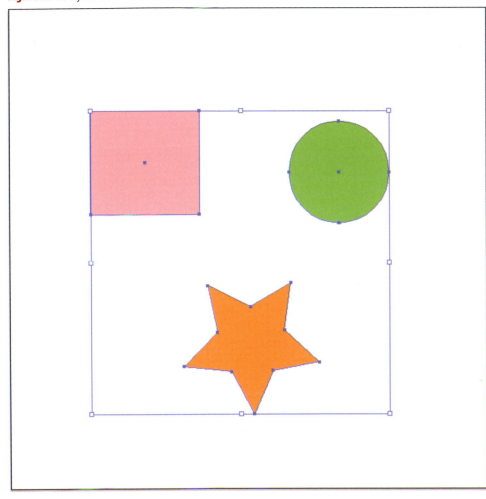

© 2015 Cengage Learning®

5. Click and drag **various handles** and note how the object is resized.

6. When you are done experimenting, undo all of the moves you made.

   The Undo command is at the top of the Edit menu.

7. Press and hold down **[Shift]**, while dragging the **top-left corner handle** to the left edge of the document.

   The object is resized proportionately.

8. Undo the move.

9. Click the **green circle** to select it.

10. Press and hold down **[Alt]** (Win) or **[option]** (Mac), then start dragging **any corner handle**.

    As you drag, the object is resized from its center.

11. While still holding down **[Alt]** (Win) **or [option]** (Mac) and dragging, press and hold **[Shift]**.

    The object is resized in proportion from its center.

12. Scale the circle to any size.

13. Undo the move.

14. Click **Select** on the Menu bar, then click **All**.

    All of the objects on the artboard are selected. The bounding box appears around all three objects, as shown in Figure 38.

    Make it a point to remember the quick key for Select All: [Ctrl][A] (Win) or ⌘ [A] (Mac).

    (continued)

15. Using the skills you learned in this lesson, reduce the size of the objects in proportion so that they are very small on the artboard, then click the artboard to deselect the objects.

Your artboard should resemble Figure 39.

16. Click **File** on the Menu bar, click **Revert**, then click **Revert** when you are prompted to confirm.

Reverting a file returns it to its status when you last saved it. You can think of it as a "super undo."

You explored various options for resizing objects, then you reverted the file.

Copy and duplicate objects

1. Click **View** on the Menu bar, then click **Hide Bounding Box**.

2. Select the **star**, then copy it, using the [Ctrl][C] (Win) or ⌘ [C] (Mac) shortcut keys.

3. Click **Edit** on the Menu bar, then click **Paste**.

A copy of the star is placed at the center of the artboard.

4. Undo the paste.

5. Click **Edit** on the Menu bar, then click **Paste in Front**.

The copy is pasted directly in front of the original star.

(continued)

Figure 39 *Resized object and contents*

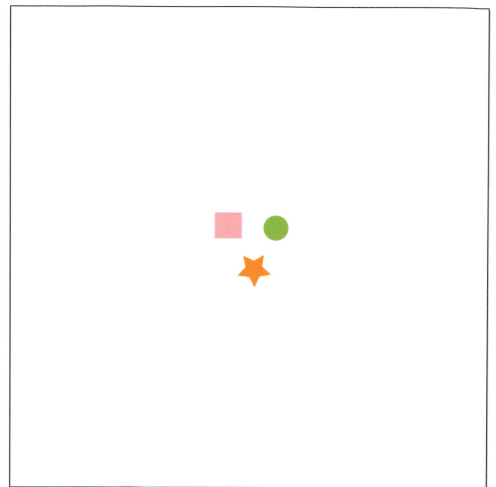

© 2015 Cengage Learning®

Figure 40 *Two stars pasted in front and in back of the original*

Lesson 3   Work with Objects and Smart Guides

6. Press **[I]** on your keypad to switch to the Eyedropper tool , then click the **pink square**.

   The star takes on the same fill and stroke colors as the square.

7. Press → on your keypad ten times.

8. Deslect all, click **Edit** on the Menu bar, then click **Paste in Back**.

   A copy of the star is pasted directly behind the original orange star that was copied.

9. Click the **Eyedropper tool** on the green circle.

10. Press and hold **[Shift]**, then press ← on your keypad one time.

11. Press and hold **[Ctrl]** (Win) or ⌘ (Mac) so that your cursor switches temporarily from the Eyedropper tool to the Selection tool, then click the artboard with the Selection tool to deselect all.

    Pressing [Ctrl] or ⌘ is a quick way to switch temporarily to the Selection tool.

12. Compare your artboard to Figure 40.

13. Click the **Selection tool** , then select the green circle.

(continued)

14. Press and hold down **[Alt]** (Win) or **[option]** (Mac), then drag a copy of the circle to the center of the square.

Your screen should resemble Figure 41.

TIP This method for creating a copy is referred to as "drag-and-drop a copy."

15. Save your work, then close the file.

You copied and pasted an object, noting that it pasted by default in the center of the artboard. You used the Paste in Front and Paste in Back commands along with arrow keys to make two offset copies of the star. You duplicated the circle with the drag-and-drop technique.

Figure 41 *Dragging and dropping a copy of the circle*

Getting to Know Illustrator

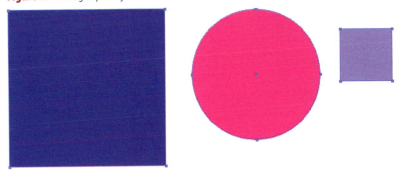

Figure 42 *Three grouped objects*

Hide, lock, and group objects

1. Open AI 1-3.ai, then save it as **Groups**.

2. Click **Object** on the Menu bar, then click **Show All**.

   This document was originally saved with hidden objects. Three objects appear. They are all selected.

3. Click **Object** on the Menu bar, then click **Group**.

4. Click the **Selection tool** [cursor icon], click **anywhere on the pasteboard** to deselect all, then click the **Pink circle**.

   As shown in Figure 42, all three objects are selected because they are grouped.

5. Click the **pasteboard** to deselect all, click the **Direct Selection tool** [cursor icon], then click the **pink circle**.

   Only the circle is selected, because the Direct Selection tool selects individual objects within a group.

6. Select all, click **Object** on the Menu bar, then click **Ungroup**.

7. Click the **Selection tool** [cursor icon], select the **small square**, click **Object** on the Menu bar, point to **Lock**, then click **Selection**.

   The object's handles disappear and it can no longer be selected.

8. Click **Object** on the Menu bar, then click **Unlock All**.

   The small square is unlocked.

   (continued)

9. Select all, click **Object** on the Menu bar, point to **Hide**, then click **Selection**.

   All selected objects disappear.

10. Click the **Object** menu, then click **Show All**.

   The three objects reappear in the same location that they were in when they were hidden.

TIP Memorize the shortcut keys for Hide/Show, Group/Ungroup, and Lock/Unlock. They are easy to remember and extremely useful. You will be using these commands over and over again when you work in Illustrator.

11. Hide the pink circle and the small square.

12. Save the file.

You revealed hidden objects, grouped them, then used the Direct Selection tool to select individual objects within the group. You ungrouped, locked, unlocked, and hid objects.

Figure 43 *Smart guide aligning square with center of artboard*

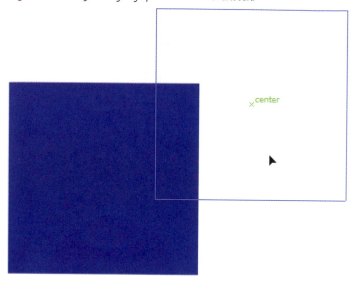

Figure 44 *Aligning the tops of two squares*

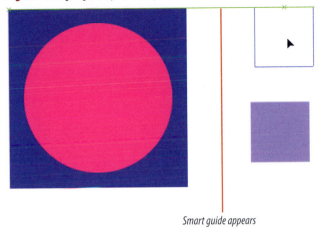

Smart guide appears

Figure 45 *Aligning bottoms of two squares*

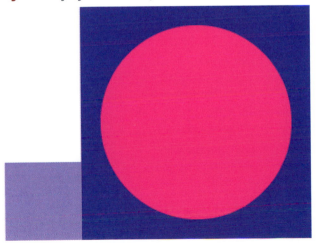

Work with smart guides

1. Click **View** on the Menu bar, then click **Smart Guides** if it is not already checked.

2. Click the **large blue square**, then try to center it visually on the page.

3. Release the mouse button when the word center appears, as shown in Figure 43.

   Smart guides use the word center to identify when the center point of an object is in line with the center point of the artboard.

4. Show the hidden objects, then hide the small square.

5. Using the same steps, align the center of the pink circle with the center of the large blue square.

6. Show the hidden small square.

7. Use smart guides to align the top of the small square with the top of the large square, as shown in Figure 44.

8. Position the small square as shown in Figure 45.

9. Save, then close the file.

You aligned an object at the center of the document and created precise relationships among three objects using smart guides.

Create
BASIC SHAPES

What You'll Do

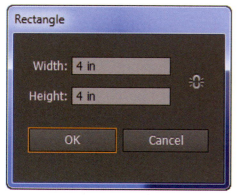

 In this lesson, you will examine the differences between bitmap and vector graphics. Then you will use the Rectangle tool to examine Illustrator's various options for creating simple vector graphics.

Getting Ready to Draw

Are you eager to start drawing? Do you want to create complex shapes, special effects, and original art? Perhaps you are a self-taught user of Adobe Illustrator, and your main interest is to graduate to advanced techniques and add a few of those cool special effects to your skill set. Good for you! Enthusiasm is priceless, and no book can teach it. So maintain that enthusiasm for this first exercise, where you'll start by creating a square. That's right. A square.

Consider for a moment that Mozart's sublime opera *Don Giovanni* is based primarily on eight notes, or that the great American novel can be reduced to 26 letters. Illustrator's foundation is basic geometric shapes, so let's start at square one...with one square.

Don't rush. As you work, keep in mind that the lessons you learn here are the foundation of every great illustration.

Bitmap Images and Vector Graphics

Before you begin drawing, you should become familiar with some basic information about computer graphics.

For starters, computer graphics fall into two main categories—bitmap images and vector graphics. **Bitmap images** are created using a square or rectangular grid of colored squares called **pixels**. Because pixels (a contraction of "picture elements") can render subtle gradations of tone, they are the most common medium for continuous-tone images—what you perceive as a photograph.

All scanned images are composed of pixels, and all "digital" images are composed of pixels. Adobe Photoshop is the leading graphics application for working with digital "photos." Figure 46 shows an example of a bitmap image.

The number of pixels in a given inch is referred to as the image's **resolution**. To be effective, pixels must be small enough to create an image with the illusion of continuous tone. Thus, bitmap images are termed **resolution-dependent**.

The important thing to remember about bitmap images is that any magnification of the image—resizing the image to be bigger— essentially means that fewer pixels are available per inch (the same number of pixels is now spread out over a larger area). This decrease

Getting to Know Illustrator

in resolution will have a negative impact on the quality of the image. The greater the magnification, the greater the negative impact.

Graphics that you create in Adobe Illustrator are vector graphics. **Vector graphics** are created with lines and curves and are defined by mathematical objects called vectors. Vectors use geometric characteristics to define the object. Vector graphics consist of **anchor points** and **line segments**, together referred to as **paths**.

For example, if you use Illustrator to render a person's face, the software will identify the iris of the eye using the mathematical definition of a circle with a specific radius and a specific location in respect to other graphics. It will then fill that circle with the color you have specified. Figure 47 shows an example of a vector graphic.

Computer graphics rely on vectors to render bold graphics that must retain clean, crisp lines when scaled to various sizes. Vectors are often used to create logos or "line art," and they are the best choice for typographical work, especially small and italic type.

As mathematical objects, vector graphics can be scaled to any size. Because they are not created with pixels, there is no inherent resolution. Thus, vector graphics are termed **resolution-independent**. This means that any graphic that you create in Illustrator can be output to fit on a postage stamp or on a billboard!

Figure 46 *Bitmap graphics*

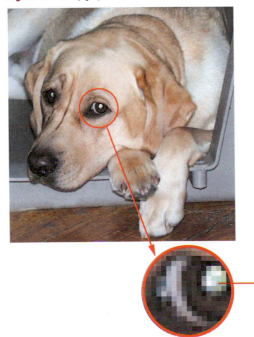

Pixels

© 2015 Cengage Learning® Image courtesy of Chris Botello.

Figure 47 *Vector graphics*

Use the Rectangle tool

1. Click **File** on the Menu bar, click **New**, create a new document that is 8" wide by 8" in height, name the file **Basic Shapes**, then click **OK**.

2. Click **File** on the Menu bar, click **Save As**, navigate to the drive and folder where your Data Files are stored, click **Save**, then click **OK** to close the Illustrator Options dialog box.

3. Click the **Default Fill and Stroke button**  on the Tools panel.

4. Click the **Swap Fill and Stroke button** on the Tools panel to reverse the default colors.

   Your fill color should now be Black and your stroke color White. The **fill color** is the inside color of an object. The **stroke color** is the color of the object's border or frame.

5. Click the **Rectangle tool** on the Tools panel.

6. Click and drag the **Rectangle tool pointer** on the artboard, then release the mouse button to make a rectangle of any size.

7. Press and hold **[Shift]** while you create a second rectangle.

   Pressing and holding [Shift] while you create a rectangle constrains the shape to a perfect square, as shown in Figure 48.

8. Create a third rectangle drawn from its center point by pressing and holding **[Alt]** (Win) or **[option]** (Mac) as you drag the **Rectangle tool pointer**.

TIP Use [Shift] in combination with [Alt] (Win) or [option] (Mac) to draw a perfect shape from its center.

You created a freeform rectangle, then you created a perfect square. Finally you drew a square from its center point.

Figure 48 *Creating a rectangle and a square*

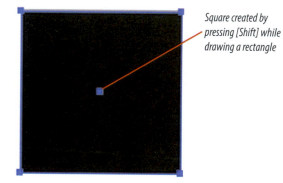

Square created by pressing [Shift] while drawing a rectangle

© 2015 Cengage Learning®

Getting to Know Illustrator

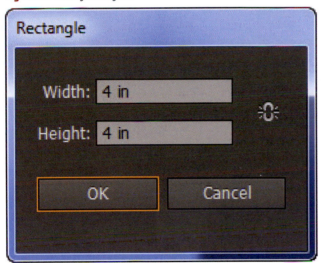

Figure 49 *Rectangle dialog box*

Use the Rectangle dialog box

1. Click **Select** on the Menu bar, then click **All** to select all of the objects.

2. Click **Edit** on the Menu bar, then click **Cut** to remove the objects from the artboard.

3. Click **anywhere on the artboard**.

   When a shape tool is selected, clicking once on the artboard opens a dialog box, which allows you to enter precise information for creating the object. In this case, it opens the Rectangle dialog box.

4. Type **4** in the Width text box, type **4** in the Height text box, as shown in Figure 49, then click **OK**.

5. Save your work.

You clicked the artboard with the Rectangle tool, which opened the Rectangle dialog box. You entered a specific width and height to create a perfect 4" square.

Apply Fill and Stroke
COLORS TO OBJECTS

What You'll Do

In this lesson you will use the Swatches panel to add a fill color to an object and apply a stroke as a border. Then you will use the Stroke panel to change the size of the default stroke.

Activating the Fill or Stroke

The Fill and Stroke buttons are on the Tools panel. To apply a fill or stroke color to an object, you must first activate the appropriate button. You activate either button by clicking it, which moves it in front of the other. When the Fill button is in front of the Stroke button, the fill is activated, as shown in Figure 50.

The Stroke button is activated when it is in front of the Fill button.

As you work, you will often switch back and forth, activating the fill and the stroke. Rather than using your mouse to activate the fill or the stroke each time, simply press [X] to switch between the two modes.

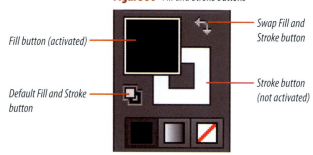

Figure 50 *Fill and Stroke buttons*

Fill button (activated)

Swap Fill and Stroke button

Default Fill and Stroke button

Stroke button (not activated)

Getting to Know Illustrator

Applying Color with the Swatches Panel

The Swatches panel, as shown in Figure 51, is central to color management in the application and a simple resource for applying fills and strokes to objects.

The Swatches panel has several preset colors, along with gradients, patterns, and shades of gray. The swatch with the red line through it is called [None] and is used as a fill for a "hollow" object. Any object without a stroke will always have [None] as its stroke color.

When an object is selected, clicking a swatch on the panel will apply that color as a fill or a stroke, depending on which of the two is activated on the Tools panel. You can also drag and drop swatches onto unselected objects. Dragging a swatch to an unselected object will change the color of its fill or stroke, depending upon which of the two is activated.

Figure 51 *Swatches panel*

Pre-set colors, gradients, patterns, and shades of gray

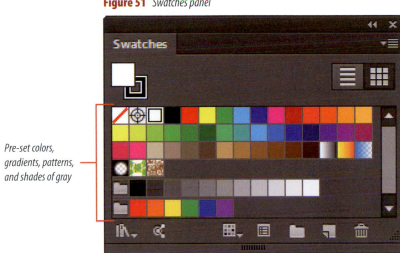

Apply fill and stroke colors

1. Verify that the new square is still selected.

2. Click the **Swatches panel icon** ⊞ in the stack of collapsed panels to open the Swatches panel.

   Your Swatches panel may already be available.

3. Click **any blue swatch** on the Swatches panel to fill the square.

   Note that the Fill button on the Tools panel is now also blue.

   TIP When you position your pointer over a color swatch on the Swatches panel, a tool tip appears that shows the name of that swatch.

4. Click the **Selection tool** ⧪ , then click **anywhere on the artboard** to deselect the blue square.

5. Drag and drop a **yellow swatch** onto the blue square.

   The fill color changes to yellow because the Fill button is activated on the Tools panel. Your colors may vary from the colors shown in the figures.

6. Press **[X]** to activate the Stroke button on the Tools panel.

7. Drag and drop the **red swatch** on the Swatches panel onto the yellow square.

   As shown in Figure 52, a red stroke is added to the square because the Stroke button is activated on the Tools panel.

   (continued)

Figure 52 *Red stroke is added to the yellow square*

Getting to Know Illustrator

Figure 53 *Yellow square without a stroke*

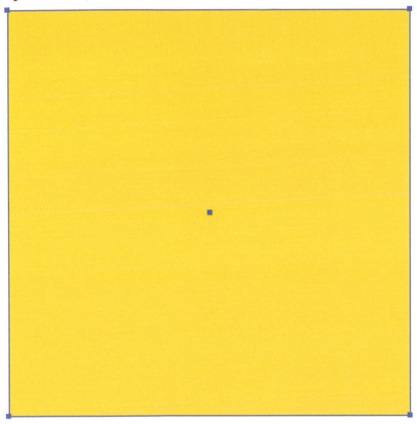

8. Click the **Stroke panel icon** ☰ in the stack of collapsed panels to display the Stroke panel.

9. Select the **square** on the artboard, click the **Weight list arrow** on the Stroke panel, then click **20 pt**.

TIP Illustrator positions a stroke equally inside and outside an object. Thus, a 20 pt stroke is rendered with 10 pts inside the object and 10 pts outside.

10. Note the Align Stroke section on the Stroke panel.

11. Click the **Align Stroke to Inside button** ⌐.

    The entire stroke moves to the inside of the square.

12. Click the **Align Stroke to Outside button** ⌐.

    The entire stroke moves to the outside of the square.

13. Click the **Align Stroke to Center button** ⌐.

    The stroke is returned to the default position, equally inside and outside the object.

14. Click **[None]** ⃠ on the Swatches panel to remove the stroke from the square.

    Your screen should resemble Figure 53.

15. Save your work.

You filled the square with blue by clicking a blue swatch on the Swatches panel. You then changed the fill and stroke colors to yellow and red by dragging and dropping swatches onto the square. You used the Stroke panel to increase the weight and change the alignment of the stroke, then removed it by choosing [None] from the Swatches panel.

Select, Move,
AND ALIGN OBJECTS

What You'll Do

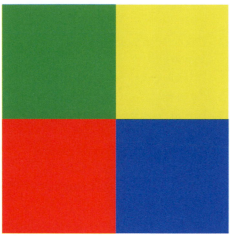

© 2015 Cengage Learning®

In this lesson, you will use the Selection tool in combination with smart guides to move, copy, and align four squares.

Selecting and Moving Objects

When it comes to accuracy, consider that Illustrator can move objects incrementally by fractions of a point—which itself is a tiny fraction of an inch! That level of precision is key when moving and positioning objects.

Before you can move or modify an Illustrator object, you must identify it by selecting it with a selection tool, menu item, or command key. When working with simple illustrations that contain few objects, selecting is usually simple, but it can become very tricky in complex illustrations, especially those containing a large number of small objects positioned closely together.

Two very basic ways to move objects are by clicking and dragging or by using the arrow keys, which by default move a selected item in 1 pt increments. Pressing [Shift] when dragging an object constrains the movement to horizontal, vertical, and 45° diagonals. Pressing [Alt] (Win) or [option] (Mac) while dragging an object creates a copy of the object.

Making a Marquee Selection

By now, you're familiar with using the Selection tool to select objects. You can also use the Selection tool to create a marquee selection, which is a dotted rectangle that disappears as soon as you release the mouse button. Any object that the marquee touches before you release the mouse button will be selected. See Figure 54.

Marquee selections are useful for both quick selections and precise selections. Make sure you practice and make them part of your skill set.

Figure 54 *Making a marquee selection*

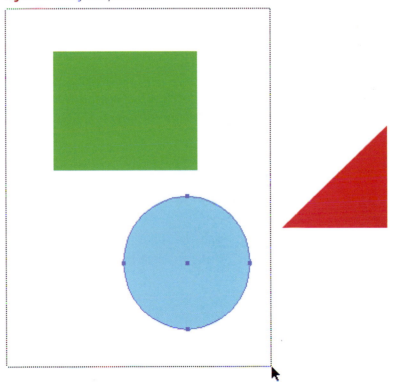

Move and position objects with precision

1. Click **View** on the Menu bar, then click **Fit Artboard in Window**.

2. Click **View** on the Menu bar, then verify that both Smart Guides and Snap to Point are selected.

TIP There will be a check next to each if they are selected. If they are not selected, click each option to select it.

Snap to Point automatically aligns anchor points when they get close together. When dragging an object, you'll see it "snap" to align itself with a nearby object or guide.

3. Click the **Selection tool** on the Tools panel, then click the **yellow square**.

4. Identify the anchor points, paths, and center point, as shown in Figure 55.

5. Move the Selection tool pointer over the **anchor points**, over the **paths that connect the points**, and over the **center point**.

6. Position the pointer over the **top-left anchor point**, click and drag so that the anchor point aligns with the top-left corner of the artboard, as shown in Figure 56, then release the mouse button.

The smart guide changes from "anchor" to "intersect" when the two corners are aligned.

You used the Selection tool in combination with smart guides to position an object exactly at the top-left corner of the artboard.

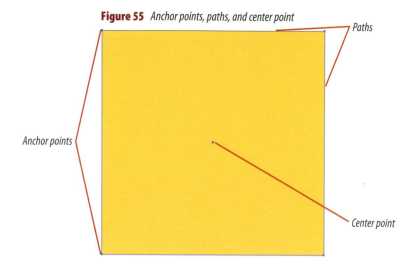

Figure 55 *Anchor points, paths, and center point*

Paths

Anchor points

Center point

Figure 56 *Intersecting two points*

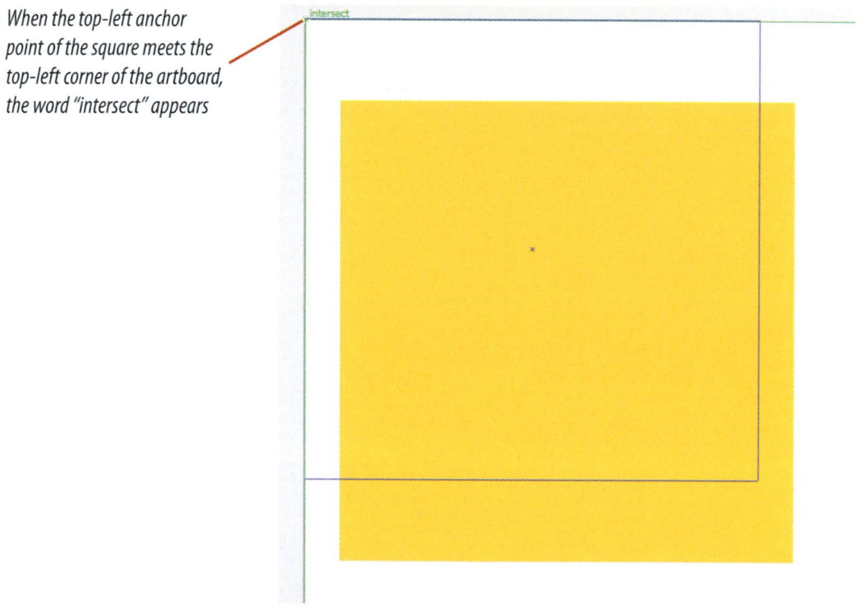

When the top-left anchor point of the square meets the top-left corner of the artboard, the word "intersect" appears

Figure 57 *Duplicating the square*

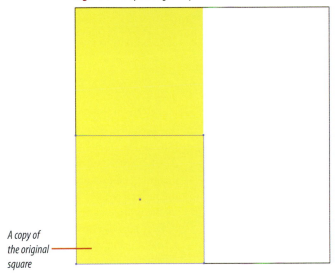

A copy of
the original —
square

Figure 58 *Four squares created using drag and drop*

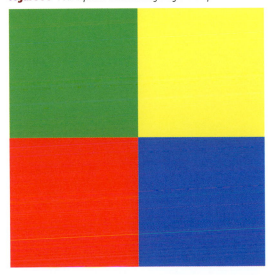

Duplicate objects using drag and drop

1. Click the **top-left anchor point** without releasing the mouse button, press and hold **[Shift] [Alt]** (Win) or **[Shift] [option]** (Mac) while dragging straight down until the top-left anchor point touches the bottom-left anchor point (the "intersect" smart guide will appear), then release the mouse button.

    When moving an object, pressing and holding [Shift] constrains the movement vertically, horizontally, or on 45° diagonals. Pressing [Alt] (Win) or [option] (Mac) while dragging an object creates a copy of the object, as shown in Figure 57.

    TIP When you press [Alt] (Win) or [option] (Mac) while dragging an object, the pointer becomes a double-arrow pointer. When two anchor points are directly on top of each other, the Selection tool pointer turns from black to white.

2. With the bottom square still selected, press and hold **[Shift],** then click the **top square** to select both items.

3. Click the **top-left anchor point** of the top square without releasing the mouse button, press and hold **[Shift] [Alt] (Win)** or **[Shift] [option]** (Mac), while dragging to the right until the top-left anchor point touches the top-right anchor point, then release the mouse button.

4. Change the fill color of each square to match the colors shown in Figure 58.

5. Save your work.

You moved and duplicated the yellow square using [Shift] to constrain the movement and [Alt] (Win) or [option] (Mac) to duplicate or "drag and drop" copies of the square.

Transform OBJECTS

What You'll Do

© 2015 Cengage Learning®

In this lesson, you will scale, rotate, and reflect objects, using the basic transform tools. You will also create a star and a triangle.

Transforming Objects

The Scale, Rotate, and Reflect tools are the fundamental transform tools. As their names make clear, the Scale and Rotate tools resize and rotate objects, respectively. When you use the tool's dialog box, the objects are transformed from their center points. This can be a useful choice because the object's position essentially doesn't change on the artboard or in relation to other objects.

Use the Reflect tool to "flip" an object over an imaginary axis. The best way to understand the Reflect tool is to imagine positioning a mirror perpendicular to a sheet of paper with a word written on it. The angle at which you position the mirror in relation to the word is the reflection axis. The reflection of the word in the mirror is the end result of what the Reflect tool does. For example, text reflected across a horizontal axis would appear upside down and inverted. Text reflected across a vertical axis would appear to be inverted and running backwards, as shown in Figure 59.

You can transform an object using the desired tool or its dialog box. Each transform tool has a dialog box where you can enter precise numbers to execute the transformation on a selected object. You can access a tool's dialog box by double-clicking the tool. Click the Copy button in the dialog box to create a transformed copy of the selected object. Figure 60 shows the Scale dialog box.

Repeating Transformations

One of the most powerful commands relating to the transform tools is Transform Again, found on the Object menu. Unfortunately, it is a command often overlooked by new users. Whenever you transform an object, selecting Transform Again repeats the transformation. For example, if you scale a circle 50%, the Transform Again command will scale the circle 50% again.

The power of the command comes in combination with copying transformations. For example, if you rotate a square 10° and copy it at the same time, the Transform Again command will create a second square rotated another 10° from the first copy. Applying Transform Again repeatedly is handy for creating complex geometric shapes from basic objects.

Figure 59 *Reflected text*

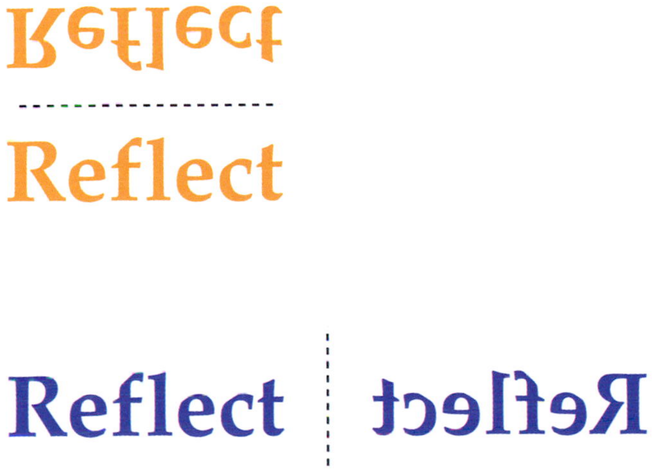

Figure 60 *Scale dialog box*

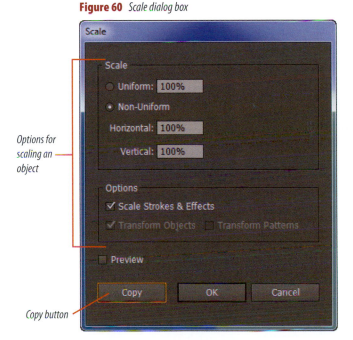

Options for scaling an object

Copy button

© 2015 Cengage Learning®

Use the Scale and Rotate tools

1. Select the **green square**, double-click the **Scale tool** , type **50** in the Scale text box, then click **OK**.

2. Click **Edit** on the Menu bar, then click **Undo Scale**.

TIP You can also undo your last step by pressing [Ctrl][Z] (Win) or ⌘ [Z] (Mac).

3. Double-click the **Scale tool** again, type **50** in the Scale text box, then click **Copy**.

    The transformation is executed from the center point; the center points of the original and the copy are aligned.

4. Fill the new square created in Step 3 with blue.

5. Double-click the **Rotate tool**, type **45** in the Angle text box, click **OK**, then click the **Selection tool**.

6. Apply a 22 pt yellow stroke to the rotated square, deselect, then compare your screen to Figure 61.

You used the Scale tool to create a 50% copy of the square, then filled the copy with blue. You rotated the copy 45°. You then applied a 22 pt yellow stroke.

Figure 61 *Scaling and rotating a square*

Getting to Know Illustrator

Figure 62 *Using the Transform Again command*

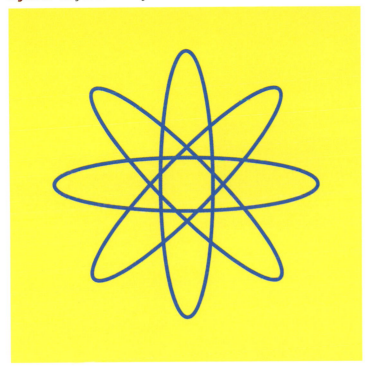

Use the Transform Again command

1. Click the **Ellipse tool** ⬭ on the Tools panel.

TIP To access the Ellipse tool, press and hold the Rectangle tool until a toolbar of shape tools appears, then click the Ellipse tool.

2. Click the **artboard**, type **3** in the Width text box and **.5** in the Height text box, then click **OK**.

3. Change the fill color to **[None]**, the stroke color to **blue**, and the stroke weight to **3 pt**.

4. Click the **Selection tool** ▷, click the **center point** of the ellipse, then drag it to the center point of the yellow square.

TIP The center smart guide appears when the two centers meet.

5. Double-click the **Rotate tool** ⟲, type **45** in the Angle text box, then click **Copy**.

6. Click **Object** on the Menu bar, point to **Transform**, then click **Transform Again**.

TIP You can also access the Transform Again command by pressing [Ctrl] [D] (Win) or ⌘ [D] (Mac).

7. Repeat Step 6 to create a fourth ellipse using the Transform Again command.

Your screen should resemble Figure 62.

8. Select the **four ellipses**, click **Object** on the Menu bar, then click **Group**.

You created an ellipse, filled and stroked it, and aligned it with the yellow square. You then created a copy rotated at 45°. With the second copy still selected, you used the Transform Again command twice, creating two more rotated copies. You then grouped the four ellipses.

Create a star and a triangle, and use the Reflect tool

1. Select the **Star tool** 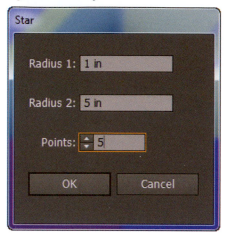, then click **anywhere on the artboard**.

   The Star tool is hidden beneath the current shape tool.

2. Type **1** in the Radius 1 text box, type **5** in the Radius 2 text box, type **5** in the Points text box, as shown in Figure 63, then click **OK**.

   A star has two radii; the first is from the center to the inner point, and the second is from the center to the outer point. The **radius** is a measurement from the center point of the star to either point.

3. Double-click the **Scale tool**, type **25** in the Scale text box, then click **OK**.

   When you create a star using the Star dialog box, the star is drawn upside down.

4. Fill the star with **white**, then apply a 5 pt blue stroke to it.

5. Click the **Selection tool**, then move the star so that it is completely within the red square.

6. Double-click the **Reflect tool**, click the **Horizontal option button**, as shown in Figure 64, then click **OK**.

   The star "flips" over an imaginary horizontal axis.

   TIP The Reflect tool is hidden beneath the Rotate tool.

7. Use the Selection tool or the arrow keys to position the star roughly in the center of the red square.

   Your work should resemble Figure 65.

   (continued)

Figure 63 *Star dialog box*

Figure 64 *Reflect dialog box*

Horizontal option button

Figure 65 *Reflecting the star horizontally*

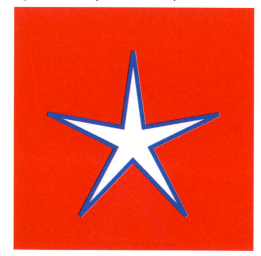

© 2015 Cengage Learning®

Getting to Know Illustrator

Figure 66 *The finished project*

TIP Arrow keys move a selected item in 1 pt increments, known as the Keyboard Increment. You can change this amount by clicking Edit (Win) or Illustrator (Mac) on the Menu bar, pointing to Preferences, clicking General, then typing a new value in the Keyboard Increment text box.

8. Click the **Polygon tool** on the Tools panel.

    The Polygon tool is hidden beneath the current shape tool on the Tools panel.

9. Click **anywhere on the blue square**.

10. Type **1.5** in the Radius text box, type **3** in the Sides text box, then click **OK**.

11. Fill the triangle with **red**.

12. Change the stroke color to **yellow** and the stroke weight to **22 pt**.

13. Position the triangle so that it is centered within the blue square.

    Your completed project should resemble Figure 66.

14. Save your work, then close Basic Shapes.

You used the shape tools to create a star and a triangle, then used the Reflect tool to "flip" the star over an imaginary horizontal axis.

Make Direct
SELECTIONS

What You'll Do

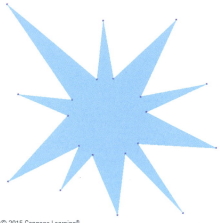

© 2015 Cengage Learning®

In this lesson, you will use the Direct Selection tool and a combination of menu commands, such as Add Anchor Points and Paste in Front, to convert existing shapes into new designs.

Using the Direct Selection Tool

The Direct Selection tool selects individual anchor points or single paths of an object. Using [Shift], you can select multiple anchor points or multiple paths. You can also select multiple points or paths by dragging a direct selection marquee. The tool also selects individual objects within a group, which can be useful for modifying just one object in a complex group. Figure 67 demonstrates the Direct Selection tool selecting one piece of a grouped object.

Clicking the center of an object with the Direct Selection tool selects the entire object. Clicking the edge selects the path segment only; the anchor points on the object all appear white, which means they are not selected. A white anchor point is not selected.

The Direct Selection tool gives you the power to distort simple objects such as squares and circles into unique shapes. Don't underestimate its significance. While the Selection tool is no more than a means to an end for selecting and moving objects, the Direct Selection tool is in itself a drawing tool. You will use it over and over again to modify and perfect your artwork.

Adding Anchor Points

As you distort basic shapes with the Direct Selection tool, you will often find that to create more complex shapes, you will need additional anchor points.

The Add Anchor Points command creates new anchor points without distorting the object. To add anchor points to an object, click the Object menu, point to Path, then click Add Anchor Points. The new points are automatically positioned exactly between the original anchor points. You can create as many additional points as you wish to use.

Turning Objects into Guides

Guides are one of Illustrator's many features that help you work with precision. Any object you create can be turned into a guide. With the object selected, click the View menu, point to Guides, then click Make Guides. Guides can be locked or unlocked in the same location. It is a good idea to work with locked guides so that they don't interfere with your

Figure 67 *Using the Direct Selection tool*

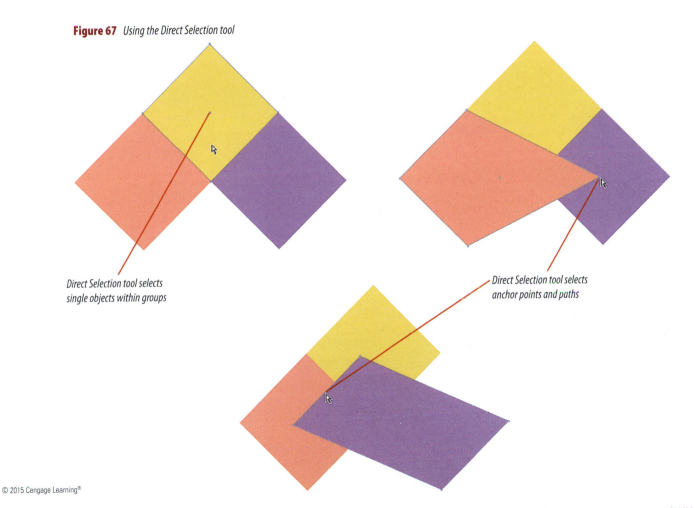

Direct Selection tool selects
single objects within groups

Direct Selection tool selects
anchor points and paths

artwork. Unlock guides only when you want to select them or delete them.

When an object is turned into a guide, it loses its attributes, such as its fill, stroke, and stroke weight. However, Illustrator remembers the original attributes for each guide. To transform a guide back to its original object, first unlock, then select the guide. Click the View menu, point to Guides, then click Release Guides.

Working with the Stacking Order

The **stacking order** refers to the order of how objects are arranged in front and behind other objects on the artboard. Every time you create an object, it is created in front of the existing objects. (Note that this discussion does not include any role of layers and the Layers panel.) You can manipulate the stacking order with the Arrange commands on the Object menu. See Table 3 below for descriptions of each Arrange command.

You can also use the **Draw Behind drawing mode** to create an object behind a selected object or at the bottom of the stacking order.

TABLE 3: ARRANGE COMMANDS			
Command	**Result**	**quick key (Win)**	**quick key (Mac)**
Bring Forward	Brings a selected object forward one position in the stacking order	[Ctrl][right bracket]	⌘ [right bracket]
Bring to Front	Brings a selected object to the very front of the stacking order—in front of all other objects	[Shift][Ctrl] [right bracket]	[Shift] ⌘ [right bracket]
Send Backward	Sends a selected object backward one position	[Ctrl][left bracket]	⌘ [left bracket]
Send to Back	Sends a selected object to the very back of the stacking order—behind all the other objects	[Shift][Ctrl] [left bracket]	[Shift] ⌘ [left bracket]

© 2015 Cengage Learning®

Deactivating Corner Widgets when Using the Direct Selection tool

When you select the Direct Selection tool and select an object on the page, it is likely that you will see small icons beside the selected object. These are corner widgets, and they are a new feature in Illustrator Creative Cloud that allows you to modify the corners of objects into round and pointed corners. We cover this extensively in this book in Chapter 4. When doing the many exercises in this book that involve using the Direct Selection tool, it is best that you deactivate corner widgets so that they don't distract from your work. To do so, click the View menu, then click Hide Corner Widget.

Figure 68 *Red square selected with the Direct Selection tool*

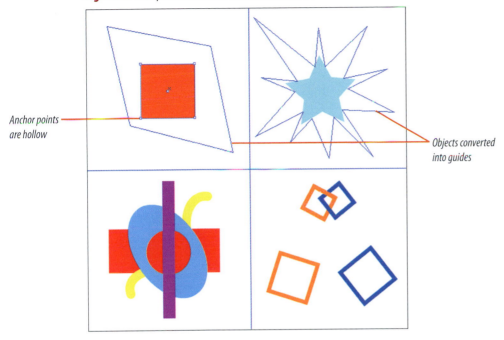

Anchor points
are hollow

Objects converted
into guides

Figure 69 *Red square distorted*

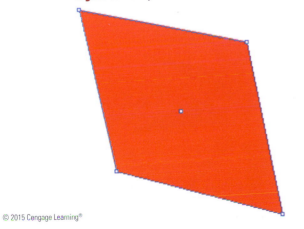

Lesson 8   Make Direct Selections

Make guides and direct selections

1. Open AI 1-4.ai, then save it as **Direct Selections**.
2. Click **View** on the Menu bar, then deactivate the Smart Guides feature.
3. Select the green polygon with the Selection tool ▸ .
4. Click **View** on the Menu bar, point to **Guides**, then click **Make Guides**.

   The polygon is converted to a guide.

TIP If you do not see the polygon-shaped guide, click View on the Menu bar, point to Guides, then click Show Guides.

5. Convert the purple starburst to a guide.
6. Click **View** on the Menu bar, point to **Guides**, verify that there is a check mark to the left of Lock Guides, then click the pasteboard to close the menu.
7. Click the **Direct Selection tool** ▸ , then click the **edge of the red square**.

   The four anchor points turn white, as shown in Figure 68.

TIP See important sidebar on page 56.

8. Click and drag the **anchor points** to the four corners of the guide to distort the square.

   Your work should resemble Figure 69.

You converted two objects to guides. You then used the Direct Selection tool to create a new shape from a square by moving anchor points independently.

Add anchor points

1. Using the Direct Selection tool 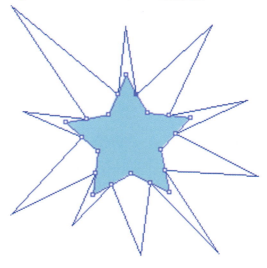, click the **center of the light blue star**, then note the anchor points used to define the shape.

2. Click **Object** on the Menu bar, point to **Path**, then click **Add Anchor Points**.

3. Click the **artboard** to deselect the star, then click the **edge of the star**.

   All the anchor points turn white and are available to be selected independently, as shown in Figure 70.

4. Move the top anchor point on the star to align with the top point of the guide that you made earlier.

5. Working clockwise, move every other anchor point outward to align with the guide, creating a ten-point starburst.

   Your work should resemble Figure 71.

6. Select and move any of the inner anchor points to modify the starburst to your liking.

You used the Add Anchor Points command and the Direct Selection tool to create an original ten-point starburst from a generic five-point star.

Figure 70 *Star selected with Direct Selection tool*

Figure 71 *Completed starburst*

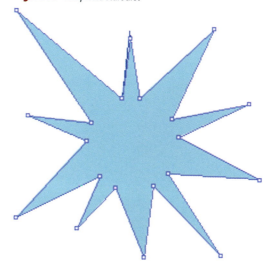

Figure 72 *Red rectangle sent to the back of the stacking order*

Figure 73 *Blue oval moved forward in the stacking order*

Use the Draw Behind drawing mode

1. Click the **Expand panels button** ◄◄ at the top of the Tools panel if necessary to display the tools in two rows.

   When the Tools panel is displayed in two rows, the three drawing modes are visible as icons at the bottom. When the panel is displayed in a single row, you need to click the Drawing Modes icon to display the tools in a submenu.

2. Note the four objects in the bottom-left quadrant of the artboard.

   The blue oval is at the back, the purple rectangle is in front of the blue oval, the curvy yellow path is in front of the purple rectangle, and the red rectangle is at the front.

3. Click the **Selection tool** ▷ , click the **red rectangle**, click **Object** on the Menu bar, point to **Arrange**, then click **Send to Back**.

   As shown in Figure 72, the red rectangle moves to the back of the stacking order.

4. Select the **yellow path**, click **Object** on the Menu bar, point to **Arrange**, then click **Send Backward**.

   The path moves one level back in the stacking order. When discussing the stacking order, it's smart to use the term "level" instead of "layer." In Illustrator, layers are different than the stacking order.

5. Select the **blue oval**, click **Object** on the Menu bar, point to **Arrange**, then click **Bring Forward**.

   As shown in Figure 73, the blue oval moves one level forward in the stacking order.

(continued)

6. Select the **purple rectangle**, then click the **Draw Behind button** 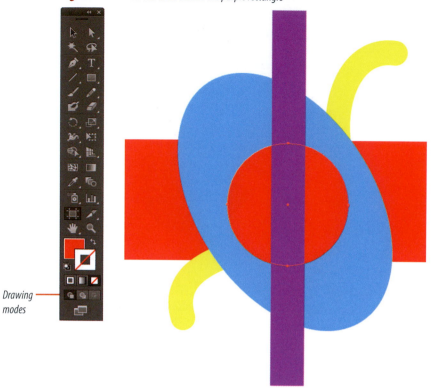 at the bottom of the Tools panel.

There are three available drawing modes: Draw Normal, Draw Behind, and Draw Inside.

7. Click the **Ellipse tool** on the Tools panel, then draw a circle at the center of the blue oval.

The circle is created behind the purple rectangle, though it still appears to be in front while it is selected. With the Draw Behind drawing mode activated, an object you draw will be positioned one level behind any selected object on the artboard. If no object is selected, the new object will be positioned at the back of the stacking order.

8. Click the **Eyedropper tool**, click the **red rectangle**, then compare your artboard to Figure 74.

The Eyedropper tool samples the fill and stroke color from the red rectangle and applies it to the selected object.

9. Click the **Draw Normal button**, then save your work.

You arranged objects on the artboard, used the Draw Behind feature, then changed the color of the circle you created.

Figure 74 *The new red circle behind the purple rectangle*

Drawing modes

Figure 75 *Completed linked squares*

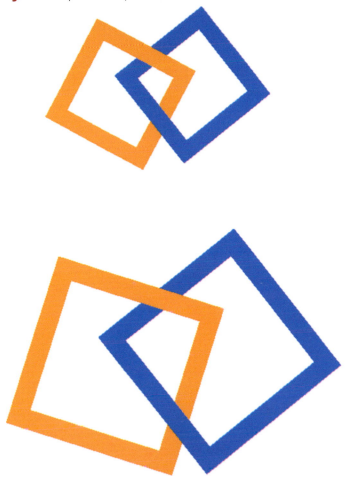

Create a simple special effect utilizing a direct selection

1. Click the **Selection tool** , overlap the large orange and blue squares so that they resemble the small orange and blue squares, then deselect.

2. Click the **Direct Selection tool** , then select the **top path segment** of the orange square.

   It will look like the whole square is selected, but you will see white anchor points in the four corners.

3. Copy the path.

4. Select the intersecting path segment on the blue square.

5. Paste in front, then save your work.

   Your work should resemble Figure 75.

6. Close the document.

   TIP Remember this technique; it's one you can use over and over again to create interesting artwork in Illustrator.

You performed a classic Illustrator trick using the Direct Selection tool. Selecting only a path, you copied it and pasted it in front of an intersecting object to create the illusion that the two objects were linked.

Work with
MULTIPLE ARTBOARDS

What You'll Do

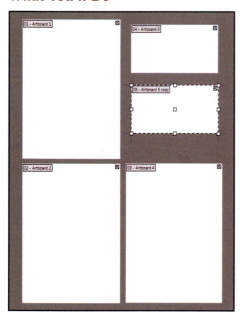

 In this lesson, you will explore various options when working with multiple artboards.

Understanding Multiple Artboards

The artboard is your workspace in an Illustrator document. Sometimes, the size of the artboard will be important to your design; sometimes it won't. For example, let's say that you're designing a logo that will be used for a variety of items such as letterhead, business cards, a poster, or a building sign. When you are creating the logo, you're just designing artwork. The size at which you're creating the artwork isn't really important, because you can resize it later to use in these different types of layouts.

At other times, the work you do in Illustrator will be at a specific size. Let's say, for example, that you're designing layouts for letterhead, business cards, and promotional postcards for the company for which you made the logo. In this case, you would need to set up your document, or the size of the artboard, at specific sizes, such as 8.5" x 11" for the letterhead, 3" x 2.5" for the business card, and 4" x 6" for the postcard.

Illustrator allows you to have anywhere from 1 to 100 artboards in a single document, depending on the size of the artboards. Using the above example, this means that you could design all three pieces in one document—no need to switch between documents for the letterhead, business card, and postcard.

Beyond this basic convenience, working with multiple artboards offers a number of important benefits. You won't have to recreate unique swatch colors or gradients; you'll only need to create them once. Paste commands are available on the Edit menu that allow you to paste an object on multiple artboards in exactly the same location—another example of the consistency that can be achieved by working in a single document.

Managing Multiple Artboards

Creating multiple artboards can be the first thing that you do when beginning a design or one of the last things you do. The New Document dialog box, shown in Figure 76, is where you define the specifics of a document, including the number of artboards.

The Width and Height values define the size of all the artboards you create at this stage, whether single or multiple, but you can resize artboards any time after creating them. Once you specify the number of artboards, you have controls for the layout of the artboards. The four buttons to the right of the Number of Artboards text box offer basic layout choices—grid by row, grid by column, arrange by row, arrange by column. The Spacing text box specifies the physical space between artboards, and the Rows value defines the number of rows of artboards in a grid.

When you click the OK button in the New Document dialog box, the document window displays all artboards, as shown in Figure 77.

Note that the top-left artboard is highlighted with a black line. This identifies the artboard as "active." As such, all View menu commands you apply affect this artboard. In other words, if you click the Fit Artboard in Window command, the active artboard is resized to fit in the document window. You can also click the Fit All in Window command to view all artboards.

When you create a new document, you can use a preset document profile in the New Document dialog box. The Document Profile menu lists a number of preset values for size, color mode, units, orientation, transparency, and resolution. This can help you set up the basic orientation for your document quickly. For example, the Web profile automatically creates an RGB document with pixels as units. By default, all new document profiles use one artboard, but you can add more in the Number of Artboards text box.

Figure 76 *New Document dialog box*

Figure 77 *Viewing multiple artboards*

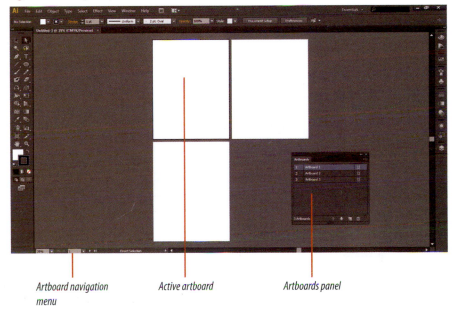

Artboard navigation menu   Active artboard   Artboards panel

The **Artboard tool**, shown in Figure 78, is your gateway to managing multiple artboards. Clicking the Artboard tool takes you to "edit artboards mode." As shown in Figure 79, all your artboards appear numbered against a dark gray background. The "selected" artboard is highlighted with a marquee. When an artboard is selected, you can change settings for it on the Control panel beneath the Menu bar, using the following options:

- Click the Presets menu to change a selected artboard to any of the standard sizes listed, such as Letter, Tabloid, or Legal.

- Click the Portrait or Landscape buttons to specify the orientation for the selected artboard.
- Click the New Artboard button to create a duplicate of the selected artboard.
- Click the Delete Artboard button to delete the selected artboard.
- Click the Name text box to enter a name for the selected artboard. This could be

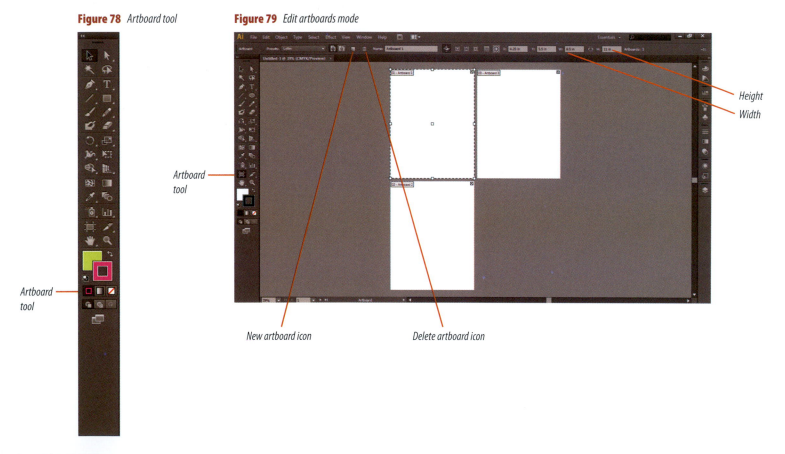

Figure 78 *Artboard tool*

Artboard tool

Figure 79 *Edit artboards mode*

Height

Width

Artboard tool

New artboard icon

Delete artboard icon

useful for managing your own work and for adding clarity when you hand your Illustrator file over to a printer or some other vendor.

- Click the Width and Height text boxes to enter different values and resize the selected artboard.

To exit edit artboards mode, press the Escape key or any other tool on the Tools panel.

Creating, Editing, and Arranging Artboards

Once you click the Artboard tool to enter edit artboards mode, you have a number of options for creating, editing and arranging artboards.

You can click the New Artboard button on the Control panel. When you do, move your cursor over the other artboards and you'll see a transparent artboard moving with the cursor, as shown in Figure 80. If you have

smart guides activated, green lines will appear to help you align the new artboard with the existing artboards. Click where you want to position the new artboard. Using this method, the new artboard button will create a new button at the size specified in the New Document dialog box.

As an alternative, you can simply click and drag with the Artboard tool to create a new artboard, as shown in Figure 81. Once you

Figure 80 *Creating with the New Artboard button*

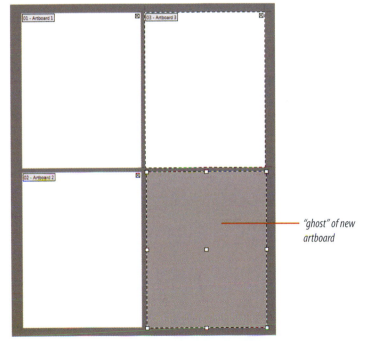

"ghost" of new artboard

Figure 81 *"Dragging out" a new artboard with the Artboard tool*

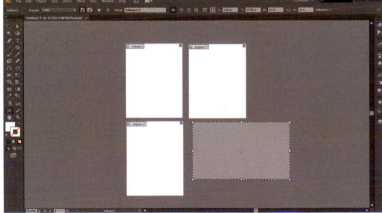

"drag out" the new artboard, you can enter a specific height and width for the artboard on the Control panel. To resize an existing artboard, first select the artboard, then enter values in the Width and Height text boxes. Figure 82 shows four artboards: letterhead, business card front, business card back, and 4 x 6 postcard. Note the Width and Height text boxes for the selected artboard.

The positioning of the artboards in the edit artboards window reflects the same layout that the artboards will be when exit edit artboards mode. You can manipulate the layout of artboards in the edit artboards window simply by clicking and dragging them as you wish. Figure 83 shows the same four artboards with a more centralized layout.

Printing Multiple Artboards

When you work with multiple artboards, you can print each artboard individually or you can compile them into one page. Usually, you'll want to print them individually, and this is easy to do in the Print dialog box. Use the forward and backward arrows in the print preview window to click through each artboard. In the Artboards section, if you click All, all artboards will print. To print only specific artboards, enter the artboard number in the Range field. To combine all artwork on all artboards onto a single page, select the Ignore Artboards option. Depending on how large your artboards are, they'll be scaled down to fit on a single page or tiled over a number of pages.

Figure 82 *Four different-sized artboards*

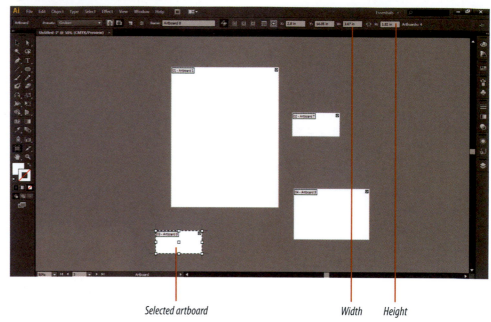

Selected artboard   Width   Height

Figure 83 *Repositioning artboards*

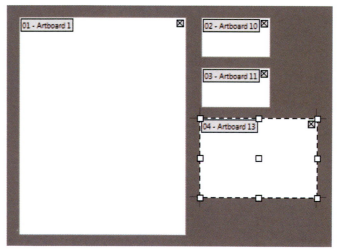

Using the Artboards Panel

You can use the Artboards panel to perform artboard operations. You can add or delete artboards, reorder and renumber them, and navigate through multiple artboards. When you create multiple artboards, each is assigned a number, and is listed with that number on the Artboards panel. If you select an artboard, you can click the up and down arrows to reorder the artboards in the panel. Doing so will renumber the artboard, but will not change its name.

Pasting Artwork on Multiple Artboards

The ability to paste copied artwork between multiple artboards is an important basic function and critical to maintain consistency between layouts. The Edit menu offers two powerful commands: Paste in Place and Paste on All Artboards. Use the Paste in Place command to paste an object from one artboard to the same spot on another. Figure 84 shows a logo pasted from the first artboard to the second. Even though the two artboards are drastically different sizes, the two logos are positioned at exactly the same distance from the top-left corner of the artboard.

The Paste on All Artboards command goes a giant step further, pasting artwork in the same position on all artboards, as shown in Figure 85.

Figure 84 *Paste in Place command used*

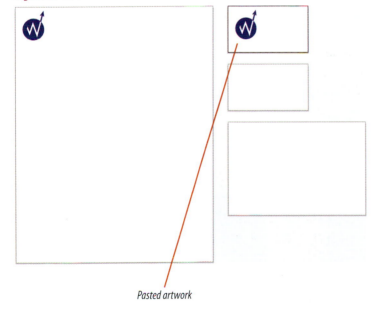

Pasted artwork

Figure 85 *Paste on All Artboards command used*

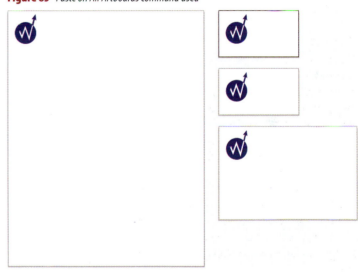

Create a new document with multiple artboards

1. Verify that no documents are open and that smart guides are activated.

TIP The Smart Guides command is on the View menu.

2. Click **File** on the Menu bar, then click **New**.

   The New Document dialog box opens.

3. Type **Winning Business Collateral** in the Name text box.

4. Set the number of artboards to **3**, then click the **Grid by Row button** 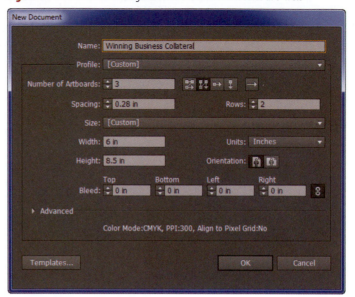.

5. Set the Spacing and Columns text boxes to **2**.

6. Set the Width to **6** and the Height to **8.5**.

7. Verify that the Units are set to Inches, then compare your dialog box to Figure 86.

8. Click **OK**.

   When you click OK, the three artboards fit in your document window, as shown in Figure 87

9. Click the **Selection tool** , then click **each artboard** to make each active.

   A black frame highlights each artboard when it is selected.

10. Click the **top-right artboard** to make it the active artboard, click **View** on the Menu bar, then click **Fit Artboard in Window**.

TIP Make a note of the quick key for this command: [Ctrl] [0] (Win) or [0] (Mac). The 0 in this shortcut key is a zero, not the letter O.

(continued)

Figure 86 *New Document dialog box set to create three artboards at 6" x 8.5"*

Figure 87 *Document with three artboards*

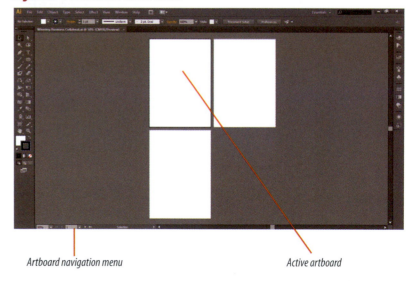

Artboard navigation menu

Active artboard

Figure 88 *Edit Artboards mode*

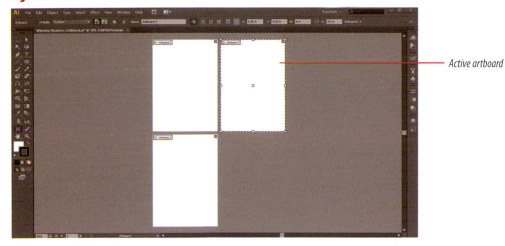

Active artboard

Figure 89 *Creating a new artboard with the New Artboard button*

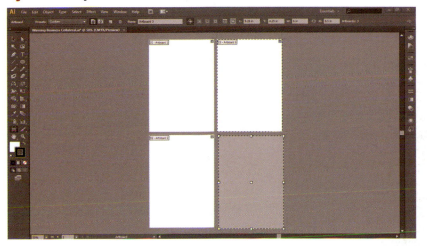

11. Click **View** on the Menu bar, then click **Fit All in Window**.

You specified settings for a new document with three artboards in the New Document dialog box. You clicked artboards in the document to activate them. You used the Fit in Window and Fit All in Window commands to view artboards.

Create and name artboards

1. Click the **Artboard tool** [icon].

   Clicking the Artboard tool switches the interface to Edit Artboards mode, shown in Figure 88. The top-right artboard is selected. All the artboards are numbered.

2. Click the **New Artboard button** [icon] on the Control panel.

3. Float your cursor over the artboards and position the new artboard as shown in Figure 89.

(continued)

4. Click to position the new artboard.

The New Artboard button creates a new artboard at the specified document size (in this case, 6" x 8.5").

5. Click the **top-right artboard**, then click the **Delete Artboard button** 🗑 on the Control panel.

TIP You can also click the small x in the upper-right corner to delete an artboard.

6. Click and drag with the **Artboard tool** ▣ to create a small new artboard, as shown in Figure 90.

(continued)

Figure 90 *"Dragging and dropping" a new artboard with the Artboard tool*

Figure 91 *New artboard created by dragging and dropping*

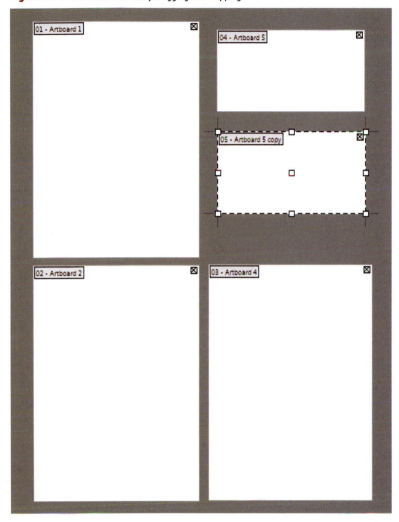

01 - Artboard 1

04 - Artboard 5

05 - Artboard 5 copy

02 - Artboard 2

03 - Artboard 4

7. Press and hold **[Alt]** (Win) or **[option]** (Mac), then drag and drop a copy of the new artboard in the space beneath it, as shown in Figure 91.

8. Click the **bottom-left artboard** to select it, then type **Bookmark** in the Name text box on the Control panel.

9. Name the bottom-right artboard **Buckslip**.

10. Name the top-left artboard **Letterhead**.

11. Name the two new objects **Biz Card Front** and **Biz Card Back** respectively.

You created a new artboard using three different methods: using the New Artboard button, using the Artboard tool, and dragging and dropping. You named all artboards.

Resize and arrange artboards

1. Click the **artboard named Bookmark** to select it, type **2** in the W (width) panel on the Control panel, then press **[Enter]** (Win) or **[return]** (Mac)

   As shown in Figure 92, the artboard is resized.

2. Resize the artboard named Buckslip to 4" wide x 6" height.

3. Resize the two business cards to 3.5" x 2."

4. Click the **Letterhead artboard**, click the **Presets menu** on the Control panel, then click **Letter**.

   The artboard is resized to 8.5" x 11"

5. Click and drag the **artboards** to arrange them as shown in Figure 93.

6. Click the **Selection tool** ![cursor] to escape Edit Artboards mode, then save the file.

You resized and arranged artboards.

Figure 92 *Resizing the Bookmark layout*

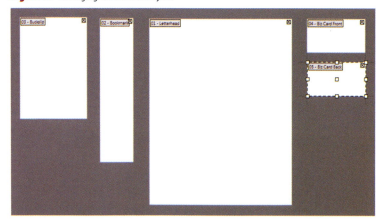

Figure 93 *Arranging the artboard layout*

Figure 94 *The Artboard Navigation menu*

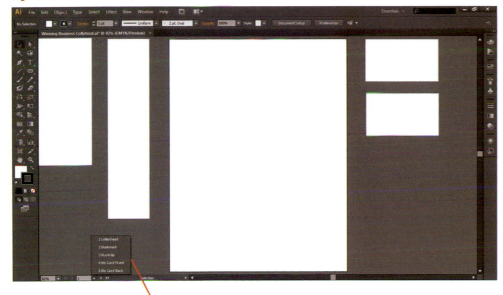

Artboard Navigation menu

Paste artwork between artboards

1. Open the file named **Winning Logo.ai**.

2. Click **Select** on the Menu bar, click **All**, click **Edit** on the Menu bar, then click **Copy**.

3. Close Winning Logo.ai.

4. In the Winning Business Collateral document, click the **Artboard Navigation menu list arrow** in the lower-left corner, then click **Letterhead**, as shown in Figure 94.

(continued)

5. Click **Edit** on the Menu bar, click **Paste**, then position the artwork as shown in Figure 95.

6. Click **Edit** on the Menu bar, then click **Copy**.

   Even though the artwork is already copied, you need to copy it again so that it is copied from this specific location.

7. Click the **Buckslip artboard** (farthest to the left) to make it the active artboard.

8. Click **Edit** on the Menu bar, then click **Paste in Place**.

   The artwork is placed in the same location, relative to the top-left corner of the artboard, on the Buckslip artboard.

   (continued)

Figure 95 *Positioning artwork*

Getting to Know Illustrator

Figure 96 *Artwork pasted on all artboards*

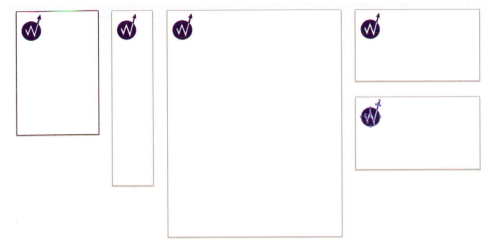

9. Click **Edit** on the Menu bar, then click **Paste on All Artboards**.
10. Click **View**, click **Fit All in Window**, then compare your screen to Figure 96.
11. Save and close Winning Business Collateral.ai.

You copied artwork, then pasted it in a specific location on one artboard. You used the Paste in Place command to paste the artwork in the same location on another artboard. You then used the Paste on All Artboards command to paste the artwork on all artboards.

Explore the Illustrator workspace.

1. Launch Adobe Illustrator.
2. Click File on the Menu bar, click Open, navigate to the drive and folder where your Chapter 1 Data Files are stored, click AI 1-5.ai, then click Open.
3. Click Window on the Menu bar, point to Workspace, then click [Essentials].
4. Click the double-arrows on the Tools panel to see two setups for the Tools panel.
5. Point to the Type tool, then press and hold the mouse button to see the Type on a Path tool.
6. View the hidden tools behind the other tools with small black triangles.
7. Click Edit (Win) or Illustrator (Mac) on the Menu bar, point to Preferences, click General, verify that Show Tool Tips is checked, then click OK.
8. Position your mouse pointer over the Direct Selection tool until its tool tip appears.
9. Click the Selection tool, then press the following keys and note which tools are selected with each key: [p], [v], [t], [i], [h], [z] [a].
10. Press [Tab] to temporarily hide all open panels, then press [Tab] again.
11. Click the Color panel icon in the stack of collapsed panels to the right of the pasteboard to open the Color panel.
12. Click the Collapse panels button at the top of the panel to minimize the panel, then click Color to open the panel again.
13. Drag the Color panel name tab to the left so it is ungrouped.
14. Click the Swatches panel icon in the stack of collapsed panels to the right of the pasteboard to open the Swatches panel.
15. Drag the Swatches panel name tab to the left so it is ungrouped.
16. Drag the Swatches panel name tab to the blank space next to the Color panel name tab, then release the mouse button.
17. Click Window on the Menu bar, then click Info.
18. Drag the Info panel name tab to the bottom edge of the Color and Swatches panels group until you see a blue horizontal line appear, then release the mouse button to dock the Info panel.
19. Click and drag the dark gray bar at the top of the panel group, found above the Color and Swatches panel name tabs, to move the docked panels.
20. Click the Info panel name tab, then drag it away from the other two panels.
21. Click Window on the Menu bar, point to Workspace, then click Reset Essentials.
22. Press [z] to access the Zoom tool.
23. Position the Zoom tool over the document window, click twice to enlarge it, press [Alt] (Win) or [option] (Mac), then click twice to reduce the document.
24. Click the Zoom Level list arrow in the lower-left corner of the document window, then click 600%.
25. Note that 600% is now listed in the document tab.
26. Double-click 800% in the Zoom Level text box, type **300**, then press [Enter] (Win) or [return] (Mac).
27. Click the Hand tool on the Tools panel, then click and drag the document window to scroll.
28. Double-click the Zoom tool.
29. Click the Selection tool, point to the center of the document window, then press and hold [Ctrl] [Spacebar] (Win) or [⌘] [Spacebar] (Mac).
30. Click three times, then release [Ctrl] [Spacebar] (Win) or [⌘] [Spacebar] (Mac).
31. Press and hold [Spacebar] to access the Hand tool, then scroll around the image.
32. Press and hold [Ctrl] [Alt] [Spacebar] (Win) or [⌘] [option] [Spacebar] (Mac), then click the mouse multiple times to reduce the view to 25%.

View and modify artboard elements.

1. Click View on the Menu bar, note the shortcut key on the Fit Page in Window command, then click Fit Page in Window.
2. Click View on the Menu bar, then note the Rulers command and its shortcut key.
3. Leave the View menu, then press [Ctrl] [R] (Win) or  [R] (Mac) several times to hide and show rulers, finishing with rulers showing.
4. Note the units on the rulers.
5. Click Edit (Win) or Illustrator (Mac) on the Menu bar, point to Preferences, then click Units.
6. Click the General list arrow to see the available measurement options, then click Picas.
7. Click OK.
8. Reopen the Units Preferences dialog box, click the General list arrow, then click Inches.
9. Click OK.
10. Select all the objects on the artboard.
11. Click View on the Menu bar, then note the Hide/Show Edges command and its shortcut key.
12. Leave the View menu, then press [Ctrl] [H] (Win) or [H] (Mac) several times to switch between hiding and showing selection marks, finishing with selection marks showing.
13. Click the View menu, point to Guides, then note the Guides commands and their shortcut keys.
14. Escape the View menu, then press [Ctrl] [;] (Win) or [;] (Mac) several times to hide and show guides, finishing with guides showing.

15. Click View on the Menu bar, then click Show Grid.
16. Press [Ctrl] ["] (Win) or ["] (Mac) several times to hide and show the grid.
17. Hide guides and the grid.
18. Click View on the Menu bar, then note the quick key command for Outline mode.

19. Enter [Ctrl] [Y] (Win) or [Y] (Mac) repeatedly to toggle between Outline and Preview modes, finishing in Preview mode, as shown in Figure 97.
20. Click Edit (Win) or Illustrator (Mac) on the Menu bar, point to Preferences, then click User Interface.

Figure 97 *Skills Review, Part 1*

21. Verify that the Open Documents As Tabs check box is checked, then click OK.
22. Save AI 1-5.ai as **Model**.
23. Open AI 1-2.ai, then click the tabs of each document several times to toggle between them, finishing with Model.ai as the active document.
24. Drag the Model.ai tab straight down approximately ½ inch.
25. Position your mouse pointer over the upper-right or bottom-right corner of the document, then click and drag towards the center of the monitor window to reduce the window to approximately half its size.
26. Position your mouse pointer over the title bar of the document, then click and drag to move Model.ai halfway down towards the bottom of your monitor screen.
27. Position your mouse pointer over the title bar of Model.ai, click and drag to position it at the top of the window beside the AI 1-2.ai tab, then release the mouse button when you see a horizontal blue bar.
28. Close AI 1-2.ai without saving changes if you are prompted.
29. Close Model.ai without saving changes if you are prompted.

Work with objects and smart guides.

1. Open AI 1-6.ai, then save it as **Object Skills**.
2. Click View on the Menu bar, then verify that the Bounding Box command is set to Show Bounding Box.
3. Click the Selection tool, then click the yellow square to select it.
4. Click View on the Menu bar, then click Show Bounding Box.
5. Click and drag various handles and note how the object is resized.
6. When you are done experimenting, undo all of the moves you made.
7. Click to select the purple circle.
8. Press and hold down [Alt] (Win) or [option] (Mac), then start dragging any corner handle.
9. While still dragging, press and hold [Shift].
10. Scale the circle to any size.
11. Undo the move.
12. Select All.
13. Using the skills you learned in this lesson, reduce the size of the objects in proportion so that they are very small on the artboard, then click the artboard to deselect the objects.

14. Click File on the Menu bar, click Revert, then click Revert when you are prompted to confirm.
15. Click the View menu, then click Hide Bounding Box.
16. Select the star, then copy it, using the [Ctrl] [C] (Win) or ⌘ [C] (Mac) shortcut keys.
17. Click Edit on the Menu bar, then click Paste to place a copy of the star at the center of the artboard.
18. Undo the paste.
19. Click Edit on the Menu bar, then click Paste in Front.
20. Press [I] on your keypad to switch to the Eyedropper tool, then click the yellow square.
21. Press the right arrow key on your keypad ten times.
22. Deselect all, click Edit on the Menu bar, then click Paste in Back.
23. Click the Eyedropper tool on the purple circle.
24. Press and hold [Shift], then press the ← on your keypad one time.
25. Press and hold [Ctrl] (Win) or ⌘ (Mac) so that your cursor switches temporarily from the Eyedropper tool to the Selection tool, then click the artboard with the Selection tool to deselect all.

26. Click the Selection tool, then select the purple circle.
27. Press and hold [Alt] (Win) or [option] (Mac), then drag a copy of the circle to the center of the square. Your screen should resemble Figure 98.
28. Save your work, then close the file.
29. Open AI 1-7.ai, then save it as **Group Skills**.
30. Click Object on the Menu bar, then click Show All.
31. Click Object on the Menu bar, then click Group.
32. Click the Selection tool, click anywhere on the pasteboard to deselect all, then click the largest blue square.
33. Click the pasteboard to deselect all, click the Direct Selection tool, then click the same square.
34. Select all, click Object on the Menu bar, then click Ungroup.
35. Deselect all.
36. Click the Selection tool, select the smallest square, click Object on the Menu bar, click Lock, then click Selection.

Figure 98 *Skills Review, Part 2*

37. Click Object on the Menu bar, then click Unlock All.
38. Select the three blue squares, click Object on the Menu bar, then click Hide.
39. Click Object on the Menu bar, then click Show All.

40. Click View on the Menu bar, then verify that Smart Guides is checked.
41. Click the large blue square, then drag it by its center point toward the center of the artboard.

42. Release the mouse button when the word center appears.
43. Using the same steps, align all the squares so that your artboard resembles Figure 99.
44. Save and close the file.

Figure 99 *Skills Review, Part 3*

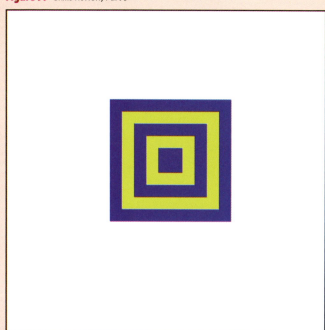

Create basic shapes and apply fill and stroke colors to objects.

1. Create a new document and name it **Flag**.
2. Make the size of the document 6" × 4".
3. Select Inches for the type of units, 1 for the number of artboards, and CMYK Color for the color mode, then click OK.
4. Click File on the Menu bar, click Save As, navigate to the drive and folder where you store your Data Files, then click Save.
5. Create a circle at the center of the artboard.
6. Click the Selection tool.
7. Set the Fill and Stroke buttons on the Tools panel to Black and [None] respectively.
8. Create a rectangle that is 3" × 1".
9. Show the Swatches panel if necessary.
10. Fill the rectangle with a light yellow.
11. Click View on the Menu bar, verify that Smart Guides are active.
12. Move the rectangle so that its top-left anchor point intersects with the top-left corner of the artboard.
13. Click the top-left anchor point, press and hold [Shift][Alt](Win) or [Shift][option] (Mac), drag straight down until the top-left anchor point touches the bottom-left anchor point (the "intersect" smart guide appears), then release the mouse button.

Transform and align objects.

1. Click Object on the Menu bar, point to Transform, then click Transform Again.
2. Repeat Step 14.
3. Change the fill color of the second and fourth rectangles to a darker yellow.
4. Save your work.
5. Select the four rectangles.
6. Double-click the Reflect tool, click the Horizontal option button, then click Copy. The four rectangles are copied on top of the original rectangles.
7. Move the four new rectangles to the right so that they align with the right side of the artboard.
8. Click the Rectangle tool, click the artboard, then create a square that is .75" x .75".
9. Apply a 1-point Black stroke and no fill to the square.
10. Click the Selection tool, click the edge of the square, then position it at the center of the artboard.
11. Use the Rotate dialog box to create a copy of the square rotated at 10°.
12. Apply the Transform Again command seven times.
13. Save your work.

Make direct selections.

1. Shift-click to select the nine black squares.
2. Click Object on the Menu bar, then click Group.
3. Scale the group of squares 200%.
4. Create a 3.75" × 3.75" circle, fill it with Orange, add a 1-point Black stroke, then position it at the center of the artboard.
5. Cut the circle from the artboard, click the group of black squares, click Edit on the Menu bar, then click Paste in Back.
6. Adjust the location of the circle as needed.
7. Click Object on the Menu bar, point to Path, then click Add Anchor Points.
8. Deselect the circle by clicking anywhere on the artboard.
9. Click the Direct Selection tool, then click the edge of the circle.
10. One at a time, move each of the four new anchor points to the center of the circle.
11. Switch to the Selection tool, then select the orange-filled shape.
12. Double-click the Rotate tool, type **22** in the Angle text box, then click Copy.
13. Apply the Transform Again command two times.
14. Save your work, then compare your illustration to Figure 100.
15. Close the Flag document.

Figure 100 *Skills Review, Part 4*

Work with multiple artboards.

1. Open AI 1-8. ai, then save it as **Artboard Skills**.
2. Click the Artboard tool.
3. Click the New Artboard button on the Control panel.
4. Float your cursor over the artboard, then position the new artboard to the right of the original.
5. Scroll to the right of the newest artboard.
6. Click and drag with the Artboard tool to create a new artboard of any size to the right of the new artboard.
7. Click the original artboard and name it **Stationery**.
8. Type **8** in the W (width) text box on the Control panel, type **10** in the H (height) text box, then press [Enter] (Win) or [return] (Mac).
9. Name the second artboard **Envelope**, then resize it to 9" wide x 3" height.
10. Name the third artboard **Business Card**, then resize it to 3.5" x 2"
11. Click the View menu, then click Fit All in Window.
12. Click and drag the artboards to arrange them as shown in Figure 101.
13. Save then close the file.

Figure 101 *Completed Skills Review*

The lady who owns the breakfast shop that you frequent knows that you are a designer and asks for your help. Her nephew has designed a sign for her store window, but she confides in you that she doesn't like it. She thinks that it's boring and "flat." She wants to redesign the sign with something that is "original" and feels more like a starburst.

1. Open AI 1-9.ai, then save it as **Window Sign**.
2. Click the Direct Selection tool, then click the edge of the star.
3. Move two of the outer anchor points of the star farther from its center.
4. Move four of the inner points toward the center.
5. Select the entire star.
6. Reflect a copy of the star across the horizontal axis.
7. Fill the new star with an orange swatch and reposition it to your liking.
8. Group the two stars.
9. Copy the group, then paste in back.
10. Fill the copies with black.
11. Using your arrow keys, move the black copies five points to the right and five points down.
12. Select only the orange star using the Direct Selection tool.
13. Copy the orange star, then paste in back.
14. Fill the new copy with black.
15. Rotate the black copy 8°.
16. Apply a yellow fill to the orange star, then apply a 1-point Black stroke to both yellow stars.
17. Save your work, then compare your illustration to Figure 102.
18. Close Window Sign.

Figure 102 *Completed Project Builder 1*

© 2015 Cengage Learning®

Getting to Know Illustrator

Iris Vision Labs has contracted with your design firm to bid on a design for their logo. Researching the company, you learn that they are a biotech firm whose mission is to develop cures for genetic blindness and vision problems. You decide to build your design around the idea of an iris.

1. Create a new document that is 6" × 6".
2. Save the document as **Iris Vision Design**.
3. Create an ellipse that is 1" wide × 4" in height, and position it at the center of the artboard.
4. Fill the ellipse with [None], and add a 1-point blue stroke.
5. Create a copy of the ellipse rotated at 15°.
6. Apply the Transform Again command 10 times.
7. Select all and group the ellipses.
8. Create a copy of the group rotated at 5°.
9. Apply a red stroke to the new group.
10. Transform again.
11. Apply a bright blue stroke to the new group.
12. Select all.
13. Rotate a copy of the ellipses 2.5°.
14. Create a circle that is 2" × 2".
15. Fill the circle with a shade of gray.
16. Remove the stroke from the circle.
17. Position the gray-filled circle in the center of the ellipses.
18. Cut the circle.
19. Select all.
20. Paste in back.
21. Save your work, then compare your illustration to Figure 103.
22. Close Iris Vision Design.

Figure 103 *Completed Project Builder 2*

The owner of Emerald Design Studios has hired you to design an original logo for her new company. She's a beginner with Illustrator, but she's created a simple illustration of what she has in mind. She tells you to create something "more sophisticated." The only other information that she offers about her company is that they plan to specialize in precise, geometric design.

1. Open AI 1-10.ai, then save it as **Emerald Logo**.
2. Select all four diamonds and group them.
3. Select the group of diamonds on the artboard, then create a 75% copy.
4. Use the Transform Again command five times.
5. Use smart guides or Outline mode to help you identify each of the seven groups.
6. Rotate one of the groups 75°.
7. Select two other groups of your choice and repeat the last transformation, using the Transform Again command.
8. Apply a dark green stroke to all groups. Figure 104 shows one possible result of multiple transformations. Your illustration may differ.
9. Save your work, then close Emerald Logo.

Figure 104 *Completed Design Project*

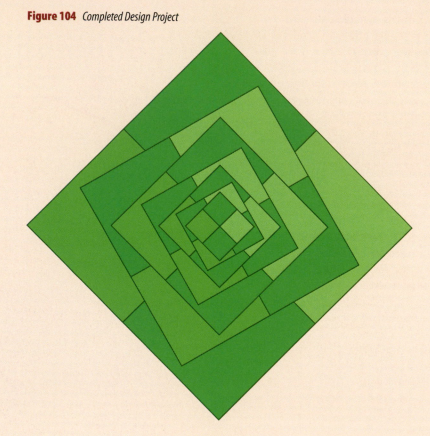

You attend a design school, and you're part of a team that is responsible for the artwork placed throughout the common areas of the school. One of the most admired professors brings you a file that he created in Illustrator, admitting that he's a beginner. You open the file and notice that the file is poorly built—everything is misaligned and uneven. After consulting with the professor, you decide that the file needs to be rebuilt from scratch.

1. Open AI 1-11.ai, then save it as **Rings**.
2. Identify the areas of the file that are misaligned and poorly constructed.
3. Pull apart the file, object by object, to see how the effect was achieved.
4. Create a "game plan" for reproducing the artwork with precision. Where's the best place to start? What's the best methodology for recreating the professor's design?
5. Work to rebuild the file, using precise methods.
6. Save your work, then compare your illustration to Figure 105.
7. Close the Rings document.

Figure 105 *Sample Portfolio Project*

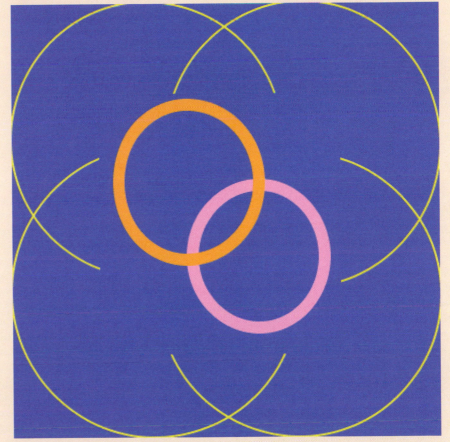

Getting to Know Illustrator

CHAPTER **2** CREATING TEXT
AND GRADIENTS

1. Create point text
2. Flow text into an object
3. Position text on a path
4. Manipulate text with the Touch Type tool
5. Create colors and gradients
6. Apply colors and gradients to text
7. Adjust a gradient and create a drop shadow
8. Apply gradients to strokes

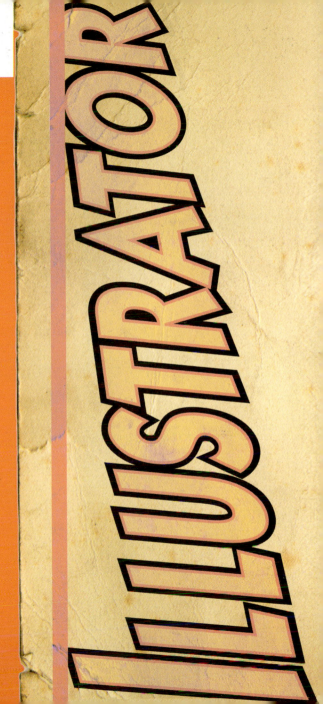

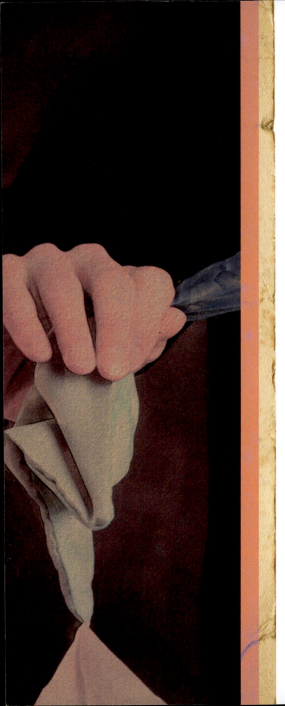

CHAPTER 2 CREATING TEXT AND GRADIENTS

Working with Text

When it comes to creating compelling and dramatic display text, no other software package offers the graphic sophistication that you'll find with Adobe Illustrator. You can quickly change fonts, font size, leading, and other text attributes with the Character panel. You can make tracking and kerning measurements with a level of precision that would satisfy even the most meticulous typographer. For the designer, Illustrator is the preeminent choice for typography. Powerful type tools offer the ability to fill objects with text, position text on curved or straight lines, and set type vertically, one letter on top of the next. Once the text is positioned, the Create Outlines command changes the fonts to vector graphics that you can manipulate as you would any other object. For example, you can apply a gradient fill to letter outlines for stunning effects.

Creating and Applying Gradient Fills

A **gradient** is a graduated blend between two or more colors used to fill an object or multiple objects. Illustrator's sophistication for creating gradients and its ease of use for applying them to objects are a dream come true for today's designers. You can create linear or radial gradients between multiple colors, then control the way they fill an object. Moreover, a single gradient can be used to fill multiple objects simultaneously! The unique gradient fills that you create can be saved with descriptive names, then imported into other Illustrator documents to be used again.

TOOLS YOU'LL USE

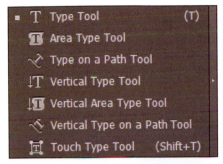

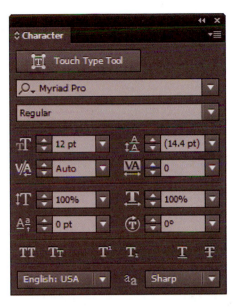

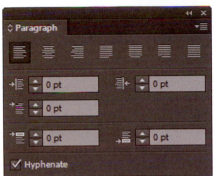

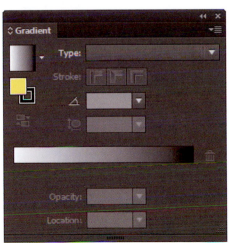

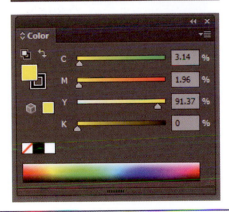

Create
POINT TEXT

What You'll Do

BERRY

 In this lesson, you will use the Type tool to create the word BERRY as display text. You will use the Character panel to format the text and perfect its appearance. You will also create a vertical version of the text.

Creating Text

You can create text anywhere on the artboard simply by selecting the Type tool, clicking the artboard, then typing. You can enter text horizontally or vertically. The ability to type vertically is rather unusual; most text-based applications don't offer this option.

Text generated by the Type tool is positioned on a path called the **baseline**. You can select text by clicking anywhere on the text or by clicking on the baseline, depending on how your Type preferences are set.

Formatting Text

The Character and Paragraph panels neatly contain all of the classic commands for formatting text. Use the Character panel to modify text attributes such as font and type size, tracking, and kerning. You can adjust the **leading**, which is the vertical space between baselines, or apply a horizontal or vertical scale, which compresses or expands selected type as shown in Figure 1. The Paragraph panel applies itself to more global concerns,

such as text alignment, paragraph indents, and vertical spaces between paragraphs.

Tracking and kerning are essential, but often overlooked, typographic operations. **Tracking** inserts uniform spaces between characters to affect the width of selected words or entire blocks of text. **Kerning** is used to affect the space between any two characters and is particularly useful for improving the appearance of headlines and other display text. Positive tracking or kerning values move characters farther apart; negative values move them closer together.

Illustrator can track and kern type down to 1/1000 of a standard em space. The width of an em space is dependent on the current type size. In a 1-point font, the em space is 1 point. In a 10-point font, the em space is 10 points. With kerning units that are 1/1000 of an em, Illustrator can manipulate a 10-point font at increments of 1/100 of 1 point! Figure 2 shows examples of kerning and tracking values.

Adjusting and Applying Hyphenation

Illustrator has a Preferences panel dedicated to hyphenation. Click Edit (Win) or Illustrator (Mac) on the Menu bar, point to Preferences, then click Hyphenation. Hyphenation in Illustrator is applied automatically based on the language dictionary that is in use. You can turn automatic hyphenation on and off or change the hyphenation default settings in the Hyphenation dialog box. To access the Hyphenation dialog box, click the Paragraph panel options button, then click Hyphenation. To turn hyphenation off, remove the check mark in the Hyphenation check box.

Hiding Objects While Working with Text

Two factors that make selecting text and other objects difficult are the number and proximity of objects in the document. Hiding objects is a simple way to avoid this problem, just don't forget they are there—they won't print if they are hidden.

The Hide Selection command is on the Object menu, as is the Show All command, which reveals all hidden objects. When hidden objects are revealed, they are all selected—which you can use to your advantage. Simply press [Shift] as you click to deselect the object you want to use, then hide the remaining objects.

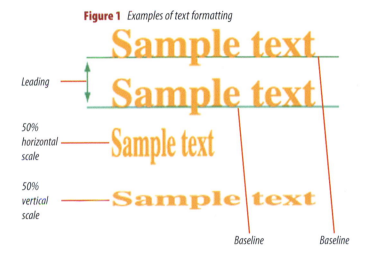

Figure 1 *Examples of text formatting*

Leading

50% horizontal scale

50% vertical scale

Sample text

Sample text

Sample text

Sample text

Baseline   Baseline

Figure 2 *Examples of kerning and tracking*

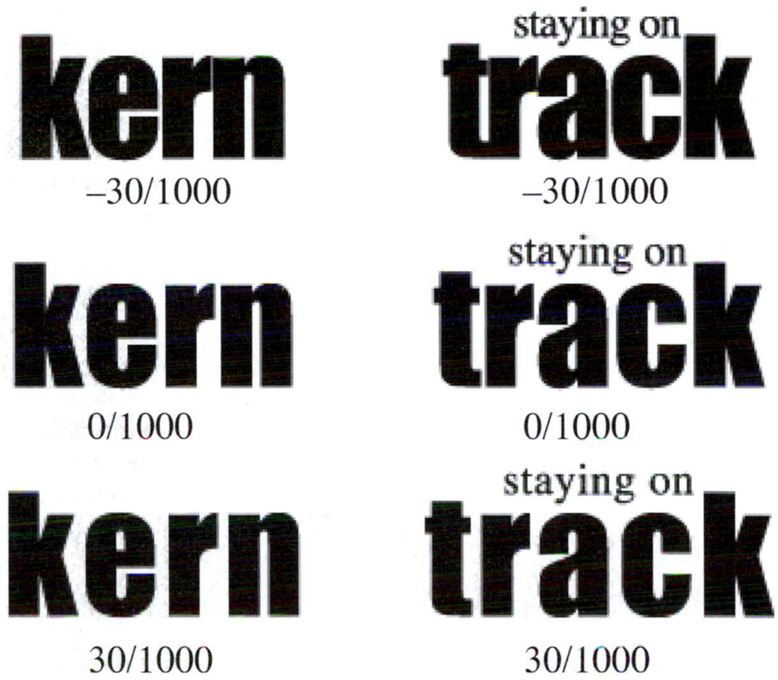

kern
−30/1000

track
−30/1000

kern
0/1000

track
0/1000

kern
30/1000

track
30/1000

Create text

1. Open AI 2-1.ai, then save it as **Berry Symposium**.

2. Click **View** on the Menu bar, then click **Hide Bounding Box** if the Bounding Box is showing.

   If the bounding box is already hidden, you won't see the Hide Bounding Box command.

3. Click the **Type tool** T, then click **anywhere on the artboard**.

4. Type **BERRY** using all capital letters.

   TIP By default, new text is generated with a black fill and no stroke. Text you create by clicking the artboard is called point text.

5. Click the **Selection tool** ⇖, then drag the **text** to the center of the artboard.

   TIP Verify that Smart Guides are not activated.

6. Click **Window** on the Menu bar, point to **Type**, then click **Character** to show the Character panel.

   TIP When a type tool is selected, you can click Character on the Control panel to display the Character panel.

7. Click the **Character panel options button** ≡, then click **Show Options** to view the entire panel as shown in Figure 3.

You used the Type tool to create the word BERRY, showed the Character panel, then expanded the view of the Character panel.

Figure 3 *Character panel*

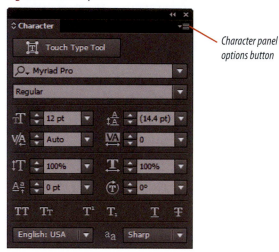

Character panel options button

Tracking and Kerning

Typography, the art of designing letterforms, has a long and rich history that extends back to the Middle Ages. With the advent of desktop publishing in the mid-1980s, many conventional typographers and typesetters declared "the death of typography." They claimed that unskilled computer users would be careless with type, and that computers would reduce typography to ugly, bitmap fonts. Cooler minds have since prevailed. The personal computer and software, such as Adobe Illustrator, have made vast libraries of typefaces available as never before. Imagine the days when the typewriter ruled with its single typeface and two point sizes as the standard for literally millions of documents, and you get a sense of the typographic revolution that has occurred in the last 30 years.

Many designers are so eager to tackle the "artwork" that they often overlook the type design in an illustration. Tracking and kerning, which are the manipulation of space between words and letters, are essential elements to good type design and are often woefully ignored.

Illustrator's precise tracking and kerning abilities are of no use if they are ignored. One good way of maintaining awareness of your tracking and kerning duties is to take note of others' oversights. Make it a point to notice tracking and kerning, or the lack thereof, when you look at magazines, posters, and especially billboards. You'll be amazed at what you'll see.

Figure 4 *Character panel*

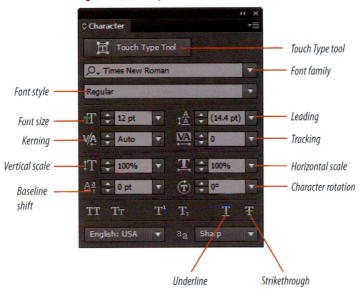

Character
Touch Type Tool
Times New Roman
Regular
12 pt
(14.4 pt)
Auto
0
100%
100%
0 pt
0°
English: USA
Sharp
Touch Type tool
Font family
Font style
Font size
Leading
Kerning
Tracking
Vertical scale
Horizontal scale
Baseline shift
Character rotation
Underline
Strikethrough

Figure 5 *Formatted text*

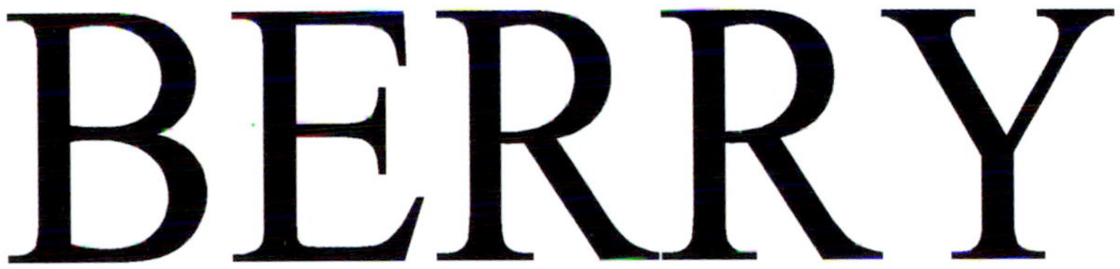

BERRY

Format text

1. Click the **Font family** (Win) or **Font menu** (Mac) **list arrow**, point to **Times New Roman** or a similar font, then click **Regular** from the Font style list arrow, as shown in Figure 4.
2. Click the **Font size text box icon**, type **142**, then press **[Enter]** (Win) or **[return]** (Mac).
3. Click the **Horizontal Scale text box icon**, type **90**, then press **[Enter]** (Win) or **[return]** (Mac).
4. Deselect all.
5. Compare your text to Figure 5.

You used the Character panel to modify the font, font size, and horizontal scaling of the word BERRY.

Track and kern text

1. Select the text if it is not already.

2. Using the Character panel, click the **Tracking icon**, then type **-30**.

TIP Click the Character panel options button, then click Show Options if you do not see the Tracking text box.

3. Click the **Type tool** 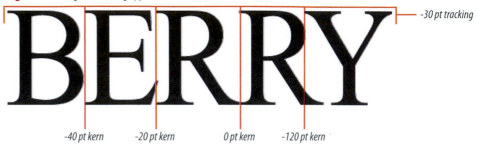, then click the cursor between the B and the E.

4. Using the Character panel, click the **up and down arrows** in the Kerning text box to experiment with higher and lower kerning values, then change the kerning value to -40.

5. Using Figure 6 as a guide, change the kerning to -20, 0, and -120 between the next three letter pairs.

6. Click the **Selection tool**, click the **Paragraph panel name tab**, then click the **Align center button**, as shown in Figure 7.

   When text is center-aligned, its anchor point doubles as its center point, which is handy for aligning it with other objects. Clicking the Align Center button centers the text inside the text box only. It does not center the text on the page.

TIP If you do not see the Paragraph panel, click Window on the Menu bar, point to Type, then click Paragraph.

7. Click **Object** on the Menu bar, point to **Hide**, then click **Selection**.

You used the Character panel to change the tracking of the word BERRY, then you entered different kerning values to affect the spacing between the four letter pairs. You center-aligned the text, then hid the text.

Figure 6 *Kerning and tracking applied to text*

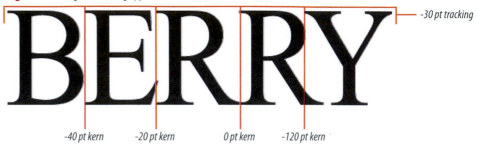

-30 pt tracking

-40 pt kern   -20 pt kern   0 pt kern   -120 pt kern

Figure 7 *Paragraph panel*

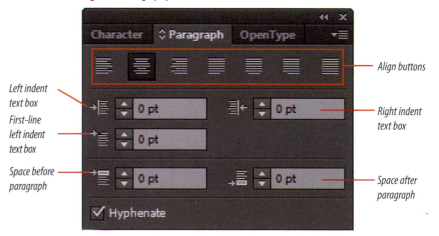

Left indent text box

First-line left indent text box

Space before paragraph

Align buttons

Right indent text box

Space after paragraph

Figure 8 *Vertical text*

B
E
R
R
Y

Using the Glyphs Panel

The Glyphs panel contains various type characters that aren't necessarily available on your keyboard. Examples of these characters include trademarks, copyright marks, accented letters, and numbers expressed as fractions. Click Window on the Menu bar, point to Type, then click Glyphs to display the Glyphs panel. To access a glyph, click the Type tool, click the artboard as you would to type any character, then double-click the glyph on the Glyph panel that you wish to use. You can zoom in or out within the panel and change the font as desired.

Create vertical type

1. Click the **Vertical Type tool** ⊥T , then click anywhere on the artboard.

TIP The Vertical Type tool is hidden beneath the Type tool.

2. Type the word **BERRY** using all capital letters.

TIP The Type tools retain the formatting attributes that were previously chosen.

3. Click the **Selection tool** ▷ , select the text, then move it to the center of the artboard.

TIP When any tool other than the Selection tool is selected on the Tools panel you can press [Ctrl] (Win) or ⌘ (Mac) to switch to the Selection tool. When you release [Ctrl] (Win) or ⌘ (Mac), the last chosen tool will be active again.

4. Using the Character panel, change the font size to 84 pt.

5. Change the tracking value to -160.

6. Verify that both the Horizontal and Vertical Scales are set to 100%, then deselect the text.

Your screen should resemble Figure 8.

7. Delete the vertical text, then save your work.

You used the Vertical Type tool to create a vertical alternative to the first word you typed. You adjusted the tracking and kerning to better suit a vertical orientation, then deleted the text.

Flow Text into
AN OBJECT

What You'll Do

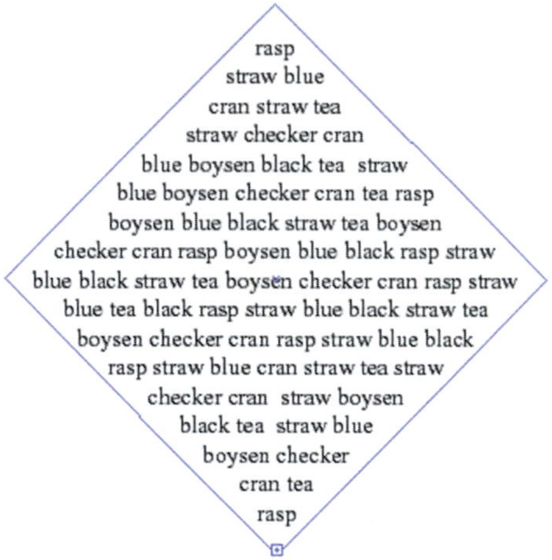

rasp
straw blue
cran straw tea
straw checker cran
blue boysen black tea straw
blue boysen checker cran tea rasp
boysen blue black straw tea boysen
checker cran rasp boysen blue black rasp straw
blue black straw tea boysen checker cran rasp straw
blue tea black rasp straw blue black straw tea
boysen checker cran rasp straw blue black
rasp straw blue cran straw tea straw
checker cran straw boysen
black tea straw blue
boysen checker
cran tea
rasp

© 2015 Cengage Learning®

 In this lesson, you will use the Area Type tool to flow text into an object.

Filling an Object with Text

Using the Area Type tool, you can flow text into any shape you can create, from circles to birds to bumblebees! Text in an object can be formatted as usual. You can change such attributes as fonts, font size, and alignment, and the text will reflow in the object as you format it. Text that you create inside an object is called **area text**.

Figure 9 shows an example of an object filled with text. Note the blue background in the

Figure 9 *An object filled with text*

To
be, or
not to be.
That is the
question. Whether
'tis nobler in the mind to suffer
the slings and arrows of outrageous fortune,
or to take arms against a sea of troubles — and by
opposing — end them. To die. To sleep.
To sleep. Perchance
to dream?
Ay, there's
the rub.

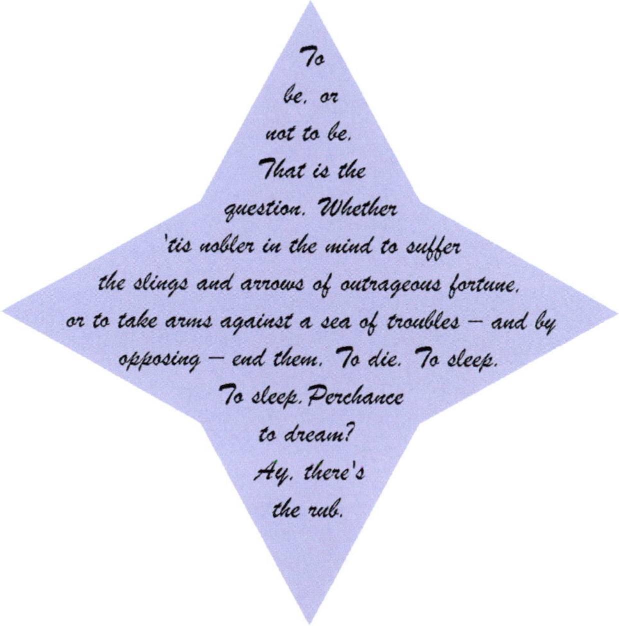

© 2015 Cengage Learning®

Creating Text and Gradients

figure. When you first flow text into an object using the Area Type tool, the object loses any fill or stroke color applied to it. However, you can add different colors to the object and the text. When you select the object with the Selection tool, any fill or stroke you choose will be applied to the text. When you select the object with the Direct Selection tool, the fill or stroke will be applied to the object.

You can also select text flowed into an object with the Type tool. You can even use the Direct Selection tool to distort the shape, and the text will reflow within the modified shape.

You'll often find that centering text in an object is the best visual solution. Figure 10 shows text aligned left and flowed into an odd-shaped object. In Figure 11, the same text is centered and fills the object in a way that is more visually pleasing.

QUICK TIP

You can underline text and strike through text using the Underline and Strikethrough buttons at the bottom of the Character panel.

Figure 10 *Text aligned left*

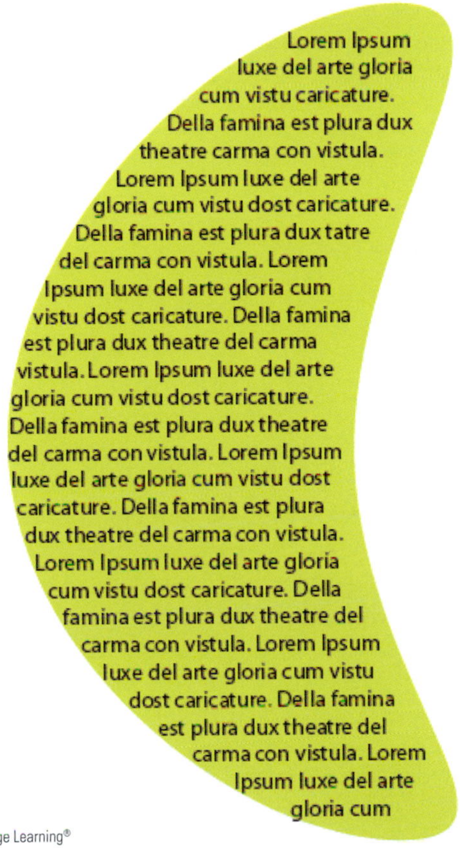
Lorem Ipsum
luxe del arte gloria
cum vistu caricature.
Della famina est plura dux
theatre carma con vistula.
Lorem Ipsum luxe del arte
gloria cum vistu dost caricature.
Della famina est plura dux tatre
del carma con vistula. Lorem
Ipsum luxe del arte gloria cum
vistu dost caricature. Della famina
est plura dux theatre del carma
vistula. Lorem Ipsum luxe del arte
gloria cum vistu dost caricature.
Della famina est plura dux theatre
del carma con vistula. Lorem Ipsum
luxe del arte gloria cum vistu dost
caricature. Della famina est plura
dux theatre del carma con vistula.
Lorem Ipsum luxe del arte gloria
cum vistu dost caricature. Della
famina est plura dux theatre del
carma con vistula. Lorem Ipsum
luxe del arte gloria cum vistu
dost caricature. Della famina
est plura dux theatre del
carma con vistula. Lorem
Ipsum luxe del arte
gloria cum

Figure 11 *Text centered in the objects*

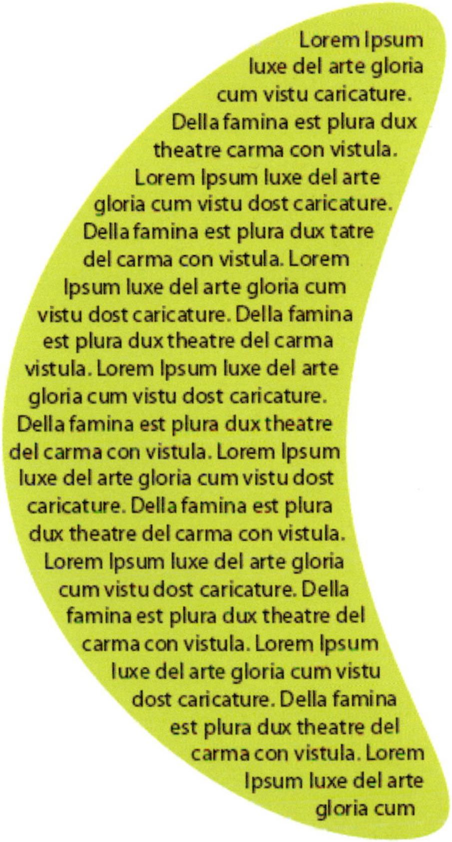
Lorem Ipsum
luxe del arte gloria
cum vistu caricature.
Della famina est plura dux
theatre carma con vistula.
Lorem Ipsum luxe del arte
gloria cum vistu dost caricature.
Della famina est plura dux tatre
del carma con vistula. Lorem
Ipsum luxe del arte gloria cum
vistu dost caricature. Della famina
est plura dux theatre del carma
vistula. Lorem Ipsum luxe del arte
gloria cum vistu dost caricature.
Della famina est plura dux theatre
del carma con vistula. Lorem Ipsum
luxe del arte gloria cum vistu dost
caricature. Della famina est plura
dux theatre del carma con vistula.
Lorem Ipsum luxe del arte gloria
cum vistu dost caricature. Della
famina est plura dux theatre del
carma con vistula. Lorem Ipsum
luxe del arte gloria cum vistu
dost caricature. Della famina
est plura dux theatre del
carma con vistula. Lorem
Ipsum luxe del arte
gloria cum

Fill an object with text

1. Open AI 2-2.ai, then save it as **Diamond Text**.
2. Select the yellow square, double-click the **Rotate tool** 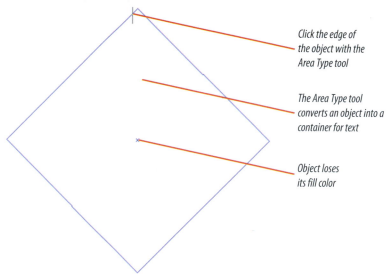, type **45** in the Angle text box, then click **OK**.
3. Click the **Area Type tool** , then click the **block of text**.

TIP The Area Type tool is hidden beneath the current type tool.

4. Click **Select** on the Menu bar, then click **All**.

TIP When you click a Type tool cursor on text and apply the Select All command, all the text is selected, but only the text. Neither the object that contains the text, nor any other text or objects on the page are selected.

5. Copy the text.
6. Click the **Selection tool** , then select the yellow square.

TIP When you are working with a Type tool, you can press [Ctrl] (Win) or ⌘ (Mac) to access the Selection tool temporarily and remain in the current Type tool mode.

7. Click the **Area Type tool** if it is not active, then click the **edge of the yellow square**.

   A flashing cursor appears and the square loses its fill color, as shown in Figure 12.

8. Paste the copied text into the square.

   Your work should resemble Figure 13.

You rotated the yellow square, then filled it with text by first copying text from another object, then clicking the edge of the square with the Area Type tool before you pasted the text into the square.

Format text in an object

1. Triple-click the **text in the object** with the Area Type tool to select all of the text in the rotated square.

(continued)

Figure 12 *Applying the Area Type tool*

Click the edge of the object with the Area Type tool

The Area Type tool converts an object into a container for text

Object loses its fill color

Figure 13 *Text pasted into an object*

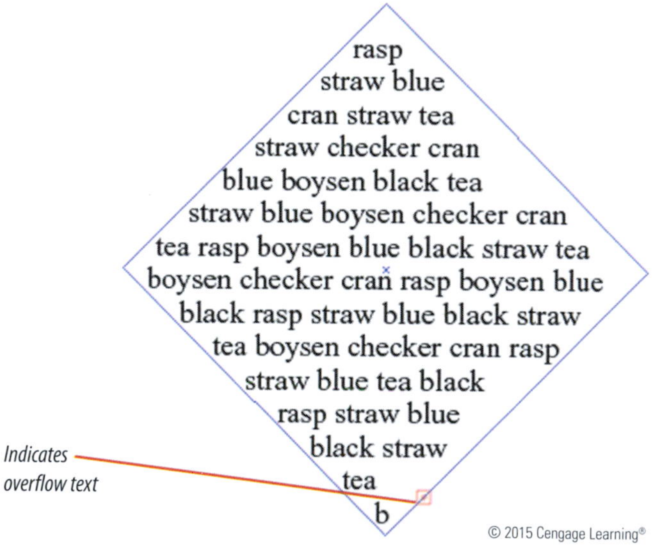

rasp
straw blue
cran straw tea
straw checker cran
blue boysen black tea
straw blue boysen checker cran
tea rasp boysen blue black straw tea
boysen checker cran rasp boysen blue
black rasp straw blue black straw
tea boysen checker cran rasp
straw blue tea black
rasp straw blue
black straw
tea
b

Indicates overflow text

Figure 14 *Centered text in an object*

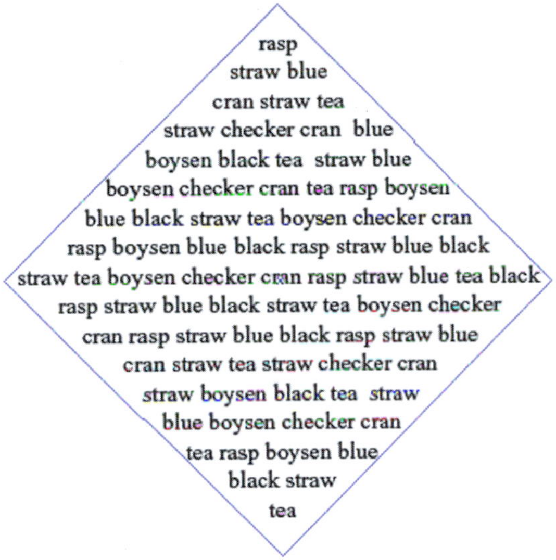

rasp
straw blue
cran straw tea
straw checker cran blue
boysen black tea straw blue
boysen checker cran tea rasp boysen
blue black straw tea boysen checker cran
rasp boysen blue black rasp straw blue black
straw tea boysen checker cran rasp straw blue tea black
rasp straw blue black straw tea boysen checker
cran rasp straw blue black rasp straw blue
cran straw tea straw checker cran
straw boysen black tea straw
blue boysen checker cran
tea rasp boysen blue
black straw
tea

Using Character and Paragraph Styles

A style is a group of formatting attributes, such as font, font size, color, and tracking, that you apply to text. You use the Character Styles panel to create and apply styles for individual words or characters, such as a footnote. You use the Paragraph Styles panel to apply a style to a paragraph. Paragraph styles include formatting options such as indents and drop caps. Using styles saves you time and keeps your work consistent. If you create styles for an Illustrator document, the styles are saved with the document and are available to be loaded for use in other documents.

2. Click the **Align center button** ☰ on the Paragraph panel.

TIP When filling an object other than a square or a rectangle with text, centering the text is often the best solution.

3. On the **Character panel**, change the font size to 9 pt.

4. Set the leading to **11**, deselect the text, then compare your work to Figure 14.
    It's OK if the line breaks in your document differ from the text in the figure.

5. Click the **Selection tool** ▷ , then click the **diamond-shaped text**.
    Both the text and the object that contains the text are selected.

6. Copy the text object.
    Both the text and the object are copied.

7. Click **Window** on the Menu bar, then click the **Berry Symposium.ai** option at the bottom of the menu to return to the Berry Symposium document tab.

TIP All open Illustrator documents are listed at the bottom of the Window menu.

8. Paste the text object into the Berry Symposium document.

9. Show guides, then align the center point of the text object with the intersection of the guides.

TIP Use the arrow keys to nudge the selection right, left, up, or down.

10. Click **Object** on the Menu bar, point to **Lock**, then click **Selection**.

11. Close the Diamond text document without saving changes, then save the Berry Symposium document.

You used the Paragraph and Character panels to format text in the object. You used the Selection tool to select the text object, then you copied and pasted it into the Berry Symposium document.

Position Text
ON A PATH

What You'll Do

three rivers

rasp
straw blue
cran straw tea
straw checker cran
blue boysen black tea straw
blue boysen checker cran tea rasp
boysen blue black straw tea boysen
checker cran rasp boysen blue black rasp straw
blue black straw tea boysen checker cran rasp straw
blue tea black rasp straw blue black straw tea
boysen checker cran rasp straw blue black
rasp straw blue cran straw tea straw
checker cran straw boysen
black tea straw blue
boysen checker
cran tea
rasp

symposium

© 2015 Cengage Learning®

 In this lesson, you will explore the many options for positioning text on a path.

Using the Path Type Tools

Using the Type on a Path tool or the Vertical Type on a Path tool, you can type along a straight or curved path. This is the most compelling of Illustrator's text effects, and it opens up a world of possibilities for the designer and typographer.

You can move text along a path to position it where you want. You can "flip" the text to make it run in the opposite direction, on the opposite side of the path. You can also change the baseline shift to modify the distance of the text's baseline in relation to the path. A positive value "floats" the text above the path, and a negative value moves the text below the path. You can modify text on a path in the same way you would modify any other text element. Figure 15 shows an example of text on a path, whereas Figure 16 shows an example of text flipped across a path.

Customizing Language Dictionaries

Illustrator comes complete with Proximity language dictionaries, which are used for spelling and hyphenation. Each dictionary contains information for standard syllable breaks for literally hundreds of thousands of words. You can assign a language to an entire document or apply a language to selected text. To apply a language to all text Choose Edit (Win) or Illustrator (Mac) on the Menu bar, point to Preferences, then click Hyphenation. Select a dictionary from the Default Language list arrow, then click OK. To assign a language to selected text, first select the text. On the Character panel, choose the appropriate dictionary from the Language menu. You may need to expand the Character panel to see the Language menu.

Figure 15 *Text on a path*

Figure 16 *Text flipped across a path*

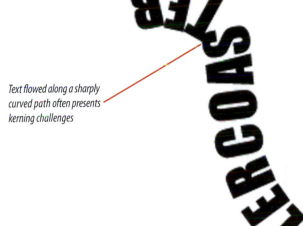

Text flowed along a sharply curved path often presents kerning challenges

Locating and Replacing Fonts Inside a Document

You can replace a given font in a document with another font using the Find Font utility. Click Type on the Menu bar, then click Find Font. All the fonts used in the document are listed. Select the name of the font you want to find; the first occurrence of the font is highlighted in the document window. Select a replacement font from the Replace with Font From list arrow. You can click Change to change just one occurrence of the selected font, or click Change All to change all occurrences of the selected font. Note that when you replace a font using the Find Font command, all other type attributes applied to the original remain applied to the replacement font.

Flow text on a path

1. Click the **Ellipse tool** 🔘, press **[Alt]** (Win) or **[option]** (Mac), then click the center of the artboard.

   Pressing [Alt] (Win) or [option] (Mac) while you click a shape tool on the artboard ensures that the center of the shape will be drawn from the point that you clicked.

2. Enter **2.9** in for the width and the height of the circle in the Ellipse dialog box, then click **OK**.

3. Click the **Type on a Path tool** 🖋, click the **Align Left button** on the Control panel, then click the edge of the circle at approximately 10 o'clock.

   A flashing cursor appears, and the circle loses its fill color.

4. Type **three rivers** in lowercase letters.

5. Click the **Selection tool** ⇱ to select the text by its baseline, verify the font is Times New Roman, then change the font size to 47 pt.

6. Compare your screen to Figure 17.

   Note the center bracket in Figure 17. Dragging the center bracket is the easiest way to move text along a path.

TIP Text flowed on a circle will often require kerning, especially when it is set at a large point size.

You created a 2.9" circle from its center, then typed along the circle's path using the Type on a Path tool. You changed the font and font size using the Character panel.

Move text along a path

1. Click **View** on the Menu bar, point to **Guides**, then click **Hide Guides**.

(continued)

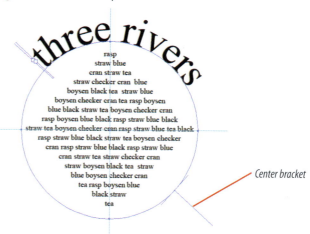

Figure 17 *Text on a circular path*

Center bracket

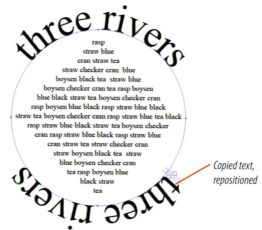

Figure 18 *Moving text on a path*

Copied text, repositioned

Figure 19 *Flipping text across a path*

Creating Text and Gradients

Figure 20 *Modifying a baseline shift*

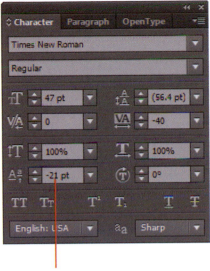

Baseline shift

Figure 21 *Flipped text positioned below the path*

2. Using the Selection tool [icon], drag the **center bracket** until the text is centered at the top of the circle.

   Moving text along a path is a touch-sensitive procedure. You will find that it's easy to "flip" the text over the baseline, and it will run inside the circle. With a little experience, you'll find that you're able to position text on a line as you desire.

3. Click **Edit** on the Menu bar, click **Copy**, click **Edit** on the Menu bar, then click **Paste in Front**.

4. Drag the **center bracket** of the copied text clockwise to move the copied text to the position shown in Figure 18.

   Your center bracket might be positioned differently on the circle and in relation to the text.

5. Drag the **center bracket** of the copied text toward the center of the circle to flip the text across the path, as shown in Figure 19, then drag the text inside the circle to position it if necessary, as shown in Figure 19.

6. Click the **Baseline shift text box** on the Character panel, type **-21**, as shown in Figure 20, then press **[Enter]** (Win) or **[return]** (Mac).

7. Click the **Type tool** [icon], select **three rivers** at the bottom of the circle, then type **symposium**.

8. Track and kern the word symposium as you think necessary.

9. Click the **Selection tool** [icon], then drag the **center bracket** to center the text at the bottom of the circle if it is not already centered.

10. Lock the two text objects, save your work, then compare your image to Figure 21.

You moved and copied text along a path, flipped its direction, changed the baseline shift, then locked both text objects.

Manipulate Text with
THE TOUCH TYPE TOOL

In this lesson, you will manipulate type with the Touch Type tool.

NEW Using the Touch Type Tool

The Touch Type tool is the newest addition to Illustrator's typing tools and has the power to truly alter what designers do with type in Illustrator. Illustrator has long held the unofficial but widely accepted title of best application for designing and manipulating type—but nevertheless there were limitations. To best understand the benefits of the Touch Type tool, it helps first to examine those limitations.

Figure 22 shows the word "bounce" set in Illustrator text. Note by the selection marks that the word is a single object. If you wanted to manipulate the text to appear as shown in Figure 23, you'd have to use the Character panel and apply baseline shifts and character rotations to each character. If you then wanted to manipulate the space between the

Figure 22 *A single text object*

bounce

Figure 23 *Text characters manipulated individually*

Creating Text and Gradients

characters, as shown in Figure 24, you'd need to kern each letter pair. Because of the tedious and time-consuming challenges of working with individual characters on one object of type, many designers instead choose to set each character as a single object, as shown in Figure 25.

The Touch Type tool allows you to scale, rotate, and move each character in a type object independently of the other characters. Rather than have to input values on the Character panel, you can manipulate individual characters by hand, scaling and repositioning by hand. It is truly revolutionary to Illustrator.

Entering the Touch Type Tool

After you've typed a word, click the Touch Type tool, then click a letter. When you do, a rectangle with five points—one on each corner and one centered at the top—appears around the character. Clicking and dragging these five points, you can scale the character uniformly, scale vertically, scale horizontally, rotate, and move the character. Figure 26 identifies what each point does to the type.

What's truly revolutionary about the Touch Type tool is that the other letters in the word move to accommodate any transformation you make. What's more, you can freely move type characters closer together or farther apart as you transform them. The Touch Type tool introduces enormous new freedom for working with type and opens the door to new possibilities and new ideas for typographical illustrations.

Figure 24 *Kerning manipulated individually*

Figure 25 *A work-around; each character is an individual object*

Figure 26 *Transform options with the Touch Type tool*

Rotate —
Vertical scale —
Move; moves the character anywhere
Uniform scale
Horizontal scale

© 2015 Cengage Learning®

Use the Touch Type tool

1. Open AI 2-3 save it as **Touch Type**, then verify that the Swatches panel is showing.

2. Click the **Touch Type tool** 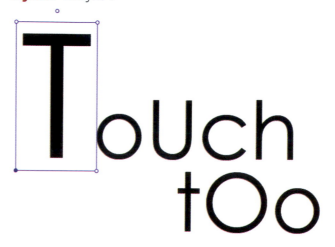, then click the first letter **T**.

    A bounding box appears around the letter.

TIP The Touch Type tool is located behind the Type tool with all the other typographical tools.

3. Click and drag the **top-right corner** of the bounding box.

    As you drag, the letter is scaled in proportion.

4. Drag until the type resembles Figure 27.

    As you drag, notice that the space between the bounding box around the letter "T" and the letter "o" next to it, does not change.

5. Position the Touch Type tool over the -left center of the letter "T" then drag.

    The letter moves independently from the other letters. No matter how far you drag the letter "T" vertically, the horizontal space between the letter "T" and the "o" is maintained.

6. Undo whatever move you made so that the type still resembles Figure 27.

7. Select the letter "**o**" with the Touch Type tool, then drag it closer to the "T," as shown in Figure 28.

    Now that both the letter "T" and the letter "o" have been manipulated by the Touch Type tool, you are able to move the letter "o" as close or as far apart to the letter "T" as you like—even overlap them.

(continued)

Figure 27 *Scaling the "T"*

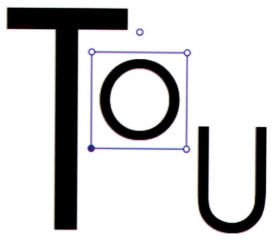

Figure 28 *Moving the "o" closer to the "T"*

Creating Text and Gradients

Figure 29 *The final illustration*

8. Click the letter "**u**," then click and drag the **lower-right point**.

   The character is scaled on the horizontal axis only.

9. Click the letter "**c**," then click and drag the **upper-left point**.

   The character is scaled on the vertical axis only.

10. Click the letter "**h**," then click and drag the point centered above it.

    The character is rotated as you drag.

11. Select the "**T**" with the Touch Type tool, then change its fill color on the Swatches panel.

12. Use the Touch Type tool to recreate the illustration shown in Figure 29.

13. Save your work, then close Touch Type.

You used the Touch Type tool to scale, rotate, and change the color of individual characters on a text object.

Create Colors
AND GRADIENTS

What You'll Do

© 2015 Cengage Learning®

In this lesson, you will use the Color panel, Gradient panel, and Swatches panel to create, name, and save colors and gradients.

Using the Gradient Panel

A **gradient** is a graduated blend between colors. The Gradient panel is the command center for creating and adjusting gradients. In the panel you will see a slider that represents the gradient you are creating or using. The slider has at least two colors. The leftmost color is the starting color, and the rightmost color is the ending color.

The colors used in a gradient are represented on the Gradient panel by small house-shaped icons called **stops**. The Gradient panel shown in Figure 30 shows a two-color gradient.

The point at which two colors meet in equal measure is called the **midpoint** of the gradient. The midpoint is represented by the diamond above the slider. The midpoint does not necessarily need to be positioned evenly between the starting and ending colors. You can change the appearance of a gradient by moving the midpoint.

The Swatches panel contains standard gradients that come with the software. To create your own original gradients, start by clicking an object filled with an existing gradient. You can then modify that existing gradient on the Gradient panel. You can change either or both the beginning and ending colors. You can change the location of the midpoint. You can also add additional colors into the gradient or remove existing colors.

You can define a gradient as linear or radial. A linear gradient can be positioned left to right, up and down, or on any angle. You can change the angle of the gradient by entering a new value in the Angle text box on the Gradient panel.

Think of a radial gradient as a series of concentric circles. With a radial gradient, the starting color appears at the center of the gradient. The blend radiates out to the ending color. By definition, a radial gradient has no angle ascribed to it.

Using the Color Panel

The Color panel, shown in Figure 31, is where you move sliders to mix new colors for fills, strokes, and gradients. You can also use the panel to adjust the color in a filled object. The panel has five color modes: CMYK, RGB, Grayscale, HSB, and Web Safe RGB. The panel will default to CMYK or RGB, depending on the color mode you choose when creating a new document.

Rather than use the sliders, you can also type values directly into the text boxes. For example, in CMYK mode, a standard red color is composed of 100% Magenta and 100% Yellow. The notation for this callout would be 100M/100Y. Note that you don't list the zero values for Cyan (C) and Black (K)—you don't list the color as 0C/100M/100Y/0K. In RGB mode (0-255), a standard orange color would be noted as 255R/128G.

NEW Changing Color Stops

There are two ways to change the color stops on a gradient. Double-clicking a color stop opens a dual Color/Swatches panel that allows you to toggle between the two by clicking the appropriate panel icon. Choose the Color panel icon to create a new color or adjust an existing color. Use the Swatches panel icon to choose an already named color.

Adding Colors and Gradients to the Swatches Panel

Once you have defined a color or a gradient to your liking, it's a smart idea to save it by dragging it into the Swatches panel or click the Color panel options arrow and select Create New Swatch. Once a color or gradient is moved into the Swatches panel, you can name it by double-clicking it, then typing a name in the Swatch Options dialog box. You cannot modify it, however. For example, if you click a saved gradient and adjust it on the Gradient panel, you can apply the new gradient to an object, but the original gradient on the Swatches panel remains unaffected. You can save the new gradient to the Swatches panel for future use.

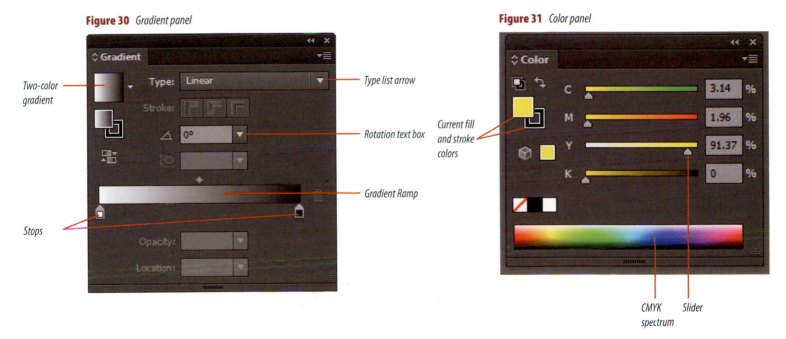

Figure 30 *Gradient panel*

Two-color gradient

Stops

Type list arrow

Rotation text box

Gradient Ramp

Figure 31 *Color panel*

Current fill and stroke colors

CMYK spectrum

Slider

Create a gradient and a color

1. Open the Berry Symposium document, if necessary, then show the guides.

2. Create a 4" circle at the center of the artboard, then apply a yellow fill to the circle.

   The most recently drawn object is automatically placed above the other objects on the artboard.

3. Hide the guides, click **Window** on the Menu bar, then click **Gradient** to open the Gradient panel if it is not already open.

4. Click the **Blended Rainbow swatch** on the Swatches panel.

   The yellow fill changes to the Blended Rainbow fill.

5. Click the **Gradient panel options button** 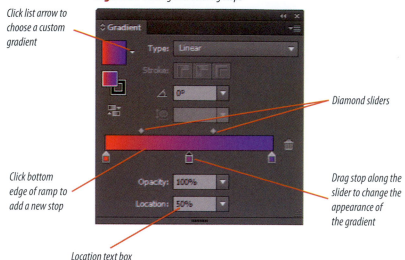, then click **Show Options** if they are not already showing.

6. Click the **yellow stop** on the Gradient Slider, and drag it straight down off the panel to delete it.

7. Delete all the stops except for the first and last stops.

TIP The changes you make to the Gradient Slider are reflected in the circle.

8. Click the **Selection tool** if it is not active, click the **bottom edge of the Gradient Slider** to add a new color stop as shown in Figure 32, then drag the **stop** along the slider until you see 50% in the Location text box on the Gradient panel, also shown in Figure 32.

TIP You can enter a value directly into the text box as an alternative to dragging the slider.

9. Drag each of the **diamond sliders**, found on top of the Gradient Slider, to the **50% mark** in the Location text box.

(continued)

Figure 32 *Adding and deleting stops*

Click list arrow to choose a custom gradient

Diamond sliders

Click bottom edge of ramp to add a new stop

Drag stop along the slider to change the appearance of the gradient

Location text box

Figure 33 *Adding the new Squash swatch to the gradient*

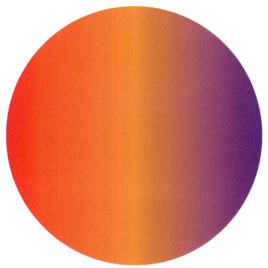

© 2015 Cengage Learning®

Creating Text and Gradients

Figure 34 *Changing the first and last colors of the gradient*

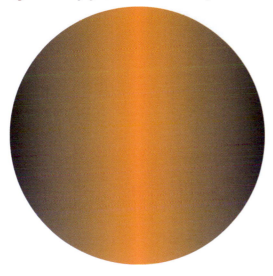

Figure 35 *Changing the middle color and the midpoint locations*

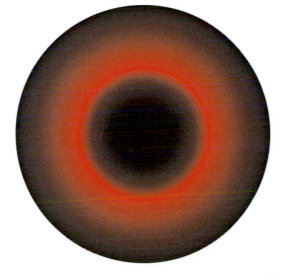

10. Verify that the new stop is selected, press and hold **[Alt]** (Win) or **[option]** (Mac), click **Squash** on the Swatches panel, then compare your circle to Figure 33.

    You must select a stop in order to change its color.

    TIP When you choose a color for a color stop from the stand-alone, standard Swatches panel, you must press [Alt] (Win) or [option] (Mac). If you don't press [Alt] (Win) or [option] (Mac), you will change the selected object's fill to a solid color.

11. Double-click the **first stop** on the Gradient Slider to open the dual Color/Swatches panel, click the **Swatches panel icon** ▦, if necessary, then click **Black**.

    TIP When you use this method to choose a color from the Swatches panel, you do not need to press [Alt] (Win) or [option] (Mac).

12. Repeat the previous step to apply Black to the third stop, then compare your circle to Figure 34.

13. Double-click the **Squash stop**, click the **Color panel icon** 🎨, if necessary, in the dual Color/Swatches panel, then drag **each slider** on the Color panel until the new CMYK values are 5C/95M/95Y/3K.

14. Click the **Type list arrow** on the Gradient panel, then click **Radial**.

15. Click the **diamond** on top of the Gradient Slider between the first two stops, then drag it to the **87% location** on the ramp.

16. Compare your circle to Figure 35.

You applied the Blended Rainbow gradient to the yellow circle. You modified the gradient by deleting stops and adding a new stop. You changed the color of the new stop, then adjusted the midpoint of the blend between the starting color and the middle color.

Add gradients and colors to the Swatches panel

1. Double-click the **Scale tool** , type **65** in the Scale text box, then click **Copy**.

2. Keeping the smaller circle selected, delete the red stop from the ramp on the Gradient panel.

3. Change the first stop to **White**, then change the ending stop to **0C/40M/50Y/0K**.

   When a stop is selected on the Gradient Slider, the color of that stop appears in the Gradient Stop Color box on the Color panel.

4. Position the midpoint at **65%**.

   Your screen should resemble Figure 36.

5. Drag the **Gradient Fill box** from the Gradient panel to the Swatches panel, as shown in Figure 37.

6. Double-click **New Gradient Swatch 1** (the gradient you just added) on the Swatches panel to open the Swatch Options dialog box.

7. Type **Pinky** in the Swatch Name text box, then click **OK**.

8. Click the **last color stop** on the Gradient Slider.

   (continued)

Figure 36 *A radial gradient with white as the starting color*

Figure 37 *Adding a gradient to the Swatches panel*

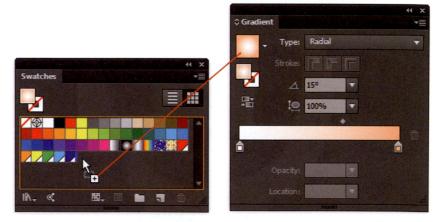

© 2015 Cengage Learning®

Creating Text and Gradients

Figure 38 *Adding a color to the Swatches panel*

Dragging the Gradient Stop Color and
Gradient Fill boxes to the Swatches panel
creates new swatches

Gradient Stop
Color box

Gradient
Fill box

When a stop is selected,
the color appears in the
Gradient Stop Color box
on the Color panel

9. Drag the **Gradient Stop Color box** from
    the Color panel to the Swatches panel to add
    this color to the Swatches panel, as shown in
    Figure 38, then name it **Pinky Ending**.

10. Click the **Selection tool**.

11. Click the **artboard** to deselect the
    smaller circle.

12. Click the **large circle**, drag the **Gradient
    Fill box** on the Gradient panel to the
    Swatches panel, then name the new gradient
    Crimson Gradient.

13. Save your work.

*You used the Gradient panel to create a new gradient. You
added the gradient fills from the two circles to the Swatches
panel and gave them descriptive names. You added a color
named Pinky Ending to the Swatches panel then saved the
Crimson Gradient to the Swatches panel.*

Apply Colors and
GRADIENTS TO TEXT

What You'll Do

In this lesson, you will apply colors to text, convert text into objects, and fill the objects with a gradient.

Applying Fills and Strokes to Text

Regardless of the fill and stroke colors shown on the Tools panel, new text is generated by default with a black fill and no stroke. To change the color of text, you must select the text by highlighting it with a type tool or switch to a selection tool. When you switch to a selection tool, the text is selected as a single object (a blue baseline and anchor point are revealed), and any color changes you make will affect the text globally. If you want to change the fill or the stroke of an individual character, you must select that character with a type tool.

Converting Text to Outlines

About the only thing you can't do to Illustrator text is fill it with a gradient. To create that effect, you first need to convert the text into objects. You can do this by selecting the text, then using the Create Outlines command on the Type menu. The letterforms, or outlines, become standard Illustrator objects with anchor points and paths that you can modify like any other object. Figure 39 shows an example of text converted to outlines.

Create Outlines is a powerful feature. Beyond allowing you to fill text with a gradient, it makes it possible to create a document with text and without fonts. This can save you time in document management when sending files to your printer by circumventing potential problems with missing fonts or font conflicts.

Once text is converted to outlines, you can no longer change the typeface. Also, the type loses its font information, including sizing "hints" that optimize letter shape at different sizes. Therefore, if you plan to scale type substantially, change its font size on the Character panel before converting to outlines.

Figure 39 *Text converted to outlines*

Apply color to text

1. Select the **two circles**, click **Object** on the Menu bar, point to **Arrange**, then click **Send to Back**.

   The two circles move behind the locked text objects.

2. Click **Object** on the Menu bar, then click **Unlock All**.

   The three text objects you created and locked are now unlocked and selected.

3. Apply the **Pinky Ending** color as a fill for the three unlocked text objects.

4. Deselect all, then lock the diamond text object.

   Your work should resemble Figure 40.

You unlocked the three text objects, filled them with the Pinky Ending color, then locked the diamond text object.

Figure 40 *Text with a new fill color*

Formatting a Story

You can use any of the shapes you create as text boxes, and you can thread, or flow, text from one object to another. When you add text to an object, it becomes a text object with an in port and an out port. To thread text, click the out port of an object that contains text, then click the in port of the object to which you want to thread the text. If the object isn't already defined as a text object, click on the path of the object.

You can also thread text by selecting an object that has type in it, then selecting the object or objects to which you want to thread the text. Click Type on the Menu bar, point to Threaded Text, then click Create. You will see icons representing threads. To view threads, choose View on the Menu bar, point to Show Text Threads, then select a linked object.

Creating Text and Gradients

Figure 41 *Outlines filled with a gradient*

Create outlines and apply a gradient fill

1. Show the guides.
2. Click **Object** on the Menu bar, then click **Show All**.
3. Select the **BERRY** text, click **Object** on the Menu bar, point to **Arrange**, then click **Bring to Front**.
4. Click **Type** on the Menu bar, then click **Create Outlines**.
5. Apply the Steel gradient swatch on the Swatches panel to fill the text outlines, then deselect the outlines.
6. Using Figure 41 as a guide, position the BERRY text outlines so that they are centered within the entire illustration, then hide the guides.
7. Save your work.

You showed the BERRY text, moved it to the front, converted it to outlines, then filled the outlines with a gradient.

Adjust a Gradient and
CREATE A DROP SHADOW

What You'll Do

© 2015 Cengage Learning®

 In this lesson, you will use the Gradient tool to modify how the gradient fills the outlines. You will then explore the effectiveness of a simple drop shadow as a design element.

Using the Gradient Tool with Linear Gradient Fills

The Gradient tool is used to manipulate gradient fills that are already applied to objects and it only affects the way a gradient fills an object.

To use the Gradient tool, you first select an object with a gradient fill. When you click the Gradient tool, the **gradient control bar** appears in the object itself, as shown in Figure 42. For linear gradients, the gradient control bar begins at the left edge and ends at the right edge by default.

You can change the length, angle, and direction of the gradient by dragging the gradient control bar.

Figure 43 shows the gradient control bar starting outside the object at the top and ending below it. Where you begin dragging and where you end dragging determines the length of the gradient from the beginning color to the ending color, even if it's outside the perimeter of the object.

Figure 42 *Gradient control bar*

Figure 43 *Changing the position of the gradient control bar*

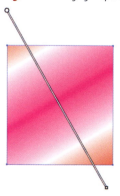

© 2015 Cengage Learning®

You can further modify how the gradient fills the object by modifying the gradient control bar itself. Click and drag the diamond-shaped endpoint of the bar to lengthen or shorten the gradient. You can also click and drag the circle-shaped starting point to move then entire bar to a different location.

When you click the gradient control bar, the color stops that compose the gradient appear, as shown in Figure 44. You can click and drag the stops right there, on the object, for precise control of how the gradient fills the object. You can change the color of the stops on the gradient control bar and even add or delete stops. To change the color of a stop, simply double-click it and the Color panel will appear.

Perhaps the best method for working with the gradient control bar is to first click and drag the Gradient tool as close as possible to where you want it to begin and end. Then, use the gradient control bar for tweaking the position of the gradient and the position of the color stops within the object.

When you float your cursor near the endpoint of the gradient control bar, the rotate icon appears, as shown in Figure 45. Click and drag to rotate the bar and the gradient within the object.

Applying Gradient Fills to Multiple Objects

If you select multiple objects then click a gradient swatch on the Swatches panel, the gradient will fill each object individually. However, with all the objects selected, you can use the Gradient tool to extend a single gradient across all of them.

When you convert text to outlines and apply a gradient fill, the gradient automatically fills

Figure 44 *Color stops on the gradient control bar*

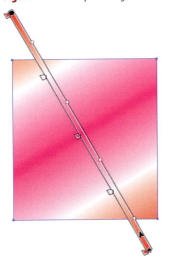

Figure 45 *Rotating the gradient control bar*

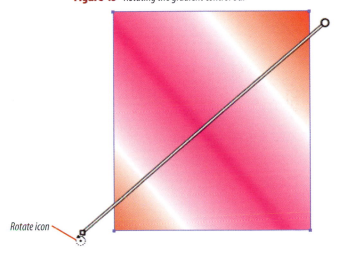

Rotate icon

each letter individually. In other words, if you fill a five-letter word with a rainbow gradient, each of the five letters will contain the entire spectrum. To extend the gradient across all the letters, drag the Gradient tool from the left edge of the word to the right edge, or vice versa. Figure 46 shows examples of different

angles and lengths of a gradient fill created with the Gradient tool.

Using the Gradient Tool with Radial Gradient Fills

With radial gradients the gradient control bar shows the length of the gradient from the

center of the circle to the outermost circle. Figure 47 shows the gradient control bar for three radial gradients.

When you click the gradient control bar on a radial gradient, a dotted line appears showing you the perimeter of the gradient, whether

Figure 46 *Using the Gradient tool*

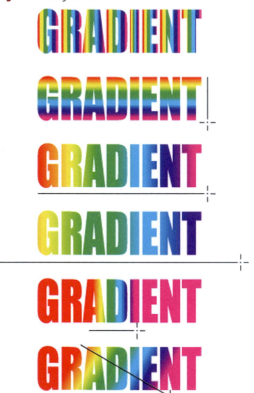

Figure 47 *Three radial gradients*

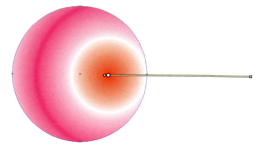

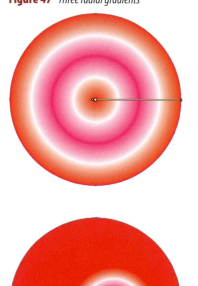

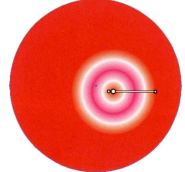

Creating Text and Gradients

that's within or outside the actual object. In Figure 48, the dotted line indicates that more of the gradient is actually outside of the object than visible within the object.

Radial gradients are not limited to concentric circles: you can also create radial gradients with concentric ellipses. To do so, click and drag the black circle on the dotted line of the radial gradient. As shown in Figure 49,

doing so will distort the concentric circles into ellipses.

Adding a Drop Shadow

Applying a shadow behind text is an effective design tool to distinguish the text from other objects and add dimension to the illustration. To apply a drop shadow to text, first copy the text, then paste the copy behind it. Fill the copy with

a darker color, then use the keyboard arrows to move it so that it is offset from the original text.

Figure 48 *Dotted line shows the perimeter of the radial gradient*

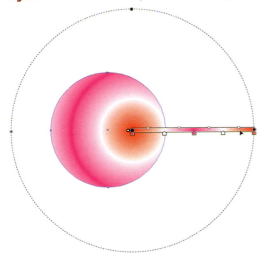

Figure 49 *Distorting the gradient*

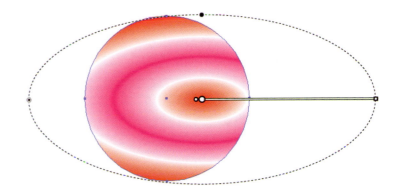

Use the Gradient tool

1. Select the **BERRY text outlines** if they are not already selected.

2. Click the **Gradient tool** [icon], then position the pointer at the top of the B.

3. Drag straight down to the bottom of the B, release the mouse button, then deselect.

TIP Pressing and holding [Shift] while you drag the Gradient tool pointer allows you to drag in a perfectly straight line.

4. Switch to the Selection tool [icon], then click the **large circle** filled with the Crimson gradient fill behind the text.

5. Click the **Gradient tool** [icon].

6. Position the color stops and the midpoints as shown in Figure 50 so that the red gradient is behind the "three rivers symposium" letters.

You used the Gradient tool to flow the gradient from top to bottom in the word BERRY. You adjusted the stops and the midpoints on the gradient control bar to perfect the gradient behind the text.

Add a drop shadow to text

1. Select the word **BERRY**.

2. Apply a 1 pt Black stroke to the outlines.

3. Copy the word, then paste in back.

4. Change the fill of the copied object to Black.

TIP Even though you can't see the copy of the text in back, it is still selected.

5. Press ↓ three times and ← three times to move the copied text 3 pts down and 3 pts to the left, as shown in Figure 51.

(continued)

Figure 50 *A highlight behind the text*

Figure 51 *Drop shadow with a 3 pt offset*

Creating Text and Gradients

Figure 52 *Drop shadows add dimension*

Figure 53 *Finished illustration*

6. Copy the word symposium, then paste in back.

7. Change the fill of the copied text to Black.

TIP Since the copy is still selected, you only need to click Black on the Swatches panel.

8. Using the arrow keys, move the copied text 2 pts down and 2 pts to the left, as shown in Figure 52.

9. Apply the same drop shadow to the three rivers text.

TIP You might find it easier to select the three rivers text if you first lock the symposium text and the symposium shadow text.

10. Unlock all, select everything on the artboard, then rotate the illustration 15°.

11. Click the **Selection tool** , then click the **artboard** to deselect all.

    Your work should resemble Figure 53.

12. Save your work, then close and save each document.

You applied a black stroke to the display text, then pasted a copy behind. You filled the copy with black, then offset the copy to create a drop shadow effect. You then applied a drop shadow to symposium and three rivers. Finally, you rotated the entire illustration.

APPLY GRADIENTS
TO STROKES

What You'll Do

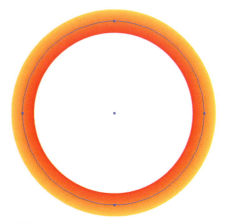

 In this lesson, you will apply gradients to strokes on objects and use the Gradient panel to determine how the gradient strokes the object.

Applying a Gradient to a Stroke

You can use the Gradient panel to apply a gradient to a stroked object and to determine how the gradient is applied. To apply the stroke, simply select the object and, with the Stroke icon activated, choose a gradient to apply to the object.

The Gradient panel offers three buttons you can use to determine how the gradient is applied to the stroke. The three options are as follows:

Within Stroke: As shown in Figure 54, the gradient moves left-to-right across the object.

Figure 54 *The within stroke option for the gradient*

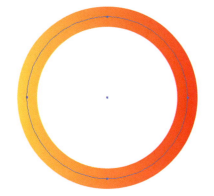

Along Stroke: As shown in Figure 55, the gradient moves clockwise around the object.

Across Stroke: As shown in Figure 56, the gradient radiates from the outside to the inside of the stroke.

If you want to specify how the stroke aligns to the object—inside, center, or outside—use the Align Stroke options on the Stroke panel before using the Gradient panel to apply a gradient to the stroke.

You cannot apply a gradient to a stroke on live type. You must first convert the type to outlines, then you will be able to apply a gradient to the stroke.

Figure 55 *The along stroke option for the gradient*

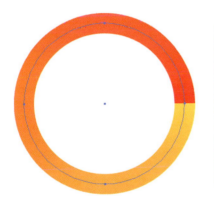

Figure 56 *The across stroke option for the gradient*

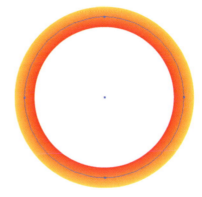

Apply gradients to strokes

1. Open AI 2-4.ai, then save it as **Gradient Strokes**.

2. Select the **triangle**, then verify that the Stroke icon is activated on the Tools panel.

3. Click the **Yellow**, **Orange**, **Blue gradient swatch** on the Swatches panel.

   The gradient is applied to the triangle.

4. Note the three Stroke buttons on the Gradient panel.

   By default, the first button—Apply gradient within stroke—is selected. As shown in Figure 57, the gradient moves from left to right across the triangle.

5. Click the **second** of the three Stroke buttons.

   As shown in Figure 58, the Apply gradient along stroke option is applied and the gradient moves clockwise around the stroke.

   (continued)

Figure 57 *The gradient applied with the default within stroke option*

Figure 58 *The along stroke option applied*

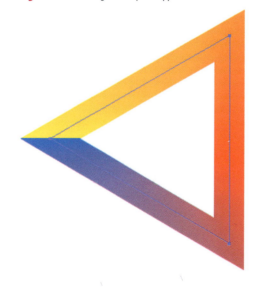

© 2015 Cengage Learning®

Creating Text and Gradients

Figure 59 *The across stroke option applied*

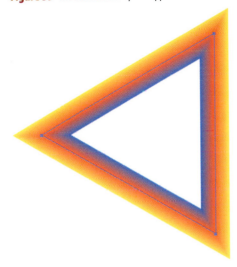

Figure 60 *Reversing the gradient on the stroke*

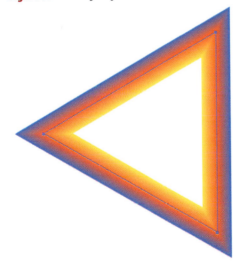

Lesson 8   Apply Gradients to Strokes

6. Click the **third** of the three Stroke buttons.

   As shown in Figure 59, the Apply gradient across stroke option is applied and the gradient radiates outward from the center of the stroke.

7. Click the **Reverse Gradient button** on the Gradient panel, then compare your screen to Figure 60.

8. Save, then close the file.

You applied a gradient to the stroke on an object, then applied two different options for how the stroke is applied. You clicked the Reverse Gradient button to reverse how the across stroke option applied the gradient.

Create point text.

1. Open AI 2-5.ai, then save it as **Restaurant Logo**.
2. Using a bold font, type **NOW OPEN** on two lines anywhere on the artboard, using all capital letters. (*Hint*: The font used in Figure 61 is Impact.)
3. Change the font size to 29 pt and the leading to 25 pt.
4. Verify that the Baseline Shift is set to 0.
5. Change the alignment to Center and the Horizontal Scale to 75%.
6. Position the text in the center of the white circle.
7. Hide the text.
8. Save your work.

Flow text into an object.

1. Copy the beige circle.
2. Paste the copy in front of it.
3. Click the Type tool, then select all of the green text at the bottom of the artboard, with the Type tool.
4. Copy the green text.
5. Click the Selection tool, then click the top beige circle.
6. Click the Area Type tool, click the edge of the top beige circle, then paste.
7. Center-align the text in the circle.
8. Change the baseline shift to -4 pts.
9. Fill the selected text with the same fill color as the beige circle (50% Orange).
10. On the Color panel, drag the Magenta slider to 40% to darken the text.
11. Hide the text.
12. Save your work.

Position text on a path.

1. Select the dark gray circle.
2. Click the Type on a Path tool, then click the top of the circle.
3. Using a bold font, type **THE HOLE-IN-ONE** in all capital letters across the top of the circle. (*Hint*: The font in Figure 61 is Arial Black. If your type appears at the bottom of the circle, drag the start or end bracket to position the type at the top of the circle. Zoom in so that you can clearly see the brackets. If you move the circle instead of the type, undo your last step and try again.)
4. Change the font size to 36 pt, set the horizontal scale to 75% and the fill color to White. (*Hint*: You may need to use a different font size, depending on the font you choose.)
5. Click the Selection tool, click Edit on the Menu bar, click Copy, click Edit on the Menu bar, click Paste in Front, then move the center bracket clockwise to position the copied text across the bottom of the circle.
6. Select the copied text with the Type tool, then type **RESTAURANT**.
7. Drag the RESTAURANT text across the path to flip its direction.
8. Apply a negative baseline shift to move the text below the path. (*Hint*: The baseline shift used in Figure 61 is -26 pts.)
9. Copy both text objects, click Edit on the Menu bar, then click Paste in Back.

10. Fill the back copies of the text with Black, then move them 2 pts up and 2 pts to the right.
11. Save your work.

Create and apply gradients.

1. Apply the White, Black Radial gradient to the small white circle.
2. Change the ending color stop on the Gradient Ramp to Smoke. (*Hint*: Press [Alt] (Win) or [option] (Mac) while you select Smoke from the Swatches panel.)
3. Save the new gradient to the Swatches panel.
4. Name it **Golf Ball**.
5. Fill the large green circle with the Golf Ball gradient.
6. Change the starting color stop to Pure Yellow.
7. Change the ending color stop to Little Sprout Green.
8. Move the midpoint to the 80% location on the Gradient Slider.
9. Save the new gradient as **The Rough**.
10. Apply a 2 pt Black stroke to the large circle and the smaller peach circle.
11. Save your work.

Adjust a gradient and create a drop shadow.

1. Click Object on the Menu bar, then click Show All.
2. Deselect all by clicking the artboard.
3. Select NOW OPEN and convert the text to outlines.
4. Fill the text with the white to black linear gradient.
5. Change the starting color stop to black.
6. Create an intermediary White color stop at the 50% mark on the Gradient Slider.

Creating Text and Gradients

7. Drag the Gradient tool starting at the top of the word NOW to the bottom of the word OPEN.
8. Change the middle color stop of the gradient to Latte.
9. Save the new gradient as **Flash**.
10. Deselect the text.
11. Delete the green text from the bottom of the artboard.
12. Convert the remaining text objects into outlines.
13. Apply a 2 pt Black stroke to the two circles in the illustration.
14. Select all, then lock all objects.

15. Save your work, compare your illustration to Figure 61, then close Restaurant Logo.

Apply gradients to strokes.

1. Open AI 2-6.ai, then save it as **Gradient Strokes to Text**.
2. Select the letter Z with the Selection tool, then verify that the Stroke icon is activated on the Tools panel.
3. Click Type on the Menu bar, then click Create Outlines.

4. Click the White to Cyan gradient swatch on the Swatches panel. The gradient is applied to the stroke.
5. Note the three Stroke buttons on the Gradient panel.
6. Click the third of the three Stroke buttons.
7. Click the Reverse Gradient button on the Gradient panel.
8. Save, then close the file.

Figure 61 *Completed Skills Review*

Creating Text and Gradients

An eccentric California real-estate mogul hires your design firm to "create an identity" for La Mirage, his development of high-tech executive condominiums in Palm Springs. Since he's curious about what you'll come up with on your own, the only creative direction he'll give you is to tell you that the concept is "a desert oasis."

1. Create a new 6" × 6" document, then save it as **Desert Oasis**.
2. Using a bold font and 80 pt for a font size, type **LA MIRAGE** in all capitals. (*Hint*: The font shown in Figure 62 is Impact.)
3. Change the horizontal scale to 80%.
4. Change the baseline shift to 0.
5. Apply a -100 kerning value between the two words.
6. Convert the text to outlines, then click the linear gradient swatch on the Swatches panel that fades white to black.
7. Using the Color panel, change the first color stop to 66M/100Y/10K.
8. Create an intermediary color stop that is 25M/100Y.
9. Position the intermediary color stop at 70% on the slider.
10. Save the gradient on the Swatches panel, and name it **Desert Sun**.
11. Drag the Gradient tool from the exact top to the exact bottom of the text.
12. Create a rectangle around the text and fill it with the Desert Sun gradient.
13. Drag the Gradient tool from the bottom to the top of the rectangle.
14. Send the rectangle to the back of the stack.
15. Apply a 1-point Black stroke to LA MIRAGE.
16. Type the tagline: a **desert oasis** in 14 pt lowercase letters.
17. Apply a tracking value of 500 or more to the tagline, then convert it to outlines.
18. Save your work, compare your image to Figure 62, then close Desert Oasis.

Figure 62 *Completed Project Builder 1*

Your friend owns Loon's Balloons. She stops by your studio with a display ad that she's put together for a local magazine and asks if you can make all the elements work together better. Her only direction is that the balloon must remain pink.

1. Open AI 2-7.ai, then save it as **Balloons**.
2. Save the pink fill on the balloon to the Swatches panel, and name it **Hot Pink**.
3. Fill the balloon shape with the White, Black Radial gradient from the Swatches panel.
4. Change the black stop on the Gradient Slider to Hot Pink.
5. Using the Gradient tool, change the highlight point on the balloon shape so that it is no longer centered in the balloon shape.
6. Copy the balloon, then paste it in front.
7. Click the Selection tool on the block of text that begins with "specializing in...," then cut the text.
8. Click the top balloon with the Selection tool, then switch to the Area Type tool.
9. Click the top edge of the top balloon, then paste.
10. Center the text and apply a -4 baseline shift.

11. Adjust the layout of the text as necessary. (*Hint*: You can force a line of text to the next line by clicking before the first word in the line you want to move, then pressing [Shift][Enter] (Win) or [Shift] [return] (Mac).)

12. Move the headline LOON'S BALLOONS so that each word is on a different side of the balloon string.
13. Apply a 320 kerning value between the two words.
14. Save your work, compare your screen to Figure 63, then close Balloons.

Figure 63 *Completed Project Builder 2*

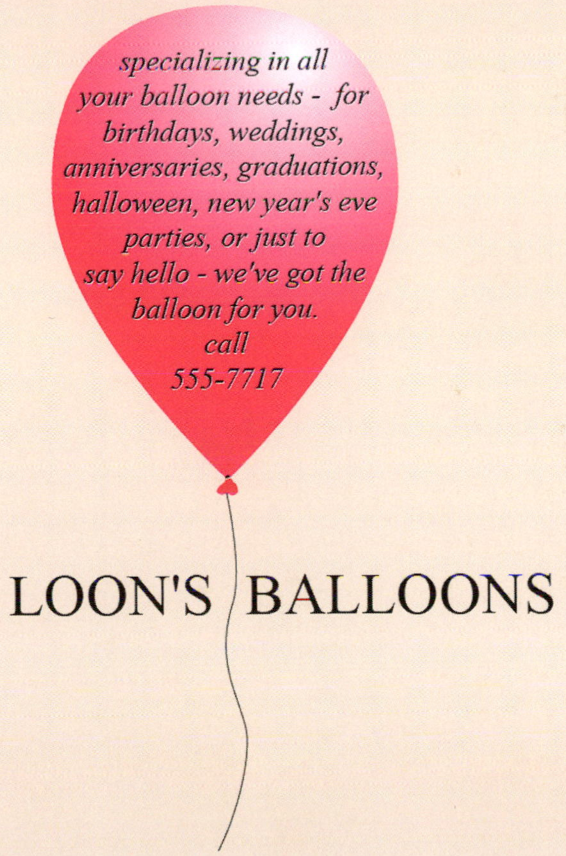

Creating Text and Gradients

You work in the marketing department of a major movie studio, where you design movie posters and newspaper campaigns. You are respected for your proficiency with typography. Your boss asks you to come up with a "teaser" campaign for the movie *Vanishing Point*, a spy thriller. The campaign will run on billboards in 10 major cities and will feature only the movie title, nothing else.

1. Create a new 6" × 6" document, then save it as **Vanish**.
2. Type **VANISHING POINT**, using 100 pt and a bold font. (*Hint*: The font used in Figure 56 is Impact.)
3. Change the horizontal scale to 55%.
4. Convert the text to outlines.
5. On the Swatches panel, click the white to black linear gradient swatch.
6. Drag the Gradient tool from the exact bottom to the exact top of the letters.
7. Copy the letters, then paste them in front.
8. Fill the copied letters in front with White.
9. Using your arrow keys, move the white letters 2 pts to the left and 8 pts up.
10. Save your work, then compare your text with Figure 64.
11. Close Vanish.

Figure 64 *Completed Design Project*

Firehouse Chili Pepper Company, a local specialty food manufacturer, has hired you to design a label for its new line of hot sauces. Since this is a new product line, they have no existing materials with which you can start.

1. Create a new 6" × 6" document, then save it as **Firehouse Chili**.

2. Search the Internet to get design ideas. Use keywords such as chili, pepper, hot sauce, barbecue, and salsa. What have other designers created to convey these concepts? Is there a broad range of ideas, or are they all pretty much different versions of the same idea? If so, can you think of something original that works?

3. Go to the grocery store and return with some samples of other products in this niche. Be sure to purchase both products that you've heard of before and products you've never heard of before. Are the known products' design concepts better than the unknown products'? Look for any correlation between the successful products and better design, if it is evident.

4. Begin brainstorming and sketching out ideas. Although there are no existing materials, the product line's name is very evocative. You should create design ideas that spring from the concepts of "firehouse" and "chili pepper," as well as from more broad-based concepts such as salsa, Mexico, and fire.

5. Use the skills that you learned in this chapter to create the label. (*Hint*: Fill text outlines with a gradient that conveys "hot." Use reds, oranges, and blacks. Use a bold font for the text so that the gradient will be clearly visible. Position the stops on the slider so that the "hot" colors are prominent in the letterforms.) Figure 65 shows one solution.

6. Save your work.

7. Close Firehouse Chili.

Figure 65 *Completed Portfolio Project*

CHAPTER 3 DRAWING AND COMPOSING AN ILLUSTRATION

1. Draw straight lines

2. Draw curved lines

3. Draw elements of an illustration

4. Apply attributes to objects

5. Assemble an illustration

6. Stroke objects for artistic effect

7. Use Image Trace

8. Use the Live Paint Bucket tool

9. Explore alternate drawing techniques

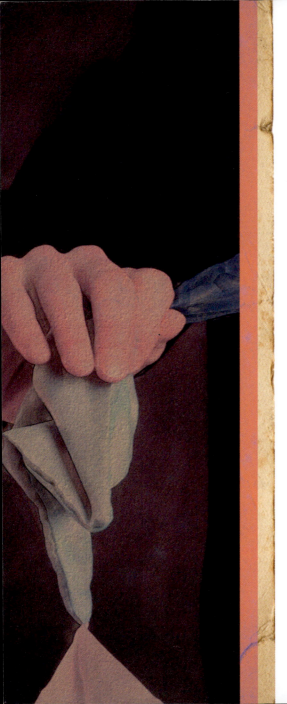

CHAPTER 3 DRAWING AND COMPOSING AN ILLUSTRATION

Drawing in Illustrator

You can create any shape using the Pen tool, which is why it's often called "the drawing tool." More precisely, the pen is a tool for drawing straight lines, curved lines, polygons, and irregularly shaped objects. It is, however, no *more* of a drawing tool than any of the shape tools but, rather, simply more versatile. Make note that *to master Illustrator, you must master the Pen tool.*

The challenges of the Pen tool are finite and can be grasped with no more than 30 minutes' study. As with many aspects of graphic design (and of life!), mastery comes with practice. So make it a point to learn Pen tool techniques. Don't get frustrated. Use the Pen tool often, even if it's just to play around making odd shapes.

All artists learn techniques for using tools such as brushes, chalk, and palette knives.

Once learned, those techniques become second nature, subconscious and unique to the artist. Ask yourself, was Van Gogh's mastery of the palette knife a triumph of his hands or of his imagination?

When you draw, you aren't conscious of how you're holding the crayon or how much pressure you're applying to the paper. Much the same goes for Illustrator's Pen tool. When you are comfortable and confident, you will find yourself effectively translating design ideas from your imagination straight to the artboard, without even thinking about the tool!

When you work with the Pen tool, you'll want complete control over your artboard. Using the Zoom tool and the New View feature, you can create custom views of different areas of your artboard, making it easy to jump to specific elements of your illustration for editing purposes.

Draw Straight
LINES

What You'll Do

© 2015 Cengage Learning®

In this lesson, you will create three new views, then explore basic techniques for using the Pen tool as you prepare to draw a complex illustration.

Viewing Objects on the Artboard

If you are drawing on paper and you want to see your work up close, you move your nose closer to the paper. Computers offer more effective options. As you have already seen, the Zoom tool is used to enlarge areas of the artboard for easier viewing. When you are working with the Pen tool, your view of the board becomes more critical as anchor points are tiny, and you will often move them in 1 point increments.

Instead of clicking the Zoom tool to enlarge the artboard, you can click and drag a **marquee** around the specific area you want to enlarge. The marquee, which is a rectangular, dotted line surrounding the area, will disappear when you release the Zoom tool, and whatever was in the marquee will be magnified as much as possible, while still fitting in the window.

The New View command allows you to save any view of the artboard. Let's say you zoom in on an object. You can save that view and give it a descriptive name, using the New View command. The name of the view is then listed at the bottom of the View menu,

so you can return to it at any time by selecting it. Saving views is an effective way to increase your productivity.

Drawing Straight Segments with the Pen Tool

You can use the Pen tool to make lines, also known as **paths**. You can also use it to create a closed shape, such as a triangle or a pentagon. When you click the Pen tool to make anchor points on the artboard, straight segments are automatically placed between the points. When the endpoints of two straight segments are united by a point, that point is called a **corner point**. Figure 1 shows a simple path drawn with five anchor points and four segments.

Perfection is an unnecessary goal when you are using the Pen tool because you can move and reposition anchor points and segments, as well as add and delete new points. You can use the Pen tool to create the general shape you have in your mind. Once the object is complete, you can use the Direct Selection tool to perfect, or tweak, the points and segments. Tweaking a finished object is always part of the drawing process.

Aligning and Joining Anchor Points

Often, you will want to align anchor points precisely. For example, if you have drawn a diamond-shaped object with the Pen tool, you may want to align the top and bottom points on the same vertical axis and then align the left and right points on the same horizontal axis to perfect the shape.

The **Average** command is a simple and effective choice for aligning points. With two or more points selected, you can use the Average command to align them on the horizontal axis, on the vertical axis, or on both the horizontal and vertical axes. Two points aligned on both the horizontal and vertical axes are positioned one on top of the other.

Why is this command named "Average?" The name is appropriate because when the command moves two points to line them up on a given axis, that axis is positioned at the average distance between the two points. Thus, each point moves the same distance.

The **Join** command unites two anchor points. When two points are positioned in different locations on the artboard, the Join command creates a segment between them. When two points are aligned on both the horizontal and vertical axes and are joined, the two points become one. Applying the Join command always results in a corner point.

You will often use the Average and Join commands in tandem. Figure 2 shows two pairs of points that have each been aligned on the horizontal axis, then joined with the Join command.

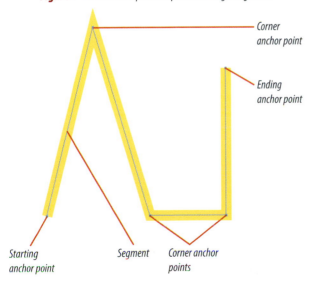

Figure 1 *Elements of a path composed of straight segments*

Corner anchor point

Ending anchor point

Starting anchor point

Segment

Corner anchor points

Figure 2 *Join command unites open points*

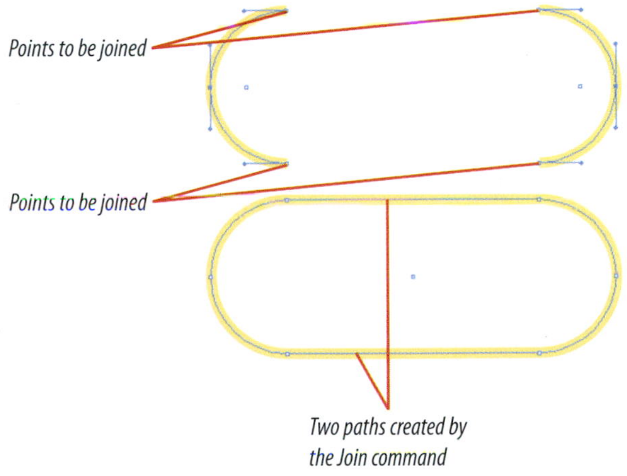

Points to be joined

Points to be joined

Two paths created by the Join command

Create new views

1. Open AI 3-1.ai, then save it as **Straight Lines**.

2. Choose the Essentials workspace, click the **Zoom tool** 🔍, then position it at the upper-left corner of the artboard.

3. Click and drag a **marquee** that encompasses the entire yellow section, as shown in Figure 3.

   The area within the selection box is now magnified.

4. Click **View** on the Menu bar, then click **New View**.

5. Name the new view **yellow**, then click **OK**.

6. Press and hold **[Spacebar]** to access the Hand tool 🖐, then drag the **artboard** upward until you have a view of the entire pink area.

7. Create a new view of the pink area, and name it **pink**.

   TIP If you need to adjust your view, you can quickly switch to a view of the entire artboard by pressing [Ctrl] [0] (Win) or ⌘ [0] (Mac), then create a new selection box with the Zoom tool.

8. Create a new view of the green area, named **mint**.

9. Click **View** on the Menu bar, then click **yellow** at the bottom of the menu.

   The Illustrator window changes to the yellow view.

   TIP You can change the name of a view by clicking View on the Menu bar, then clicking Edit Views.

You used the Zoom tool to magnify an area of the artboard. You then named and saved the three views.

Figure 3 *Drag the Zoom tool to select what will be magnified*

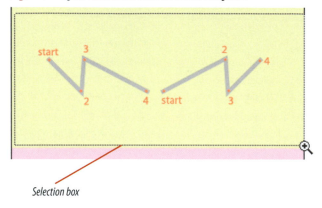

Selection box

Drawing and Composing an Illustration

Figure 4 *Four anchor points and three segments*

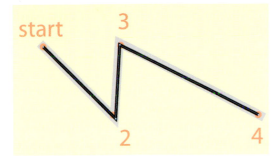

Figure 5 *Click the path with the Pen tool to add a new point*

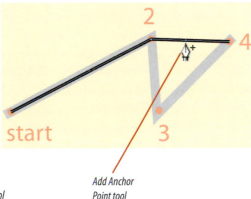

Add Anchor
Point tool

Figure 6 *Move an anchor point with the Direct Selection tool*

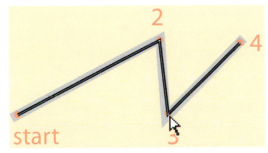

Draw straight lines

1. Verify that you are still in the yellow view, then click the **Pen tool** 🖊.

2. Open the Swatches panel and set the fill color to **[None]** and the stroke color to **Black**, then open the Stroke panel and set the stroke weight to **1 pt**.

3. Using Figure 4 as a reference, click **position 1 (start)**.

4. Click **position 2**, then note how a segment is automatically drawn between the two anchor points.

5. Click **position 3**, then click **position 4**.

TIP If you become disconnected from the current path you are drawing, undo your last step, then click the last anchor point with the Pen tool and continue.

6. Press and hold **[Ctrl]** (Win) or ⌘ (Mac) to switch to the Selection tool ▶, then click the **artboard** to stop drawing the path and to deselect it.

   You need to deselect one path before you can start drawing a new one.

7. Release **[Ctrl]** (Win) or ⌘ (Mac), click **position 1 (start)** on the next path, then click **position 2**.

8. Skip over position 3 and click **position 4**.

9. Using Figure 5 as a guide, position the Pen tool 🖊 anywhere on the segment between points 2 and 4, then click to add a new anchor point.

TIP When the Pen tool is positioned over a selected path, the Add Anchor Point tool 🖊⁺ appears.

10. Click the **Direct Selection tool** ▶, then drag the **new anchor point** to position 3, as shown in Figure 6.

Using the Pen tool, you created two straight paths.

Close a path and align the anchor points

1. Click **View** on the Menu bar, then click **pink**.

2. Click the **Pen tool** ✏, click the **start/end position** at the top of the polygon, then click **positions 2 through 6**.

3. Position the Pen tool ✏ over the first point you created, then click to close the path, as shown in Figure 7.

4. Switch to the **Direct Selection tool** ▶, click **point 3**, press and hold **[Shift]**, then click **point 6**.

TIP You use the [Shift] key to select multiple points.

Anchor points that are selected appear as solid blue squares; anchor points that are not selected are white or hollow squares.

5. Click **Object** on the Menu bar, point to **Path**, then click **Average**.

6. Click the **Horizontal option button** in the Average dialog box, then click **OK**.

The two selected anchor points align on the horizontal axis, as shown in Figure 8.

7. Select both the start/end point and point 4.

8. Use the Average command to align the points on the vertical axis.

9. Select both point 2 and point 5, then use the Average command to align the points on both axes, as shown in Figure 9.

You drew a closed path, then used the Average command to align three sets of points. You aligned the first set on the horizontal axis, the second on the vertical axis. You aligned the third set of points on both axes, which positioned them one on top of the other.

Figure 7 *Close a path at its starting point*

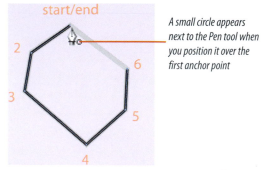

A small circle appears next to the Pen tool when you position it over the first anchor point

Figure 8 *Two points aligned on the horizontal axis*

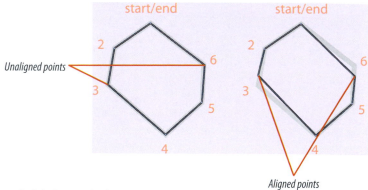

Unaligned points

Aligned points

Figure 9 *Averaging two points on both the horizontal and vertical axes*

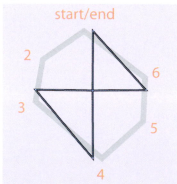

Figure 10 *Cutting points also deletes the segments attached to them*

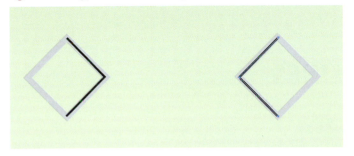

Figure 11 *Join command unites two distant points with a straight segment*

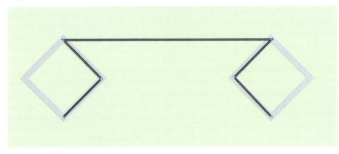

Figure 12 *Joining the two open anchor points on an open path closes the path*

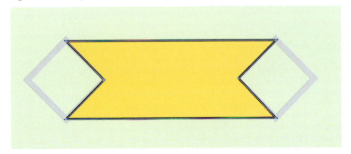

Join anchor points

1. Switch to the mint view of the artboard.

2. Use the Pen tool 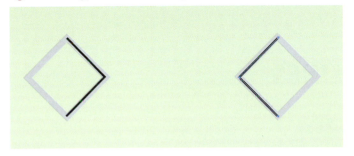 to trace the two diamond shapes.

   TIP Remember to deselect the first diamond path with the Selection tool before you begin tracing the second diamond.

3. Click the **left anchor point** of the first diamond with the Direct Selection tool , click **Edit** on the Menu bar, then click **Cut**.

   Cutting points also deletes the segments attached to them.

4. Cut the right point on the second diamond.

   Your work should resemble Figure 10.

5. Select the **top point** on each path.

6. Click **Object** on the Menu bar, point to **Path**, then click **Join**.

   The points are joined by a straight segment, as shown in Figure 11.

   TIP The shortcut key for Average is [Ctrl] [Alt] [A] (Win) or [option] [⌘] [J] (Mac) and for Join is [Ctrl] [J] (Win) or [⌘] [J] (Mac).

7. Join the two bottom points.

8. Apply a yellow fill to the object, then save your work.

   Your work should resemble Figure 12.

9. Close the Straight Lines document.

You drew two closed paths. You cut a point from each path, which deleted the points and the segments attached to them, creating two open paths. You used the Join command, which drew a new segment between the two top points and the two bottom points on each path. You then applied a yellow fill to the new object.

Draw CURVED LINES

What You'll Do

© 2015 Cengage Learning®

In this lesson, you will use the Pen tool to draw and define curved paths, and you will learn techniques to draw lines that abruptly change direction.

Defining Properties of Curved Lines

When you click to create anchor points with the Pen tool, the points are connected by straight segments. You can "draw" a curved path between two anchor points by *clicking and dragging* the Pen tool to create the points instead of just clicking. Anchor points created by clicking and dragging the Pen tool are known as **smooth points**.

When you use the Direct Selection tool to select a point connected to a curved segment, you will expose the point's **direction lines**, as shown in Figure 13. The angle and length of the direction lines determine the arc of the curved segment. Direction lines are editable. You can click and drag the **direction points**, or handles, at the end of the direction lines to reshape the curve. Direction lines function

Figure 13 *Direction lines define a curve*

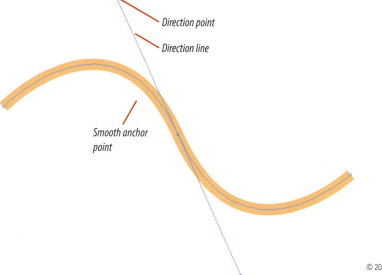

Direction point

Direction line

Smooth anchor point

© 2015 Cengage Learning®

only to define curves and do not appear when you print your document.

A smooth point always has two direction lines that move together as a unit. The two curved segments attached to the smooth point are both defined by the direction lines. When you manipulate the direction lines on a smooth point, you change the curve of both segments attached to the point, always maintaining a *smooth* transition through the anchor point.

When two paths are joined at a corner point, the two paths can be manipulated independently. A corner point can join two straight segments, one straight segment and one curved segment, or two curved segments. That corner point would have zero, one, or two direction lines, respectively. Figure 14 shows examples of smooth points and corner points.

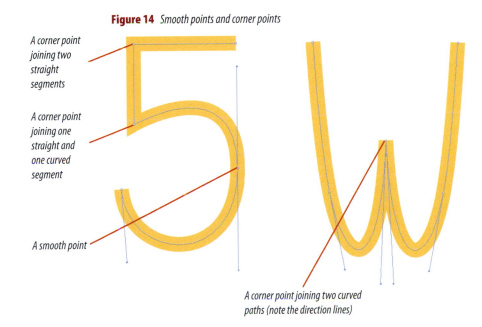

Figure 14 *Smooth points and corner points*

A corner point joining two straight segments

A corner point joining one straight and one curved segment

A smooth point

A corner point joining two curved paths (note the direction lines)

When a corner point joins one or two curved segments, the direction lines are unrelated and are often referred to as "broken." When you manipulate one, the other doesn't move.

Converting Anchor Points

The Anchor Point tool changes corner points to smooth points and smooth points to corner points.

To convert a corner point to a smooth point, you click and drag the Anchor Point tool on the anchor point to *pull out* direction lines. See Figure 15.

The Anchor Point tool works two ways to convert a smooth point to a corner point, and both are very useful when drawing.

When you click directly on a smooth point with the Anchor Point tool, the direction lines disappear. The two attached segments lose whatever curve defined them and become straight segments, as shown in the middle circle in Figure 16.

Figure 15 *Converting a corner point to a smooth point*

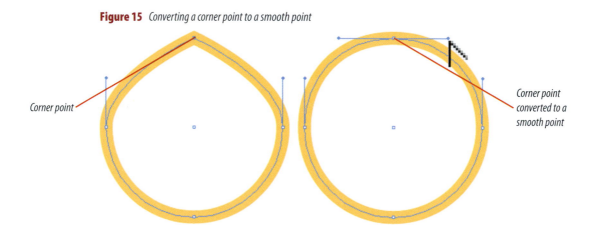

Corner point

Corner point converted to a smooth point

You can also use the Anchor Point tool on one of the two direction lines of a smooth point. The tool "breaks" the direction lines and allows you to move one independently of the other as shown in the third circle in Figure 16. The smooth point is converted to a corner point that now joins two unrelated curved segments.

Once the direction lines are broken, they remain broken. You can manipulate them independently with the Direct Selection tool; you no longer need the Anchor Point tool to do so.

Toggling Between the Pen Tool and Selection Tools

Drawing points and selecting points go hand in hand so and you will often need to switch back and forth between the Pen tool and one of the selection tools. Clicking from one tool to the other on the Tools panel is unnecessary and will impede your productivity. To master the Pen tool, you must incorporate the keyboard command for "toggling" between the Pen tool and the selection tools. With the Pen tool selected, press [Ctrl] (Win) or ⌘ (Mac), which will switch the Pen tool to the Selection tool or the Direct Selection tool, depending on which tool you used last.

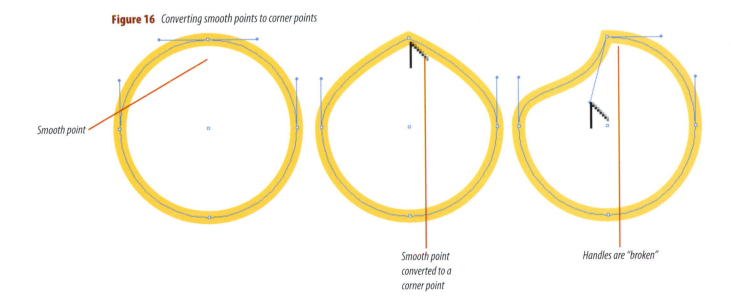

Figure 16 *Converting smooth points to corner points*

Smooth point

Smooth point converted to a corner point

Handles are "broken"

Draw and edit a curved line

1. Open AI 3-2.ai, then save it as **Curved Lines 1**.

2. Click the **Pen tool** , then position it over the first point position on the line.

3. Click and drag upward until the pointer is at the center of the purple star, then release the mouse button.

4. Position the Pen tool over the second point position.

5. Click and drag down to the red star, then release the mouse button.

6. Using the same method, trace the remainder of the blue lines, as shown in Figure 17.

7. Click the **Direct Selection tool** .

8. Select the **second anchor point**.

9. Click and drag the **direction handle** of the top direction line to the second purple star, as shown in Figure 18, then release the mouse button.

   The move changes the shape of both segments attached to the anchor point.

10. Select the **third anchor point**.

11. Drag the **bottom direction handle** to the second red star, as shown in Figure 19, then release the mouse button.

12. Manipulate the direction lines to restore the curves to their appearance in Figure 17.

13. Save your work, then close the Curved Lines 1 document.

You traced a curved line by making smooth points with the Pen tool. You used the Direct Selection tool to manipulate the direction lines of the smooth points and adjust the curves. You then used the direction lines to restore the line to its original curves.

Figure 17 *Smooth points draw continuous curves*

Figure 18 *Moving one direction line changes two curves*

Click the Direct Selection tool on any smooth point to expose its direction lines

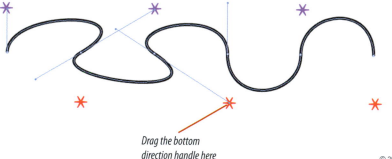

Figure 19 *Round curves are distorted by moving direction lines*

Drag the bottom direction handle here

© 2015 Cengage Learning®

Drawing and Composing an Illustration

Figure 20 *Smooth points converted to corner points*

Figure 21 *Smooth points restored from corner points*

Convert anchor points

1. Open AI 3-3.ai, then save it as **Curved Lines 2**.
2. Click **View** on the Menu bar, then click **View #1**.
3. Click the **Direct Selection tool** anywhere on the black line. Make note of the location of the six existing anchor points that become visible.
4. Click **Object** on the Menu bar, point to **Path**, then click **Add Anchor Points**.

   Five anchor points are added that do not change the shape of the line.
5. Click the **Anchor Point tool** , then click **each of the five new anchor points**.

TIP The Anchor Point tool is hidden beneath the Pen tool.

   The smooth points are converted to corner points, as shown in Figure 20.
6. Click **the six original anchor points** with the Anchor Point tool.
7. Position the Anchor Point tool over the sixth anchor point from the left.
8. Click and drag the **anchor point** to the purple star.

   The corner point is converted to a smooth point.
9. Using Figure 21 as a guide, convert the corner points to the left and right of the new curve.

You added five new anchor points to the line, then used the Anchor Point tool to convert all 11 points from smooth to corner points. You then used the Anchor Point tool to convert three corner points to smooth points.

Draw a line with curved and straight segments

1. Click **View** on the Menu bar, then click **View #2**.

2. Click the **Pen tool** 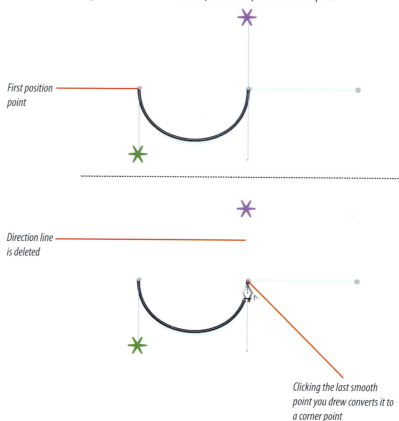, position it over the first point position, then click and drag down to the green star.

3. Position the Pen tool over the second point position, then click and drag up to the purple star, as shown in the top section of Figure 22.

4. Click the **second anchor point**.

    The direction line you dragged is deleted, as shown in the lower section of Figure 22.

5. Click the **third point position** to create the third anchor point.

6. Position the Pen tool over the third anchor point, then click and drag a direction line up to the green star.

7. Position the Pen tool over the fourth point position, then click and drag down to the purple star.

8. Click the **fourth anchor point**.

9. Position the Pen tool over the fifth position, then click.

10. While the Pen tool is still positioned over the fifth anchor point, click and drag a direction line down to the green star.

11. Finish tracing the line, then deselect the path.

You traced a line that has three curves joined by two straight segments. You used the technique of clicking the previous smooth point to convert it to a corner point, allowing you to change the direction of the path.

Figure 22 *Click to convert an open smooth point to a corner point*

First position point

Direction line is deleted

Clicking the last smooth point you drew converts it to a corner point

Drawing and Composing an Illustration

Figure 23 *Use the Anchor Point tool to "break" the direction lines and redirect the path*

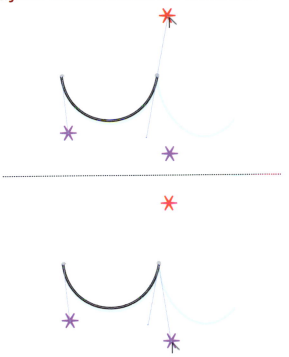

The Pencil, Smooth, and Path Eraser Tools

When drawing paths, be sure to experiment with the Pencil, Smooth, and Path Eraser tools, which are grouped together on the Tools panel. You can draw freehand paths with the Pencil tool and then manipulate them using the Direct Selection tool, the Smooth tool, the Path Eraser tool or the Path Reshape feature on the Pen tool or Anchor Point tool. The Smooth tool is used to smooth over line segments that are too bumpy or too sharp. The Path Eraser tool looks and acts just like an eraser found at the end of a traditional pencil; dragging it over a line segment erases that part of the segment from the artboard. The Pencil tool draws freehand lines or straight lines. Press and hold [Shift] while dragging the Pencil tool to draw horizontal and vertical straight lines and diagonal lines with a 45-degree angle.

Reverse direction while drawing

1. Click **View** on the Menu bar, then click **View #3**.

2. Click the **Pen tool** 🖋, position it over the first point position, then click and drag down to the purple star.

3. Position the Pen tool 🖋 over the second point position, then click and drag up to the red star, as shown in the top section of Figure 23.

4. Press and hold **[Alt]** (Win) or **[option]** (Mac) to switch to the Anchor Point tool ⌐, then click and drag the **direction handle** on the red star down to the second purple star, as shown in the lower section of Figure 23.

   TIP Press [Alt] (Win) or [option] (Mac) to toggle between the Pen and the Anchor Point tools.

5. Release [Alt] (Win) or [option] (Mac), then continue to trace the line using the same method.

   TIP If you switch between the Pen tool and the Anchor Point tool using the Tools panel instead of using [Alt] (Win) or [option] (Mac), you will disconnect from the current path.

6. Save your work, then close the Curved Lines 2 document.

You used the Anchor Point tool to "break" the direction lines of a smooth point, converting it to a corner point in the process. You used the redirected direction line to define the next curve in the sequence.

Draw Elements of
AN ILLUSTRATION

What You'll Do

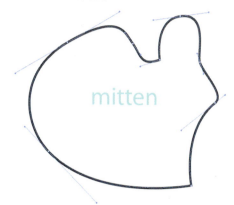

mitten

© 2015 Cengage Learning®

In this lesson, you will draw 14 elements of an illustration. By tracing previously drawn elements, you will develop a sense of where to place anchor points when drawing a real-world illustration.

Starting an Illustration

Getting started with drawing an illustration is often the hardest part. Sometimes the illustration will be an image of a well-known object or a supplied sketch or a picture. At other times, the illustration to be created will exist only in your imagination. In either case, the challenge is the same: How do you translate the concept from its source to the Illustrator artboard?

Drawing from Scratch

Drawing from scratch means that you start with a new Illustrator document and create the illustration, using only the Illustrator tools. This approach is common, especially when the goal is to draw familiar items such as a daisy, fish, or sun.

Illustrator's shape tools (such as the Ellipse tool) combined with the transform tools (such as the Rotate tool) make the program very powerful for creating geometric designs from scratch. The Undo and Redo commands allow you to experiment, and you will often find yourself surprised by the design you end up with!

Typographic illustrations—even complex ones—are often created from scratch.

Many talented illustrators and designers are able to create complex graphics off the cuff. It can be an astounding experience to watch an illustrator start with a blank artboard and, with no reference material, produce sophisticated graphics with attitude, expression, and emotion, as well as unexpected shapes and subtle relationships between objects.

Tracing a Scanned Image

Using the Place command, it is easy to import a scanned image into Illustrator. For complex illustrations, especially those of people or objects with delicate relationships, such as maps or blueprints, many designers find it easier to scan a sketch or a photo and import it into Illustrator as a guide or a point of reference.

Tracing a scanned image is not "cheating." An original drawing is an original drawing, whether it is first created on a computer or on a piece of paper. Rather than being a negative, the ability to use a computer to render a sketch is a fine example of the revolutionary techniques that illustration software has brought to the art of drawing. Figure 24 shows an illustration created from scratch in Illustrator, and Figure 25 shows a scanned sketch that will be the basis for the illustration you will create throughout this chapter.

Figure 24 *An illustration created from scratch*

Figure 25 *Place a scanned sketch in Illustrator, and you can trace it or use it as a visual reference*

Draw a closed path using smooth points

1. Open AI 3-4.ai, then save it as **Snowball Parts**.

2. Click **View** on the Menu bar, then click **Arm**.

3. Verify that the fill color is set to [None] and the stroke color is set to Black.

4. Click the **Pen tool** , position it over point 1, then click and drag a direction line to the green star on the right side of the 1.

5. Go to position 2, then click and drag a direction line to the next green star.

TIP Watch the blue preview of the new segment fall into place as you drag the Pen tool. This will help you understand when to stop dragging the direction line.

6. Using the same method, continue to draw points 3 through 6, then compare your screen to Figure 26.

7. Position the Pen tool over point 1.

8. Press and hold **[Alt]** (Win) or **[option]** (Mac), then click and drag to position the ending segment and close the path.

You drew a curved path. To close the path, you used a corner point, which allowed you to position the ending segment without affecting the starting segment.

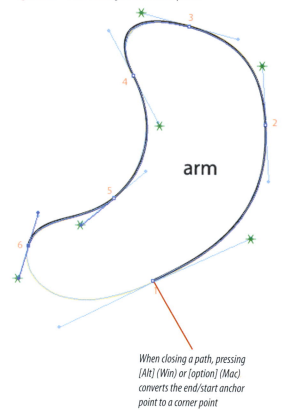

Figure 26 *Points 1 through 6 are smooth points*

arm

When closing a path, pressing [Alt] (Win) or [option] (Mac) converts the end/start anchor point to a corner point

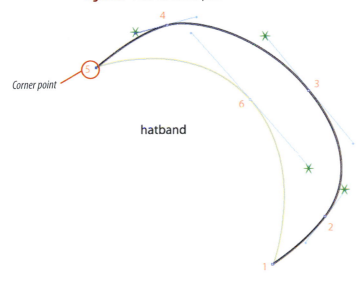

Figure 27 *Point 5 is a corner point*

Corner point

hatband

Begin and end a path with a corner point

1. Click **View** on the Menu bar, then click **Hatband**.
2. Verify that the fill color is set to [None] and the stroke color is set to Black.
3. Click the **Pen tool** , then click **position 1** to create a corner point.
4. Draw the next two curved segments for positions 2 and 3, using the green stars as guides.
5. Position the Pen tool   over position 4, then click and drag to the green star.
6. Click **position 5** to create a corner point, as shown in Figure 27.
7. Position the Pen tool   over position 6, then click and drag to the green star.
8. Click **position 1** to close the path with a corner point.
9. Click the **Selection tool** , then deselect the path.

You began a path with a corner point. When it was time to close the path, you simply clicked the starting point. Since the point was created without direction lines, there were no direction lines to contend with when closing the path.

Redirect a path while drawing

1. Click **View** on the Menu bar, then click **Nose**.

   The Nose view includes the nose, mouth, eyebrow, and teeth.

2. Click the **Pen tool** , then click **point 1** on the nose to start the path with a corner point.

3. Create smooth points at positions 2 and 3.

   The direction of the nose that you are tracing abruptly changes at point 3.

4. Press and hold **[Alt]** (Win) or **[option]** (Mac) to switch to the Anchor Point tool, then move the top direction handle of point 3 down to the red star, as shown in Figure 28.

5. Release [Alt] (Win) or [option] (Mac) to switch back to the Pen tool, click and drag **position 4** to finish drawing the path, click the **Selection tool**, then deselect the path.

   The nose element, as shown in Figure 29, is an open path.

Tracing the nose, you encountered an abrupt change in direction, followed by a curve. You used the Anchor Point tool to redirect the direction lines on point 3, simultaneously converting point 3 from smooth to corner and defining the shape of the curved segment that follows.

Figure 28 *Use the Anchor Point tool to redirect the path*

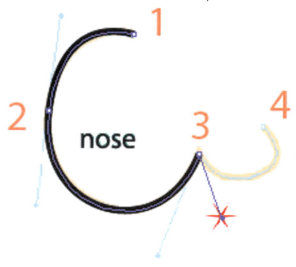

Figure 29 *Nose element is an open path*

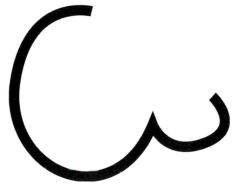

Drawing and Composing an Illustration

Figure 30 *Use a scanned sketch as a reference or for tracing*

Place a scanned image

1. Click **View** on the Menu bar, then click **Fit All in Window**.
2. Click **File** on the Menu bar, then click **Place**.
3. Navigate to the drive and folder where your Data Files are stored.
4. Click **Snowball Sketch.tif**, then click **Place**.

   A scan of the Snowball Sketch illustration is placed in a bounding box at the center of the artboard.
5. Use the Scale tool to scale the placed file 115%.

TIP You can apply all of the transform tools to placed files.

6. Click the **Selection tool** , move the placed file into the scratch area, then lock it.
7. Draw the remaining elements of the illustration, referring to the sketch in the scratch area or to Figure 30 for help. Save your work after you complete each element.

TIP The mouth, eyebrow, and teeth are located in the Nose view.

You placed a file of a scanned sketch to use as a reference guide. You scaled the object, dragged it to the scratch area, locked it, then drew the remaining elements of the illustration.

Apply Attributes
TO OBJECTS

What You'll Do

© 2015 Cengage Learning®

You will create four new colors on the Color panel and apply each to one of the illustration elements. Using the Eyedropper tool, you will paint the remaining items quickly and easily.

Using the Eyedropper Tool

In Illustrator, **attributes** are formatting that you have applied to an object to affect its appearance. Typographic attributes, for example, would include font, leading, and horizontal scale. Artistic attributes include the fill color, stroke color, and stroke weight.

The Eyedropper tool is handy for applying *all* of an object's attributes to another object. Its icon is particularly apt. The Eyedropper tool "picks up" an object's attributes, such as fill color, stroke color, and stroke weight.

> **QUICK TIP**
>
> You can think of the Eyedropper tool as taking a sample of an object's attributes.

The Eyedropper tool is particularly useful when you want to apply one object's attributes

to another. For example, if you have applied a blue fill with a 3.5 pt orange stroke to an object, you can easily apply those attributes to new or already-existing objects. Simply select the object that you want to format, then click the formatted object with the Eyedropper tool.

This is a simple example, but don't underestimate the power of the Eyedropper tool. As you explore more of Illustrator, you will find that you are able to apply a variety of increasingly complex attributes to objects. The more complex the attributes, the more the Eyedropper tool reveals its usefulness.

You can also use the Eyedropper tool to copy type formatting and effects between text elements. This can be especially useful when designing display type for headlines.

Adding a Fill to an Open Path

You can think of the letter O as an example of a closed path and the letter U as an example of an open path. Although it seems a bit strange, you are able to add a fill to an open path just as you would to a closed path.

The program draws an imaginary straight line between the endpoints of an open path to define where the fill ends. Figure 31 shows an open path in the shape of a U with a red fill. Note where the fill ends. For the most part, avoid applying fills to open paths. Though Illustrator will apply the fill, an open path's primary role is to feature a stroke. Any effect that you can create by filling an open path you can also create with a more effective method by filling a closed path.

Figure 31 *A fill color applied to an open path*

Apply new attributes to closed paths

1. Verify that nothing is selected on the artboard.

2. Open the Color panel, then create a royal blue color on the Color panel.

3. Fill the arm with the royal blue color, then change its stroke weight to 6 pt.

TIP Use the views at the bottom of the View menu to see and select each element with which you need to work. The mouth, eyebrow, and teeth are located in the Nose view.

4. Deselect the arm, then create a deep red color on the Color panel.

5. Fill the hatband with the deep red color, then change its stroke weight to 3 pt.

6. Deselect the hatband, then create a flesh-toned color on the Color panel that is 20% Magenta and 56% Yellow.

7. Fill the head with the flesh tone; don't change the stroke weight.

8. Fill the pompom with White; don't change the stroke weight.

9. Fill the mouth with Black; don't change the stroke weight.

10. Compare your work with Figure 32.

You applied new attributes to five closed paths by creating three new colors, using them as fills, then changing the stroke weight on two of the objects.

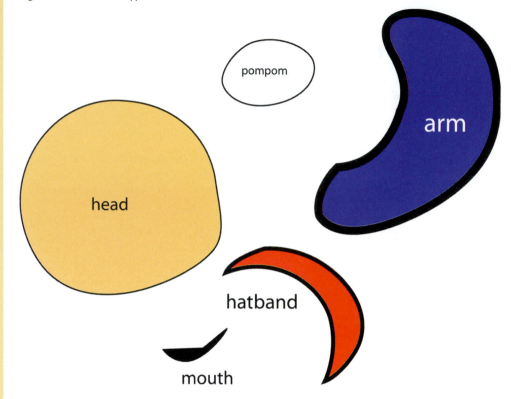

Figure 32 *New attributes applied to five elements*

Figure 33 *Use the Eyedropper tool to apply the attributes of one object to another with one click*

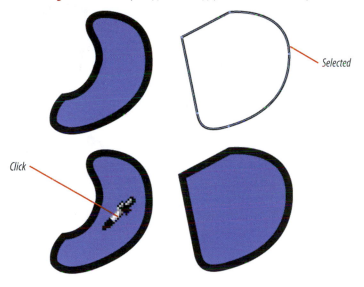

Selected

Click

Figure 34 *All elements ready to be assembled*

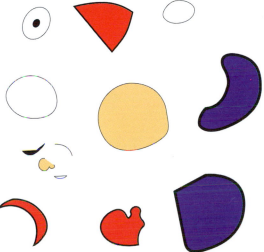

© 2015 Cengage Learning®

Copy attributes with the Eyedropper tool

1. Select the **torso**.
2. Click the **Eyedropper tool** 🖉, then click the **blue arm**.

   As shown in Figure 33, the torso takes on the same fill and stroke attributes as the arm.
3. Switch to the **Selection tool** ▸, select the **hat**, click the **Eyedropper tool** 🖉, then click the **hatband**.
4. Using any method you like, fill and stroke the remaining objects using the colors shown in Figure 34.
5. Save your work.

You applied the attributes of one object to another by first selecting the object to which you wanted to apply the attributes, then clicking the object with the desired attributes with the Eyedropper tool.

Assemble an
ILLUSTRATION

What You'll Do

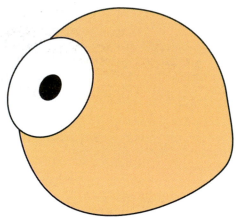

 In this lesson, you will arrange the elements that you drew in Lesson 4 to create a composed illustration.

Assembling an Illustration

Illustrator's basic stacking order design is sophisticated enough to compose any illustration. Assembling an illustration with multiple objects will test your fluency with the stacking order commands: Bring to Front, Send to Back, Bring Forward, Send Backward, Paste in Front, Paste in Back, Group, Lock, Unlock All, Hide, and Show All. The sequence in which you draw the elements determines the stacking order (newer elements are in front of older ones), so you'll almost certainly need to adjust the stacking order when assembling the elements. Locking and hiding placed elements will help you to protect the elements when they are positioned correctly.

Figure 35 *Eye positioned on the head*

Figure 36 *Second eye is a copy of the first*

Drawing and Composing an Illustration

Figure 37 *Nose pasted in front of the left eye*

The nose behind
the left eye

The nose in front
of the left eye

Figure 38 *Eyebrow positioned over the right eye*

Figure 39 *All elements in position*

Assemble the illustration

1. Select and copy all the elements on the artboard.

2. Create a new CMYK Color document that is 9" × 9", then save it as **Snowball Assembled**.

3. Paste the copied elements into the Snowball Assembled document.

4. Deselect all objects, select the **head**, click **Object** on the Menu bar, point to **Arrange**, then click **Send to Back**.

5. Group the eye and the iris, then position the eye on the head as shown in Figure 35.

6. Click the **eye**, press **[Alt]** (Win) or **[option]** (Mac), then drag to create a copy of it, as shown in Figure 36.

7. Position the nose on the face, cut the nose, select the left eye, then paste in front.

   The nose is pasted in the same position, but now it is in front of the eye, as shown in Figure 37.

8. Select the **teeth**, then bring them to the front.

9. Position the teeth over the mouth, then group them.

10. Position the mouth and the teeth on the head, and the eyebrow over the right eye, as shown in Figure 38.

11. Finish assembling the illustration, using Figure 39 as a guide, then save your work.

TIP Use the Object menu and the Arrange menu command to change the stacking order of objects as necessary.

You assembled the illustration, utilizing various commands to change the stacking order of the individual elements.

Stroke Objects for
ARTISTIC EFFECT

What You'll Do

© 2015 Cengage Learning®

 In this lesson, you will experiment with strokes of varying weight and attributes, using options on the Stroke panel. You will then apply pseudo-strokes to all of the objects to create dramatic stroke effects.

Defining Joins and Caps

In addition to applying stroke weights, you use the Stroke panel to define other stroke attributes, including joins and caps, and whether a stroke is solid or dashed. Figure 40 shows the Dashed Line utility and Caps on the Stroke panel.

Caps are applied to the ends of stroked paths. The Stroke panel offers three choices: Butt Cap, Round Cap, and Projecting Cap.

Choose Butt Cap for squared ends and Round Cap for rounded ends. Generally, round caps are more appealing to the eye.

The projecting cap applies a squared edge that extends the anchor point at a distance that is one-half the weight of the stroke. With a projecting cap, the weight of the stroke is equal in all directions around the line. The projecting cap is useful when you align two anchor points at a right angle, as shown in Figure 41.

Figure 40 *Stroke panel*

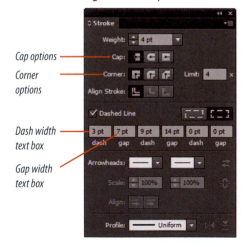

Cap options
Corner options
Dash width text box
Gap width text box

Figure 41 *Projecting caps are useful when segments meet at right angles*

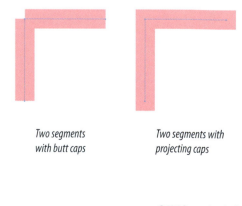

Two segments with butt caps

Two segments with projecting caps

© 2015 Cengage Learning®

When two stroked paths form a corner point, **joins** define the appearance of the corner. The default is a miter join, which produces stroked lines with pointed corners. The round join produces stroked lines with rounded corners, and the bevel join produces stroked lines with squared corners. The greater the weight of the stroke, the more apparent the join will be, as shown in Figure 42.

Defining the Miter Limit

The miter limit determines when a miter join will be squared off to a beveled edge. The miter is the length of the point from the inside to the outside. The length of the miter is not the same as the stroke weight. When two stroked paths are at an acute angle, the length

of the miter will greatly exceed the weight of the stroke, which results in an extreme point that can be very distracting.

QUICK TIP

You can align a stroke to the center, inside, or outside of a path using the Align Stroke buttons on the Stroke panel.

The default miter limit is 4, which means that when the length of the miter reaches 4 times the stroke weight, the program will automatically square it off to a beveled edge. Generally, you will find the default miter limit satisfactory, but remain conscious of it when you draw objects with acute angles, such as stars and triangles. Figure 43 shows the impact of a miter limit on a stroked star with acute angles.

Creating a Dashed Stroke

A dashed stroke is like any other stroked path in Illustrator, except that its stroke has been broken up into a sequence of dashes separated by gaps. The Stroke panel offers you the freedom to customize dashed or dotted lines by entering the lengths of the dashes and the gaps between them in the six dash and gap text boxes. You can create a maximum of three different sizes of dashes separated by three different sizes of gaps. The pattern you establish will be repeated across the length of the stroke.

When creating dashed strokes, remain conscious of the cap choice on the Stroke panel. Butt caps create familiar square dashes,

Figure 42 *Three types of joins*

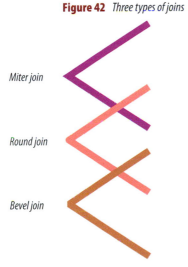

Miter join

Round join

Bevel join

Figure 43 *Miter limit affects the length of stroked corner points*

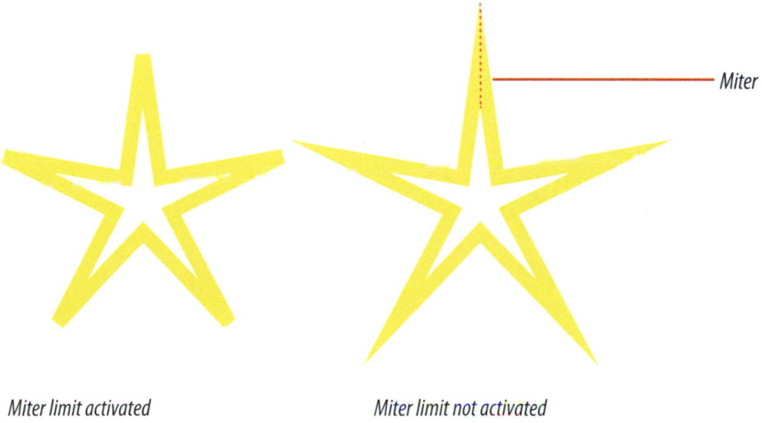

Miter

Miter limit activated

Miter limit not activated

© 2015 Cengage Learning®

and round caps create rounded dashes. Creating a dotted line requires round caps. Figure 44 shows two dashed lines using the same pattern but with different caps applied.

Improving the Appearance of a Dashed Stroke

The Stroke panel offers a helpful option for dashed lines. The options, identified in Figure 44 as Exact Dashes and Adjust Dashes, affect how dashes are distributed along a stroked path or the edge of a stroked object. Figure 45 shows each option. The red rectangle is an example of the Exact Dashes option. The dashes are distributed around the edge of the rectangle with the exact measurements input in the Stroke panel, regardless of the resulting appearance. In this case, the appearance leaves a bit to be desired. All four corners look different and, in the bottom-right corner, two dashes are actually overlapping.

The blue rectangle is an example of the Adjust Dashes option. Though the measurements for the dashed stroke are the same as those input for the red rectangle, here the Adjust Dashes option automatically adjusts the position and gaps of the dash so that the corners all look the same and the overall dashed effect is balanced.

Creating Pseudo-Stroke Effects

Strokes around objects, especially black strokes, often contribute much to an illustration in terms of contrast, dimension, and dramatic effect. A classic technique that designers have used since the early versions of Illustrator is the "pseudo-stroke," or false stroke. Basically, you place a black-filled copy behind an illustration element, then distort the black element with the Direct Selection tool so that it "peeks" out from behind the element in varying degrees.

This technique, as shown in Figure 46, is relatively simple to execute and can be used for dramatic effect in an illustration.

Figure 44 *Caps are an important factor in determining the appearance of a dashed line*

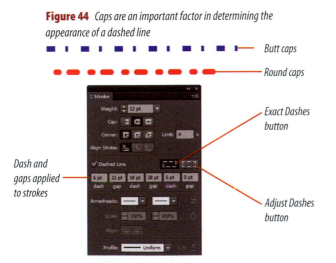

Butt caps

Round caps

Dash and gaps applied to strokes

Exact Dashes button

Adjust Dashes button

Figure 45 *The Exact Dashes and Adjust Dashes options applied to a stroked object*

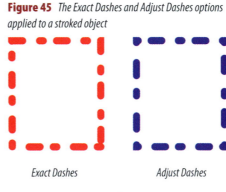

Exact Dashes   Adjust Dashes

Figure 46 *The "pseudo-stroke" effect*

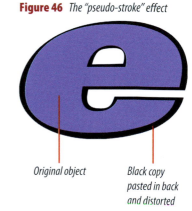

Original object

Black copy pasted in back and distorted

Drawing and Composing an Illustration

Figure 47 *Bevel joins applied to paths*

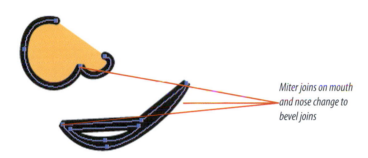

Miter joins on mouth and nose change to bevel joins

Figure 48 *Round joins applied to paths*

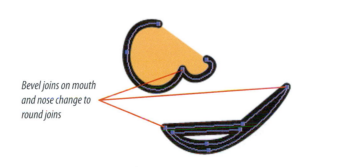

Bevel joins on mouth and nose change to round joins

Modify stroke attributes

1. Select the **eyebrow**, the **nose**, and the **mouth**.
2. Click **Select** on the Menu bar, then click **Inverse**.

   The selected items are now deselected, and the deselected items are selected.
3. Hide the selected items, then open the Stroke panel.
4. Select all, then change the stroke weight to 3 pt.
5. Click the **Stroke panel options button** , click **Show Options** if options are hidden, then click the **Round Cap button** .

   The caps on open paths are rounded.
6. Click the **Bevel Join button** .

   The miter joins on the mouth and nose change to a bevel join, as shown in Figure 47.
7. Click the **Round Join button** .

   The bevel joins on the mouth and nose change to round joins, as shown in Figure 48.
8. Remove the stroke from the teeth.

TIP Use the Direct Selection tool to select the teeth, since they are grouped with the mouth.

You hid elements so you could focus on the eyebrow, nose, and mouth. You applied round caps to the open paths and round joins to the corner points.

Create a dashed stroke

1. Show all objects, then select all.

2. Deselect the snowball, then hide the selected items.

   The snowball should be the only element showing.

3. Select the snowball, then change the stroke weight to 4 pt.

4. Click the **Dashed Line check box** on the Stroke panel.

5. Experiment with different dash and gap sizes.

6. Toggle between butt and round caps.

   The dashes change from rectangles to ovals.

7. Enter 1 pt dashes and 4 pt gaps.

8. Click the **Round Cap button** , verify that the Adjust Dashes option is activated, then compare your snowball to the one shown in Figure 49.

9. Show all of the objects that are currently hidden.

You applied a dashed stroke to the snowball object and noted how a change in caps affected the dashes.

Figure 49 *Creating a dashed stroke using the Stroke panel*

Drawing and Composing an Illustration

Figure 50 *Pompom with the pseudo-stroke effect*

Figure 51 *Completed illustration*

Create pseudo-strokes

1. Select the **pompom**, copy it, then paste in back.

2. Apply a black fill to the copy.

TIP The copy is still selected behind the original white pompom, making it easy to apply the black fill.

3. Click the **white pompom**, then remove the stroke.

4. Lock the white pompom.

5. Using the Direct Selection tool , select the **bottom anchor point** on the black copy.

6. Use the arrow keys to move the anchor point 5 pts down.

   The black copy is increasingly revealed as its size is increased beneath the locked white pompom.

7. Move the left anchor point 4 pts to the left.

8. Move the top anchor point 2 pts up, then deselect.

   Your work should resemble Figure 50.

9. Using the same methods and Figure 51 as a reference, create distorted black copies behind all the remaining elements except the torso, the mouth, and the eyebrow.

10. Save your work, then close Snowball Assembled.

You created black copies behind each element, then distorted them, using the Direct Selection tool and the arrow keys, to create the illusion of uneven black strokes around the object.

Use Image
TRACE

What You'll Do

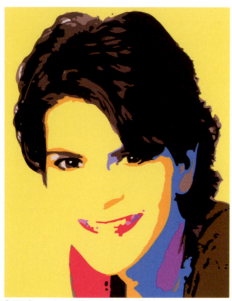

© 2015 Cengage Learning® Image Courtesy of Chris Botello.

 In this lesson, you will use Image Trace.

Using Image Trace

Image Trace is a feature that converts a bitmap image into a vector image so that you can modify it as you would a vector graphic.

When you place and select an image, the Image Trace button becomes available on the Control panel. Click the triangle beside the Image Trace button to expose the Image Trace menu, shown in Figure 52. Image

Figure 52 *Tracing presets in the Image Trace menu*

Trace offers a number of new and traditional tracing presets that give you different results. These presets include Line Art, Sketched Art, Black and White Logo, and 16 Colors.

In addition to the options in the Image Trace menu, you can use the Image Trace panel, shown in Figure 53. Here, you can click the Preset list arrow to choose which type of preset you want to use to trace the bitmap. Click the Preview check box to see previews of your results as you click on different presets.

Figure 53 *Image Trace panel*

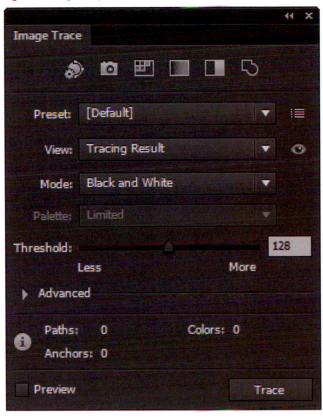

The Image Trace panel is dynamic: so long as the Preview option is activated, the selected image will update with any changes you make in the panel. Click the View menu to see the Tracing Results, or switch to Outline view to see just the paths being created by the tracing utility. Drag the Colors slider to increase or reduce the number of colors available to the resulting trace. Figure 54 shows the traced image reduced to just two colors and visible with both the tracing result and the outline.

Figure 54 *Traced image*

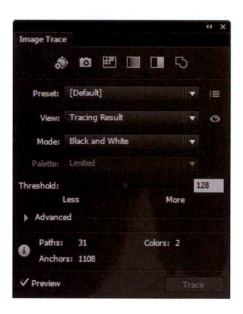

Drawing and Composing an Illustration

Tracing a Line-Art Sketch

Figure 55 shows a magic marker sketch of a dog that has been scanned into Photoshop and placed in Illustrator. Figure 56 shows the artwork after it has been traced using the Sketched Art preset in the Image Trace panel. Not much difference, you say? Images can be deceiving: though the artwork in Figures 55 and 56 appears similar, they couldn't be more different, because the artwork in Figure 56 is a vector graphic that has been traced from the bitmap graphic shown in Figure 55.

Figure 55 *Bitmap graphic placed in Illustrator*

Figure 56 *Traced graphic*

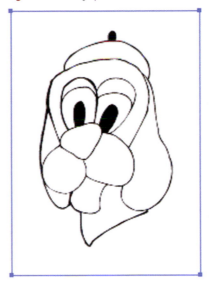

Tracing a Photograph

You use Image Trace to trace a bitmap photo the same way you trace a sketch. With photographic images especially, the presets list can be used to create some really interesting illustration effects. Figure 57 shows four different vector graphics, each traced with a different preset and with different color settings.

Figure 57 *Four traced graphics*

Drawing and Composing an Illustration

Expanding a Traced Graphic

After Image Trace has been executed, the Expand button becomes available on the Control panel. In order to select and modify the paths and points that make up the new vector graphic, you must first click the Expand button. Once expanded, the illustration is available to be selected and modified, as shown in Figure 58.

Especially when tracing photographs, the Image Trace utility creates illustrations with complex relationships between different paths. Working with expanded tracing results will often test your skills for working with paths.

Figure 58 *Four traced graphics*

Managing Assets with the Links Panel

Whenever you link to or embed artwork from another file, such as a TIFF file from Photoshop, that file will be listed on the Links panel along with any metadata that has been saved with the file. The Links panel shows a thumbnail of the artwork and the filename to help you identify the file. The Links panel also uses icons to indicate the artwork's status, such as whether the link is up to date, the file is missing, or the file has been modified since you placed it. You can use the Links panel to see and manage all linked or embedded artwork. To select and view a linked graphic, select a link and then click the Go To Link button, or choose Go To Link on the Links panel menu. The file will appear centered in the window.

When you place an image, the Control panel lists the name of the placed file, its color mode (usually RGB, CMYK, or Grayscale) and its resolution in PPI (pixels per inch). The resolution listing is the effective resolution—that is, it's the resolution of the file as its size in Illustrator. If you scale a placed image up, its effective resolution goes down, and the resolution listing on the Control panel will update to show the decrease. In the converse, if you scale a placed image down, it's effective resolution increases.

Click on the file name on the Control panel to reveal a menu of options, shown in Figure 59. These commands help you to manage the link to the placed file. For example, click Go To Link, and the placed file will be centered in your window; this can be very helpful when working with many images. Click Edit Original and the placed file will open in its native application. Click Relink to reestablish the link to the placed image if you've moved it to a different location on your computer or server.

Figure 59 *Link options on the Control panel*

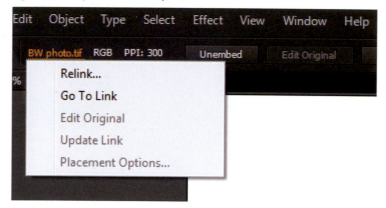

Drawing and Composing an Illustration

These commands are all available on the Links panel, shown in Figure 60. Note the yellow triangle with the exclamation point, which indicates that the placed file has been modified in its native application since being placed. In other words, the original is different from the placed file. Click the Update Link icon on the Links panel or on the Control panel to update the link and bring the placed file in synch with the original file.

Embedding Placed Images

Another important option on the control bar is the **Embed** button. When you place a file, that file is not automatically a part of the Illustrator file. Instead a link is created from Illustrator to that file. If you were to move the Illustrator file to a different computer—or email it to a friend–the placed image would not be available when the file is opened on the other computer. The link would be broken. For this reason, many designers choose to click the Embed button; doing so is like copying and pasting the placed file into the Illustrator document. The placed image no longer links to an original; it is in the Illustrator document and saved with the Illustrator document.

Note that when you click Embed, the file name of the placed image no longer appears on the Control panel. Instead, the panel lists the word Embedded. If you position your cursor over the word Embedded, a tool tip appears saying "No file associated with this image." In other words, there's no longer a link associated with this embedded image.

QUICK TIP

To unembed an image, click Unembed on the Control panel or click the Links panel options button, then click Unembed. You will be prompted to save the image to your hard drive.

Figure 60 *Links panel*

Use Image Trace to trace a sketch

1. Open AI 3-5.ai, then save it as **Image Trace Sketch**.

   The file contains a placed marker sketch that was scanned in Photoshop.

2. Click the **Selection tool** 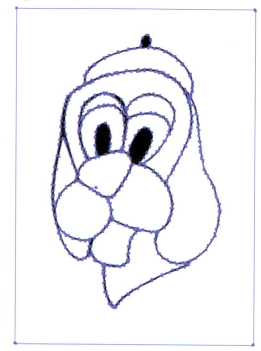, then click the **placed graphic**.

   When the placed graphic is selected, the Image Trace button on the Control panel becomes visible.

3. Click the **Image Trace button**.

   A progress bar appears while the placed image is being traced. Once completed, the Expand button appears on the Control panel.

4. Click the **Expand button**.

   As shown in Figure 61, the traced graphic is expanded into vector objects.

5. Deselect all, then using the Direct Selection tool, select and fill the illustration with whatever colors you like. Figure 62 shows one example.

6. Save your work, then close the Image Trace Sketch document.

You used the Image Trace utility on the Control panel to convert a placed sketch into vector objects.

Figure 61 *Expanded artwork*

Figure 62 *One example of the painted illustration*

Drawing and Composing an Illustration

Figure 63 *Previewing the results*

Figure 64 *Reducing the results to four colors*

Figure 65 *Coloring the expanded artwork*

© 2015 Cengage Learning® Image Courtesy of Chris Botello.

Use Image Trace to trace a photo

1. Open AI 3-6.ai, then save it as **Image Trace Photo**.

   The file contains a placed image that was scanned into Photoshop.

2. Zoom in on the photo, click the **Selection tool**, select the **graphic**, then open the Image Trace panel from the Window menu.

3. Click the **Preset list arrow**, then click **Line Art**.

4. Click the **Mode list arrow**, then click **Grayscale**.

5. Click the **Preview check box** if necessary.

   Your panel and image should resemble Figure 63.

6. Click the **Mode list arrow**, then click **Color**.

7. Drag the **Colors slider** to **4**, then compare your result to Figure 64.

8. Click the **Expand button** on the Control panel, then deselect all.

9. Click the **Direct Selection tool**, then select and fill the objects that make up the illustration. Figure 65 shows one example.

10. Save your work, then close Image Trace Photo.

You used the Image Trace panel to explore various tracing and color options, watching the result update dynamically.

Use the Live Paint
BUCKET TOOL

What You'll Do

© 2015 Cengage Learning®

 In this lesson, you will use the Live Paint Bucket tool and the Live Paint Selection tool, learn about regions and edges, and paint live paint groups.

Using the Live Paint Features

When Adobe launched the Live Paint Bucket tool, they called it "revolutionary," and that was not an overstatement. The Live Paint Bucket tool breaks all the fundamental rules of Illustrator, and creates some new ones. For that reason, when you are working with the Live Paint Bucket tool, it's a good idea to think of yourself as working in Live Paint mode, because Illustrator will function differently with this tool than it will with any other.

QUICK TIP

The Live Paint Bucket tool is located behind the Shape Builder tool.

Essentially, the Live Paint Bucket tool is designed to make painting easier and more intuitive. It does this by changing the basic rules of Illustrator objects. In Live Paint mode, the concept of "objects" no longer applies—you can fill and stroke negative spaces. The Live Paint Bucket tool uses two object types called regions and edges. **Regions** and **edges** are comparable to fills and strokes, but they are "live." As shown in Figure 66, where two regions overlap, a third region is created and can be painted with its own color. Where two edges overlap, a third edge is created. It too can be painted its own color.

Adobe likes to say that Live Paint is intuitive—something that looks like it should be able to be filled with its own color can indeed be filled with its own color. As long as you have the Live Paint Bucket tool selected, selected objects can be filled using the new rules of Live Paint mode. Once you leave Live Paint mode, the paint that you have applied to the graphic remains part of the illustration.

Figure 66 *Identifying regions and edges in an illustration*

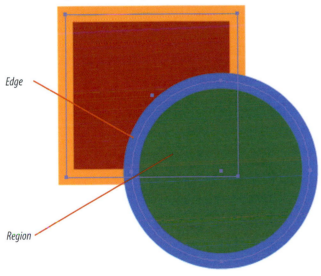

Edge

Region

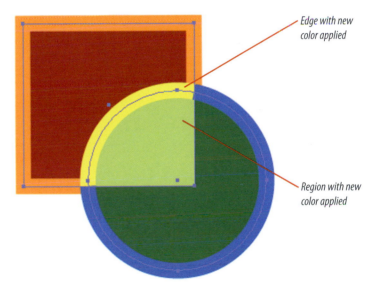

Edge with new color applied

Region with new color applied

Live Painting Regions

Figure 67 shows three selected rectangles that overlap each other. The selection marks show various shapes created by the overlap. As stated earlier, these overlapping areas or shapes are called regions. To fill the regions, you must first select all the objects that you want to paint. Click the Live Paint Bucket tool, click a color on the Swatches panel, then click a region that you want to fill. As shown in Figure 68, when you position the Live Paint Bucket tool pointer over

a region, that region is highlighted. Click the Live Paint Bucket tool and the region is filled, as shown in Figure 69.

As shown in Figure 70, each region can be filled with new colors. But that's not all that the Live Paint Bucket tool has to offer. The "live" part of Live Paint is that these regions are now part of a **Live Paint group**, and they maintain a dynamic relationship with each other. This means that when any of the objects is moved, the overlapping area changes shape and fill

accordingly. For example, in Figure 71, the tall thin rectangle has been moved to the left. Note how the overlapping regions have been redrawn and how their fills have updated with the move.

Figure 67 *Three overlapping selected rectangles*

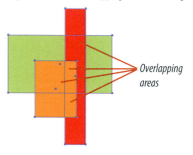

Overlapping areas

Figure 68 *Positioning the Live Paint Bucket tool pointer*

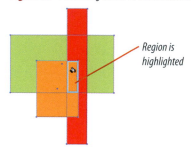

Region is highlighted

Figure 69 *Filling a region with a new color*

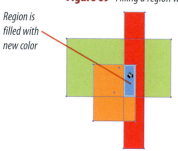

Region is filled with new color

Figure 70 *Filling multiple regions*

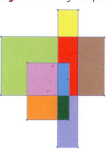

Figure 71 *Moving an object in a Live Paint group*

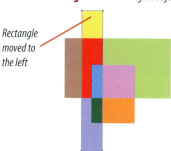

Rectangle moved to the left

© 2015 Cengage Learning®

Painting Virtual Regions

The intuitive aspect of Live Paint mode goes one step further with virtual regions. Figure 72 shows six Illustrator paths; each path is selected and has a 1-point black stroke and no fill. This simple illustration provides a perfect example of the powers of the Live Paint Bucket tool.

Imagine trying to fill the four center polygons created by the overlapping strokes in "classic"

Illustrator without the Live Paint Bucket tool. This seemingly simple goal would actually be a really tough challenge. You'd need to create four polygons that align perfectly with the shapes created by the overlapping strokes because without the shapes, you'd have nothing to fill. And, because the strokes are so thin, you'd need those polygons to align exactly with the strokes. Finally, if you moved any of the strokes, you'd need to modify the polygons to match the new layout.

With the Live Paint Bucket tool, the regions that are created by the intersection of the paths are able to be filled as though they were objects. Figure 73 shows four regions that have been filled with the Live Paint Bucket tool.

In this case, as in the case of the overlapping rectangles, the dynamic relationship is maintained. Figure 74 shows the paths moved, and the filled regions redrawn and their fills updated.

Figure 72 *Six paths*

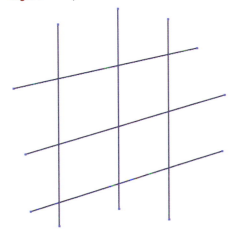

Figure 73 *Four filled regions between paths*

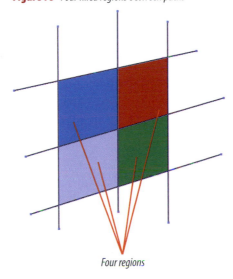

Four regions

Figure 74 *Moving paths in a Live Paint group*

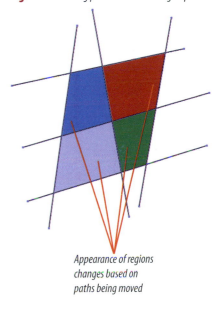

Appearance of regions changes based on paths being moved

Inserting an Object into a Live Paint Group

New objects can be inserted into a Live Paint group. To do so, switch to the Selection tool, then double-click inside any of the regions of the group. As shown in Figure 75, a gray rectangle appears around the group,

indicating that you are in insertion mode. Once in **insertion mode**, you can then add an object or objects to the group.

As shown in Figure 76, another tall rectangle has been added to the group. It can now be painted with the Live Paint Bucket tool as part of the Live Paint group. Once you've added all that you want to the Live Paint group,

exit insertion mode by double-clicking the Selection tool outside of the Live Paint group.

Expanding a Live Paint Group

When you are done colorizing a Live Paint group, you have the option of using the Expand command to release the Live Paint group into its component regions. Simply

Figure 75 *Viewing the art in insertion mode*

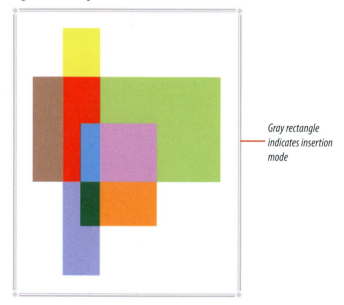

Gray rectangle indicates insertion mode

Figure 76 *Adding an object to the Live Paint group*

New object is added to the Live Paint group

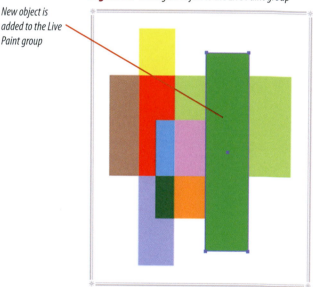

Drawing and Composing an Illustration

select the Live Paint group, then click the Expand button on the Control panel. Each region will be converted to an ordinary Illustrator object.

Live Painting Edges

In Live Paint mode, just as regions are akin to fills, edges are akin to strokes. With the Live Paint Bucket tool, you can paint edges as well as regions.

Figure 77 shows two overlapping objects, each with a 6-point stroke. To paint edges (strokes), you must first double-click the Live Paint Bucket tool, then activate the Paint Strokes check box in the Live Paint Bucket Options dialog box, as shown in Figure 78.

When activated, the Live Paint Bucket tool will paint either regions or edges, depending on where it's positioned.

When you position the Live Paint Bucket tool over an edge, its icon changes to a paint brush icon. The edge is highlighted and paintable as though it were its own object, as shown in Figure 79.

Figure 77 *Two overlapping rectangles*

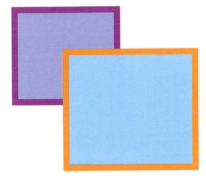

Figure 78 *Specifying the Live Paint Bucket tool to paint strokes (edges)*

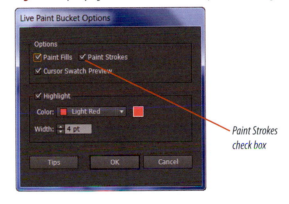

Paint Strokes check box

Figure 79 *Painting edges*

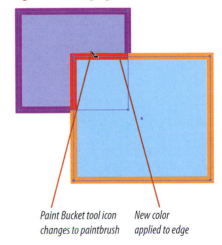

Paint Bucket tool icon changes to paintbrush

New color applied to edge

Use the Live Paint Bucket tool

1. Open AI 3-7.ai, then save it as **Live Paint Circles**.

2. Open the Swatches panel, fill the top circle with red, fill the left circle with green, then fill the right circle with blue.

3. Select all, double-click the **Live Paint Bucket tool** to open the Live Paint Bucket Options dialog box, verify that both the Paint Fills and Paint Strokes check boxes are checked, then click **OK**.

TIP The Live Paint Bucket tool may be behind the Shape Builder tool on the Tools panel.

4. Click any of the orange swatches on the Swatches panel.

    Note that because you are in Live Paint mode, none of the selected objects changes to orange when you click the orange swatch.

5. Position the Live Paint Bucket tool pointer over the red fill of the red circle, then click.

6. Click any pink swatch on the Swatches panel, position the Live Paint Bucket tool pointer over the area where the orange circle overlaps the blue circle, then click.

    As shown in Figure 80, the region of overlap between the two circles is filled with pink.

(continued)

Figure 80 *Painting the region that is the overlap between two circles*

Drawing and Composing an Illustration

Figure 81 *Viewing seven painted regions*

Figure 82 *Viewing 12 painted edges*

© 2015 Cengage Learning®

Lesson 8   Use the Live Paint Bucket Tool

7. Using any colors you like, fill all seven regions so that your artwork resembles Figure 81.

8. Change the Stroke button on the Tools panel to any purple, position the Live Paint Bucket tool pointer over any of the black strokes in the artwork, then click.

   When positioned over a stroke, the Live Paint Bucket tool pointer changes to a paintbrush icon.

9. Using any color you like, change the color of all 12 edges then deselect all so that your artwork resembles Figure 82.

(continued)

10. Deselect all, click the **Direct Selection tool** ▶, then, without pulling them apart, drag the circles in different directions, noting that the components of the Live Paint group maintain a dynamic relationship as shown in Figure 83.

11. Select all, click **Expand** on the Control panel, deselect all, then pull out all of the regions so that your artwork resembles Figure 84.

    The illustration has been expanded into multiple objects.

12. Save your work, then close the Live Paint Circles document.

You used the Live Paint Bucket tool to fill various regions and edges of three overlapping circles. You then moved various components of the Live Paint group, noting that they maintain a dynamic relationship. Finally, you expanded the Live Paint group, which changed your original circles into multiple objects.

Figure 83 *Exploring the dynamic relationship between regions in a Live Paint group*

Figure 84 *Dissecting the expanded Live Paint group*

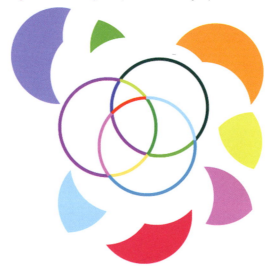

Drawing and Composing an Illustration

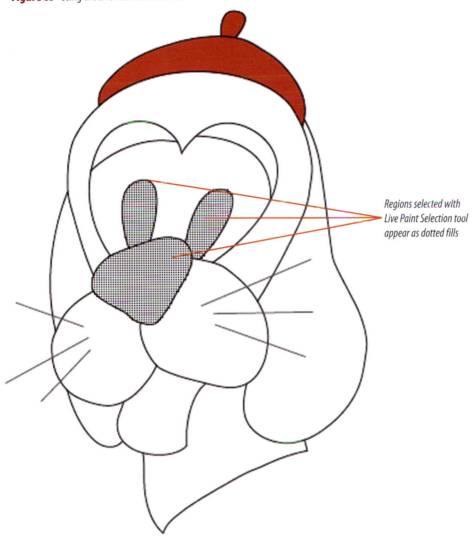

Figure 85 *Using the Live Paint Selection tool*

Regions selected with Live Paint Selection tool appear as dotted fills

Use the Live Paint Bucket tool to paint an illustration

1. Open AI 3-8.ai, then save it as **Live Paint Dog**.

2. Click the **Selection tool** , then click the different colored strokes so that you understand how the illustration has been drawn.

   The illustration has been created with a series of open paths. The only closed path is the nose.

3. Select all, then change the stroke color of all the paths to Black.

4. Click the **Live Paint Bucket tool** , then click a red swatch on the Swatches panel.

   Note that because you are in Live Paint mode, none of the selected objects changes to red when you click the red swatch.

5. Fill the hat and the knot at the top of the hat with red, then click **Black** on the Swatches panel.

6. Click the **Live Paint Selection tool** , click the **nose**, press and hold **[Shift]**, click the **left eye**, then click the **right eye**.

   Your illustration should resemble Figure 85.

TIP When you select multiple areas with the Live Paint Selection tool, the areas are filled with a dot pattern until you apply a color.

7. Click **Black** on the Swatches panel.

8. Using the same method, select both eyelids, then fill them with a lavender swatch.

(continued)

9. Click the **Live Paint Bucket** tool , click a yellow swatch on the Swatches panel, then paint the illustration so that your illustration resembles Figure 86.

   Note the small areas between the whiskers that must be painted yellow.

10. Using the Live Paint Bucket tool , paint the right jowl light brown, paint the left jowl a darker brown, then paint the tongue pink.

11. Click the **Stroke button** on the Tools panel to activate the stroke, then click a gray swatch on the Swatches panel.

12. Double-click the **Live Paint Bucket tool** , click the **Paint Stroke check box** in the Live Paint Bucket Options dialog box if it is not already checked, then click **OK**.

(continued)

Figure 86 *Painting the yellow regions*

Drawing and Composing an Illustration

Figure 87 *Viewing the finished artwork*

13. Paint the edges that draw the whiskers.

TIP You will need to click 14 times to paint the
six whiskers.

14. Deselect, compare your work to Figure 87,
save your work, then close the Live Paint
Dog document.

*You used the Live Paint Bucket tool to fill regions created by the
intersection of a collection of open paths. You also used the tool
to paint edges.*

Explore Alternate
DRAWING TECHNIQUES

What You'll Do

 In this lesson, you will learn some new and fun drawing techniques including how to reshape a path with the Anchor Point tool and how to change Pencil tool settings to draw the way you want to.

Reshaping Path Segments with the Anchor Point Tool

Along with its ability to convert anchor points from smooth to corner and vice versa, the Anchor Point tool can also convert path segments from straight to curved. In fact, the Anchor Point tool is so powerful that you can use it as an alternate to dragging directional handles to modify a curve. Instead you can just click and drag any segment to reshape it and position it as you like.

Figure 88 shows a shape created from a simple rectangle. No directional handles were manipulated to create these curves. Instead, the original straight segments were curved and reshaped using the Anchor Point tool.

When you're creating paths with the Pen tool, you can access the Anchor Point tool and the path segment reshape function simply by pressing [Alt] (Win) or [option] (Mac).

In practice, you'll likely use a combination of both methods—dragging directional handles and dragging path segments—but you'll find that the Anchor Point tool adds a more freehand, intuitive option.

Figure 88 *A curved object reshaped from a simple rectangle*

Drawing with the Pencil Tool

With the widespread use of tablets and pen styluses, advances in Illustrator's Pencil tool are making the tool a great option for drawing in Illustrator by hand. For many designers, it's become a real alternative to the Pen tool.

Setting specific options is important for making the tool practical or drawing. In Figure 89, note that the Fidelity slider is set to Smooth. At this setting, relatively uneven lines you draw using your stylus and tablet will smooth out automatically.

Figure 90 shows a relatively uneven line being drawn with the Pencil tool. Figure 91 shows the same path once the Pencil tool is lifted. The path is automatically smoothed out and anchor points are added at necessary locations.

Figure 89 *Pencil Tool Options dialog box*

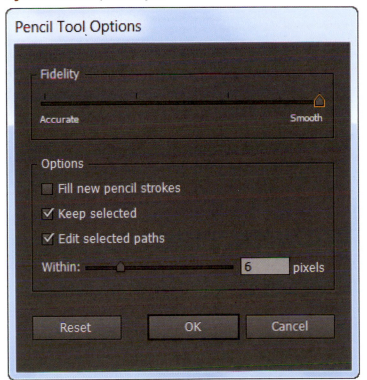

Figure 90 *Rough line being drawn*

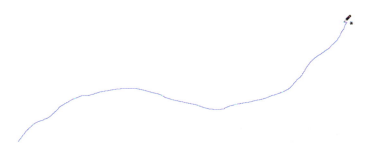

Note the Keep selected option in Figure 89. When this option is activated, you can add to a path you've already drawn by floating over an open anchor point and continuing your drawing with the Pencil tool. Essentially, this allows you to draw on your screen with the Pencil tool as you would on a piece of paper with a real pencil.

The Edit selected paths option is a critical one that has a big effect on how the Pencil tool works. It's one you'll might have to activate and deactivate to draw certain types of artwork.

Figure 92 shows a simple, hand-drawn circle done with the Pencil tool. If you want to draw

Figure 91 *Rough line smoothed automatically*

Figure 92 *Simple circle*

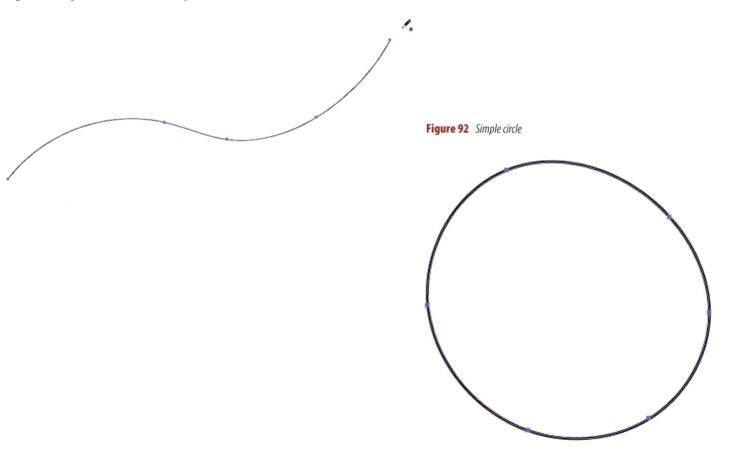

© 2015 Cengage Learning®

Drawing and Composing an Illustration

a line across the circle, as shown in Figure 93, you must do so with the Edit selected paths option *deactivated*. If the Edit option is activated, drawing the line across the circle will actually edit the circle and redraw it with the new line, as shown in Figure 94.

On the other hand, the Edit selected paths option can be very useful for doing just that … editing paths while you draw. If you want to tweak a line, simply draw over it and the path will redraw with the new line.

Figure 93 *Circle with line drawn across it*

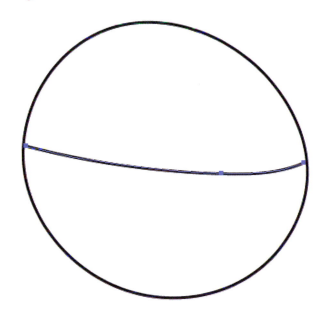

Figure 94 *Circle redrawn with new line*

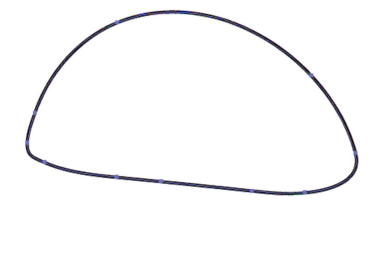

Reshape path segments with the Anchor Point tool

1. Open AI 3-9.ai, then save it as **Reshape Path**.

2. Click the **Anchor Point tool** 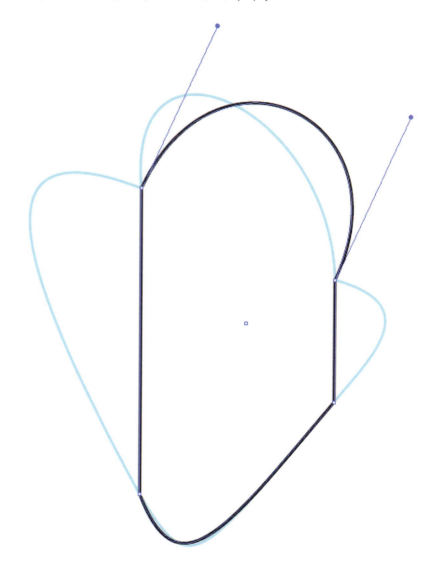.

   The Anchor Point tool is behind the Pen tool.

   TIP You can access the Anchor Point tool by pressing [Shift][C] on your keypad.

3. Drag the **bottom path segment** as many times as necessary to align it to the blue line.

   In this exercise, you will drag only path segments; don't drag any anchor points or any directional handles.

4. Drag the **right segment** to align it to the blue line.

5. Drag the **top segment** up then, as you're dragging, press the [**Shift**] key and keep dragging.

   With the [Shift] key pressed, the directional handles are even and the oval is balanced on both sides.

6. Position the path so that it resembles Figure 95.

7. Drag the **oval** left so that it aligns with the blue path.

8. Click the **Pen tool** .

9. Press and hold [**Alt**] (Win) or [**option**] (Mac).

   The tool changes to the Anchor Point tool.

10. Reshape the remaining paths to match the blue shape.

11. Save your work, then close Reshape Path.

You used the Anchor Point tool to reshape an object.

Figure 95 *Reshaping the segment with the [Shift] key in play*

Drawing and Composing an Illustration

Figure 96 *Pencil Tool Options dialog box*

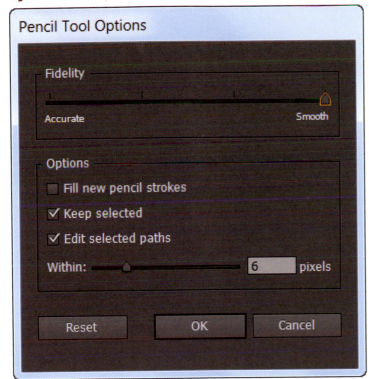

Draw with the Pencil tool

1. Open AI 3-10.ai, then save it as **Pencil Tool**.
2. Set the Fill color to None, set the Stroke color to Black, then set the stroke weight to 2 points.
3. Double click the **Pencil tool** , then compare your Pencil tool Options dialog box to Figure 96.

   Note that Fidelity is set to Smooth and that the Keep selected and Edit selected paths options are both activated.
4. Click **OK**, then zoom in on the top path on the artboard.

   (continued)

5. Trace the first half circle slowly, then release the mouse button.

As you draw, the path is very jagged and rough, but when you release the mouse button, the path is smoothed out. As shown in Figure 97, the path is created with the minimum number of anchor points necessary.

6. Float over the end point, then draw the second half circle.

Because the Keep selected option is activated, the second segment you draw is connected to the first to create a single path.

7. Finish drawing the top path.

8. Zoom in on the middle path on the artboard.

9. Trace the first half-circle, don't lift your stylus, press and hold [**Shift**], then trace the straight horizontal line so that your path resembles Figure 98.

10. Using the same method, complete the trace in one move.

(continued)

Figure 97 *Smooth path created with Pencil tool*

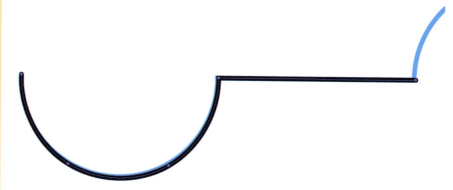

Figure 98 *Straight segment added to curved segment*

Drawing and Composing an Illustration

Figure 99 *Editing the path with the Pencil tool*

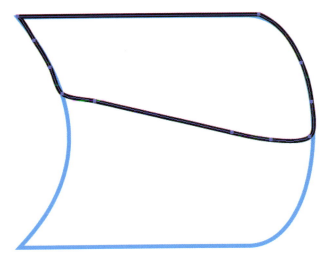

11. Zoom in on the path at the bottom of the artboard, then select it with the Selection tool ⬐ .

    The path was drawn with the Pencil tool.

12. Click the **Pencil tool** 🖊 , then draw a path from a point on the left segment to a point on the right segment.

    As shown in Figure 99, because the Edit selected paths option is activated, the object is edited and redrawn with the new path.

13. Save your work, then close Pencil Tool.

You used the Pencil tool to trace different paths. You introduced the Shift key to trace straight paths along with curved paths. With the Edit selected paths option activated, you edited a path by drawing a segment across an existing object.

Draw straight lines.

1. Open AI 3-11.ai, then save it as **Mighty Montag**.
2. Place Montag Sketch.tif into the Montag document; you will need to navigate to the drive and folder where your Data Files are stored to find it.
3. Position the sketch in the center of the artboard, then lock it.
4. Set the fill color to [None] and the stroke to 1 pt black.
5. Use the Pen tool to create a four-sided polygon for the neck.
6. Draw six whiskers.
7. Save your work.

Draw curved lines.

1. Using the Pen tool, draw an oval for the eye.
2. Draw a crescent moon shape for the eyelid.
3. Draw an oval for the iris.
4. Save your work.

Draw elements of an illustration.

1. Trace the left ear.
2. Trace the hat.
3. Trace the nose.
4. Trace the left jowl.
5. Trace the right jowl.
6. Trace the tongue.
7. Trace the right ear.
8. Trace the head.
9. Save your work.

Apply attributes to objects.

1. Unlock the placed sketch and hide it.
2. Fill the hat with a red swatch.
3. Fill the right ear with 9C/18M/62Y.
4. Fill the nose with black.
5. Fill the eye with white.
6. Fill the tongue with salmon.
7. Using Figure 100 as a guide, use the colors on the Swatches panel to finish the illustration.
8. Save your work.

Assemble an illustration.

1. Send the neck to the back of the stacking order, then lock it.
2. Send the head to the back, then lock it.
3. Send the left ear to the back, then lock it.
4. Bring the hat to the front.
5. Bring the right ear to the front.
6. Select the whiskers, group them, then bring them to the front.
7. Select the tongue, then cut it.
8. Select the right jowl, then apply the Paste in Back command.
9. Bring the nose to the front.
10. Select the eye, the eyelid, and the iris, then group them.
11. Drag and drop a copy of the eye group. (*Hint*: Press and hold [Alt] (Win) or [option] (Mac) as you drag the eye group.)
12. Select the right jowl.
13. On the Color panel add 10% K to darken the jowl.
14. Use the Color panel to change the fills on other objects to your liking.
15. Save your work.

Stroke objects for artistic effect.

1. Make the caps on the whiskers round.
2. Change the whiskers' stroke weight to .5 pt.
3. Unlock all.
4. Select the neck and change the joins to round.
5. Apply pseudo-strokes to the illustration. (*Hint*: Copy and paste the elements behind themselves, fill them with black, lock the top objects, then use the Direct Selection tool to select anchor points on the black-filled copies. Use the arrow keys on the keyboard to move the anchor points. The black copies will peek out from behind the elements in front.)
6. Click Object on the Menu bar, then click Unlock All.
7. Delete the Montag Sketch file behind your illustration.
8. Save your work, compare your illustration to Figure 100, then close Mighty Montag.

Figure 100 *Completed Skills Review, Part 1*

Drawing and Composing an Illustration

Use Image Trace.

1. Open AI 3-12.ai, then save it as **Skills Trace Photo**.
2. Zoom in on the photo, click the Selection tool, select the graphic, then open the Image Trace panel.
3. Click the Preset list arrow, then click Line Art.
4. Click the Mode list arrow, then click Grayscale.
5. Click to activate the Preview option if necessary.
6. Click the Mode list arrow, then click Color.
7. Drag the Colors slider to 6.
8. Click the Expand button on the Control panel, then deselect all.
9. Click the Direct Selection tool, then select and fill the objects that make up the illustration. Figure 101 shows one example.
10. Save your work, then close Skills Trace Photo.

Figure 101 *Completed Skills Review, Part 2*

Use the Live Paint Bucket tool.

1. Open AI 3-13.ai, then save it as **Live Paint Skills**.

2. Open the Swatches panel, fill the top circle with Orange, fill the left circle with blue, then fill the right circle with purple.

3. Select all, then double-click the Live Paint Bucket tool to open the Live Paint Bucket Options dialog box, verify that both the Paint Fills and Paint Strokes check boxes are checked, then click OK.

4. Click any yellow swatch on the Swatches panel.

5. Position the Live Paint Bucket tool pointer over the orange fill of the orange circle, then click.

6. Click any pink swatch on the Swatches panel, position the Live Paint Bucket tool pointer over the area where the yellow circle overlaps the purple circle, then click.

7. Using any colors you like, fill the remaining five regions with different colors.

8. Click the Stroke button on the Tools panel, click any blue swatch on the Swatches panel, position the Live Paint Bucket tool pointer over any of the black strokes in the artwork, then click.

9. Using any color you like, change the color of all 12 edges then deselect all.

10. Click the Direct Selection tool, then, without pulling them apart, drag the circles in different directions noticing that they stay grouped, as shown in Figure 102.

11. Save your work, then close Live Paint Skills.

Figure 102 *Completed Skills Review, Part 3*

The owner of The Blue Peppermill Restaurant has hired your design firm to take over all of their marketing and advertising, saying they need to expand their efforts. You request all of their existing materials, such as slides, prints, digital files, brochures, and business cards. Upon examination, you realize that they have no vector graphic version of their logo. Deciding that this is an indispensable element for future design and production, you scan in a photo of their signature peppermill, trace it, and apply a blue fill to it.

1. Create a new 6" × 6" document, then save it as **Peppermill**.
2. Place the Peppermill.tif file into the Peppermill Vector document. (*Hint*: The Peppermill.tif file is in the Chapter 3 Data Files folder.)
3. Scale the placed image 150%, then lock it.
4. Set your fill color to [None], and your stroke to 2 pt black.
5. Using the Zoom tool, create a selection box around the round element at the top of the peppermill to zoom in on it.
6. Using the Pen tool, trace the peppermill, adjusting your view as necessary to see various sections of the peppermill as you trace, then fill it with a blue swatch.
7. When you finish tracing, tweak the path if necessary, then save your work.
8. Unlock the placed image and cut it from the document.
9. Save your work, compare your illustration to Figure 103, then close Peppermill.

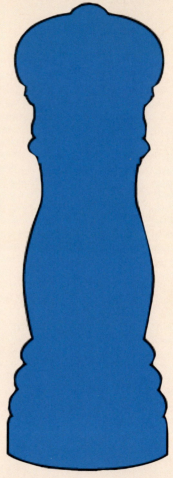

Figure 103 *Completed Project Builder 1*

You work at a children's library that has recently been remodeled. They've asked you to create a mural theme with interesting shapes of bright colors for the freshly painted walls. You create a sample in Illustrator to present to the staff—a single theme that can be modified to create multiple versions of the artwork.

1. Open AI 3-14.ai, then save it as **Tic Tac Toe**.
2. Select all, then change the stroke colors to black.
3. Click the Live Paint Bucket tool, select a fill color, then click in any of the squares.
4. Fill each of the squares with a different color, then deselect all.
5. Click the Direct Selection tool, then change the angles of the black paths. Figure 104 shows one possible result.
6. Save your work, then close Tic Tac Toe.

Figure 104 *Completed Project Builder 2*

Drawing and Composing an Illustration

Your design firm is contacted by a company called Stratagem with a request for a proposal. They manufacture molds for plastic products. The terms of the request are as follows: You are to submit a design for the shape of the bottle for a new dishwashing liquid. You are to submit a single image that shows a black line defining the shape. The line art should also include the nozzle. The size of the bottle is immaterial. The design is to be "sophisticated, so as to be in visual harmony with the modern home kitchen." The name of the product is "Sleek."

1. Go to the grocery store and purchase bottles of dishwashing liquid whose shape you find interesting.
2. Use the purchases for ideas and inspiration.
3. Sketch your idea for the bottle's shape on a piece of paper.
4. Scan the sketch and save it as a TIFF file.
5. Create a new Illustrator document, then save it as **Sleek Design**.
6. Place the scan in the document, then lock it.
7. Trace your sketch, using the Pen tool.
8. When you are done tracing, delete the sketch from the document.
9. Tweak the line to define the shape to your specifications.
10. Use the Average dialog box to align points to perfect the shape.
11. Save your work, compare your illustration to Figure 105, then close Sleek Design.

Figure 105 *Completed Design Project*

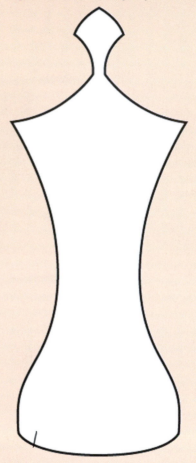

© 2015 Cengage Learning®

Note to Instructors: The central point of this exercise—a discussion of shapes and their role in the history of mankind—can be had with or without screening *2001: A Space Odyssey*. Should you choose not to show the film, simply omit questions 1 and 2. Rephrase Question 8 so that individuals are instructed to draw any abstract shape from their own imaginations.

The classic sci-fi movie, *2001: A Space Odyssey*, includes a 20-minute "Dawn of Man" sequence that begins millions of years ago with a group of apes, presumably on the African plains. One day, *impossibly*, a tall, black, perfectly rectangular slab appears out of nowhere on the landscape. At first the apes are afraid of it, afraid to touch it. Eventually, they accept its presence.

Later, one ape looks upon a femur bone from a dead animal. With a dawning understanding, he uses the bone as a tool, first to kill for food, and then to kill another ape from an enemy group. Victorious in battle, the ape hurls the bone into the air. The camera follows it up, up, up, and—in one of the most famous cuts in film history—the image switches from the white bone in the sky to the similar shape of a white spaceship floating in space.

1. How do you feel upon first seeing the "monolith" (the black rectangular slab)? Were you frightened? Do you sense that the monolith is good, evil, or neutral?
2. How would you describe the sudden appearance of the straight-edged, right-angled monolith against the landscape? What words describe the shapes of the landscape in contrast to the monolith?
3. Do you think perfect shapes exist in nature, or are they created entirely out of the imagination of human beings?
4. If perfect shapes exist—if they are real—can you name one example? If they are not real, how is it that humankind has proven so many concepts in mathematics that are based on shapes, such as the Pythagorean Theorem?
5. What advancements and achievements of humankind have their basis in peoples' ability to conceive of abstract shapes?
6. Can it be said legitimately that the ability to conceive abstract shapes is an essential factor that distinguishes humankind from all the other species on the planet?
7. Create a new document, then save it as **Shape**.
8. In Adobe Illustrator, draw any shape that you remember from the opening sequence, except the monolith. Did you render a shape based on the bone?
9. Save your work, compare your results to Figure 106, which is one possible result, then close Shape.

Figure 106 *Completed Portfolio Project*

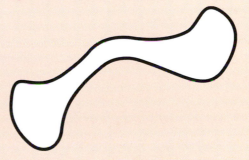

CHAPTER 4 TRANSFORMING AND DISTORTING OBJECTS

1. Transform objects
2. Offset and outline paths
3. Create compound paths
4. Work with the Pathfinder panel
5. Apply round corners to objects
6. Use the Shape Builder tool
7. Create clipping masks

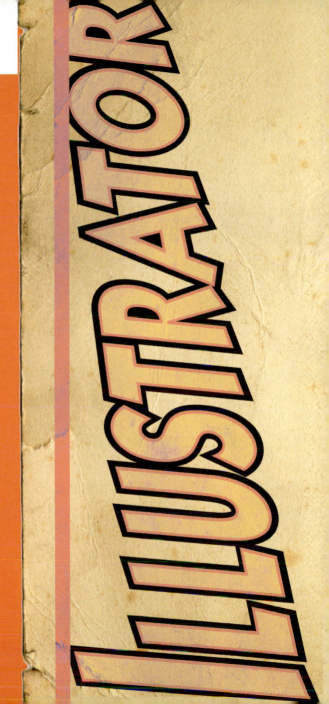

CHAPTER 4 TRANSFORMING AND DISTORTING OBJECTS

Putting It All Together

Think about a conventional toolbox. You've got a hammer, nails, a few different types of screwdrivers, screws, nuts, bolts, a wrench, and probably some type of measuring device. That set of tools could be used to build anything from a birdhouse to a dollhouse to a townhouse to the White House.

A carpenter uses tools in conjunction with one another to create something, and that something is defined far less by the tools than by the imagination of the carpenter. But even the most ambitious imagination is tempered by the demands of knowing which tool to use and when.

Illustrator offers a number of sophisticated transform "tools" on the Tools panel, and the metaphor is apt. Each tool provides a basic function, such as a rotation, scale, reflection, precise move, or precise offset. It is you, the designer, who uses those tools in combination with menu commands and other features to realize your vision. And like the carpenter, your ability to choose the right tool at the right time will affect the outcome of your work.

This is one of the most exciting aspects of working in Illustrator. After you learn the basics, there's no blueprint for building an illustration. It's your skills, your experience, your smarts, and your ingenuity that lead you toward your goal. No other designer will use Illustrator's tools quite the same way you do. People who appreciate digital imagery understand this salient point: Although the tools are the same for everyone, the result is personal—it's *original*.

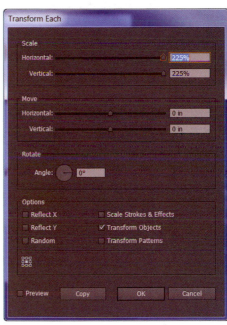

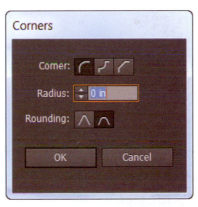

Transform
OBJECTS

What You'll Do

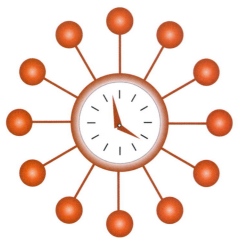

 In this lesson, you will explore options for transforming objects with the transform tools.

Defining the Transform Tools

When you change an object's size, shape, or position on the artboard, Illustrator defines that operation as a transformation. Transforming objects is a fundamental operation in Illustrator, one you will perform countless times.

Because transformations are so essential, Illustrator provides a number of methods for doing them. As you gain experience, you will naturally adopt the method that you find most comfortable or logical.

The Tools panel contains five transform tools: Rotate, Scale, Reflect, Shear, and Free Transform. The Rotate tool rotates an object or a group of objects around a fixed point. The Scale tool enlarges and reduces the size of objects. The Reflect tool "flips" an object across an imagined axis, usually the horizontal or the vertical axis, however, you can define any diagonal as the axis for a reflection. In Figure 1, the illustration has been flipped to create the illusion of a reflection in a mirror.

Figure 1 *The Reflect tool flips an image horizontally or vertically*

The Shear tool slants—or skews—an object on an axis that you specify. By definition, the Shear tool distorts an object. Of the five transform tools, you will probably use the Shear tool the least, although it is useful for creating a cast shadow or the illusion of depth.

Finally, the Free Transform tool offers you the ability to perform quick transformations and distort objects in perspective.

Defining the Point of Origin

All transformations are executed in relation to a fixed point. In Illustrator, this point is called the **point of origin**. For each transform tool, the default point of origin is the selected object's center point. However, you can change that point to another point on the object or to a point elsewhere on the artboard. For example, when a majorette twirls a baton, that baton is essentially rotating on its own center. By contrast, the petals of a daisy rotate around a central point that is not positioned on any of the petals themselves, as shown in Figure 2.

Figure 2 *All transformations are executed from a point of origin*

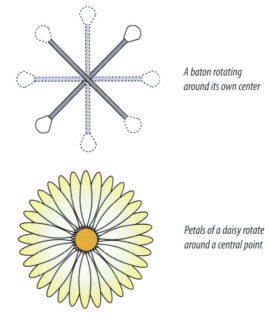

A baton rotating around its own center

Petals of a daisy rotate around a central point

There are four basic methods for making transformations with the transform tools. First, select an object, then do one of the following:

- Click a transform tool, then click and drag anywhere on the artboard. The object will be transformed using its center point as the default point of origin.
- Double-click the transform tool, which opens the tool's dialog box. Enter the values you want to use to execute the transformation, then click OK. You may also click Copy to create a transformed copy of the selected object. The point of origin for the transformation will be the center point of the selected object.
- Click a transform tool, then click the artboard. Where you click the artboard defines the point of origin for the transformation. Click and drag anywhere on the artboard, and the selected object will be transformed from the point of origin that you clicked.
- Click a transform tool, Press [Alt] (Win) or [option] (Mac), then click the artboard. The tool's dialog box opens, allowing you to enter precise values for the transformation. When you click OK or Copy, the selected object will be transformed from the point of origin that you clicked.

QUICK TIP

If you transform an object from its center point, then select another object and apply the Transform Again command, the point of origin has not been redefined, and the second object will be transformed from the center point of the first object.

Working with the Transform Again Command

An essential command related to transformations is Transform Again. Whenever you execute a transformation, such as scale or rotate, you can repeat the transformation quickly by using the Transform Again command. This is also true for moving an object. Using the Transform Again command will move an object the same distance and angle entered in the last step. The quickest way to use the Transform Again command is to press [Ctrl] [D] (Win) or ⌘ [D] (Mac). To remember this quick key command, think "D for *duplicate*."

A fine example of the usefulness of the Transform Again command is the ease with which you can make incremental transformations. For example, let's say you have created an object to be used in an illustration, but you haven't decided how large the object should be. Simply scale the object by a small percentage—say 5%—then press the quick key for Transform Again repeatedly until you are happy with the results. The object gradually gets bigger, and you can choose the size that pleases your eye. If you transform again too many times, and the object gets too big, simply undo repeatedly to decrease the object's size in the same small increments.

Using the Transform Each Command

The Transform Each command allows you to transform multiple objects individually, as shown in Figure 3. The Transform Each dialog box offers options to move, scale, rotate, or reflect an object, among others. All of them will affect an object independent of the other selected objects.

Without the Transform Each command, applying a transformation to multiple objects simultaneously will often yield an undesired effect. This happens because the selected objects are transformed as a group in relation to a single point of origin and are repositioned on the artboard.

Figure 3 *Multiple objects rotated individually*

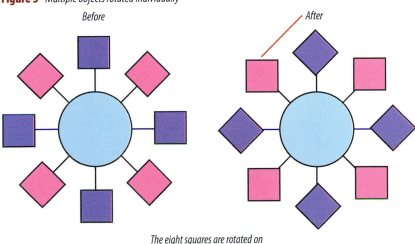

Before

After

The eight squares are rotated on their own center points

Using the Free Transform Tool

When you click the Free Transform tool, an eight-handle bounding box appears around the selected object or objects. You can move the handles to scale or distort the object. You can click and drag outside the bounding box to rotate the selection. With the Free Transform tool, transformations always use the selected object's center point as the point of origin for the transformation.

In general, the role of the Free Transform tool is to make quick transformations by clicking and dragging; some designers prefer it to the individual Scale and Rotate tools, especially for making inexact transformations. However, the Free Transform tool has a powerful ability to distort objects in very interesting ways.

Moving the handles on the Free Transform tool in conjunction with certain keyboard commands allows you to distort an object or distort in perspective, as shown in Figure 4. You start by dragging any handle on the bounding box, then to distort in perspective, you must apply the following *after* you start dragging a handle:

- Press and hold [Shift][Alt][Ctrl] (Win) or [Shift][option] ⌘ (Mac) to distort in perspective
- Press and hold [Shift][Ctrl] (Win) or [Shift] ⌘ (Mac) to distort the selection

When you click the Free Transform tool, the Free Transform menu appears, as shown in Figure 5. The Free Transform menu offers four button controls to execute the transformations described above. If you click the top button, named Constrain, the object will be scaled in proportion. Note, however, that you can just hold the [Shift] key when transforming to achieve the same result.

The second button, Free Transform, is the default setting. With this button selected, the Free Transform tool works as it always has. The third button is Perspective Distort. When it is activated, the object will scale in perspective. The fourth button is called Free Distort. When it is activated, all four corner points move independently, allowing you to distort the object at will.

The method you use is up to you. Some designers like the simple ease of use that the menu buttons offer, while others like the hands-on use of alternating keyboard commands. In this lesson, you'll practice the keyboard commands, since that is the trickier method of the two.

Figure 4 *Use the Free Transform tool to distort objects in perspective*

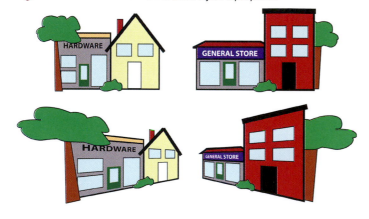

Figure 5 *Free Transform tool options*

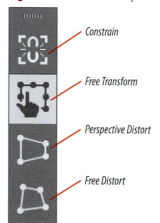

Constrain

Free Transform

Perspective Distort

Free Distort

© 2015 Cengage Learning®

Transforming and Distorting Objects

Using the Transform Panel

The Transform panel displays information about the size, orientation, and location of one or more selected objects. You can type new values directly into the Transform panel to modify selected objects. All values on the panel refer to the bounding boxes of the objects, whether the bounding box is visible or not. You can also identify on the Transform panel the reference point on the bounding box from which the object will be transformed. To reflect an object vertically or horizontally using the Transform panel, click the Transform panel options button, then choose the appropriate menu item, as shown in Figure 6.

Figure 6 *Transform panel*

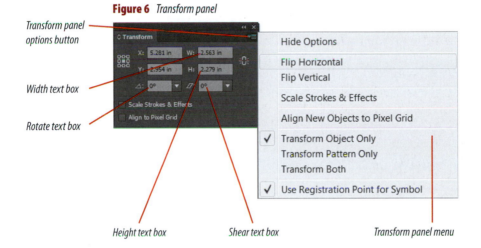

Transform panel options button

Width text box

Rotate text box

Height text box

Shear text box

Transform panel menu

Rotate an object around a defined point

1. Open AI 4-1.ai, then save it as **Mod Clock**.

2. Click the **Selection tool** , click the **brown line**, then click the **Rotate tool** .

3. Press and hold **[Alt]** (Win) or **[option]** (Mac), then click the **bottom anchor point of the line** to set the point of origin for the rotation.

   With a transform tool selected, pressing [Alt] (Win) or [option] (Mac) and clicking the artboard defines the point of origin and opens the tool's dialog box.

4. Enter **30** in the Angle text box, then click **Copy**.

5. Press **[Ctrl] [D]** (Win) or ⌘ **[D]** (Mac) ten times so that your screen resembles Figure 7.

   [Ctrl] [D] (Win) or ⌘ [D] (Mac) is the quick key for the Transform Again command.

6. Select all **12 lines**, group them, send them to the back, then hide them.

7. Select the **small orange circle**, click **View** on the Menu bar, then click **Outline**.

(continued)

Figure 7 *12 paths rotated at a point*

Understanding X and Y Coordinates

The X and Y coordinates of an object indicate the object's horizontal (X) and vertical (Y) locations on the artboard. These numbers, which appear on the Transform panel and the Control panel, represent the horizontal and vertical distance from the upper-left corner of the artboard. The current X and Y coordinates also depend on the specified reference point. Nine reference points are listed to the left of the X and Y Value text boxes on the Transform panel. Reference points are those points of a selected object that represent the four corners of the object's bounding box, the horizontal and vertical centers of the bounding box, and the center point of the bounding box.

© 2015 Cengage Learning®

Figure 8 *12 circles rotated around a central point of origin*

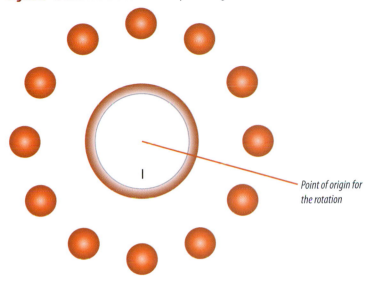

Point of origin for
the rotation

Figure 9 *Completed illustration*

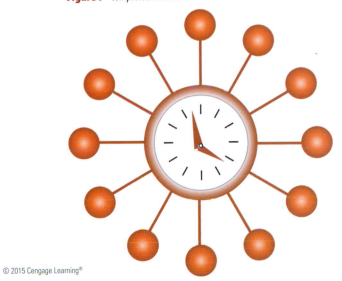

8. Click the **Rotate tool** 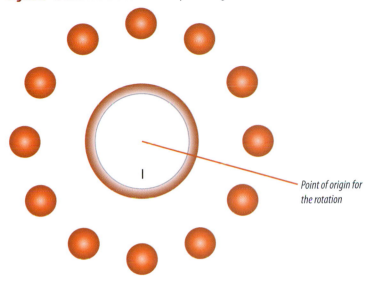, press and hold
   [Alt] (Win) or **[option]** (Mac), then click the
   center point of the larger circle to set the
   point of origin for the next rotation.

   The small circle will rotate around the center
   point of the larger circle.

TIP   Outline mode is especially useful for rotations
      because center points are visible and easy to target
      as points of origin.

9. Enter **30**, click **Copy**, apply the Transform
   Again command ten times, then switch to
   Preview mode.

10. Your screen should resemble Figure 8.

11. Select the **small black vertical dash**, then
    transform again 11 times.

    The dash is also rotated around the center point
    of the larger circle, since a new point of origin
    has not been set.

12. Unlock the hands in the scratch area, then
    move them onto the clock face.

13. Show all, then deselect all to reveal the 12
    segments, as shown in Figure 9.

14. Save your work, then close the Mod
    Clock document.

*You selected a point on the brown line, then rotated 11 copies
of the object around that point. Second, you defined the point
of origin for a rotation by clicking the center point of the larger
circle, then rotated 11 copies of the smaller circle and the dash
around that point.*

Use the Shear tool

1. Open AI 4-2.ai, then save it as **Shear**.

2. Select all, copy, paste in front, then fill the copy with the swatch named Graphite.

3. Click the **Shear tool** 🔁 .

TIP The Shear tool is hidden behind the Scale tool.

4. Press and hold **[Alt]** (Win) or **[option]** (Mac), then click the **bottom-right anchor point** of the letter R to set the origin point of the shear and open the Shear dialog box.

5. Enter **45** in the Shear Angle text box, verify that the Horizontal option button is checked, then click **OK**.

6. Your screen should resemble Figure 10.

7. Click the **Scale tool** 🔲 .

8. Press **[Alt]** (Win) or **[option]** (Mac), then click any bottom anchor point or segment on the sheared objects to set the point of origin for the scale and open the Scale dialog box.

9. Click the **Non-Uniform option button**, enter **100** in the Horizontal text box, enter **50** in the Vertical text box, then click **OK**.

10. Send the sheared objects to the back.

11. Apply a 1 pt black stroke to the orange letters, deselect, then compare your screen to Figure 11.

12. Save your work, then close the Shear document.

You created a shadow effect using the Shear tool.

Figure 10 *Letterforms sheared on a 45° axis*

The objects are sheared on a 45° angle in relation to a horizontal axis

Figure 11 *Shearing is useful for creating a cast-shadow effect*

The shadow is "cast" from the letters in the foreground

Transforming and Distorting Objects

Figure 12 *Use the Reflect tool for illustrations that demand exact symmetry*

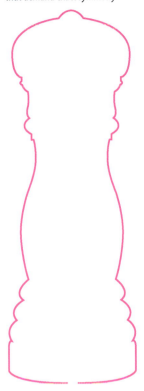

Figure 13 *Selecting two anchor points with the Direct Selection tool*

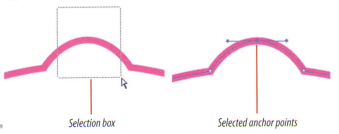

Selection box   Selected anchor points

Use the Reflect tool

1. Open AI 4-3.ai, then save it as **Reflect**.
2. Select all, then zoom in on the top anchor point.
3. Click the **Reflect tool** 🔲.

   The Reflect tool is hidden behind the Rotate tool.
4. Press **[Alt]** (Win) or **[option]** (Mac), then click the **top anchor point** to set the point of origin for the reflection.
5. Click the **Vertical option button**, then click Copy.

   A copy is positioned, reflected across the axis that you defined, as shown in Figure 12.
6. Deselect all, then click the **Direct Selection tool** 🔲.
7. Using Figure 13 as a guide, drag a selection box around the top two anchor points to select them.

TIP One of the anchor points is directly on top of the other because of the reflected copy.

8. Click **Object** on the Menu bar, point to **Path**, click **Average**, click the **Both option button**, then click **OK**.
9. Click **Object** on the Menu bar, point to **Path**, then click **Join**.
10. Select the bottom two anchor points, average them on both axes, then join them to close the path.
11. Save your work, then close the Reflect document.

You created a reflected copy of a path, then averaged and joined two pairs of open points.

Use the Free Transform tool to distort in perspective

1. Open AI 4-4.ai, then save it as **Distort in Perspective**.

2. Press **[Ctrl] [A]** (Win) or ⌘ **[A]** (Mac), then click the **Free Transform tool** .

   The Free Transform tool is visible even if selection edges are hidden.

3. Click and begin dragging the **upper-right handle** directly to the right, then, while still dragging, press and hold **[Shift] [Ctrl]** (Win) or **[Shift]** ⌘ (Mac) and continue dragging, releasing your mouse when you are halfway to the edge of the artboard.

4. Compare your result to Figure 14.

   The illustration is distorted; the upper-right corner is moved to the right. The other three corners do not move.

5. Click **Edit** on the Menu bar, then click **Undo Perspective**.

   The way this command is listed is a bit of a misnomer. You distorted the illustration, but you did not distort in perspective. To be more specific, the command should say "Undo Distort."

   (continued)

Figure 14 *Distorting the illustration*

Transforming and Distorting Objects

Figure 15 *Distorting the illustration in perspective*

Figure 16 *Illustration distorted in complex perspective*

6. Click and start dragging the **upper-right handle** directly to the right, then, while still dragging, press and hold **[Shift] [Ctrl] [Alt]** (Win) or **[Shift] [option]** ⌘ (Mac) and continue dragging.

7. Release the mouse button when you are halfway to the edge of the artboard, then compare your result to Figure 15.

   The illustration is distorted with a different perspective.

8. Click and drag the **upper-left corner** straight down, then, while dragging, press and hold **[Shift] [Ctrl] [Alt]** (Win) or **[Shift] [option]** ⌘ (Mac) and continue dragging until your illustration resembles Figure 16.

9. Save your work, then close Distort in Perspective.

You used keyboard combinations first to distort the illustration, then to distort it in perspective.

Offset and
OUTLINE PATHS

What You'll Do

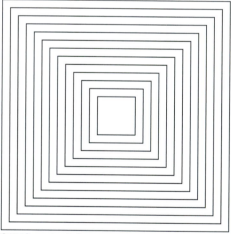

© 2015 Cengage Learning®

In this lesson, you will use the Offset Path command to create concentric squares and the Outline Stroke command to convert a stroked path into a closed path.

Using the Offset Path Command

Simply put, the Offset Path command creates a copy of a selected path set off by a specified distance. The Offset Path command is useful when working with closed paths—making concentric shapes or making many copies of a path at a regular distance from the original.

Figure 17 shows two sets of concentric circles. **Concentric** refers to objects that share the same center point, as the circles in both sets do. The set on the left was made with the Scale tool, applying an 85% scale and copy to the outer circle, then repeating the transformation ten times. Note that with each successive copy, the distance from the copy to the previous circle decreases. The set on the right was made by offsetting the outside circle -.125", then applying the same offset to each successive copy. Note the different effect.

When you offset a closed path, a positive value creates a larger copy outside the original; a negative value creates a smaller copy inside the original.

Transforming and Distorting Objects

Using the Outline Stroke Command

The Outline Stroke command converts a stroked path into a closed path that is the same width as the original stroked path. This operation is useful if you want to apply a gradient to a stroke. It is also a useful design tool, allowing you to modify the outline of an object more than if it were just a stroke. Also, it is often easier to create an object with a single heavy stroke and then convert it to a closed path than it is to try to draw a closed path directly, as shown with the letter S in Figure 18.

Figure 17 *Two sets of concentric circles*

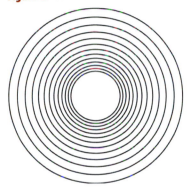
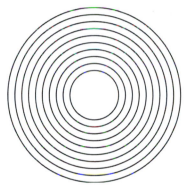

Concentric circles produced by the Scale tool

Concentric circles produced by the Offset Path command

Figure 18 *The Outline Stroke command converts a stroked path to a closed object*

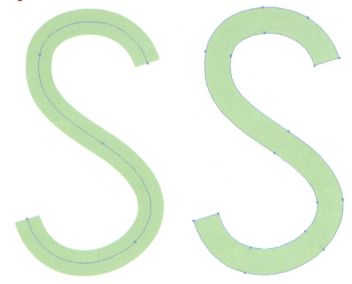

Offset a path

1. Open AI 4-5.ai, then save it as **Squares**.

2. Select the square.

3. Click **Object** on the Menu bar, point to **Path**, then click **Offset Path**.

4. Enter **-.125** in the Offset text box, then click **OK**.

TIP Be sure that your Units preference is set to Inches in the General section of the Units Preferences.

A negative value reduces the area of a closed path; a positive value increases the area.

5. Apply the Offset Path command with the same value four more times.

TIP The Transform Again command does not apply to the Offset Path command because it is not one of the transform tools.

6. Deselect all, save your work, compare your screen to Figure 19, then close the Squares document.

You used the Offset Path command to create concentric squares.

Figure 19 *Concentric squares created with the Offset Path command*

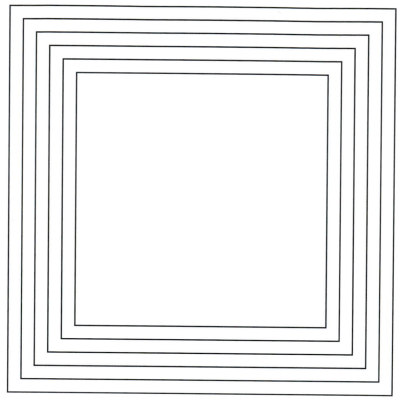

Transforming and Distorting Objects

Figure 20 *The Outline Stroke command converts any stroked path into a closed path*

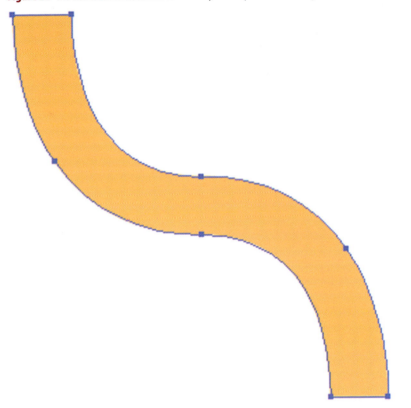

Convert a stroked path to a closed path

1. Open AI 4-6.ai, then save it as **Outlined Stroke**.

2. Select the **path**, then change the weight to 36 pt.

3. Click **Object** on the Menu bar, point to **Path**, then click **Outline Stroke**.

   The full weight of the stroke is converted to a closed path, as shown in Figure 20.

4. Save your work, then close the Outlined Stroke document.

You applied a heavy weight to a stroked path, then converted the stroke to a closed path, using the Outline Stroke command.

Create Compound
PATHS

What You'll Do

 In this lesson, you will explore the role of compound paths for practical use and for artistic effects.

Defining a Compound Path

Practically speaking, you make a compound path to create a "hole" or "holes" in an object. As shown in Figure 21, if you were drawing the letter "D," you would need to create a hole in the outlined shape, through which you could see the background. To do so, select the object in back (in this case, the black outline that defines the letter) and the object in front (the yellow object that defines the hole) and apply the Make Compound Path command. When compounded, a "hole" appears where the two objects overlap.

The overlapping object still exists, however. It is simply *functioning* as a transparent hole in conjunction with the object behind it. If you move the front object independently, as shown in Figure 22, it yields an interesting result. Designers have seized upon this effect and have run with it, creating complex and eye-catching graphics, which Illustrator calls compound shapes.

It is important to understand that when two or more objects are compounded, Illustrator defines them as *one* object. This sounds strange at first, but the concept is as familiar

Transforming and Distorting Objects

to you as the letter D. You identify the letter D as a single object although it is drawn with two paths—one defining the outside edge, the other defining the inside edge.

Compound paths function as groups. You can select and manipulate an individual element with the Direct Selection tool, but you cannot change its appearance attributes independently. Compound paths can be released and returned to their original component objects by applying the Release Compound Path command.

Figure 21 *The letter D is an example of a compound path*

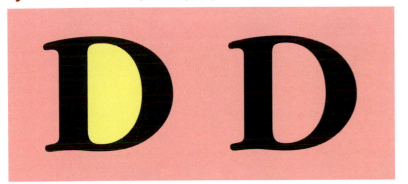

Figure 22 *Manipulating compound paths can yield interesting effects*

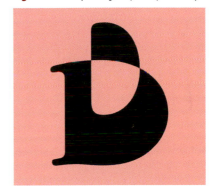

Create compound paths

1. Open AI 4-7.ai, then save it as **Simple Compound**.

2. Cut the red circle in the middle of the illustration, then undo the cut.

   The red circle creates the illusion that there's a hole in the life-preserver ring.

3. Select the **red background object**, then change its fill to the Ocean Blue gradient on the Swatches panel.

   The illusion is lost; the red circle no longer seems to be a hole in the life preserver.

4. Select both the **white "life preserver" circle** and the **red circle** in the center.

5. Click **Object** on the Menu bar, point to **Compound Path**, then click **Make**.

   As shown in Figure 23, the two circles are compounded, with the top circle functioning as a "hole" in the larger circle behind it.

6. Move the background object left and right, and up and down behind the circles.

   The repositioned background remains visible through the compounded circles.

7. Deselect all, save your work, then close the Simple Compound document.

You selected two concentric circles and made them into one compound path, which allowed you to see through to the gradient behind the circles.

Figure 23 *A compound path creates the effect of a hole where two or more objects overlap*

U.S.S. MINNOW

U.S.S. MINNOW

Transforming and Distorting Objects

Figure 24 *A simple compound path*

Figure 25 *A more complex compound path*

Each of the five small circles is scaled, using its own center point as the point of origin

Figure 26 *Simple compound paths can yield stunning visual effects*

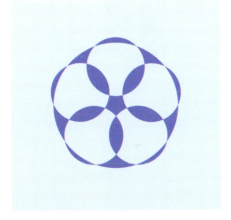

Create special effects with compound paths

1. Open AI 4-8.ai, then save it as **Compound Path Effects**.

2. Select all.

   The light blue square is locked and does not become part of the selection.

3. Click **Object** on the Menu bar, point to **Compound Path**, then click **Make**.

4. Deselect, click the **Direct Selection tool** , then click the **edge** of the large blue circle.

5. Click the **center point** of the circle, then scale the circle 50% so that your work resembles Figure 24.

6. Click **Select** on the Menu bar, then click **Inverse**.

7. Click **Object** on the Menu bar, point to **Transform**, then click **Transform Each**.

8. Enter **225** in the Horizontal and Vertical text boxes in the Scale section of the Transform Each dialog box, click **OK,** then deselect all.

   Your work should resemble Figure 24.

9. Using the Direct Selection tool , click the **edge of the center circle**, click its **center point** to select the entire circle, then scale the circle 120%.

10. Apply the Transform Again command twice, then compare your screen to Figure 26.

11. Deselect all, save your work, then close Compound Path Effects.

You made a compound path out of five small circles and one large circle. You then manipulated the size and location of the individual circles to create interesting designs.

Work with the
PATHFINDER PANEL

What You'll Do

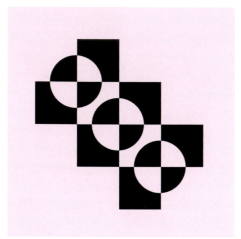

© 2015 Cengage Learning®

In this lesson, you will use shape modes and pathfinders to create compound shapes from simple shapes.

Defining a Compound Shape

Like a compound path, a **compound shape** is two or more paths that are combined in such a way that "holes" appear wherever paths overlap.

The term "compound shape" is used to distinguish a complex compound path from a simple one. Compound shapes generally assume an artistic rather than a practical role. To achieve the effect, compound shapes tend to be composed of multiple objects. You can think of a compound shape as an illustration composed of multiple compound paths.

Understanding Essential Shape Modes and Pathfinders

Shape modes and **pathfinders** are preset operations that help you combine paths in a variety of ways. They are useful operations for creating complex or irregular shapes from basic shapes. In some cases, they are a means to an end in creating an object. In others, the operation they provide will be the end result you want to achieve. Shape modes and pathfinders can be applied to overlapping objects using the Effect menu or the Pathfinder panel.

For the purposes of drawing and creating new objects, the following five shape modes and pathfinders are essential; compare each with Figure 27.

Unite shape mode Converts two or more overlapping objects into a single, merged object.

Minus Front shape mode Where objects overlap, deletes the frontmost object(s) from the backmost object in a selection of overlapped objects.

Intersect shape mode Creates a single, merged object from the area where two or more objects overlap.

Minus Back pathfinder The opposite of Minus Front; deletes the backmost object(s) from the frontmost object in a selection of overlapped objects.

Divide pathfinder Divides an object into its component filled faces. Illustrator defines a "face" as an area undivided by a line segment.

Figure 27 *Five essential shape modes and pathfinders*

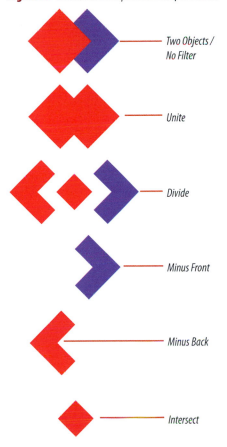

Two Objects / No Filter

Unite

Divide

Minus Front

Minus Back

Intersect

Using the Pathfinder Panel

The Pathfinder panel contains ten buttons for creating compound shapes, as shown in Figure 28. As you learned earlier, a compound shape is a complex compound path. You can create a compound shape by overlapping two or more objects, then clicking one of the four shape mode buttons in the top row of the Pathfinder panel, or clicking the Pathfinder panel list arrow, then clicking Make Compound Shape. The four shape mode buttons are Unite, Minus Front, Intersect, and Exclude. When you apply a shape mode button,

the two overlapping objects are combined into one object with the same formatting as the topmost object in the group before the shape mode button was applied. After applying a shape mode button, the resulting objects in the compound shape can be selected and formatted using the Direct Selection tool. You can also press [Alt] (Win) or [option] (Mac) when you click a shape mode button. Doing so results in a compound shape whose original objects can be selected and formatted using the Direct Selection tool.

Applying Shape Modes

Figure 29 shows a square overlapped by a circle.

If you apply the Minus Front shape mode button, the resulting object is a compound shape, as shown in Figure 30. Notice the overlapped area is deleted from the square. The circle, too, is deleted. The result is a simple reshaped object.

If you took the same two overlapping shapes shown in Figure 29, but this time pressed [Alt] (Win) or [option] (Mac) when

Figure 28 *Pathfinder panel*

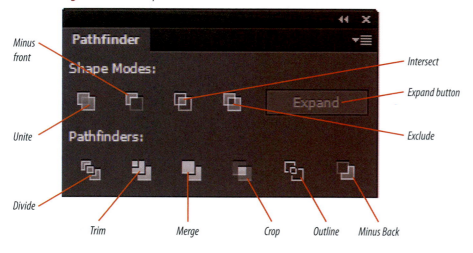

Minus front

Unite

Intersect

Expand button

Exclude

Divide

Trim

Merge

Crop

Outline

Minus Back

Figure 29 *Two overlapping objects*

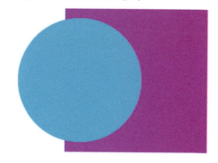

Transforming and Distorting Objects

applying the Minus Front shape mode button, the circle would not be deleted but would function as a hole or a "knockout" wherever it overlaps the square, as shown in Figure 31. The relationship is dynamic: You can move the circle independently with the Direct Selection tool to change its effect on the square and the resulting visual effect.

Figure 32 shows a group of objects converted into a compound shape using the Make Compound Shape command on the Pathfinder panel.

Releasing and Expanding Compound Shapes

You can release a compound shape, which separates it back into individual objects.

To release a compound shape, click the Pathfinder panel options button, then click Release Compound Shape. Expanding a compound shape is similar to releasing it, except that it maintains the shape of the compound object. You cannot select the original individual objects. You can expand a compound shape by selecting it, and then clicking the Expand button on the Pathfinder panel.

Figure 30 *Applying the Minus Front shape mode without [Alt] (Win) or [option] (Mac)*

Figure 31 *Applying the Minus Front shape mode with [Alt] (Win) or [option] (Mac)*

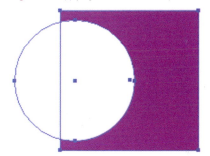

Figure 32 *A compound shape*

Apply the Unite shape mode

1. Open AI 4-9.ai, then save it as **Heart Parts**.

2. Click **Window** on the Menu bar, then click **Pathfinder**.

3. Select **both circles**, then click the **Unite button** 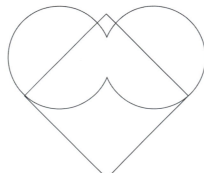 on the Pathfinder panel.

   The two objects are united.

4. Move the diamond shape up so that it overlaps the united circles, as shown in Figure 33.

5. Click the **Delete Anchor Point tool** , then delete the top anchor point of the diamond.

6. Select all, press and hold **[Alt]** (Win) or **[option]** (Mac), click the **Unite button** , then deselect all.

   Your screen should resemble Figure 34.

7. Remove the black stroke, then apply a red fill to the new object.

8. Draw a rectangle that covers the "hole" in the heart, then fill it with black, as shown in Figure 35.

9. Select all, press **[Alt]** (Win) or **[option]** (Mac), then click the **Unite button** .

   The heart turns black.

10. Double-click the **Scale tool** , then apply a non-uniform scale of 90% on the horizontal axis and 100% on the vertical axis.

You created a single heart-shaped object from two circles and a diamond shape using the Unite shape mode.

Figure 33 *A diamond shape in position*

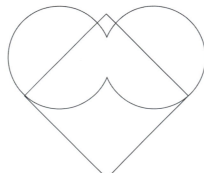

Figure 34 *The diamond shape and the object behind it are united*

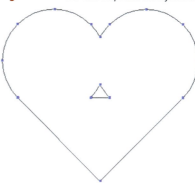

Figure 35 *A heart shape created by applying the Unite shape mode to three objects*

Transforming and Distorting Objects

Figure 36 *Circle overlaps the square*

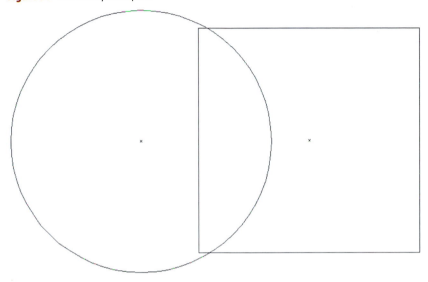

Figure 37 *Right circle is a reflected copy of the left one*

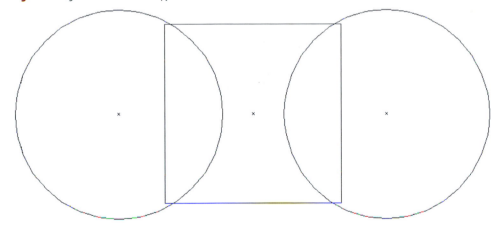

Lesson 4   Work with the Pathfinder Panel

Apply the Minus Front shape mode

1. Rotate the black heart shape 180°, then hide it.

2. Create a square that is 1.5" × 1.5" without a fill color and with a 1 pt black stroke.

3. Create a circle that is 1.75" in width and height.

4. Switch to Outline mode.

5. Move the circle so that it overlaps the square, as shown in Figure 36.

6. Verify that the circle is still selected, click the **Reflect tool** , press **[Alt]** (Win) or **[option]** (Mac), then click the **center point** of the square.

7. Click the **Vertical option button**, click **Copy**, then arrange the three objects so that your work resembles Figure 37.

8. Select all, then click the **Minus Front button** on the Pathfinder panel.

(continued)

9. Switch to Preview mode, then apply a black fill to the new object.

10. Show all, then overlap the new shape with the black heart shape to make a spade shape.

11. Select all, click the **Unite button** , then deselect.

   Your work should resemble Figure 38.

You overlapped a square with two circles, then applied the Minus Front shape mode to delete the overlapped areas from the square. You used the Unite button to unite the new shape with a heart-shaped object to create a spade shape.

Figure 38 *The final shape, with all elements united*

Working with the Align Panel

The Align panel offers a quick and simple solution for aligning selected objects along the axis you specify. Along the vertical axis, you can align selected objects by their rightmost, leftmost, or center point. On the horizontal axis, you can align objects by their topmost point, center point, or bottommost point. You can also use the panel to distribute objects evenly along a horizontal or vertical axis. In contrasting the Align panel with the Average command, think of the Average command as a method for aligning anchor points and the Align panel as a method for aligning entire objects.

When you align and distribute objects, you have the choice of aligning them to a selection, a key object, or the artboard. If you want to align or distribute objects using the artboard, you must first define the artboard area using the Artboard tool on the Tools panel. Click the Align To list arrow on the Align panel, then click Align to Artboard. Resize the artboard as desired. Finally, choose the alignment setting you need on the Align panel.

Transforming and Distorting Objects

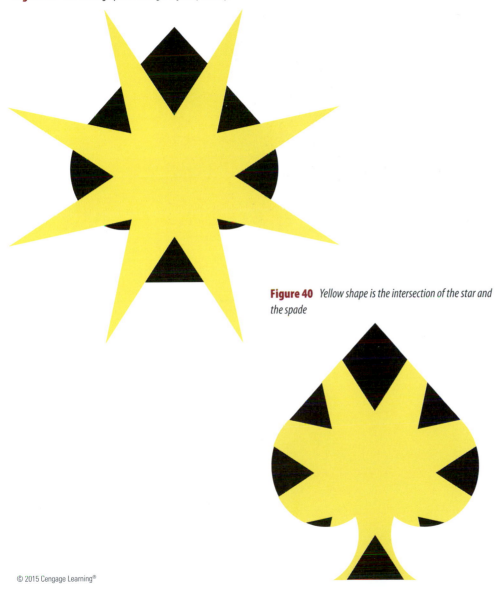

Figure 39 *Use the Align panel to align objects precisely*

Figure 40 *Yellow shape is the intersection of the star and the spade*

Apply the Intersect shape mode

1. Click the **Star tool** ⭐, then click the **artboard**.
2. Enter **1** in the Radius 1 text box, **3** in the Radius 2 text box, and **8** in the Points text box, then click **OK**.
3. Apply a yellow fill to the star and no stroke.
4. Use the Align panel to align the center points of the two objects so that they resemble Figure 39.
5. Copy the black spade, then paste in front.

   Two black spades are now behind the yellow star; the top one is selected.
6. Press and hold **[Shift]**, then click to add the star to the selection.
7. Click the **Intersect shape mode button** 🔲 on the Pathfinder panel.

   The intersection of the star and the copied spade is now a single closed path. Your work should resemble Figure 40.

   Save your work, then close Heart Parts.

You created a star, then created a copy of the black spade-shaped object. You used the Intersect shape mode button to capture the intersection of the two objects as a new object.

Apply the Divide pathfinder

1. Open AI 4-10.ai, then save it as **Divide**.

2. Select the **red line**, then double-click the **Rotate tool** .

3. Enter **30** in the Angle text box, then click **Copy**.

4. Repeat the transformation four times.

5. Select all, then click the **Divide button** on the Pathfinder panel.

   The blue star is divided into 12 separate objects, as defined by the red lines, which have been deleted. See Figure 41.

6. Deselect, click the **Direct Selection tool**, select the left half of the top point, press **[Shift]**, then select every other object, for a total of six objects.

7. Apply an orange fill to the selected objects.

8. Select the inverse, then apply a yellow fill so that your work resembles Figure 42.

9. Save your work, then close the Divide document.

You used six lines to define a score pattern, then used those lines and the Divide pathfinder to break the star into 12 separate objects.

Figure 41 *Blue star is divided into 12 objects by the Divide pathfinder*

Figure 42 *Divide pathfinder is useful for adding dimension*

Transforming and Distorting Objects

Figure 43 *An example of the Exclude shape mode*

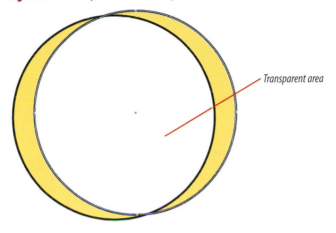

Transparent area

Figure 44 *An example of the Intersect shape mode*

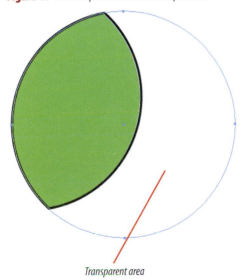

Transparent area

Lesson 4 Work with the Pathfinder Panel

Create compound shapes using the Pathfinder panel

1. Open AI 4-11.ai, then save it as **Compound Shapes**.

2. Click **View** on the Menu bar, then click **Yellow**.

3. Select the **two yellow circles**, press [**Alt**] (Win) or [**option**] (Mac), then click the **Exclude button** on the Pathfinder panel.

   The area that the top object overlaps becomes transparent.

4. Deselect, click the **Direct Selection tool**, then move either circle to change the shape and size of the filled areas.

   Figure 43 shows one effect that can be achieved.

5. Select **Green** from the View menu, select the two green circles, press [**Alt**] (Win) or [**option**] (Mac), then click the **Intersect button** on the Pathfinder panel.

   The area not overlapped by the top circle becomes transparent.

6. Deselect, then use the Direct Selection tool to move either circle to change the shape and size of the filled area.

   Figure 44 shows one effect that can be achieved.

7. Save your work, then close the Compound Shapes document.

You applied shape modes to two pairs of circles, then moved the circles to create different shapes and effects.

Create special effects with compound shapes

1. Open AI 4-12.ai, then save it as **Compound Shape Effects**.

2. Select all, press **[Alt]** (Win) or **[option]** (Mac), then click the **Exclude button** 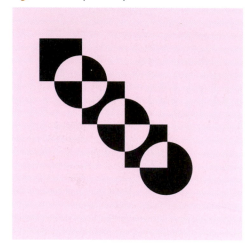 on the Pathfinder panel.

   Your work should resemble Figure 45.

3. Deselect all, click the **Direct Selection tool** , select the **three squares**, then move them to the right, as shown in Figure 46.

   (continued)

Figure 45 *A compound shape*

Figure 46 *A compound shape*

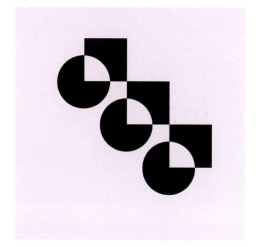

Transforming and Distorting Objects

Figure 47 *A compound shape*

Figure 48 *A compound shape*

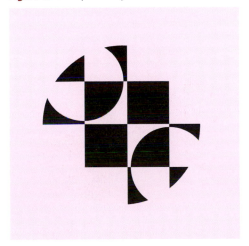

4. Drag and drop a copy of the three squares, as shown in Figure 47.

TIP Use [Shift] [Alt] (Win) or [Shift] [option] (Mac) to drag and drop a copy at a 45-degree angle or in straight vertical or horizontal lines.

5. Scale each circle 150% using the Transform Each command.

6. Scale the center circle 200%, then bring it to the front of the stacking order.

7. Press **[Alt]** (Win) or **[option]** (Mac), then click the **Intersect button** on the Pathfinder panel.

   Figure 48 shows the results of the intersection. Your final illustration may vary slightly.

TIP The topmost object affects all the objects behind it in a compound shape.

8. Save your work, then close Compound Shape Effects.

You made three squares and three circles into a compound shape by excluding overlapping shape areas. You then manipulated the size and location of individual elements to create different effects. Finally, you enlarged a circle, brought it to the front, then changed its mode to Intersect. Only the objects that were overlapped by the circle remained visible.

Apply Round
CORNERS TO OBJECTS

What You'll Do

In this lesson you will apply round corners to artwork using the Corners dialog box. You will also learn about the options in the Corners dialog box.

Applying Round Corners

Round corners are an essential component of any designer's tool kit. Figure 49 shows a five-point star, like one you'd see on the American flag. Note the five pointy points; it's serious, and to some degree it says 'don't mess with me.' With its mathematical basis and sharp points, a star is regal, which is why it's often used to convey majesty and supremacy.

Figure 50 shows the same star with round corners. It's remarkable what an emotional effect changing from pointy corners to round corners has on the object. Suddenly the object is cute, it's playful. It's almost cartoonish, like an animated character or a sponge toy a child could play with in the bathtub.

Round corners make objects fun, playful, comical, and cute. When you round corners in Illustrator, you are working with widgets, small circles that appear at every corner, as shown in Figure 51. To view widgets, you must select the object with the Direct Selection tool. If you do not see widgets, click the View menu and choose Show Corner Widget.

Figure 49 *Star with pointy points*

Figure 50 *Star with round corners*

© 2015 Cengage Learning®

When you click and drag the widget, all the corners of the object are rounded as you drag. You may have a situation in which you only want to round one corner, not all of them, on a given object. To do so, first select *only* the anchor point of the corner you wish to round with the Direct Selection tool, then drag its associated widget. Using this method, you can apply differently rounded corners to every point on the object.

If you want to apply a specific corner radius to a point, rather than click and drag to create the rounded corner, simply double-click the widget. This opens the Corners dialog box where you can enter a specific radius, as shown in Figure 52. You can also specify two other types of corners: Inverted Round and Chamfer.

QUICK TIP

You can also enter a specific radius for a corner by clicking Corners on the Control panel.

Don't forget that you can apply round corners to type after you've converted the text to outlines. This is a great option for creating fun, friendly letter shapes.

Figure 51 *Corner widgets visible on objects*

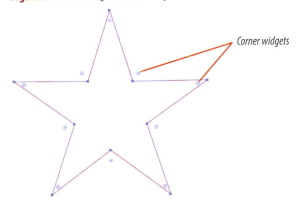

Corner widgets

Figure 52 *Corners dialog box with options for corners*

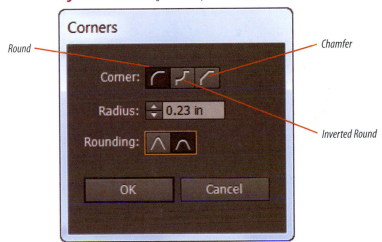

Round

Chamfer

Inverted Round

Apply corners to an object

1. Open AI 4-13.ai, save it as **Round Corners**, click **View** on the menu bar, then click **Show Corner Widget**.

   If the command reads Hide Corner Widget, do nothing; the corner widget is already showing.

2. Click the **Direct Selection tool** , then click the interior of the blue shape to select the object.

   As shown in Figure 53, corner widgets appear at every corner of the selected object.

   TIP If you find corner widgets distracting, you can hide them using the Hide Corner Widget command on the View menu.

3. Click and drag the **topmost corner widget** toward the center of the object.

   As you drag, all the corners on the object become increasingly rounded.

4. Drag until the object resembles Figure 54.

5. Press and hold **[Alt]** (Win) or **[option]** (Mac) then click any corner widget.

   The round corners change to inverted round corners.

   (continued)

Figure 53 *Corner widgets visible on the object*

Figure 54 *Round corners applied to the object*

Transforming and Distorting Objects

Figure 55 *Chamfer corners applied to the object*

6. While still holding [Alt] (Win) or [option] (Mac), click the **corner widget** again.

   As shown in Figure 55, the inverted round corners change to chamfer corners. Each time you press and hold [Alt] (Win) or [option] (Mac) and click a corner widget, the corner cycles through the three types of corner options in the Corners dialog box.

   TIP The word chamfer is based on a cut made in woodcutting and is similar to a beveled edge.

7. While still holding [Alt] (Win) or [option] (Mac), click the **corner widget** again.

   The chamfer corners change to round corners.

8. Drag the **corner widget** away from the center of the object.

   The object is restored to its original shape.

9. Save your work.

You dragged corner widgets with the Direct Selection tool to create round corners, then modified the corners from round to inverted round to chamfer. You then removed the specialized corners from the object.

Apply specific corner measurements to individual points on an object

1. Deselect all, then select the **top anchor point** on the blue object with the Direct Selection tool 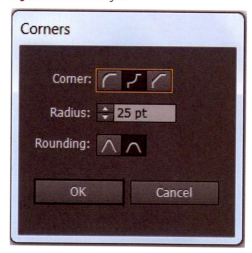.

2. Click and drag the **corner widget** toward the center of the object to create a round corner.

   Note that the radius of the corner is identified in the Corners section of the Control panel, as shown in Figure 56.

3. Double-click the **corner widget**.

   The Corners dialog box opens.

4. Enter **25** in the Radius text box, then click **OK**.

5. Select the **anchor point** at the bottom of the blue object.

6. Double-click the **corner widget**, enter **25** in the Radius text box, then click **OK**.

7. Select both of the **orange objects**.

8. Double-click any **corner widget**.

9. Enter **25** in the Radius text box, then click **OK**

10. Select the **far left** and **far right anchor points** on the blue object with the Direct Selection tool.

11. Double-click either of the two corner widgets, click the **Inverted Round option**, enter **25** in the Radius text box, then compare your Corners dialog box to Figure 57.

(continued)

Figure 56 *Corners text box on the Control panel*

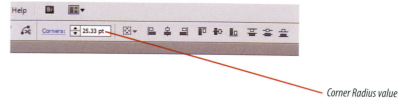

Corner Radius value

Figure 57 *Corners dialog box*

Transforming and Distorting Objects

Figure 58 *Final artwork with corners applied to all anchor points*

12. Click **OK**, deselect all, then compare your artwork to Figure 58.

13. Save your work, then close the file.

You applied a corner to individual points on an object, then used the Corners dialog box to apply the exact same corner style to other points on the object and to other objects.

Lesson 5 Apply Round Corners to Objects

Use the Shape
BUILDER TOOL

What You'll Do

© 2015 Cengage Learning®

 In this lesson, you use the Shape Builder tool to create new shapes from overlapping objects.

Understanding the Shape Builder Tool

The Shape Builder tool is grouped on the Tools panel with the Live Paint Bucket. This makes sense because the tool functions in a similar manner to the Live Paint Bucket.

The Shape Builder tool is designed to help you create new objects from overlapping objects. Comparing it to the Live Paint Bucket (covered in Chapter 3) can help you understand its role.

Where the Live Paint Bucket fills closed paths created by overlapping objects, the Shape Builder tool creates new closed paths from overlapping objects. From this perspective, you can think of the Shape Builder tool as a combination of the Live Paint Bucket and the Pathfinder tools.

Figure 59 shows eight orange-filled circles overlapping. The Shape Builder tool is selected on the Tools panel, and a pink fill

Figure 59 *Specifying objects to be created with the Shape Builder tool*

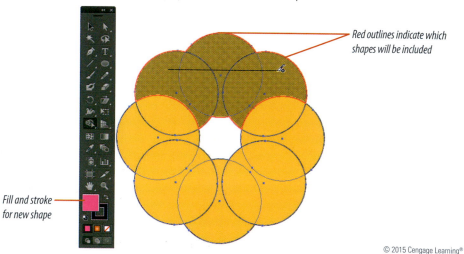

Red outlines indicate which shapes will be included

Fill and stroke for new shape

© 2015 Cengage Learning®

Transforming and Distorting Objects

and black stroke has been chosen on the Tools panel. Closed objects are highlighted when the Shape Builder tool is dragged across them.

In Figure 60, those objects are united into a single object with the pink fill and a black stroke. Note that this is not something you could do with the Unite pathfinder. The Unite pathfinder would have united the three whole circles, but, as shown in this example, the Shape Builder tool created a single object from overlapping components of the circles.

In Figure 61, the Shape Builder tool has been dragged to the negative space in the center so that it will be added to the merged object.

In addition to creating new objects, the Shape Builder tool also deletes closed paths from overlapping objects. To delete an object with the Shape Builder tool, press and hold [Alt] (Win) or [option] (Mac), then click or drag over the objects you want to delete. Note the minus sign beside the Shape Builder tool icon in Figure 62. Upon release, the objects are deleted, as shown in Figure 63.

Figure 60 *New object created with the Shape Builder tool*

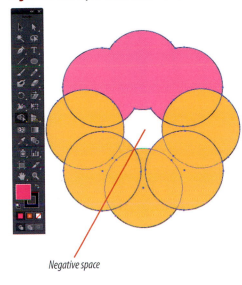

Negative space

Figure 61 *Adding the negative space to the object*

Figure 62 *Specifying objects to be deleted*

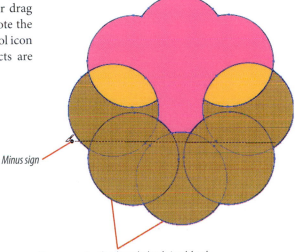

Minus sign

Shapes are not outlined in red when being deleted

Figure 63 *Illustration after deletion*

Create objects with the Shape Builder tool

1. Open AI 4-14.ai, then save it as **Shape Builder**.
2. Select all, then click the **Shape Builder tool**  .
3. Set the fill and stroke color to Pink and None, respectively.

   Your artboard should resemble Figure 64. Even though the yellow circles are selected, when you set the foreground color to a different color, the circles don't change color.

4. Click and drag to highlight the objects shown in Figure 65.

   When you release the mouse button, the objects are united as a single object.

5. Click and drag to highlight the objects shown in Figure 66.

   Because you included the first pink object, the objects are united into a single object, as shown in Figure 67.

6. Save your work.

You dragged with the Shape Builder tool to create a new object.

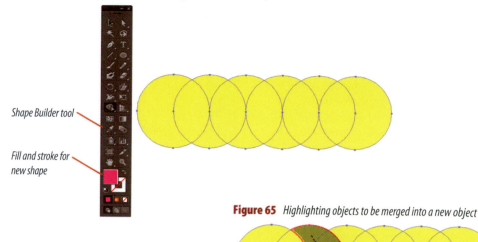

Figure 64 *Selecting a fill color for the Shape Builder tool*

Shape Builder tool

Fill and stroke for new shape

Figure 65 *Highlighting objects to be merged into a new object*

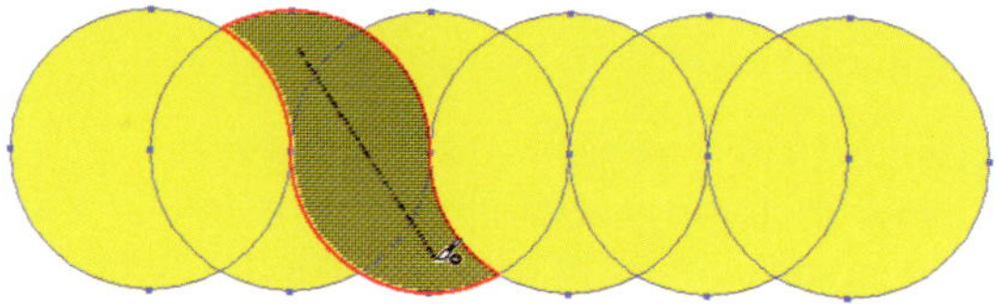

Figure 66 *Adding more objects to the new shape*

Start dragging within first shape

Figure 67 *The new shape*

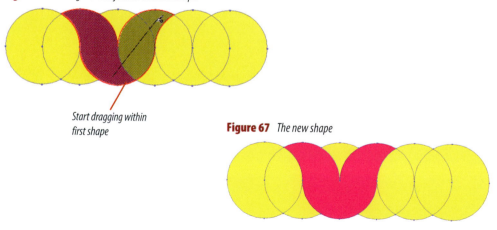

© 2015 Cengage Learning®

Figure 68 *Highlighting shapes to be deleted*

Figure 69 *The final shape*

Delete objects with the Shape Builder tool

1. Verify that the entire illustration is selected.

2. Press and hold **[Alt]** (Win) or **[option]** (Mac), then drag the **Shape Builder tool** over the objects shown in Figure 68.

   When you release, the objects are deleted.

3. Press and hold **[Shift] [Alt]** (Win) or **[Shift] [option]** (Mac), then drag the **Shape Builder tool** over all the yellow objects to the right of the pink shape.

   Adding the Shift key to the combination allows you to drag a selection square to highlight more objects.

4. Press and hold **[Alt]** (Win) or **[option]** (Mac), then click the **last remaining yellow object**.

   Your result should resemble Figure 69.

5. Save your work, then close the file.

You used the Shape Builder tool to delete objects.

Create Clipping
MASKS

 In this lesson, you will explore the role of clipping masks for practical use and for artistic effects.

Defining a Clipping Mask

Clipping masks are used to yield a practical result. And as with compound paths, that practical result can be manipulated to create interesting graphic effects.

Practically speaking, you use a clipping mask as a "window" through which you view some or all of the objects behind the mask in the stacking order. When you select any two or more objects and apply the Make Clipping Mask command, the *top object* becomes the mask and the object behind it becomes "masked." You will be able to see only the parts of the masked object that are visible *through* the mask, as shown in Figure 70. The mask crops the object behind it.

Using Multiple Objects as a Clipping Mask

When you select multiple objects and apply the Make Clipping Mask command, the top object becomes the mask. Since every object has its own position in the stacking order, it stands to reason that there can be only one top object.

If you want to use multiple objects as a mask, you can do so by first making them into a compound path because Illustrator regards compound paths as a single object. Therefore, a compound path containing multiple objects can be used as a single mask.

Creating Masked Effects

Special effects with clipping masks are, quite simply, fun! You can position as many objects as you like behind the mask and position them in such a way that the mask crops them in visually interesting (and eye-popping!) ways. See Figure 71 for an example.

Using the Draw Inside Drawing Mode

The Draw Inside drawing mode does just what its name implies: it allows you to create one object within the perimeter of another object. Drawing one object inside another is essentially the same thing as creating a clipping mask. When you draw an object inside another, the two objects behave the same way any two objects behave in a clipping set. The relationship can be undone with the Clipping Mask/Release command. The big difference between using the Draw Inside drawing mode and making a clipping mask is that the Draw Inside option can involve only two objects.

Figure 70 *Clipping mask crops the object behind it*

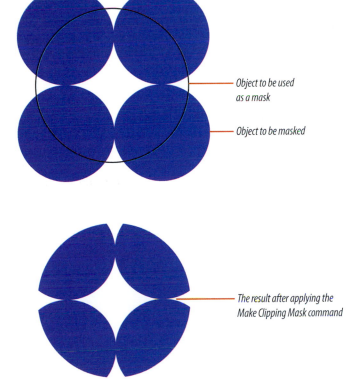

Object to be used
as a mask

Object to be masked

The result after applying the
Make Clipping Mask command

Figure 71 *Masks can be used for stunning visual effects*

Create a clipping mask

1. Open AI 4-15.ai, then save it as **Simple Masks**.
2. Click **View** on the Menu bar, then click **Mask 1**.
3. Move the rectangle so that it overlaps the gold spheres as shown in Figure 72.
4. Apply the Bring to Front command to verify that the rectangle is in front of all the spheres.
5. Select the **seven spheres** and the **rectangle**.
6. Click **Object** on the Menu bar, point to **Clipping Mask**, then click **Make**.
7. Deselect, then compare your screen to Figure 73.
8. Click **View** on the Menu bar, then click **Mask 2**.
9. Select the **three circles**, then move them over the "gumballs."

   The three circles are a compound path.
10. Select the **group of gumballs** and the **three circles**, then apply the Make Clipping Mask command.
11. Deselect, click **Select** on the Menu bar, point to **Object**, then click **Clipping Masks**.
12. Apply a 1 pt black stroke to the masks. Your work should resemble Figure 74.
13. Save your work, then close the Simple Masks document.

You used a rectangle as a clipping mask. Then, you used three circles to mask a group of small spheres, and applied a black stroke to the mask.

Figure 72 *Masking objects must be in front of objects to be masked*

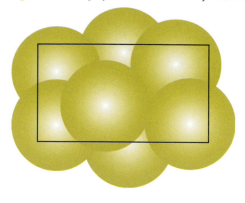

Figure 73 *The rectangle masks the gold spheres*

Figure 74 *A compound path used as a mask*

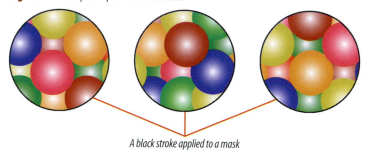

A black stroke applied to a mask

Figure 75 *Lining up the letter g*

Figure 76 *Positioning the magnifying glass*

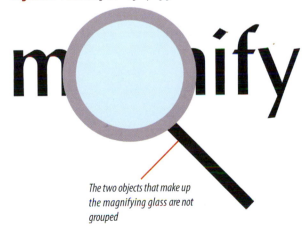

The two objects that make up the magnifying glass are not grouped

Lesson 7   Create Clipping Masks

Apply a fill to a clipping mask

1. Open AI 4-16.ai, then save it as **Magnify**.

2. Move the large text over the small text so that both letters *g* align as shown in Figure 75.

3. Select the **smaller text**, then hide it.

4. Select the **magnifying glass** and the **handle**, then drag them over the letter *g*, as shown in Figure 76.

5. Deselect all, select only the **circle** and the **text**, click **Object** on the Menu bar, point to **Clipping Mask**, then click **Make**.

   The circle is the masking object.

6. Deselect, click **Select** on the Menu bar, point to **Object**, then click **Clipping Masks**.

7. Use the Swatches panel to apply a light blue fill and a gray stroke to the mask.

   (continued)

8. Change the weight of the stroke to 8 pt, so that your work resembles Figure 77.

9. Show all, deselect, then compare your screen to Figure 78.

10. Select the **mask** only, press and hold **[Shift]**, then click the **magnifying glass handle**.

11. Press the **arrow keys** to move the magnifying glass.

    As you move the magnifying glass left and right, it gives the illusion that the magnifying glass is enlarging the text. This would make for an interesting animation in a PDF or on a web page.

12. Save your work, then close the Magnify document.

You used the circle in the illustration as a clipping mask in combination with the large text. You added a fill and a stroke to the mask, creating the illusion that the small text is magnified in the magnifying glass.

Figure 77 *A fill and stroke are applied to a mask*

The mask

By default, a fill is positioned behind the masked elements, and the stroke is in front of the mask

Figure 78 *Large text is masked by the magnifying glass*

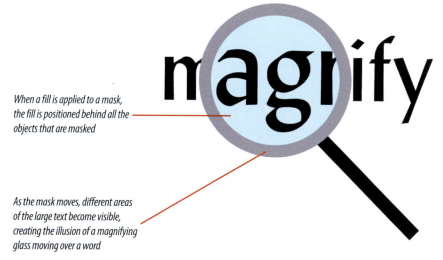

When a fill is applied to a mask, the fill is positioned behind all the objects that are masked

As the mask moves, different areas of the large text become visible, creating the illusion of a magnifying glass moving over a word

Transforming and Distorting Objects

Figure 79 *Outlined text used as a mask*

Figure 80 *Curvy object in position to be masked by the letters*

Figure 81 *Object behind the mask is selected*

The rectangle behind
the mask is selected

Lesson 7   Create Clipping Masks

Use text as a clipping mask

1. Open AI 4-17.ai, then save it as **Mask Effects**.
2. Select the **four letters** that make the word MASK.

   The word MASK was converted to outlines and ungrouped.
3. Make the four letters into a compound path.
4. With the compound path still selected, select the **rectangle** behind it.
5. Apply the Make Clipping Mask command, then deselect.
6. Save your work, then compare your text to Figure 79.

You converted outlines to a compound path, then used the compound path as a mask.

Use a clipping mask for special effects

1. Position the curvy object with the gradient fill over the mask, as shown in Figure 80.
2. Cut the curvy object.
3. Use the Direct Selection tool to select the original **rectangle** behind the mask.

TIP Click slightly above the mask until you see the rectangle selected, as shown in Figure 81.

(continued)

4. Paste in front, then deselect so that your screen resembles Figure 82.

The object is pasted in front of the masked rectangle and behind the mask.

5. Click the **Selection tool** , select the **purple dotted line**, position it over the letter K, then cut the purple dotted line.

6. Select the **mask (rectangle)** with the Direct Selection tool , click **Edit** on the Menu bar, then click **Paste in Front**.

7. Using the same technique, mask the other objects on the artboard in any way that you choose.

When finished, your mask should contain all of the objects, as shown in Figure 83.

TIP Add a stroke to the mask if desired.

8. Save and close Mask Effects.

You created visual effects by pasting objects behind a mask.

Use the Draw Inside drawing mode

1. Open AI 4-18.ai, save it as **Draw Inside**, click the **Selection tool** , then select the **blue square** at the top of the document.

When you select the blue square, by default the Fill and Stroke buttons on the Tools panel take on the object's colors, which, in this case, are Blue and None.

2. Click the **Draw Inside button** on the Tools panel, then click the **Ellipse tool** .

Because you must have an object selected to use the Draw Inside drawing mode, the object you draw will always be the same fill and stroke color

(continued)

Figure 82 *Curvy object is masked by the letters*

Figure 83 *Pasting multiple objects behind a mask yields interesting effects*

© 2015 Cengage Learning®

Transforming and Distorting Objects

Figure 84 *Drawing the yellow ellipse inside the blue square*

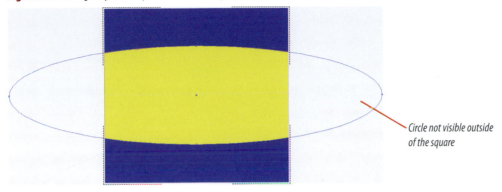

Circle not visible outside of the square

Figure 85 *Drawing the pink ellipse inside the outlines via the Paste command*

as the object you're drawing into. You can make them different colors only after you draw inside.

3. Draw an ellipse that overlaps the blue square, making it approximately the same size as the pink ellipse already on the artboard.

4. With the ellipse still selected, change its fill color to yellow.

   Figure 84 shows one example of how the ellipse is drawn within the blue square. Dotted lines around the four corners of the blue square indicate that it is functioning as a mask for the ellipse. As long as you stay in Draw Inside drawing mode, any object you create will be drawn inside the blue square.

5. Click the **Draw Normal button** 🔲 on the Tools panel, select the word **MASK**, click the **Type menu**, then click **Create Outlines**.

6. With the outlines still selected, click the **Object menu**, point to **Compound Path**, click **Make**, then fill them with any green swatch on the Swatches panel.

7. Defined as a compound path, the letter outlines are now a single object into which you can draw.

8. Select the **pink ellipse**, cut it, select the **MASK outlines**, then click the **Draw Inside button** 🔲.

   Dotted lines appear around the MASK outlines, indicated they can be drawn into.

9. Click the **Edit menu**, click **Paste**, then move the ellipse so that it overlaps the MASK outlines as shown in Figure 85.

10. Save your work, then close Draw Inside.ai.

You used the draw inside drawing mode to create objects within other objects and within outlined text.

Transform objects.

1. Open AI 4-19.ai, then save it as **Transform Skills**.
2. Select "DIVIDE."
3. Scale the text objects non-uniformly: Horizontal = 110% and Vertical = 120%.
4. Rotate the text objects 7°.
5. Shear the text objects 25° on the horizontal axis.
6. Save your work.

Offset and outline paths.

1. Ungroup the text outlines.
2. Using the Offset Path command, offset each letter -.05".
3. Save your work.

Work with the Pathfinder panel.

1. Select all.
2. Apply the Divide pathfinder.

3. Fill the divided elements with different colors, using the Direct Selection tool.
4. Select all, then apply a 2-point white stroke. (*Hint*: Enlarge the view to see the effect better.)
5. Save your work, compare your image to Figure 86, then close the Transform Skills document.

Figure 86 *Completed Skills Review, Part 1*

Create compound paths.

1. Open AI 4-20.ai, then save it as **Compounded**.
2. Select all, press [Alt] (Win) or [option] (Mac), then click the Exclude button on the Pathfinder panel.
3. Deselect, then click the center of the small square with the Direct Selection tool.
4. Rotate a copy of the small square 45°.
5. Save your work, compare your image to Figure 87, then close the Compounded document.

Use the Shape Builder tool.

1. Open AI 4-21.ai, then save it as **Shape Builder Skills**.
2. Select all, then set the fill color on the objects to None so that you can see the shapes being created by the overlapping.
3. Click the Shape Builder tool.
4. Set the fill and stroke color to a shade of light blue and None, respectively.

(*Hint*: Even though the circles are selected, when you set the foreground color to a different color with the Shape Builder tool, the circles don't change color.)

5. Click and drag to highlight the objects shown in Figure 88. When you release the mouse button, the objects are united as a single object.
6. Change the fill color on the Tools panel to a shade of red.

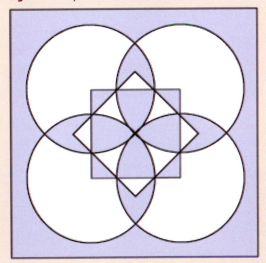

Figure 87 *Completed Skills Review, Part 2*

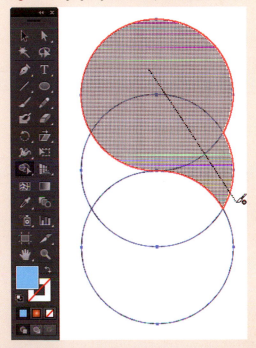

Figure 88 *Highlighting with the Shape Builder tool*

© 2015 Cengage Learning®

7. Click and drag to highlight the remaining objects shown in Figure 89.
8. Click the Selection tool, then click the artboard to deselect both objects.
9. Click the top blue object, then drag it away from the red object.
10. Save your work, then close Shape Builder Skills.

Create clipping masks.

1. Open AI 4-22.ai, then save it as **Masked Paths**.
2. Position any three of the letters on the right side of the canvas over the artwork on the left.
3. Hide the three letters you didn't choose.

Figure 89 *Highlighting the remaining shapes*

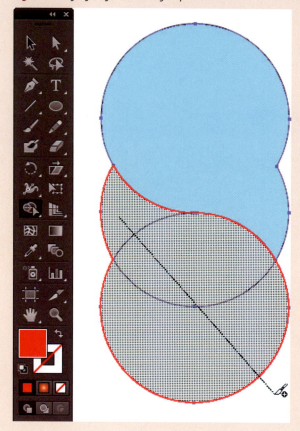

4. Select the three letters over the artwork, click Object on the Menu bar, point to Compound Path, then click Make.
5. Select everything on the artboard.
6. Click Object on the Menu bar, point to Clipping Mask, then click Make.

7. Deselect all.
8. Click Select on the Menu bar, point to Object, then click Clipping Masks.
9. Add a 1.5 pt black stroke to the selection.

10. Compare your results to Figure 90, which shows one potential result.
11. Save your work, then close Masked Paths.ai.

Figure 90 *Completed Skills Review, Part 3*

Transforming and Distorting Objects

You are entering a contest to design a new stamp. You have decided to use a picture of Tom Sawyer, which you have placed in an Illustrator document. You have positioned text over the image. Now, to complete the effect, you want to mimic the perforated edges of a stamp.

1. Open AI 4-23.ai, then save it as **Tom Sawyer Stamp**.
2. Select all the circles, then make them into a compound path.
3. Add the rectangle to the selection.
   (*Hint*: The rectangle is behind the circles in the stacking order.)
4. Apply the Minus Front shape mode, then deselect all.
5. Save your work, compare your image to Figure 91, then close Tom Sawyer Stamp.

Figure 91 *Completed Project Builder 1*

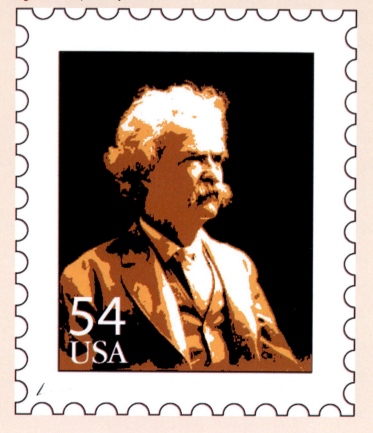

Transforming and Distorting Objects

You're contracted to design the logo for Wired Gifts, which is an online gift site. Your concept is of a geometric red bow. You feel that your idea will simultaneously convey the concepts of gifts and technology.

1. Open AI 4-4.ai, then save it as **Wired**.
2. Switch to Outline mode.
3. Select the small square, click the Rotate tool, press and hold [Alt] (Win) or [option] (Mac), then click the center of the large square.
4. Type 15 in the Angle text box, then click Copy.
5. Repeat the transformation 22 times.
6. Delete the large square at the center.
7. Switch to Preview mode.
8. Select all, then fill all the squares with Caribbean Blue. (*Hint*: The color swatches on the Swatches panel in this file have been saved with names.)
9. Apply the Divide pathfinder to the selection.
10. Fill the objects with the Red Bow gradient.
11. Delete the object in the center of the bow. (*Hint*: Use the Direct Selection tool to select the object.)
12. Select all, then remove the black stroke from the objects.
13. Save your work, compare your illustration with Figure 92, then close Wired.

Figure 92 *Completed Project Builder 2*

Transforming and Distorting Objects

You're an illustrator for a small town quarterly magazine. You're designing an illustration to accompany an article titled "A Walk Down Main Street." You decide to distort the artwork in perspective to make for a more interesting illustration.

1. Open AI 4-5.ai, then save it as **Main Street Perspective**.
2. Select all of the buildings on the left, then click the Free Transform tool.
   (*Hint*: The selection marks are hidden, but the Free Transform tool is nevertheless visible. Having selection marks hidden will help you to see the artwork better as you distort it.)
3. Click and begin dragging the upper-right handle straight down.
4. While still dragging, press and hold [Shift] [Ctrl] [Alt] (Win) or [Shift] ⌘ (Mac) and continue dragging until you like the appearance of the artwork.
5. Release the mouse button.
6. Click and drag the middle-left handle to the right to reduce the depth of the distortion.
   Figure 93 shows one possible result.
7. Using the same methodology, distort the buildings on the right in perspective.
   Figure 94 shows one possible solution.
8. Save your work, then close Main Street Perspective.

Figure 93 *Distorting the left of the illustration*

Figure 94 *Completed Design Project*

© 2015 Cengage Learning®

You are the design department manager for a toy company, and your next project is to design a dartboard that will be part of a package of "Safe Games" for kids. The target market is boys and girls ages six to adult. You will design the board but not the darts.

1. Create a new document and name it **Dartboard**.
2. Search the Internet for pictures of dartboards.
3. Research the sport of throwing darts. What are the official dimensions of a dartboard? Is there an official design? Are there official colors?
4. Decide which colors should be used for the board, keeping in mind that the sales department plans to position it as a toy for both girls and boys.
5. Using the skills you learned in this chapter and Figure 95 as a guide, design a dartboard.
6. Save your work, compare your image to Figure 95, then close Dartboard.

Figure 95 *Completed Portfolio Project*

Transforming and Distorting Objects

CHAPTER **5** **WORKING WITH**
LAYERS

1. Create and modify layers
2. Manipulate layered artwork
3. Work with layered artwork
4. Create a clipping set

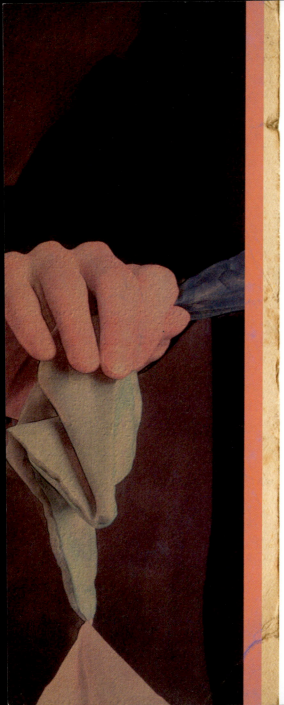

CHAPTER

WORKING WITH
LAYERS

Designing with Layers

When you're creating complex artwork, keeping track of all the items on the artboard can become a challenge. Small items hide behind larger items and it may become difficult to find, select, and work with them. The Layers panel solves this problem because you can organize your work by placing objects or groups of objects on separate layers. Artwork on layers can be manipulated and modified independently from artwork on other layers. The Layers panel also provides effective options to select, hide, lock, and change the appearance of your work. In addition, layers are an effective solution for storing multiple versions of your work in one file.

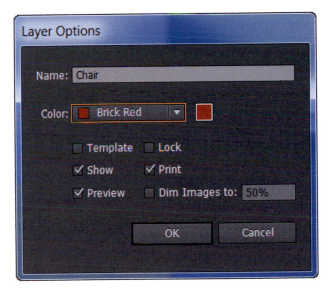

Create and Modify
LAYERS

What You'll Do

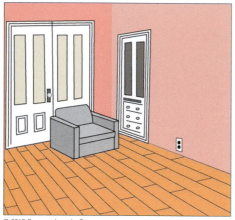

© 2015 Cengage Learning®

In this lesson, you will create new layers and explore options on the Layers panel for viewing, locking, hiding, and selecting layers and layered artwork.

Creating Layers and Sublayers

Layers are a smart solution for organizing and managing a complex illustration. For example, if you were drawing a map of your home state, you might put all the interstate freeways on one layer, the local freeways on a second layer, secondary roads on a third layer, and all the text elements on a fourth layer.

As the name suggests, the Layers panel consists of a series of layers. By default, every Illustrator document is created with one layer, called Layer 1. As you work, you can create new layers and move objects into them, thereby segregating objects and organizing your work. The first object that is placed on Layer 1 is placed on a sublayer called <Path>. Each additional object placed on the same layer is placed on a separate <Path> sublayer.

On the Layers panel, each layer has a **thumbnail**, or miniature picture, of the objects on that layer. Thumbnails also display the artwork that is positioned on each of the individual sublayers of a layer. You can change the size of the rows on the Layers panel by choosing a new size in the Layers Panel Options dialog box. Click the Layers panel options button, then click Panel Options. Layers and sublayers can also be given descriptive names to help identify their contents.

The stacking order of objects on the artboard corresponds to the hierarchy of layers on the Layers panel. Artwork in the top layer is at the front of the stacking order, while artwork in the bottom layer is in the back. The hierarchy of sublayers corresponds to the stacking order of the objects within a single layer.

Illustrator offers two basic ways to create new layers and sublayers. You can click the New Layer or New Sublayer command on the Layers panel menu, or you can click the Create New Layer or Create New Sublayer button on the Layers panel. Figure 1 shows a simple illustration and its corresponding layers on the Layers panel.

Duplicating Layers

In addition to creating new layers, you can duplicate existing layers by clicking the Duplicate command on the Layers panel

Figure 1 *Layers panel*

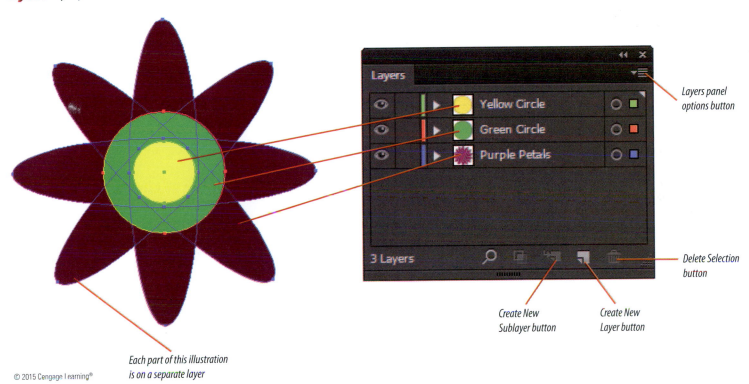

Layers panel options button

Delete Selection button

Create New Sublayer button

Create New Layer button

Each part of this illustration is on a separate layer

© 2015 Cengage Learning®

menu or by dragging a layer or sublayer onto the Create New Layer button on the Layers panel. When you duplicate a layer, all of the artwork on the layer is duplicated as well. Note the difference between this and copying and pasting artwork. When you copy and paste artwork, the copied artwork is pasted on the same layer.

Setting Layer Options

The Layer Options dialog box offers a wealth of options for working with layered artwork, many of which are not available to you unless you are working with layers. You can name a layer, and you can also set a selection color for the layer. When an object is selected, its selection marks will be the same color as specified for the layer, making it easy to differentiate layers of artwork on the artboard.

Also in the Layer Options dialog box are options for locking, unlocking, showing, and hiding artwork on the layer. When you lock a layer, all the objects on the layer are locked and protected. When the Show check box is checked, all the artwork that is contained in the layer is displayed on the artboard. When the Show check box is not checked, the artwork is hidden.

The Preview option displays all the artwork on a layer in Preview mode. When the Preview option is not activated, the artwork is displayed in Outline mode. Thus, with layers, some elements on the artboard can be in Preview mode, while others are in Outline mode.

The Print option allows you to choose whether or not to print a layer. This feature is useful for printing different versions of the same illustration. The Dim Images to option reduces the intensity of bitmap images that are placed on the artboard. Dimming a bitmap often makes it easier to trace an image.

Use the Template option when you want to trace the artwork on a layer to create a new illustration. By default, a template layer is locked and cannot be printed.

Buttons on the Layers panel represent ways to lock, unlock, hide, and show artwork on each layer, making it unnecessary to use the Layer Options dialog box to activate these functions. Clicking the Eye icon (the tool tip will display "Toggles Visibility" when you mouse over it) lets you hide and show layers, and the Lock icon lets you lock and unlock layers.

Selecting Artwork on Layers and Sublayers

The easiest way to select a layer is to click the layer name or the layer thumbnail. Selecting a layer is referred to as "targeting" a layer. When you select an object on the artboard, its layer is selected (highlighted) on the Layers panel, and the Indicates Selected Art icon (or Selected art icon for brevity) appears, as shown in Figure 2. Selecting a layer or sublayer on the Layers panel does not select the artwork on that layer.

Changes that you make to layers on the Layers panel affect the artwork on those layers. For example, if you delete a layer, the artwork on the layer will be deleted. The artwork on a layer will be duplicated if the layer is duplicated. Changing a layer's position in the layers hierarchy will move the artwork forward or backward in the stacking order.

Duplicating the artwork on the artboard does not duplicate the layer that the artwork is on. If you delete all the artwork on a layer, you are left with an empty layer. *A layer is never automatically created, copied, or deleted because of something you do to the artwork on the layer.*

The same is *not* true for sublayers. If you delete or copy artwork that is on a sublayer, the *sublayer* is deleted or copied, respectively.

Selecting All Artwork on a Layer

The Select All command makes it easy to select every object on the artboard in one step. At times, however, you will want to select every object on a layer or sublayer, but not every object on the artboard. To select all the artwork on a single layer or sublayer, select the **layer target** to the left of the Selected art icon, shown in Figure 2. You can also press and hold [Alt] (Win) or [option] (Mac) and click the layer. All objects on that layer will become selected on the artboard.

Selected art icon

Layer target (click to select all art on layer)

Selection marks for chair are red, the Chair layer's assigned color

Create a new layer

1. Open AI 5-1.ai, then save it as **Living Room**.

2. Open AI 5-2.ai, then save it as **Showroom**.

   You will work with two documents during this lesson.

3. Click the **Selection tool** , select the **chair**, then copy it.

4. Click the **Living Room.ai document tab** to activate the Living Room document.

   TIP Using the Window menu is another way to switch between open documents.

5. Click the **Layers panel icon** in the stack of collapsed icons on the right to open the Layers panel if it is not already open.

   The Layers panel shows two layers. The Empty room layer contains the artwork you see on the artboard. The objects on the Foreground layer are hidden.

6. Click the **Create New Layer button** on the Layers panel.

   A new layer named Layer 3 appears above the Foreground layer.

7. Click **Edit** on the Menu bar, then click **Paste**.

   The chair artwork is pasted into Layer 3.

8. Position the chair on the artboard as shown in Figure 3.

You created a new layer using the Create New Layer button on the Layers panel, then pasted an object onto that new layer.

Figure 3 *Chair positioned on its own layer*

Thumbnail of chair artwork on Layer 3

© 2015 Cengage Learning®

Figure 4 *Layer Options dialog box*

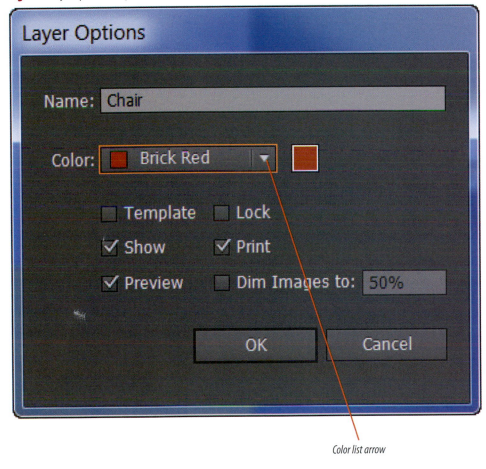

Color list arrow

Name a layer and change a layer's selection color

1. Double-click the words **Layer 3**.

   The words highlight.

2. Type **Chair** to rename the layer.

3. Double-click the **Chair layer**.

4. Click the **Color list arrow**, click **Brick Red**, as shown in Figure 4, then click **OK**.

   Note that the selection marks on the chair are now red, reflecting the new selection color for the Chair layer.

5. Deselect the chair.

You used the Layer Options dialog box to rename Layer 3 and assign it a new selection color.

Lesson 1 Create and Modify Layers

Select items on a layer and lock a layer

1. Click the **chair** with the Selection tool .

   Note that the Selected art icon appears on the Layers panel when the chair is selected, as shown in Figure 5.

   TIP The Selected art icon is the same color as its layer.

2. Deselect the chair.

   The Selected art icon disappears.

3. Press **[Alt]** (Win) or **[option]** (Mac), then click the **Chair layer** on the Layers panel.

   The chair artwork is selected.

4. Click either of the two mauve walls in the illustration.

   When an object is selected on the artboard, the layer on which the selected object is placed is highlighted on the Layers panel.

5. Double-click the **Empty room layer**, click the empty **Lock icon box** , then click **OK**.

   The Lock icon appears on the Empty room layer, indicating that all the objects on the Empty room layer are locked. See Figure 6.

   You noted the relationship between a selected item and its corresponding layer on the Layers panel. You activated the Selected art icon and selected the artwork on the Chair layer. You then locked the Empty room layer.

Figure 5 *Selected art icon identifies the layer of a selected object*

Selected art icon

Figure 6 *Lock icon identifies a locked layer*

Lock icon

Figure 7 *Foreground layer is locked and hidden*

The absence of the Eye icon indicates this layer is hidden

The Lock icon indicates that this layer is locked

Show and hide layers

1. Double-click the **Foreground layer**.
2. Click the **Color list arrow**, then click **Grass Green**.
3. Click the **Show check box**, then click **OK**.

   The objects on the Foreground layer become visible, and the Eye icon 👁 appears on the Foreground layer.
4. Click the **Eye icon** 👁 on the Foreground layer to hide the objects.
5. Click the empty **Eye icon** box ☐ on the Foreground layer to show the objects.

TIP The Eye and Lock icons appear as empty gray squares in their off state.

6. Click the empty **Lock icon** box ☐ on the Foreground layer.

   The Lock icon 🔒 appears.
7. Click the **Eye icon** 👁 on the Foreground layer to hide the objects.

   Your Layers panel should resemble Figure 7.
8. Save your work.

You used the Eye icon on the Layers panel to toggle between showing and hiding the artwork on two layers. You also locked the Foreground layer.

Manipulate Layered
ARTWORK

What You'll Do

© 2015 Cengage Learning®

In this lesson, you will learn methods for manipulating layers to change the display of layered artwork. You will change the order of layers on the panel, merge layers, work with sublayers, and move objects between layers.

Changing the Order of Layers and Sublayers

The hierarchy of the layers on the Layers panel determines how objects on the artboard overlap. All the objects on a given layer are behind the objects on the layer above it and in front of the objects on the layer beneath it. Multiple objects within a given layer overlap according to their stacking order and you can reposition them with the standard stacking order commands.

To change the position of a layer or sublayer in the hierarchy, simply drag it up or down on the panel. A thick horizontal line identifies where the layer will be repositioned, as shown in Figure 8. When you reposition a layer, its sublayers move with it.

Merging Layers

When you have positioned artwork to your liking using multiple layers and sublayers, you will often want to consolidate those layers to simplify the panel. First, you must select the layers that you want to merge. Press [Ctrl] (Win) or ⌘ (Mac) to select multiple layers. Once you have selected the layers that

you want to merge, apply the Merge Selected command on the Layers panel menu. When you merge layers, all the artwork from one or more layers moves onto the layer that was last selected before the merge.

Be careful not to confuse merging layers with condensing layers. Condensing layers is simply the process of dragging one layer into another. The repositioned layer becomes a sublayer of the layer into which it was dragged.

Defining Sublayers

Whenever you have one or more objects on a layer, you have **sublayers**. For example, if you draw a circle and a square on Layer 1, it will automatically have two sublayers—one for the square, one for the circle. The layer is comprised of its sublayers.

As soon as the first object is placed on a layer, a triangle appears to the left of the layer name, indicating that the layer contains sublayers. Click the triangle to expand the layer and see the sublayers, then click it again to collapse the layer and hide the sublayers.

Working with Sublayers

When you place grouped artwork into a layer, a sublayer is automatically created with the name <Group>. A triangle appears on the <Group> sublayer, which, when clicked, exposes the sublayers—one for every object in the group, as shown in Figure 9.

Dragging Objects Between Layers

Sublayers are easy to move between layers; you simply drag and drop a sublayer from one layer to another.

You can move artwork from one layer to another by dragging the Selected art icon. Select the artwork on the artboard that you want to move; the layer is selected, and the Selected art icon appears. Drag the button to the destination layer or sublayer, as shown in Figure 10. If you drag the Selected art icon to a layer, the artwork becomes the top sublayer in the layer. If you drag the Selected art icon to a sublayer, the artwork is grouped with the object already on the sublayer.

You have two other options for moving objects between layers. You can simply cut and paste artwork from one layer to another by selecting the object that you want to move, cutting it from the artboard, selecting the layer on which you wish to place it, then pasting. You can also use the Send to Current Layer command. Select the artwork you want to move, click the name of the destination layer to make it the active layer, click Object on the Menu bar, point to Arrange, then click Send to Current Layer. Clearly, these two methods are more time-consuming; your best option is to simply drag the Selected art icon.

Figure 8 *Changing the order of layers*

Moving a layer on the Layers panel

Figure 9 *A Group sublayer*

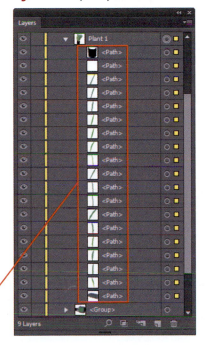

Each object in a group is placed on its own sublayer

Figure 10 *Dragging a sublayer to another layer*

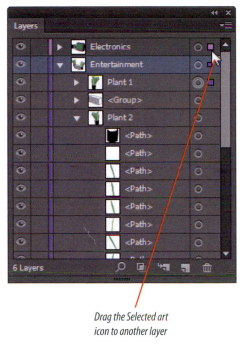

Drag the Selected art icon to another layer

Change the hierarchy of layers

1. Switch to the Showroom document, copy the rug, then return to the Living Room document.

2. Press **[Ctrl]** (Win) or ⌘ (Mac), then click the **Create New Layer button**  on the Layers panel.

    Pressing [Ctrl] (Win) or ⌘ (Mac) creates a new layer at the top of the layer list.

3. Click **Edit** on the Menu bar, then click **Paste**.

    The rug is pasted into the new layer because it is the active, or targeted, layer.

4. Name the new layer **Rug**, set the layer color to **yellow**, then position the rug artwork with a corner of it hanging slightly off the artboard, as shown in Figure 11.

5. Click and drag the **Rug layer** and position it below the Chair layer, as shown in Figure 12, then release the mouse.

    The rug artwork is now positioned below the chair artwork.

You created a new layer at the top of the Layers panel. You pasted artwork into that layer, then moved the layer below another layer in the hierarchy so that the artwork on the two layers overlapped properly on the artboard.

Figure 11 *The Rug layer is at the top of the layers hierarchy*

Figure 12 *Changing the hierarchy of layers*

Gray line appears beneath the Chair layer

© 2015 Cengage Learning®

Working with Layers

Figure 13 *Sculpture artwork positioned on top of the end table*

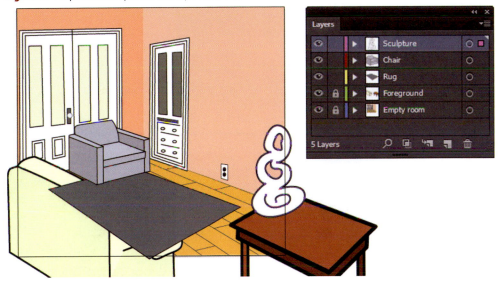

Merge layers

1. Switch to the Showroom document, copy the sculpture, then return to the Living Room document.

2. Press **[Ctrl]** (Win) or ⌘ (Mac), then click the **Create New Layer button** 🔲.

3. Paste the sculpture into the new layer, then name the layer **Sculpture**.

TIP Assign a unique color to this and all other layers you create in this lesson.

4. Show the Foreground layer, then position the sculpture artwork on the brown end table, as shown in Figure 13.

5. Deselect the sculpture, then drag the **Foreground layer** above the Sculpture layer on the Layers panel.

6. Unlock the Foreground layer.

7. Click the **Sculpture layer** to select it, press **[Ctrl]** (Win) or ⌘ (Mac), then click the **Foreground layer**.

   When merging layers, the last layer selected becomes the merged layer.

8. Click the **Layers panel options button**, then click **Merge Selected**.

   The objects from both layers are merged into the Foreground layer; the Sculpture layer is deleted.

TIP Layers must be showing and unlocked in order to be merged.

9. Compare your screen to Figure 14.

   Don't worry that your sculpture is temporarily behind the table.

You merged the Sculpture and the Foreground layers.

Figure 14 *Foreground and Sculpture layers merged*

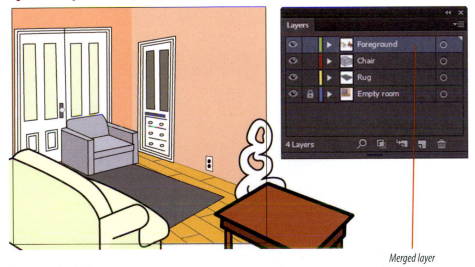

Merged layer

Lesson 2   Manipulate Layered Artwork

Work with sublayers

1. Expand the Foreground layer by clicking the **triangle** 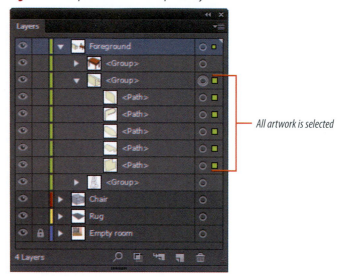 to the left of the layer.

   Three sublayers, all named <Group>, are revealed.

2. Expand the sofa <Group> sublayer by clicking the **triangle** to the left of it.

   The five paths that compose the sofa are revealed.

3. Select the **sofa artwork** on the artboard.

   The Selected art icon appears for each of the selected paths, as shown in Figure 15.

4. Click the **triangle** to the left of the sofa <Group> sublayer to collapse it, then deselect the sofa.

5. Double-click the **sofa <Group> sublayer**, then name it **Sofa**.

6. Name the sculpture sublayer **Sculpture**, then name the end table sublayer **End Table**.

7. Move the Sculpture sublayer above the End Table sublayer so that your Layers panel resembles Figure 16.

   Notice that the sculpture artwork is on top of the end table.

8. Click the **triangle** to the left of the Foreground layer to hide the three sublayers.

9. Hide the Foreground layer.

You viewed sublayers in the Foreground layer. You then renamed the three sublayers in the Foreground layer and rearranged the order of the Sculpture and the End Table sublayers.

Figure 15 *Each path in the sofa <Group> sublayer is selected*

All artwork is selected

Figure 16 *Sculpture sublayer moved above the End Table sublayer*

Working with Layers

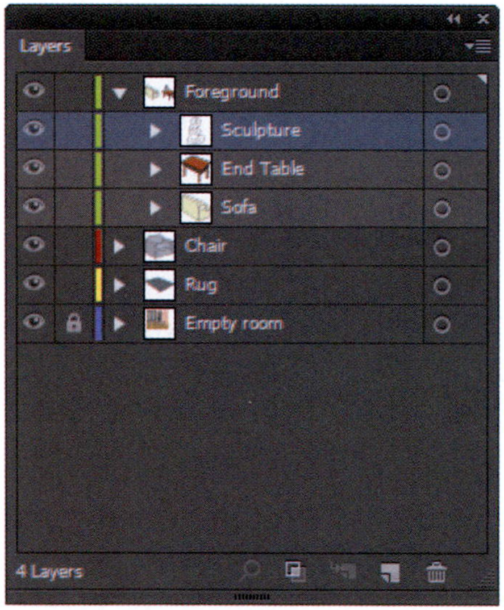

Figure 17 *Cabinet and plant are on the same layer*

Figure 18 *Moving the Plant 2 sublayer*

Plant 2 sublayer

Figure 19 *The reflected copy of the plant in position*

The new plant is positioned behind the cabinet

Figure 20 *The reflected copy of the plant, scaled and pruned*

Create new sublayers

1. Switch to the Showroom document, copy the cabinet, then return to the Living Room document.

2. Press **[Ctrl]** (Win) or ⌘ (Mac), then click the **Create New Layer button** 🔲.

3. Name the new layer **Entertainment**, select **Violet** as the layer color, then click **OK**.

4. Paste the cabinet artwork into the new layer.

5. Copy the plant from the Showroom document, then paste the plant artwork into the Entertainment layer.

6. Position the cabinet artwork and the plant artwork as shown in Figure 17.

7. Deselect all, expand the Entertainment layer, then select the **plant artwork** on the artboard.

8. Double-click the **Reflect tool** 🔧, click the **Vertical option button**, then click **Copy**.

   The reflected copy of the plant is placed on a new sublayer above the original plant sublayer.

9. Rename the new sublayer **Plant 2**.

10. Move the Plant 2 sublayer to the bottom of the Entertainment sublayer hierarchy, as shown in Figure 18.

11. Click the **Selection tool** ▸, then move the new plant artwork into the position shown in Figure 19.

12. Scale the new plant artwork 85%, delete or move some leaves on it so that it's not an obvious copy of the original plant, then compare your screen to Figure 20.

You created and moved new sublayers.

Move objects between layers

1. Switch to the Showroom document, copy the electronics images, then return to the Living Room document.

2. Create a new layer at the top of the hierarchy, name it **Electronics**, choose Magenta as its color, then click **OK**.

3. Paste the electronics on the Electronics layer, then position the electronics artwork on the cabinet.

   The plant on the right needs to be positioned in front of the electronics for the visual to be realistic.

4. Name the top sublayer in the Entertainment layer **Plant 1**, then select the **Plant 1 artwork** on the artboard.

   The Selected art icon appears in the Plant 1 sublayer.

5. Drag the **Selected art icon** from the Plant 1 sublayer to the Electronics layer, as shown in Figure 21.

   The Plant 1 sublayer moves into the Electronics layer. The Plant 1 sublayer automatically becomes the top sublayer in the Electronics layer.

6. Switch to the Showroom document, copy the Matisse, return to the Living Room document, then create a new layer at the top of the hierarchy, named **Matisse**.

7. Paste the Matisse artwork into the new layer, then position it as shown in Figure 22.

   (continued)

Figure 21 *Moving a sublayer from one layer to another*

Drag the Selected art icon to the Electronics layer

Figure 22 *The Matisse in position on its own layer*

© 2015 Cengage Learning®

Working with Layers

Figure 23 *Moving the Matisse layer into the Electronics layer*

White hand with
small rectangle

The Matisse layer
becomes a sublayer of
the Electronics layer

Figure 24 *The lamp and table in position*

New Table and
Lamp layers

Lesson 2   Manipulate Layered Artwork

8. Drag the **Matisse layer** on top of the
Electronics layer.

A white hand with a small rectangle appears
when you drag the Matisse layer on top of the
Electronics layer, as shown in Figure 23. The
Matisse layer is moved into the Electronics layer
as the topmost sublayer.

9. Create new layers for the lamp and the table,
copy and paste the lamp and table artwork
from the Showroom document to the new
layers, then position the artwork so that your
illustration resembles Figure 24.

10. Save your work.

*You created a new layer named Electronics, dragged the Plant
1 sublayer into the Electronics layer by dragging its Selected art
icon to the Electronics layer. You then moved the Matisse layer
into the Electronics layer by dragging it on top of the Electronics
layer and created new layers for the table and the lamp.*

Work with Layered
ARTWORK

What You'll Do

© 2015 Cengage Learning®

▶ *In this lesson, you will explore options for managing your work using the Layers panel.*

Using the View Buttons on the Layers Panel

The view options available on the Layers panel make working with layers a smart choice for complex illustrations. You can target specific viewing options to each layer in the document. Without layers, your options for viewing your work are limited to the Hide and Show All commands on the Object menu.

The Eye icon makes it easy to change what can be seen on the artboard. Clicking this icon once hides all the artwork on a layer, and the icon disappears. Clicking the empty gray square where the icon was shows all of the artwork on the layer, and the Eye icon reappears. Pressing [Alt] (Win) or [option] (Mac) and clicking the Eye icon once shows all layers. Clicking a second time hides all layers except for the layer you clicked.

Pressing [Ctrl] (Win) or ⌘ (Mac) and clicking the Eye icon toggles between Outline and Preview modes and all the artwork on the layer will switch between outlined and filled objects. Pressing [Alt] [Ctrl] (Win) or [option] (Mac) and clicking the Eye icon switches all other layers between Outline and Preview modes.

Importing a Photoshop File with Layers

When you use the Open command to import a layered Photoshop file into Illustrator CC, you have the option to open that file with its layers intact. In the Photoshop Import Options dialog box that appears, click the Convert Layers to Objects option button, then click OK. Display the Illustrator Layers panel and you will see that Illustrator has preserved as much of the Photoshop layer structure as possible.

Locating an Object on the Layers Panel

With complex illustrations, layers and sublayers tend to multiply—so much so that you will often find it easiest to work with collapsed layers, those in which you hide the sublayers. Sometimes it can be difficult to identify an object's layer or sublayer, especially if there are multiple copies of the object in the illustration. The Locate Object command offers a simple solution. Select an object on the artboard, click the Layers panel options button, then click Locate Object. The layers expand, revealing their sublayers, and the selected object's layer or sublayer is selected.

Reversing the Order of Layers

Another option that the Layers panel offers for managing your artwork is the ability to reverse the order of layers. Select the layers whose order you want to reverse. Press [Shift] to select multiple contiguous (those next to each other on the panel) layers. Press [Ctrl] (Win) or [⌘] (Mac) to select multiple noncontiguous layers. Click the Layers panel options button, then click Reverse Order.

Making Layers Nonprintable

The ability to choose whether or not to print the artwork on a specific layer is useful, especially during the middle stages of producing an illustration. For example, you could print just the text elements and give them to a copy editor for proofing. You could

print just the elements of the illustration that are ready to be shown to the client, holding back the elements that still need work. See Figure 25 for the Print option in the Layer Options dialog box.

Another value of the print option is the ability to print different versions of a document. Let's say you're working on the design of a poster for a client, and you've finalized the artwork but you're still undecided about the typeface for the headline after narrowing down the choices to five typefaces. You could create five layers, one for the headline formatted in each typeface. Then you would print the

illustration five times, each with a different headline. This is a smart and simple way to produce comps quickly.

Exporting Illustrator Layers to Photoshop

You can export Illustrator layers to Photoshop. Click File on the Menu bar, click Export, then choose Photoshop (PSD) as the file format. When the Photoshop Export Options dialog box opens, verify that the Color Model is set to CMYK and that the Write Layers option button is selected. Click OK to export the layers to a Photoshop document.

Figure 25 *Print option in the Layer Options dialog box*

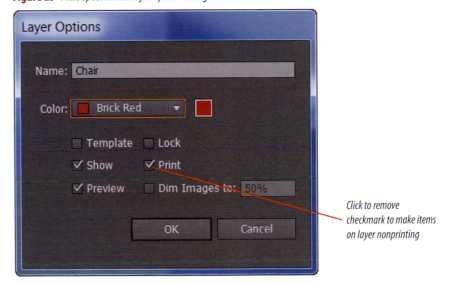

Click to remove checkmark to make items on layer nonprinting

Explore view options on the Layers panel

1. Collapse the Electronics and Entertainment layers, then hide them.

2. Press and hold **[Alt]** (Win) or **[option]** (Mac), then click the **Eye icon**  on the Chair layer.

   All of the layers are displayed.

3. Using the same keyboard commands, click the **Eye icon** on the Chair layer again.

   All layers, except for the Chair layer, are hidden.

4. Using the same keyboard commands, click the **Eye icon** (in its off state) on the Chair layer again so that all of the layers are displayed.

5. Move the Foreground layer to the top of the hierarchy.

6. Press **[Ctrl]** (Win) or ⌘ (Mac), then click the **Eye icon** on the Chair layer.

   The artwork on the Chair layer switches to Outline mode.

7. Using the same keyboard commands, click the **Eye icon** on the Chair layer again.

8. Press **[Alt] [Ctrl]** (Win) or **[option]** ⌘ (Mac), then click the same **Eye icon**.

   The artwork on every layer, except for the Chair layer, switches to Outline mode, as shown in Figure 26.

9. Using the same keyboard commands, click the **Eye icon** again.

You learned keyboard commands to explore view options on the Layers panel.

Figure 26 *The Chair layer shown in Preview mode and all other layers shown in Outline mode*

Working with Layers

Figure 27 *Duplicating the Lamp layer*

To duplicate a layer and its contents, drag it on top of the Create New Layer button

Figure 28 *Positioning the second lamp*

Lesson 3   Work with Layered Artwork

Locate, duplicate, and delete layers

1. Select the **Plant 2 artwork** on the artboard.
2. Click the **Layers panel options button**, then click **Locate Object**.

   The Entertainment layer expands, as does the Plant 2 sublayer.

   TIP The Locate Object command is useful when you are working with collapsed layers or with many layers and sublayers.

3. Collapse the Entertainment layer.
4. Select the **Lamp layer**, then drag it on top of the Create New Layer button 📲, as shown in Figure 27.

   The Lamp layer and its contents are duplicated onto a new layer that is created above the original lamp layer. The copied lamp artwork is positioned directly on top of the original lamp artwork.

5. Position the duplicated lamp artwork on the artboard, as shown in Figure 28.
6. Drag the **Lamp copy layer** to the Delete Selection button 🗑 on the Layers panel.

You used the Locate Object command to identify a selected object's position on the Layers panel. You duplicated a layer, then deleted it.

Dim placed images

1. Hide all layers, then create a new layer at the top of the hierarchy, named **Photo**.

2. Click **File** on the Menu bar, then click **Place**.

3. Navigate to the drive and folder where your Data Files are stored, click **Living Room Original.tif**, then click **Place**.

   The source for the illustration is placed on its own layer.

4. Align the photo with the top-left corner of the artboard, as shown in Figure 29.

5. Double-click the **Photo layer**, click the **Dim Images to check box**, type **50** in the Dim Images to text box, then click **OK**.

   The placed image is less vivid.

TIP Dimming a placed image is useful for tracing.

You created a new layer, placed a photo on the new layer, then used the Layer Options dialog box to dim the photo 50%.

Figure 29 *The source of the illustration, placed on its own layer*

Figure 30 *Using a layer for a message to the printer*

Printer: Use photo for reference if necessary. Thank you!
Call me at 555-1234 if any problems.

Exclude specific layers from printing

1. Create a new layer at the top of the hierarchy, named **Message**.
2. Using any font you like, type a message for the printer, as shown in Figure 30.
3. Convert the message text to outlines. Double-click the **Message layer**, remove the check mark from the Print check box, then click **OK**.

   The Message layer will not print to any output device.

   TIP When a layer is set not to print, its name is italicized on the Layers panel.

4. Make the Photo layer nonprintable.
5. Hide the Message and Photo layers.
6. Make all the other layers visible.
7. Save your work.

You created a new layer called Message, typed a message for the printer, then designated the Message and Photo layers as nonprintable. You then displayed all of the layers except for the Message and Photo layers.

Create a
CLIPPING SET

What You'll Do

© 2015 Cengage Learning®

In this lesson, you will create a clipping mask on a sublayer that will mask the other sublayers in the layer.

Working with Clipping Sets

Adobe uses the terms "clipping mask" and "clipping path" interchangeably. The term **clipping set** is used to distinguish clipping paths used in layers from clipping paths used to mask nonlayered artwork. There's no difference; it's just terminology. Essentially, the term "clipping set" refers to the clipping mask *and* the masked sublayers as a unit.

The following rules apply to clipping sets:

- The clipping mask and the objects to be masked must be in the same layer.
- You cannot use a sublayer as a clipping mask, unless it is a <Group> sublayer. However, the top sublayer in a layer becomes the clipping mask if you first select the layer that the sublayer is in, then create the clipping mask.

- The top object in the clipping set becomes the mask for every object below it in the layer.
- A <Group> sublayer can be a clipping set. The top object in the group will function as the mask.
- Dotted lines between sublayers indicate that they are included in a clipping set.

Flattening Artwork

When you apply the Flatten Artwork command, all visible objects in the artwork are consolidated in a single layer. Before applying the command, select the layer into which you want to consolidate the artwork. If you have a layer that is hidden, you will be asked whether to make the artwork visible so that it can be flattened into the layer or delete the layer and the artwork on it.

Figure 31 *The new <Path> sublayer*

The rectangle is placed on a new sublayer called <Path>, on top of the other sublayers in the Foreground layer

Figure 32 *Clipping path masks only the objects on its own layer*

© 2015 Cengage Learning® Photo Courtesy of Chris Botello.

Clipping path

Lesson 4 Create a Clipping Set

Create clipping sets

1. Select the **Foreground layer**, click the **Rectangle tool** ▢ , then create a rectangle that is 6.5" wide by 6" tall.

2. Position the rectangle so that it aligns exactly with the edges of the artboard.

3. Apply a black stroke to the rectangle and no fill color.

4. Expand the Foreground layer.

 The rectangle, identified as <Path>, is at the top of the sublayers, as shown in Figure 31.

5. Click the **Make/Release Clipping Mask button** ▣ on the Layers panel.

 Any path on the Foreground layer that is positioned off the artboard is masked. The part of the rug that extends beyond the artboard is not masked, because it is not in the same layer as the clipping path. The lamp, too, extends beyond the artboard and is not masked, as shown in Figure 32.

You created a rectangle, then used it as a clipping path to mask the sublayers below it in its layer.

Copy a clipping mask and flatten artwork

1. Click the **Layer target button** ⊙ on the **<Clipping Path> sublayer** to select the artwork.

2. Click **Edit** on the Menu bar, click **Copy**, click **Edit** on the Menu bar again, then click **Paste in Front**.

   A new sublayer named <Path> is created. The rectangle on the <Clipping Path> sublayer is duplicated on the new <Path> sublayer and can be used to mask other layers.

3. Drag the **Selected art icon** ▣ on the <Path> sublayer down to the Rug layer, as shown in Figure 33.

4. Expand the Rug layer to see the new <Path> sublayer, select the **Rug layer**, then click the **Make/Release Clipping Mask button** ▣.

   Compare your Layers panel to Figure 34. The <Path> sublayer becomes the <Clipping Path> sublayer, and the rectangle on the <Clipping Path> sublayer is used to mask the rug on the artboard.

(continued)

Figure 33 *Moving the copy of the rectangle to the Rug layer*

Drag the Selected art icon to the Rug layer

Figure 34 *Using the duplicate rectangle to mask the rug*

The <Path> sublayer becomes the <Clipping Path> sublayer, and the rectangle on the <Clipping Path> sublayer is used to mask the rug on the artboard

Figure 35 *Completed illustration*

Lesson 4 Create a Clipping Set

5. Select the **lamp artwork** on the artboard, drag the **Selected art icon** on the Lamp layer to the Sculpture sublayer of the Foreground layer, then deselect all.

   The lamp artwork moves to the Sculpture sublayer and is therefore masked. Deselect the lamp and your illustration should resemble Figure 35.

TIP When you drag the Selected art icon from one layer to another, the selected artwork moves to the new layer, but the layer does not move.

6. Select the **empty Lamp layer**, then click the **Delete Selection button** on the Layers panel.

7. Click **File** on the Menu bar, then click **Save**.

8. Select the **Foreground layer**, click the **Layers panel options button**, click **Flatten Artwork**, then click **Yes** when you are asked whether or not you want to discard the hidden art on the hidden layers.

9. Click **File** on the Menu bar, click **Save As**, then save the file as **Living Room Flat**.

   Note that we saved the flattened version as a separate file and saved the original Living Room.ai file with all layers intact. Whenever you flatten a layered document, save the flattened version as a copy so that you can preserve your original layered file.

10. Close Showroom.ai and Living Room flat.ai, saving any changes if prompted.

You made a copy of the rectangle, moved the copied rectangle to the Rug layer, then made it into a clipping path to mask the rug artwork. You then moved the lamp artwork into the Sculpture sublayer, which masked the lamp. You deleted the empty Lamp layer and flattened all of the artwork on the Foreground layer.

Create and modify layers.

1. Open AI 5-3.ai, then save it as **Gary**.
2. Create a new layer at the top of the layer hierarchy, named **Text**.
3. Create a new layer at the top of the layer hierarchy, named **Gary Garlic**.
4. Rename Layer 2 **Body Parts**.
5. Save your work.

Manipulate layered artwork.

1. Move the garlic artwork into the Gary Garlic layer.
2. Move the three text groups onto the Text layer.
3. Merge the Background layer with the Box Shapes layer so that the Box Shapes layer is the name of the resulting merged layer. (*Hint*: Click the Background layer, press [Ctrl] (Win) or [⌘] (Mac), click the Box Shapes layer, click the Layers panel options button, then click Merge Selected.)
4. Move the Body Parts layer to the top of the layer hierarchy.
5. Save your work.

Work with layered artwork.

1. View each layer separately to identify the artwork on each.
2. Using Figure 36 as a guide, assemble Gary Garlic.
3. Merge the Gary Garlic and Body Parts layers so that the resulting merged layer will be named Body Parts.
4. Select all the artwork on the Body Parts layer, then group the artwork.
5. Save your work.

Create a clipping set.

1. Target the Box Shapes layer.
2. Create a rectangle that is 5" wide by 8" in height.
3. Position the rectangle so that it is centered on the artboard.
4. With the rectangle still selected, expand the Box Shapes layer on the Layers panel.
5. Click the Make/Release Clipping Mask button on the Layers panel.
6. Reposition the masked elements (text and box parts) so that your illustration resembles Figure 36.
7. Save your work, then close Gary.

Figure 36 *Completed Skills Review*

You are designing an outdoor sign for Xanadu Haircutters, a salon that recently opened in your town. You are pleased with your concept of using scissors to represent the X in Xanadu, and decide to design the logo with different typefaces so that the client will feel she has some input into the final design.

1. Open AI 5-4.ai, then save it as **Xanadu**.
2. Create a new layer, then move the ANADU headline into that layer.
3. Make four duplicates of the new layer.
4. Change the typeface on four of the layers, for a total of five versions of the logo type.
5. Rename each type layer, using the name of the typeface you chose.
6. Rename Layer 1 **Xanadu Art**.
7. View the Xanadu Art layer five times, each time with one of the typeface layers, so that you can see five versions of the logo.
8. Save your work, compare your illustration with Figure 37, then close Xanadu.

Figure 37 *Completed Project Builder 1*

Working with Layers

You are the Creative Director for a Los Angeles design firm that specializes in identity packages for television networks. One of your most important projects this week is delivering the first round of comps for a new cable channel, Milty TV. Your art directors have come up with two concepts—one dark, one light. You decide to bring each to the client with two options for typography, for a total of four comps.

1. Open AI 5-5.ai, then save it as **Milty TV**.
2. Select the four pieces of artwork that comprise the television at the top of the artboard, then group them.

3. Group the four pieces of artwork at the bottom of the artboard, then cut them.
4. Create a new layer, name it **Orange**, then paste the artwork.
5. Position the orange artwork exactly on top of the blue artwork on the artboard so that it is covered.
6. Rename Layer 1 **Blue**, then duplicate the layer and name it **Blue Two**.
7. Duplicate the Orange layer, then name it **Orange Two**.
8. Deselect all, use the Direct Selection tool to select the large M on the Orange Two layer, change its typeface to Cooper Std, then hide the two Orange layers.

(*Hint*: If you do not have Cooper Std as a typeface, choose another one.)
9. Select the Blue Two layer, change the M to Cooper Std, then hide it.
10. View each of the four layers separately. You created two versions of each design.
11. Save your work, compare your Orange Two layer to Figure 38, then close Milty TV.

Figure 38 *Completed Project Builder 2*

Working with Layers

You are a freelance designer, working out of your house. The owner of the town's largest plumbing company, Straight Flush, has hired you to redesign his logo. He gives you an Illustrator file with a design created by his son. You study the logo, then decide that it lacks cohesion and focus.

1. Open AI 5-6.ai, then save it as **Straight Flush**.
2. Group the elements of each playing card together.
3. Create four new layers.
4. Move each card to the layer with the corresponding number in the layer name.
5. Select all the layers, click the Layers panel options button, then click Reverse Order.
6. Reposition the cards on each layer so that they are in order, directly behind the ace.
7. Adjust the layout of the cards to your liking to create a new layout for the logo.
8. Save your work, compare your illustration with Figure 39, then close Straight Flush.

Figure 39 *Completed Design Project*

You are a fabric designer for a line of men's clothing. You are asked to supervise a team that will design new patterns for men's ties. Now that you have studied working with layers, how would you approach building a file that shows three patterns for a tie?

1. Open AI 5-7.ai, then save it as **Tie Pattern**.
2. Select various objects to see how the file has been built.
3. Ask yourself how the document would be more practical if it were built with layers.
4. How many masks would be required to show the three patterns?
5. How many layers would be required?
6. Redesign the document with layers so that the three patterns are all in one clipping set with one tie shape functioning as the mask.
7. Save your work, compare your Layers panel with Figure 40, then close Tie Pattern.

Figure 40 *Completed Portfolio Project*

CHAPTER **1**

INTEGRATING ILLUSTRATOR, PHOTOSHOP, AND INDESIGN

1. Copy and paste from Illustrator to Photoshop
2. Export layers from Illustrator to Photoshop
3. Create a Chisel Hard Emboss layer style
4. Create a Stamp Visible layer
5. Create a Smooth Emboss layer style
6. Create and apply a gradient overlay to a layer style
7. Create a Pillow Emboss layer style
8. Copy layer styles between layers
9. Add an Outer Glow layer style
10. Apply blending modes
11. Create an InDesign output file

CHAPTER 1

INTEGRATING ILLUSTRATOR, PHOTOSHOP, AND INDESIGN

Introduction

Adobe Photoshop and Adobe Illustrator have always been closely related—so much so that many users refer to them as "sister" applications. Adobe added InDesign as the much-needed layout component, thus creating the Adobe trinity of Photoshop, Illustrator, and InDesign.

With Photoshop and Illustrator bundled together with InDesign, the relationship between the Adobe trinity is seamless—and powerful. In this chapter, you'll explore some very important techniques for integrating the three applications. Starting with an Illustrator file, you'll export layers to Photoshop, and use the Illustrator artwork as a basis for a stunning Photoshop illustration. Then, you'll use InDesign as a layout and output solution to create a PDF file of the illustration, complete with crop marks, bleeds and printer's marks.

Working together, the power of all three software applications is magnified. This chapter will help you begin to see how the three Creative Cloud applications work together as one entity, providing all the solutions you need for designing and producing great graphics.

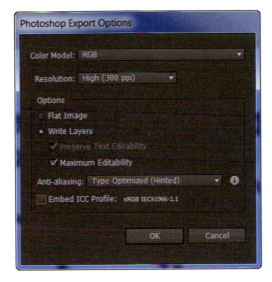

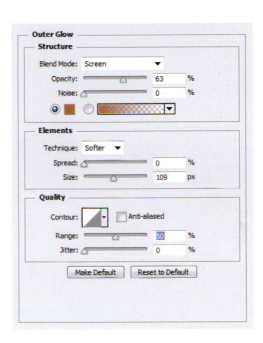

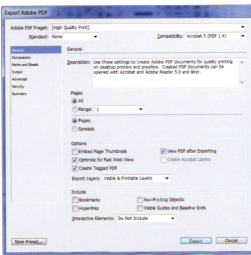

Copy and Paste from
ILLUSTRATOR TO PHOTOSHOP

What You'll Do

In this lesson, you will explore three options for placing an Illustrator graphic into Photoshop.

Moving Graphics Between Programs

Adobe Illustrator is an articulate and powerful software package, but many professional designers are so Photoshop-oriented that they completely ignore Illustrator. They tell themselves that Photoshop can do everything that Illustrator can do—and that's just not true.

Illustrator offers many smart and sophisticated options for working with paths and typography. Incorporate Illustrator into your skills set, and you'll soon find that you're producing typography and graphics that are more interesting and sophisticated than what most other designers are coming up with in Photoshop. That's a sweet edge to have in the competitive world of graphic design.

The key, of course, is moving graphics from Illustrator into Photoshop—into the photographic artwork. Using Illustrator, it's as easy as Copy/Paste.

Figure 1 *Pasting art from Illustrator into Photoshop*

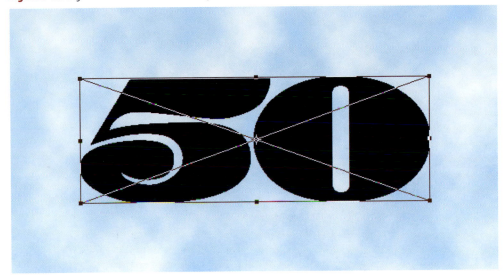

Pasting from Illustrator to Photoshop

When pasting from Illustrator to Photoshop, it's a good idea to keep the File Handling & Clipboard preferences as they are set in Step 2. With these settings, you are offered the Paste dialog box when you paste Illustrator artwork into Photoshop. Without these settings, copied artwork is automatically rasterized when pasted in Photoshop.

AICB stands for Adobe Illustrator Clipboard. The phrase (no transparency support) refers to the fact that the artwork you are copying from Illustrator will be flattened when pasted—in other words, you're not copying layers. This is not a problem for most Illustrator artwork, especially artwork which, as in this case, you are using as simple base art for Photoshop.

Copy and paste from Illustrator to Photoshop

1. Open AI 1-1.ai in Illustrator, click **Edit** (Win) or **Illustrator** (Mac) on the Menu bar, point to **Preferences**, then click **File Handling & Clipboard**.

2. In the Clipboard on Quit section, verify that the PDF and the AICB (no transparency support) check boxes are both checked and that only the Preserve Paths option button is selected, then click **OK**.

3. Click the **Selection tool** , select the two numbers, then copy them.

4. Start Photoshop, open PS 1-2.psd in Photoshop, then save it as **Paste from Illustrator**.

5. Display the Layers panel, if necessary.

6. Click **Edit** on the Menu bar, then click **Paste**.

   The Paste dialog box appears, offering you four options for pasting. We will explore the Pixels, Path, and Shape Layer options in this chapter.

7. Click the **Pixels option button**, then click **OK**.

   As shown in Figure 1, the artwork is pasted in a bounding box, which can be resized, rotated, and so on.

   (continued)

8. Click the **Move tool** , then click **Place** in the dialog box that appears.

   When you paste as pixels, the result of the paste is a bitmap graphic, which is pasted as a new layer. No vector information is pasted with the graphic.

9. Delete the new layer.

10. Click **Edit** on the Menu bar, click **Paste**, click the **Path option button**, then click **OK**.

    As shown in Figure 2, the path from Illustrator is pasted; a new layer is not created.

11. Click **Window** on the Menu bar, click **Paths**, then note that the path was pasted as a new Work Path on the Paths panel.

12. Click below the Work Path on the Paths panel to turn the Work Path off.

    The path disappears.

(continued)

Figure 2   *Pasting an Illustrator path as a path in Photoshop*

Integrating Illustrator, Photoshop, and InDesign

Figure 3 *Pasting an Illustrator path as a shape layer in Photoshop*

13. Change the foreground color to any red swatch on the Swatches panel.

14. Paste again, click the **Shape Layer option button**, then click **OK**.

    As shown in Figure 3, the artwork is pasted as a shape layer and uses the foreground color as its fill.

    Shape layers are vector graphics positioned on layers in a Photoshop document. As vectors, they can be scaled and otherwise transformed without any loss in quality. This makes shape layers ideal for handling paths from Illustrator.

15. Save your work, close AI 1-1.ai, then close the Paste from Illustrator document.

You explored three options for pasting Adobe Illustrator graphics in Adobe Photoshop: pasting as pixels, pasting as a path, and pasting as a shape layer.

Export Layers from
ILLUSTRATOR TO PHOTOSHOP

What You'll Do

In this lesson, you will export a layered Illustrator file as a layered Photoshop file.

Never forget that Photoshop and Illustrator are remarkably compatible. Incorporating the power of Illustrator into your Photoshop skills set expands your overall skills set as a designer exponentially. Indeed, when you are as fluent in Illustrator as you are in Photoshop, you'll find that much of the artwork you want to create in Photoshop is often best started in Illustrator, with all of its great drawing tools and precise typographical abilities.

With each upgrade, Adobe has strived to make Photoshop and Illustrator more and more compatible. One of the best features of that compatibility is the ability to export layered artwork from Illustrator to Photoshop while maintaining the layer structure created in Illustrator. This is an amazing feature and bravo to Adobe for putting it in place. Once you've created layered artwork in Illustrator, this powerful option allows you to target those layers individually after the artwork has been exported to Photoshop. In other words, you maintain the same working relationship with the artwork from one application to the other.

Figure 4 *Export dialog box*

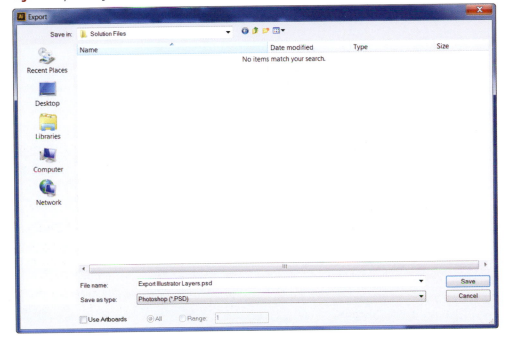

Export layers from Illustrator to Photoshop

1. Open AI 1-3.ai in Adobe Illustrator, then save it as **Export Illustrator Layers**.

   TIP Click OK to accept the defaults in the Illustrator Options dialog box.

2. Display the Layers panel, click the **Selection tool** then pull the individual pieces of the illustration apart, keeping an eye on the Layers panel.

3. Click **File** on the Menu bar, click **Revert**, then click **Revert** in the dialog box that follows.

4. Click **File** on the Menu bar, then click **Export**.

5. Click the **Save as type list arrow** (Win) or the **Format list arrow** (Mac) in the Export dialog box, then click **Photoshop (*.PSD)** (Win) or **Photoshop (psd)** (Mac), as shown in Figure 4.

   TIP Note that the file to be exported is automatically named with the .psd extension: Export Illustrator Layers.psd.

(continued)

6. Click **Export**.

The Photoshop Export Options dialog box opens.

7. Click the **Color Model list arrow**, click **RGB**, click the **Resolution list arrow**, then click **High (300 ppi)**.

It is important to understand that, with this export, you are creating a Photoshop file. The choices you made in this step determine the color model of the file—RGB—and the resolution of the file—300 ppi.

8. In the Options section, click the **Write Layers option button** to select it, click the **Maximum Editability check box** to select it, then make sure that the Embed ICC Profile check box is not selected so that your dialog box resembles Figure 5.

With these choices, you have specified that you want to save or "write" the layers from the Illustrator file to the Photoshop file and that you want the artwork to be anti-aliased in the Photoshop file.

(continued)

Figure 5 *Photoshop Export Options dialog box*

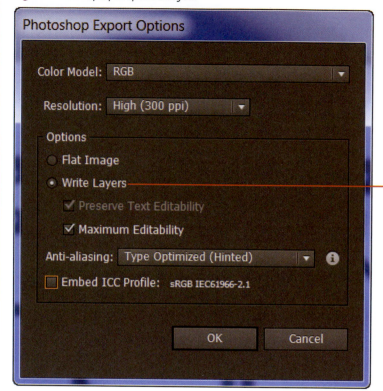

Write Layers option specifies that Illustrator layers will be exported

Figure 6 *Illustrator artwork and layers exported to Photoshop*

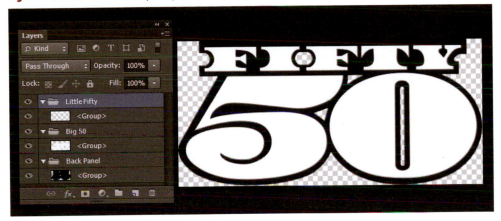

Applying a Feather to a Selection

When you apply a feather to a selection then delete the selected pixels, remember that the pixels at the edge of the selection are not deleted entirely—because of the feather. Sometimes, as in this case, deleting twice is a good move. When working with a larger selection and a higher feather value, you might want to delete three times.

9. Click **OK**, then close the Illustrator document.

10. Switch to Photoshop, then open Export Illustrator Layers.psd.

11. Notice that the layers from Illustrator—including their layer names—were exported onto the Photoshop Layers panel, as shown in Figure 6.

12. Close Export Illustrator Layers.psd.

You exported a layered Illustrator file as a layered Photoshop file. When you opened the file in Photoshop, you saw that all the layers and layered artwork in Illustrator were exported to the Photoshop file.

Create a Chisel Hard
EMBOSS LAYER STYLE

What You'll Do

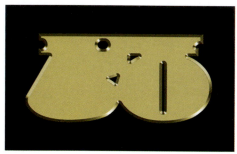

In this lesson, you will use a Bevel & Emboss layer style to apply a chiseled edge to the artwork.

Chisel Hard Emboss, the first of many layer styles you'll experiment and work with in this chapter, creates a dramatic, three-dimensional effect. A chisel is anything but a gentle tool, and this layer style delivers exactly what its name implies: a chiseled effect with a hard edge. Chisel Hard Emboss, a subset of the Bevel & Emboss layer style, is a very useful layer style, one that you will use often, especially when you want to create the effect of a hard metal edge.

Create a Chisel Hard Emboss layer style

1. Open PS 1-4.psd, then save it as **Fifty 50**.

2. Hide the Little Fifty layer and the Big 50 layer, then target the **Back Panel layer**.

3. Change the name of the layer from Back Panel to **Chisel Hard Emboss**.

4. Click **Layer** on the Menu bar, point to **Layer Style**, then click **Bevel & Emboss**.

5. Verify that the Preview check box is checked, then move the dialog box so that you can see as much of the artwork as possible.

(continued)

Saving Settings for Layer Styles

Once you've specified settings for a layer style, Photoshop allows you to make those settings the default for that type of layer style. This can be enormously useful for saving time from entering the same settings over and over, and it helps you to be sure that your work is consistent. For example, let's say you design a monthly newsletter for a client, and in that newsletter all the photos have a drop shadow. You could save the settings for the drop shadow as a default that you can use time and time again. You can save default settings for every layer style so, theoretically, you could have a default Bevel & Emboss, a default Inner Shadow, a default Outer Glow, etc. Once you've entered settings, simply click the Make Default button in the Layer Style dialog box. Click the Reset to Default button at any time to restore the original Photoshop defaults for the style.

6. Verify that Style is set to Inner Bevel in the Structure section.

7. Click the **Technique list arrow**, then click **Chisel Hard**.

8. Drag the **Size slider** to 29, then experiment by dragging the slider to different values.

9. Return the **Size slider** to 29.

10. Type **42** in the Angle text box.

    The angle determines the angle that the light source strikes the artwork.

11. Experiment with various angle values, then return to **42**.

12. Click the **Gloss Contour list arrow**, then click **Ring** (the second thumbnail in the second row).

    Gloss contours are preset curves—just like the curves you use to color correct an image— that dramatically affect the contrast and the appearance of the layer effect. Explore the other contours, but be sure to return to Ring.

    (continued)

Figure 7 *Bevel & Emboss settings in the Layer Style dialog box*

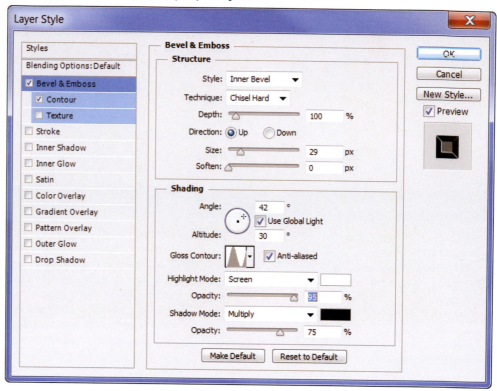

Figure 8 *Effect of applying the Chisel Hard Inner Bevel layer style*

13. Click the **Anti-aliased check box**, and note the effect on the artwork.

14. For a dramatic effect, increase the contrast by dragging the **Highlight Mode Opacity slider** to 95%.

15. Click the **Contour check box** directly beneath the Bevel & Emboss check box in the Styles section on the left.

    Like a gloss contour, the Contour check box applies a preset curve.

16. Compare your Layer Style dialog box to Figure 7.

17. Click **OK**, then compare your canvas to Figure 8.

18. Save your work.

You used a Bevel & Emboss layer style to apply a chiseled edge to the artwork.

Create a Stamp
VISIBLE LAYER

What You'll Do

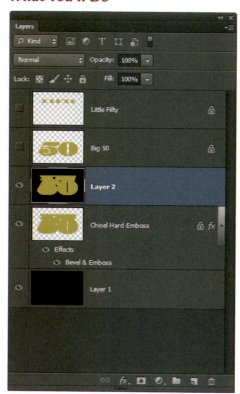

In this lesson, you will use the Stamp Visible command to create a copy of the entire canvas as a flattened layer.

A Stamp Visible layer copies the entire canvas in its current status, then creates a new layer with the artwork flattened onto one layer.

When you're working with complex layered art, a Stamp Visible layer can be very effective for putting all of your artwork on one layer, then working from there to apply new effects. Note the word "visible" in the term. When you create a Stamp Visible layer, the entire canvas is copied. Thus, only the visible artwork will be included in the new layer. Artwork on hidden layers will not be "stamped."

Figure 9 *Using the Stamp Visible command*

Copy of all
visible layers

Create a Stamp Visible layer

1. Verify that the Chisel Hard Emboss layer is targeted on the Layers panel and that the Bevel & Emboss layer style is showing.

2. Press [**Shift**][**Alt**][**Ctrl**][**E**] (Win) or [**Shift**][**option**] ⌘ [**E**] (Mac).

   This keyboard sequence is called Stamp Visible. As shown in Figure 9, it takes a picture of the document in its current visible state, then places it in a new layer. You have created a merged copy without merging the Chisel Hard Emboss layer style on its original layer.

3. Click the **Magic Wand tool** ![magic wand icon], set the Tolerance to **0**, click to select the **Anti-alias** and **Contiguous check boxes** on the Options bar, then click to select the **gold interior** of the artwork in the new layer.

4. Click **Select** on the Menu bar, then click **Inverse**.

5. Press **Delete** to delete the selected pixels.

6. Deselect, then save your work.

You used a keyboard command to create a Stamp Visible layer, thus creating a copy of the canvas as flattened artwork on a layer. You then used the Magic Wand tool to select a specific area of the flattened artwork and removed all other pixels.

Create a Smooth
EMBOSS LAYER STYLE

What You'll Do

▶ *In this lesson, you will use the Bevel & Emboss layer style again to create a different effect.*

In the early days of computer graphics, naysayers dismissed computer-generated art as automated and monotonous. Their idea was that you take some artwork, run a filter, and what you get is what you get. Of course, that is an extremely limited view of computer graphics. What it overlooks is that computer graphic design is not about "running a filter"—anybody can do that.

Computer graphic design is about knowing all the utilities that you have at your disposal and, even more challenging, knowing how and when to use those tools to create an image that you have in your imagination. This lesson will provide you with a great example of using two different layer styles—each from the same dialog box—and making them work in tandem to create unique artwork.

Figure 10 *Settings for the Smooth Emboss layer style*

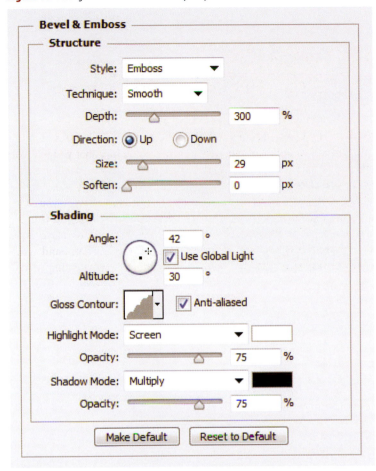

1. Rename Layer 2 **Smooth Emboss**, then verify that nothing is selected on the canvas.

2. Create a Bevel & Emboss layer style.

3. Set the Style to **Emboss**, set the Technique to **Smooth**, then set the Depth to **300**.

4. Drag the **Size slider** to **29**.

5. Click the **Gloss Contour list arrow**, then click **Rounded Steps**, the fifth icon in the second row.

6. Click the **Anti-aliased check box**, compare your Layer Style dialog box to Figure 10, then click **OK**.

TIP For the exercises in this chapter, and usually for all the gloss contours you apply in your own work, activate the Anti-aliased option.

(continued)

7. Hide the Chisel Hard Emboss layer so that you can see the Smooth Emboss layer on its own.

As shown in Figure 11, the Smooth Emboss effect is dramatically different than the Chisel Hard Emboss effect. Both feature a beveled edge, but where the Chisel Hard Emboss effect features a hard, shiny edge, the Smooth Emboss effect presents a much softer edge—thus the term Smooth Emboss.

(continued)

Figure 11 *Smooth Emboss effect*

Figure 12 *Viewing the relationship between the two layer styles*

8. Show the Chisel Hard Emboss layer, then hide and show the Smooth Emboss layer.
9. Show both embossed layers, then compare your canvas to Figure 12.

You used the Bevel & Emboss layer style to create a smooth emboss effect.

Create and Apply a Gradient
OVERLAY TO A LAYER STYLE

What You'll Do

 In this lesson, you will apply a gradient overlay to the artwork.

In most illustrations in which gradients are utilized, the gradient is often an element that calls attention to itself. By its very nature, it has movement—the shift from one color to other colors—and that movement is often noticeable. In this lesson, you're going to use a gradient overlay for a very subtle effect: to enrich the Smooth Emboss you created in the previous lesson. You'll see how the gradient overlay adds complexity to the layer style effect and how it contributes to the metallic effects that are the key to this illustration. But there's a little twist. As you go through the later lessons in this chapter, you'll see that the gradient overlay will be covered mostly by other elements. In the final version of the illustration, it will be interesting for you to note the very subtle role that this gradient overlay ultimately plays.

Integrating Illustrator, Photoshop, and InDesign

Figure 13 *Adding a gradient overlay*

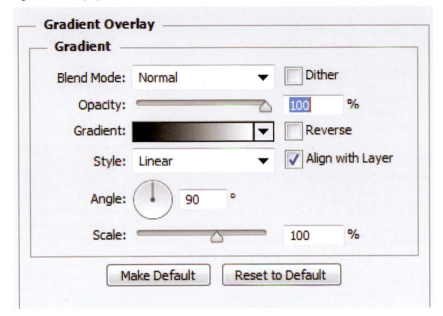

Create and apply a gradient overlay to a layer style

1. Double-click the **Effects sublayer** in the Smooth Emboss layer group.

   The Layer Style dialog box opens.

2. Click the words **Gradient Overlay** in the Styles section to highlight it.

   As shown in Figure 13, a default black-and-white gradient is applied to the Smooth Emboss layer style. Note its effect on the Smooth Emboss.

3. Click the **black-and-white gradient** in the Gradient section.

4. Double-click the **first color stop** on the bottom of the gradient ramp, type **41** in the R, G, and B text boxes, then click **OK**.

5. Double-click the **second color stop**, type **140** in the R, G, and B text boxes, then click **OK**.

6. Click the **gradient ramp** anywhere between the two color stops to add a third color stop.

7. Drag the **new color stop** left until the Location text box value is 20.

8. Double-click the **new color stop**, type **150** in the R, G, and B text boxes, then click **OK**.

9. Click to the right of the new color stop to add a fourth, then drag it until the Location text box value is 43.

(continued)

10. Double-click the **new color stop**, type **36** in the R, G, and B text boxes, then click **OK**.

11. Click to the right of the new color stop to add a fifth, then drag it until the Location text box value is 63.

12. Double-click the **new color stop**, type **200** in the R, G and B text boxes, then click **OK**.

    This color stop is the lightest.

13. Click to the right of the new color stop to add a sixth, then drag it until the Location text box value is 81.

14. Double-click the **new color stop**, type **14** in the R, G, and B text boxes, then click **OK**.

    Your Gradient Editor dialog box should resemble Figure 14.

15. Type **Smooth Emboss Overlay** in the Name section, then click **New**.

    The new gradient appears as a thumbnail in the Presets section.

16. Click **OK** to close the Gradient Editor dialog box.

    The new gradient appears in the Gradient section and is applied to the Smooth Emboss layer style.

    (continued)

Figure 14 *Specifications for the gradient*

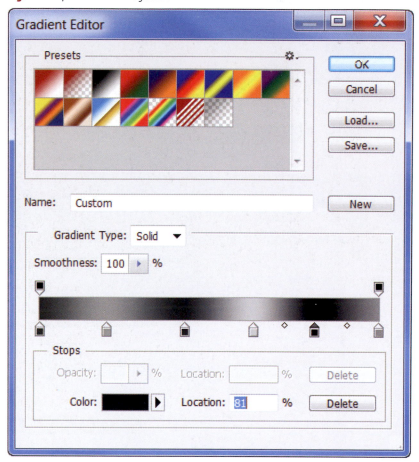

Figure 15 *Finished gradient layer style*

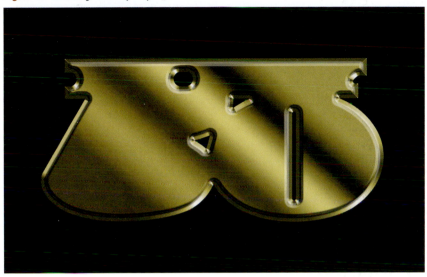

17. Click the **Blend Mode list arrow**, then click **Luminosity**.

    The Luminosity blending mode applies the brightness values of the gradient to the artwork beneath.

18. Click **OK** to close the Layer Style dialog box.

    A new sublayer named Gradient Overlay appears beneath Bevel & Emboss in the Smooth Emboss layer group.

19. Double-click **Gradient Overlay** in the Smooth Emboss layer group to edit it in the Layer Style dialog box.

20. Type **51** in the Angle text box.

21. Experiment with the Scale slider.

22. Drag the **Scale slider** to **92**, click **OK**, then compare your artwork to Figure 15.

    The often-overlooked Scale slider reduces or enlarges the gradient overlay within the layer style and can be useful for positioning the gradient in a way that is just right for the illustration.

You applied a gradient overlay to the artwork, creating the gradient itself and determining the direction that it was applied.

Create a Pillow
EMBOSS LAYER STYLE

What You'll Do

▶ *In this lesson, you will use the Bevel & Emboss layer style to apply a Pillow Emboss effect to the artwork.*

This lesson demonstrates how exporting layers from Illustrator really pays off. You're going to apply yet another layer style, but this time, you are going to apply it to a new piece of artwork. You will apply a layer style to a foreground component created for this layered illustration. Keep an eye out for how the layer style adds an entirely new dimension to the illustration, and keep in mind that the basis for the effect was the foreground and background components that were exported from Illustrator.

Figure 16 *Settings for the Pillow Emboss effect*

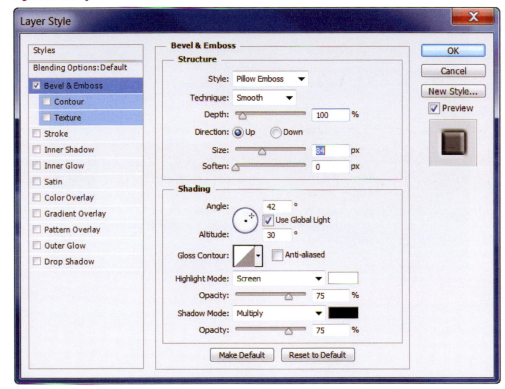

1. Show the layer named **Big 50**, then change its name to **Pillow Emboss**.
2. Create a **Bevel & Emboss** layer style.
3. Click the **Style list arrow**, then click **Pillow Emboss**.
4. Verify that the Technique is set to Smooth and that the Depth is set to 100%.
5. Experiment with the Size slider to get a good sense of the Pillow Emboss effect.
6. Drag the **Size slider** to 84, then compare your dialog box to Figure 16.

(continued)

7. Click **OK**, then compare your artwork to Figure 17.

8. Hide and show the Pillow & Emboss layer to see the effect.

(continued)

Figure 17 *Results of the Pillow Emboss effect*

Figure 18 *Viewing the Pillow Emboss layer style only*

9. Hide the Smooth Emboss and Chisel Hard Emboss layers to see the Pillow Emboss effect against the black background, then compare your canvas to Figure 18.

   With the Pillow Emboss effect, the highlight is offset outside of the artwork. In this case, the highlight is gray/silver because the highlight in the Bevel & Emboss Layer Style dialog box is set to white. Rather than change that, we will add a Hue/Saturation adjustment later in the exercise.

10. Show the Smooth Emboss and Chisel Hard Emboss layers, then save your work.

You used the Bevel & Emboss layer style again, this time to apply a Pillow Emboss effect to the artwork.

Copy Layer Styles
BETWEEN LAYERS

What You'll Do

 In this lesson, you will copy layer styles from one layer to another layer.

A fundamental part of working with layers involves duplicating: duplicating layers and copying layer styles and adjustment layers. This is something you'll do over and over again in your work.

Take layer styles, for example. Rather than create new styles from scratch every time, simply copy an existing style.

Figure 19 *Illustration with the top text embossed*

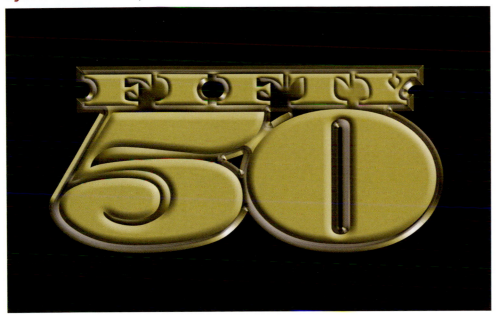

Choosing Resolution

It's a good idea to choose the highest resolution for the exported file. In Photoshop, you can always reduce the resolution if you want. Remember the first rule of changing resolution in Photoshop: It is always better, from an image quality standpoint, to reduce the resolution of a Photoshop file than it is to increase the resolution.

Copy layer styles between layers

1. Show the **Little Fifty layer**, then save your work.
2. Press and hold [**Alt**] (Win) or [**option**] (Mac), then drag the **Effects sublayer** in the Pillow Emboss layer group to the Little Fifty layer.

   Dragging the Effects sublayer copies all the layer styles to the new destination.

TIP The Size setting on the Pillow Emboss layer style that you copied is too large for the Little Fifty artwork.

3. Double-click the **Bevel & Emboss** layer style on the Little Fifty layer.
4. Drag the **Size slider** to 46, click **OK**, then compare your artwork to Figure 19.
5. Hide and show the Little Fifty and the Pillow Emboss layers, then save your work.

You copied layer styles from one layer to another, then adjusted the styles to suit the smaller artwork.

Add an Outer Glow
LAYER STYLE

What You'll Do

 In this lesson, you will add an Outer Glow layer style behind the existing artwork.

Outer Glow is one of the more popular and practical layer styles, used to create both subtle and dramatic effects. Glows also have a practical use. When you're working with layered artwork, adding a glow to an object is a good way to distinguish it from other objects behind it. In the case of this illustration, you'll use an Outer Glow layer style to create the effect that the metallic letters are so shiny that they glow.

Figure 20 *Outer Glow Layer Style dialog box*

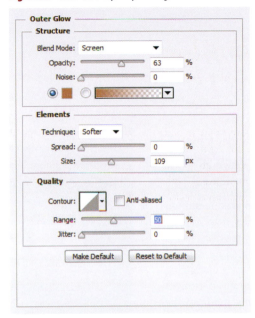

Figure 21 *Outer glow behind artwork*

Add an Outer Glow layer style

1. Target the **Chisel Hard Emboss layer**.
2. Click **Layer** on the Menu bar, point to **Layer Style**, then click **Outer Glow**.
3. In the Structure section, click the **Set color of glow color box**.

   The Color Picker opens.
4. Type **182** in the R text box, **115** in the G text box and **75** in the B text box, then click **OK**.
5. Enter the settings in the Layer Style dialog box shown in Figure 20, then click **OK**.
6. Compare your artwork to Figure 21, then save your work.

You added an Outer Glow layer style behind all the artwork.

Apply Blending
MODES

What You'll Do

 In this lesson, you will add adjustment layers with blending modes to create dramatic effects.

When designing complex artwork—especially eye-popping artwork like this illustration—blending modes play an important role in creating dramatic visual effects. The Overlay section of the blending modes menu on the Layers panel offers modes that increase contrast and saturation, making them especially useful for creating shiny metallic effects. One of the best methods for applying blending modes is to create an adjustment layer then apply the blending mode to the adjustment layer.

Figure 22 *Clipped adjustment layers on the Layers panel*

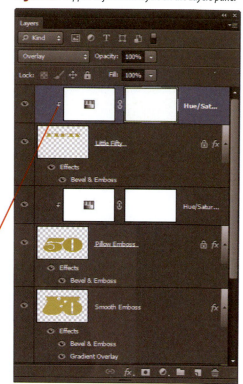

Second clipped adjustment layer

Integrating Illustrator, Photoshop, and InDesign

Figure 23 *Final artwork*

1. Target the **Pillow Emboss** layer, click the **Layer menu**, point to **New Adjustment Layer**, then click **Hue/Saturation**.

2. Click the **Use Previous Layer to Create Clipping Mask check box**, then click **OK**.

3. On the Properties panel, click the **Colorize check box**, set the Hue slider to **51**, set the Saturation slider to **42**, then set the Lightness slider to **+50**.

4. On the Layers panel, click the **Blending Mode list arrow**, then click **Overlay**.

5. Using the same method, create a clipped adjustment with the same settings and the same blending mode above the **Little Fifty** layer.

   Your Layers panel should resemble Figure 22, and the new adjustment layer should be targeted as shown in the figure.

6. Click the **Create new fill or adjustment layer** button , then click **Hue/Saturation**.

7. On the Properties panel, click the **Colorize check box**, set the Hue slider to **51**, set the Saturation slider to **42**, then set the Lightness slider to **+15**.

8. On the Layers panel, click the **Blending Mode list arrow**, then click **Hard Light**.

   Because the layer is the top layer and because it is not clipped, the blending mode affects all the artwork on the canvas.

9. Compare your artwork to Figure 23.

10. Save your work, then close Fifty 50.psd

You added Hue/Saturation adjustment layers with blending modes applied to them to make a more vivid and metallic illustration.

Create an InDesign
OUTPUT FILE

What You'll Do

> In this lesson, you will create a layout for the Fifty 50.psd file in InDesign and import the file with a bleed.

It is often the case that when you have a high-resolution Photoshop file, you won't need to actually import it into InDesign for output. Photoshop is perfectly capable of executing many of the same output solutions as InDesign. For example, Photoshop can output a file as a PDF, as a JPEG or as a TIFF. However, in a professional working environment, designers often import finished Photoshop artwork into a layout that contains the company's logo, date/time information, client information, and so on. You might also import a Photoshop file into an InDesign layout so that you can export a PDF with crop marks, color bars, and other printer's marks.

Figure 24 *New Document dialog box*

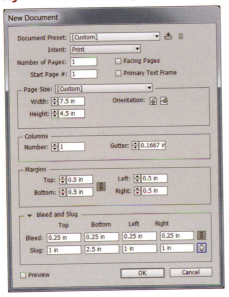

Figure 25 *Positioning the slug information*

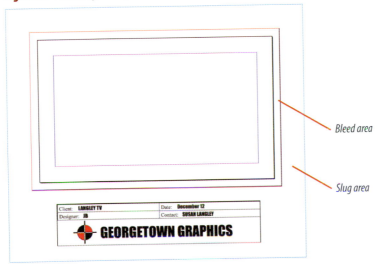

Bleed area

Slug area

Create a new InDesign document

1. Start InDesign.

2. Click **File** on the Menu bar, point to **New**, then click **Document**.

3. Type **1** in the Number of Pages text box, then verify that the Facing Pages check box is not checked.

4. Type **7.5** in the Width text box, press **Tab**, type **4.5** in the Height text box, then click the **Landscape Orientation** button.

5. If necessary, expand the Bleed and Slug section.

6. Enter the values shown in Figure 24, then click **OK**.

   You are creating a 2.5" slug area below the document that you will use to position document information.

7. Open the file named Slug.indd from the drive and folder where you store your Data Files.

8. Select all, copy, then close Slug.indd.

9. Paste the slug in the position shown in Figure 25.

10. Save the file as **Fifty 50 Output**.

You created a new document, then pasted slug information into the slug area at the bottom of the document.

Import artwork

1. Click the **Rectangle Frame** tool 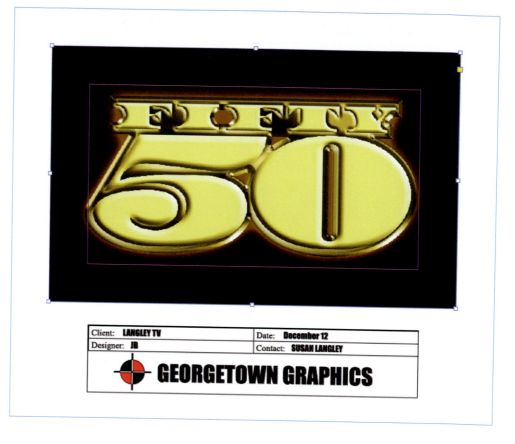, then draw a rectangle that extends to the red bleed guides on all four sides.

2. Click **File** on the Menu bar, click **Place**, navigate to the drive and folder where your Data Files are stored, then import the Fifty 50.psd file you created in an earlier lesson.

3. Click **Object** on the Menu bar, point to **Fitting**, then click **Fit Content to Frame**. Your layout should resemble Figure 26.

4. Hide the guides.

5. Save your work.

You created a frame with the Rectangle Frame tool, then placed a Photoshop image in it.

Figure 26 *Placing the artwork*

Integrating Illustrator, Photoshop, and InDesign

Figure 27 *General window of the Export Adobe PDF dialog box*

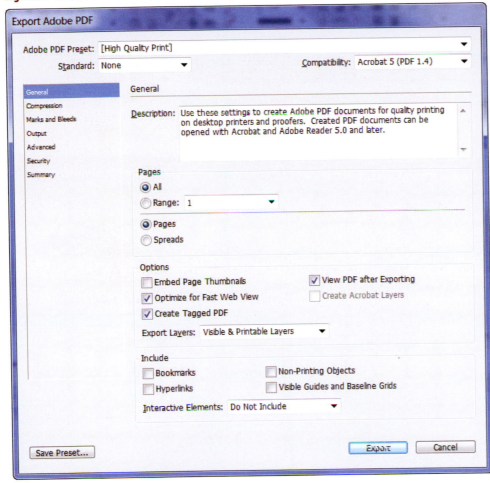

Export a PDF

1. Click **File** on the Menu bar, then click **Export**.

   The Export dialog box opens.

2. Click the **Save as type list arrow** (Win) or the **Format list arrow** (Mac), then click **Adobe PDF (Print)**.

   By default, the filename changes to Fifty 50 Output.pdf.

3. Click **Save**.

   The Export Adobe PDF dialog box opens.

4. Click the **Adobe PDF Presets list arrow**, then click **[High Quality Print]**.

5. Click the **View PDF after Exporting check box**, so that your dialog box resembles Figure 27.

   (continued)

Lesson 11 Create an InDesign Output File

DESIGN COLLECTION 1-39

6. In the left-hand column, click **Compression**.

7. Enter the data shown in the Color Images section so that your dialog box resembles Figure 28.

8. In the left column, click **Marks and Bleeds**, click the **All Printer's Marks check box**, then click **Bleed Marks** to remove the check mark.

9. Type **.5** in the Offset text box.

10. In the Bleed and Slug area of the dialog box, verify that the Include Slug Area check box is checked.

   This means that the entire slug area and the items in the slug area will be included and visible in the exported .pdf file.

11. Verify that the Use Document Bleed Settings check box is checked.

   This means that the file will be exported with the bleed settings you specified when you created the document.

   (continued)

Figure 28 *Compression window of the Export Adobe PDF dialog box*

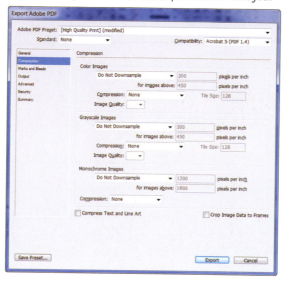

Figure 29 *Marks and Bleeds window of the Export Adobe PDF dialog box*

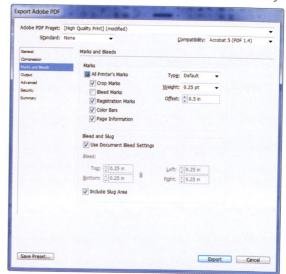

Integrating Illustrator, Photoshop, and InDesign

Figure 30 *Viewing the PDF*

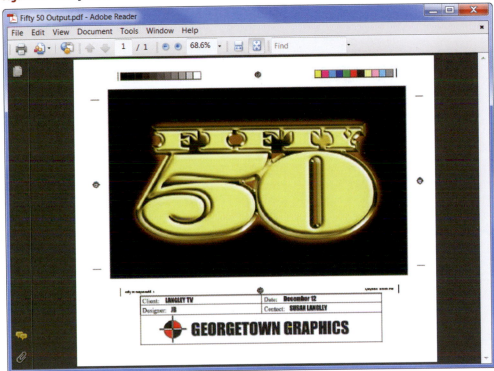

12. Click the **Save Preset** button.

The settings you entered will export a PDF with no compression—a print-ready document. Rather than entering these settings every time you want to deliver a high-res document to a printer, saving a preset makes these settings available as a preset in the Adobe PDF Presets menu at the top of the dialog box.

13. Type **Zero Compression**, then click **OK**.

14. Click **Export**.

Because you clicked the View PDF after Exporting check box, Adobe Reader should launch automatically showing you the PDF.

15. Compare your screen to Figure 30.

Figure 30 shows the exported PDF opened in Adobe Reader.

16. Close Adobe Reader.

17. Save the InDesign file, then close it.

Your exported an InDesign document as a PDF.

Export layers from Illustrator to Photoshop.

1. Open AI 1-5.ai in Adobe Illustrator, then save it as **Jazz Export**.
2. Show the Layers panel, click the Selection tool, then pull the individual pieces of the illustration apart, keeping an eye on the Layers panel.
3. Note the names of the four layers.
4. Click File on the Menu bar, click Revert, then click Revert in the dialog box that follows.
5. Click File on the Menu bar, then click Export.
6. Click the Save as type list arrow (Win) or the Format list arrow (Mac) in the Export dialog box, then click Photoshop (*.PSD) (Win) or Photoshop (psd) (Mac).
7. Click Export.
8. Click the Color Model list arrow, click RGB, then click the High (300 ppi) option button.
9. In the Options section, click the Write Layers option button, then click the Maximum Editability check box.
10. Click OK, then close the Illustrator document.
11. Open Jazz Export.psd in Photoshop.

12. Notice that the layers from Illustrator, including their names, were exported.
13. Close Jazz Export.psd.

Work with layer styles in Photoshop.

1. Open PS 1-6.psd, then save it as **Jazz 2096**.
2. Change the foreground color to 128R/128G/128B.
3. Hide the Red and Orange layers.
4. Fill the Blue layer with the foreground color.
5. Click the Add a layer style button on the Layers panel, then click Bevel & Emboss.
6. Verify that the Style is set to Inner Bevel, click the Technique list arrow, then click Chisel Hard.
7. Slowly drag the Size slider to 16, and watch the effect on the artwork as you drag.
8. In the Shading section, verify that the Use Global Light check box is checked, set the Angle to 45, then set the Altitude to 30.
9. Click OK, then fill the Green layer with the foreground color.

10. Click the Add a layer style button on the Layers panel, then click Inner Shadow.
11. Verify that the Blend Mode is set to Multiply, the Opacity is set to 75%, and that the Angle is set to 45.
12. Drag the Distance slider to 11, drag the Choke slider to 14, then drag the Size slider to 16.
13. Click the words Pattern Overlay on the left side of the dialog box.
14. Click the Pattern list arrow, then click the pattern named Woven. (*Hint*: If you don't see the Woven pattern, click the Pattern list arrow, click the arrow in the Pattern preview window, click Patterns, then click OK to load the Pattern swatches.)
15. Click the Blend Mode list arrow, click Multiply, set the Opacity to 60%, then click OK.
16. Make the Orange layer visible, select the Orange layer, then fill it with the foreground color.
17. Click the Add a layer style button on the Layers panel then click Bevel & Emboss.

18. Verify that the Style is set to Inner Bevel, click the Technique list arrow, then click Chisel Hard.
19. Drag the Size slider to 9.
20. Click the Gloss Contour list arrow, click Ring, then click the Anti-aliased check box to activate it.
21. Click OK, then compare your artwork to Figure 31.
22. Make the Red layer visible, select the Red layer, then fill it with the foreground color.

23. Click the Add a layer style button on the Layers panel, then click Inner Shadow.
24. Enter the settings shown in Figure 32, then click OK.
25. Click the Create new fill or adjustment layer button on the Layers panel, then click Solid Color.
26. Create a color that is 147R/55G/144B, then click OK.
27. Clip the new fill layer into the Red layer.

28. Double-click the Bevel & Emboss effects layer on the Orange layer.
29. Click the Gloss Contour list arrow, click Linear, then click OK.
30. Target the Color Fill 1 layer.
31. Press [Shift][Alt][Ctrl][E] (Win) or [Shift][option][⌘][E] (Mac).

Figure 31 *The second Bevel & Emboss effect*

Figure 32 *Inner Shadow settings in the Layer Style dialog box*

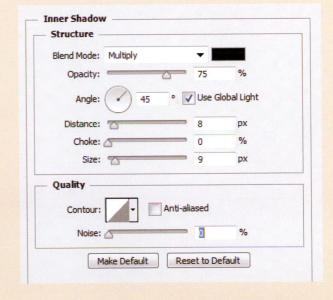

Integrating Illustrator, Photoshop, and InDesign

32. Name the new layer **Stamp Visible**, then set its blending mode to Overlay.
33. Compare your artwork to Figure 33.
34. Save your work, then close Jazz 2096.

Create an InDesign output file.

1. Open ID 1-7.indd, then save it as **Jazz 2096 Output**.
2. Verify that the Control panel is showing.
3. Click the Rectangle tool, then draw a rectangle anywhere on the page.
4. On the Control panel, with the rectangle still selected, click the upper-left reference point.

5. Type **-.125** in the X Location text box, type **-.125** in the Y Location text box, type **10.25** in the W text box, type **6.25** in the H text box, then press Enter (Win) or return (Mac).
6. Verify that the rectangle has no fill or stroke.
7. Click File on the Menu bar, click Place, navigate to the folder where you store your Data Files, then click the Jazz 2096.psd file.
8. Click Object on the Menu bar, point to Fitting, then click Fit Content to Frame.
9. Hide the guides.

10. Save your work.
11. Click File on the Menu bar, then click Export.
12. Click the Save as type list arrow (Win) or the Format list arrow (Mac), then click Adobe PDF (Print). (*Hint*: By default, the filename changes to Jazz 2096 Output.pdf.)
13. Click Save.
14. Click the Adobe PDF Preset list arrow, then click [High Quality Print].
15. Click the View PDF after Exporting check box.
16. In the left-hand column, click Compression.

Figure 33 *Completed Skills Review, Part 1*

17. Enter the data shown in Figure 34.
18. In the Left column, click Marks and Bleeds, then click the All Printer's Marks check box.
19. Verify that Use Document Bleed Settings and Include Slug Area are both checked.
20. Type **.5** in the Offset text box.

21. Click Export, then compare your PDF to Figure 35. (*Hint*: If you get a warning dialog box stating that the color settings of the document should be changed, ignore the warning and click to continue with the same settings.)

22. Close Adobe Reader.
23. Save the InDesign file, then exit InDesign.

Figure 34 *Compression window of the Export Adobe PDF dialog box*

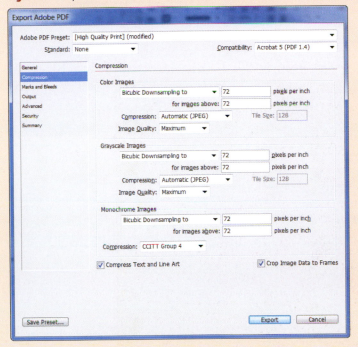

Figure 35 *Viewing the PDF*

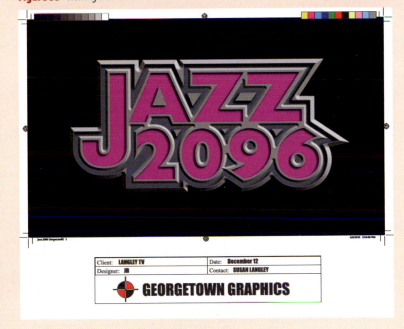

As part of your job at a prepress service company, you open customers' documents, preflight them, then output them to film. Starting on a new project, you open the customer's InDesign layout and note that the job ticket says that this page is to be printed at letter size. You notice immediately that the document has been built to letter size, but the customer failed to create bleeds.

1. Open ID 1-8.indd, then save it as **Multiple Bleeds**.
2. Verify that you are in Normal view so that guides are showing.
3. Open the Document Setup dialog box.
4. Type **.125** in all four Bleed text boxes, then click OK.
5. Click the Selection tool, select the large background graphic, then drag the frame's four corners to the bleed guide on all four sides.
6. Click Object on the Menu bar, point to Fitting, then click Fit Content to Frame.
7. Select the Windmill Silhouette.psd graphic in the lower-left corner, then drag the left and bottom sides of the frame to the left and bottom sides of the bleed guide.
8. Select the Windmills Color.psd graphic on right side of the layout, then drag the right side of the frame to the right side of the bleed guide.
9. Click Object on the Menu bar, point to Fitting, then click Fit Content to Frame.
10. Deselect all, compare your work to Figure 36, save your work, then close Multiple Bleeds.indd.

Figure 36 *Completed Project Builder 1*

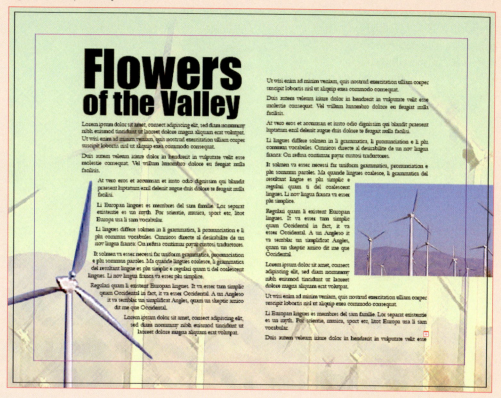

You have set type to be used in Photoshop for a complex layered project incorporating layer styles. To create the layers for the multi-layered project, you decide to apply the Offset Path command on the type, then position the new paths on different layers so that they can be exported to Photoshop.

1. Open AI 1-9.ai, then save it as **Offsetting Jazz**.
2. Select all, click Object on the Menu bar, point to Path, then click Offset Path.
3. In the Offset Path dialog box, type **.06** in in the Offset text box.

4. Verify that Joins is set to Miter and that Miter Limit is set to 4, then click OK.
5. On the Layers panel, move the selection to the Orange layer.
6. Fill the selection with an orange swatch on the Swatches panel, and do not deselect.
7. Keep the Orange layer targeted, then hide the Red layer.
8. With the Orange layer still targeted, open the Pathfinder panel, then click the Unite button on the Pathfinder panel, so that your artwork resembles Figure 37.
9. Open the Offset Path dialog box, note that the settings haven't changed, then click OK.

10. On the Layers panel, move the selection to the Green layer, then fill it with a green swatch from the Swatches panel.
11. Open the Offset Path dialog box, note that the settings haven't changed, then click OK.
12. On the Layers panel, move the selection to the Blue layer, then fill it with a blue swatch from the Swatches panel.
13. Show the Red layer, deselect all, then compare your artwork to Figure 38.
14. Save your work, then close Offsetting Jazz.ai.

Figure 37 *Offset artwork on the Orange layer*

Figure 38 *Completed Project Builder 2*

You designed a logo for a T-shirt for a women's clothing line, and they liked it so much they've come back to you for more work. This time, they want to incorporate the same phrase into jewelry, a pendant for a necklace that says LUCK BE A LADY. They tell you that—for production reasons—all the letters need to be touching, so that it is one unit. They also tell you that the piece needs to have a metallic frame around the letters. They will use your illustration to establish a look before going into production.

1. Open PS 1-10.psd, then save it as **Pink Lady**.
2. Create a new layer above the Background layer, then name it **Back Tray**.
3. Press and hold [Ctrl] (Win) or [⌘] (Mac), then click the Layer thumbnail to load the selection of the Lady layer.

4. Press and hold [Shift][Ctrl] (Win) or [Shift] [⌘] (Mac), then click the Layer thumbnail to load and add the selection of the Luck layer so that you have a selection of both layers.
5. Target the Back Tray layer.
6. Click Select on the Menu bar, point to Modify, then click Expand.
7. Type **18** in the Expand By dialog box, then click OK.
8. Click Edit on the Menu bar, then click Fill.
9. Click the Use list arrow, choose 50% Gray, verify that the Opacity is set to 100%, then click OK.
10. Deselect all.
11. Create a Bevel & Emboss layer style.
12. Set the Style to Inner Bevel, set the Technique to Chisel Hard, set the Depth to 100, then set the Size to 10 pixels.
13. Click the Use Global Light check box, then set the Angle to 120.
14. Change the Gloss Contour to Gaussian, verify that the Anti-aliased check box is not checked, then click OK.

15. Target the Lady layer, then add a Bevel & Emboss layer style.
16. Set the Style to Pillow Emboss, set the Technique to Smooth, set the Depth to 100, then set the Size to 29 pixels.
17. Verify that the Use Global Light check box is checked, that the Angle is set to 120, then click OK.
18. Target the Luck layer, then add a Bevel & Emboss layer style.
19. Set the Style to Pillow Emboss, set the Technique to Chisel Hard, set the Depth to 100, then set the Size to 10 pixels.
20. Verify that the Use Global Light check box is checked and that the Angle is set to 120.
21. Set the Gloss Contour to Cove-Deep, then click OK.
22. Compare your artwork to Figure 39, save your work, then close Pink Lady.psd.

Figure 39 *Completed Design Project*

You've been contacted by a women's clothing company. They've asked you to design type for a T-shirt that reads LUCK BE A LADY. They tell you that the T-shirt will print only on white or pink cloth, and that it's targeted to younger women and teens. They ask you to come up with something "shiny and feminine, but not soft."

1. Open PS 1-11.psd, then save it as **Luck Be a Lady**. (*Hint*: The typeface used in the document is Bellevue.)
2. Target the Pink layer, then add a Bevel & Emboss layer style.
3. Set the Style to Inner Bevel, set the Technique to Chisel Hard, set the Depth to 100, then set the Size to 32 pixels.
4. Verify that the Use Global Light check box is checked and that the Angle is set to 120.
5. Set the Gloss Contour to Ring.
6. Drag the Shadow Mode Opacity slider to 50%, then click OK.
7. Target the Black layer, then add a Bevel & Emboss layer style.
8. Set the Style to Outer Bevel, set the Technique to Chisel Hard, set the Depth to 161, then set the Size to 10 pixels.
9. Verify that the Use Global Light check box is checked and that the Angle is set to 120.
10. Click OK, then compare your artwork to Figure 40.
11. Save your work, then close Luck Be a Lady.psd.

Figure 40 *Completed Portfolio Project*

3D Extrusion
A tool for turning a 2-dimensional object (such as type) into a 3-dimensional object. Allows for rotation, rolling, panning, sliding, and scaling.

— A —

Absorption
Occurs when light strikes an object and is absorbed by the object.

Actions
Indicate what happens when the specific interactive event occurs—usually when someone clicks a button.

Active layer
The layer highlighted on the Layers panel. The active layer's name appears in parentheses in the image window title bar.

Additive colors
A color system in which, when the values of R, G, and B (red, green, and blue) are 0, the result is black; when the values are all 255, the result is white.

Additive primary colors
Refers to the fact that Red, Green, and Blue light cannot be broken down themselves but can be combined to produce other colors.

Adjustment layer
An additional layer for which you can specify individual color adjustments. The adjustment layer allows you to temporarily alter a layer before making the adjustment permanent.

Adjustment panel
Visible panel that makes creation of adjustment layers easy.

Adobe Bridge
A stand-alone application that can be used for file management tasks such as opening, viewing, sorting, and rating files.

Adobe Configurator
A stand-alone program (available as a download) that lets you create your own panels.

Adobe Creative Cloud
A fee-based membership service that includes Creative Cloud tools, Adobe Touch Apps, services, plus new products and services as they are released.

Adobe DNG
See Digital Negative Format.

Adobe Mini Bridge
A less-powerful (and smaller) version of Bridge that opens within the Photoshop window.

Align
To position objects in specific relationship to each other on a given axis.

Alpha channel
Selections made in Photoshop that have been saved with a descriptive name, and which can be loaded into an InDesign document.

Altitude
A Bevel and Emboss setting that affects the amount of visible dimension.

Ambient light
Determines how an object is lit globally.

Anchored objects
Objects created and used as text characters within a block of text.

Angle
In the Layer Style dialog box, the setting that determines where a drop shadow falls relative to the text.

Animation effects
Let you make objects move and fade, appear and disappear, in your exported layout.

Anti-aliasing
Partially fills in pixel edges, resulting in smooth-edge type. This feature lets your type maintain its crisp appearance and is especially useful for large type.

Area text
Text that you create inside an object.

Arrange
To adjust the position of an object in the stacking order.

Arrangement
How objects are positioned in space, relative to one another.

Art brushes
A brush style that stretches an object along the length of a path.

Artboard tool
Gateway to working with multiple artboards.

Asymmetrical balance
When objects are placed unequally on either side of an imaginary vertical line in the center of the page.

Attributes
Formatting which has been applied to an object that affects its appearance.

Attribution (cc by)
The simplest of all Creative Commons licenses, in which any user (commercial or non-commercial) can distribute, modify, or enhance your work, provided you are credited.

Attribution No Derivatives (cc by-nd)
Your work can be distributed by others, but not modified and in its entirety, with you being credited.

Attribution Non-Commercial (cc by-nc)
Your work can be distributed, modified, or enhanced, with credit to you, for non-commercial purposes only. Derivative works do not have to be licensed.

Attribution Non-Commercial No Derivatives (cc by-nc-nd)
This is the most restrictive license category. Redistribution is allowed as long as credit is given. The work cannot be modified or used commercially.

Attribution Non-Commercial Share Alike (cc by-nc-sa)
Your work can be distributed, modified, or enhanced, with credit to you, for non-commercial purposes only, but must be licensed under the identical terms. All derivative work must carry the same license, and be non-commercial.

Attribution Share Alike (cc by-sa)
The same as Attribution, except that the new owner must create their license under the same terms you used.

Autoflow
The automatic threading of text through multiple text frames.

B

Background color
Used to make gradient fills and to fill in areas of an image that have been erased. The default background color is white.

Balance colors
Process of adding and subtracting colors from those already existing in a layer.

Base color
The original color of an image.

Baseline
An invisible line on which type rests.

Baseline shift
The distance type appears from its original position.

Bevel
The angle that one surface makes with another when they are not at right angles.

Bevel join
Produces stroked lines with squared corners.

Bitmap
A geometric arrangement of different color dots on a rectangular grid.

Bitmap graphics
Images that are created by pixels in a program like Photoshop. Every digital image and scanned graphic is a bitmap graphic.

Bitmap images
Graphics created using a grid of colored squares called pixels.

Bitmap mode
Uses black or white color values to represent image pixels; a good choice for images with subtle color gradations, such as photographs or painted images.

Bitmap type
Type that may develop jagged edges when enlarged.

Bleed marks
Marks that define the bleed size.

Bleeds
Areas of the layout that extend to the trim size.

Blend
A series of intermediate objects and colors between two or more selected objects.

Blend color
The color applied to the base color when a blending mode is applied to a layer.

Blend steps
Controls how smoothly shading appears on an object's surface and is most visible in the transition from the highlight areas to the diffusely lit areas.

Blending modes
An InDesign feature that allows you to create different transparency and color effects where two or more objects overlap. In Photoshop, preset filters that control how colors blend when two objects overlap.

Blur filters
Used to soften a selection or image.

Book
In InDesign, a collection of two or more InDesign documents, which are paginated as a single book.

Bounding box

Always rectangular, the frame that defines the horizontal and vertical dimensions of the graphic.

Bridge

See Adobe Bridge.

Brightness

The measurement of relative lightness or darkness of a color (measured as a percentage from 0% [black] to 100% [white]).

Bristle Brush

Brush style that mimics traditional media like watercolors.

Butt caps

Squared ends of a stroked path.

Buttons

Perform actions when the InDesign document is exported to SWF or PDF formats. Clicking a button could take you to a different page in the document, or it could open a website, or it could play a movie, a sound, or an animation. Buttons you create are listed and formatted in the Buttons panel.

— C —

Calligraphic brushes

Brush style that applies strokes that resemble those drawn with a calligraphic pen.

Camera Raw

Allows you to use digital data directly from a digital camera. The file extension that you see will vary with each digital camera manufacturer. The Camera Raw feature allows you to make additional adjustments to images.

Canvas size

The full editable area of an image that can be increased or decreased in size using the Canvas Size command on the Image menu.

Caps

Define the appearance of end points when a stroke is added to a path. The Stroke panel offers three types of caps: butt, round, and projecting.

Cell

A rectangle in a table row or column.

Channels

Used to store information about the color elements contained in each channel.

Character panel

Helps you control type properties. The Toggle the Character and Paragraph panels button is located on the options bar when you select a Type tool.

Clipboard

Temporary storage area, provided by your operating system, for cut and copied data.

Clipping mask

An object whose area crops objects behind it in the stacking order.

Clipping path

A graphic you draw in Photoshop that outlines the areas of the image to be shown when the file is placed in a layout program like InDesign.

Clipping set

Term used to distinguish clipping paths used in layers from clipping paths used to mask non-layered artwork.

Closed path

Continuous lines that do not contain end points.

Cloud computing

Allows you to share files with others in a virtual environment.

CMYK

Cyan, Magenta, Yellow, and Black; four inks essential to professional printing.

CMYK image

An image using the CMYK color system, containing at least four channels (one each for cyan, magenta, yellow, and black).

CMYK mode

Color mode is based on colors being partially absorbed as the ink hits the paper and then being partially reflected back to your eyes.

Color bars

Used to maintain consistent color on press.

Color gamut

Refers to the range of colors that can be printed or displayed within a given color model.

Color mode

Used to determine how to display and print an image. Each mode is based on established models used in color reproduction. Represents the amount of color data that can be stored in a given file format, and determines the color model used to display and print an image. Determines the number and range of colors displayed.

Color model

Determines how pigments combine to produce resulting colors.

Color Picker

A sophisticated dialog box for specifying colors.

Color Range command

Used to select pixels having a particular color in an existing image or layer.

Color separation

Result of converting an RGB image into a CMYK image; the commercial printing process of separating colors for use with different links.

Color stops
Colors added to a gradient located between the starting and ending colors.

Color tools
Circle icons in the Live Color dialog box which represent the colors for the loaded harmony rule.

Column break
A typographic command that forces text to the next column.

Columns
Vertical page guides often used to define the width of text frames and body copy. Also, in a table, the vertical arrangement of cells.

Combination graph
A graph that uses two graph styles to plot numeric data; useful for emphasizing one set of data in comparison to others.

Compositing
Combining images from sources such as other Photoshop images, royalty-free images, pictures taken from digital cameras, and scanned artwork.

Compound path
Two or more paths that define a single object. When overlapped, the overlapped area becomes a negative space. Closed paths joined using the Make Compound Path command to create one complete path. You create compound paths when you want to use one object to cut a hole in another object.

Compound shape
A term used to distinguish a complex compound path from a simple one. Compound shapes generally assume an artistic rather than a practical role.

Condition set
A snapshot of the current visibility of applied conditions to text; Allows you to set multiple conditions simultaneously.

Content Management Application
A framework to organize and access electronic content, such as Adobe Bridge.

Contiguous
Items that are next to one another.

Copyright
The right of an author or creator of a work to copy, distribute, and modify a thing, idea, or image; a type of intellectual property.

Corner point
An anchor point joining two straight segments, one straight segment, and one curved segment, or two curved segments.

Creative Commons licenses
Licensing of intellectual property without the use of lawyers or expensive fees by Creative Commons, a non-profit organization that offers free licenses and legal tools used to mark creative work.

Crisp
Anti-aliasing setting that gives type more definition and makes it appear sharper.

Crop
To exclude part of an image. Cropping hides areas of an image without losing resolution quality.

Crop marks
Short, thin lines that define where artwork is trimmed after it is printed.

Custom graph design
Artwork used to replace traditional columns, bars, or markers in Illustrator graphs.

D

Darken Only option
Replaces light pixels with darker pixels.

Dashed strokes
Strokes that consist of a series of dashes and gaps, created and formatted using the Stroke panel.

Data merge
When a data source containing fields and records is merged with a target document to create personalized documents.

Defringe command
Replaces fringe pixels with the colors of other nearby pixels.

Derivative work
A new, original product that includes content from a previously existing work.

Deselect
A command that removes the marquee from an area so it is no longer selected.

Digital camera
A camera that captures images on electronic media (rather than film). Its images are in a standard digital format and can be downloaded for computer use.

Digital image
A picture in electronic form. It may be referred to as a file, document, picture, or image.

Digital Negative Format
An archival format for camera raw files that contains the raw image data created within a digital camera as well as its defining metadata. Also called *Adobe DNG*.

Direction handle
The round blue circle at the top of the direction line that you drag to modify a direction line.

Direction lines

Two lines attached to a smooth point. Direction lines determine the arc of the curved path, depending on their direction and length.

Distance

Determines how far a shadow falls from the text. This setting is used by the Drop Shadow and Bevel and Emboss styles.

Distort filters

Create 3-dimensional or other reshaping effects. Some of the types of distortions you can produce include Glass, Pinch, Ripple, Shear, Spherize, Twirl, Wave, and ZigZag.

Distributing

Positioning objects on a page so that they are spaced evenly in relation to one another.

Dock (noun)

The dark gray bar to the left of the collection of panels or buttons. The arrows in the dock are used to maximize and minimize the panels.

Dock (verb)

To connect the bottom edge of one panel to the top edge of another panel so that both move together.

Document grid

An alignment guide to which objects can be aligned and snapped.

'Drag & drop' a copy

Pressing [Alt](Win) or [option](Mac) when moving an object; creates a copy of the object.

Drawing mode

Functionality option in which you can draw behind or inside of existing objects.

Drop cap

A design element in which the first letter or letters of a paragraph are increased in size to create a visual effect.

Drop Shadow

A style that adds what looks like a colored layer behind the selected type or object. The default shadow color is black.

Drop Zone

A blue outline area that indicates where a panel can be moved.

Duotone mode

Color mode used to create grayscale images using monotones, duotones, tritones, and quadtones.

Dynamic preview

An InDesign feature in which the entirety of a placed graphic, including areas outside a graphics frame, can be seen as the graphic is being moved.

——————— **E** ———————

Edge

Similar to a stroke, an edge is a new shape or area created by the overlap of Illustrator objects when the Live Paint Bucket tool is applied. Edges appear as strokes but can be filled with color using the Live Paint Bucket tool.

Effect

A type of appearance attribute which alters an object's appearance without altering the object itself.

Effective resolution

The resolution of a placed image based on its size in the layout.

Em space

A type of white space inserted into a text box. The width of an em space is equivalent to that of the lowercase letter m in the current typeface and type size.

En space

A type of white space inserted into a text box. The width of an en space is equivalent to that of the lowercase letter n in the current typeface and type size.

Ending color

The last color in a gradient.

Envelopes

Objects that are used to distort other objects into the shape of the envelope object.

Event

The specific interactive occurrence that triggers the action of a button.

Extrude

To add depth to an object by extending it on its Z axis. An object's Z axis is always perpendicular to the object's front surface.

Extrude & Bevel effect

A 3D effect that applies a three-dimensional effect to two-dimensional objects.

——————— **F** ———————

Facing pages

Two pages in a layout that face each other, as in an open magazine, book, or newspaper.

Fair use doctrine

Allows a user to make a copy of all or part of a work within specific parameters of usage, even if permission *has not* been granted.

Fastening point

An anchor within the marquee. When the marquee pointer reaches the initial fastening point, a small circle appears on the pointer, indicating that you have reached the starting point.

Feather
A method used to control the softness of a selection's edges by blurring the area between the selection and the surrounding pixels.

Fields
Labels in a data source that categorize information in the records of a database, which are placed in a target document to specify how to do a data merge.

File versioning
A feature that allows you to store multiple versions of your work.

Fill
A color you apply to the inside of an object.

Filters
Used to alter the look of an image and give it a special, customized appearance by applying special effects, such as distortions, changes in lighting, and blurring.

Flatten Artwork
Consolidating all layers in a document into a single layer.

Flattening
Merging all visible layers in a layered document. Reduces file size.

Font
Characters with a similar appearance.

Font family
Represents a complete set of characters, letters, and symbols for a particular typeface. Font families are generally divided into three categories: serif, sans serif, and symbol.

Foreground color
Used to paint, fill, and stroke selections. The default foreground color is black.

Frame edges
Visible edges of frames; when frames are selected, edges are automatically highlighted.

Frames
Rectangular, oval, or polygonal shapes that you use for a variety of purposes, such as creating a colored area on the document or placing text and graphics.

Fuzziness
Similar to tolerance, in that the lower the value, the closer the color pixels must be to be selected.

G

Gamut
The range of displayed colors in a color model.

GIF
A standard file format for compressing images by lowering the number of colors available to the file.

Gloss contour
A Bevel and Emboss setting that determines the pattern with which light is reflected.

Glyphs
Alternate versions of type characters; usually used for symbols like trademarks, etc.

Gradient
A graduated blend between two or more colors.

Gradient fill
A type of fill in which colors appear to blend into one another. A gradient's appearance is determined by its beginning and ending points. Photoshop contains five gradient fill styles.

Gradient presets
Predesigned gradient fills that are displayed in the Gradient picker.

Graph
A diagram of data that shows relationships among a set of numbers.

Graph type
A dialog box that provides a variety of ways to change the look of an Illustrator graph.

Graphic
An element on a page that is not text. In an InDesign document, refers to a bitmap or vector image.

Graphic Styles
Named sets of appearance attributes.

Graphics frames
Rectangles in which you place imported artwork.

Graphics tablet
An optional hardware peripheral that enables use of pressure-sensitive tools, allows you to create programmable menu buttons and maneuver faster in Photoshop.

Grayscale image
Can contain up to 256 shades of gray. Pixels can have brightness values from 0 (black) to white (255).

Grayscale mode
Uses up to 256 shades of gray, assigning a brightness value from 0 (black) to 255 (white) to each pixel.

GREP style
A style that is applied to patterns of text, such as a telephone number, based on code.

Gridify
To position frames into a grid pattern in one move, using tool and keypad combinations.

Gridify Behaviors
Various gridify moves accomplished using various tool and keypad combinations.

Guides
Horizontal and vertical lines that you create to help you align objects. Guides appear as light blue lines.

Gutter
The space between two columns.

————————— **H** —————————

Handles
Small boxes that appear along the perimeter of a selected object and are used to change the size of an image.

Harmony Rule
Sets of complimentary colors in the Color Guide, which work well together and help you choose colors for your illustration.

Hexadecimal values
Sets of three pairs of letters or numbers that are used to define the R, G, and B components of a color.

Highlight Intensity
Controls how intense a highlight appears.

Highlight Mode
A Bevel and Emboss setting that determines how pigments are combined.

Highlight Size
Controls how large the highlights appear on an object.

History panel
Contains a record of each action performed during a Photoshop session. Up to 1000 levels of

Undo are available through the History panel (20 levels by default).

Hue
The color reflected from/transmitted through an object and expressed as a degree (between 0° and 360°). Each hue is identified by a color name (such as red or green).

Hyperlinks
Interactive text that jumps to other pages in a document, another document, an email address or to a website.

————————— **I** —————————

Image map
A graphic with areas defined as links for the Internet.

Imageable area
The area inside the dotted line on the artboard which represents the portion of the page that a standard printer can print.

Image-editing program
Used to manipulate graphic images that can be posted on websites or reproduced by professional printers using full-color processes.

Index
An alphabetized list of terms in a book, which references the page or pages on which the items are mentioned.

In port
A small box in the upper-left corner of a text frame that you can click to flow text from another text frame.

Insertion mode
The drawing mode in Illustrator that allows you to add a new object to a live paint group.

A gray rectangle surrounding a live paint group indicates Insertion mode is active.

Intellectual property
An image or idea that is owned and retained by legal control.

Interpolation
The process by which Photoshop creates new pixels in a graphic to maintain an image's resolution.

Isolation mode
A work mode in Illustrator in which a selected group appears in full color, while all the remaining objects on the artboard are dimmed and non-selectable.

————————— **J** —————————

Joins
Define the appearance of a corner point when a path has a stroke applied to it as miter, round, or bevel.

JPEG
A standard file format for compressing continuous tone images, gradients, and blends.

————————— **K** —————————

Kerning
Controlling the amount of space between two characters.

Keyboard increment
The distance that a single press of an arrow key moves a selected item; editable as a preference.

Keyboard shortcuts
Combinations of keys that can be used to work faster and more efficiently.

Kuler

A web-hosted application that lets you create, save, share, and download color-coordinated themes for use in images. It can be accessed from a browser, the desktop, or Adobe products such as Photoshop or Illustrator.

L

Landscape orientation

An image with the long edge of the paper at the top and bottom.

Layer (Photoshop)

A section within an image on which objects can be stored. The advantage: Individual effects can be isolated and manipulated without affecting the rest of the image. The disadvantage: Layers can increase the size of your file.

Layer comp

A variation on the arrangement and visibility of existing layers within an image; an organizational tool.

Layer group

An organizing tool you use to group layers on the Layers panel. (Sometimes referred to as *nested layers*.)

Layer style

An effect that can be applied to a type or image layer.

Layer thumbnail

Contains a miniature picture of the layer's content, and appears to the left of the layer name on the Layers panel.

Layers (Illustrator)

A solution for organizing and managing a complex illustration by segregating artwork.

Layers panel

Displays all the individual layers within an active image. You can use the Layers panel to create, delete, merge, copy, or reposition layers.

Leading

The amount of vertical space between lines of type.

Libraries

Files you create that appear as a panel in your InDesign document for organizing and storing graphics. Also called Object Libraries.

Lighten Only option

Replaces dark pixels with light pixels.

Lighting Effects filter

Applies lighting effects to an image.

Lighting Intensity

Controls the strength of the light on the object. The range for lighting intensity is 0-100, with 100 being the default.

Linear gradient

A gradient which can fill an object from left to right, top to bottom, or on any angle.

Live paint group

A live paint group is created when the Live Paint Bucket tool is applied to selected objects. All of the resulting regions and edges are part of the live paint group and share a dynamic relationship.

Logo

A distinctive image used to identify a company, project, or organization. You can create a logo by combining symbols, shapes, colors, and text.

Luminosity

The remaining light and dark values that result when a color image is converted to grayscale.

M

Margin Guides

Page guides that define the interior borders of a document.

Marquee

A series of dotted lines indicating a selected area that can be edited or dragged into another image.

Mask

A feature that lets you protect or modify a particular area; created using a marquee.

Master items

All objects on the master page that function as a place where objects on the document pages are to be positioned.

Master pages

Templates that you create for a page layout or for the layout of an entire publication.

Match Color command

Allows you to replace one color with another.

Matte

A colorful box (often without shine) placed behind an object that makes the object stand out.

Menu bar

Contains menus from which you can choose commands.

Merged document

A target document which has been merged with records from a data source.

Merging layers

Process of combining multiple image layers into one layer.

Mesh lines
Paths that crisscross a mesh object, joined at their intersections by mesh points.

Mesh object
A single, multicolored object in which colors can flow in different directions and transition gradually from point to point.

Mesh patch
The area between four mesh points.

Mesh points
Diamond-shaped points that function like anchor points to which you can assign color.

Metadata
Descriptive standardized information about a file, including the author's name, copyright, and associated keywords.

Miter join
Produces stroked lines with pointed corners.

Miter limit
Determines when a Miter join will be squared off to a beveled edge.

Monitor calibration
A process that displays printed colors accurately on your monitor.

Monotype spacing
Spacing in which each character occupies the same amount of space.

Motion presets
Pre-defined animations that you can apply quickly and easily to objects in your layout.

Multiply
An essential blending mode in which the colors of overlapping objects create an effect that is similar to overlapping magic markers.

N

Named color
Any color that you create in the New Color Swatch dialog box.

Nested styles
Paragraph styles that contain two or more character styles within the paragraph style.

Non-destructive effects
Applied effects such as glows, shadows, bevels, and embosses that do not permanently change the graphic to which they are applied.

Non-process Inks
Special pre-mixed inks that are printed separately from process inks.

Normal mode
Screen mode in which all page elements, including margin guides, ruler guides, frame edges and the pasteboard are visible.

O

Object layer
A layer containing one or more images.

Object Libraries
See Libraries.

Objects
Text or graphic elements such as images, blocks of color and even simple lines that are placed in an InDesign document.

Offset
The distance that text is repelled from a frame. Also, the specified horizontal and vertical distance a copy of an object will be from the original. The distance that an object is moved from a starting location to a subsequent location.

Offset path
A command that creates a copy of a selected path repositioned at a specified distance.

Opacity
Determines the percentage of transparency. Whereas a layer with 100% opacity will obstruct objects in the layers beneath it, a layer with 1% opacity will appear nearly transparent.

Opacity Mask
Function that allows selective control of where an object is transparent.

Optimization
A process by which a file's size is reduced through standard color compression algorithms.

Open path
A path whose end points are not connected.

Optical center
The point around which objects on the page are balanced; occurs approximately 3/8ths from the top of the page.

Options bar
Displays the settings for the active tool. The options bar is located directly under the Menu bar, but can be moved anywhere in the workspace for easier access.

Orientation
Direction an image appears on the page: portrait or landscape.

Orphans
Words or single lines of text at the bottom of a column or page that become separated from the other lines in a paragraph.

Outline stroke

A command that converts a stroked path into a closed path that is the same width as the original stroked path.

Outlined text

A command that changes text in a document to standard vector graphics.

Outline type

Type that is mathematically defined and can be scaled to any size without its edges losing their smooth appearance. Also known as a *vector font*.

Out-of-gamut indicator

Indicates that the current color falls beyond the accurate print or display range.

Out port

A small box in the lower right corner of a text frame that flows text out to another text frame when clicked.

Override

To modify a master page item on a document page.

Overset text

Text that does not fit in a text frame.

— P —

Page information

A type of printer's marks that includes the title of the InDesign document.

Page size

See Trim size.

Page transitions

Display classic video transition effects, such as dissolve, push, or wipe, when you're moving from page to page in an exported SWF or PDF document.

Panel well

An area where you can assemble panels for quick access.

Panels

Small windows that can be moved and are used to verify settings and modify images. Panels contain named tabs, which can be separated and moved to another group. Each panel contains a menu that can be viewed by clicking the Panel options button in its upper-right corner.

PANTONE

The standard library of non-process inks.

Paragraph return

Inserted into the text formatting by pressing [Enter] (Win) or [return] (Mac). Also called a hard return.

Pasteboard

The area surrounding the document.

Pathfinders

Preset operations that combine paths in a variety of ways; useful for creating complex or irregular shapes from basic shapes.

Paths

Straight or curved lines created with vector graphics.

Pattern brushes

A brush style that repeats a pattern along a path.

Pattern fill

Multiple objects used as a fill for an object; the object is filled by repeating the artwork.

PDF

Acronym for Portable Document Format. As a PDF, an original Illustrator file is complete and self-contained. Useful for emailing Illustrator artwork to others who don't have Illustrator installed.

Perspective Grid

Grid and functionality that allows you to draw and copy objects in a fixed perspective.

Pica

12 points, or 1/6 of an inch.

Picture package

Shows multiple copies of a single image in various sizes, similar to a portrait studio sheet of photos.

Pixel

Nickname for picture element; a single-colored square that is the smallest component of a bitmap graphic.

Pixel aspect ratio

A scaling correction feature that automatically corrects the ratio of pixels displayed for the monitor in use. Prevents pixels viewed in a 16:9 monitor (such as a widescreen TV) from looking compressed when viewed in a 4:3 monitor (nearly-rectangular TV).

Point of origin

The point from which an object is transformed; by default, the center point of an object, unless another point is specified.

Point text

Text that you create by clicking the artboard.

Points

Unit of measurement for font sizes. Traditionally, one inch is equivalent to 72.27 points. In PostScript measurement, one inch is equivalent to 72 points. The default Photoshop type size is 12 points.

Portrait orientation

An image with the short edge of the paper at the top and bottom.

PostScript
A programming language created by Adobe that optimizes printed text and graphics.

Preferences
Used to control the Photoshop environment using your specifications.

Preflight
Refers to checking out a document before it's released to a printer or downloaded to an output device.

Presentation mode
A screen mode in which all non-printing elements, panels, and Application bar are invisible and the page is centered and sized against a black background so that the entire document fits in the monitor window.

Preview file
A low-resolution version of the placed graphic file. As such, its file size is substantially smaller than the average graphic file.

Preview mode
A screen mode in which all non-printing page elements are invisible.

Preview panel
Shows a preview of animations in your document.

Printer's marks
Include crop marks, bleed marks, registration marks, color bars, and page information.

Process colors
Colors you create (and eventually print) by mixing varying percentages of cyan, magenta, yellow, and black (CMYK) inks.

Process inks
Cyan, Magenta, Yellow, and Black ink; the fundamental inks used in printing.

Process tints
Colors that can be printed by mixing varying percentages of CMYK inks.

Profile
Defines and interprets colors for a color management system.

Project scope
The work that needs to be accomplished to deliver a project, the complexity of which can be discussed using three variables—performance, time and cost.

Projecting cap
Produces a squared edge that extends the anchor point of a stroked path by a distance that is 1/2 the weight of the stroke.

Proof setup
Lets you preview your image to see how it will look when printed on a specific device.

Properties panel
Panel on which the characteristics of Adjustment layers are modified.

Proportional spacing
The text spacing in which each character takes up a different amount of space, based on its width.

Pull quote
A typographical design solution in which text is used at a larger point size and positioned prominently on the page.

Q

Quick Selection tool
Tool that lets you paint a selection from the interior using a brush tip, reducing rough edges and blockiness.

R

Radial gradient
A series of concentric circles, in which the starting color appears at the center of the gradient, then radiates out to the ending color.

Rasterize
The process of converting a type layer to a bitmapped image layer.

Recolor Artwork
An Illustrator utility that offers you the ability to affect color in an entire illustration dynamically—rather than fill objects with various colors individually.

Records
Rows of information organized by fields in a data source file.

Refine Edge option
Button found on the options bar of a variety of tools that allows you to improve the size and edges of a selection.

Reflection
Occurs when light strikes an object and 'bounces' off the object.

Region
Similar to a fill, a region is a new shape or area created by the overlap of Illustrator objects. Regions are created when the Live Paint Bucket tool is applied.

Registration marks
Marks that align color-separated output.

Registration swatch
The swatch you should use as the fill color for slug text so that it appears on all printing plates.

Relief
The height of ridges within an object.

Rendering intent
The way in which a color-management system handles color conversion from one color space to another.

Resolution
The number of pixels in a given inch of a bitmap graphic.

Resolution-independent
Refers to a graphic which can be scaled with no impact on image quality. Usually refers to vector graphics.

Resulting color
The outcome of the blend color applied to the base color.

Revolve
Another method that Illustrator provides for applying a 3D effect to a 2D object by "sweeping" a path in a circular direction around the Y axis of the object.

RGB
Red, Green and Blue; the additive primary colors of light.

RGB image
Image that contains three color channels (one each for red, green, and blue).

RGB mode
Color mode in which components are combined to create new colors.

Rich black
A process tint that is 100% Black plus 50% Cyan; used to print deep, dark black areas of a printed page.

Round cap
Produces a stroked path with rounded ends.

Round join
Produces stroked lines with rounded corners.

Row
In a table, the horizontal arrangement of cells.

Ruler Guides
Horizontal and vertical rules that you can position anywhere in a layout as a reference for positioning elements.

Rulers
Onscreen markers that help you precisely measure and position an object. Rulers can be displayed using the View menu.

Rules
Horizontal, vertical or diagonal lines on the page used as design elements or to underline text.

 S

Sampling
A method of changing foreground and background colors by copying existing colors from an image.

Sans serif fonts
Fonts that do not have tails or strokes at the end of characters; commonly used in headlines.

Saturation
The strength or purity of the color, representing the amount of gray in proportion to hue (measured as a percentage from 0% [gray], to 100% [fully saturated]). Also known as *chroma*.

Save As
A command that lets you create a copy of the open file using a new name.

Scale
The size relationship of objects to one another.

Scanner
An electronic device that converts print material into an electronic file.

Scatter brush
A brush style which disperses copies of an object along a path.

Scope creep
A condition in which a project seems to have lost its way.

Scratch area
The area outside the artboard where objects may be stored for future use; objects on the scratch area will not print.

Screen frequency (line screen)
The number of printer dots or halftone cells per inch used to print grayscale images or color separations.

Screen Mode
Options for viewing documents, such as Preview, Normal, and Presentation mode.

Sections
Pages in a document where page numbering changes.

Selection
An area in an image that is surrounded by a selection marquee and can then be manipulated.

Semi-autoflow
A method for manually threading text through multiple frames.

Serif fonts
Fonts that have a tail, or stroke, at the end of some characters. These tails make it easier for the eye to recognize words; therefore, serif fonts are generally used in text passages.

Glossary

Shading
Collection of Bevel and Emboss settings that determine lighting effects.

Shadow Mode
Bevel and Emboss setting that determines how pigments are combined.

Shape Builder tool
Complex tool that allows you to unite multiple objects as a single object.

Sharp
Anti-aliasing setting that displays type with the best possible resolution.

Sharpen More filter
Increases the contrast of adjacent pixels and can focus blurry images.

Sharpness
An element of composition that draws the viewer's eye to a specific area.

Sidecar file
A separate file that contains metadata and can be applied to other files as a template.

Silhouette
A selection you make in Photoshop using selection tools, such as the Pen tool.

Size
Determines the clarity of a drop shadow.

Slice
Divided artwork to be output as individual and, therefore, smaller files.

Slug
A note you include on your document for a printer. A slug usually contains special instructions for outputting your document.

Slug area
The area for a slug, positioned outside of the document's trim size, so that it will be discarded when the document is trimmed.

Smart Filter
A filter applied to a Smart Object and allows for nondestructive editing of the object(s).

Smart Guides
A feature that displays vertical or horizontal guides that appear automatically when you draw a shape or move an object and are helpful in its positioning. Also, non-printing words that appear on the artboard and identify visible or invisible objects, page boundaries, intersections, anchor points, etc.

Smart Object
A combination of objects that has a visible indicator in the bottom-right corner of the layer thumbnail. Makes it possible to scale, rotate, and wrap layers without losing image quality.

Smooth
Anti-aliasing setting that gives type more rounded edges.

Smooth points
Anchor points created by clicking and dragging the Pen tool; the path continues uninterrupted through the anchor point.

Snap to point
Automatically aligns points when they get close together.

Snippet
An XML file with an .inds file extension that contains complete representation of document elements, including all formatting tags and document structure.

Soft proof
The way an image looks on specific calibrated hardware using a color management system.

Soft return
In typography, using the Shift key in addition to the Enter (Win) or [return] (Mac) key to move text onto the following line without creating a new paragraph.

Source
The image containing the color that will be matched.

Spot colors
Non-process inks that are manufactured by companies; special pre-mixed inks that are printed separately from process inks.

Spread
Determines the width of drop shadow text. Also refers to facing pages.

Spring-loaded keyboard shortcuts
A feature that lets you temporarily change the active tool by pressing and holding the key that changes to another tool.

Square-up
The default placement of a Photoshop file in InDesign that includes the entire image with background.

Stacking order
Refers to the hierarchical order of objects on a level. Also the hierarchy of objects on the artboard, from frontmost to backmost.

Starting color
The first color in a gradient.

State
An entry on the History panel, or the individual steps in an action in the Actions panel.

Status bar

A utility on the artboard that contains a list arrow menu from which you can choose a status line with information about the current tool, the date and time, the amount of free memory, or the number of undo operations. Also the area located at the bottom of the program window (Win) or the work area (Mac) that displays information such as the file size of the active window and a description of the active tool.

Stroke

A color applied to the outline of an object.

Stroke weight

The thickness of a stroke, usually measured in points.

Stroking the edges

The process of making a selection or layer stand out by formatting it with a border.

Strong

Anti-aliasing setting that makes type appear heavier, much like the bold attribute.

Structure

A Bevel and Emboss setting that determines the size and physical properties of the object.

Style

In type, a collection of formatting attributes that can be saved and applied to specific characters or a paragraph. When creating a customized object, there are eighteen predesigned styles that can be applied to buttons.

Subtractive colors

A color system in which the full combination of cyan, magenta, and yellow absorb all color and produce black.

Subtractive primary colors

Cyan, Magenta and Yellow; the term subtractive refers to the concept that each is produced by removing or subtracting one of the additive primary colors and that overlapping all three pigments would absorb all colors.

Swatches panel

Contains available colors that can be selected for use as a foreground or background color. You can also add your own colors to the Swatches panel.

Symbol fonts

Used to display unique characters (such as $, ÷, or ™).

Symbol instance

A single usage of a symbol.

Symbol instance set

Symbol instances created with the Symbol Sprayer tool.

Symmetrical balance

When objects are placed equally on either side of an imaginary vertical line in the center of the page.

T

Table of Contents (TOC)

A list of divisions in a book and the pages on which they start, generated in InDesign by styles applied to headings and subheadings.

Tables

Rectangles in horizontal rows and vertical columns that organize information.

Tabs

A command that positions text at specific horizontal locations within a text frame.

Target

When sampling a color, the image that will receive the matched color.

Target document

An InDesign file containing text that will be seen by all recipients as well as placeholders representing fields in a data source with which it will be merged.

Target layer

The layer selected on the Layers panel.

Targeting

Clicking a layer on the Layers panel to select it.

Text frames

Boxes drawn with the Type tool in which you type or place text.

Text insets

In a text frame, the distance the text is from the frame edge.

Threading

Linking text from one text frame to another.

Thumbnail

Contains a miniature picture of the layer's content, appears to the left of the layer name, and can be turned on or off.

Tick marks

Short lines that extend out from the value axis of a graph and aid viewers in interpreting the meaning of column height by indicating incremental values on the value axis.

Tile

Artwork, usually square, used repeatedly in a pattern fill.

Tiling

The process of repeating a tile as a fill for a pattern.

Timing panel

Command central for controlling when animated objects play.

Tint

In InDesign, a lighter version of a given color.

Title bar
At the top of the Illustrator window; contains the name of the document, magnification level, and color mode. In Photoshop, displays the program name and filename of the open image. The title bar also contains buttons for minimizing, maximizing, and closing the image.

Tolerance
The range of pixels that determines which pixels will be selected. The lower the tolerance, the closer the color is to the selection. The setting can have a value from 0–255.

Tone
The brightness and contrast within an image.

Tools panel
Contains tools for frequently used commands. On the face of a tool is a graphic representation of its function. Place the pointer over each button to display a tool tip, which displays the name or function of that button. An arrow in the lower-right of the button face indicates other similar tools in the group.

Tracking
The process of inserting or removing uniform spaces between text characters to affect the width of selected words or entire blocks of text.

Transform
The act of moving, scaling, skewing, or rotating an object.

Transmission
Occurs when light strikes an object and passes through the object.

Transparency blend space
Setting that applies to managing color for transparency in your InDesign layout.

Trim marks
Like crop marks, define where a printed image should be trimmed; used to create multiple marks for multiple objects on a page that are to be trimmed.

Trim size
The size to which a printed document will be cut when it clears the printing press.

Tweaking
Making small, specific improvements to artwork or typography.

Type
Text, or a layer containing text. Each character is measured in points. In traditional measurement, one inch is equivalent to 72.27 points.

Type area select
An Illustrator preference which allows the user to select text simply by clicking anywhere in the text.

Type spacing
Adjustments you can make to the space between characters and between lines of type.

Typeface
See Font.

——————— U ———————

Unnamed colors
Any colors you create that aren't saved to the Swatches panel.

——————— V ———————

Variation
A group of swatches loaded by the Color Guide panel when you select an object on the artboard and then choose a harmony rule.

Vector font
Fonts that are vector-based type outlines, which means that they are mathematically defined shapes. Also known as *outline type*.

Vector graphics
Artwork created entirely by geometrically defined paths and curves. Usually created and imported from Adobe Illustrator.

Vectors
Straight or curved paths defined by geometrical characteristics, usually created and imported from a drawing program.

Vignette
A feature in which the border of a picture or portrait fades into the surrounding color at its edges.

Vignette effect
A feature that uses feathering to fade a marquee shape.

Visible light
Light waves that are visible to the human eye.

Visual hierarchy
The order in which the eye understands what it is seeing.

——————— W ———————

Warping type
A feature that lets you create distortions that conform to a variety of shapes.

Web Gallery
In Bridge, contains a thumbnail index page of all exported images, the actual JPEG images, and any included links.

Web-safe colors
The 216 colors that can be displayed on the web without dithering.

White light
Refers to the concept that natural light on Earth appears to people as not having any dominant hue.

Widget
Tool that can be used to change a 3D object.

Widows
Words or single lines of text at the top of a column or page that become separated from the ther lines in a paragraph.

Working space
Tells the color management system how RGB and CMYK values are interpreted.

Workspace
The entire window, from the Menu bar at the top of the window, to the status bar at the bottom border of the program window.

Workspace switcher
List arrow on the Menu bar that lets you switch between defined workspaces.

Z

Zero point
By default, the upper-left corner of the document; the point from which the location of all objects on the page is measured.

Zoom text box
A utility in the lower-left corner of the Illustrator window that displays the current magnification level.

Note: Page numbers preceded by IL refer to Illustrated chapters; those preceded by IND refer to InDesign chapters; those preceded by INT refer to the Integration chapter; those preceded by PS refer to Photoshop chapters.

across stroke option, Gradient panel, IL 2–39

active layer, PS 3–8

    inserting layers beneath, PS 3–12

Add Anchor Points command, IL 1–58—59, IL 1–62

additive colors, PS 5–5, PS 5–6

adjusting color saturation, PS 5–5

adjustment layers, PS 3–4

    adding, INT 1–35

Adobe Bridge. See Bridge

Adobe Configurator, PS 1–23

Adobe Creative Cloud. See Creative Cloud

Adobe Exchange, PS 2–7

Adobe Generator, PS 3–9

Adobe Illustrator Clipboard (AICB), INT 1–5

Adobe Mini Bridge. See Mini Bridge

Adobe Output Module, PS 2–27

Adobe Photoshop. See Photoshop

Adobe Typekit. See Typekit

Align panel, IL 4–30, IND 4–8—10

aligning

    anchor points, IL 3–5, IL 3–8

    objects with Align panel, IL 4–30

aligning and distributing objects on a page, IND 4–4—19

    fills and strokes, IND 4–4—6, IND 4–12—13

Gap tool, IND 4–11, IND 4–16—17

Live Distribute technique, IND 4–1—11, IND 4–14—16

    Step and Repeat command, IND 4–6—7, IND 4–13—14

along stroke option, Gradient panel, IL 2–39

altering images, ethical implications, PS 1–28

altitude setting, Bevel and Emboss style, PS 6–20

anchor point(s), IL 1–41

    adding, IL 1–58—59, IL 1–62

    aligning and joining, IL 3–5, IL 3–8—9

    changing appearance, IL 3–11

    converting, IL 3–12—13, IL 3–15

    hiding, IL 2–35

    removing from paths, IL 3–5

Anchor Point tool, reshaping path segments, IL 3–55, IL 3–62

angle, drop shadows, PS 6–13

angle setting

    Bevel and Emboss style, PS 6–20

    drop shadows, PS 6–14

Anti-alias setting, Magnetic Lasso tool, PS 4–13

anti-aliasing, PS 6–16—19

    applying, PS 6–18

    methods, PS 6–17

    undoing, PS 6–19

    when to apply, PS 6–16

Apply Color button, IND 5–12—13

Apply Gradient button, IND 5–12—13

Apply Master to Pages command, IND 3–34—35

Apply None button, IND 5–13

area text, IL 2–10

Arrange commands, IL 1–60, IND 4–24—25

Arrange Documents button, IL 1–22

Arrange menu, IND 4–20

arrangement, PS 1–27

arranging multiple artboards, IL 1–70, IL 1–76

artboard(s)

    multiple. See multiple artboards

    resizing, IL 1–76

Artboard Navigation menu, IL 1–77

Artboards panel, IL 1–71

.arw file format, PS 1–5

assembling illustrations, IL 3–28—29

assets, generating from layers, PS 3–9

asymmetrical balance, PS 1–28

attributes

    applying to objects, IL 3–24—27, IL 3–26—27

    strokes, modifying, IL 3–33

attribution licenses, Creative Commons, PS 1–31

attribution no derivatives licenses, Creative Commons, PS 1–31

attribution non-commercial licenses, Creative Commons, PS 1–31

attribution non-commercial no derivatives licenses, Creative Commons, PS 1–31

attribution non-commercial share alike licenses, Creative Commons, PS 1–31

attribution share alike licenses, Creative Commons, PS 1–31

Autocorrect feature, IND 2–31

autoflowing text, IND 4–46—47, IND 4–49—50

automatic page numbering, IND 3–25—26, IND 3–29—30

Average command, IL 3–5

background color, PS 5–6
    changing using Color panel, PS 5–7
    changing using Eyedropper tool, PS 5–9
    setting, PS 5–7

Background layers, PS 3–4
    converting image layers into, PS 3–6—7

balancing
    colors, PS 5–28, PS 5–31
    objects, PS 1–28

base color, PS 5–27

baseline, IL 2–4, IND 2–5, PS 6–9

baseline shift, PS 6–9

Behance, PS 2–6

Bevel and Emboss style, PS 6–20
    adding with Layer menu, PS 6–22
    modifying settings, PS 6–23

settings, PS 6–20

bitmap color mode, PS 5–6

bitmap (.bmp) file format, PS 1–5

bitmap font, PS 6–4

bitmap images, IL 1–40—41, IND 4–32, PS 5–2

Black & White command, PS 5–22

black shadow text, IND 5–16, IND 5–21—22

bleed(s), IND 1–5

blemishes, correcting. *See* imperfections, correcting

blend color, PS 5–27

blending modes, PS 3–9, PS 5–27, PS 5–30
    applying, INT 1–34—35
    components, PS 5–27
    list, PS 5–28

blurring images, PS 6–24—25

blurry images, fixing, PS 5–26

.bmp (bitmap) file format, PS 1–5

borders, PS 5–16—17

bounding boxes, IL 1–27—28, IND 4–10, IND 4–33

Bridge
    creating PDFs, PS 2–27
    creating Web Gallery, PS 2–29
    filtering, PS 1–15, PS 2–11
    finding files, PS 1–9—10
    housekeeping tasks, PS 2–8
    opening files using Folders panel, PS 1–12
    rating files, PS 1–15
    resetting preferences, PS 1–10
    uses, PS 1–10

brightness
    adjusting in images, PS 5–29
    color, PS 5–5

Brightness/Contrast dialog box, PS 5–29

Bring Forward command, IL 1–60, IND 4–20

Bring to Front command, IL 1–60, IND 4–20

bulleted and numbered lists, IND 2–34—37
    creating, IND 2–34, IND 2–36
    modifying, IND 2–34—35, IND 2–37

Camera Raw format, PS 1–5

canvas size, PS 1–11

caps, strokes, IL 3–30—31

captions based on metadata, creating, IND 4–44

channels, PS 5–5

character(s), kerning, PS 6–8, PS 6–10

Character panel, IL 1–8, IL 1–9, IL 2–2, IL 2–7, IND 1–7, IND 2–5, PS 6–8
    formatting paragraphs, IND 2–20
    formatting text, IND 2–4, IND 2–8—10
    modifying text attributes, IND 2–11—12
    scaling text, IND 2–6
    searching for fonts, IND 2–8—10

character spacing, PS 6–8

character style(s), IL 2–13, IND 2–24, IND 2–26—27
    applying, IND 2–27
    creating, IND 2–26—27, PS 6–9

Character Style Options dialog box, PS 6–11

Character Styles panel, IND 2–24, IND 2–25, PS 6–9

Check Spelling dialog box, IND 2–30—31

Chisel Hard Emboss layer style, INT 1–12—15

clicking and dragging, IL 3–10

Clipboard, PS 4–2

clipping groups. *See* clipping mask(s)

clipping mask(s), IL 4–46—53

    applying fills, IL 4–49—50

    creating, IL 4–48

    defining, IL 4–46

    Draw Inside drawing mode, IL 4–47, IL
        4–52—53

    multiple objects used as, IL 4–46

    special effects, IL 4–47, IL 4–51—52

    text used as, IL 4–51

Clipping Mask/Release command, IL 4–47

clipping paths, wrapping text around graphics,
    IND 4–36—37

clipping sets, IL 5–26—29

    copying, IL 5–28—29

    creating, IL 5–27

    flattening artwork, IL 5–26, IL 5–29

closed paths

    converting stroked paths to, IL 4–19

    drawing using smooth points, IL 3–20

closing

    files. *See* closing files

    panels, IL 1–8

    paths, IL 3–8

closing files, PS 1–25

    closing all files without exiting Photoshop,
        PS 1–24

    exiting vs., PS 1–24

cloud computing, PS 2–4—5

CMYK color mode, PS 5–6

CMYK inks, IND 5–4

collapsing panels, IL 1–8

color(s), IND 5–1—37, PS 5–1—34

    adding to Swatches panel, IL 2–23, IL 2–26—27

    additive, PS 5–5, PS 5–6

    adjusting saturation, PS 5–5

    applying to objects, IND 5–12—13, IND 5–18

    applying to text, IND 5–15, IND 5–20

    applying with Swatches panel, IL 1–45

    background. *See* background color

    black shadow text, IND 5–16, IND 5–21—22

    brightness, PS 5–5

    changing selection color on layers, IL 5–9

    creating, IL 2–24—25

    Default Fill and Stroke button, IND 5–12,
        IND 5–19

    deleting swatches, IND 5–16—17, IND 5–23

    ending, IND 5–30

    existing, changing type color using, PS 6–7

    fill. *See* fill(s)

    foreground. *See* foreground color

    gradients. *See* gradient(s)

    guides, margins, and columns, IND 3–8,
        IND 3–18

    identifying layers with, PS 3–19

    layers, IND 4–22

    matching, PS 5–32—33

    modifying swatches, IND 5–16, IND 5–23

    named, IND 5–4, IND 5–16

    Paper swatch, IND 5–14

    printing images, PS 2–23

process. *See* process colors

psychology, PS 5–4

sample, creating gradients, PS 5–20

saturation, PS 5–5

selecting using Color Picker, PS 5–10, PS 5–12

selecting using Swatches panel, PS 5–11,
    PS 5–12

selections based on, PS 4–18

spot. *See* spot colors

starting, IND 5–30

stroke. *See* stroke(s)

subtractive, PS 5–6

Swap Fill and Stroke button, IND 5–19

theme, changing, PS 1–21

type, changing, PS 6–7

unnamed, IND 5–6—7, IND 5–11, IND 5–17

Color Balance dialog box, PS 5–28, PS 5–31

Color blending mode, PS 5–28

Color Burn blending mode, PS 5–28

Color Dodge blending mode, PS 5–28

color images, converting to grayscale images,
    PS 5–24

color labels, applying to page thumbnails,
    IND 1–25, IND 1–27

color management systems, PS 5–7

color mode(s), PS 5–2

    bitmap, PS 5–6

    CMYK, PS 5–6

    converting grayscale images to, PS 5–22,
        PS 5–24

    duotone, PS 5–6

    grayscale, PS 5–6

color mode(s) (*continued*)

   HSB, PS 5–5

   Lab, PS 5–5

   RGB, PS 5–5—6

   selecting, PS 5–4

color models, PS 5–2, PS 5–4

Color panel, IL 2–23, IND 5–10, IND 5–11, IND 5–12, PS 5–8

   changing background color, PS 5–7

Color Picker, IND 5–18, PS 5–10, PS 5–11, PS 5–12, PS 6–4, PS 6–13

color range(s), PS 3–15—16

Color Range command, PS 4–19, PS 4–20

Color Range dialog box, PS 3–15, PS 3–16

Color Range tool, Magic Wand tool vs., PS 4–21

color separation, PS 5–6

Color Settings dialog box, PS 5–7

color stops, IL 2–22, IND 5–30, IND 5–31

   changing, IL 2–23

color tint frames, IND 3–19—20

colorizing grayscale images, PS 5–23, PS 5–25

Colors slider, Image Trace panel, IL 3–38

column break(s), inserting with text frames, IND 4–47, IND 4–52

Column Break command, IND 4–47

column guides, locking, IND 3–8

column(s), text

   color, IND 3–8, IND 3–18

   modifying, IND 3–6, IND 3–14

commands. *See also specific command names*

   choosing, PS 1–16

complexity, projects, PS 2–7

compositing, PS 4–2

composition, PS 1–26—27

compound paths, IL 4–20—23

   creating, IL 4–20—22

   special effects with, IL 4–23

compound shapes

   creating, IL 4–33

   defining, IL 4–24

   expanding, IL 4–27

   releasing, IL 4–27

   special effects using, IL 4–34—35

concluding work sessions, PS 1–24

condensing layers, IL 5–12

conditional text, IND 3–16

Configurator, PS 1–23

content indicator, IND 4–34

contrast

   adding emphasis using, PS 2–28

   adjusting, PS 5–29

Contrast setting, Magnetic Lasso tool, PS 4–13

Control panel, IND 3–9

   placed images, IL 3–42

   setting up documents, IND 3–9

converting layers, PS 3–6—7

copying. *See also* duplicating

   clipping sets, IL 5–28—29

   layer styles between layers, INT 1–30—31

   objects, IL 1–28—29, IL 1–34—36, IND 1–29, IND 1–32—33

   selections, PS 4–9

copying and pasting

   graphics, IND 4–35

   from Illustrator to Photoshop, INT 1–4—7

copyright, PS 1–29—30

corner(s), round. *See* round corners

corner points, IL 3–4

   beginning and ending paths with, IL 3–21

corner widgets, deactivating, IL 1–60

Corners dialog box, IL 4–37

correcting

   imperfections. *See* imperfections, correcting

   selection errors, PS 4–6

   spelling errors, PS 6–10

Create a new layer button, PS 3–8

Create Guides command, IND 3–7

Create New Layer button, IL 5–5

Create new paragraph style button, PS 6–9

Create New Sublayer button, IL 5–5

Create Outlines command, IL 2–2, IL 2–28—29

creating graphics

   advanced text features. *See* text

   Pen tool. *See* Pen tool

Creative Cloud, PS 2–4—5

   managing, PS 2–4—5

   sharing images with Behance, PS 2–6

   Sync feature, PS 2–5

Creative Cloud apps, updates, PS 1–24

Creative Commons licenses, PS 1–31

Creative.adobe.com, PS 2–4

Crisp setting, anti-aliasing, PS 6–17

cropping images, PS 3–14

.cr2 file format, PS 1–5

.crw file format, PS 1–5

curved lines, drawing. *See* drawing curved lines

Customize Style Import option button, IND 3–48

customizing

    gradient fills, PS 5–19

    workspace, IL 1–5, IND 1–5, IND 1–11, PS 1–18

cutting and pasting artwork between layers,
    IL 5–13

cutting selections, PS 4–9

Darken blending mode, PS 5–28

dashed strokes, IL 3–31—32, IL 3–34

data merges, IND 2–26

.dcm (dicom) file format, PS 1–5

.dcr file format, PS 1–5

.dcs file format, PS 1–5

deactivating corner widgets, IL 1–60

default display, changing, PS 1–21

Default Fill and Stroke button, IND 5–12, IND 5–19

defringing selections, PS 3–15, PS 3–17

Delete Anchor Point tool, IL 3–5

Delete Swatch command, IND 5–16, IND 5–17,
    IND 5–23

deleting. *See also* removing

    layers, IL 5–23, PS 3–11, PS 3–13

    objects with Shape Builder tool, IL 4–45

    selections, PS 4–9

    states from History panel, PS 2–15, PS 6–19

    swatches, IND 5–16—17, IND 5–23

depth of field, PS 1–28

derivative works, PS 1–29, PS 1–30

deselecting, selections, PS 4–9, PS 4–11

deselecting selections, PS 4–5

design, print vs. web, PS 1–26

devices, monitor, PS 2–18

dicom (.dcm) file format, PS 1–5

Difference blending mode, PS 5–28

digital cameras, PS 1–25

    Camera Raw format. *See* Camera Raw format

digital images, PS 1–2

dimming placed images on layers, IL 5–24

Direct Selection tool, IL 1–58—59, IND 4–33

    adding anchor points, IL 1–58—59, IL 1–62

    deactivating corner widgets, IL 1–60

    special effect, IL 1–65

direction lines, IL 3–10—11

direction points, IL 3–10

displaying. *See also* viewing

    changing default display, PS 1–21

    document grids, IL 1–22, IND 1–20—21

    documents, PS 1–21

    frame edges, IND 1–15, IND 1–19—20

    images, modes, PS 1–20

    layer thumbnails, PS 3–4

    layers, IL 5–11, PS 2–13, PS 2–14

    panels, PS 1–17, PS 1–22

    ruler guides, IL 1–22, IND 1–20

    rulers, IL 1–22, IND 1–18

    selection marks, IL 1–17, IL 1–22

Dissolve blending mode, PS 5–28

distance, drop shadows, PS 6–13

distance setting, drop shadows, PS 6–14

Distort filters, PS 6–24

distributing objects. *See* aligning and distributing
    objects on a page

Divide pathfinder, IL 4–32

Divide shape mode, IL 4–25

.dnf file format, PS 1–5

dock(s), PS 1–17

docking panels, IL 1–10, IND 1–8, IND 1–11

document(s)

    arranging, IL 1–22

    InDesign, creating, INT 1–37

    merged, IND 2–26

    multi-page, viewing, IND 3–12

    multiple. *See* multiple documents

    navigating, IND 1–24—27

    sections, IND 3–50, IND 3–52—53

    setting up. *See* setting up documents

    target, IND 2–26

    toggling between, IL 1–24—25

    types, IND 3–5

document grids, IL 1–16, IL 1–22, IND 1–15

    hiding and displaying, IND 1–20—21

    setting up, IND 1–21

Document Info panel, IL 1–12

Drag and Drop feature, IND 2–32

dragging

    frame handles with keyboard combinations,
        IND 1–28

    layers to change order, IND 4–23

    objects between layers, IL 5–13

dragging and dropping, IL 1–29
    applying color to objects, IND 5–12, IND 5–18
    applying master pages to document pages, IND 3–34
    duplicating objects, IL 1–51
Draw Behind drawing mode, IL 1–60, IL 1–63—64
Draw Inside drawing mode, clipping masks, IL 4–47
drawing
    curved lines. *See* drawing curved lines
    Draw Behind drawing mode, IL 1–60, IL 1–63—64
    illustrations. *See* drawing illustrations
    lines with curved and straight segments, IL 3–16
    Pencil tool, IL 3–59—61, IL 3–63—65
    preparing for, IL 1–40
    reshaping path segments with Anchor Point tool, IL 3–55, IL 3–62
    reversing direction during, IL 3–17
    straight lines. *See* drawing straight lines
drawing curved lines, IL 3–10—17
    converting anchor points, IL 3–12—13, IL 3–15
    defining properties of curved lines, IL 3–10—12
    reversing direction while drawing, IL 3–17
    toggling between Pen tool and selection tools, IL 3–13
drawing illustrations, IL 3–18—23
    beginning and ending paths with corner points, IL 3–21

closed paths using smooth points, IL 3–20
    redirecting paths, IL 3–22
    from scratch, IL 3–18
    starting, IL 3–18
    tracing scanned images, IL 3–19, IL 3–23
drawing straight lines, IL 3–4—9
    aligning and joining anchor points, IL 3–5, IL 3–8—9
    creating new views, IL 3–4, IL 3–6
    Pen tool, IL 3–4—5
Dreamweaver, jumping between Photoshop and, PS 1–5
.drf file format, PS 1–5
drop caps, IND 2–17, IND 2–23
drop shadows, IL 2–35, IL 2–36—37, PS 6–12—15
    adding, PS 6–14
    controlling, PS 6–13
    modifying settings, PS 6–15
    settings, PS 6–14
drop zones, PS 1–17
due dates, PS 2–9
duotone color mode, PS 5–6
duotone images, PS 5–23
duplicating. *See also* copying; copying and pasting
    layers, IL 5–5—6, IL 5–23, IND 4–21, PS 3–18
    master pages, IND 3–27
    objects, IL 1–34—36, IND 1–32—33
    objects using dragging and dropping, IL 1–51
dynamic preview, IND 4–34
dynamic spell checking, IND 2–31

edges, Live Paint Bucket tool, IL 3–46—47, IL 3–51
Edit Artboards mode, IL 1–73
editing
    curved lines, IL 3–14
    multiple artboards, IL 1–70, IL 1–76
editing text, IND 2–30—33
    Autocorrect feature, IND 2–31
    complex documents, IND 4–48
    Drag and Drop feature, IND 2–32
    Find/Change command, IND 2–30, IND 2–32
    spell checking, IND 2–30—31, IND 2–33
effects. *See* special effects; *specific effects*
electronic mail (e-mail), IND 2–6—7
Elliptical Marquee tool, PS 4–5
em dashes, IND 3–36—37
em spaces, IND 3–26
Embed button, IL 3–43
embedding placed images, IL 3–43
emphasis, adding using contrast, PS 2–28
en dashes, IND 3–36—37
en spaces, IND 3–26
ending color, IND 5–30
ending work sessions, PS 1–24
enlarging images, Loupe tool, PS 1–8
.eps (Photoshop EPS) file format, PS 1–5
.erf file format, PS 1–5
errors. *See also* imperfections, correcting
    selection, correcting, PS 4–6
    spelling, correcting, PS 6–10
ethics, altering images, PS 1–28
Exchange, PS 2–7

Exclusion blending mode, PS 5–28

exiting
    closing vs., PS 1–24
    Photoshop, PS 1–25

expanding
    compound shapes, IL 4–27
    Live Paint groups, IL 3–50—51
    panels, IND 1–8
    traced graphics, IL 3–41—43

Export dialog box, INT 1–9

exporting
    layers from Illustrator to Photoshop,
        INT 1–8—11
    layers to Photoshop, IL 5–21
    PDFs, INT 1–39—41
    resolution for exported files, INT 1–31

.exr (Open EXR) file format, PS 1–5

Extensible Metadata Platform (XMP) standard
    format, PS 2–8

Eyedropper tool, IL 3–24, IL 3–27
    changing background color, PS 5–9

facing pages, IND 3–4

Fade command, PS 5–27

Fade dialog box, PS 5–30

fair use doctrine, PS 1–29, PS 1–30

fastening points, PS 4–5

feather(s), applying to selections, INT 1–11

Feather setting, Magnetic Lasso tool,
    PS 4–13

field(s), IND 2–26

field of view, PS 1–28

file(s)
    closing, PS 1–24, PS 1–25
    filtering using Bridge, PS 1–15
    finding, PS 1–9—10
    flattening, PS 1–4
    opening. See opening files
    rating using Bridge, PS 1–15
    saving, PS 1–8, PS 1–13
    sidecar, PS 2–8
    uploading to Creative Cloud web site, PS 2–5

file formats
    Camera Raw. See Camera Raw format
    changing using Save As command, PS 1–14
    supported by Photoshop, PS 1–5

File Handling & Clipboard preferences, INT 1–5

File Info dialog box, PS 2–24

file versioning, PS 2–4—5

fill(s), IND 4–4—6, IND 4–12—13
    adding to open paths, IL 3–25
    applying, IL 1–46
    applying to objects, IND 5–12—13, IND 5–18
    applying to text, IL 2–28, IL 2–30, IL 2–31
    clipping masks, IL 4–49—50
    gradient. See gradient(s); gradient fills; linear
        gradients; radial gradients
    Paper vs. None, IND 5–14

Fill button, IND 4–4—5, IND 5–12, IND 5–13,
    IND 5–19
    activating, IL 1–44

Filmstrip view, clicking thumbnails, PS 1–8

filter(s), PS 5–26—27, PS 5–30
    Distort, PS 6–24

softening filter effects, PS 5–27
    type. See filter(s), type

filter(s), type, PS 6–24—27
    applying to type layers, PS 6–26
    blurring images, PS 6–24—25
    distort, PS 6–24
    modifying filter settings, PS 6–27
    multiple, PS 6–26
    neon glow, PS 6–27
    relief, PS 6–24

Filter panel, PS 1–10

filtering
    Bridge, PS 1–15, PS 2–11
    Isolation Mode, PS 3–10
    layers, PS 2–12—13

Find Font utility, IL 2–15

Find/Change command, IND 2–30, IND 2–32

Find/Change dialog box, IND 2–31

finding. See also searching
    files, PS 1–9—10
    fonts, IL 2–15, PS 6–5
    layers, IL 5–21, IL 5–23

Fitting commands, IND 4–36

Flash 3D (.fl3) file format, PS 1–5

flattening
    artwork, IL 5–26, IL 5–29
    files, PS 1–4, PS 3–2, PS 3–19

flipping selections, PS 4–22

"floating" document windows, IND 1–23

floating documents, changing to tabbed
    documents from, PS 1–14

floating images, PS 1–18

flowing text into objects, IL 2–10—13

.fl3 (Flash 3D) file format, PS 1–5

focus, maintaining, PS 5–13

Folders panel, opening files, PS 1–12

font(s), PS 6–2
    acquiring, PS 6–5
    bitmap, PS 6–4
    finding, PS 6–5
    locating and replacing, IL 2–15
    missing, finding, PS 6–6
    number to use, PS 6–17
    readability, PS 6–5
    sans serif, PS 6–4, PS 6–5
    searching for, IND 2–8—10, IND 2–14—15
    serif, PS 6–4, PS 6–5
    symbol, PS 6–4
    vector, PS 6–4
    warnings, IND 1–8

font families, IND 2–9—10, PS 6–4

font list, IND 2–4

footnotes
    formatting, IND 2–14
    inserting automatically, IND 2–13

foreground color, PS 5–6
    setting, PS 5–6

formatting
    footnotes, IND 2–14
    paragraphs. *See* formatting paragraphs
    text. *See* formatting text

formatting paragraphs, IND 2–16—23
    Character panel, IND 2–20

drop caps, IND 2–17, IND 2–23
    indents, IND 2–16—17, IND 2–19
    Paragraph panel, IND 2–16—17, IND 2–20
    returns, IND 2–18—19, IND 2–23
    vertical spacing between paragraphs,
        IND 2–19, IND 2–21
    widows and orphans, IND 2–18

formatting text, IL 2–4, IL 2–6—8, IL 2–30,
    IND 2–4—15
    Character panel, IND 2–4, IND 2–8—10
    kerning and tracking text, IND 2–6—7,
        IND 2–12
    leading, IND 2–5
    modifying attributes, IND 2–11—12
    scaling text horizontally and vertically,
        IND 2–6
    searching for fonts, IND 2–8—10, IND
        2–14—15
    subscript characters, IND 2–7
    superscript characters, IND 2–7, IND 2–13
    underlining text, IND 2–7, IND 2–13—14

frame(s), IND 1–15, IND 4–1—53
    aligning and distributing objects. *See* aligning
        and distributing objects on a page
    graphics. *See* graphics frames
    stacking and layering objects. *See* layer(s)
    text. *See* text frames
    wrapping text around, IND 3–51,
        IND 3–54—55

frame edges, IND 1–15
    hiding and showing, IND 1–19—20

frame handles, dragging with keyboard
    combinations, IND 1–28

frame-based grids, setting up, IND 1–21

framing, PS 1–28

Free Transform tool, IL 4–4, IL 4–5, IL 4–8,
    IL 4–14—15

Frequency setting, Magnetic Lasso tool, PS 4–13

Full Screen Mode, PS 1–20

fuzziness setting, Color Range command, PS 4–19

Gap tool, IND 4–11, IND 4–16—17

Gaussian Blur filter, PS 6–24—25

General Preferences dialog box, IL 1–31

Generator, PS 3–9

GIF or .gif (Graphics Interchange Format) file
    format, PS 1–5

gloss contour setting, Bevel and Emboss style,
    PS 6–20

glyphs, IND 2–25

Glyphs panel, IL 2–9, IND 2–25

Go To Page command, IND 1–24

Google Earth (.kmz) file format, PS 1–5

GPU (graphics processing unit), Open GL, PS 6–22

gradient(s), IL 2–22, IND 5–30—37
    adding to Swatches panel, IL 2–23,
        IL 2–26—27
    applying, IND 5–32, IND 5–35—36
    applying to multiple objects, IL 2–33—34
    applying to strokes, IL 2–38—41
    creating, IL 2–24—25, IND 5–30—31,
        IND 5–33—34

extending across multiple objects, IND 5–36—37

linear. *See* linear gradients

modifying, IND 5–32, IND 5–36—37

radial. *See* radial gradients

starting and ending colors, IND 5–30

stops. *See* color stops

gradient control bar, IL 2–32

Gradient Editor dialog box, PS 5–19

gradient effect, grayscale images, PS 5–23

Gradient Feather tool, IND 5–32

gradient fills, PS 5–6, PS 5–18—21

applying, IL 2–2, PS 5–21

creating, IL 2–2

creating from sample colors, PS 5–20

customizing, PS 5–19

Gradient Map dialog box, PS 5–23

gradient overlays, layer styles, INT 1–22—25

Gradient panel

applying gradients to strokes, IL 2–38—41

modifying gradient fills, IND 5–32, IND 5–36, IND 5–37

Gradient Ramp, IND 5–30, IND 5–31, IND 5–32

Gradient Swatch tool, IND 5–32, IND 5–35—37

Gradient tool, IL 2–36, PS 5–18—21

applying gradient fills, PS 5–21

creating gradients from sample colors, PS 5–20

customizing gradients, PS 5–19

linear gradients, IL 2–32—33

radial gradients, IL 2–34—35

graphic file formats supported by Photoshop, PS 1–5

graphics. *See also* illustrations

bitmap, IL 1–40—41, IND 4–32, PS 5–2

copying and pasting, IND 4–35

definition, IND 4–32

graphics frames vs., IND 4–33

moving between programs, INT 1–4—7

moving within graphics frame, IND 4–34—35, IND 4–39—41

resizing, IND 4–35

resolution. *See* image resolution

resolution-dependent, IL 1–40. *See also* bitmap graphics

resolution-independent, IL 1–41. *See also* vector graphics

vector, IL 1–41, IND 4–32

wrapping text around, IND 4–36—37, IND 4–43—45

graphics frames, IND 3–7, IND 4–32—45

content indicator, IND 4–34

copying and pasting graphics, IND 4–35

Fitting commands, IND 4–36

graphics vs., IND 4–33

moving graphics within, IND 4–34—35, IND 4–39—41

placing graphics in documents, IND 4–32—33, IND 4–38—39

resizing, IND 4–41—42

resizing graphics, IND 4–35

selecting, IND 4–33—34

wrapping text around, IND 4–36—37, IND 4–43—45

Graphics Interchange Format (GIF or .gif) file format, PS 1–5

graphics processing unit (GPU), Open GL, PS 6–22

grayscale color mode, PS 5–6

grayscale images, PS 5–22

adjustments, PS 5–22—23

colorizing, PS 5–23, PS 5–25

converting color images to, PS 5–24

converting to color mode, PS 5–22, PS 5–24

Group command, IL 1–29

grouping

items on layers, IND 4–30—31

objects, IL 1–29, IL 1–37, IND 1–29, IND 1–30, IND 1–33—34

panels, IL 1–9, IL 1–10, IND 1–7

Grow command, PS 4–14

guides, IND 3–7—8, PS 3–5, PS 4–7—8. *See also* Smart Guides

adding to master pages, IND 3–15—16

color, IND 3–8, IND 3–18

column, locking, IND 3–8

creating, IND 3–7

locking, PS 4–8

turning objects into, IL 1–59—60, IL 1–61

Hand tool, IL 1–16, IL 1–21, IND 1–13—14, IND 1–17

handles
    changing appearance, IL 3—11
    selections, PS 4—19
Hard Light blending mode, PS 5—28
hard returns, IND 2—18—19
hardware requirements
    Mac OS, PS 1—7
    Windows, PS 1—6
.hdr (Radiance) file format, PS 1—5
headlines, placeholders for, IND 3—28—29
Healing Brush tool, PS 4—19, PS 4—23
Help system, PS 2—2, PS 2—16—21
    finding information in Adobe reference titles,
        PS 2—18
    finding information using Search,
        PS 2—20
    finding new features, PS 2—21
    Support Center vs., PS 2—19
    topics, PS 2—16
hexadecimal values, PS 5—9
Hide Selection command, IL 2—5
hiding
    anchor points, IL 2—35
    document grids, IL 1—22, IND 1—20—21
    frame edges, IND 1—15, IND 1—19—20
    layer thumbnails, PS 3—4
    layers, IL 5—11, PS 2—13, PS 2—14
    objects, IL 1—29, IL 1—38, IND 1—29, IND 1—33,
        IND 1—34—35
    objects while working with text, IL 2—5
    panels, PS 1—22
    ruler guides, IL 1—22, IND 1—20

rulers, IL 1—22, IND 1—18
    selection marks, IL 1—17, IL 1—22
hierarchy. See also order
    visual, PS 2—14
highlight(s), correcting, PS 5—29
highlight mode setting, Bevel and Emboss style,
    PS 6—20
History panel, PS 2—13
    deleting states, PS 2—15, PS 6—19
Horizontal Type tool, PS 6—28
housekeeping tasks, Bridge and Mini Bridge, PS 2—8
HSB color mode, PS 5—5
hue, PS 5—5
Hue blending mode, PS 5—28
Hue/Saturation dialog box, PS 5—25
hyphenation, IL 2—5
    language dictionaries, IL 2—14
Hyphenation Settings dialog box, IND 2—18

illustrations
    assembling, IL 3—28—29
    drawing. See drawing illustrations
    painting using Live Paint Bucket tool,
        IL 3—55—57
Illustrator
    copying and pasting to Photoshop from,
        INT 1—4—7
    exporting layers to Photoshop from, INT
        1—8—11
    opening files in previous versions, IL 1—11
image(s). See also graphics; illustrations
    altering, ethical implications, PS 1—28

assigning keywords, PS 2—8—9, PS 2—10
bitmap, IL 1—40—41, IND 4—32, PS 5—2
blurring, PS 6—24—25
borders, PS 5—16—17
created in Microsoft Office programs, PS 1—5
cropping, PS 3—14
digital, PS 1—2
displaying, modes, PS 1—20
duotone, PS 5—23
enlarging using Loupe tool, PS 1—8
filling type with, PS 6—20
flattening, PS 3—2, PS 3—19
floating, PS 1—18
grayscale. See grayscale images
importing, PS 1—11
manipulating, PS 5—26
modifying using layers, PS 3—2
non-contiguous, selecting, PS 1—10
opening. See opening images
printed vs. on-screen, PS 2—23
printing, PS 2—23
rendering, PS 6—21
repurposing, PS 2—10
resizing. See resizing graphics
resolution. See resolution
resolution-independent, IL 1—41. See also
    vector graphics
scanned, opening, PS 1—8
sharing with Behance, PS 2—6
sources, PS 1—2
vector, IL 1—41, IND 4—32
viewing. See viewing images

image layers, PS 3–4

image resolution, IL 1–40—41

    choosing, INT 1–31

Image Size dialog box, PS 1–11

Image Trace, IL 3–36—45

    embedding placed images, IL 3–43

    expanding traced graphics, IL 3–41—43

    line-art sketches, IL 3–39, IL 3–44

    photographs, IL 3–40, IL 3–45

Image Trace panel, IL 3–37—38

image-editing software, PS 1–4

imperfections, correcting, selections, PS 4–19,
    PS 4–23

Import Options dialog box, IND 3–48

importing

    artwork, INT 1–38

    graphics with spot colors, IND 5–25,
        IND 5–27—29

    images, PS 1–11

    Photoshop files with layers, IL 5–20

    Word or RTF files, mapping style names,
        IND 3–48

in port, IND 3–44

increments, rulers, setting, IND 1–18—19

indents, paragraphs, IND 2–16—17, IND 2–19

InDesign

    opening InDesign CC files in earlier versions,
        IND 1–10

    output files, INT 1–36—41

    overview, IND 1–2

Info panel, IND 3–9, PS 5–8

information overload, PS 1–16

inks

    mixed ink swatches, IND 5–28

    process, IND 5–4

Insert Break Character command, IND 4–47

Insertion mode, IL 3–50

installing Output Module, PS 2–27

intellectual property, PS 1–28, PS 1–29, PS 1–30

Intent menu, IND 3–5

Interface Preferences dialog box, IND 1–16

Intersect shape mode, IL 4–25, IL 4–31

Isolation Mode filtering, PS 3–10

join(s), strokes, IL 3–30—31

Join command, IL 3–5

joining anchor points, IL 3–5, IL 3–9

jpg; jpe; jpeg (Joint Photographic Experts Group)
    file format, PS 1–5

.kdc file format, PS 1–5

Keep Options command, IND 2–18

kerning, IL 2–4, IL 2–6, IL 2–8, IND 2–6—7,
    IND 2–12, PS 6–8

keyboard

    applying color to objects, IND 5–12

    dragging frame handles, IND 1–28

    selecting text, IND 2–5

    viewing commands, IND 1–21

keyboard shortcuts. *See also* power user shortcuts

    creating, PS 1–18

    defining one's own, IL 1–21

    lack of case sensitivity, IL 1–7

    learning, PS 1–18

navigating Layers panel, PS 3–9

    spring-loaded, PS 1–18

    tools, IL 1–6—7, PS 1–18

    view commands, IL 1–20

    Zoom tool, IL 1–14—15

Keyboard Shortcuts and Menus dialog box,
    PS 1–18

Keyboard Shortcuts dialog box, IL 1–21

keywords, assigning to images, PS 2–8—9,
    PS 2–10

Keywords panel, PS 1–10

.kmz (Google Earth) file format, PS 1–5

Kuler, PS 5–10

    mobile app, PS 5–14

    using from Photoshop, PS 5–15

    using from web browser, PS 5–14

Lab color mode, PS 5–5

landscape orientation, PS 2–23

language dictionaries, hyphenation, IL 2–14

Lasso tool, PS 4–5

layer(s), IL 5–1—29, IND 4–20—31, PS 2–2,
    PS 2–12, PS 3–1—24

    active, PS 3–8, PS 6–18

    adding, PS 3–8—9, PS 3–12, PS 3–13

    adjusting opacity, PS 3–22

    adjustment. *See* adjustment layers

    applying styles, PS 6–13

    changing order, IL 5–12, IL 5–14, IL 5–21,
        PS 3–5

    changing selection color, IL 5–9

    clipping sets. *See* clipping sets

layer(s) (*continued*)

   colors, IND 4–22

   condensing, IL 5–12

   converting, PS 3–6—7

   copying layer styles between, INT 1–30—31

   creating, IL 5–4—5, IL 5–8, IND 4–20

   defringing contents, PS 3–15, PS 3–17

   deleting, IL 5–23, PS 3–11, PS 3–13

   dimming placed images, IL 5–24

   displaying and hiding, PS 2–13, PS 2–14

   duplicating, IL 5–5—6, IL 5–23, IND 4–21, PS 3–18

   exporting from Illustrator to Photoshop, INT 1–8—11

   exporting to Photoshop, IL 5–21

   filtering, PS 2–12—13

   generating assets from, PS 3–9

   grouping items on, IND 4–30—31

   identifying with color, PS 3–19

   importance, PS 3–2

   importing Photoshop files with, IL 5–20

   inserting layers beneath active layer, PS 3–12

   Isolation Mode filtering, PS 3–10

   layer comps, PS 3–20, PS 3–22

   layer groups. *See* layer groups

   Layers panel. *See* Layers panel

   locating, IL 5–21, IL 5–23

   locking, IL 5–10, IND 4–20—21

   making nonprintable, IL 5–21, IL 5–25

   manipulating layers and objects on layers, IND 4–22—23

   maximum number, PS 3–2

   merging, IL 5–12, IL 5–15, PS 3–8

   modifying images using, PS 3–2

   moving, PS 2–15

   moving objects between, IL 5–13, IL 5–18—19

   naming, IL 5–6, IL 5–9, PS 3–10

   organizing, PS 3–5

   positioning objects on, IND 4–27—28

   printing, IL 5–6

   rasterizing, PS 3–8

   renaming, PS 3–22

   reversing order, IL 5–21

   selecting artwork, IL 5–6, IL 5–7, IND 4–23

   selecting items, IL 5–10

   selecting objects behind other objects, IND 4–23

   setting options, IL 5–6

   showing and hiding, IL 5–11

   stacking order, IND 4–20, IND 4–22, IND 4–23, IND 4–24—25, IND 4–29

   Stamp Visible, INT 1–16—17

   sublayers. *See* sublayers

   target, IND 4–22

   targeting, IND 4–22—23

   template, IL 5–6

   types, PS 3–4—5

   view options on Layers panel, IL 5–20, IL 5–22

layer comps, PS 3–20

   creating, PS 3–22

Layer Comps panel, PS 3–20, PS 3–22

layer groups, PS 3–18

   creating, PS 3–21

   moving layers to, PS 3–21

   organizing layers into, PS 3–18—19

Layer menu, adding layers, PS 3–12

Layer Options dialog box, IL 5–6, IL 5–21, IND 5–21

layer style(s), PS 6–12

   Chisel Hard Emboss, INT 1–12—15

   copying between layers, INT 1–30—31

   gradient overlays, INT 1–22—25

   Outer Glow, INT 1–32—33

   Pillow Emboss, INT 1–26—29

   saving settings, INT 1–13

   Smooth Emboss, INT 1–18—21

Layer Style dialog box, INT 1–14, PS 6–15, PS 6–22

layer target, IL 5–6

layer thumbnails, PS 3–4

Layers panel, IL 5–4—5, IND 4–20—21, IND 4–26, PS 2–12, PS 3–4

   adding layers, PS 3–13

   navigating, PS 3–9

   view options, IL 5–20, IL 5–22

leading, IL 2–4, IND 2–5, PS 6–8

learning keyboard shortcuts, PS 1–18

letter spacing, adjusting, PS 6–8

licenses, Creative Commons, PS 1–31

Lighten blending mode, PS 5–28

line(s)

   with curves and straight segments, drawing, IL 3–16

   drawing. *See* drawing curved lines; drawing straight lines

line screen, PS 2–18

line segments, IL 1–41

line spacing, PS 6–8

Line tool, IND 3–10

linear gradients, IL 2–22, IND 5–31, IND 5–32, IND 5–33—34

  Gradient tool, IL 2–32—33

line-art sketches, tracing, IL 3–39, IL 3–44

links, warnings, IND 1–8

Links panel, IL 3–43

  managing assets, IL 3–41

lists. *See* bulleted and numbered lists

Live Distribute technique, IND 4–1—11, IND 4–14—16

Live Paint Bucket tool, IL 3–46—57

  edges, IL 3–46—47, IL 3–51

  expanding Live Paint groups, IL 3–50—51

  illustrations, IL 3–55—57

  inserting objects into Live Paint groups, IL 3–50

  painting virtual regions, IL 3–49

  regions, IL 3–46—48

  Shape Builder tool compared, IL 4–42

Live Paint groups, IL 3–48

  expanding, IL 3–50—51

  inserting objects, IL 3–50

Live Paint Selection tool, IL 3–48

Load Master Pages command, IND 3–25

loading

  master pages, IND 3–25

  selections, PS 4–11

locating. *See* finding; searching

locking

  column guides, IND 3–8

  guides, PS 4–8

  layers, IL 5–10, IND 4–20—21

  objects, IL 1–29, IL 1–37, IND 1–29—30, IND 1–34

  transparent pixels, PS 5–16—17

logos, PS 1–4

Loupe tool, PS 1–8

luminosity, PS 5–22

Luminosity blending mode, PS 5–28

Mac OS

  hardware requirements, PS 1–7

  right-clicking, PS 3–13

  starting Photoshop, PS 1–7

Magic Wand tool, PS 4–18, PS 4–21

  Color Range tool vs., PS 4–21

  selecting, PS 4–18, PS 4–21

Magnetic Lasso tool, PS 4–5

  creating selections, PS 4–12

  settings, PS 4–13

Make Clipping Mask command, IL 4–46

Make Compound Path command, IL 4–20

mapping style names when importing Word or RTF files, IND 3–48

margin(s)

  color, IND 3–8, IND 3–18

  modifying, IND 3–6, IND 3–14

  specifying width, IND 3–5

margin guides, IND 1–14—15

marquee(s), IL 3–4, PS 3–14, PS 3–15, PS 4–14—17

  changing size, PS 4–14, PS 4–16

modifying, PS 4–14, PS 4–15

moving, PS 4–14, PS 4–16

marquee selections, IL 1–49

masked effects, clipping masks, IL 4–47

master items, IND 3–7

  detaching, IND 3–39, IND 3–43

  modifying, IND 3–40—42

  overriding, IND 3–38—39, IND 3–40

master pages, IND 3–6—7, IND 3–24—33

  adding guides, IND 3–15—16

  applying to document pages, IND 3–34—37

  automatic page numbering, IND 3–25—26, IND 3–29—30

  based on another, creating, IND 3–27, IND 3–30—31

  blank, creating, IND 3–32—33

  creating master items on, IND 3–7

  detaching master items, IND 3–39, IND 3–43

  duplicating, IND 3–27

  em and en dashes, IND 3–36—37

  inserting space between characters, IND 3–26, IND 3–29

  loading, IND 3–25

  modifying margins and number of columns, IND 3–14

  modifying master items, IND 3–40—42

  new, creating, IND 3–24

  overriding master items, IND 3–38—39, IND 3–40

  placeholders for headlines, IND 3–28—29

  removing local overrides, IND 3–43

Match Color command, PS 5–32

Match Color dialog box, PS 5–33
matching colors, PS 5–32—33
Measurement Log, PS 4–8
measurement scale, PS 4–8
measuring type size, PS 6–4—5
menu(s), choosing commands, PS 1–16
Menu bar, PS 1–16
    opening files, PS 1–12
Merge Selected command, IL 5–12
merged documents, IND 2–26
merging layers, IL 5–12, IL 5–15, PS 3–8
metadata, PS 2–8
    creating captions based on, IND 4–44
Metadata panel, PS 1–10
Microsoft Office programs, images created in, PS 1–5
midpoint, gradients, IL 2–22
Mini Bridge, PS 1–8
    housekeeping tasks, PS 2–8
    opening files, PS 1–13
    uses, PS 1–10
    window, PS 1–13
Minus Back shape mode, IL 4–25
Minus Front shape mode, IL 4–25, IL 4–26—27,
    IL 4–29—30
miter limit, IL 3–31
mixed ink swatches, IND 5–28
mode(s), displaying images, PS 1–20
Mode command, PS 5–4
monitors
    image resolution, PS 2–18
    printed vs. on-screen images, PS 2–23

monotype spacing, PS 6–8
Move Pages command, IND 3–14
Move tool
    changing selected tools into, PS 4–7
    positioning selections, PS 4–10
moving
    graphics between programs, INT 1–4—7
    graphics within graphics frame,
        IND 4–34—35, IND 4–39—41
    layers, PS 2–15
    layers to layer groups, PS 3–21
    objects. See moving objects
    panels, PS 1–17
    selections, PS 3–14, PS 3–17, PS 4–9, PS 4–10,
        PS 4–13
    text along a path, IL 2–16—17
moving objects, IL 1–49, IL 1–50
    between layers, IL 5–13, IL 5–18—19
.mrw file format, PS 1–5
multi-page documents, viewing, IND 3–12
multiple artboards, IL 1–66—79
    arranging, IL 1–70, IL 1–76
    Artboards panel, IL 1–71
    creating new artboards, IL 1–69—70,
        IL 1–72—75
    editing, IL 1–70, IL 1–76
    managing, IL 1–66—69
    pasting artwork on, IL 1–71, IL 1–77—79
    printing, IL 1–70
multiple documents, IND 1–22—23
    open, IND 1–16

    working with, IL 1–19—20, IL 1–24—25
multiple filters, PS 6–26
multiple objects
    extending gradients across, IND 5–36—37
    used as clipping masks, IL 4–46
Multiply blending mode, PS 5–28

named colors, IND 5–4, IND 5–16
naming layers, IL 5–6, IL 5–9, PS 3–10
navigating
    documents, IND 1–24—27
    Layers panel, PS 3–9
navigation keys, Presentation mode, IND 1–15
Navigator panel, PS 2–24
.nef file format, PS 1–5
Neon Glow filter, PS 6–27
New Artboard button, IL 1–69, IL 1–73
New Character Style dialog box, IND 2–26
New Color Swatch dialog box, IND 5–4, IND 5–5
New dialog box, PS 1–5
New Document dialog box, IND 3–4—5,
    IND 3–13, INT 1–37
New Gradient Swatch dialog box, IND 5–30,
    IND 5–33
New Group dialog box, PS 3–21
New Layer command, IL 5–5
New Layer Comp dialog box, PS 3–20, PS 3–22
New Layer dialog box, PS 3–12
New Master command, IND 3–24
New Master dialog box, IND 3–32
New Mixed Ink Group command, IND 5–28

New Paragraph Style dialog box, IND 2–28

New Section dialog box, IND 3–50, IND 3–52

New Sublayer command, IL 5–5

New View command, IL 3–4

New Workspace dialog box, PS 1–23

Next Page Number command, IND 4–48

non-contiguous images, selecting, PS 1–10

None fill, IND 5–14

None setting, anti-aliasing, PS 6–17

Normal mode, IND 1–15

.nrw file format, PS 1–5

Numbering & Sections Options command, IND 3–50

.obj (Wavefront) file format, PS 1–5

objects, IL 1–17

    aligning. *See* aligning and distributing objects
        on a page

    aligning with Align panel, IL 4–30

    applying attributes, IL 3–24—27

    applying colors, IND 5–12–13, IND 5–18

    applying fill and stroke, IL 1–44—47

    behind other objects, selecting, IND 4–23

    copying, IL 1–28—29, IL 1–34—36,
        IND 1–29, IND 1–32—33

    creating with Shape Builder tool, IL 4–44

    deleting with Shape Builder tool, IL 4–45

    distributing on pages. *See* aligning and
        distributing objects on a page

    duplicating, IL 1–34—36

    effects. *See* special effects; *specific effects*

    fills. *See* fill(s)

flowing text into, IL 2–10—13

    grouping, IL 1–29, IL 1–37, IND 1–29,
        IND 1–30, IND 1–33—34

    hiding, IL 1–29, IL 1–38, IND 1–29, IND 1–33,
        IND 1–34—35

    hiding while working with text, IL 2–5

    inserting into Live Paint groups, IL 3–50

    locking, IL 1–29, IL 1–37, IND 1–29—30,
        IND 1–34

    moving, IL 1–49

    moving between layers, IL 5–13, IL 5–18—19

    multiple, used as clipping masks, IL 4–46

    positioning, IL 1–50

    positioning on layers, IND 4–27—28

    resizing, IL 1–27—28, IL 1–32—34,
        IND 1–28—29, IND 1–31—32

    round corners. *See* round corners

    selecting, IL 1–48, IL 1–49

    stacking order, IL 1–60

    transforming. *See* transforming objects

    turning into guides, IL 1–59—60, IL 1–61

    X and Y coordinates, IL 4–10

Offset Path command, IL 4–16, IL 4–18

opacity, PS 3–2

    adjusting, PS 3–22

    drop shadows, PS 6–14

    settings, PS 5–30, PS 6–14

Open As command, PS 1–9

Open dialog box, PS 1–8, PS 1–12

Open EXR (.exr) file format, PS 1–5

Open GL, PS 6–22

opening files, PS 1–8—9

    Illustrator files in previous versions, IL 1–11

    InDesign CC files in earlier versions, IND 1–10

    using Folders panel in Bridge, PS 1–12

    using Menu bar, PS 1–12

    using Mini Bridge, PS 1–13

opening images, PS 4–6

    scanned images, PS 1–8

optical center, PS 1–28

Optical Margin Alignment, IND 2–17

options bar, PS 1–17

order

    layers, changing, IL 5–12, IL 5–14, IL 5–21,
        PS 3–5

    layers, reversing, IL 5–21

.orf file format, PS 1–5

orientation, paper, PS 2–23

orphans, IND 2–18

out port, IND 3–44

Outer Glow layer style, INT 1–32—33

outline(s), converting text to, IL 2–28—29,
    IL 2–31

Outline mode, IL 1–18

Outline Stroke command, IL 4–17

outline type, PS 6–4

Output Module, installing, PS 2–27

Overlay blending mode, PS 5–28

overriding

    master items, IND 3–38—39, IND 3–40

    removing local overrides, IND 3–43

overset text, IND 3–45

page(s)
  aligning and distributing objects. *See* aligning
    and distributing objects on a page
  applying thumbnail color labels, IND 1–25,
    IND 1–27
  facing, IND 3–4
  master. *See* master pages
page continuation notations, IND 4–47—48,
  IND 4–53
page numbering
  automatic, IND 3–25—26, IND 3–29—30
  placeholders for page numbers, IND 3–25—26
  setting starting number, IND 3–5—6
page sizes, IND 3–4
Pages panel, IND 1–25, IND 3–7
panel(s), IL 1–8—10, IND 1–5—11, PS 1–17.
    See also specific panels; specific panels
  closing, IL 1–8
  collapsing, IL 1–8
  creating your own, PS 1–23
  displaying, PS 1–17
  docking, IL 1–10, IND 1–8, IND 1–11
  expanding, IND 1–8
  grouping, IL 1–9, IL 1–10, IND 1–7
  hiding, PS 1–22
  moving, PS 1–17
  separating, PS 1–17
  showing, PS 1–22
panel groups, PS 1–17
Panel options button, PS 1–17
Panel Options dialog box, IND 1–27, IND 3–36
paper, orientation, PS 2–23

Paper fill, IND 5–14
Paper swatch, IND 5–14
paragraph(s), spanning or splitting columns,
  IND 4–48
Paragraph panel, IL 1–8, IL 1–9, IL 2–8,
  IND 1–6—7, IND 2–4
  formatting paragraphs, IND 2–16—17,
    IND 2–20
paragraph returns, IND 2–18—19
paragraph style(s), IL 2–13, IND 2–24—25
  applying, IND 2–29
  choosing, IND 2–25
  creating, IND 2–28, PS 6–9
Paragraph Style Options dialog box, PS 6–9
Paragraph Styles panel, IND 2–24—25, IND 2–28,
  PS 6–9
Paste dialog box, INT 1–5
Paste in Back command, IL 1–28
Paste in Front command, IL 1–28
Paste in Place command, IL 1–28, IL 1–71,
  PS 4–6
Paste on All Artboards command, IL 1–71
pasteboard, IND 1–5
pasting. *See also* copying and pasting; cutting and
    pasting artwork between layers
  artwork on artboards, IL 1–71, IL 1–77—79
  from Illustrator to Photoshop, INT 1–5
  selections, PS 4–9
  text, without formatting, IND 2–4
path(s), IL 1–41
  beginning and ending with corner points,
    IL 3–21

  closed. *See* closed paths
  closing, IL 3–8
  compound. *See* compound paths
  creating, PS 6–29
  moving text along, IL 2–16—17
  offsetting, IL 4–16, IL 4–18
  open, adding fills, IL 3–25
  positioning text on, IL 2–14—17
  redirecting, IL 3–22
  removing anchor points, IL 3–5
  reshaping segments with Anchor Point tool,
    IL 3–55, IL 3–62
  stroked, converting to closed path, IL 4–19
  text on, PS 6–28—29
Path Eraser tool, IL 3–14
pathfinder(s), IL 4–24—25
Pathfinder panel, IL 4–24—35
  compound shapes. *See* compound shapes
  creating compound shapes, IL 4–33
  pathfinders, IL 4–24—25, IL 4–32
  releasing and expanding compound shapes,
    IL 4–27
  shape modes. *See* shape modes
PC Paintbrush (.pcx) file format, PS 1–5
.pct (PICT file) file format, PS 1–5
.pcx (PC Paintbrush) file format, PS 1–5
PDF(s)
  creating from Photoshop files, PS 2–28
  creating using Bridge, PS 2–27, PS 2–28
  exporting, INT 1–39—41
  saving files, PS 2–28
.pdf (Photoshop PDF) file format, PS 1–5

Pen tool, IL 3–2, IL 3–58
    drawing straight lines, IL 3–4—5
    toggling between selection tools and,
       IL 3–13
Pencil tool, IL 3–17, IL 3–59—61, IL 3–63—65
photographs, tracing, IL 3–40, IL 3–45
photography. *See* Camera Raw format; digital
       cameras
Photoshop
    copying and pasting from Illustrator to,
       INT 1–4—7
    exiting, PS 1–25
    exporting layers from Illustrator to,
       INT 1–8—11
    exporting layers to, IL 5–21
    features, PS 1–4
    importing files with layers, IL 5–20
    jumping between Dreamweaver and, PS 1–5
    new features in Photoshop CC, PS 2–21
    64-bit version, PS 1–19
    starting, PS 1–5
Photoshop EPS (.eps) file format, PS 1–5
Photoshop Export Options dialog box, INT 1–10
Photoshop (.psd) file format, PS 1–5
Photoshop PDF (.pdf) file format, PS 1–5
picas, PS 6–4
PICT file (.pct, .pic, or .pict) file format, PS 1–5
Pillow Emboss layer styles, INT 1–26—29
Pixar (.pxr) file format, PS 1–5
pixels, IL 1–40—41, PS 1–4, PS 2–18, PS 3–6,
    PS 5–2
    transparent, locking, PS 5–16—17

Place command, IND 3–44, IND 4–32—33
Place Embedded command, PS 3–16
Place Linked command, PS 3–16
placed images, layers, dimming, IL 5–24
placeholder(s)
    for headlines, IND 3–28—29
    for page numbers, IND 3–25—26
placeholder frames
    graphics. *See* graphics frames
    text, IND 3–17
placing. *See also* moving
    text, IND 3–44, IND 3–46—48
platforms, Photoshop, PS 1–2. *See also* Mac OS;
    Windows
point(s), PS 6–4—5
point of origin, IL 4–5—6, IND 3–11
Polygonal Lasso tool, PS 4–5
portrait orientation, PS 2–23
positioning objects, IL 1–50
PostScript, PS 6–4
power user shortcuts, PS 1–32, PS 2–30, PS 3–24,
    PS 4–26, PS 5–34, PS 6–30
preferences, IL 1–19, IL 1–26, IND 1–15—16,
    PS 1–8—9
    Bridge, resetting, PS 1–10
    File Handling & Clipboard, INT 1–5
    setting, IL 1–31—32, PS 1–21
Preferences dialog box, IND 2–11, PS 1–8—9,
    PS 1–21
Presentation mode, IND 1–15
Preview mode, IL 1–18, IND 1–15
Preview panel, PS 1–10

print design, web design vs., PS 1–26
Print dialog box, PS 2–23, PS 2–26
printing
    color handling, PS 2–23
    images, PS 2–23
    layers, IL 5–6
    making layers nonprintable, IL 5–21,
       IL 5–25
    modifying settings, PS 2–26
    multiple artboards, IL 1–70
    printed vs. on-screen images, PS 2–23
    viewing, PS 2–2
process colors, IND 5–4—11
    Color panel, IND 5–10, IND 5–11
    saving on Swatches panel, IND 5–11
    swatches, IND 5–6, IND 5–8—9
    tints, IND 5–4—5
    unnamed colors, IND 5–6—7, IND 5–11
process inks, IND 5–4
project(s), visual hierarchy, PS 2–14
project complexity, PS 2–7
project management
    basics, PS 2–11
    principles, PS 2–9
project scope, PS 2–9
Proof Setups, PS 2–26
proportional spacing, PS 6–8
.psd (Photoshop) file format, PS 1–5
pseudo-stroke effects, IL 3–32, IL 3–35
.ptx file format, PS 1–5
pull quotes, IND 2–16—17
.pxr (Pixar) file format, PS 1–5

Quick Apply, IND 2–25

Quick Selection tool, PS 4–15, PS 4–17, PS 4–21

quotes, pull, IND 2–16—17

radial gradients, IL 2–22, IND 5–30—31,
    IND 5–34
    Gradient tool, IL 2–34—35

Radiance (.hdr, .rgbe, or .xyze) file format, PS 1–5

.raf file format, PS 1–5

rasterizing
    layers, PS 3–8
    type, PS 6–24

rating files, Bridge, PS 1–15

raw formats, PS 1–5

readability, fonts, PS 6–5

records, IND 2–26

Rectangle dialog box, IL 1–43

Rectangle tool, IL 1–42

Rectangular Marquee tool, PS 4–5
    creating selections, PS 4–9

Red Eye tool, PS 4–22

redirecting paths, IL 3–22

Redo command, IL 3–18

Reflect dialog box, IL 1–56

Reflect tool, IL 1–52, IL 1–56—57, IL 4–4—5,
    IL 4–13

reflowing text, IND 4–50—51

regions, Live Paint Bucket tool, IL 3–46—48

Release Compound Path command, IL 4–21

releasing compound shapes, IL 4–27

relief effect, PS 6–24

removing. *See also* deleting
    anchor points paths, IL 3–5

renaming layers, PS 3–22

rendering
    images, PS 6–21
    intents, PS 5–7

replacing fonts, IL 2–15

Repoussé, PS 6–21

repurposing, PS 2–10

resizing
    artboards, IL 1–76
    graphics. *See* resizing graphics
    graphics frames, IND 4–41—42
    objects, IL 1–27—28, IL 1–32—34,
        IND 1–28—29, IND 1–31—32

resizing graphics, IND 4–35, PS 1–11
    enlarging using Loupe tool, PS 1–8
    marquees, PS 4–14, PS 4–16

resolution
    images. *See* image resolution
    images vs. device or printer, PS 2–18

resolution-dependent images, IL 1–40. *See also*
    bitmap images

resolution-independent images, IL 1–41. *See also*
    vector graphics

resource allocation, PS 2–9

Restore Default Workspaces button, PS 1–21

resulting color, PS 5–27

returns, IND 2–18—19, IND 2–23
    hard, IND 2–18—19
    soft, IND 2–19

reversing order of layers, IL 5–21

RGB color mode, PS 5–5—6

.rgbe (Radiance) file format, PS 1–5

right-clicking, PS 3–13

Rotate tool, IL 1–52, IL 1–54, IL 4–4

rotating
    objects, around defined point,
        IL 4–10—11
    spread views, IND 3–26

round corners, IL 4–36—41
    applying, IL 4–36—39
    applying specific corner measurements to
        individual points, IL 4–40—41

RTF files, mapping style names when importing,
    IND 3–48

ruler(s), IL 1–16, IL 1–22—23, IND 1–14,
    PS 1–18, PS 3–6
    hiding and showing, IND 1–18
    setting units and increments preferences,
        IND 1–18—19

ruler coordinates, PS 5–7

ruler guides, IL 1–16, IND 1–14
    hiding and showing, IND 1–20

sampling, PS 4–19, PS 5–6

sans serif fonts, PS 6–4, PS 6–5

saturation, colors, PS 5–5

Saturation blending mode, PS 5–28

Save As command
    changing file formats, PS 1–14
    Save command compared, PS 1–10—11

Save As dialog box, PS 1–13, PS 3–23

Save command, Save As command compared, PS 1–10—11

Save Document Preset button, IND 3–5

Save Selection dialog box, PS 4–11

saving
    files, PS 1–8, PS 1–13
    PDF files, PS 2–28
    process colors on Swatches panel, IND 5–11
    selections, PS 4–11
    settings for layer styles, INT 1–13

scale, PS 1–27

Scale dialog box, IL 1–53

Scale tool, IL 1–52, IL 1–54, IL 4–4

Scale X Percentage text box, IND 4–35

Scale Y Percentage text box, IND 4–35

scaling text horizontally and vertically, IND 2–6

scanned images
    blurry, fixing, PS 5–26
    opening, PS 1–8
    tracing, IL 3–19, IL 3–23

scanners, PS 1–25

Scitex CT (.sct) file format, PS 1–5

Screen blending mode, PS 5–28

screen frequency, PS 2–18

screen modes, IL 1–18, IND 1–15, IND 1–21—22
    toggling, IL 1–24

scrolling, IND 1–13—14, IND 1–24

.sct (Scitex CT) file format, PS 1–5

Search text box, PS 2–20

searching. *See also* finding
    for fonts, IND 2–8—10, IND 2–14—15, PS 6–5

sections, documents, IND 3–50, IND 3–52—53

Selected items icon, IND 4–23

selecting
    artwork on layers, IL 5–6, IL 5–7, IND 4–23
    Color Range command, PS 4–19, PS 4–20
    colors. *See* selecting colors
    graphics frames, IND 4–33—34
    items on layers, IL 5–10
    Magic Wand tool. *See* Magic Wand tool
    non-contiguous images, PS 1–10
    objects, IL 1–48, IL 1–49
    objects behind other objects, IND 4–23
    Quick Selection tool, PS 4–21
    by shape, PS 4–4—13
    text, keyboard commands, IND 2–5
    tools, IND 1–6, PS 1–19—20
    using color, PS 4–18

selecting colors
    using Color Picker, PS 5–10, PS 5–12
    using Swatches panel, PS 5–11, PS 5–12

selection(s), PS 3–14—17, PS 4–1—26
    adding to, PS 4–15
    applying feathers, INT 1–11
    complex, moving, PS 4–13
    copying, PS 4–9
    correcting errors, PS 4–6
    creating, PS 4–4—5, PS 4–9, PS 4–12
    cutting, PS 4–9

defringing, PS 3–15, PS 3–17

deleting, PS 4–9

deselecting, PS 4–5, PS 4–9, PS 4–11

fastening points, PS 4–5

fixing imperfections, PS 4–19, PS 4–23

flipping, PS 4–22

handles, PS 4–19

loading, PS 4–11

making, PS 3–14

marquess. *See* marquee(s)

mastering, PS 4–12

matching colors using, PS 5–32

moving, PS 3–14, PS 3–17, PS 4–9, PS 4–10, PS 4–13

pasting, PS 4–9

placing, PS 4–6—7

saving, PS 4–11

selecting by shape, PS 4–4

subtracting from, PS 4–15

transforming, PS 4–19

vignettes, PS 4–24—25

selection marks, IL 1–22
    hiding and showing, IL 1–17

Selection tool, IND 4–33

selection tools, PS 3–15, PS 4–2, PS 4–5
    choosing, PS 4–19
    by shape, PS 4–5
    toggling between Pen tool and, IL 3–13

semi-autoflowing text, IND 4–46

Send Backward command, IL 1–60, IND 4–20

Send to Back command, IL 1–60, IND 4–20

Send to Current Layer command, IL 5–13

separating panels, PS 1–17

serif fonts, PS 6–4, PS 6–5

setting up documents, IND 3–1—55

    color tint frames, IND 3–19—20

    colors of guides, margins, and columns,
        IND 3–8, IND 3–18

    conditional text, IND 3–16

    Control panel, IND 3–9

    creating new documents, IND 3–4—5,
        IND 3–12—14

    guides. *See* guides

    Line tool, IND 3–10, IND 3–21

    master pages. *See* master pages

    modifying margins and columns, IND 3–6,
        IND 3–14

    placeholder text frames, IND 3–17

    setting starting page number, IND 3–5—6

    Transform panel, IND 3–8—9

    transforming objects, IND 3–10—11,
        IND 3–22—23

shading setting, Bevel and Emboss style,
    PS 6–20

shadow(s). *See also* drop shadows

    correcting, PS 5–29

shadow mode setting, Bevel and Emboss style,
    PS 6–20

Shadow/Highlight dialog box, PS 5–29

shape(s), selecting by, PS 4–4—13

Shape Builder tool, IL 4–42—45

    creating objects, IL 4–44

deleting objects, IL 4–45

    Live Paint Bucket tool compared,
        IL 4–42

shape modes, IL 4–24—25

    applying, IL 4–26—27, IL 4–28—31

sharing images, Behance, PS 2–6

Sharp setting, anti-aliasing, PS 6–17

Sharpen filters, PS 5–27

Sharpen More filter, PS 5–27

sharpness, PS 1–26

Shear tool, IL 4–4, IL 4–5, IL 4–12

shortcut keys. *See* keyboard; keyboard shortcuts

Show Bounding Box button, IL 1–27

showing. *See* displaying

sidecar files, PS 2–8

Single Column Marquee tool, PS 4–5

Single Row Marquee tool, PS 4–5

size. *See also* resizing; resizing graphics

    canvas, PS 1–11

    drop shadows, PS 6–13

    marquees, changing, PS 4–14, PS 4–16

    type, measuring, PS 6–4—5

size setting, drop shadows, PS 6–14

Smart Cursor, IND 1–35

Smart Guides, IL 1–30, IL 1–39, IND 1–30,
    IND 1–35—37, PS 4–10

Smart Text Reflow, IND 3–47

Smooth Emboss layer styles, INT 1–18—21

Smooth tool, IL 3–14

Soft Light blending mode, PS 5–28

soft proof, PS 2–26

spacing, vertical, between paragraphs, IND 2–19,
    IND 2–21

special effects

    clipping masks, IL 4–47, IL 4–51—52

    compound paths, IL 4–23

    compound shapes, IL 4–34—35

    filters. *See* filter(s)

spell checking, IND 2–30—31, IND 2–33

spelling errors, correcting, PS 6–10

splash screen, PS 1–5

spot colors, IND 5–24—29

    creating swatches, IND 5–25, IND 5–26

    importing graphics, IND 5–25, IND 5–27—29

Spot Healing Brush tool, PS 4–24

spread, drop shadows, PS 6–13

spread setting, drop shadows, PS 6–14

spreads, IND 1–24

    rotating view, IND 3–26

spring-loaded keyboard shortcuts, PS 1–18

.srf file format, PS 1–5

.sr2 file format, PS 1–5

stacking order, IL 1–60, IND 4–20, IND 4–22,
    IND 4–23, IND 4–24—25, IND 4–29

Stamp Visible layers, INT 1–16—17

Star dialog box, IL 1–56

starting color, IND 5–30

starting Photoshop, PS 1–5

    Mac OS, PS 1–7

    Windows 7, 8, or 8.1, PS 1–6

states, deleting from History panel, PS 2–15,
    PS 6–19

status bar, PS 1–18

Step and Repeat command, IND 4–6—7, IND 4–13—14

Step Backward command, PS 6–19

Story Editor, IND 4–48

straight lines, drawing. *See* drawing straight lines

Strikethrough button, IL 2–11

stroke(s), IL 3–30—35, IND 4–4—6, IND 4–12—13

    applying, IL 1–46—47

    applying gradients, IL 2–38—41

    applying to objects, IND 5–12—13, IND 5–18

    applying to text, IL 2–28, IL 2–30

    dashed, IL 3–31—32, IL 3–34

    joins and caps, IL 3–30—31

    miter limit, IL 3–31

    modifying attributes, IL 3–33

    pseudo-stroke effects, IL 3–32, IL 3–35

Stroke button, IND 4–5, IND 5–12, IND 5–13, IND 5–19

    activating, IL 1–44

Stroke dialog box, PS 5–17

Stroke panel, IND 4–5—6

    cap options, IL 3–30

    dashed lines, IL 3–32

stroke weight, IND 4–5

stroked paths, converting to closed path, IL 4–19

stroking edges, PS 5–16—17

Strong setting, PS 6–17

structure setting, Bevel and Emboss style, PS 6–20

style(s), IND 2–24—29

    applying to active layer, PS 6–13

    choosing, IND 2–25

    layers, PS 6–12

    mapping style names when importing Word or RTF files, IND 3–48

    Quick Apply, IND 2–25

    type, PS 6–8—9

Style Mapping button, IND 3–48

sublayers, IL 5–16

    automatic creation, IL 5–13

    changing order, IL 5–12

    creating, IL 5–4—5

    defining, IL 5–12

    new, creating, IL 5–17

    selecting artwork on, IL 5–6, IL 5–7

subscript characters, IND 2–7

subtractive colors, PS 5–6

superscript characters, IND 2–7, IND 2–13

Support Center, Help system vs., PS 2–19

Swap Fill and Stroke button, IND 5–19

swatch(es)

    mixed ink, IND 5–28

    process colors, IND 5–6, IND 5–8—9

    spot colors, creating, IND 5–25, IND 5–26

    tints, IND 5–9

Swatch Options dialog box, IND 5–16, IND 5–17

Swatches panel, IL 1–8, IND 5–6, IND 5–11, IND 5–12, IND 5–30, PS 5–11

    adding colors and gradients, IL 2–23, IL 2–26—27

adding new colors, PS 5–13

applying color, IL 1–45

changing type color, PS 6–7

selecting colors, PS 5–12

symbol fonts, PS 6–4

symmetrical balance, PS 1–28

Sync feature, PS 2–5

tabbed documents, changing to floating documents from, PS 1–14

Tagged Image Format (.tif or .tiff) file format, PS 1–5

Targa (.tga or .vda) file format, PS 1–5

target, matching colors, PS 5–32

target documents, IND 2–26

target layer, IND 4–22

targeting layers, IND 4–22—23

tasks, PS 2–9

template layers, IL 5–6

text, IND 2–1—37. *See also* document(s); paragraph(s); type

    applying color to, IND 5–15, IND 5–20

    applying fills and strokes, IL 2–28, IL 2–30, IL 2–31

    area, IL 2–10

    autoflowing, IND 4–46—47, IND 4–49—50

    black shadow, IND 5–16, IND 5–21—22

    bulleted and numbered lists. *See* bulleted and numbered lists

    as clipping masks, IL 4–51

    conditional, IND 3–16

text (*continued*)
    converting to outlines, IL 2–28—29, IL 2–31
    creating, IL 2–4, IL 2–6
    editing. *See* editing text
    flowing into objects, IL 2–10—13
    footnotes. *See* footnotes
    formatting. *See* formatting text
    hiding objects while working with, IL 2–5
    hyphenation, IL 2–5
    moving along a path, IL 2–16—17
    overset, IND 3–45
    pasting without formatting, IND 2–4
    on path, PS 6–28—29
    placing, IND 3–44, IND 3–46—48
    positioning on a path, IL 2–14—17
    reflowing, IND 3–47, IND 4–50—51
    selecting, keyboard commands, IND 2–5
    semi-autoflowing, IND 4–46
    styles. *See* style(s)
    threading, IND 3–44—45, IND 3–48—49.
        See also autoflowing text
    Touch Type tool, IL 2–18—21
    underlining, IL 2–11
    vertical type, IL 2–9
    wrapping. *See* wrapping text
text frames, IND 3–7, IND 4–46—53
    autoflowing text, IND 4–46—47, IND 4–49—50
    inserting column breaks, IND 4–47, IND 4–52

    inserting page continuation notations, IND 4–47—48, IND 4–53
    placeholder, IND 3–17
    reflowing text, IND 4–50—51
    semi-autoflowing text, IND 4–46
.tga (Targa) file format, PS 1–5
theme color, changing, PS 1–21
threading text, IND 3–44—45, IND 3–48—49.
    See also autoflowing text
3D extrusion, PS 6–21
    applying, PS 6–23
    memory requirement, PS 6–21
Threshold slider, Image Trace panel, IL 3–38
thumbnails, IL 5–5
    clicking in Filmstrip view, PS 1–8
    layer, PS 3–4
    viewing using Bridge, PS 1–10
.tif or .tiff (Tagged Image Format) file format, PS 1–5
tints, IND 5–4—5
    swatches, IND 5–9
toggling
    documents, IL 1–24—25
    screen modes, IL 1–24
    between selection tools and Pen tool, IL 3–13
Tolerance setting, Magic Wand tool, PS 4–18
tone, PS 1–26
tool(s). *See also specific tools*
    adding to Tool Preset picker, PS 1–21
    selecting, IND 1–6, PS 1–19—20
    shortcut keys, PS 1–18

Tool Preset picker
    adding tools, PS 1–21
    selecting tools, PS 1–20
Tool Preset picker panel, PS 1–22
Tools panel, IL 1–5—7, IL 1–11, IND 1–5—6, IND 1–9—10, IND 5–12, PS 1–17
Touch Type tool, IL 2–18—21
tracing images
    Image Trace. *See* Image Trace
    scanned images, IL 3–19, IL 3–23
tracking, IL 2–4, IL 2–6, IL 2–8, PS 6–8
    text, IND 2–6—7, IND 2–12
Transform Again command, IL 4–7, IND 3–11, IND 3–22—23
Transform Again tool, IL 1–53, IL 1–55
Transform Each command, IL 4–7
Transform panel, IL 4–9, IND 3–8—9
transforming objects, IL 1–52—57, IL 4–4—15, IND 3–10—11, IND 3–22—23
    methods, IL 4–6
    multiple objects, IL 4–7
    point of origin, IL 4–5—6
    Reflect tool, IL 1–52, IL 1–56—57
    repeated, IL 4–7
    repeating transformations, IL 1–53, IL 1–55
    rotating objects, IL 4–10—11
    Scale and Rotate tools, IL 1–52, IL 1–54
    tools, IL 4–4—5, IL 4–7—9, IL 4–12—15
trim size, IND 3–4
Twirl dialog box, PS 6–25

type, PS 1–4, PS 6–1—30
adding effects, PS 6–12
anti-aliasing. *See* anti-aliasing
applying special effects using filters.
See filter(s), type
Bevel and Emboss style. *See* Bevel and Emboss
style
changing color, PS 6–7
creating, PS 6–6
filling with imagery, PS 6–20
fonts. *See* font(s)
measuring size, PS 6–4—5
modifying, PS 6–6
outline, PS 6–4
purpose, PS 6–2
rasterizing, PS 6–24
styles, PS 6–8—9
using on web, PS 6–16
type layers, PS 3–4
Type on a Path tool, IL 2–14, IND 2–19
Type Preferences dialog box, IL 1–19
type spacing, PS 6–8
Type tool, IL 1–16, IND 2–4
typefaces, PS 6–2
Typekit, IND 2–10, PS 2–7, PS 6–5, PS 6–6

underlining text, IL 2–11, IND 2–7,
IND 2–13—14
Undo command, IL 3–18, PS 6–19
undoing actions, PS 6–19
unembedding images, IL 3–43

unit(s), rulers, IL 1–16, IL 1–22
setting, IND 1–18—19
Unite shape mode, IL 4–25, IL 4–28
units of measurement, PS 3–6
Units Preferences dialog box, IL 1–16, IL 1–22,
IL 1–31
unnamed colors, IND 5–6—7, IND 5–11,
IND 5–17
Unsharp Mask filter, PS 5–26
update(s), Creative Cloud apps, PS 1–24
Update dialog box, PS 1–24
updating layer comps, PS 3–20
uploading files to Creative Cloud web site, PS 2–5
User Dictionary, IND 2–31

.vda (Targa) file format, PS 1–5
vector font, PS 6–4
vector graphics, IL 1–41, IND 4–32
vertical type, IL 2–9
Vertical Type on a Path tool, IL 2–14
viewing. *See also* displaying
commands, shortcut keys, IND 1–21
images. *See* viewing images
layers, IL 5–20, IL 5–22
multi-page documents, IND 3–12
printing, PS 2–2
thumbnails, using Bridge, PS 1–10
viewing images, PS 2–2
multiple views, PS 2–22—23
vignette(s), PS 4–24—25
creating, PS 4–24, PS 4–25

vignette effects, PS 4–24—25
virtual regions, painting, IL 3–49
visual hierarchy, PS 2–14

warnings, links and fonts, IND 1–8
warping type, PS 6–28
Wavefront (.obj) file format, PS 1–5
web design, print design vs., PS 1–26
Web Gallery, creating using Bridge, PS 2–29
white space, PS 1–27
widgets, IL 4–36—37, PS 6–21
widows, IND 2–18
Width setting, Magnetic Lasso tool, PS 4–13
Wind dialog box, PS 6–25
Windows
hardware requirements, PS 1–6
versions 7, 8, or 8.1, starting Photoshop,
PS 1–6
within stroke option, Gradient panel, IL 2–38
Word files, mapping style names when importing,
IND 3–48
work sessions, concluding, PS 1–24
workspace, IL 1–4—13, IND 1–4—11,
PS 1–16—23
areas, IND 1–4
customizing, IL 1–5, IND 1–5, IND 1–11,
PS 1–18, PS 1–23
elements, PS 1–17—18
modifying, PS 3–12
panels, IND 1–5—11
pre-defined, IND 1–4

workspace (*continued*)
    switching between, IL 1–4—5, IND 1–4—5
wrapping text
    around a frame, IND 3–51, IND 3–54—55
    around graphics, IND 4–36—37, IND 4–43—45

X coordinate, IL 4–10, PS 5–8
XMP (Extensible Metadata Platform) standard
    format, PS 2–8
.xf file format, PS 1–5
.xyze (Radiance) file format, PS 1–5

Y coordinate, IL 4–10, PS 5–8

zoom factor, PS 1–17
Zoom tool, IL 1–14—15, IL 1–21, IND 1–12—13,
    IND 1–17—18, PS 2–22, PS 2–25